STUDIES IN EARLY *ḤADĪTH* LITERATURE

WITH A CRITICAL EDITION OF SOME EARLY TEXTS

STUDIES IN EARLY *HADĪTH* LITERATURE

With a Critical Edition of Some Early Texts

By
Dr Muḥammad Muṣṭafā al-Aʻẓamī

Islamic Book Trust
Kuala Lumpur

This edition 2000
by
Islamic Book Trust
607 Mutiara Majestic, 6th floor,
Jalan Othman, 46000 Petaling Jaya,
Malaysia.
email: ibtkl@pd.jaring.my

ISBN 983-9154-21-4

Distributed by
A.S.Noordeen,
G. P.O.Box 10066, 50704 Kuala Lumpur.
Tel: 603 40236003 Fax 603 40213675

Printed in Malaysia by
Percetakan Zafar Sdn. Bhd

To my father,

who diverted my course of study from Mathematics to *Ḥadīth*, but did not live long enough to share the joy of the first fruit.

ACKNOWLEDGMENTS

I wish to express my gratitude to my supervisor, Dr. R. B. Serjeant, who first introduced me to the University of Cambridge while he was at London University, and later on agreed to supervise my research; Professor A. J. Arberry, who gave me his time generously and offered me much useful advice and assistance, and wrote the foreword for this work; H. H. Shaikh ʻAlī b. ʻAbd Allāh Āl-Thānī, the former Ruler of Qaṭar and H. H. Aḥmad b. ʻAlī Āl-Thānī , the Ruler of Qaṭar, whose personal interest in Arabic manuscripts gave me the opportunity to discover many most valuable ones; while the compilation of this work is due to H. H. Shaikh Qāsim b. Ḥamad Āl-Thānī , Minister of Education, who granted me a generous period of leave for study and ordered the Public Library, Doha, to supply all the available material, on the subject. His personal interest ensured that there were no official hinderances to the study: to Professor Muḥammad Ḥamīdullāh, for advising me to benefit from the experience of Western scholars and supplying me with many invaluable microfilms; to Shaikh Nāṣir al-Dīn al-Albānī, who placed his extensive knowledge of rare manuscripts at my disposal; to Miss Malak Hanāno, who kindly copied some passages for me from *Tārīkh Dimashq* and supplied the photo-copies of various important manuscripts; to Shaikh Aḥmad al-Mānī', Cultural Attaché, Sa'ūdī, Embassy, Cairo, and Mr. Fuwad Sayyed of Egyptian Library Cairo for supplying some important microfilms; to Mr. Ma'lūf for translating some chapters of the French version of *Muh. Stud.* by Goldziher; to Maulana Sa'īd Aḥmad Akbarabadi, Dean of the Faculty of Theology, Muslim University Aligarh, for his sincere advice and supervision of my first research work; to Mr. Martin Hinds of the Middle East Centre, and Miss J. Thompson of the University Library Cambridge for correcting my English; to Mr. M. A. Baig, Mrs. Taylor and Mrs. Barnes for typing this manuscript; to Mr. Z. Baig and Mr. K.S. Bashir Ahmad of the Eastern Bank, Doha, for going through the proof and indexing the book, to Mr. Adil Aqil of Dar al-Irshad, Beirut, and Mr. Gebrail Fatté of Catholic Press, Beirut, for the service they have rendered in printing this book; and finally to Mr. Abdul Badi' Saqar the Director and all the staff of the Public Library, who supplied me with all the required materials, and to Mr. Zuhair al-Shāwīsh for publishing the book.

FOREWORD

Pembroke College,
Cambridge.
16 February 1967.

No doubt the most important field of research, relative to the study of Hadith, is the discovery, verification, and evaluation of the smaller collections of Traditions antedating the six canonical collections of al-Bukhari, Muslim and the rest. In this field Dr Azmi has done pioneer work of the highest value, and he has done it according to the exact standards of scholarship. The thesis which he presented, and for which Cambridge conferred on him the degree of Ph.D., is in my opinion one of the most exciting and original investigations in this field of modern times.

Professor A.J.Arberry

LIST OF ABBREVIATIONS

PERIODICALS.

A.J.S.L.	:	American Journal of Semitic Languages and Literatures.
E.I.	:	Encyclopaedia of Islam.
J.A.S.B.	:	Journal of the Asiatic Society of Bengal.
J.N.E.S.	:	Journal of Near Eastern Studies.
J.R.A.S.	:	Journal of the Royal Asiatic Society.
I.C.	:	Islamic Culture.
M.E.J.	:	The Middle East Journal.
M.W.	:	The Muslim World.

BOOKS.

Abū Yūsuf	:	Abū Yūsuf, *al-Radd 'alā Siyar al-Auzā'ī.*
A.D.	:	Abū Dāwūd, *Sunan.*
Aghānī	:	Al-Isfahānī, *Aghānī.*
Amwāl	:	Ibn Sallām, *Amwāl.*
Annales	:	Al-Ṭabarī, *Annales.*
A.Y.	:	Abū Yūsuf, *Āthār.*
Bagh.	:	Al-Khaṭīb al-Baghdādī, *Tārīkh Baghdād.*
Bājī	:	Al-Bājī (in manuscripts).
Bayān	:	Ibn 'Abd al-Barr, *Jāmi'.*
BU	:	Al-Bukhārī, *Ṣaḥīḥ.*
BTK	:	Al-Bukhārī, *Tārīkh Kabīr.*
BTS	:	Al-Bukhārī, *Tārīkh Ṣaghīr.*
Daraquṭnī	:	Daraquṭnī, *Sunan.*
Dārimī	:	*Sunan.*
Dūlābī	:	Dūlābī, al-Kunā.
Faqīh	:	Al-Khaṭīb al-Baghdādī, *Al-Faqīh* (Ms.).
Fasawī	:	Al-Fasawī, *Tārīkh* (Ms.).
Fihrist	:	Ibn al-Nadīm, *Fihrist.*
Fischer	:	Al-Dhahabī, *Biographien*, ed. by Fischer.

Guillaume	:	*The Traditions of Islam.*
Ḥanbal	:	Ibn Ḥanbal, *Musnad.*
Ḥuffāẓ	:	Al-Dhahabī, *Tadhkirat al-Ḥuffāẓ.*
'Ilal	:	Ibn Ḥanbal, *'Ilal* (Ms. and printed).
'Ilm	:	Abū Khaithamah, *'Ilm* (Ms.).
I.M.	:	Ibn Mājah, *Sunan.*
Imlā	:	Al-Sam'ānī, *Die Methodik.*
Iṣābah.	:	Ibn Ḥajar, *Iṣābah.*
Islām	:	Al-Dhahabī, *Tārīkh Islām.*
Istī'āb	:	Ibn 'Abd al-Barr, *Istī'āb.*
Ja'd	:	'Alī b. Ja'd, *Musnad* (Ms.).
Jāmi'	:	Al-Khatīb al-Baghdādī, *Al-Jāmi'* (Ms.).
Kāmil	:	Ibn 'Adī, *Al-Kāmil* (Ms.).
Khaithamah	:	Ibn Abū Khaithamah, *Tārīkh* (Ms.).
Kharāj	:	Abū Yūsuf, *Kharāj.*
Khazrajī	:	Al-Khazrajī, *Khulāṣat Tahdhīb.*
Khuzaimah	:	Ibn Khuzaimah, *Ṣaḥīḥ* (Ms.).
Kifāyah	:	Al-Khatīb al-Baghdādī, *Kifāyah.*
Law	:	Schacht, *Introduction to Islamic Law.*
Lisān	:	Ibn Ḥajar, *Lisān al-Mīzān.*
Madkhal	:	Al-Ḥākim, *al-Madkhal.*
Majrūḥīn	:	Ibn Ḥibbān, *Al-Majrūḥīn* (Ms.).
Mālik	:	Mālik b. Anas, *Muwaṭṭa'.*
Ma'rifah	:	Al-Ḥakīm, *Ma'rifat.*
Mashāhīr	:	Ibn Ḥibbān, *Mashāhīr.*
Mīzān	:	Al-Dhahabī, Mīzān al-I'tidāl.
Mudallisīn	:	Ibn Ḥajar, *Ṭabaqāt al-Mudallisīn*
Muntaqā	:	Ibn Jarūd, *Al-Muntaqā.*
MU	:	Muslim b. al-Ḥajjāj, *Ṣaḥīḥ.*
Mustadrak	:	Al-Ḥākim, *Al-Mustadrak.*
Nas	:	Nasa'ī, *Sunan.*
Nubalā	:	Al-Dhahabī, *Siyar a'lām al-Nubalā'* (Ms. and printed).
Origin	:	Schacht, *Origins of Muh. Jurisprudence.*
Qaisarānī	:	Ibn al-Qaisarānī, *Al - Jam'a bain Rijāl...*
Rāmhurmuzī	:	Al-Rāmhurmuzī, *al-Muḥaddith...* (Ms.).
Rāzī	:	Ibn Abū Ḥātim, *Al - Jarḥ...*
Risālah	:	Shāfi'ī, *Al-Risālah.*
Sa'd	:	Ibn Sa'd, *Ṭabaqāt.*
Sharaf	:	Al-Khaṭīb al-Baghdādī, *Sharaf* ... (Ms.).
Sharḥ 'Ilal	:	Ibn Rajab, *Sharḥ 'Ilal* ... (Ms.).
Tahd.	:	Ibn Ḥajar, *Tahdhīb* ...

Ta'jīl	: Ibn Ḥajar, *Ta'jīl al-Manfa'ah.*
Tamyīz	: Muslim b. Al-Ḥajjāj, *Tamyīz* (Ms.).
Taqrīb	: Ibn Ḥajar, *Taqrīb.*
Taqyīd	: Al-Khaṭīb al-Baghdādī, *Taqyīd al-'Ilm.*
Tawsat	: Al-Ṭabarānī, *Al-Mu'jam Al-Awsaṭ* (Ms.).
Thiqāt	: Ibn Ḥibban, *Thiqāt* (Ms.).
Tirmidhī	: Al-Tirmidhī, *Al-Jāmi'.*
Ṭkabīr	: Al-Ṭabarānī, *Al-Mu'jam al-Kabīr* (Ms.).
Tṣaghīr	: Al-Ṭabarānī, *Al-Mu'jam al-Ṣaghīr.*
Usd al-Ghābah	: Ibn al-Athīr, *Usd al-Ghābah.*
Wāsiṭ	: Al-Wāsiṭī, *Tārikh Wāsiṭ* (Ms.).
Zanjuwaih	: Zanjuwaih, *Amwāl* (Ms.).
Ziriklī	: Al-Ziriklī, *Al-A'lām.*
Zur'ah	: Abū Zur'ah, *Tārīkh* (Ms.).

CONTENTS

Page

INTRODUCTION xvii

PART ONE

CHAP. I. Literary activities in Pre- and Early Islamic Arabia 1
The Art of writing in Pre-Islamic Arabia .. 1
Schools and other literary activities in Pre-Islamic Arabia 1
The Art of writing in Arabia in Early Islam 3
Educational policy of the Prophet 3
The outcome of the Educational policy 5
Arabic literature in the first century of the *Hijrah* 6
Goldziher and Nicholson's conception of this literature 8
Goldziher's conception of early Muslim Community 9
Other forms of literary Activity 15
Private-Public Libraries 16

CHAP. II. Recording of *Aḥādīth:* An Argument 18
The Prophet and the writing of *Aḥādīth* 22
Misinterpretation of Early Scholars' Statements about recording of *Aḥādīth* 25

CHAP. III. Pre-Classical *Ḥadīth Literature* 28
The terms *Kitāb*, *Nuskhah*, etc. and their meanings 28
Information concerning Pre-Classical *Ḥadīth* Literature 31
The Classification of the Literary period 31
Dating of Scholars' Lives 32

Writings of and from the Companions 34
Writings of and from the first century Successors 60
Writings of and from Scholars covering late first and early second centuries 74
Writings of and from the early second century Scholars 106

CHAP. IV. *Taḥammul al-'Ilm* (the learning and transmitting of *Ḥadīth*) 183
The Teachers 183
Memorising the *Aḥādīth* of the Prophet in early days 184
The appearance of the books 185
The *Aṭrāf* system and its effect 185
The curricula of education in the first century 186
Teaching of *Aḥādīth* according to *Shuyūkh* .. 186
The Method of teaching 188
a) Oral recitation of *Aḥādīth* by the teacher .. 188
b) Reading from books 189
c) Questions and answers 191
d) Dictating the *Aḥādīth* 192
The method of dictation 193
The *Mustamlīs* 194
To select someone for writing 195
The employment of scribes for writing *Aḥādīth* 196
The correction of written copies 196
The writing materials 197
Students: their ages 197
The number of students 199
School buildings 199

CHAP. V. The Book 200
Material for writing 200
The method of writing on the paper 201
Diacritical signs, dotting and other kinds of punctuation 203
Stealing of Material 204
Adding external Material in the body of a Book 204
Books and the problems of authorship 205

Schacht and the authenticity of Mūsā b. 'Uqbah's authorship of *Maghāzī* 207

CHAP. VI. *Isnād* 212
The Beginning of *Isnād* 212
The Beginning of *Isnād* in *Ḥadīth* Literature 212
Orientalists and *Isnād* 213
Professor Schacht and *Isnād* 215
Material for the study of *Isnād* 218
Schacht and the study of *Isnād* in legal literature 218
The methods of quoting traditions of early lawyers 219
The conclusion 222
Flourishing of *Isnāds* in the later part 222
Refutation of Schacht's theory of flourishing of *Isnāds* 232
General conclusion about the growth of *Isnāds* 236
Schacht and the authenticity of *Isnāds*...... 237
Argument about Schacht's examples of the arbitrary character of *Isnāds* 238
Difficulties in the "Projecting Back" theory of Schacht 242
Schacht and the *Isnād* of Mālik and Nāfi' .. 244
Final Conclusion 246

CHAP. VII. *Aḥādīth* 248
The authenticity of *Ḥadīth*............ 248
Schacht and the authenticity of *Ḥadīth* 248
An outline of early legal activities of the first and second centuries A.H. as given by Schacht. 249
Schacht's conception of the Nature of Law in Islām 251
Schacht's 'ancient schools of law' and the birth of an opposition party in their chronological setting 252
Schacht and "the growth of legal traditions in the literary period" 253
Argument about Schacht's examples of the growth of legal traditions 254
Schacht as the critic of *Ḥadīth* on material grounds 260

Wensinck as the critic of the tradition of Five pillars of Islam on material ground — a refutation 267

CHAP. VIII. The Edited Texts 269
The manuscripts and their authors 269
The method of editing 270
Nuskhah of Suhail, authorship 271
Authenticity of the work 273
The second manuscript, *Ḥadīth* 'Ubaid Allāh b. 'Umar 275
The authorship of the work 275
The authenticity of the work 275
The third manuscript, *Aḥādīth* Abī al-Yamān 277
The authorship of the work 277
The authenticity of the work 277
Muḥammad b. Muslim b. 'Ubaid Allāh b. Shihāb al Zuhrī, his life and works 278
His education 279
His literary career 280
Al-Zuhrī's relations with his students 283
Al-Zuhrī and the diffusion of Knowledge .. 284
His attitude towards the Writing down of *Ḥadīth* 284
Al-Zuhrī and his critics 287
Al-Zuhrī and the Umayyads 288
Did al-Zuhrī provide a substitute for the pilgrimage? Refutation of al-Ya'qūbī and Goldziher 289

APPENDICES

I. The meaning of the words *Ḥaddathanā*, etc. 293
II. The problem of enormous numbers of *Ḥadīth* 301
III. *Nuskhah* of Zubair b. 'Adī (a part of it) 306
IV. A folio from *Maghāzī* of Ibn Isḥāq 307
V. A folio from *Ṣaḥīḥ* of Ibn Khuzaimah 308

BIBLIOGRAPHY 311

GENERAL INDEX 323

Part Two, Arabic Section (the edited texts and commentary)

INTRODUCTION

Ḥadīth literature is the richest source for the investigation of early Islamic History. It provides material for an understanding of the legal, cultural and religious ideas of those early centuries.

Ḥadīth is also the repository of the *Sunnah* of the Prophet, which is the second principal source of Islamic legislation.

Western scholars have devoted much more time to Islamic literature, history and other subjects than to *Ḥadīth.* The first and the last significant attempt was made by Ignas Goldziher. He published the result of his research, *Muhammedanische Studien*, in 1890. Since then it has been the fundamental source for the study of *Ḥadīth* in the West. After the lapse of three-quarters of a century, Professor Schacht tried to investigate the legal *aḥādīth.* Apart from this there are some articles and a few books which have dealt with the subject in passing. There is only one book in English relating to the subject: *The Traditions of Islam* by A. Guillaume, which contains no original idea and draws mostly on Goldziher's work. Since the publication of the work of Goldziher, many valuable manuscripts of the first and second century of the *Hijrah* have been discovered and some of them have been published. Quite obviously, many theories and conclusions of Goldziher now need to be changed or modified. Had he been aware of these documents, he would, most probably, have formed some other theories.

Apart from his translation of *Mishkāt,* Professor Robson contributed several valuable articles in this field. He was able to modify some traditional ideas of Western scholars but he himself was influenced by Professor Schacht's recent works, in particular *The Origins of Muhammadan Jurisprudence.* Had it not been so, he might have been able to contribute much more.

Professor Schacht's way of thinking concurs with that of Margoliouth and Goldziher and carries their theories still further, without paying any attention to recent discoveries of manuscripts or research. In this connection I would like to borrow the expression of Professor Gibb. He writes in the Preface to *Mohammedanism*, describing the need for a new work on Mohammadanism instead of a revised edition of the original work of Professor D. S. Margoliouth, "Between one generation and the next, the bases of judgment necessarily suffer some change. They are modified firstly in the material or scientific sense, by the discovery of new facts and the increase of understanding which result from the broadening and deepening of research. If this were all, it might well be met by minor additions or alterations in the text. More important, however, is the change in the spiritual and imaginative sense. Every work of this kind reflects not only the factual knowledge but also the intellectual and emotional limitations of its period, even when every effort is made to eliminate prejudgments and prejudice. No generation in our changing world sees the problems of life, society, or belief in terms of the thought or values of the previous generation; and the gulf which separates the outlook of 1911 from the outlook of 1946 is one which has rarely been equalled in so short a space of human history". Since the writing of this preface another twenty years have elapsed, yet Professor Schacht still thinks in terms of Goldziher and Marolíouth.

Most Western scholars have praised Professor Schacht's works and have paid very high tribute to him. But much attention does not seem to have been paid to the method of Schacht's research, or to checking his conclusions and relevant references. The conclusions of the present study are in marked contrast to his. So, inevitably I have had to check and investigate his results. It is not my intention to study his work critically and in detail, nor have I sufficient time to do this. But it seems that a thorough study would reveal weaknesses in his work.

*
* *

My work, as it stands, consists of two parts. The first part comprises eight chapters and five appendices.

First, there is a brief survey of the literary activities in Pre- and Early Islamic Arabia. Then follows a discussion of whether or not the recording of the *aḥādīth* was permitted by the Prophet. Later on a comprehensive survey of the pre-classical *Ḥadīth* literature is attempted.

The third chapter, covering some one hundred and fifty pages, provides information about the thousands of books circulating among scholars in the pre-classical period. It records also the common practice of utilizing written documents. This proliferation of books raised the number of *aḥadīth* from a few thousand to three-quarters of a million. *Muḥaddithūn* had their own terminology, such as *'Ḥaddathanā, 'Akhbaranā, aḥādīth Mauḍū'ah,* etc. as well as their own method of numbering *Ḥadīth* which has not been fully understood by recent scholars of the east and west, consequently it has given rise to considerable confusion.

In this context the method of education in early *Muḥaddithūn* circles, their ways of handling the documents and the criteria for it was not sufficient for a document to be genuine in its material; was not sufficient for a document to be genuine in its material; it must also be obtained through the proper method. This is clear from Appendix III the *Nuskhah* of Zubair bin 'Adī. This booklet is classified as *Nuskhah Mauḍū'ah,* yet about one quarter of its contents are to be found in the *Ṣaḥīḥ* works of Bukhārī and Muslim, and a good many in other classical collections.

In Chapter V, the writing materials and the problems of authorship and other related subjects are discussed.

Chapter Six and Seven are based to a great extent on the conclusions of the second part of my work.

The sixth Chapter deals with *isnād,* its beginning and its authenticity. The seventh Chapter deals with the authenticity of *Ḥadīth.*

In Appendix No. 1, I have tried to explain the meaning of the terms *Akhbaranā, Ḥaddathanā,* etc. The evidence collected there makes it clear that these terms were used as a means of transmitting *aḥadīth* from one man to another, either in the form of books, or by dictation or reading from a written work, or by recitation. Oral transmission of *Ḥadīth* and aural receiving is only one of several methods.

There were about a dozen manuscripts at my disposal whose authors belong to the early half of the second century, the editing of which would have presented no major difficulties. Later, it was found necessary to confine the work to one and to study it exhaustively in order to achieve some concrete results. I chose the smallest one which is derived from Abū Hurairah, who has been unjustly criticised by some modern scholars. A search was made for these materials among the printed works of *ḥadīth* and in some manuscripts.

As a result dozens, and even hundreds, of references were found for a single *ḥadīth.* The spread of *ḥadīth,* the increasing numbers of narrators and the variety of their localities provide more than sufficient proof for the acceptance of the method of *isnād* as genuine and as commencing from the very early days of Islam, and not in the second and third centuries of the *Hijrah.*

In this connection some theories of Schacht are scrutinized, and the effort of modern scholars in the criticism of *Ḥadīth* is assessed.

In Part Two, there is an edited version of Suhail's manuscript. Two other important manuscripts are included, one of them belonging to Nāfi' (d. 117), and the other to al-Zuhrī (d. 124). As these were the sources utilized by Mālik in his work *Muwaṭṭa',* only references to *Muwaṭṭa'* or the works of their two colleagues Sufyān b. 'Uyaynah and Juwairīyah b. Asma' are given. They provide scope for a further study of Mālik's sources as well as an opportunity to examine the method of handling the materials: e.g., to what extent these works were true to the original wording, and, if changes were made, then to what extent the sense was affected by such changes.

In Chapter 8, the manuscripts and their authors are discussed. There is a lengthy discussion about al-Zuhrī as some modern scholars have attacked him severely without any justification. This chapter shows the lack of any basis for the charges made against him and proves that they are historically impossible to substantiate.

Finally, the work is somewhat lengthy; there were many important issues needing clarification without which further progress in the study of *Ḥadīth* was almost impossible. The work, therefore, has had to be extended as it would hardly have been possible to eliminate some chapters without damaging its unity. In doing so I have sought as much brevity as was possible.

PREFACE

In October 1966, this dissertation was submitted to the University of Cambridge for the degree of Ph.D. Since then a great deal of new material has come into my possession, which I intended to utilize with a view to extending the work. At the same time, I have been asked by many a scholar to publish the findings of my research as early as possible, and to devote my time to the clarification of other important issues. Utilization of new material would, no doubt, have entailed further delay in the publication of this thesis; hence this work is going to the press in its original form with a few additions and alterations here and there, particularly with regard to the language.

Now that I am free from the work of revision, I hope soon to be able to discuss the weakness of Schacht's Origins of Muhammadan Jurisprudence which I have dealt with, as briefly as the subject and space allowed, in chapters vi and vii of this book, which undoubtedly needs further investigation.

This dissertation is, most probably, the first work of its kind in this field of study and it is hoped that it will open new horizons for further research and help eliminate many prevalent misunderstandings that have resulted from a lack of proper understanding of the true nature of the *Ḥadīth* literature.

By its very nature, this book (particularly some of its chapters) follows an expanding area of research on the subject and does not claim to be the final word. It shall always be my endeavour to improve and enlarge upon this subject and to cooperate with those who have similar aims and interests. I shall, therefore, be grateful to the scholars and readers for their suggestions and criticisms for further improvement.

Public Library — M.M.A.

Doha, Nov. 1967

PART ONE

CHAPTER I

LITERARY ACTIVITIES IN PRE- AND EARLY ISLAMIC ARABIA

THE ART OF WRITING IN PRE-ISLAMIC ARABIA.

It is said that at the time of the advent of Islām, there were only seventeen persons in Makkah who knew how to write[1]. This statement sounds strange in view of the fact that Makkah was a cosmopolitan city, a barter-market and a junction of caravan routes. The figure limiting the learned persons to seventeen appears, therefore, to be an underestimate.

Schools and Other Literary Activities in Pre-Islamic Arabia.

In Pre-Islamic Arabia there were some schools, for example, in Makkah, al-Ṭā'if[2], Anbār[3], Ḥīrah[4], Dūmat al-Jandal[5], Madīnah[6], and in the tribe of Hudhail[7], where boys and girls learned together the skills of reading and writing.

There were some literary activities as well. Tribes used to record the poems of their tribal poets[8], and sometimes even historical

1. Ibn 'Abd Rabbih, *'Iqd,* iv, 157; Balādhurī, *Futūḥ,* 580; Ibn Qutaibah, *Mukhtalif al-Ḥadīth,* 366; see also Sa'd, iii, i, 77; 148; compare with Lammens, *Mecque,* pp. 103-145.

2. Balādhurī, *Futūḥ,* 579.

3. Ibn Qutaibah, *'Uyūn al-akhbār,* i, 43, Ibn 'Abd al-Barr, *al-Qaṣd wa al-Umam,* 22.

4. Balādhurī, *Futūḥ,* 579; Ibn 'Abd al-Barr, *op. cit.,* 22.

5. Ibn Ḥabib, *Muḥabbar,* 475.

6. Balādhurī, *Futūḥ,* 583.

7. Ibn Qutaibah, *'Uyūn al-Akhbār,* iv, 103; see also al-Maidāni, *Amthāl,* ii, 47.

8. Nāṣir al-Asad, *Maṣādir al-Shi'r al-Jāhilī,* pp. 107-133. Especially, pp. 122-133 where he has collected some 20 references from different poems for

incidents[1]. There were some occasional writings, such as promissary notes[2], personal letters[3] and tribal agreements[4]. There was also some religious literature, e.g., The Book of Daniel[5], which is mentioned in several sources, books of wisdom[6] and tables of genealogy[7]. Was there any translation of the Bible in the early days of Islam? Ruth says, "According to Barhebraeus the gospels had been translated into Arabic for Amīr 'Amr b. Sa'd by John I . . . who came to the Archepiscopal Throne in A.D. 631 and died in 648. Is the Amīr referred to 'Amr b. Sa'īd al-Ashdak . . . who was put to death 70/690 . . ."[8]. The statement of Barhebraeus and the suggestion of Ruth cannot be accepted. The father of 'Amr was born in 624 A.D.[9]. This means that 'Amr was born about 640 A.D., if not later, and thus he was only eight years old when the Bishop, John I, died; and a book of such a nature could not have been translated for a child not more than eight years old. Another argument against the acceptance of the statement of Barhebraeus is that it was the period of 'Umar 634-644 A.D., which covered the time of John I, and it is hard to believe that this could happen in his time. He himself had a copy of Daniel and was rebuked for it by the Prophet, and later on 'Umar himself once beat the man who copied Daniel[10]. The attitude of the community towards reading other Scriptures was no less harsh than that of 'Umar[11].

So, summing up, it is possible that the verses containing prayers were translated; otherwise we find that Waraqah b. Naufal

---

the recording of poetry in Pre-Islamic Arabia; see also Krenkow, *The Use of Writing for the Preservation of Ancient Arabic Poetry.* A volume of Or. St. presented to E.G. Browne, pp. 261-68.

1. Nāṣir al-Asad, *op. cit.,* 165.
2. Ḥamīdullāh, *Wathā'iq,* No. 181, Clause 10.
3. *Aghānī,* ii, 180; v, 118.
4. See for details, Nāṣit al-Asad, *op. cit.,* 66.
5. *Taqyīd,* 51-52.
6. Al-Sijistānī, *al-Mu'ammarūn,* 17; 18; 19; 69 cited by Nāṣir al-Asad, *op. cit.,* 166; Ibn Hishām, *Sīrah,* 285.
7. Nāṣir al-Asad, *op cit.,* 165; see also Sa'd, iv, i, 32-3. *Aghānī,* iv, 237. It gives a hint for their recording of the tribal genealogy.
8. Ruth, *Libraries in Umaiyad Period, A.J.S.L.,* Vol. Liv. p. 49.
9. *Tahd.,* vii, 38.
10. *Taqyīd,* 51-2.
11. *Taqyīd,* 56-57. But for the fair treatment of Scripture see *Iṣābah,* No. 8431.

used to write the Bible in *al-'Ibrāniyah*[1]. However, all this written material was not such as to foster a popular desire for literacy, and generally the people did not feel any necessity to learn to read and write.

THE ART OF WRITING IN ARABIA IN EARLY ISLAM.

Read in the name of thy Lord who created,
Created Man of a blood-clot
Read and thy Lord is Most Bounteous,
Who taught by the Pen,
Taught Man, that which he knew not[2].

This is the first revelation made by God to the Prophet Muḥammad. There is no record to show that he ever studied reading and writing; and it is generally believed that he remained illiterate throughout his life[3]. Therefore, this very first revelation gives a clue to the forthcoming activities of the Prophet in the field of education.

Educational Policy of the Prophet.

The Prophet was quite aware of the importance of education. This is why, before he migrated to Madīnah, he sent Muṣ'ab b.

---

1. BU, *Bad' al-Waḥy,* 1, see also, *I'tiṣām,* 25. *Tauḥīd,* 51, but in some other *riwāyāt* the word *al-'Arabiyah* occurs instead of *al-'Ibrāniyah.* As he knew both languages, he might have written in both languages or this might be and old discrepancy in copying the text. For more details see Kilgour, *The Gospel in many years,*pp. 10-11 where it is mentioned that, "The first version of Christian Scripture in Arabic dates from the eighth century . . ." Also, M.J. de Goeje, *Quotations from the Bible in the Qoran and the Tradition* where he agrees with Nöldeke that, "No Arabic version of the Bible, or parts of the Bible, existed either in the time of the Prophet or at the time of the fathers of the Mohammedan church". *Semitic Studies,* p. 185, in memory of Rev. Dr. A. Kohut, Berlin, 1897.

2. *Al-Qur'ān,* xcvi, 1-5.

3. Nicholson, in his book, *A Literary History of the Arabs,* p. 151, says, "The question whether the Prophet could read and write is discussed by Nöldeke . . . who leaves it undecided . . . It appears that he [the Prophet] wished to pass for illiterate, with the object of confirming the belief in his inspiration: "Thou" (Muḥammad) "wert not used to read any book before this (the *Koran*) nor to write it with thy right hand; else the liars would have doubted (*Koran,* xxix, 47)." The above-quoted verse by Nicholson gives the impression that the Prophet never read or wrote anything in the past; therefore, there could be no question of wishing to pass for illiterate with the object of confirming the belief in his inspiration.

'Umair and Ibn Umm Maktūm to teach his few followers[1]. After his arrival at Madīnah, the Prophet, first of all built a mosque, part of which was meant for a school, and from the very early days 'Abd Allāh b. Sa'īd b. al-'Āṣ was appointed to teach the pupils how to write[2]. He was killed in the battle of Badr. However, the victory of Badr brought a good number of prisoners of war and, "...Ransoms for the prisoners of Badr varied; for some of them, the ransom was to teach children how to write"[3].

There were also other people appointed as teachers of writing[4].

In the second year of the *Hijrah* at least one new school was opened[5]. There were nine mosques in the city of Madīnah[6], and most probably they were used as schools as well.

The most important and interesting thing in this field is the sermon of the Prophet regarding his educational policy. He ordered the illiterate and literate to co-operate with each other and admonished those who did not learn from their neighbours and those who did not teach their neighbours. Furthermore, he threatened with punishment those who would not learn[7]. It looks as if special significance was given to the art of writing. In a *ḥadīth* which is recorded by many compilers, the teaching of writing is described as the duty of a father towards his son[8].

Deputations arriving from outlying distance were given into the custody of Madinites, not only for the provision of board and lodging but also for education. The Prophet used to ask them questions to discover the extent of their learning[9].

Education of Non-Madinites.

Sending teachers outside Madīnah was one of the main features of the policy of the Prophet; at least forty of the teachers

1. Fasawī, iii, 193 b.
2. *Iṣābah,* No. 1777.
3. *Amwāl,* 116; also Sa'd, ii, 14; Ḥanbal, i, 14; Ḥanbal, i, 247; *Mustadrak,* ii, 140.
4. e.g. 'Ubādah b. Ṣāmit; see Ḥanbal, v, 315.
5. Sa'd, iv, 150.
6. Balādhurī, *Ansāb,* i, 273.
7. Haithamī, *Majma' al-Zawā'id,* i, 164; al-Kattānī, *Tarātīb al-Idāriyah,* I, 41-2.
8. Al-Kattānī, *op. cit.,* ii, 239-40
9. Ḥanbal, iv, 206.

who were on their way to Bi'r Ma'ūnah were murdered[1]. Many others were sent to Najrān[2] and the Yemen[3]. In the ninth year of the *Hijrah* a man was appointed to organise education in the Yemen[4]. The other factor, which helped in the diffusion of knowledge, was the influence of the *aḥādīth* of the Prophet, according to which un-paid teaching is the duty of every learned man, and withholding knowledge is a punishable sin. In contrast mention of many rewards for both teachers and students is made in other *aḥādīth*[5].

The outcome of the Educational Policy.

As a result of this policy education spread so fast that very soon after the *Hijrah*, the *Qur'ān* prescribed that every transaction on credit, however small its amount, should be written down and attested by at least two witnesses[6].

Another proof of this achievement is the long list of secretaries who wrote for the Prophet permanently or occasionally. They number about fifty[7]. Many of them were engaged in special sectors such as correspondence with tribal chiefs, keeping account of *Zakāt* and other kinds of taxes, agricultural products, etc.[8], with, perhaps, one chief secretary who used to carry out the job of any absentee[9] and who was the seal-keeper of the Prophet, responsible for answering letters and other business matters within three days[10]. In

---

1. Balādhurī, *Ansāb,* i, 375.
2. Sa'd, iii, 299.
3. Ḥanbal, iii, 212; iv, 397; Dūlābī, *Al-Kunā,* i, 19.
4. *Annales,* i, 1852-3.
5. See: *for free teaching,* Ḥanbal, v, 315; *for Rewards of Learning,* Ḥanbal, iv, 239; 240; 154; v, 196; *'Ilm,* 2b; *for Punishment for the Hiding of Knowledge,* Tirmidhī, *'Ilm,* 3. For more details, see Ḥamidullāh, *Educational System in the Time of the Prophet, I.C.,* 1939, pp. 48-59.
6. *Al-Qur'ān,* ii, 282.
7. Al-Kattānī, *Tarātīb Idāriyah,* I, 115-117, where forty-two names are mentioned, few more could be added on the list from *al-Wathā'q al-Siyāsiyah.*
8. For details see, e.g. *Annales,* ii, 836; Balādhurī, *Futūḥ,* 581-83; al-Mas'ūdī, *al-Tanbīh wa al-Ishrāf,* 282-4; Ibn 'Abd Rabbih, *'Iqd,* iv, 161-62; Ibn Miskawaih, *Tajārib al-Umam,* i, 291-2; al-Jahshiyārī, *al-Wuzarā',* 12-13; al-Kattānī, *op. cit.,* i, 121-4.
9. Al-Jahshiyārī, *op. cit.,* 12-13; Ibn 'Abd Rabbih, *op. cit.,* 161-2.
10. Ibn Miskawaih, *op. cit.,* i, 292; Ibn 'Abd Rabbih, *op cit.,* 161-2.

the effort to correspond with non-Arabs even foreign languages and their scripts were learnt[1].

Many books have been written on the secretaries of the Prophet[2] which throw light on the Secretarial side of the government of the Prophet. Writing was taught to women and many names are given of women who knew how to write[3].

There are also several instances of interesting advice given by the Prophet on the art of letter-writing, revision after completion, dotting ambiguous letters, and drying writings by means of sand.[4]

ARABIC LITERATURE IN THE FIRST CENTURY OF THE *hijrah*.

The literature of the early days of *Khilāfah* and the early Umayyad period either perished long ago or was incorporated in the encyclopaedic literature of the Abbasid period.

From the scanty material at our disposal we may sketch a variety of subjects covered by the writers in the period referred to, both non-religious and religious.

Non-religious subjects:

1. Poetry[5].
2. Proverbs[6].
3. Pre-Islamic History[7].

---

1. Ḥanbal, v, 186; Balādhurī, *Futūḥ,* 583; Sijistānī, *Maṣāḥif,* 3; Qalqashandī, *Subḥ al-A'shā,* i, 165.
2. For detail see Kattānī, *op. cit.,* i, 124-25.
3. Sa'd, viii, 220; Balādhurī, *Futūḥ,* 580-81.
4. For examples: Advice of the Prophet on: *Revising after Writing,* Ṣūlī, *Adab al-Kuttāb,* 165.

For *Dusting of Letters,* Ibn Mājah, *Adab,* 49; see also Maidāni, *op. cit.,* ii, 47.

Dotting Ambiguous Letters, Jāmi', 55b; see also Ṣūlī, *op. cit.,* 57; Ibn 'Abd Rabbih, *op. cit.,* iv, 173. *For Early Invention of Diacritical Dots see,* Farrā', *Ma'ānī al-Qur'ān,* i, 172-3; A. Grohman, *from The World of Arabic Papyri,* p. 82; G. C. Miles, *Early Islamic Inscriptions near Tā'if in the Ḥijāz, J.N.E.S.,* 1948, p. 240; Nāṣir al-Asad, *op. cit.,* 34-41.

5. See Nāṣir al-Asad, *op. cit.,* 155-164.
6. *Fihrist,* 89-90.
7. *Fihrist,* 89. See also 'Ubaid b. Sharyah and Wahb b. Munabbih, in *GAL,* i, 250-2 by Brockelmann, Arabic Translation by al-Najjār.

4. Genealogy[1].
5. Medicine[2].
6. Mineralogy[3].

Religious subjects:

1. The Holy Qur'ān[4].
2. Early commentary on *al-Qur'ān*[5].
3. Collections of *aḥādīth*[6].
4. Books on acts of worship[7].
5. Books on Inheritance and other topics of law[8].
6. Booklets on *Zakāt* and Taxation[9].
7. Biography of the Prophet, and the early history of the Caliphs.

It seems as if in the period referred to works on the biography of the Prophet and on other historical topics were in a very advanced stage. We find that work on the biography of the Prophet was begun by the Companions[10]. 'Abdallāh b. 'Amr b. al-Āṣ recorded many historical events. It is possible still to trace his work in the *aḥādīth* narrated by 'Amr b. Shu'IB (d. 118 A.H.) as he utilized his great grand-father 'Abd Allāh b. 'Amr's books[11]. 'Urwah (d. 93 A.H.) in his biography of the Prophet names his authority and most probably he had obtained the information in writing. There are works mentioned here and there on a single topic of the *Sīrah,* e.g., Memorandum on the Servants of the

---

1. *Supra,* p. 2.
2. Ibn Abū Uṣaibiy'ah, *Ṭabaqāt al-Aṭibbā',* i, 163; 164; Ibn Qifṭī, *Tarih al-Ḥukamā,* 324; Ibn Juljul, *Ṭabaqāt al-Aṭibbā',* p. 61.
3. Al-Bīrūnī, *al-Jamāhir fi Ma'rifat al-Jawāhir,* cited by Ruth, *A.S.J.L.,* Vol. LIV, p. 60. See also Art. Khālid b. Yazīd, in *E.I.*
4. *For its copying,* see Sijistāni, *al-Maṣāḥif,* 19; *Nubalā',* i, 341; iii, 248-9.
   For sending outside Madīnah, Sijistānī, *op. cit.,* 19.
   For Revising after Copying, Ḥanbal, iv, 216.
   For copying as a trade, Dūlābī, i, 155-6; Sijistāni, *op. cit.,* 130-1.
5. See *infra,* Ibn 'Abbās, Ubai b. Ka'b, Sa'īd b. Jubair, Qatādah in the third chapter of this work.
6. See chapter iii of this work.
7. See *infra,* Jābir b. 'Abd Allāh, and Abū Rāfi', in chapter III.
8. See *infra,* Zaid b. Thābit, al-Sha'bī, Ibn 'Abbās, in the third chapter and al-Zuhrī, in the eighth chapter.
9. *Infra,* pp. 48; 49; 58.
10. See for example, ṬKabīr, iii, 176.
11. See *infra,* 'Amr b. Shu'aib, p. 44.

Prophet[1], a book on the ambassadors of the Prophet to different rulers and chieftains with their negotiations[2]. There are references to the collections of the Prophet's letters in a very early period[3]. Interest in historical writing was not confined to the biography of the Prophet, as is shown by the compilation of the history of the battle between 'Alī and Mu'āwiyah[4].

All the above-mentioned subjects and many others were covered by authors who were born within the lifetime of the Prophet and were historically connected with him. Furthermore, all these topics are Islamic in their very nature and are written in prose, not in poetry.

Goldziher and Nicholson's conception of this literature.

Professor R. A. Nicholson, quoting Goldziher's *Muhhamedanische Studien,* II, p. 203 sqq.[5], says, "Concerning the prose writers of the period [the Umayyad Dynasty] we can make only a few general observations, inasmuch as their works have almost entirely perished. In this branch of literature the same secular, non-Muhammadan spirit prevailed which has been mentioned as characteristic of the poets who flourished under the Umayyad dynasty, and of the dynasty itself"[6]. He further quotes from Goldhizer the names of two scholars who were encouraged by the court of Damascus to historical studies — they are, 'Abīd b. Sharyah and Wahb b. Munabbih —, then gives two more names of *Maghāzī* writers: Mūsā b. 'Uqbah and Ibn Isḥāq. Later, he mentions al-Zuhrī as collecting the *Ḥadīth,* and *Kitābu 'l-Zuhd* (Book of Asceticism) by Asad b. Mūsā (749 A.D.)[7]. Quoting Goldziher's *Muhammedanische Stud.,* II, p. 72 f, J. Schacht says, "Goldziher has pointed out that those traditions that were current in the Umayyad period, were hardly concerned with law but rather with ethics, asceticism, eschatology, and politics"[8]. This assumption,

1. Sa'd, i, ii, 179-80.
2. *Annales,* i, 1560.
3. See *infra,* 'Amr b. Ḥazm, in the third chapter and relative foot notes.
4. See *infra,* Ibn Abū Rāfi', scribe of 'Alī b. Abū Ṭālib, in the third chapter of this book, who composed the book on this subject. His work is mentioned not only in Shi'ite sources but it is also confirmed by *Sunnī* sources. For quotations from this work see, e.g., ṬKabīr, i, 144a; 216a.
5. See also Goldziher, *History of classical Arabic Lit.,* p. 31.
6. *A Literary History of the Arabs,* p. 246. See also 'Alī 'Abd al-Qādir, *Naẓrah 'Ammah,* i, 113.
7. Nicholson, *op. cit.,* p. 247.
8. J. Schacht, *A Revaluation of Islamic Traditions, J.R.A.S.,* 1949, p. 148.

which was put forward by Goldziher and is accepted by Schacht and other scholars, is based on a misconception of the literary history of the Umayyad period, and perhaps the latter conception of Goldziher is based on the copy of Kitab al-Zuhd by Asad b. Mūsā, which is mentioned by him, but which does not belong to the period referred to. Asad b. Mūsā was born in the early Abbasid period in 132 A.H. and died in 212 A.H.[1].

Goldziher's conception of the early writings and literatures of the Umayyad period is a natural outcome of his observance of the religious conditions of that time. It is not the purpose of the present study to criticize his work *Muhd. Studien,* which is thought to be an indispensable work for the study of *Ḥadīth.* Nevertheless, as he is a scholar of good repute, a mistake which he commits necessarily misleads a number of other scholars[2]. And, as it is the only serious work, apart from Schacht's on *ḥadīth,* it becomes necessary in some vital issues, to look at Goldziher's conclusions.

Before commenting any further on Goldziher's work, it would be better to bring together his deductions, with the relevant references provided by him. Following is a summary of his conception of Islam with regard to the first century after the *Hijrah*[3].

Goldziher's conception of early Muslim Community.

1. The Muslim community's sheer ignorance of Islam as a religious practice as well as a dogma.

2. Islam was unable to incorporate its customs within a systematic ideology.

The basis of Goldziher's conclusions — His references and deductions.

1. The people were fighting in the name of Islam, and even built mosques, yet in Syria they did not know that only five prayers a day were an obligatory duty, and for this knowledge they had to refer to an old Companion of the Prophet (p. 30/3)[4].

---

1. *Tahd.,* I, 260.

2. For example see his remarks on al-Zuhrī concerning the mosque of Jerusalem, and their impact on the following writers:
   a) Buhl, F., Art. *Al-Kuds,* in *E.I.,* ii, 1098.
   b) Guillaume, *Traditions of Islam,* 47-8.

3. Goldziher, *Muh. Stud.,* ii, 28-31.

4. The first number denotes the page of *Muh. Stud.* and the second number to the references of Goldziher.

عن ابن محيريز ان رجلا من بنى كنانة يدعى المخدجى سمع رجلا بالشام يدعى ابا محمد يقول : « ان الوتر واجب » قال المخدجى فرحت إلى عبادة بن الصامت فاخبرته فقال عبادة : كذب ابو محمد . سمعت رسول الله صلعم يقول : خمس صلوات كتبهن الله على العباد فمن جاء بهن لم يضيع منهن شيئا استخفافا بحقهن كان له عند الله عهد ان يدخله الجنة ومن لم يات بهن فليس له عند الله عهد ان شاء عذبه وان شاء ادخله الجنة . ابو داود السنن . الحديث رقم / ١٤٢٠

2. The people had no idea how to perform prayers (p. 30/1).

باب من صلى بالناس وهو لا يريد إلا ان يعلمهم صلاة النبى صلى الله عليه وسلم

. . . عن ابى قلابه جاءنا مالك بن الحويرث فى مسجدنا هذا فقال إنى لأصلى بكم وما اريد الصلاة . اصلى كيف رأيت النبى صلعم يصلى . خ اذان ٤٥

3. Therefore it is not strange if the tribe of Banū 'Abd al-Ashhal had only a slave to act as their *Imām* for prayers (p. 30/4).

ابو سفيان الاسدى . قيل مولى بنى عبد الاشهل روى عن ابى هريرة ومروان بن الحكم... عن داود بن الحصين كان ابو سفيان يؤم بنى عبد الاشهل وفيهم ناس من الصحابة . تهذيب ١٢ / ١١٣

4. They were so ignorant that when Ibn 'Abbās asked the Baṣrites to pay *Ṣadaqāt al-Fiṭr,* they did not know of *Ṣadaqāt al-Fiṭr,* and were helped by some Madinites (29/4).

عن الحسن : قال خطب ابن عباس فى آخر رمضان على منبر البصرة فقال « اخرجوا صدقة صومكم » . فكان لم يعلموا.

فقال من ههنا من اهل المدينة ؟ قوموا الى اخوانكم فعلموهم فانهم لا يعلمون . . . ابو داوود الرقم / ١٦٢٢

قال محمد محى الدين معلقاً على هذه الرواية . واخرجه النسائى وقال : « الحسن لم يسمع من ابن عباس » وهذا الذى قاله النسائى هو الذى قاله الامام محمد وعلى بن المدينى وغيرهما من الائمة .

5. The Arabs in this period were so little accustomed to Islamic conceptions that it was necessary to begin by teaching Muslims that one should not say, *as-Salām 'Alā Allāh* (30/6).

. . . حدثنى شقيق عن عبدالله قال كنا اذا جلسنا مع رسول الله صلى الله عليه وسلم فى الصلاة قلنا السلام على الله من عباده ... فقال رسول الله صلى الله عليه وسلم لا تقولوا السلام على الله فان الله هو السلام ولكن اذا جلس احدكم فليقل التحيات لله ... النسائى باب تخير الدعاء (سهو ٤١ ؛ ايضاً ٤٣)

6. And what can one expect of religious knowledge from a generation in which the people stood in the pulpit reading poetry and believing that it was the *Qur'ān* (30/7).

عوانة بن حكم ... من علماء الكوفيين . راوية للاخبار ... قال عوانة فيما يروى عنه هشام بن الكلبي قال خطبنا عتبة بن النهاس العجلى فقال ما احسن شيئاً قاله الله عز وجل فى كتابه : ليس حى على المنون بباق ... قال فقمت اليه فقلت الله عز وجل لم يقل هذا وانما قاله عدى بن زيد . قال : قاتله الله . ما ظننته إلا من كتاب الله . توفى عوانه سنة ١٤٧ . ابن النديم. الفهرست ص ٩١

7. The official influence and activity in the fabrication of *Ḥadīth* goes back to a very early period. The alleged instruction given by Mu'āwiyah to al-Mughīrah, to denounce 'Alī and his followers, to drive them away and not to listen to them *as a source of aḥādīth,* always to praise 'Uthmān and his followers, to have close contact with them, and *to listen to them as a source of aḥādīth,* was an official statement to encourage the production and diffusion of *aḥādīth* hostile to 'Alī and in favour of 'Uthmān. (35/1).

من وصية معاوية للمغيرة . . « لا تتحم عن شتم على وذمه والترحم على عثمان والاستغفار له . والعيب على اصحاب على والاقصاء لهم وترك الاستماع منهم » الطبري . التاريخ ٢ / ١١٢

The first drawback in the setting of this picture is the complete omission of any reference which could shed some light on educational activities in early days.

Moreover there are many important issues based on the book *al-'Uyūn wa al-Ḥadā'iq* by an unknown author, as well as on some other Shi'ite sources, which he should have read critically for anti-Umayyad sentiments, to appreciate their true value.

Furthermore, he takes a single incident and enlarges it to cover the whole century as well as the entire dynasty. It is difficult to agree with him on any of these issues.

If one were to utilize the technique of Goldziher's research and his method of generalization, one might draw the following picture of 20th-century Europe:

1. Western Society is so corrupt that it uses holy churches for unholy purposes.[1].

1. Drugs were passed at the meeting of church youth club. Daily Mirror, Apr. 17, 1967.

2. People are so demoralised that they force 8 to 10 year old girls to earn their living as whores[1].

3. There is no security, society being infested with gangsters and racketeers, and people live in constant danger to life and property[2].

4. They are so cruel that they practice infanticide[3].

The obvious absurdity of these conclusions is sufficient to demonstrate the invalidity of Goldziher's technique of research and his method of generalization.

Even if we were to accept his generalizations, it would be almost impossible to follow him to his extreme conclusions, because the references provided by him do not justify his assumptions.

AN ANALYSIS OF GOLDZIHER'S REFERENCES AND DEDUCTIONS.

I shall now discuss Goldziher's deductions in their numerical order as referred to in the preceding pages. Every student of Islamic law is aware of the difference of opinions of the scholars regarding the Prayer of *Witr,* whether it is a *wājib* prayer, or a *Sunnah* one, etc. This difference exists even today[4], and the same kind of argument is used by the scholars up to now. Can we assume that the whole Muslim world is ignorant of the fact that there are only five prayers a day? Furthermore, the Syrians used to go to Makkah for the pilgrimage and according to Goldziher, 'Abd al-Malik, being afraid of political upsets in the time of Iban al-Zubair, wanted to prevent them from pilgrimage[5]. There must have been a considerable number of them otherwise 'Abd al-Malik would not have been afraid of them.

So the Syrians who attended *Ḥajj* every year did know the prayer — *Ṣalāt* — with certainty. So how can one suggest, on the basis of the above-mentioned text, that the Syrians did not know the numbers of the daily prayers?

---

1. A man used two sisters of 8 and 10 for the purpose of procuration. *The Times,* Apr. 22, 1967.
2. Criminals in England steal £500,000 weekly, *Daily Telegraph,* May 2, 67.
3. A City leads in legal abortions. *The Sunday Times* Page 3, 5th Feb. 67.
4. See for example: (a) *Al-Fiqh 'alā al-Madhāhib al-Arba'ah,* 246-250.
   (b) Ibn al-Humām, *Fatḥ al-Qadīr,* Vol. i, 300-303.
5. Goldziher, *Muh. Stud.,* pp. 35-37.

The second quotation is even more irrelevant to his conclusion. According to Ibn Sa'd[1], Mālik b. al-Ḥuwairith was ordered by the Prophet to teach the people how to pray. Therefore, he probably went to various mosques to show the correct performance of *Ṣalāt.* Not only the heading of al-Bukhārī gives this impression, agreeing with IBN Sa'd, but even the wording of the statement itself confirms this. He prayed only to give an example to those present, not at an obligatory prayer-time, nor to find fault with those who were praying and to accuse them of mistakes. It is a very strange conclusion that if someone teaches, then the whole community must be ignorant; yet if there is no mention of the educational and instructional activities of that period Goldziher accuses the ruling dynasty of secular and non-Muhammadan spirit[2].

3. Banū 'Abd Ashhal lived in Madīnah or in its suburbs. This was the tribe of Sa'd b. Mu'ādh[3]. Abū Rāfi' says that the Prophet used to visit Banū 'Abd Ashhal after the *'Āṣr* prayer and speak to them; sometimes the meetings and discussions even continued till the *Maghrib* prayer[4].

In this case a number of these people must have known how to pray. This tribe was not in too remote a desert to have been unable to find an *Imām* and to find only a slave to lead the prayers. This tribe was in the very heart of Madīnah, of which Goldziher himself has a good opinion[5]. Would it not be more reasonable to interpret this incident to mean that even the client of a tribe could be the *Imām* in prayer if he was equipped with sufficient knowledge of Islam?

4. This statement is a *mursal* one. Its authenticity is challengeable. Even if it is an authentic statement, it was a single incident. How could an isolated instance be used as inclusively as is suggested by Goldziher? There were more than fifty famous Companions who had settled down in the city. Among them were Abū Mūsā al-Ash'arī, Anas b. Mālik, Qabīṣah b. al-Mukhāriq, etc.[6]. Al-Ḥasan al-Baṣrī says that 'Abd Allāh b. Mughaffal was one of the

1. Sa'd, vii, 1, 29-30.
2. Nicholson, *Literary History of the Arabs,* 246, quoting Goldziher's *Muh. Stud.*, p. 203 sqq.
3. Ḥumaidī, Tr. No. 1197; Ibn Ḥazm, *Djamharat al-Ansāb,* p. 319.
4. Ṭkabīr, 1, 66a.
5. Goldziher, *op. cit.,* 31.
6. *Mashāhīr,* 37-42.

ten who were sent by 'Umar b. al-Khaṭṭāb to teach the Basrites[1] Therefore, even if it had happened, it should not be used for generalization.

5. The conclusion is irrelevent. The Arab society with whom the Prophet was dealing was pagan. The new religion and its method of worship were totally new to these people and, as there were no precedents, they had to learn everything however trivial it might otherwise appear. This particular case concerns the Companions of the Prophet who were learning from him, so it cannot be taken as a proof of general ignorance of Islamic conceptions.

6. Quotation No. 6 implies that the Governor, 'Utbah b. al-Nahhās al-'Ijlī, did not know the *Qur'ān,* and was so ignorant that he recited poetry maintaining that it was a part of the *Qur'ān.* The statement seems to be doubtful. As Ibn al-Kalbī, the narrator of this incident, had Shi'ite tendencies, and the same may be said of 'Awānah, while 'Utbah was *'Uthmānī* and pro-Umayyad, the whole story appears doubtful. The other reason for doubt is the age of 'Utbah bin al-Nahhās al-'Ijlī.

At the time of the assassination of the Caliph *'Uthmān* (d. 35), 'Utbah was the governor of Ḥulwān[2]. Al-Mughīrah, while going to see Mu'āwiyah in 45 A.H., appointed 'Utbah governor of Kūfah[3]. After this date, he is not mentioned by Ṭabarī. In the year 11 A.H., he took Part in the *Riddah* War[4]. Therefore it would be safe to assume that he must have been at least twenty years of age at that time, and that if he lived to the common age of about sixty years, he might have died somewhere about 50 A.H.

'Awānah, most probably, might have been born somewhere about 85 A.H.[5] and could not have been in a position to criticize the governor till he was fifteen or twenty years of age. Bearing all this in mind, one could only assume that this event took place at the beginning of the second century, when 'Utbah was probably one hundred and ten years of age. It is questionable that a man of such an age could be appointed a governor even supposing that he lived that long.

---

1. *Nubalā,* ii, 345; the other member of the team was 'Imrān b. Ḥuṣain, *Nubalā,* ii, 363.
2. *Annales,* i, 3058.
3. *Annales,* ii, 72.
4. *Annales,* i, 1971.
5. *Fihrist,* 91, where his death is mentioned in 147 A.H.

7. It is a well-known fact that there had been wars between Umayyads and Alides. Every government, even now in every country, employs people who are thought to be loyal to the regime, and suppresses rebels. Similar measures were taken by the Umayyads. But in the entire quotation there is neither an official nor an unofficial statement alleging fabrication of the *aḥādīth* and the diffusion of them. Mu'āwiyah says, "denounce 'Alī, and those who assassinated the Caliph 'Uthmān, and pray for 'Uthmān . . ." etc. There seems to be nothing wrong in this attitude, except for his denunciation of 'Alī. There is not a single word giving the slightest hint of any fabrication of *aḥādīth.*

Going through Goldziher's references, one reaches the conclusion that his picture of the religious knowledge and practice of the first century of the *Ḥijrah* is incomplete and unbalanced. Therefore, his other conclusions, on the above-mentioned assumptions, are baseless. He is quite wrong in his belief that prose writing in the Umayyad period was secular and non-Muhammadan. The bulky literature of *Ḥadīth* in the Umayyad period, as is shown in the third Chapter of the present study, compels us to reject this assumption. The claim is based on incomplete knowledge of the period and the arbitrary judgment that religious people were against the Umayyads. If a few incidents can be given to prove that the pious were against them, a more lengthy list could be provided of those who worked for the Umayyads and by any standard the Abbasids were no better, if not much worse, than the Umayyads. It is the duty of a historian to be more cautious when he writes on the Umayyads, as the entire literature available for the subject is the product of the anti-Umayyad period.

Other Forms of Literary Activity.

At the time of the Prophet, people used to copy whatever he dictated. Many Companions had copies of his letters dispatched to different people. It is not clear whether this was done under his instruction or on a personal initiative.

There were some kinds of records kept even at the time of the Prophet. Once he ordered a statistical list to be made of those who embraced Islam. The list contained some 1,500 names[1].

---

1. BU, *Jihād,* 181.

Those who were recruited for any military expedition even in the time of the Prophet were also registered[1]. It was 'Umar who introduced the system of registers at the state level and this may be reckoned as the beginning of systematic official records. He had all the treaties with the tribes or foreign governments preserved in a box, *Tābūt*[2].

There was a house attached to Caliph 'Uthmān's house for the preservation of *Qirṭās*. Marwān was hidden there by Fāṭimah bint Sharīk, and thus his life was saved[3] while the Caliph 'Uthmān was assassinated. It might have been a state-paper depository. Later on Ṭabarī mentions *Bait al-Qarāṭīs* (State-Paper House) in connection with the assassination of 'Amr b. Sa'īd, in 69 A.H.[4]. Towards the end of the first century, *Qirṭās* was even distributed to governors for official use[5].

Private—Public Libraries.

In the middle of the first century of the *Hijrah*, we find a man called 'Abd al-Ḥakam b. 'Amr al-Jumaḥī, who established a public library which contained *Kurrāsāt* (books) on various subjects, different kinds of games and a place to hang the mantles. People were free to use the library for reading or for amusement[6].

At the same time there was the library of Ibn Abū Lailā, which contained only the Holy *Qur'ān* and people gathered there for recitation[7].

There is another library mentioned in the possession of Khālid b. Yazīd b. Mu'āwiyah[8]; but it is not the earliest record of anything like a public library as was supposed by Krenkow, because the libraries of 'Abd al-Ḥakam and Ibn Abū Lailā most probably existed at an earlier date than this library.

There may have been some other libraries which are unknown to us because this information is scattered far and wide,

1. BU, *Jihād,* 140, *Nikāh,* 111, MU, *Ḥajj,* 424, Ibn Mājah, *Manāsik,* 7.
2. Maqrīzī, *Khiṭaṭ,* i, 295.
3. Balādhūrī, *Ansāb,* i, 22.
4. *Annales,* ii, 790.
5. Ibn 'Abdal-Ḥakam, *Sīrat 'Umar b. 'Abd al-'Azīz,* p. 64.
6. *Aghānī,* iv, 253.
7. Sa'd, vi, 75.
8. Krenkow, Art. *Kitābkhāna,* in *E.I.*, Vol. ii, 1045.

and there is no special chapter on early libraries in the sources available.

However, the existence of these libraries in such early times gives us sufficient proof of the presence of early intellectual activities during the Umayyad period. It was neither a secular, nor a non-Muhammaden literary period, as we are given to understand by Goldziher. Had it been so, there could not have been such a tremendous achievement in every field in the early Abbasid period.

CHAPTER II

RECORDING OF "AḤĀDĪTH": AN ARGUMENT

According to the general belief, *aḥādīth* were orally transmitted at least for one hundred years[1]. 'Umar b. 'Abd al-'Azīz was the first who asked Abū Bakr b. Muḥammad b. 'Amr b. Ḥazm[2], al-Zuhrī[3] and others[4] to collect *aḥādīth* and al-Zuhrī was the first who recorded them[5]. On the authenticity of this statement, there are differences of opinion among orientalists. Muir accepts it with the remark that there are no authentic remains of any such compilation of an earlier date than the middle of the 2nd century of the *Hijrah*[6]. While Guillaume in referring to this statement says, "The *ḥadīth* must be regarded as an invention"[7], Ruth also refers to Guillaume and some other scholars who doubt the trustworthiness of the report[8]. Goldziher and Schacht have rather harsh opinions. Schacht says, "On the tendency underlying this spurious

---

1. See for oral transmission of Ḥadīth about 100 years and late recording in II century: Abū Ṭālib al-Makkī, *Qūt al-Qulūb,* i, 159; *Ḥuffāẓ,* i, 144; Ibn Ḥajar, *Hady al-Sārī,* i, 17; *Fatḥ al-Bārī,* i, 208; H. Khalīfah, *Kashf al-Ẓunūn,* i, 637; al-Kattānī, *Risālah Mustaṭrafah,* 3; Zahw, *al-Ḥadīth wal-Muḥaddithūn,* 127; Dhahabī, *Tafsīr wa al-Mufassirūn,* i, 140-41; Rashīd Riḍā, *Manār,* x 768; Abū Rayyah, *Aḍwā' 'alā al-Sunnah,* 207; Nicholson, *Literary History of Arabs,* 144; for recording and making collections after a few hundred years, Justice Muḥammad Shāfi' as cited in *The Tarjumān, Risālat,* No. Lahore, 1961, p. 267.
2. Sa'd, viii, 353; BTS, 105; Dārimī, i, 126; *Taqyīd,* 105; al-Kattānī, *Risālah Mustaṭrafah,* 3.
3. Khaithamah, iii, 126a; Ibn 'Abd al-Barr, *Jāmi' Bayān al-'Ilm,* i, 76.
4. Ibn Ḥajar, *Fatḥ al-Bārī,* i, 207-8; al-Kattānī, *op. cit.,* 4.
5. Khaithamah, iii, 126b; Ibn 'Asākir, *Tārīkh Dimashq,* xv, 400a as cited by Eche, in *Taqyīd,* 5. See also M. 'Abd al-Rāziq, *Tamhīd li-Tārīkh al-Falsafah al-Islāmiyah,* 198.
6. Muir, *Life of Mahomet,* xxx-xxxi.
7. Guillaume, *Traditions,* 19.
8. Ruth, *Early libraries, A.J.S.L.,* Vol. Lii, 248.

tradition, see Goldziher, *Muh. Stud.* II, 210 f., and Mirzā Kazem Beg, in *J.A.*, 4th Ser., XV, 168''[1].

He further says, "Hardly any of these traditions, as far as matters of religious law are concerned, can be considered authentic; they were put into circulation . . . from the first half of the second century onwards''[2].

It is not strange that Schacht should maintain this attitude regarding the authenticity of 'Umar b. 'Abd al-'Azīz's statement, because he believes that almost all the legal *aḥādīth* were invented long after the death of 'Umar b. 'Abd al-'Azīz, and, therefore, there cannot be a question of transmitting *aḥādīth* orally, let alone recording them.

The general belief in the late recording of *aḥādīth* and oral transmissions for more than 100 years was due to the information provided by the *muḥaddithūn* themselves.

The names of the earliest compilers in *ḥadīth* provided by *muḥaddithūn* belong to the mid-second or the later half of the 2nd century of the *Hijrah*[3].

It is not clear who was the first who furnished this information, but later on all the scholars, even al-Dhahabī and Ibn Ḥajar, repeated the old statement without scrutinizing it, even though they themselves had provided ample evidence in their writings against this common belief.

This theory of the recording of *ḥadīth* in the 2nd century was the result of many misconceptions:

1. Misinterpretation of the words: *Tadwīn, Taṣnīf and Kitābah* which were understood in the sense of recording.

2. The terms *Ḥaddathanā, Akhbaranā, 'An,* etc., which were generally believed to be used for oral transmissions.

3. The claim of the powers of unique memory of the Arabs, so that they had no need to write down anything.

4. *Aḥādīth* against recording *aḥādīth.*

---

1. *Origin,* 62, footnote 3.
2. Schacht, *Introduction to Islamic Law,* 34; see also. *Origin,* 149.
3. *Islām,* VI, 5-6; Rāmhurmuzī, 78b; Ḥājī Khalīfah, *Kashf al-Zunūn,* 637; Yūsuf b. Taghrī Bardī, *Nujūm Zāhirah,* i, 351; al-Kattānī, *Risālah Mustaṭrafah,* 6-7.

These points will be discussed systematically.

1. *Meaning of Tadwīn.*

Tadwīn and *Taṣnīf* do not mean writing down. According to Tāj al-'Arūs, *Dīwān* means a collection of Booklets, *(al-Dīwān Mujtama' al-Ṣuḥuf). Tadwīn* means collection *(Dawwanahū, Tadwīnan, Jama'ahū),* and *Taṣnīf* means classification according to the subjects.

The statement that اول من دون العلم ابن شهاب الزهرى was mostly understood and generally translated as meaning that the first who wrote down *aḥādīth* was al-Zuhrī; but he was neither the first recorder of *aḥādīth* nor the first compiler or composer, as we shall see later on.

2. The term *Ḥaddathanā, Akhbaranā* and *'An* etc., and their meanings will be discussed in appendix No. 1[1].

3. *Unique Memory.* It is a fact that all human beings do not have equal powers of memory or ability. Any human capacity can be improved by exercise to a certain extent. Arabs used to recite their poems from memory; they may thus have developed this power. There might have been some people with an excellent memory while others had a bad one. Therefore, to claim that depending on their powers of memory they did not need to write things down is disputable. At the same time it is also wrong to doubt the powers of memory. I have found a rare example of this in the memory of Mr. Stanley Adams about whom the Times reports, "His acute business sense and remarkable memory – after one reading of the stock exchange list he was reputed to be able to quote every price – led to many appointments over a vast range of business interests"[2]. Churchill's memory is another example.

4. THE *aḥādīth* AGAINST WRITING DOWN THE *aḥādīth*.

In *Taqyīd al-'Ilm,* al-Khaṭīb al-Baghdādī deals with the subject of the recording of *aḥādīth* at length concerning whether or not it was prohibited by the Prophet. The first part of the book is mainly concerned with the disapproval of writing; and the first

---

1. See *infra,* appendix No. I.
2. *The Daily Times,* obituary columns, June 4, 1965.

chapter of this part mainly contains *aḥādīth* from the Prophet, forbidding writing of anything except the *Qur'ān*[1].

In the second chapter he mentions the names of 6 Companions who disapproved the recording of the *aḥādīth* of the Prophet[2]. They are:

Abū Sa'īd al-Khudrī.
'Abd Allāh b. Mas'ūd.
Abū Mūsā al-Ash'arī.
Abū Hurairah.
'Abd Allah b. 'Abbās.
'Abd Allāh b. 'Umar.

In chapter 3, he provides a list of Successors which contains 12 names of persons who were supposed to be against writing down *aḥādīth*[3]. They are:

Al-A'mash.
'Abīdah.
Abū al-'Āliyah.
'Amr b. Dīnār.
Al-Ḍaḥḥāk.
Ibrāhīm al-Nakha'ī.
Abū Idrīs.
Manṣūr.
Muḥammad b. Sīrīn.
Mughīrah.
Al-Qāsim b. Muḥammad.
'Ubaid Allāh b. 'Abd Allāh.

In part two, chapter 1, he gives the names of al-Ash'arī, Ibn Mas'ūd and Ibn 'Awn who were against writing of *Ḥadīth* besides the name of the Caliph 'Umar b. al-Khaṭṭāb, who consulted the Companions over the recording of the *ḥadīth* officially and after their full support he disapproved of it[4]. But almost all of them had written down *aḥādīth* and in many cases had sent them to others. Full details will be found in the third chapter of this work, under

1. *Taqyīd*, 29-35.
2. *Taqyīd*, 36-44.
3. *Taqyīd*, 45-48.
4. *Taqyīd*, 49-57.

the very name of the scholars who are supposed to be against the writing of *aḥādīth*.

There now remain *aḥādīth* from the Prophet which forbid writing down of *Ḥadīth*[1], and these need investigating.

THE PROPHET AND THE WRITING OF AḤADĪTH.

The *aḥādīth* against the recording of *aḥādīth* are transmitted by three Companions; 1. Abū Sa'īd al-Khudrī, 2. Abū Hurairah and 3. Zaid b. Thābit.

The *ḥadīth* of Abū Sa'īd al-Khudrī had two different versions. One of them is transmitted by 'Abd al-Raḥmān b. Zaid[2]. The authorities agree unanimously that he was a weak narrator, and according to al-Ḥakīm and Abū Nu'aim he transmitted even false *aḥādīth*; and in the words of Ibn Ḥibbān, "He used to reverse *aḥādīth,* without knowing it, and put the full *isnād* for interrupted ones, so he deserved to be abandoned"[3]. Therefore, the *ḥadīth* of Abū Sa'īd al-Khudrī transmitted by 'Abd al-Raḥmān b. Zaid is weak and unacceptable.

The same 'Abd al-Raḥmān b. Zaid occurs in the *ḥadīth* of Abū Hurairah[4]. Therefore, this *ḥadīth* is also weak and unacceptable. The third companion is Zaid b. Thābit. His *ḥadīth* is *Mursal.* The transmitter from Zaid is al-Muṭṭalib b. 'Abd Allāh who did not meet Zaid[5]. So, this *ḥādīth* is not acceptable. Furthermore, *ḥadīth* from Zaid has two versions. In one of them, his disapproval of the writing of *ḥadīth* is based on the order of the Prophet[6], while in another statement it is said that he disapproved of it because the written materials were his personal opinions[7]. Therefore, this statement does not confirm his disapproval of the recording of the *aḥādīth* of the Prophet.

Now there is only one *ḥadīth* transmitted by Abū Sa'īd al-Khudrī, which reads, "Do not write from me anything except the *Qur'ān* and whoever has written anything from me other than the

1. *Taqyīd*, 29-35.
2. *Taqyīd*, 32-33.
3. *Tahd.*, vi, 177-79.
4. *Taqyīd*, 33-35.
5. *Tahd.*, x, 179.
6. *Taqyīd*, 35.
7. *Nubalā*, ii, 313; Ibn Sa'd, ii, ii, 117.

Qur'ān should erase it"[1]. Even this *ḥadīth,* which is transmitted by Abū Sa'īd al-Khudrī on the authority of the Prophet, is disputed among scholars. According to al-Bukhārī and others, it is the statement of Abū Sa'īd himself, that is erroneously attributed to the Prophet[2]. But it seems to be a *ḥadīth* coming from the Prophet, and it actually meant that nothing should be written with the *Qur'ān* on the same sheet, because this might lead someone to conclude that sentences or words written in the margin or between lines belonged to the *Qur'ān*[3]. It should be remembered that this order was given in the period when the *Qur'ān* was being revealed and when the text itself was incomplete. Otherwise, there does not appear to be any sound reason to forbid the writing of *aḥādīth.*

The Prophet himself sent hundreds of letters. Many of them were very lengthy, containing the formulae for prayers and worship[4]. According to the *Qur'an* the Prophet's conduct and deeds should be followed by the community[5]. The *Qur'ān* itself demands a record of credit transactions[6]. Therefore, it looks as if there were no general instructions not to record the *aḥādīth,* though it might have been explained by some of the scholars in this way.

On the other hand there is clear evidence to show that the Prophet approved of recording *aḥādīth*[7]. Further, we find that quite a number of Companions recorded *aḥādīth* and among them were those people who were responsible for transmitting *ḥadīth* which forbade its recording[8]. Bearing all this in mind one arrives at the conclusion that the Prophet's disapproval of writing *aḥādīth* most probably meant the writing of the *Qur'ān* and non-Qur'ānic material on the same sheet[9] because that might have led to misun-

---

1. *Taqyīd,* pp. 29-32; MU, *Zuhd* 72; *Bayān,* i, 63.
2. Ibn Ḥajar, *Fatḥ al-Bārī,* i, 208; see also al-Yamānī, *al-Anwār al-Kāshifah,* 43; also Rāmhurmuzī, 37b. He says that if the tradition is *Maḥfūẓ,* then it was in the early days of *Hijrah.*
3. See al-Khaṭṭābī, *Ma'ālim al-Sunan,* iv, 184; al-Ṣan'ānī, *Tauḍīḥ al-Afkār,* ii, 366.
4. See for detail, Ḥamīdullāh, *al-Wathā'iq al-Sīyāsiyah,* pp. 3-283 where he has given the ample references.
5. *Sūrah,* xxxiii, 21.
6. *Sūrah,* ii, 282.
7. See *infra,* 'Abd Allāh b. 'Amr. p. 43-4; An Ansarite, p. 50. Abū Shāh, p.40.
8. *Infra,* Abū Mūsā, p. 39; Abū Sa'īd, p. 39-40.
9. Ibn Ḥajar, *Fatḥ al-Bārī,* i, 218.

derstanding. There is another theory that people were forbidden to write down *aḥādīth* in early days because all attention should be paid to the *Qur'ān* and its preservation, and that later on, when there was no danger of neglecting the *Qur'ān,* the previous order was abrogated and permission was given to write *aḥādīth*[1].

Among the scholars, Sayed Rashīd Riḍā held an opposite theory. In his conception, the writing of *ḥadīth* was allowed in the early days of Islam and was forbidden at a later period[2].

This was the natural outcome of his view of the legal value of the *ḥadīth.* In his theory, the Prophet did not mean to make his *aḥādīth* an everlasting legal source or part of *Dīn*[3]. Therefore the Prophet forbade the writing down of the *aḥādīth.* This order was strictly observed by the Companions. So, the Righteous Caliphs did not write, let alone consider publishing *ḥadīth.* Moreover the senior Companions were even against the imparting of *Ḥadīth.* The Successors did not have any *Ṣaḥīfah* from the Companions and they recorded only when they were asked to do so by the Governors[4]. Rashīd Riḍā describes all *aḥādīth* coming from the Prophet and the Companions in favour of the recording of *ḥadīth,* however authentic they may be, as defective and weak or designed to serve a special purpose[5]. Whereas, in fact, there are among them *aḥādīth* which were universally accepted among the scholars as authentic. Meanwhile he gathers all the defective, weak, *Mursal* and *Maqṭū' aḥādīth,* even those that had nothing to do with the interdiction of writing, and treats them as authentic and in the sense of interdiction[6].

It is not the aim of the present study to explore the legal validity of the *Sunnah.* But going through the historical data and the cross-references to hundreds of statements one finds oneself bound to reject Riḍā's hypothesis totally. The theory is based on superficial study of *ḥadīth* literature. No scholar can find a

1. Ibn Qutaibah, *Tāwīl Mukhtalif al-Ḥadīth,* 365; al-Khaṭṭābī, *Ma'ālim al-Sunnan,* iv, 184; Ibn al-Qayyim, *Tahdhīb al-Sunan,* v, 245; Aḥmad Shākir, *Alfiyat al-Suyūṭī,* 146; *Al-Bā'ith al-Ḥathīth,* 148-9; Maudūdī, *Tarjumān,* Risalat Number, 1961, pp. 329-330.
2. Rashīd Riḍā, *Review on early compilation, Al-Manār,* x, 767.
3. Rashīd Riḍā, *op. cit.,* 768.
4. Rashīd Riḍā, *op. cit.,* 768.
5. Rashīd Riḍā, *op. cit.,* 765-6.
6. Rashīd Riḍā, *op. cit.,* 767-768. See also Abū Rayyah, *Aḍwā' 'alā al-Sunnah al-Muḥammadiyah,* pp. 42-43.

single authentic *ḥadīth* forbidding the writing of *aḥādīth* save the one of Abū Sa'īd al-Khudrī, and even this is challenged by scholars of the stature of al-Bukhārī[1].

A glance at the 3rd chapter of this work would be sufficient to refute Rashīd Riḍā's claim that the Companions and the senior Successors did not copy out *aḥādīth*.

Even if we accept Rashīd Riḍā's verdict that the *aḥdīth* were copied out by the order of the Caliph, 'Umar b. 'Abd al-'Azīz, it was not blasphemy. The *Qur'ān* itself was copied out and published by order of the Caliph 'Uthmān. He sent four copies of the *Qur'ān* to the provincial capitals[2], so that the people should recite strictly in accordance with them[3]. If these copies were meant for mass education they would have been insufficient by any standard. Therefore, even the learning of the *Qur'ān* was based on memorizing and private copying. The task was carried out by both means: by government appointed teachers[4] and by volunteer scholars[5]. The same method was adopted for the diffusion of *ḥādīth*[6]. Hence the assumption of Rashīd Riḍā that the Righteous Caliphs and the Companions did not write down *aḥādīth* or make any arrangement for their publication has no real basis.

MISINTERPRETATION OF EARLY SCHOLARS' STATEMENTS.

There have been many scholars who copied *aḥādīth* but sometimes disliked doing so. They gave reasons for their attitudes which were not based on the Prophet's order and in many cases the reasons were omitted. Sometimes when the statements were given in full they were interpreted as against writing, without any serious consideration.

Some examples:

1. It is reported that Ibrāhīm al-Nakha'ī was against writing; the reason he gave for his dislike was: "whoever writes depends on

1. Ibn Ḥajar, *Fatḥ al-Bārī,* i. 208.
2. This figure is accepted by Abū Rayyah, *op. cit.,* 206, so I am taking this hypothesis for further discussion.
3. Al-Yamānī, *op. cit.,* 45.
4. e.g. Abū al-Dardā', *Nubalā,* ii, 2.
5. e.g. Abū 'Abd al-Raḥmān al-Sulamī, *'Ilal,* i, 37.
6. Sa'd, iii, I, 201; Ḥanbal, i, 48.

it''[1]. Early scholars considered books bad stores of knowledge[2]; and the best store was one which was kept in memory and could be utilized anywhere and at any time.

2. The name of 'Āmir al-Sha'bī has been given in the lists of those against writing[3]. If one reads his statement carefully one must reach the conclusion that al-Sha'bī was not against writing. We have two of his statements on the subject. In one of them he says, ''I neither wrote with black on white nor did I ask any man to repeat a *ḥadīth* twice to me.''[4] The purpose of this statement is to show his great power of memory so that he never needed to ask anyone to repeat a *ḥādīth,* and to hear it only once was sufficient for him to memorize it. The statement has no connection with the subject of recording of *ḥādīth.* n another statement he advises his students to write down everything they hear from him, if they did not have paper they were even asked to write on walls[5].

Therefore, to present these two statements in such a way as to prove that he was first against writing and then in its favour[6] is extremely ingenious as an explanation but extremely doubtful as an argument.

Summing up the argument, al-Khaṭīb describes reasons for disliking recording[7]. He gives several reasons but there is no evidence that the interdiction of writing was based on any Prophetic order. Many scholars who disliked writing at one time or another purely on personal prejudice, nevertheless committed *aḥādīth* to writing.

The *aḥādīth* related from the Prophet concerning the interdiction of writing were precautions required by a specific set of circumstances motivated by the care, lest the *Qur'ān* be mixed with non-Qur'anic material. The writing of *aḥādīth* by a vast number of Companions[8] is itself a proof that the prohibition of writing of *aḥādīth* (if any) was neither a general, nor a permanent order.

---

1. Sa'd, vi, 189.
2. *Taq yīd,* 58.
3. *Taqyīd,* 48, footnote by Eche; Maḥammad 'Ajjāj, *al-Sunnah Qabl al-Tadwīn,* p.323.
4. *'Ilm,* 11b.
5. *Taq yīd,* 100.
6. Muḥammad 'Ajjāj, *op. cit.,* 325.
7. *Taq yīd,* 57.
8. For detail of their writings, see *infra,* 3rd chapter.

In the 2nd and 3rd chapters of the 2nd part of *al-Taqyīd,* al-Khatīb gives some examples of those who drote down *aḥādīth* but ordered that these be erased on their death. He also gives examples of those who regretted having erased the *aḥādīth.*[1]

In the 3rd part, al-Khatīb gives details of *aḥādīth* coming from the Prophet in favour of recording; then he provides the list of Companions, Successors and others who recorded *aḥādīth*[2]. It is hoped the next chapter of this work will be more comprehensive than al-Khatīb's in this respect.

Before concluding this chapter, one need mention only one more point. Going through all these statements on the writing of the *Ḥadīth* or its interdiction, Goldziher deduced from them a strange conclusion. In short, that there were two groups in the early days of Islam; a) *Ahl al-Ḥadīth,* who were pro-*Ḥadīth,* and b) *Ahl al-Rāi'*, who were anti-*Ḥadīth. Ahl al-Rāi* forged traditions relating to the interdiction of writing, so that they could prove untrustworthiness of the *Ḥadīth* and get rid of it. This was against the interest of *Ahl al-Ḥadīth,* so they invented *aḥādīth* in favor of recording, to prove its trustworthiness[3].

A glance at the names of the scholars – who are said to be against writing – is sufficient to refute this conclusion of Goldziher. The most famous Scholars, who were supposed to be extremists against writing, were Ibn Sīrīn and 'Abīdah who were *muḥaddithīn.* Among the most famous *Fuqahā'* who wrote down and were in favour of recording of the *aḥādīth* were *Ahl al-Rāi* as Ḥammād, Ibrāhīm, Al-A'mash, al-Zuhrī, Abū Ḥanifah, Abū Yūsuf, Mālik and al-Thaurī. Secondly there were no *Fuqahā'* at that time without a sound knowledge of *aḥādīth.* A *muḥaddith* might not have been a *Faqīh,* but a *Faqīh* was – at that time – a *muḥaddith* versed in the science of analogy.

1. *Taqyīd,* 58-63.
2. *Taqyīd,* 64-113.
3. Goldziher, *Muhd Stud,* ii, 194 sqq. as quoted by Y. Eche, *Taqyīd,* margin note 16.

CHAPTER III

PRE-CLASSICAL "ḤADĪTH" LITERATURE

Before giving details of the literary activities of the early *Muḥaddithīn,* it is necessary to discuss the problems with which the chapter is concerned.

1. The terms of *Nuskhah, Ṣaḥīfah, Kitāb, Risālah* etc., and their meanings.
2. Classification of literary period.
3. Methods employed to establish dates of birth and death of scholars.

THE TERM *Kitāb, Nuskhah,* etc.

The word *Kitāb* generally has two meanings, a letter or a book. In many cases the context helps to make clear a possible ambiguity as to whether it means a book or a letter. In some cases even context does not give any clue. As a general rule we may decide that whenever this word occurs in reference to the Companions' writings — with a few exceptions e.g. 'Abd Allāh b. 'Amr b. al-'Āṣ, Ibn 'Abbās, Jābir etc., — it may be taken in the sense of a letter, while in the writings of the Successors, it should be taken as meaning a book[1], except where the context suggests another meaning. I do not mean that the word *Kitāb* when translated as a 'letter' means a personal letter unrelated to educational activities. These letters were, in fact, the genesis of the later work.

1. This differenciation in translation is based on the volume of their literary activities.

Nuskhah AND *Ṣaḥīfah.*

These two words were used, it appears to me, synonymously. Al-Dhahabī says, Hammām has a famous *Nuskhah* from Abū Hurairah — "*Nuskhah Mashhūrah*"[1], while the same work is mentioned by the name of *Ṣaḥīfah Hammām*[2].

Nuskhah.

This word means "copy" and perhaps the word is derived from the very practice of copying out *aḥādīth* from teachers' books. It is interesting to note that they sometimes use two words: *Al-Aṣl* and *Nuskhah.* Ibn Bashkuwāl describes 'Abd al-Raḥmān b. Muḥammad as saying, "He did not lend his *Al-Aṣl* (original books), and if someone requested him persistently, then he used to give it to a scribe who copied it and revised it, then handed it to the borrower"[3]. One more example may be added to clarify this point. Abū Ja'far says that Ibn Lahī'ah brought his books before the scholars and dictated to the students. Some of them were good at writing while others committed many mistakes. Later Ibn Lahī'ah did not produce his books. So anyone who wanted *aḥādīth* from him used to go to his students to copy out the book and to read it to Ibn Lahī'ah. Therefore, the *aḥādīth* of anyone who found a correct copy of the book فمن وقع على نسخة صحيحة were correct, otherwise there were many discrepancies[4].

Ibn Abū Ḥātim al-Rāzī says that Ibn Wahb and Ibn al-Mubārak used to follow the original books — *Uṣūl* — of Ibn Lahī'ah, while others used to write down from copies — *Nusakh* —[5].

Thus the word *Nuskhah* may have derived from the fact that the students used to copy out from teachers' books. As it was coppied on sheets — *Ṣaḥīfah* or *Ṣuḥuf* — the word *Ṣaḥīfah* was employed as well. *Ṣaḥīfah* was known to Arabs even before Islām[6].

---

1. *Ḥuffāẓ*, i, 89.
2. See *Ṣaḥīfah Ḥammām*, edited by M. Ḥamīdullāh. For further example of synonymous usage, *Tahd.*, xi, 253, and 254 for Ṣaḥifah/Nuskhah of Ibn Mauhab.
3. Ibn Bashkuwāl, *al-Ṣilah*, 299.
4. Fasawī, iii, 136b.
5. Rāzī, ii, ii, 147-8.
6. Nāṣir al-Asad, *Muṣādir al-Shi'r*, pp. 70-71; 133.

word is also used in the *Qur'ān,* e.g. *Ṣuḥuf Ibrāhīm wa Mūsā*[1]. Though the word originally means a sheet, yet it was not used in its strict sense and was sometimes employed for a booklet. The *Ṣaḥīfah* of Hammām, for instance, contains 138 *aḥādīth* and covers a space of 18 pages in print[2]. There are ample references describing the number of *aḥādīth* contained in a certain *Ṣaḥīfah*[3]. There was another famous *Ṣaḥīfah* of 'Abd allāh b. 'Amr b. al-'Āṣ, called *al-Ṣaḥīfah al-Ṣādiqah,* which consisted of hundreds of *aḥādīth*[4], which, obviously, could not be written on a single sheet. Therefore, the word *Ṣaḥīfah* or *Nuskhah* means a book or booklet.

Kurrāsah. This word means a booklet or a note-book.

Risālah.

This word also means a letter as well as a book. We find a reference to the word *Risālah* in the statement of Ibn Sīrīn, saying that the *Risālah* of Samurah to his son contained much knowledge[5]. The portion of this *Risālah,* which is still preserved in *Mu'jam* of al-Ṭabarānī, indicates that the *Risālah* was a lengthy one[6]. Another book which bears the name of *Risālah* is that of al-Shāfi'ī, which covers some 600 pages[7]. On the basis of these facts, therefore, in this chapter the terms *Ṣaḥīfah, Risāla, Huskhaḥ* and *Kitāb* will be translated as 'book'. The nature of the books in most cases is not specified. A book might contain 5 or 500 or 5000 *aḥādīth.*

---

1. *The Qur'ān, Sūrah* 87, verse 18, 19; for further usage see Fuwād 'Abd al-Bāqī, *Mu'jam al-Mufahras,* p. 403.
2. See *Ṣaḥīfah Hammām,* Arabic edition, Damascus, pp. 29-47.
3. See for example:
   (i) *Nuskhah of Bishr* from Zubair about 150 *aḥādīth, Mīzān,* i, 316.
   (ii) Nuskhah of Mughīrah about 100 *aḥādīth, Kāmil,* i, 316b.
   (iii) Nuskhah in the possession of Ibn Mahdī containing only 4 *aḥādīth, Kāmil,* i, 36a.
4. 'Ajjāj, *Sunnah Qabl al-Tadwīn,* pp. 349-50, giving a number of 1,000 *aḥ ādīth,* citing *Usd al-Ghābah,* but his reference does not agree with his deduction, see *Usd al-Ghābah,* iii, 233.
5. *Tahd.,* iv., 236.
6. Ṭkabīr, iii, 220-226.
7. Al-Shāfi'ī, *al-Risālah,* ed. Aḥmad Shākir.

INFORMATION CONCERNING PRE-CLASSICAL ḤADĪTH LITERATURE AND THE METHOD OF ITS ARRANGEMENT IN THIS CHAPTER.

As a general rule, the books are recorded under the names of the scholars from whom the students derived their written collections. Usually the method by which the material was collected by the students is not disclosed, whether the students copied it out from particular books or recorded from dictations or lectures, or compiled their collections from memory in the later periods. This last method was very rare and wherever a reference has been found to this practice, it has been described as such.

In short, where a student is described as having written *aḥādīth* of a certain scholar, his name is listed under the name of that scholar.

Here I have tried to utilize the explicit references to writings or written records, without utilizing the logical approach.

One point remains to be clarified in this context. There is not a single chapter in any book dealing with *aḥādīth* where one may find references to the early books on *aḥādīth.* The books are mentioned here and there, especially when the scholars criticize someone or compare two Scholars, A and B. Then sometimes they say that 'A' was *Ṣāḥib Kitāb.* This means that 'B' was famous for his memory while 'A' depended mainly on books; meanwhile, whether or not 'B' was in possession of books is not disclosed. In this statement "*Kāna Ṣāḥib Kitāb*" does not mean that he had only one book, he might have had 10 or 20 books, but in this context it is only used in the sense of dependence upon the book. Yet according to English it must be translated to mean 'he had a book'. Wherever a sentence of this type occurs in this chapter, it usually has the meaning that the man depended on books. Where the context requires any other meaning it has been specified.

THE CLASSIFICATION OF THE LITERARY PERIOD.

I have tried to cover the literary activities concerning *ḥadīth* up to about 150 A.H. The main point of interest in confining the period of research within this limit relates to the fact that during this period books began to appear in voluminous quantities. The pattern of composing books changed from the mere recording of *aḥādīth* at random or composing of booklets on a single topic, to cumulative writings incorporating scores of topics in one book e.g.

Muwaṭṭa' of Ibn Abū Dhi'b, *Muwaṭṭa'* of Mālik, the books of Ibn Juraij, Ibn Isḥāq, Ibn Abū 'Arūbah, Ma'mar b. Rāshid, al-Auzā'ī, Sufyān al-Thaurī, and so forth. Most of these authors died about 150-160 A.H. In later periods, this material was utilized by the classical authors, and edited with the utmost care, as is clear from the style of Muslim b. al-Ḥajjāj, al-Bukhārī, etc.

I have divided this period somewhat arbitrarily. It is the aim of the chapter to throw some light on the early literature of *ḥadīth,* with special reference to the first and second century A.H. separately. Classification on this basis is very difficult and therefore arbitrary. There were many people who were born in the early first century and lived for a considerable period into the second century as well. Therefore, I have divided the scholars and their activities as follows:

1. The writings and works of the Companions.

2. The writings and works of the Successors who lived mostly in the first century.

3. The writings and works of the scholars whose literary careers cover the later part of the first century as well as considerable period of the second century of the *Hijrah.* In this class I have listed all the scholars who were born up to or about 65 A.H., maintaining that the 35 years time and over before the end of the century was sufficient for them to begin their literary career in the later part of the first century.

4. The writings and works of the scholars who were born between 70 A.H. and 110 A.H. on the assumption that every one in this category had sufficient time for literary work, up to 150 A.H. The activities of the 1st and 2nd groups and roughly half of the 3rd, belong to the first century and the rest to the early second century.

Dating of Scholars' Lives.

In this classification the dates of birth and death are essential. In some cases both dates are given by historians, while in other cases no date is given or only one of the two dates is given. Sometimes different dates of birth or death of the same person are given, e.g. al-Zuhrī is said to have been born in 50, 51, 56, 58 and to have died in 123, 124 or 125 etc[1]. In such contradictory cases

1. Fischer, 73-4.

one of the dates has been arbitrarily chosen. It is doubtful whether, if I had investigated all the statements of their births and deaths, I would have been able to reach any definite conclusion. Moreover, as I shall be dealing with what amounts to about 500 Scholars such an investigation would be excessively lengthy as well as fruitless.

If only the date of death is given, I have either subtracted from it 60 to 65 years as an average span of a man's life, to establish the approximate date of birth. Or I have gone through the names of his teachers and tried to recognize the one who died earliest and then subtracted 20 from this date as being the average age for the beginning of the study of *ḥadīth.* In most cases the Scholars must have been born much earlier than the assumed dates, but there is no adequate means of ascertaining the actual dates. For example, if a man narrated *aḥādīth* from Ḥasan al-Baṣrī (d. 110), we may say with a fair amount of confidence that the man was born about 90 A.H., as according to the customs of the time, they usually began to learn *ḥadīth* in their twenties[1]. Moreover, such a student would not necessarily have gone to a teacher on his death-bed. He might have attended the lectures well before the death of his teacher and may have accompanied him for years.

This supposition cannot be contradicted on the basis of the practice of the later periods when people began to take children as young as 2 and 3 years to listen to the reading of certain books[2], because those books had been compiled a long time before and it became a fashion to have an authority to transmit them with *Isnād ʻĀlī.*

Where no date of birth or death of a scholar is available, the above mentioned method is utilized to establish an approximate date of birth, i.e. going through his teachers to find out an approximate birth date then adding about 65 years to obtain a rough date of his death. So, if a man transmitted from Nāfi' (d. 117) then the *Rāwī* may have been born about 95 A.H. and have lived to (95 +65) about 160 A.H.

---

1. See *infra,* chapter iv, pp. 197-8.
2. See for example Qāsim b. Ja'far heard *Kitāb al-Sunan* for the first time while he was in this second year. *Kifāyah,* 64.

I. WRITINGS OF AND FROM THE COMPANIONS

1. Abū Ayyūb al-Anṣārī, Khālid b. Zaid (d. 52 A.H.)[1].

The following derived *aḥādīth* from him in written form:

1. His nephew. Abū Ayyūb wrote down some *aḥādīth* and sent them to his nephew[2].

2. Another member of his family Ayyūb b. Khālid b. Ayyūb related a collection of *aḥādīth* from his father who related them from his grand-father. The collection consists of 112 *aḥādīth*[3].

It is not clear whether the collection was made by Abū Ayyūb himself, by his son, or by his grand-son.

2. Abū Bakr al-Ṣiddīq. The First Caliph (13. A.H.).

It is said that he wrote down 500 *aḥādīth* of the Prophet. Later on he was reported to have burnt them saying that he might have heard these *aḥādīth* from men who, he thought, were trustworthy, but who, as a matter of fact, were not[4]. Al-Dhahabī describes this statement as false[5]. In fact Abū Bakr was the man most closely attached to the Prophet. Had he wanted to make a collection of *aḥādīth,* he would not have needed a medium between him and the Prophet. Many scholars have quoted this statement without examining its authenticity or referring to its refutation[6]. It is quoted by Abū Rayyah as evidence against the writing down of *aḥādīth*[7]. Had it been authentic, it would have been a proof of early writing of *aḥādīth,* as the burning of the *Ṣaḥīfah* was for quite different reasons. It implies also that at the time of writing he did not know the interdiction of the Prophet.

---

1. Khazrajī, 86.
2. Ḥanbal, v, 413.
3. Ḥanbal, v, 423.
4. *Ḥuffāẓ,* i, 5; 'Alī al-Muttaqī, *Kanz al-'Ummāl,* v, 237.
5. *Ḥuffāẓ,* i, 5; where he says, *La Yaṣiḥḥ* other scholars also rejected its *isnād.* See 'Alī al-Muttaqī, *op. cit.,* v, 237.
6. Ḥamīdullāh, *Ṣaḥifah Hammām,* 28-9; Gīlānī, *Tadwīn Ḥadīth,* 285; 'Ajjāj, *al-Sunnah qabl al-Tadwīn,* 309-10; Abū Rayyah, *Aḍwā' 'alā al-Sunnah,* 42.
7. Abū Rayyah, *op. cit.,* 42.

The following derived *aḥādīth* from Abū Bakr in written form:

1. 'Amr b. al-'Āṣ. Abū Bakr sent a letter to 'Amr b. al-'Āṣ, which contained *aḥādīth*[1].

2. Anas b. Mālik. Abū Bakr wrote a letter – *Kitāb* – on taxation for Anas b. Mālik, who was the governor of al-Baḥrain. This booklet seems to be a copy of the Prophet's letter – *Kitāb* – concerning the rates of *Zakāt*[2].

3. Abu Bakrah al-Rhaqafī, Nufai' b. Masrūḥ (d. 51 A.H.)[3].

He sent a letter to his son, the Governor of Sijistān, which contained the Prophet's sayings relating to the business of justice[4].

4. Abu Hind al-Dārī[5]. Makḥūl wrote down *aḥādīth* from him[6].

5. Abu Hurairah (19 B.H. - 59 A.H.)[7].

He joined the Prophet at Khaibar in the year 7 A.H. He had no occupation or any interest other than gaining knowledge. He lived in Madīnah depending upon the Prophet for his food and other necessities. He accompanied the Prophet for four years[8]. This is the period between his arrival at Khaibar and the death of the Prophet. According to some other statements he accompanied the Prophet for three years[9]. He was sent to Bahrain[10] with 'Alā' al-Ḥaḍramī. Thus, if we subtract this period of absence from four years, it becomes three years.

According to Abū Rayyah he accompanied the Prophet for only 21 months[11]. He thinks that 'Alā' remained as Governor of Baḥrain till he died during the Caliphate of 'Umar, who then appointed Abū Hurairah in his place. But historical facts are against this assumption. 'Alā' himself was discharged from his duties, and in 9 A.H. the post was filled by Abān b. Sa'īd[12]. Most probably Abū Hurairah also left the office at that time and returned to

1. Ṭkabīr, i, 5a.
2. BU, *Zakāt*, 33; 34; 35; 38; *Ḥiyal*, 3; Ibn Mājah, *Zakāt*, 10; A.D. *ḥadīth* No. 1567; Ibn Jārūd, *Muntaqā, ḥadīth* No. 342; Ḥanbal, i, 11; *Taqyīd*, 87.
3. *Istī'āb*, No. 2877.
4. Ḥanbal, v, 36; MU, *Aqḍiyah*, 16; Nas, ii, 307; Dāraquṭnī, 512.
5. *Iṣābah*, iv, 212.
6. N. Abbot. *Studies in Arabic Literary Papyri*, ii, 238.
7. *Istī'āb*, No. 3208, p. 1772.
8. *Nubalā*, ii, 426.
9. Sa'd, iv, ii, 54; *Nubalā*, ii, 426.
10. *Nubalā*, ii, 429.
11. Abū Rayyah, *Shaikh al-Maḍīrah*, 45.
12. *Nubalā*, i, 189.

Madīnah. We find him at the end of the year 9 A.H. at Makka in the pilgrimage[1]. This is the claim of Abū Hurairah, and his statement is attested to by 'Abd Allāh b. 'Abbās as well[2]. So there is no sound reason to reject this statement and to believe that 'Alā' held the office continuously[3]. Even if 'Alā' had held the office, there would not have been any logical obligation to prevent Abū Hurairah's departure from 'Alā.

Here, it is better to clarify two more points raised by Abū Rayyah, who charged Abū Hurairah with favouring the Umayyads, yet was unable to produce any authentic *ḥadīth* from Abū Hurairah against 'Alī and in favour of the Umayyads. Abū Rayyah himself gives us *aḥādīth* transmitted by Abū Hurairah in favor of 'Alī and against the Umayyads[4]. If we go through the *Nuskhah* of Suhail, *ḥadīth* No. 14, we find Abū Hurairah giving 'Alī a place even higher than 'Umar in the battle of Khaibar. Thus it is inconceivable that he was against 'Alī. To interpret all these *aḥādīth* , as is done by Abū Rayyah[5], in the sense that he circulated them in order to blackmail Mu'āwiyah is ridiculous. Equally ridiculous is the claim of Abū Rayyah and others in which they state that Abū Hurairah used to eat with Mu'āwiyah and to pray with 'Alī[6], as it was historically impossible[7].

Abū Rayyah doubts Abū Hurrairah's honesty and bases his verdict on the practice of 'Umar, as he distributed the money which he brought from Baḥrain[8]. But this was the usual practice of 'Umar with many other Governors[9].

Abū Hurairah lived only three years with the Prophet, yet he transmitted more *aḥādīth* than any other Companion. According

1. Balādhurī, *Ansāb al-Ashrāf,* i, 383; Khaithamah, iii, 76a.
2. Khaithamah, iii, 76b.
3. Abū Rayyah, *Shaikh al-Maḍīrah,* 45.
4. *Ibid.,* 125, 142.
5. Abū Rayyah, *op, cit., 126.*
6. Abū Rayyah, *op. cit.,* 30.
7. See for its condemnation by Ṭāhā Ḥusain, *The Daily Jamhūriyah,* 25.11.1958 as it is published by Zakariyā 'Alī Yūsuf in *Difā' an al-Ḥadīth,* p.114.
8. Abū Rayyah, *op. cit.,* pp. 147-8.
9. Balādhurī, *Futūḥ al-Buldān,* i, 257. For other examples, see 'Umar's practice with Sa'd b. Abū Waqqās; Sa'd, iii, ii, 105; and with Khālid b. al-Walīd, *Nubalā,* i, 273; and with Abū Mūsā al-Ash'arī, Ibn 'Abd Rabbih, *'Iqd,* i, 52; and with al-Ḥārith b. Ka'b, *ibid.*; and with Mu'ādh b. Jabal, *Nubalā,* i, pp. 325-6.

According to Ibn al-Jauzī, there are 5374 *aḥādīth* transmitted by him in Musnad Baqī and 3848 *aḥādīth* in the Musnad of Ibn Ḥanbal. According to Aḥmad Shākir, after substracting repeated *aḥādīth,* there remain 1579 *aḥādīth* transmitted by Abū Hurairah[1]. In a period of three years he observed and learnt some 1500 traditions, which are a mixture of verbal and practical *Sunnah.* This does not seem to be a large number, although both in his life-time as well as in the later period he was charged with having transmitted a vast number of *aḥādīth.* Yet all those who have criticized him, have praised him one time or another[2].

We are not sure whether or not he had any written collection of *aḥādīth* in his early life, but mention is made in a later period of the books he had in his possession:

1. Ḥasan b. 'Amr al-Damarī saw many books of *aḥādīth* in Abū Hurairah's possession[3].

2. It is said that Bashīr b. Nahīk made his collection, copying the book of Abū Hurairah, but the *Isnād* of this statement is somewhat defective[4].

The following derived *aḥādīth* from him in written form:

1. 'Abd al-'Azīz b. Marwān. He had almost all the *aḥādīth* of Abū Hurairah in written form[5].

2. Abū Ṣāliḥ al-Sammān. He transmitted from Abū Hurairah and others. Al-A'mash wrote down 1000 *aḥādīth* from him[6] and Ibrāhīm al-Nakha'ī (d. 96) made his collection of Abū Hurairah's *aḥādīth* through al-A'mash-Abū Ṣāliḥ-Abū Hurairah[7]. It is not mentioned whether or not Abū Ṣāliḥ himself had any

---

1. Aḥmad Shākir, *Sharḥ alfiyat al-Suyūṭī,* 220-21.
2. See e.g. Ibn 'Umars saying, Sa'd, iv, i, 63; Ṭalḥah b. Ubaid Allāh's saying, *'Ilal,* i, 72. See also the saying of 'Āishah where she objected to his method of imparting traditions, not the traditions themselves. Ibn Ḥibbān, *Saḥīḥ,* i, 101.
3. Ibn Ḥajar, *Fatḥ al-Bārī,* i, 217; al-Kattānī, *Trātīb,* ii, 246; *'Ilal,* 120a.
4. *Sharḥ 'Ilal,* 54b.
5. Sa'd, vii, ii, 157; erroneously Ḥamīdullāh mentioned it under 'Umar b. 'Abd al-'Azīz. See *Ṣaḥīfah Hammām,* 39.
6. Ja'd, 80.
7. *'Ilal,* i, 140.

written collection, but his son Suhail had a written collection from him. Therefore, most probably Abū Ṣāliḥ had a written collection from Abū Hurairah.

3. 'Aqbah b. Abū al-Ḥasnā'. He transmitted a book *(Nuskhah)* from Abū Hurairah. A copy of this *Nuskhah* was in the possession of al-Dhahabī[1].

4. Bashīr b. Nahīk. He made his collection from Abū Hurairah, and presented the book to him and even obtained Abū Hurairah's permission to transmit it[2].

5. Hammām b. Munabbih. He transmitted from Abū Hurairah a *Ṣaḥīfah* (book) which has been edited and published[3].

6. Marwān B. Ḥakam. He made a collection of Abū Hurairah's *aḥādīth*. It was copied by Abū al-Za'zā[4].

7. Muḥammad b. Sīrīn. The book was written on an old parchment, and it began: "This is what Abū Hurairah imparted to us: Abū al-Qāsim (The Prophet) said so, Abū al-Qāsim said so. There were circles after every ten *aḥādīth*. There were sayings of Abū Hurairah separately". The book was in the possession of Yahyā b. Sīrīn, because in his later days Muḥammad b. Sīrīn did not like to have any sort of books[5].

8. Sa'īd al-Maqburī. Muḥammad b. 'Ajlān had the book of Sa'īd which he had compiled from Abū Hurairah[6].

9. 'Ubaid Allāh b. 'abd Allāh b. Mauhab al-Taimī. His son related a *Nuskhah* (book) from him most of which consisted of defective *aḥādīth*[7].

---

1. *Mīzān,* iii, 85.
2. Sa'd, vii, i, 162; *'Ilal,* i, 43; Abū Khaithamah, *'Ilm,* 11a; 11b; Fasawī, iii, 264b; *'Ilal Tirmidhī,* ii, 239; Rāmhurmūzī, 63b; *Kifāyah,* 275; *Taqyīd,* 101; *Jāmi',* 138b; *Sharḥ 'Ilal,* 54b; 60b; *Islām,* iii, 345; *Tahd.,* i, 470.
3. *Ṣaḥīfat Hammām,* edited by Dr. Muḥammad Ḥamīdullāh, 1961, 5th edition, Hyderabad Deccan, India.
4. *Nubalā,* ii, 431; Ibn Kathīr, *Bidāyah,* viii, 106.
5. Fasawī, iii, 14b; *Imlā,* 173; *Jāmi',* 56b.
6. *Thiqāt,* 599; *Tahd.,* ix, 342.
7. *Majrūḥīn,* 250b; *Tahd.,* xi, 254; see also page 253.

5. Abū Mūsā al-Ash'arī, 'Abd Allāh b. Qais (d. 42)[1].

It is reported that he was not in favour of writing down *ḥādīth*. He even erased the writing of his students[2].

'Abd Allāh b. 'Abbās derived *aḥādīth* from him in written form. Abū Mūsā wrote some *aḥādīth* and sent them to 'Abd Allāh b. 'Abbās[3].

6. Abū Rāfi' (d. before 40 A.H.)[4].

The following derived *aḥādīth* from him in written form:

'Abd Allāh b. 'Abbās. He used to go to Abū Rāfi' and ask him about the Prophet's deeds and sayings on certain occasions. Then he or his slaves would write the answers.[5]

Abū Bakr b. 'Abd al-Raḥmān b. Hishām. Abū Rāfi' gave him a booklet (*Kitāb*) which described the Prophet's method of commencing prayers and invocation of God[6].

7. Abū Sa'īd al-Khudrī, Sa'd b. Mālik (d. 74 A.H.)[7].

Abū Sa'īd is the main narrator of a *ḥādīth* from the Prophet which forbade the writing down of *ḥadīth*[8]. He did not agree with his students who wanted to make written collections of *aḥādīth*[9], but he himself transcribed *aḥādīth*[10]. Once he was informed about a *Fatwā* (legal decision) of Ibn 'Abbās which was against the Prophet's *ḥadīth*; then he said to his informer: "We shall write to him, then he will not give these decisions to anybody"[11]. It is not known whether or not he wrote but Ibn 'Abbās later changed

1. *Istī'āb,* No. 3193.
2. Rāmhurmuzī, 36b; *Taqyīd,* 39-41.
3. Ḥanbal, iv, 396; 414.
4. Khalifah, Ṭabaqat, I, 19; see also *Istī'āb,* No. 2948.
5. *Taqyīd,* 91-92; *Iṣābah,* No. 4781; al-Kattānī, *Trātīb,* ii, 247.
6. *Kifāyah,* 330-31.
7. *Istī'āb,* No. 2997.
8. MU, *Zuhd,* 72; *Taqyīd,* 29-33.
9. *Taqyīd,* 36-38.
10. *Taqyīd,* 93; Ibn al-Qayyim, *Tahdhīb al-Sunan,* v, 248.
11. Ḥanbal, iii, 60.

his Fatwā. Had he written the letter, it would probably have referred to the Prophet's *ḥadīth.*

8. Abū Shāh, a Yamanite.

He heard the sermon of the Prophet at Mecca in 8 A.H., on the occasion of its conquest. He requested the Prophet to have this sermon taken down in written form. The Prophet ordered someone: "Write it for Abū Shāh"[1].

9. Abū Umāmah, Ṣudai b. 'Ajlān (10 B.H. - 81 A.H.)[2].

Al-Ḥasan b. Jābir asked him about the recording of *ḥadīth* and he approved of it[3].

Al-Qusim al-Shami, perhaps, recorded *aḥādīth* from him.[4]

10. Abd Allāh b. 'Abbās (3 B.H. - 68 A.H.)[5].

He was a cousin of the Prophet. He was known for a keen mind and love of knowledge. After the death of the Prophet he asked one of his Ansari friends to join him in seeking knowledge. This man laughed at him and left him. So Ibn 'Abbās devoted himself to learning[6].

Ruth states that "he is one of the few Meccans reputed to have been able to write before the days of Islām"[7], though he was born in the Islamic period!

He used to sit outside the doors of the Companions in very hot and windy weather. When they saw him, they would say: "O cousin of the Prophet...if you had sent someone we would have come to you". The usual reply of Ibn 'Abbās was, 'No, I must come to you'. Then he used to ask for *aḥādīth*[8].

He was so eager for knowledge that he would ask as many as 30 Companions about a single incident[9].

---

1. Ḥanbal, II, 238; BU, *'Ilm,* 39; *Luqṭah,* 7; *Diyāt,*[8]; MU, *Ḥajj,* 447; Tirmidhi, ii, 110; A.D. *ḥadīth,* No. 4505; *Muntaqā,* No. 508; Rāmhurmazi, 34a; *Kifāyah,* 53; *Isti'āb,* No. 3028.
2. *Isti'āb,* No. 1237.
3. Sa'd, vii, ii, 132; Dārimī, 1, 127; *Taqyīd,* 98.
4. Abdur Razāq, Al-Musannaf 1, 50-1.
5. *Isti'āb,* No. 1588; *Iṣābah,* 4781.
6. Sa'd, ii, ii, 121; Fasawī, ii, 173a; Ṭ kabīr, v, 139a. *Iṣābah,* II, 323, No 4781; *Jāmi',* 24a.
7. Ruth, *Umayyad Libr., A.S.J.L.,* liv, p. 49.
8. Sa'd, ii, ii, 121; Fasawī, ii, 173a.
9. *Nubalā,* iii, 231.

His recording of aḥādīth.

It seems that he wrote what he heard[1] and sometimes even employed his slaves for this purpose[2]. After prayers he would sit down to recite the *Qur'ān* with his slaves behind him. If he found any verse which needed investigation of its meaning he repeated it and the slaves noted it down; then he used to inquire about it[3].

His method of teaching.

His lectures covered most of the knowledge and the subjects of those days. It seems that he fixed certain days for certain subjects, e.g. one day for law, the next day for commentary on the *Qur'ān*, the third day for *al-Maghāzī,* (war) etc.[4] At the time of the pilgrimage his teaching circle was much enlarged[5]. He even had an interpreter to translate the questions and answers for non-Arabs[6].

There are some statements giving the impression that he disapproved of the writing of *ḥadīth*[7]. On the other hand there are statements encouraging the recording of *ḥadīth*[8]. If we bear in mind his personal literary activities while he was learning and afterwards when he was teaching, we need to explain his discouragement of writing for some other reason than the prophet's prohibition. He had a copy of the legal judgements of 'Alī, and copied it for one of his students[9]. At more advanced age when his eyes failed him, people used to read his books to him[10]. Later, some of his books were in the possession of his slave-student Kuraib, who entrusted them to Mūsā b. 'Uqbah[11].

---

1. Sa'd, ii, ii, 123; *Taqyīd,* 92.
2. Al-Kattānī, *Tarātīb,* ii, 247.
3. Fasawī, ii, 172b.
4. Sa'd, ii, ii, 122; *Nubalā,* iii, 235; see also Sa'd, ii, ii, 121; *Usd al-Ghābah,* iii, 193; *Iṣābah,* ii, 234. See for his lengthy discussions, Sa'd, vi, 79; Dulābī, ii, 126.
5. *Istī'āb,* No. 1588.
6. BU, *Aḥkām,* 40.
7. *'Ilal,* i, 394; Khaithamah, iii, 52a; *Taqyīd,* 42-43.
8. *'Ilal,* i, 42; *Taqyīd,* 92.
9. MU, *Introduction,* p. 13.
10. *'Ilal Tirmidhī,* ii, 238; *Kifāyah,* 263; *Nubalā,* iii, 238.
11. Sa'd, v, 216; Khaithamah, iii, 111 a-b.

The following derived *aḥādīth* from him in written form:

'Ali b. Abdullāh b. 'Abbās[1].

'Amr b. Dīnār[2].

Al-Ḥakam b. Miqsam[3].

Ibn Abū Mulaikah[4].

'Ikrimah. He transmitted the commentary on the *Qur'ān* as well[5].

Kuraib[6].

Mujāhid[7].

Najdah, a Kharijite. He asked certain questions and Ibn 'Abbās answered them saying that people were accusing him of correspondence with a Kharijite, "If I were not afraid of hiding the knowledge (and of the severe punishment) I would not have replied to him"[8].

Sa'īd b. Jubair[9].

11. 'Abd Allāh b. Abū Awfā (d. 86)[10].

The following derived *aḥādīth* from him in written form:

Sālim, the scribe of 'Abd Allāh. Ibn Abū Awfā, wrote to 'Umar b. 'Ubaidullāh, recording some *aḥādīth.* Sālim made a copy of them and transmitted them[11].

Sālim provided a copy of those *aḥādīth* for one of his friends on request[12].

---

1. Ibn Sa'd, v, 216.
2. Fasawī, iii, 5b; *Zur'ah,* 78b.
3. Al-Sakhawi, Fathul Mughīth II, 138.
4. Ḥanbal, i, 343; 351; BU, ii, 116; MU, *Introd.,* pp. 13-14.
5. *Fihrist,* 34.
6. Sa'd, v, 216; Khaithamah, iii, 111 a-b.
7. *Fihrist,* 33; Dhahabī, *Tafsīr wa al-Mufassirūn,* i, 104, quoting Ibn Taymīyah.
8. *Amwāl,* 333-35; Ḥanbal, i, 224; 248; 294; 308; MU, *Jihād,* 137-141; Nas, ii, 177; *Muntaqā, aḥādīth,* No. 1085; 1086; Zanjuwaih, 124 a-b; Marwazī, *al-Sunnah,* 44; Ṭkabīr, v, 159 a-b.
9. Sa'd, vi, 179; *'Ilal,* i, 50; 394; Fasawī, ii, 166b; *Zura'h,* 119a; Darimī, i, 128; *Taqyīd,* 102. Rāmhurmuzī, 35a; 35b. Tāwūs Testifies Sa'īd's writing in the presence of Ibn 'Abbās, Rāmhurmuzī, 35b.
10. *Usd al-Ghābah,* iii, 122.
11. MU, *Jihād,* 20; al-Qaisarānī, 189; *Tahd.,* iii, 431.
12. Ḥanbal, iv, 353-54.

'Umar b. 'Ubaidullāh. 'Abd Allāh b. Abū Awfā wrote some *aḥādīth* of the Prophet regarding the law of war and sent them to 'Umar[1].

12. ABD ALLĀH B. 'AMR B. AL-'ĀṢ (27 B.H. - 63 A.H.)[2].

He embraced Islam before his father[3] and emigrated to Madinah after 7 A.H. He knew the Hebrew language as well[4]. found some books of *Ahl Al-Kitāb* at Yarmūk and used to read them[5] and even transmitted some knowledge from them. Perhaps he studied these books with Sarij of al-Yarmūk, a *Kitābī* in his early days[6].

His Literary Activities.

He came to know that Companions of the Prophet were writing *aḥādīth*[7]. This information aroused his curiosity and he began to write everything he heard from the Prophet. Some of his colleagues objected to his writing down everything, because sometimes the Prophet might have been in an angry mood and he might have uttered something which was not necessarily meant for the record. On this point 'Abd Allāh requested the Prophet's permission to write and made the point clear asking whether he could record everything at every stage. He was told he could[8].

He named his book *al-Sahīfah al-Ṣādiqah*[9]. He wrote some *aḥādīth* which were taught by the Prophet to Abū Bakr at the

---

1. BU, *Tamannā,* 8; *Jihād,* 22; 32; 112 with good detail; MU, *Jihād,* 20; *Mustadrak,* ii, 78; *Usd al-Ghābah,* iii, 122; *Kifāyah,* 336-37.
2. *Usd al-Ghābah,* iii, 235 with different dates regarding his birth.
3. *Nubalā,* iii, 54.
4. Sa'd, vii, ii, 189.
5. Ḥanbal, ii, 195; *Huggāz,* i, 36; *Nubalā,* iii, 54; for transmission of knowledge from these books see e.g. *Annales,* i, 464-5; Ibn 'Abd al-Ḥakam, *Futūḥ Miṣr,* pp. 1, 35.
6. *Iṣābah,* No. 3669.
7. Rāmhurmuzī, 36a; al-Haithamī, *Majma' al-Zawā'id,* i, 152.
8. Sa'd, ii, ii, 125; iv, ii, 8; vii, ii, 189; Ḥanbal, ii, 162; 192; 207; 215; *Wāsiṭ,* 162; Dūlābī, i, 144; see also *Nubalā,* iii, 54; *Istī'āb,* No. 1618; *Islām,* iii, 38; testimony of Abū Hurairah about his writing, Ḥanbal, ii, 403; BU, *'Ilm,* 39; Rāmhurmuzī, 34b.
9. Sa'd, iv, ii, 8-9; vii, ii, 189; Dārimī, i, 127; *Taqyīd,* 84; *Nubalā,* iii, 58; Rāmhurmuzī, 34b.

request of the latter[1]. He also collected legal decisions (*Fatāwā*) of 'Umar[2]. He had a fair collection of books[3], and probably compiled some booklets on early history, *Maghāzī* and the biography of the Prophet[4]. He used to dictate *aḥādīth* to his students[5].

The following derived *aḥādīth* from him in written form:

Abdullāh b. Rabāḥ al-Anṣārī[6].

'Abd al-Raḥmān[7].

Abū Sabrah. 'Abd Allāh dictated to him[8].

'Abd al-Raḥmān b. Salamah al-Jumaḥī[9].

Sālim, servant of 'Abdullāh[10].

Shu'aib b. Muḥammad b. 'Abd Allāh, grand-son of 'Abd Allāh b. 'Amr. Later on 'Amr b. Shu'aib, great grandson of 'Abd Allāh came into possession of all these books[11].

Shufai b. Māti'. He had two books from 'Abd Allāh[12].

13. 'Abd Allah b. Mas'ūd (d. 32 A.H.)[13].

It is reported that he was against the recording of *ḥadīth*, and that he even erased one of the books[14].

Written Collections.

Ibn Masud says that in the life-time of the Prophet they used to write only the *Qur'ān, Tashahhud* and *Istikhārah* prayer[15]. But

1. Ḥanbal, ii, 196.
2. Dāraquṭnī, 453.
3. *Ḥuffāẓ*, i, 36; see also Ḥanbal, ii, 176.
4. Ṭkabīr, iii, 176.
5. 'Ajjāj, *Sunnah qabl al-Tadwīn*, 351, citing Ibn 'Asākir, vi, 49.
6. Ḥanbal, ii, 192.
7. Sakhāwī, *Fatḥ al-Mughīth*, p. 216. It is not clear the name mentioned there referred to him or to 'Ibn 'Umar.
8. Ḥanbal, ii, 162-163; 199; *Mustadrak*, i, 75.
9. Fasawī, iii, 163b. He wrote down *aḥādīth* and after memorizing erased them.
10. Baihaqī, Sunan, vi, 16; read with Ḥanbal, ii, 183.
11. *Mīzān*, iii, 264-7; *Tahd.*, viii, 49-50; 53; Tirmidhī, i, 43; Ibn Ḥajar, *Ṭabaqāt al-Mudallisīn*, ii.
12. Maqrīzī, *Khiṭaṭ*, ii, 332.
13. *Istī'āb*, No. 994.
14. *Taqyīd*, 53-56.
15. *'Ilal*, i, 322; *Muṣannaf* of Ibn Abū Shaibah, 45b.

there should not be any discrimination between the recording of *Tashahhud* and other *aḥādīth.*

His son brought a book and swore by God that it was his father's book in his own hand-writing[1].

14. 'ABD ALLĀH B. 'UMAR B. AL-KHAṬṬĀB (10 B.H. - 74 A.H.)[2].

He transmitted a large number of *aḥādīth,* and was so strict in relating them that he did not allow the order of a word to be changed even though it would not have altered the meaning[3].

He was very famous for strictly following the Prophet's path, even in insignificannt matters[4]. Therefore his actions were taken as a model[5].

He did not take part in political crises and prayed behind anyone of the victorious[6], yet never agreed with their manners, and even rebuked al-Ḥajjāj in the presence of thousands of men[7].

He had books[8]. One *Kitāb* which belonged to 'Umar, and was in his possession, was read to him by Nāfi' several times[9]. Once when a man asked him to write down all the *aḥādīth* for him, 'Abd Allāh replied that it was too much for him to write. Then he gave the man a piece of advice for his behaviour[10].

The following derived *aḥādīth* from him in written form:

Jamīl b. Zaid al-Ṭā'ī. He went to Madīnah, perhaps after the death of Ibn 'Umar, and collected his *aḥādīth* from various sources[11].

Nāfi' client of Ibn 'Umar[12].

---

1. *Bayān,* i, 72. See also I Bukhārī, Juz' al-Qirāt, 12.
2. Sa'd, iv, 137.
3. Sa'd, iv, 106
4. *Nubalā,* iii, 141.
5. Sa'd, iv, 106; see also Sa'd, iv, 114; 116.
6. Sa'd, iv, 110; 125.
7. Sa'd, iv, 117.
8. BTK, i, i, 325; Bājī, 97b; *Jāmi',* 101a: *Nubalā,* iii, 160.
9. *Amwāl,* 393; Zanjuwaih, 134b.
10. Khaulānī, *Tarīkh Dāriyā,* 46; *Nubalā,* iii, 148.
11. BTK, i, ii, 215; Jamīl Saw Ibn 'Umr, Sa'd, iv, 128.
12. Ḥanbal, ii, 29; see also *Bagh.,* x, 406; *Islām,* v, 11.

Sa'īd b. Jubair[1].

'Abd al-'Azīz b. Marwān[2].

'Abd al-Malik b. Marwān[3].

'Ubaid Allah b. 'Umar[4].

'Umar b. 'Ubaid Allāh[5].

One of his friends in Syria[6].

It is said that he was against the transcription of *ḥadīth*[7]. This assumption is based on the statement of Ibn Jubair that he was asking Ibn 'Umar some questions which were written in a booklet; had Ibn 'Umar known it, it would have been the end of their relations[8]. But it is a mere impression of Ibn Jubair while Ibn 'Umar's practice is quite against this assumption[9].

15. 'Abd Allāh b. al-Zubair (2 A.H. - 73 A.H.)[10].

'Abd Allāh b. 'Utbah derived *aḥādīth* from him in written form:

Ibn Al-Zubair wrote a letter to him concerning some legal decisions and quoted *aḥādīth* of the Prophet in it[11].

16. 'Āishah, Umm al-Mūminīn (d. 58)[12].

A very large number of *aḥādīth* is transmitted by her. It is certain that she knew how to read; but it is difficult to say whether or not she knew how to write. It is mentioned many times that she was asked questions and wrote answers; but the word *Katabat* might be used even if the letters were dictated by her.

She transmitted two letters, – *Kitābān* – of the Prophet which were found in the case of his sword[13].

1. *Taqyīd,* 103.
2. Ḥanbal, ii, 152; Sa'd, iv, i, 110, where it is Hārūn instead of Marwān.
3. *Kāmil,* i, 379a.
4. Khatīb, Faqīh, 143-4.
5. Ḥanbal, ii, 45.
6. Ḥanbal, ii, 90.
7. *Taqyīd,* 44.
8. *Taqyīd,* 44; Rāmhurmuzī, 36a.
9. Khaulānī, *Tārīkh Dāriyā,* 46; *Nubalā,* iii, 148.
10. Khazrajī, 167.
11. Ḥanbal, iv, 4; see also Dāraquṭnī, p. 464 (commentary).
12. *Usd al-Ghābah,* v, 504.
13. Dāraquṭnī, 343.

The following derived *aḥādīth* from her in written form:

Mu'āwiyah. He wrote to 'Ā'ishah several times asking her to write down some *aḥādīth* for him and she sent them to him in written form[1].

'Urwah, her nephew. He used to write down her *aḥādīth*[2].

Zayād b. Abū Sufyān. He wrote to her asking for some *aḥādīth*. We know her answer; but it is not clear whether she wrote it or not[3].

17. 'ALĪ B. ABŪ ṬĀLIB (23 B.H. - 40)[4].

He was one of the scribes of the Prophet. The Prophet once dictated to him and he wrote on a large piece of parchment on both sides[5].

He had a *Ṣaḥīfah* from the Prophet which is mentioned in various statements, such as those of:

Abū Juḥaifah[6].

Abū al-Tufail[7].

Al-Ashtar[8].

Al-Ḥārith b. Suwaid[9].

Jariyah b. Qudāmah[10].

Qais b. 'Abbād[11].

Ṭāriq b. Shihāb[12].

---

1. Ḥanbal, vi, 87; Khaithamah, III, 44b.
2. *Kifāyah,* 205.
3. MU, *Ḥajj, ḥadīth,* No. 369 (p.959).
4. Ziriklī, v, 107.
5. *Imlā,* 12; Rāmhurmuzī, 76a.
6. Ḥanbal, i, 79; A.D. *ḥadīth,* No. 4530; *Muntaqā,* No. 794; Nas, ii, 241; *Ṭawsat,* I, 42b.
7. Ḥanbal, i, 118; 152; Khaithamah, iii, 34a.
8. Ḥanbal, i, 119; Dāraquṭnī, 330.
9. Ḥanbal, i, 151.
10. Khaithamah, iii, 62b.
11. *Amwāl,* 185; *Mustadrak,* ii, 141.
12. Ḥanbal, i, 100; for further reference to *Ṣaḥīfah* see BU, *'Ilm,* 39; *Jizyah,* 10; *Farā'iḍ,* 21; *I'tiṣām,* 5; *Diyāt,* 24; MU, *Ḥajj,* 467, *'Itq,* 20; Zanjuwaih, 65b.

He had the *Kitāb* of the Prophet on *Zakāt* and Taxation[1] and encouraged students to write down *aḥādīth*[2].

The following derived *aḥādīth* from him in written form:

'Abd Allāh b. 'Abbās who had the legal decisions of 'Alī in written form[3].

'Aṭā' b. Abū Ribāḥ[4].

Al-Ḥārith b. al-A'war[5].

Ḥasan b. 'Alī who had 'Alī's legal decisions in written form[6].

Ḥujr b. 'Adī[7].

Khilās b. 'Amr al-Ḥajarī[8].

Mujāhid[9].

Al-Sha'bī[10].

Suwaid b. Mugrin[11].

18. 'AMR B. ḤAZM (d. after 50)[12].

He was appointed by the Prophet as a governor of Najrān[13]. He had a letter (*Kitāb*) from the Prophet containing the times of the prayers, methods of prayer, ablution, booty, taxation, *zakāt*, *Diyāt* etc. . . [14].

He edited the letters of the Prophet, which were transmitted by his son and have been published with the book of Ibn Ṭūlūn[15].

---

1. Ḥanbal, i, 141; BU, *Khums,* 5; *Taqyīd,* 88-89.
2. Sa'd, vi, 116; *'Ilal,* i, 42; *Taqyīd,* 89.
3. MU, *Muqaddimah,* 13-14.
4. Khaithamah, iii, 24b; Rāzī, *Introduction,* 130; *Sharḥ 'Ilal,* 62b.
5. Sa'd, vi, 116; Rāmhurmuzī, 35a.
6. *'Ilal,* i, 104.
7. Sa'd, vi, 154.
8. *Kāmil,* i, 327a; Bājī, 53a; *Mīzān,* i, 658; *Islām,* iii, 364; Rāzī, i, ii, 402; *Tahd.,* iii, 176-177; see also *'Ilal,* i, 114; Baihaqī, Sunan, vi, 43.
9. Khaithamah, iii, 24b.
10. Rāzī, *Introduction,* 130.
11. Shāfa'ī, al-umm, vii, 158.
12. *Usd al-Ghabah,* iv, 99.
13. *Iṣābah,* ii, 525, No. 5812.
14. Rāzī, iii, i, 224-5; Ḥamīdullāh, *Wathā'iq Sīyāsiyah,* No. 105; 'Aṭā b. Abū Ribāḥ read this letter. Rāmhurmuzī, 58a.
15. Ibn Ṭūlūn, *I'lām al-Sā'īlīn 'an Kutub Sayyid al-Mursalīn,* 48-52. There have been other attempts to collect the letters of the Prophet, e.g. 'Urwah, in Zanjuwaih, 67b-71a, also Ibn 'Abbās, see Zaila'ī, *Naṣb al-Rāyah,* iv, 420, they were not left and abandoned as was alleged by Margoliouth in his work *Early Development of Muhammedanism,* p. 20.

19. ANAS B. MĀLIK (10 B.H. - 93)[1].

He was ten years old when the Prophet moved to al-Madīnah and served the Prophet his entire life in this city.

There is a long list of his students who transmitted *aḥādīth* or made their own collection from him. As he lived till the end of the first century of the *Hijrah* his circle of students became very wide. Some false books and *aḥādīth* are also attributed to him.

He advised his sons to write *aḥādīth* of the Prophet and to learn them[2]. He used to say, "We do not value the knowledge of those who have not written it down"[3]. Here knowledge means *aḥādīth* of the Prophet.

His Books.

Hubairah b. 'Abd al-Rahmān says, "When Anas b. Mālik imparted the *aḥādīth* many people gathered and he brought books and gave them to the people saying,'I heard these *aḥādīth* from the Prophet, then I wrote them down and read them to him[4]'."

The following derived *aḥādīth* from him in written form:

Very many students wrote from him in al-Wāsiṭ[5].

'Abd Allāh b. Dīnār had a lengthy book from him[6].

'Abd al-Malik b. 'Umair[7].

Anas b. Sīrīn. Anas b. Mālik wrote *Sunnat 'Umar*[8] for him concerning taxation.

Ḥumaid[9].

Ibrāhīm b. Hudbah had a *Nuskhah* —book—from him[10].

---

1. *Iṣābah,* No. 277.
2. Sa'd, vii, i, 14. Rāmhurmuzī, 34b; *'Ilm,* 10a; *Sharaf,* 56b; *Taqyīd,* 96.
3. *Taqyīd,* 96.
4. *Wāsiṭ,* 38; Fasawī, 363a; Rāmhurmuzī, 34b, where his reading to the Prophet is not mentioned.
5. *Bagh.,* viii, 259.
6. *Ma'rifah,* 10.
7. *Thiqāt,* 438.
8. *Amwāl,* 532-3.
9. *Imlā,* 90; *Jāmi',* 117b; see also *Majrūḥīn,* 23b.
10. *Ma'rifah,* 9.

Kathīr b. Salīm[1].

Mūsā b. 'Abd Allāh al-Ṭawīl[2].

Al-Taimī[3].

Forged copies.

Abān[4].

Al-'Alā b. Zaid[5].

Dīnār b. 'Abd Allāh al-Ahwāzī[6].

Khālid b. 'Ubaid al-Baṣrī[7].

Kharāsh b. 'Abd Allāh[8].

20. AN ANSARITE, ANONYMOUS.

He complained to the Prophet of the weakness of his memory, saying he could not remember what he had heard from the Prophet. The Prophet replied, "Be helped by the right hand"[9]. It is not known whether he recorded or not but probably he did so.

21. ASMĀ' BINT 'UMAIS (d. after 40 A.H.)[10].

She had a collection of *aḥādīth* of the Prophet[11].

22. AL-BARĀ' B. 'ĀZIB (d. 72) [12].

Students used to write down *aḥādīth* in his lectures[13], and used to sit one behind another[14].

---

1. *Tahd.*, ii, 57.
2. *Ma'rifah,* 10.
3. Ja'd, 157.
4. See *infra* Abān, pp. 106-7.
5. *Tahd.*, viii, 183; Mizān, iii, 99.
6. Ibn Khair, *Fihrist,* 161-2.
7. *Tahd., iii,* 105.
8. Ibn Khair, *Fihrist,* 162; still preserved in Shahīd 'Alī Library, Istanbul; see also Ḥumaidī, *Jadhwat al-Muqtabis,* 131.
9. Tirmidhī, *'Ilm,* 12; Haithamī, *Majma' al-Zawā'id,* i, 152, but both *Isnāds* are defective.
10. Khazrajī, 420.
11. Ya'qūbī, *Tārīkh,* ii, 114.
12. Khazrajī, 39.
13. *'Ilal,* i, 42; *'Ilm,* 11b; Dārimī, i, 128; *Taqyīd,* 105.
14. *'Ilal,* i, 37.

23. AL-ḌAḤḤĀK B. SUFYĀN AL-KILĀBĪ.

He wrote a letter to 'Umar concerning inheritance contrary to the Caliph's opinion. He quoted the Prophet's letter to this effect[1].

24. AL-DAḤḤĀK B. QAIS B. KHĀLID (killed in 65 A.H.[2]).

Qais b. al-Haitham derived *aḥādīth* from him in written form.

Al-Daḥḥāk wrote him a letter which contained *aḥādīth* from Prophet[3].

Only these *aḥādīth* werc transmitted through him in the Musnad of Ibn Ḥanbal.

25. FĀTIMAH DAUGHTER OF THE PROPHET (d. 11 A.H.).

She wrote down some *aḥādīth* of the Prophet[4].

26. FĀTIMAH DAUGHTER OF QAIS[5].

The following derived *aḥādīth* from her in written form:

Abū Salamah. He wrote down her *aḥādīth* as she dictated[6].

Usamah b. Zaid. His wife Fātima sent him a letter describing the condition of the Prophet[7].

27. ḤASAN B. 'ALĪ (3 A.H. - 50 A.H.)[8].

He advised his sons and nephews to write down *aḥādīth*[9] and had a book[10]. It is not clear whether it contained *aḥādīth* only from 'Alī or from someone else as well.

---

1. Ibn Mājah, *ḥadīth*, No. 2642; see also, *Risālah* of al-Shāfi'ī, 426; *Muntaqā*, No. 966; Ḥamīdullāh, *Wathā'iq*, No. 228.
2. Usd al-Ghābah, III, 37-8.
3. Ḥanbal, iii, 453, see also *Iṣābah*, ii, 199, *Usd al-Ghābah*, iii, 37.
4. Ḥanbal, vi, 283, see also al-Kharā'iṭī, *Makārim al-Akhlāq*, 37 cited by Yūsuf al-Eche in the footnote of *Taqyīd*, 99, *Ṭkabīr*, v, 127b.
5. *Usd al-Ghābah*, v, 526-7.
6. Ḥanbal, vi, 413; MU, *Ṭalāq*, 39, pp. 1114-1121; Sa'd, viii, 200-1.
7. Sa'd, iv, i, 47.
8. Khazrajī, 67.
9. *'Ilal*, 97b; *Kifāyah*, 229.
10. *'Ilal*, i, 104.

28. 'ITBĀN B. MĀLIK (died in the time of Mu'āwiyah)[1].

He was imparting *aḥādīth,* and Anas b. Mālik was so impressed by some of them that he told his son to write them down[2].

29. JĀBIR B. 'ABD ALLĀH B. 'AMR (16 B.H. - 78)[3].

He was the last of the companions who died in al-Madīnah[4] and was the compiler of a booklet on Pilgrimage[5].

Many students made their collections of *aḥādīth* from him. Among them were:

'Abd Allāh b. Muḥammad b. 'Aqīl[6].

Abū Sufyān[7].

'Aṭā[8].

Ḥasan al-Baṣrī[9].

Ibn al-Ḥanafīyah[10].

Muḥammad b. 'Alī[11].

Muḥammad b. Muslim, Abū al-Zubair (d. 126.) He had two books from Jābir, one transmitted by al-Laith b. Sa'd[12], and the other he had heard himself from Jābir.

Mujāhid[13].

Qatādah b. Di'āmah[14].

Al-Sha'bī[15].

Sulaimān b. Qais al-Yashkurī (d. 70-80). He wrote a *Ṣaḥīfah*

---

1. *Isti'āb,* No. 2019.
2. MU, *Imān,* 54, Rāmhurmazī, 35a, *Taqyīd,* 94-5.
3. *Mashāhīr,* 11.
4. *Tahd.,* ii. 43.
5. *Ḥuffāz,* i, 37.
6. *Kāmil,* ii, 113b; Rāmhurmuzī, 35a; *Islām,* vi, 90; *Mīzān,* ii, 484.
7. *'Ilal,* 120a; Rāzī, ii, i, 475; *Mīzān,* ii, 342.
8. BU. BUYU', 112. Ḥanbal, iii, 326.
9. *Tahd.,* ii, 267.
10. *Kāmil,* ii, 113b.
11. *Kāmil,* ii, 113b; Rāmhurmuzī, 35a, *Taqyīd,* 104.
12. *Tahd.,* ix, 442; Ibn Ḥajar, *Ṭabaqāt al-Mudallisīn,* 21; see also, Fasawī, ii, 18b; iii, 41a; 139a.
13. Sa'd, v, 344; Fasawī, iii, 269a.
14. BTK, iv, i, 186; Fasawī, III, 204b; 81b; Rāzī, ii, i, 136; iii, ii, 135; *Sharḥ 'Ilal,* 36a; *Tahd.,* viii, 353.
15. Rāzī, ii, i, 136.

from Jābir[1]. Later on it was transmitted by many scholars. Wahb. b. Munabbih[2].

30. Jābir b. Samurah (d. 74)[3].

He wrote down some *aḥādīth* and sent them to 'Āmir b. Sa'd[4].

31. Jarīr b. 'Abd Allāh al-Bajalī (d. 54 A.H.)[5].

He wrote down some *aḥādīth* in a letter and sent them to Mu'āwiyah[6].

32. Mu'ādh b. Jabal (20 B.H. - 18 A.H.)[7].

Mūsā b. Ṭalḥah said that he had a copy of *Kitāb* of Mu'ādh from the Prophet concerning *Ṣadaqāt*[8].

Ibn 'Ā'idh had books from him[9].

Ṭāwūs transmitted some of Mu'ādh's judgement from a book[10].

33. Mu'āwiyah b. Abū Sufyān (d. 60 A.H.)[11].

He wrote a letter to Marwān and related a *ḥadīth* from the Prophet[12]. He asked several companions e.g.: 'Ā'ishah and Mughīrah to write down *aḥādīth* for him[13].

He had literary tastes and ordered 'Ubaid b. Sharyah narratives about Pre-Islamic History and poetry etc.[14] to be written down.

He used to teach the people *aḥādīth* of the Prophet[15], and wrote to Abdur Rahman b. Shibl asking him to teach the people *aḥādīth* of the Prophet[16].

1. *'Ilal*, i, 316; Fasawī, iii, 81b; Rāzī, ii, i, 136; *Tahd.*, iv, 215.
2. *Tahd.*, i, 316.
3. *Iṣābah*, No. 1018.
4. MU, *Faḍā'il*, 45.
5. Khazrajī, 52.
6. Ḥanbal, iv, 361; Baihaqī, *Sunan*, ix, 41.
7. *Usd al-Ghābah*, iv, 378.
8. Zanjuwaih, 189a; see also Ḥanbal, v, 228.
9. Rāmhurmuzī, 56a.
10. 'Abdur Razzāq, *al-Muṣannaf*, x, 373-4; Sa'īd b. Manṣur, *sunan*, iii, ii, 245.
11. *Iṣābah*, No. 8070.
12. Ḥanbal, iv, 94.
13. See under 'Ā'ishah and Mughīrah in this chapter.
14. 'Ubaid b. Sharyah, *Akhbār 'Ubaid*, printed with *al-Tījān*, pp. 311-488 in Hyderabad Deccan, 1347.
15. Al-Kishshi, *sunan*, 49a.
16. *ibid*, 39a.

34. AL-MUGHĪRAH B. SHU'BAH (d. 50)[1].

Mu'āwiyah asked Mughīrah to write some *aḥādīth* for him. So he wrote them down and sent them to Mu'āwiyah[2].

35. MUḤAMMAD B. MASLAMAH AL-ANṢARĪ (31 B.H. - 46 A.H.)[3].

After his death a booklet (*Ṣaḥifah*) was found attached to his sword containing *aḥādīth*[4].

36. AL-NU'MĀN B. BASHĪR (64 A.H.)[5].

The following derived *aḥādīth* from him in written form:

Qais b. al-Haitham. Al-Nu'mān wrote some *aḥādīth* and sent them to him[6].

Ḥabīb b. Sālim, scribe of al-Nu'mān, wrote some *aḥādīth* of al-Nu'mān and sent them to his son Yazīd b. Nu'mān[7]. Daḥḥak b. Qais[8].

37. RĀFI' B. KHADĪJ (12 B.H. - 74)[9].

He had a statement of the Prophet in writing concerning the sanctuary of al-Madīnah[10].

38. SA'D B. 'UBĀDAH (d. 15)[11].

Sa'd knew the art of writing even in Pre-Islamic days[12]. He collected *aḥādīth* in a book; later on a *ḥadīth* from this book was transmitted by a member of his family[13].

---

1. *Iṣābah,* No. 8181.
2. BU, *Adhān,* 155; *Da'wāt,* 18; *Qadr,* 12; *Zakāt,* 53; *I'tiṣām,* 3; MU, *Aqḍiyah,* 13; *Masājid,* 137-8. Nas, i, 197; A.D. *ḥadīth,* No. 1500; Ḥanbal, iv, 245; 247; 249; 250; 254; Dūlābī, ii, 66, Rāzī, i, ii, 357; *Ṭawsaṭ,* i, 216b.
3. *Usd al-Ghābah,* iv, 331.
4. Rāmhurmuzī, 56a.
5. Khazrajī, 345.
6. Ḥanbal, iv, 277.
7. Ḥanbal, iv, 273.
8. Ibn Khuzaimah, 193b.
9. *Iṣābah,* No. 2526.
10. Ḥanbal, iv, 141; see also Ḥamīdullāh, *al-Wathā'iq al-Siyāsiyah,* p. 21.
11. Khazrajī, 114.
12. Sa'd, iii, ii, 142.
13. Ḥanbal, v, 285; Ṭkabīr, iii, 85a; see also *Thiqāt,* 396; *Mashāhīr,* 130; Ibn Ḥajar *Ta'jīl al-Manfa'ah,* 36; 314.

39. Sahl b. Sa'd al-Sadī (9 B.H. - 91 A.H.)[1].

Salamah b. Dīnār, Abū Ḥāzim collected Sahl's *aḥ ādīth* which were transmitted by Ibn Abū Ḥāzim[2].

40. Salmān al-Fārisī (c. 32)[3].

He wrote some *aḥādīth* and sent them to Abū al-Dardā'[4].

41. Samurah b. Jundub (d. 59)[5].

He wrote his *aḥādīth* and later on they were transmitted by many scholars.

The following derived *aḥādīth* from him in writing:

Al-Ḥasan al-Baṣrī. He also transmitted Samurah's book[6].

Muḥammad b. Sīrīn. He knew Samurah's book and praised it[7]. It is not clear whether or not he obtained this book from Samurah.

Sulaimān b. Samurah. He transmitted a lengthy book from his father[8]. A part of this work is still preserved in *Mu'jam al-Kabīr* of al-Ṭabarānī[9].

42. Subai'ah al-Aslamiyah.

The following derived *aḥādīth* from her in written form:

'Amr b. 'Utbah.

---

1. Khazrajī, 133.
2. *Kāmil,* iii, 4b; see also Rāzī, ii, ii, 382; Ibn Ḥajar, *Hādy al-Sārī,* ii, 185; *Tahd.,* vi, 333.
3. *Iṣābah,* No. 3357.
4. *Mīzān,* iv, 546.
5. *Iṣābah,* No. 3475.
6. *'Ilal,* i, 322; Fasawī, iii, 269a; Sa'd, vii, i, 115; Nas, i, 205; Bājī 8a; *Tahd.,* ii, 267; 269. See also, Ṭkabīr, iii; 208-215 where a portion of this work is preserved.
7. *Tahd.,* iv, 236.
8. A.D. *ḥadīth,* No. 1562; Dāraquṭnī, 214.
9. Ṭkabīr, iii, 220-226.

Masrūq. 'Amr b. 'Utbah and Masrūq wrote to her asking for the *aḥādīth* of the Prophet regarding *'Iddat.* She wrote a letter to them giving a full account of events and relevant teachings of the Prophet[1].

43. SHADDĀD B. AUS B. THĀBIT (17 B.H. - 58)[2].

He was a nephew of the poet Ḥassān b. Thābit.

On his way to pilgrimage he dictated *aḥādīth* to two of his companions[3].

44. SHAMGHŪN AL-AZDĪ, AL-ANṢĀRĪ.

He had some books (*Suḥuf*). He was the first to write on both sides of papyrus which he pressed and sewed together[4].

45. UBAI B. KA'B (d. 22)[5].

One of the oldest companions of the Prophet, he was famous for his Quranic knowledge.

The following transmitted his books or made their own collections from him:

Rufai' B. Mihrān (d. 91). He transmitted a lengthy book of commentary on the Holy *Qur'ān* from Ubai b. Ka'b[6].

Samurah and 'Imrān differed about some actions of the Prophet concerning prayer; then they wrote to Ubai who in turn confirmed Samurah's sayings[7].

46. 'UMAR B. AL-KHAṬṬĀB. THE SECOND CALIPH (c. B.H. 40 - 23 A.H.).

It is said on the authority of 'Urwah that 'Umar wanted to have *aḥādīth* written and compiled under the patronage of the

---

1. Ibn Mājah, *ḥadīth,* No. 2028; see also BU, *Maghāzī,* 10; MU, *Ṭalāq,* 56; Qaisarānī, 341; *Kifāyah,* 337; *Tahd.,* viii, 75.
2. *Iṣābah,* No. 3847.
3. *Nubalā,* ii, 333.
4. *Iṣābah,* No. 3921.
5. *Iṣābah,* No. 32.
6. Muḥammad al-Dhahabī, *al-Tafsīr wal-Mufassirūn,* i, 115, quoting Ibn Taymiyah.
7. Ḥanbal, v, 7.

Government. He consulted the Companions who unanimously agreed to his proposal. However, he reconsidered the matter thoroughly and then disapproved of it[1]. Accordinng to Yaḥyā b. Ja'dah, he even sent a circular demanding that everyone who had written a collection should burn it[2]. Somewhat similar to this, is a statement of al-Qāsim b. Muḥammad[3]. All these three statements are *Mursal.* The links between 'Umar and the narrators are unknown.

The transmitters of 'Urwah's statement are:

Ibn Wahb – Yūnus – Al-Zhurī – 'Urwah – 'Umar.

Abū al-Yamān – Shu'aib – Al-Zhurī – 'Urwah – 'Umar.

A. Razzāq – Ma'mar – Al-Zhurī – 'Urwah – 'Umar.

Qabīṣah – Al-Thaurī – Ma'mar – Al-Zuhurī – 'Urwah –

Al-Firyābī – Al-Thaurī – Ma'mar – Al-Zuhrī – 'Urwah – Ibn 'Umar – 'Umar[4].

It is now clear that al-Firyābī's colleague, Qabīṣah did not mention Ibn 'Umar, nor did the other pupils of Ma'mar or any other student of Al-Zuhrī. Therefore, it was al-Firyābī who inserted the name of Ibn 'Umar erroneously. Hence, it is a *mursal ḥadīth* and the authority of this statement is questionable. The other point is that, although schools had been established for the teaching of the Holy *Qur'ān*, and teachers had been sent here and there[5], yet written copies of the *Qur'ān* were not provided for these centres. Therefore it is difficult to believe that 'Umar would have given priority to the recording of the *aḥādīth* while the sacred book itself needed attention.

Nevertheless, if we accept the statement without any argument, as a genuine one, then it would be clear that the writing of *ḥadīth* was not considered to be against the order of the Prophet, otherwise these Companions would not have agreed unanimously with 'Umar on the subject.

It is also incorrect to say that he did not want anything to be written except the *Qur'ān*. He asked the governor of Kūfah to

---

1. *Taqyīd,* 49; see also, Sa'd, iii, i, 206.
2. *Taqyīd;* 52-3.
3. *Taqyīd,* 52.
4. *Taqyīd,* 49-51.
5. See for details, Shiblī Nu'mānī, *al-Fārūq,* pp. 371-75.

write down certain poetry[1], and even allowed Anṣār to write down their poems of the Islamic and Pre-Islamic periods[2]. He introduced the system of registers in official business[3].

It is assumed that he was against the imparting of *aḥādīth*[4], and detained Ibn Mas'ūd, Abū Dharr and Abū al-Dardā', as they imparted *aḥādīth* in great number[5].

The number of *aḥādīth* narrated by them are 848, 280 and 179 respectively[6]. The last two numbers are very small. 'Umar himself sent Ibm Mas'ūd[7] and Abū al-Dardā[8] as teachers to Kūfah and Damascus respectively, and praised the former very much. It is also reported that he advised Companions to reduce the imparting of *aḥādīth*, for the sake of the *Qur'ān,* and in the same statement he informed them about ablution. It looks as if he suggested they should impart *aḥādīth* regarding practical life[9], and not to tell the stories of war (Maghāzī) which might have been a very interesting subject of *Quṣṣāṣ* in those days. As he sent instructors to teach the *Qur'ān* and *Sunnah* to the people[10], how could he have forbidden the people from learning *Sunnah*? On the other hand it is also reported that he encouraged the writing of *aḥādīth*[11].

He used to quote *aḥādīth* from the Prophet in his official letters[12]. Furthermore, it looks as if he collected several documents from the Prophet, concerning financial matters and taxation, and put them together[13]. This was, later on, in the possession of Ibn 'Umar and was read to him by his servant Nāfi', several times[14].

---

1. *Annales,* iii, 2359.
2. *Aghānī,* iv, 140-1.
3. Sa'd, iii, v, 202-3.
4. *'Ilal,* i, 62-3.
5. *Mustadrak,* i, 110.
6. Ibn Ḥazm, *Jawāmi', al-Sīrah,* 276-277.
7. Sa'd, vi, 7; Fasawī, iii, 166b.
8. *Nubalā,* ii, 248.
9. Dārimī, i, 85.
10. Ḥanbal, i, 48; Sa'd, iii, i, 201; 243.
11. *Taqyīd,* 88; *Mustadrak,* i, 106.
12. BU, *Libās,* 25; MU, *Libās,* 12; 14; Ḥanbal, i, 28; 36; 46; 50; Dāraquṭnī, 461.
13. A.D. *ḥadīth* No. 1568-1570; *Muwaṭṭa',* pp. 257-259.
14. BTK, i, i, 218.

47. Usaid B. Ḥuḍair[1].

He wrote some legal *aḥādīth* of the Prophet and sent them to Marwān[2].

48. Wāthilah B. al-Asqua'(22 B.H. - 83)[3].

He dictated *aḥādīth* to his pupils[4].

49. Zaid B. Arqam (d.66)[5].

He wrote down *aḥādīth* in a letter and sent them to Anas b. Mālik[6].

50. Zaid B. Thābit (d.45).

He learnt Hebrew and other languages and used to write for the Prophet in Arabic and non-Arabic languages as well[7]. It is reported that he was against the writing down of *aḥādīth*. When Marwān wrote down his *aḥādīth* without his knowledge, he imparted a *ḥadīth* from the Prophet in which the recording of *aḥādīth* was prohibited[8]. But the narrator of this *ḥadīth* is al-Muṭṭalib b. Ḥanṭab, who never saw Zaid, so it is invalid. Meanwhile there is another narrator Al-Sha'bī who claims that the written material was not the *aḥādīth* of the Prophet, but the personal opinions and decisions of Zaid, so he said, "Marwān, excuse me, it is my opinion"[9]. This might be the case, but it is difficult to accept because we have positive evidence of his attitude contrary to what has been said e.g.

On the request of the Caliph 'Umar, he wrote his judicial opinion concerning the share of grand-fathers in inheritance and handed it to 'Umar[10].

---

1. *Iṣābah*, No. 539.
2. Ḥanbal, iv, 226.
3. *Usd al-Ghābah*, vi, 77.
4. *Nubala*, iii, 259; *Imlā*, 13; *Mīzān*, iv, 145; *Jāmi'*, 113b see also Ibn Mufliḥ, *Ādāb Shar'iyah*, ii, 125, cited by Eche in the margin of *Taqyīd*, 99.
5. Tahd, iii 395.
6. Hanabal, iv, 370; 374; Tirmidhī, ii, 230; see also, *Tahd.*, iii, 394.
7. Sa'd, ii, ii, 115.
8. *Taqyīd*, 35.
9. *Nubalā*, ii, 313; Sa'd, ii, ii, 117.
10. Dāraquṭnī, 464.

He compiled the first book on *Farā'iḍ*[1]; the book was transmitted by Qabīṣah[2] and his own son Khārijah b. Zaid[3], and its introductory page is still preserved in *Mu'jam* of al-Ṭabārānī[4].

The following derived *aḥādīth* from him in written form:

Abū Qilābah[5].

Unnamed students. Kathīr b. Ṣalt saw people writing in his presence[6].

Kathīr b. Aflaḥ. He used to record the lectures of Zaid[7].

II. WRITINGS OF AND FROM THE FIRST CENTURY SUCCESSORS

1. ABRĀN B. 'UTHMĀN (c. 20 - 105)[8].

He is one of the earliest compilers of *al-Maghāzī*. Al-Mughīrah b. 'Abd al-Raḥmān had a copy of this book, which was read to him, and he advised his sons to learn it[9].

2. 'ABD ALLĀH B. HURMUZ (c. 40 - c. 100).

He transmitted *aḥādīth* from Abū Hurairah[10] and wrote *aḥādīth* which he sent to Tamīm al-Jaishānī[11].

3. 'ABD ALLĀH B. MUḤAMMAD B. 'ALĪ, ABŪ HĀSHIM (c. 50 - 99)[12].
He transmitted *aḥādīth* from his father (d. 73) etc.

---

1. Fasawī, ii, 148b; *Nubalā,* ii, 312.
2. 'Ilal, i, 236.
3. Ibn Khair, *Fihrist,* 263.
4. Ṭkabīr, iii, 419. See also Ibn 'Asākir, *Tārīkh Dimashq,* v, 448, cited by Yusaf al-Eche in the margin of *Taqyīd,* 99.
5. *Kāmil,* i, 208b.
6. Khaithamah, iii, 6b.
7. *Taqyīd,* 102,
8. Horovitz, *The earliest biographies,* I.C., 1927, pp. 536-7; *Tahd.,* i, 97.
9. Sa'd, v, 156; Fischer, 76.
10. *Ḥanbal,* ii, 531.
11. *Ḥanbal,* ii, 531.
12. *Tahd., vi, 16.*

Muḥammad b. ‘Alī b. ‘Abd Allāh b. ‘Abbāh had his books[1].

4. ‘Abd Allāh b. Rabāḥ al-Anṣarī (c. 10 - about 90)[2]

He transmitted from Ubai b. Ka‘b (d.22).

The following derived *aḥādīth* from him in writing:

Abū ‘Imrān[3].

‘Abd al-Malik b. Ḥabīb al-Azdī[4].

5. ‘Abd Allāh b. Sakhbarah al-Azdī (c. 1 - c. 65)[5].

He transmitted *aḥādīth* from ‘Umar (d.23) etc.
‘Abd al-Karīm b. Abū al-Mukhāriq derived *aḥādīth* from him in written form[6].

6. ‘Abd al-Rahmān b. ‘Abd Allāh b. Mas‘ūd (c. 25 - c. 79)[7].

He transmitted a few *aḥādīth* from his father (d.33) and from ‘Alī etc. His son Ma‘n had a book written by him which contained *aḥādīth* and sayings of Ibn Mas‘ūd[8].

7. ‘Abd al-Raḥmān b. ‘Āidh (c. 1 - c. 80)[9].

He transmitted from Mu‘ādh b. Jabal (d.18) and his books were very much respected in Ḥimṣ[10]. He went to Iraq where many students of al-Kūfah and al-Baṣah derived *aḥādīth* from him in writing[11].

1. Sa‘d, v, 241; Khaithamah, iii, 116a; *Tahd.*, vi, 16.
2. *Tahd.*, v, 207.
3. *Ḥanbal*, ii, 192; ‘Ilm, 2.
4. *Tahd.*, vi, 389.
5. *Tahd.*, v,231. He died in the governorship of ‘Ubaid b. Ziyād (28-67).
6. Khaithamah, iii, 200b.
7. *Tahd.*, vi, 216.
8. Fasawī, iii, 215.
9. *Tahd.*, vi, 204.
10. Fasawī, iii, 118a; *Tahd*, vi, 204; see also for distribution of his books among the soldirs, Fasawī, iii, 118a.
11. *Mashāhīr*, 113.

8. 'ABD AL-RAḤMĀN B. GHANM (c. 1 - 78)[1].

Maisarah had *aḥādīth* from him in written form[2].

9. 'ABD AL-RAḤMĀN B. MULL, ABŪ 'UTHMĀN AL-NAHDĪ (35 B.H. 95)[3].

Sulaimān al-Taimī had *aḥādīth* from him in written form[4].

10. 'ABĪDAH B. 'AMR AL-SALMĀNĪ (c. 10 B.H. - 72)[5].

He had many books, but was afraid that someone might make some mistakes in dealing with them; so on his death-bed he willed that they should either be burnt or erased[6]. He ordered one of his students, Ibrāhīm, who was writing in his presence, not to retain any book from him permanently[7].

There is a conflicting statement of Ibn Sīrīn in which it is reported that he not only disliked writing but also the reading of books[8]. Yet the same person — Ibn Sīrīn — says that he used to have *Aṭrāf* and ask 'Abīdah those *aḥādīth*[9]. Furthermore, Shuraiḥ used to write him if he had some difficulties[10]. On considering these statements, one arrives at the conclusion that he was not against the writing of *aḥādīth*. It is quite possible that at certain times and in certain cases he disapproved of it, because methods of teaching were always changing.

11. Abū al-Malīḥ b. Usāmah al-Hudhalī (c. 35 - 98)[11].

He used to write down *aḥādīth*[12].

---

1. *Tahd,* vi, 251. There is controversy about his companionship. It seems that he was born in the time of the Prophet, but did not see him.
2. Rāmhurmuzī, 55b.
3. *Tahd.*, vi, 278.
4. BU, *Adab,* 22.
6. Fasawī, iii, 183a; Khaithamah, iii, 186b; 189b; *'Ilal,* i, 43; Sa'd, vi,
7. *'Ilal,* i, 42; 180b; Zur'ah, 130a.
8. *'Ilal,* i, 42.
9. *'Ilal,* i, 387.
10. *Tahd.*, vii, 84.
11. *Tahd.*, xii, 246 in footnote.
12. Rāmhurmuzī, 35a.

12. ABŪ QILĀBAH - 'ABD ALLĀH B. ZAID AL-BASRĪ (c. 40 - 104)[1].

He was in favour of writing *aḥādīth*[2]. At the time of his death, he had many books which were entrusted to Ayyūb who paid about 15 dirhams for their carriage[3], which amounted to about a pony load[4].

The following derived *aḥādīth* from him in writing:

Ayyūb[5].

Qatādah[6].

Yaḥyā b. Abū Kathīr[7].

13. ABŪ SALAMAH B. 'ABD AL-RAḤMĀN (32 - 104)[8].

He used to take students from the school to his house and dictate *aḥādīth* to them[9].

Yaḥyā b. Abū Kathīr transmitted a *Nuskhah* from him [10].

14. 'ĀMIR B. 'ABD ALLĀH B. MAS'ŪD (c. 25 - c. 83)[11].

He wrote some *aḥādīth* of the Prophet and some practices of Ibn Mas'ūd and sent them to Yaḥyā b. Abȳ Kathīr[12].

15. 'ĀMIR B. SHARĀḤIL B. 'ABD AL-SHA'BĪ (19 - 103)[13].

He is one of the earliest compilers; perhaps being a judge he was compelled to compile. He depended mostly on his memory and

---

1. *Tahd.*, v, 226.
2. *Taqyīd*, 103.
3. Sa'd, vii, ii, 17; *'Ilal*, i, 394; Rāmhurmuzī, 51a. *Ḥuffāẓ*, i, 82.
4. Fasawī, ii, 145b.
5. Sa'd, vii, i, 135; vii, ii, 17; *'Ilal*, i, 77; 295; 394; BU, *Ṭib*, 26; Zur'ah, 71b; Fasawī, iii, 24a; 272a; *Kāmil*, 1, 208b; Rāmhurmuzī, 51a; *Kifāyah*, 257; 352; *Ḥuffāẓ*, 1, 82.
6. Al-Khaulānī, *Tārīkh Dāriyā*, 62.
7. *Tahd.*, xi, 270.
8. *Tahd.*, xii, 116.
9. *'Ilal*, i; 247; *Bagh.*, i, 218.
10. *Majrūḥīn*, 96a.
11. *Tahd.*, v, 75.
12. Ṭkabīr, v, 97 a-b about 1½ pages.
13. Sa'd, vi, 178; *Tahd.*, v, 68.

said that he never wrote anything nor asked anyone to repeat *aḥādīth*[1], as if a single hearing were sufficient to memorize them. Naturally, he forgot much[2]. Accordingly, he advised his students to write down everything and if the materials were not available, to write even on the wall[3].

At present we have references to his work as follows:

Kitāb al-Farā'iḍ — book on inheritance[4].

Kitāb al-Jarāḥāt[5].

Kitāb al-Ṭalāq[6].

Ṣadaqāt. He dictated three scrolls about *Ṣadaqāt* and *Farā'iḍ*[7] and had a collection of *aḥādīth* concerning Law - *Fiqh* - which were read to him[8]. It is not clear whether it was one of his above mentioned works or something else. Probably he had a book of al-*Maghāzī* as well[9].

16. 'AṬĀ' B. YASĀR AL-HILĀLĪ (19 - 103)[10].

He had a book which was read by 'Umar b. Isḥāq b. Yasār[11].

17. AL-DAḤḤĀK B. MUZĀḤIM (c. 40 - 105)[12].

He had a commentary on the *Qur'ān*[13] and dictated the book on *al-Manāsik* to Ḥusain b. 'Aqīl[14].

---

1. Sa'd, vi, 174; Rāzī, iii, i, 323; Rāmhurmazī, 36b; *Bagh.*, xii, 229; *Tahd.*, vi, 67.
2. *Bagh.*, xii, 229.
3. Sa'd, vi, 174; *'Ilm*, 11b; Rāmhurmazī, 35b; 36a; *Taqyīd*, 100.
4. Fasawī, iii, 252b; Rāzī, iv, i, 41; *Tahd.*, ix, 177, See also *'Ilad*, i, 340, *Bagh.*, xii, 232.
5. *Bagh.*, xii, 232.
6. Rāmhurmuzī, 78a; 78a-b; *Jāmi'*, 189a.
7. *'Ilal*, i, 340.
8. *'Ilal*, 153b, *Kifāyah*, 264; see also Rāmhurmuzī, 44a;
9. *Bagh.*, xii, 230; see also *Tahd.*, x, 40; Rāzī, iv, i, 361.
10. *Tahd.*, vii, 218.
11. Ḥanbal, vi, 333; al-Bannā, *al-Fatḥ al-Rabbānī*, ii, 67; Ibn Ḥajar, *Ta'jīl al-Manfa'ah*, 296.
12. *Tahd.*, iv, 454.
13. *Fihrist*, 34; see also Rāzī, i, ii, 319.
14. *'Ilal*, i, 43.

18. DHAKWĀN ABŪ ṢĀLIḤ AL-SAMMĀN (c. 20 - 101[1].

He was *Maulā* of Juwairiyah bint Qais.

The following derived *aḥādīth* from him in writing:

Al-A'mash derived 1000 *aḥādīth* from him in writing[3].

Suhail son of Dhakwan wrote down *aḥādīth* from him[4].

19. ḤĀRITH B. 'ABD ALLĀH AL-A'WAR (c. 15 - 65)[5].

He wrote down *aḥādīth* from 'Alī b. Abū Ṭālib[6] and had many books[7]. The following derived *aḥādīth* from him in writing:

'Abd al-A'lā al-Tha'libī[8].

Abū Isḥāq al-Sabī'ī[9].

20. ḤIBBĀN B. JAZI AL-SULAMĪ (c. 35 - c. 100)[10].

He transmitted *aḥādīth* from Abū Hurairah and others.

Muṭarrif b. 'Abd al-Raḥmān had a *Nuskhah* from him[11].

21. ḤUMRĀN B. ABĀN (c. 10 B.H. - after 75 A.H.)[12].

He met Abū Bakr (d. 13).

The people of Baṣrah derived *aḥādīth* from him in writing.[13].

22. IBRĀHĪM B. YAZĪD AL-NAKH'Ī AL-A'WAR (47 - 96)[14].

He was against writing *aḥādīth* and is reported to have

---

1. *Tahd,* iii, 220, He was in Madīnah at the time of the assassination of the Caliph 'Uthmān, Rāzī, i, ii, 451. See also Khaithamah, iii, 112a.
2. Ibn Qutaiban, *Ma'ārif,* 478.
3. Ja'd, 80; see also *'Ilal,* i, 140.
4. See *infra,* Suhail in this chapter.
5. *Mīzān,* i, 437.
6. Sa'd, vi, 116.
7. Rāzīm im iim 78.
8. Rāzī, iii, i, 26.
9. *Mīzān,* i, 435; *Tahd.,* VIII, 65.
10. *Tahd.,* ii, 171.
11. Eāzī, i, ii, 268.
12. Khazrajī, 79.
13. *Thiqāt,* 171.
14. *Tahd.,* i, 178.

said, "Anyone who writes depends on his writing"[1]. He meant that he who writes does not remember what he has written.

The following derived *aḥādīth* from him in writing:

Ḥammād B. Abū Sulaimā (d. 119)[2].

Qatādah wrote to him asking some questions concerning foster relationships, and Ibrāhīm replied quoting *aḥādīth* from the Prophet and many Companions[3].

23. 'IKRIMAH CLIENT OF IBN 'ABBAS (c. 25 - 105)[4].

According to his statement, his master Ibn 'Abbās used to put shackles on 'Ikrimah's feet to teach him the Holy *Qur'ān* and the *Sunnah*[5]. He had books[6]. He was a great traveller and went to different countries. He was very famous for his commentary on the *Qur'ān*[7].

The following derived *aḥādīth* from him in writing:

'Amr b. 'Abd Allāh[8].

Ayyūb[9].

Ḥusain b. Qais[10].

Ibn Juraij, perhaps wrote *aḥādīth* from him and chided Yaḥyā b. Ayyūb, who did not write from 'Ikrimah, that he had in this way lost two-thirds of his knowledge[11].

Jābir b. Zaid[12].

'Uthmān b. Ghiyāth[13].

Salamah b. Wahram[14]

---

1. Sa'd ,vi, 189.
2. Ja'd, 26; Sa'd, vi, 232; *Ilal*, i, 43; Fasawī, 183a, see also Sa'd, vi, 190; *'Ilal*, I, 295, *Taqyīd*, footnote, 110, where Eche erroneously confused Hammād b. Salamah and Hammād b. Abū Sulaimān.
3. Nas, ii, 82; Rāmhurmuzī, 48b.
4. *Tahd.*, vii, 270-71.
5. Sa'd v, 212.
6. Rāzī, iii, i, 244; *Mīzān*, iii, 295; *Tahd.*,viii, 61.
7. Rāzī, iii, ii, 9.
8. Rāzī, iii, i, 244; *Mīzān*, iii, 295; *Tahd., viii, 61.*
9. *Annales, Supl.*, iii, 2484; Rāzī, iii, ii, 8.
10. *Majrūḥīn*, 83b.
11. *Tahd.*, vii, 266; see also the commentary on the *Sunan* of Dāraquṭnī. 448.
12. *Mīzān*, iii, 93.
13. Rāzī, *Introd.*, 236; *Tahd.*, vii, 147.
14. Mīzān, ii, 193.

Numerous scholars of the Yeman and of the eastern zone of the Caliphate[1].

24. JĀBIR B. ZAID AL-AZDĪ (c. 30 - 93)[2].
His students wrote *aḥādīth* from him[3].

25. KATHĪR B. MURRAH AL-ḤAḌRAMĪ (c. 15 - c. 75)[4].

'Abd al-'Azīz b. Marwān asked him to write *aḥādīth*[5]. It is not clear whether or not he fulfilled the request, but most probably he did.

26. KHĀLID B. MA'DĀN B. ABŪ KURAIB AL-KALĀ'Ī (c. 30 - 103)[6].

He wrote *aḥādīth* in the form of a book which was kept covered[7].

Baḥīr b. Sa'īd had a book from him[8].

Jumai' b. Thaub al-Shāmī transmitted a *Nuskhah* from him[9].

27. KURDŪS B. 'ABBĀS AL-THA'LABĪ (c. 10 B.H. - c. 60 A.H.).

He transmitted *aḥādīth* from Ibn Mas'ūd (d. 33) etc.[10]. It is mentioned that he used to read books[11].

28. LĀḤIQ B. ḤUMAID - ABŪ MIJLAZ (c. 35 - 100)[12].

Yaḥyā found a book containing *aḥādīth* from Lāḥiq[13].

---

1. *Annales, Supl.*, iii, 2485.
2. Sa'd, vii, i, 133. Here his death is mentioned 103; but according to al-Bukhārī and Ibn Ḥibbān, it is 93 A.H. See *Tahd.*, ii, 38.
3. Sa'd, vii, i, 131.
4. *Tahd.*, viii, 429.
5. Sa'd, vii, ii, 157.
6. *Tahd.*, iii, 119.
7. *Ḥuffāz*, i, 81; *Tahd.*, iii, 119.
8. *Ḥuffāz*, i, 158.
9. *Kāmil*, i, 224b - 225a.
10. *Tahd.*, viii, 431.
11. Rāzī, iii, ii, 175; *Tahd.*, viii, 432.
12. *Tahd.*, xi, 172.
13. Tāzī, *Introd.*, 243.

29. MAMṬŪR AL-ḤABASHĪ, ABŪ SALLĀM (c. 40 - c. 105).

He transmitted from Nu'mān b. Bashīr etc. Makḥūl and al-Auzāī' related from him[1].

Yaḥyā b. Abū Kathīr had his book[2].

30. MIQSAM B. BUJRAH (c. 40 - 101)[3].

The following derived *aḥādīth* from him in writing:

Al-Ḥakam (d. 115)[4].

'Uthmān al-Mushāhid wrote two *Ṣaḥīfah* from him relating to *al-Maghāzī*[5].

31. MU'ĀDHAH BINT 'ABD ALLĀH AL-ADWIYAH (c. 20 - 83)[6].

She transmitted *aḥādīth* from 'Alī (d. 40) etc.

Yazīd al-Rashk had her *aḥādīth* in written form, and Shu'bah copied out her books from Yazīd's copies[7].

32. MUGHĪTH B. SUMAI (c. 10 - c. 80).

He transmitted *aḥādīth* from 'Umar, Abū Mas'ūd etc.[8] and had books[9].

33. MUḤAMMAD B. 'ALĪ B. ABŪ ṬĀLIB - IBN AL-ḤANAFIYAH (c. 15 - 73)[10].

---

1. *Tahd.*, x, 296.
2. Fasawī, iii, 268b; Khaithamah, iii, 58b; *Jāmi'*, 136a.
3. *Tahd.*, x, 289.
4. Ja'd 23; *'Illal*, i, 192; Fasawī, iii, 183a; Khaithamah, iii, 31a; Rāzī, *Introd.*, 130; *Tahd.*, 11, 434; x, 289.
5. *'Ilal*, 119b; i, 5.
6. *Tahd.*, xii, 452 (footnote).
7. *Kafāyah*, 229.
8. *Tahd.*,x, 255.
9. *Tahd.*, x, 255.
10. *Tahd.*, ix, 354 with great controversy about his death from 73 to 93.

'Abd al-A'lā b. 'Āmir al-Tha'labī transmitted a book from him in writing[1].

34. MUJĀHID B. JABR AL-MAKKĪ (21 - 102)[2].

He compiled a commentary on the *Qur'ān* which was copied by many scholars[3].

The following derived *aḥādīth* from him in writing:

Abū Yaḥyā al-Kunāsī[4].

Al-Ḥakam b. 'Utaibah[5].

Ibn Abū Najīḥ[6].

Ibn Juraij[7].

Ibn 'Uyaynah[8].

Laith b. Abū Sulaim[9].

Mayyāḥ b. Sarī'[10].

Al-Qāsim b. Abū Bazzah[11].

35. MUḤAMMAD B. JUBAIR (before 100 A.H.)[12]

Abū Bakr wrote *aḥādīth* from him[13].

36. AL-QĀSIM B. MUḤAMMAD (35 - 105)[14].

The following transcribed *aḥādīth* from him:

Abū Bakr b. Muḥammad b. Ḥazm[15].

Ṭalḥah b. 'Abd al-Malik al-Ailī[16].

---

1. Sa'd, vi, 233; *'Ilal,* 129b; i, 227; Fasawī, iii, 262a; Rāzī, *Introd.,* 71; iii, i, 26; *Tahd.,* vi, 94.
2. *Tahd.,* x, 43.
3. *'Ilal,* i, 44; Khaithamah, iii 27a; *Taqyīd,* 105.
4. *Taqyīd,* 105.
5. BTK, i, ii, 330, *Mashāhīr,* 146; *Thiqāt* 585; *Tahd.,* ii, 434.
6. *Thiqāt,* 506, 585; *Mashāhīr,* 146; *Tahd.,* vi, 54; see also Khaithamah, iii, 36b; Rāzī, ii, ii, 203; iv, ii, 51; *Kifāyah,* 215; *Tahd.,* vi, 54.
7. *Thiqāt,* 506, 585; *Tahd.,* vi, 54.
8. *Thiqāt,* 585; *Masāhīr,* 146. He transmitted book of Mujāhid by *Tadlīs.*
9. *Thiqāt,* 585; *Mashāhīr,* 146.
10. *Majrūḥīn,* 220b.
11. *Thiqāt,* 505; 585; *Mashāhīr,* 146.
12. *Tahd.,* ix, 91-2.
13. Sa'd, i, i, 39.
14. *Tahd.,* viii, 335.
15. *Tahd.,* xii, 39.
16. Rāmhurmuzī, 63b.

37. Rufai' b. Mihrān, Abū al-'Ākiyah al-Riyāḥī (10 B.H. - 90)[1].
90)[1].

He was born in the pre-Islamic era.

He wrote a commentary on the *Qur'ān*[2] and had *aḥāhīth* concerning Prayer, divorce, and the Pilgrimage (*Manāsik*) in writing[3]. He encouraged Abū Khaladah to write his *ahādīth*[4].

38. Sa'īd b. Fairūz al-Ṭā'ī (c. 30 A.H. - 83 A.H.)[5].

He had some *aḥādīth* in written form[6].

39. Sa'īd b. Jubair al-Asdī (46 - 95)[7].

He used to write *aḥādīth* and the knowlege of Ibn 'Abbās, Ibn 'Umar etc.,[8]. He compiled a commentary on the *Qur'ān*[9] which was transmitted by the following scholars:

Abd al-Malik b. Marwān[10].

'Aṭā' b. Dīnār[11].

'Azrah[12].

Al-Daḥḥāk[13].

Qatādah[14].

---

1. *Tahd.*,iii, 285.
2. Al-Kattānī, *Tarātib al-Idārīyah,* ii, 264 citing *Sharḥ al-Shifā'* for al-Qāḍī, 'Ayāḍ, i, 175.
3. *'Ilal,* 176b; *Jāmi',* 189b.
4. Rāmhurmuzī, 32b.
5. *Tahd.*, iv, 73.
6. *Amwāl,* 11.
7. *Tahd.*, iv, 13.
8. Sa'd, vi, 179.
9. *Fihrist,* 34.
10. Rāzī, iii, i, 332; *Tahd.*, vii, 198-9.
11. Rāzī, iii, i, 332; *Mīzān,* iii, 70; *Tahd.*, vii, 198.
12. Sa'd, vi, 186; Fasawī, iii, 326b; *Jāmi',* 57b.
13. Sa'd, vi, 210.
14. *'Ilal,* 160b.

40. Sālim b. Abū al-Ja'd (c. 15 B.H. - 100 A.H.)[1].

He used to write *aḥādīth*[2].

41. Sulaimān b. Qais al-Yashkurī (c. 30 between 70-80)[3].

He transmitted from Abū Sa'īd al-Khudrī etc., He used to write *aḥādīth*[4].

42. Shahr b. Ḥaushab al-Ash'arī (c. 20 - 100) [5].

'Abd al-Ḥamīd b. Bahrām transmitted a *Nuskhah* from him[6].

43. Shaqīq b. Salamah al-Asdī (7 B.H. after - 82 A.H.)[7].

Sufyā al-Thaurī had his *aḥādīth* in written form[8]. Sufyān was not a pupil of Shaqīq. He might have obtained this collection from his father who was a pupil of Shaqīq.[9].

44. Sharāḥīl b. Shuraḥbīl (c. 1 A.H. - c. 60).

He died in the reign of Mu'āwiyah (60 A.H.)[10] His students wrote *aḥādīth* from him[11].

45. 'Ubaid Allāh b. Abū Rāfi' (c. 15 - c. 80).

He was the scribe of the Caliph 'Alī[12] and transmitted *aḥādīth* from him and others. He composed a book on the war between 'Alī and Mu'āwiyah[13].

---

1. Bājī, 156b.
2. Sa'd, vi, 203; Khaithamah, iii, 88a; 155a; Rāmhurmuzī, 35b; *Taqyīd*, 108; 109; *Sharḥ 'Ilal*, 33a.
3. *Tahd*, iv, 215.
4. *Taqyīd*, 108.
5. *Tahd.*, iv, 371. See also *Bagh.*, xi, 59.
6. Khazrajī, 187. See also Rāzī, iii, i, 9; *Bagh.*, 59.
7. *Tahd.*, iv, 362.
8. *Bagh.*, ix, 160.
9. *Tahd.*,iv, 362.
10. *Thiqāt*, 221; *Tahd.*, iv, 319.
11. *Thiqāt*, 221.
12. *Tahd.*, vii, 10-11.
13. Tūsī, *Fihrist*, p. 202, see for quotations from this work in *Sunnī* sources, e.g. Ṭkabīr, i, 109b; 215b; 227b; 282a-b.

46. UM AL-DARDĀ' - HUJAIMAH (c. 15 - after 81)[1].

She wrote some *aḥādīth* for Sulaimān b. Zaitūn[2].

47. 'UMAR B. 'ABD AL-'AZĪZ (63 - 101)[3].

He wrote some *aḥādīth* and sent them to 'Abd al-Malik b. Ṭufail al-Jazarī who in turn transmitted them[4].

48. 'URWAH B. AL-ZUBAIR (22 - 93)[5].

He had a literary mind and taste and did not participate in the political turbulance of his period. His relations with the Umayyads were, however, amicable.

He began to write *aḥādīth* in the early stages of his life. We know that he wrote down *aḥādīth* of 'Ā'ishah[6]. Some of his books were destroyed which caused him great distress and sorrow throughout his life[7].

He taught *aḥādīth* systematically[8] and used to dictate *aḥādīth* to his students[9]. He was aware of the importance of revising after writing and we find his advice concerning this[10]. Furthermore, he emphasised the recollection of *aḥādīth* and refreshing the memory[11].

His Literary Career.

He is, perhaps, one of the first writers who compiled the comprehensive biography of the Prophet. The pattern set by him as well as the material he collected was followed and used by the later compilers such as al-Zuhrī etc. Going through al-Ṭabaranī's quotations, it looks as if the book was a large one.

---

1. *Tahd.*, xii, 467.
2. Zur'ah, 41b.
3. *Tahd.*, vii, 477.
4. *Tahd.*, vii, 476.
5. Ziriklī, v, 17, quoting *Nubalā*.
6. *Kifāyah*, 205.
7. Sa'd, v, 133; Rāmhurmuzī, 35b - 36a; Fischer, 41, 47; *Tahd.*, vii, 183.
8. Fasawī, ii, 178a-b.
9. *Imlā*, 78.
10. *Imlā*, 79.
11. Khaithamah, iii, 98b; Fasawī, ii, 178a-b.

Here are some extracts of the headings in this book collected from the first volume of al-Ṭabarānī's *al-Mu'jam al-Kabīr,* which gives some idea of the nature and size of the work.

The names of the Persons who were killed in the battle of Badr. I, 38a.

Those who were killed in the battle of al-Yamāmah from Al-Anṣār. I, 40a; 85a; 89b; 93b.

Those who were killed in the battle of Ḥunain from Quraish. 89a-b.

Those who were killed in the battle of Jisr al-Madā'in. I, 93b.

The Quaraishites who were killed in the battle of Khaibar. I, 99b.

The Names of Aṣḥāb al-'Aqabah. I, 118a.

Those who were murdered at Bi'r Ma'ūnah. I, 24a etc.

Battle of Khandaq. I, 95b.

Battle of Ajnādīn. I, 93b.

Al-Ṭabarī has preserved some lengthy passages from this work as well[1].

This book has been transmitted by various students and it was quite possible that it differed according to the transmitter, as compilers always adds new material and revises the previous work. The following versions can be traced:

Abū al-Aswad — 'Urwah[2].

Hishām b. 'Urwah — 'Urwah[3].

Al-Zuhrī — 'Urwah[4].

Yaḥyā b. 'Urwah - 'Urwah[5].

---

1. See for example: al-Ṭabarī, *Annales,* i, 1180; 1224-5; 1284-8; 1634-6; 1654; 1669-70. See also i, 1529; 1534; 1549 and 1551.

2. See for extracts, e.g. Ḥanbal, ii, 320; al-Balādhurī, *Futūḥ,* 41; 83, 96; Ṭabarānī, *al-Mu'jam al-Kabīr,* as mentioned above.

3. Ḥanbal, vi, 212; *Annales,* as quoted under footnote No. 1, of this page.

4. Ḥanbal, iv 323-26; 328-31; BU, *Maghāzī* 35; *Aḥkām* 26; Ṭ kabīr x, 243a-244b; *Annales,* i, 1529; 1534; 1549; 1551.

5. *Annales,* i, 1185, 1188.

Apart from the *Sīrah* work, the following derived *aḥādīth* from him in writing:

'Abd al-Malik b. Marwān[1].

Hishām, his son[2].

Hubaira[3].

49. YAḤYĀ B. AL-JAZZĀR AL-'URANĪ (c. 20 - c. 80).

He transmitted from 'Alī (d. 40) etc.[4].

Al-Ḥakam b. 'Utaibah had his *aḥādīth* in writing[5].

III. WRITINGS OF AND FROM SCHOLARS COVERING LATE FIRST AND EARLY SECOND CENTURIES

1. 'ABDAH B. ABŪ LUBĀBAH AL-GHĀḌIRĪ (c. 50 - after 123)[6].

He transmitted *aḥādīth* from Ibn 'Umar (d. 74) etc. Qatādah wrote *aḥādith* and sent them to him[7]. It is reported that he disliked the writing of *aḥādīth*[8].

2. 'ABD AL-'AZĪZ B. SA'ĪD B. SA'D B. 'UBĀDAH (c. 50 - c. 110).

His father was one of the group of younger Companions.

'Abd al-Ghafūr b. 'Abd al-'Azīz al-Wasiṭī transmitted a *Nuskhah* from him[9].

3. 'ABD ALLĀH B. ABŪ BAKR B. ḤAZM AL-ANṢĀRĪ (65 - 135)[10].

He wrote down some *aḥādīth* and sent them to Ibn Juraij[11]. It seems that 'Abd Allāh had a book on al-Maghāzī which was transmitted by his nephew 'Abd al-Malik b. Muḥammad b. Abū Bakr[12].

---

1. Sa'd, viii, 6-7; *Annales,* i, 1180; 1284-8; 1634-6; 1654; 1669-70 etc.
2. Fasawī, ii, 263a; Khaithamah, iii, 39a; 138b; 141a.
3. Sa'd, viii, 6-7.
4. *Tahd.,* xi, 191.
5. *Bag.,*vii, 348; *Kifāyah,* 112; *Tahd.,* ii, 305. See also *Kifāyah,* 220.
6. *Tahd.,* vi, 462.
7. Al-Qaisarānī, 335.
8. *'Ilal,* i, 310.
9. *Thiqāt,* 266.
10. *Tahd.,* v, 165; Khazrajī, 163.
11. Ḥanbal, iv, 56; see for detail, *Ṭakabīr,* iii, 196b.
12. *Bagh,* x, 409. See also *Tahd.,*vi 388. Ibn al-Nadīm attributes this book to 'Abd al-Mālik, *Fihrist,* 226.

4. ʻABD ALLĀH B. ʻAUN AL-BAṢRĪ (66-151)[1].

It is said that he did not write down *aḥādīth*[2], but according to ʻUthmān b. Abū Shaibah his book was perfect[3]. It is possible that he was not in favour of writing down traditions in lectures, but that one could memorize what was said in the lecture and later write down from memory. Perhaps this was his own practice too. He wrote to Nafiʻasking for *aḥādīth* and received them in written form[4].

The following derived *aḥādīth* from him in writing:

Haudhah b. Khalīfah[5].

Ismāʻīl[6].

Khālid b. Ḥārith[7].

Muʻādh b. Muʻādh[8].

Muḥammad b. Abū ʻAdi[9].

Salīm b. Akhḍar[10].

Yaḥyā al-Qaṭṭān[11].

5. ABD ALLĀH B. BISHR - AL-KĀTIB (c. 50 - c. 115).

He transmitted from ʻUrwah al-Bāriqī, the first judge of Kūfah[12].

Shuʻbah wrote *aḥādīth* from him[13].

6. ʻABD ALLĀH B. BURAIDAH AL-ASLAMĪ (15 - 115)[14].

Husain al-Muʻallim was invited by Maṭar-al-Warrāq to write down ʻAbd Allāh's *aḥādīth*, and so they attended the lecture[15].

---

1. *Tahd.*, v, 347-8; Khazarajī, 177.
2. Rāmhurmuzī, 36b.
3. *Tahd.*, v, 349.
4. BTK, iii, i, 3; MU, *Jihād,* i; Balādhurī, *Ansāb,* i, 342; *Mustadrak,* I, 15.
5. Saʻd, vii, ii, 80.
6. *ʻIlal,* i, 379.
7. Rāzī, Introd. 248; iv, ii, 150.
8. Rāzī, Introd. 248; iv, ii, 150.
9. *ʻIlal,* 98a.
10. *ʻIlal,* i, 372.
11. Rāzī, Introd. 248; iv, ii, 150.
12. *Tahd.*, vii, 178.
13. *Kifāyah,* 231.
14. *Tahd.*, v, 158.
15. *Jāmiʻ,* 136a.

Al-Ḥussain b. Wāqid al-Marwazī transmitted a *Nuskhah* from him[1].

7. 'Abd Allāh b. Dhakwān - Abū al-Zinād (64 - 130)[2].

He had a book[3] and compiled many works[4].

The following derived *aḥādīth* from him in writing:

'Abd al-Raḥmān b. Abū al-Zinād. He transmitted from his father *Kitāb al-Fuqahā' al-Sab'ah*[5].

Mālik had a *Ṣaḥīfah* from him[6].

Al-Mughīrah[7].

Shu'āib b. Abū Ḥamzah[8].

Sufyān[9].

Warqā'[10].

8. 'Abd Allāh b. 'Isā b. Abū Lailā al-Anṣārī (c. 65 - 135)[11].

He transmitted from his grandfather Ibn Abū Lailā (d. 83).

Zaid b. 'Alī wrote down some *aḥādīth* from him[12].

9. 'Abd Allāh b. Muḥammad b. 'Aqīl (c. 55 - 142)[13].

He transmitted from Ibn 'Umar (d. 74) etc. 'Ubaid Allāh b. 'Amr al-Raqqī had his book[14].

10. 'Abd al-Raḥmān b. Hurmuz al-A'raj (c. 40 - 117)[15].

He transmitted from Abū Hurairah (d. 59) etc.

---

1. *Ma'rifah*, 165.
2. *Tahd.*, v, 204.
3. *Tahd.*, v, 205; *Imlā,* 173; *Thiqāt*, 507; *Mashāhīr*, 135.
4. See, Sa'īd b. Manṣūr, Sunan iii, i, 2-12; Abd ur Rāzza *Muṣannaf,* viii, 338.
5. *Tahd.*, vi, 172; *Bagh.*, x, 230; see also *Imlā,* 173.
6. *Majrūḥīn,* 109b.
7. *'Ilal,* 109a.
8. Zur'ah, 67b.
9. *Kifāyah*, 354.
10. *Mīzān,* ii, 133; see also Rāzī, introduction 154; *Tahd.*, xi, 114; *'Ilal,* 166a; *Mīzān,* iv, 332.
11. *Tahd.*, v, 352.
12. *'Ilal,* 97b.
13. *Tahd.*, vi, 15.
14. Rāzī, ii, ii, 329.
15. *Tahd.*, v, 291.

The following derived *aḥādīth* from him in writing:

Anonymous[1].

Abū Zinād[2]

'Ikrimah[3].

Nāfi' al-Qārī[4].

Yazīd b. Abū Ḥabīb[5].

Al-Zhurī[6].

11. 'ABD AL-RAḤMĀN B. SĀBIṬ (c. 35 - 118)[7].

He transmitted from 'Ā'shah (d. 57) and others.

Jābir b. Zaid wrote *aḥādīth* from him[8].

12. ABŪ BAKR B. MUḤAMMAD B. 'AMR. B. ḤAZM AL-ANṢĀRĪ (c. 50 - 117)[9].

On the command of 'Umar b. 'Abd al-'Azīz he wrote the *aḥādīth* from 'Amrah bint 'Abd al-Raḥmān, Qāsim b. Muḥammad and others[10]. When his son was asked about these books he stated that they were lost[11].

13. AL-'ALĀ' B. 'ABD AL-RAḤMĀN (c. 50 - 139)[12].

He transmitted from Ibn 'Umar (d. 74) etc. and had *Nusakh*[13] which were famous in al-Madīnah[14]. He used to say

1. Sa'd, v, 209
2. Rāmhurmuzī, 77b; *Jāmi'*, 56b; *Imlā*, 173; see also *Kāmil*, i, 316b; iii, 117a-b.
3. Fasawī, ii, 209b.
4. *Kāmil*, ii, 52b.
5. *Kifāyah*, 355. Someone put a book in his trustee which contained *aḥādīth* from al-A'raj.
6. Fasawī, ii, 209b.
7. *Tahd.*, vi, 181.
8. *Taqyīd*, 109.
9. *Tahd.*, xii, 39.
10. Fasawī, ii, 216a; 132a; Rāzī, introd. 21; iv, II, 337; Fischer 90; see also *'Ilal*, i, 12; *Taqyīd*, 105-6; Darimī, i, 126; Sa'd, viii, 353.
11. *Tahd.*, xii, 39.
12. *Tahd.*, viii, 187.
13. *Kāmil*, ii, 278b.
14. *Tahd.*, vii, 187.

to those who wanted to copy a part of his book that they must copy completely or they should not copy at all[1].

1. Yūsuf b. 'Abd al-Raḥmān transmitted a *Nuskhah* from him[2].

14. 'ALĪ B. 'ABD ALLĀH B. 'ABBĀS (40 - 117)[3].

He had books[4].

15. 'ALĪ B. YAZĪD AL-ALHĀNĪ (c. 50 - about 110)[5].

He had many books[6].

'Ubaid Allāh b. Zahr transmitted a *Nuskhah* from him[7].

16. 'AMR. B. 'ABD ALLĀH - ABŪ ISḤĀQ AL-SABĪ'Ī (29 - 127)[8].

He had books which were utilized by his son and grandson.

The following derived *aḥādīth* from him in writing:

Al-A'mash[9].

'Abd al-Ghaffār b. al-Qāsim[10].

'Abd al-Kabīr b. Dīnār[11].

Isrā'īl[12].

Nūḥ b. Abū Maryam[13].

Shu'bah[14].

Yūnus[15].

---

1. Ibn Qutaibah, *Ma'ārif* 491.
2. *Kāmil,* i, 316b.
3. *Tahd.*, vii, 358.
4. Abū 'Awānah, *Musnad,* ii, 340.
6. *Tahd.*, vii, 397.
7. *Tahd.*, vii, 12.
8. *Tahd.*, viii, 65-6.
9. *'Ilal,* i, 104; Rāmhurmuzī, 37a; *Taqyīd,* 112.
10. Ṭkabīr, vi, 261a.
11. *Ma'rifah,* 165.
12. Fasawī, iii, 49a; *Tahd.*, i, 262.
13. *Ma'rifah,* 164.
14. *Kifāyah,* 220.
15. *Tahd.*, xi, 434.

17. 'AMR. B. DĪNĀR AL-MAKKĪ (c. 50 - 126)[1].

He wrote tradition from Ibn 'Abbās[2].

Students used to write his opinions also, of which he disapproved saying, "They ask our opinions, when we tell them, they write them as if they were marks on a stone. We may have opinions against them tomorrow[3]."

The following derived *aḥādīth* from him in written form:

Abū 'Amr b. al-'Alā'[4].

Ayyūb[5].

Ḥammād b. Zaid[6].

Ibn 'Uyaynah[7].

Nephew of 'Amr[8].

Al-Walīd b. Al-Walīd[9].

18. 'ĀṢIM B. 'UMAR B. QATĀDAH (c. 50 - 120)[10].

He transmitted from Jābir b. 'Abd Allāh (d. 73) etc. He had books on *Al-Maghāzī* and *Siyar*[11].

19. AL-ASWAD B. QAIS AL-BAJALĪ (c. 50 - c. 125).

He transmitted from Jundub b. 'Abd Allāh (d. c. 65) etc., and Ibn 'Uyaynah etc., transmitted from him[12].

'Abīdah b. Ḥumaid had *aḥādīth* of Aswad in written form[13].

---

1. *Tahd.*, vii, 30. He was over 70 years when he died.
2. Fasawī, iii, 5b.
3. Sa'd, v, 353; Khaithamah, iii, 34b; Fasawī, iii, 5a.
4. Sa'd, vii, ii, 42.
5. Sa'd, vii, ii, 42; *'Ilal,* i, 20; Zur'ah, 72a; 91a; Khaithamah, iii, 35a; *Jāmi'*, 144.
6. Sa'd. vii. ii, 42.
7. Ja'd, 213; Rāzī, introd. 34; ii, i, 226; *Kāmil,* i, 32a; *Kifāyah* 60; 231; see also *'Ilal,* i, 20; Zur'ah, 72a; Khaithamah, iii, 35a.
8. Fasawī, iii, 233a-b.
9. *Majrūḥīn,* 237b.
10. *Tahd.*, v, 54.
11. Dr. Jawād 'Alī, *Mawārid Tārīkh alṬabarī, Majallah al-Majma' al-'Ilmī al-'Irāqī,* vol. iii, i, 38-39.
12. Khazrajī, 32; *Tahd.*, i, 341.
13. *'Ilal,* i, 384.

20. 'AṬĀ' B. ABŪ MUSLIM AL-KHURĀSĀNĪ (60 - 135)[1].

He compiled a commentary on the holy *Qur'ān*[2].

Ibn Juraij had the commentary on the *Qur'ān* from him in writing[3].

21. 'AṬĀ' B. ABŪ RABĀḤ (27 - 117)[4].

He encouraged students to transcribe *aḥādīth* and even helped them in their writings with paper and ink etc.[5].

The following derived *aḥādīth* from him in writing:

Anonymous[6].

Ḥaushab b. 'Aqīl[7].

Hishām b. Ḥassān[8].

Ibn Juraij[9].

Mu'āwiyah b. 'Abd al-Karīm al-Thaqafī[10].

Qais b. Sa'd[11].

Ya'qūb b. 'Aṭā'[12].

Yazīd b. Abū Ḥabīb. 'Aṭā' wrote *aḥādīth* and sent them to him[13].

Zakariyā b. Isḥāq al-Makkī[14].

---

1. *Kāmil,* ii, 329b.
2. Ḥājī Khalīfah, *Kashf al-Zunūn,* 453.
3. Khaithamah, iii, 40a; __*'ilal Tirmidhī,* ii, 239; *Kifāyah,* 315: *Sharḥ 'ilal,* 59a; *Tahd.,* vii, 214.
4. *Tahd.,* vii, 202-3.
5. Rāmhurmuzī, 35b. See also, Dārimī, i, 125.
6. Khaithamah, iii, 30a.
7. *Tahd.,* xi, 37.
8. Fasawī, iii, 274b; see also *Tahd.,* xi, 37.
9. Tirmidhī, *'Ilal,* ii, 238.
10. *Tahd.,* x. 214.
11. *Tahd.,* vii, 244.
12. Rāzī, i, ii, 593; *Tahd.,* iii, 329; see also Rāzī, introd. 39.
13. BU. *Buyū',* 112; *Tafsīr An'ām* 6.
14. Rāzī, *introd.,* 39; i, ii, 593; *Tahd.,* iii, 329.

22. ʻAUF B. ABŪ JAMĪLAH (59 - 146)[1].

The following derived *aḥādīth* from him in writing:

ʻAbbād b. ʻAbbād[2].

Bunḍār[3].

Haudhah[4].

Hushaim[5].

23. ʻAUN B. ʻABD ALLĀH B. ʻUTBAH (c. 40 - about 110)[6].

He transmitted from Abū Hurairah (d. 59) etc., and wrote some *aḥādīth* for Ya'qūb al-Ashajj[7].

24. AYYŪB B. ABŪ TAMĪMAH AL-SAKHTIYĀNĪ (68 - 131)[8].

He wrote *aḥādīth* in great quantities. According to Ibn Sa'd, he was a collector of *Ḥadīth*[9].

The following transcribed *aḥādīth* from him:

ʻAbd al-Ṣamad. He had incomplete memoranda from Ayyūb, and completed them after Ayyūb's death[10].

ʻAbd al-Wārith. He wrote Ayyūb's *aḥādīth* from memory after the death of his teacher[11].

Ḥammād b. Zaid[12].

Ḥusain b. Wāqid (d. 159)[13].

Ibn ʻUlayyah[14].

---

1. *Tahd.*, vii, 167.
2. *ʻIlal,* i, 376.
3. *Mīzān,* iii, 305; *Tahd.*, viii, 167.
4. Sa'd, vii, ii, 80.
5. *ʻIlal,* i, 353.
6. *Tahd.*, viii, 173.
7. Rāmhurmuzī, 58b.
8. Sa'd, vii, ii, 17.
9. Sa'd, vii, ii, 14; *Tahd.*, i, 398.
10. Fasawī, iii, 37b.
11. Fasawī, iii, 37b.
12. *Tahd.*, iii, 11.
13. *Thiqāt,* 438.
14. *ʻIlal,* i, 379; Zur'ah, 76a.

Ibrahīm b. Yazīd (d. 150)[1].
Mālik b. Anas[2].

25. ḤABĪB B. SĀLIM AL-ANṢĀRĪ (c. 40 - c. 110).
He transmitted from Abū Hurairah (d. 59) etc.[3].
The following transcribed *aḥādīth* from him:
Qatādah. Ḥabīb sent him some *aḥādīth* in written form[4].
Yazīd b. Nu'mān. Ḥabīb wrote down some *aḥādīth* and sent them to Yazīd[5].

26. ḤABĪB B. ABŪ THĀBIT (c. 45 - 119)[6].
He wrote only one *ḥadīth*[7].

27. ḤAFS B. SULAIMĀN AL-TAMĪMĪ AL-MINQARĪ (c. 65 - 130)[8].
He had books which were read by Ash'ath b. 'Abd al-Malik[9].

28. AL-ḤAKAM B. 'UTAIBAH B. AL-KINDĪ (50 - 115)[10].
Shu'bah had some *aḥādīth* from him in writing[11].

29. ḤAMMĀD B. ABŪ SULAIMĀN (c. 60 - 120)[12].
He transmitted from Anas b. Mālik (d. 93) and others.
The following transcribed *aḥādīth* from him:
Abū Ḥanīfah[13].
Ḥammad b. Salamah[14].

---

1. *Majrūḥīn,* 33b.
2. Bājī, 24a; *Tahd.,* i, 398.
3. *Tahd.,* ii, 184.
4. Nas, ii, 89; see also Ḥanbal, iv, 276.
5. Ḥanbal, iv, 273.
6. Sa'd vi, 224; *Tahd.,* ii, 179.
7. Sa'd, vi, 223.
8. Khazrajī, 74.
9. Sa'd, vii, ii, 35.
10. *Tahd.,* ii, 434.
11. *Kifāyah,* 220; *Bagh.,* ix, 260; *Islām,* vi, 193.
12. *Tahd.,* iii, 17.
13. Rāzī, iv, i, 450.
14. Ja'd, 439.

Hishām[1].

Muḥammad b. Jābir al-Yamāmī[2].

Shu'bah[3].

30. Al-Ḥasan b. Yasār al-Baṣrī (21 - 110)[4].

He transmitted from very many companions and got many books from them[5]. He himself had many books[6]. He used to write to Ibn Al-Musayyab whenever he was confronted with difficult problems[7].

He dictated his commentary on the *Qur'ān*[8] to his pupils and even wrote *aḥādīth* for the people[9].

The following derived *aḥādīth* from him in written form:

Anonymous[10].

Anonymous[11].

Ḥafṣ al-Minqarī[12].

Ḥaushab b. 'Aqīl[13].

Hishām b. Ḥassān al-Azdī[14].

Hishām b. Ziyād[15].

Ḥumaid b. Abū Ḥumaid al-Ṭawīl[16].

Ḥusain Abū Sufyān b. Ḥusain al-Wāsiṭī. Ḥasan dictated to him[17].

Khālid al-'Abd[18].

---

1. Ja'd, 439.
2. Rāzī, iv, i, 450.
3. *Islām,* vi, 193.
4. *Tahd.*, ii, 266.
5. *Annales, Dhail,* iii, 2489; *Tahd.*, ii, 267; 269.
6. *Annales, Dhail,* iii, 2492; Sa'd, vii, i, 127; see also Sa'd, vii, i, 116; *Taqyīd,* 101; *Jāmi',* 101a.
7. *Ḥuffāẓ,* i, 47.
8. *Mukhtaṣar Jāmi' Bayān al-'Ilm of Ibn 'Abd al-Barr,* p. 37.
9. *Taqyīd,* 102.
10. *Kifāyah,* 318.
11. Dāraquṭnī, 204.
12. Rāzī, iv, ii, 58; Sa'd, vii, ii, 35; *Tahd.*, xi, 39.
13. *Tahd.*, xi, 37.
14. *Tahd.*, xi. 35.
15. Rāzī, iv, ii, 58.
16. *'Ilal,* i, 15; Fasawī, iii, 24a; Sa'd, vii, ii, 17; *Tahd.*, iii, 39; *Kifāyah,* 236; see also *Mīzān,* i, 610.
17. BTK, i, ii, 380.
18. BTS. 181; Rāzī, i, ii, 364; *Kāmil,* I, 312b; *Majrūḥīn,* 94b.

Mu'āwiyah b. 'Abd al-Karīm al-Thaqafī[1].
Sahl b. Ḥuṣain b. Muslim al-Bāhilī[2].
Yūnus b. 'Ubaid[3].

31. HISHĀM B. 'URWAH (61 - 146)[4].
His father instructed him to copy *aḥādīth* and to revise them[5].
The following transcribed *aḥādīth* from him:
Anonymous[6].
Ibn Juraij[7].
Ja'far b. Rabī'ah[8].
Khālid b. al-Ḥārith[9].
Laith b. Sa'd Hishām wrote some *aḥādīth* for him[10].
Ma'mar. His *Ṣaḥīfah* from Hishām had only four *aḥādīth*[11].
Nūḥ b. Abū Maryam[12].
'Ubaid b. Al-Qāsim transmitted a forged *Nuskhah* from him[13].
Yaḥyā[14].

32. ḤUṢAIN B. 'ABD AL-RAḤMĀN AL-SULAMĪ (43 - 136)[15].
The following wrote *aḥādīth* from him:
'Alī b. 'Āṣim[16].
Hushaim. He wrote down nearly all the *aḥādīth* of Ḥuṣain[17].

---

1. *Tahd.*, x, 214.
2. Sa'd, vii, i, 127; *'Ilal*, i, 89; *Annales, Dhail*, iii, 2492.
3. Rāzī, iv, ii, ɔ8.
4. *Tahd.*, xi, 51; see also *Mīzān*, iv, 302.
5. *Imlā*, 78-9.
6. Sa'd, v, 362; Ibn Qutaibah, *Ma'ārif*, 488.
7. Sa'd, v, 362; Fasawī, iii, 263b; al-Tirmidhī, *'Ilal*, ii, 239; Ibn Qutaibah, *Ma'ārif*, 488; *Kifāyah*, 320.
8. *Kifāyah*, 343.
9. Nas, i, 66.
10. BU, *Bad' al-Khalq*, 11; *Manāqib*, 24; *Kifāya*, 344.
11. *Kāmil*, i, 36a.
12. *Ma'rifah*, 164.
13. *Mīzān*, iii, 21; *Tahd.*, vii, 73.
14. Fasawī, iii, 43a; Khaithamah, iii, 138b; 141a.
15. *Tahd.*, ii, 382; Khazrajī, 73.
16. *Jāmi'*, 175a.
17. *Wāsiṭ*, 74.

Ibn Idrīs[1].

Nūḥ b. Abū Maryam transmitted a *Nuskhah* from him[2].

A group of students read his book to him[3].

33. ḤUYAY B. HĀNĪ - ABŪ QABĪL (c. 25 - 128)[4].

Ibn Lahī'ah had a book from him[5].

34. IBRĀHĪM B. 'ABD AL-A'LĀ AL-JU'FĪ (c. 60 - c. 125).

He transmitted from Suwaid B. Ghaflah (d. 80) and others[6]. Among his transmitters were Isrā'īl and al-Thaurī.

Isra'il derived *aḥādīth* from him in written form:

Shu'bah wrote to him, asking him to send 'Abd al-A'la's *aḥādīth* written in his own hand. So he wrote them and sent them to him[7].

35. IBRĀHĪM B. JARĪR B. 'ABD ALLĀH AL-BAJALĪ (c. 40 - before 120)[8].

Sharīk had *aḥādīth* from him in writing[9].

36. IBRĀHĪM B. MUSLIM AL-HAJARĪ (c. 65 - c. 130).

He transmitted *aḥādīth* from 'Abd Allah b. Abū Awfā (d. 86) and others[10]. Ibn 'Uyaynah says that when he visited Ibrahīm al-Hajarī, he brought all his books to Ibn 'Uyaynah who put them in order for the old man[11]. Ibn 'Uyaynah explained to him which book was from 'Abd Allāh, which was from the Prophet, and which one was from 'Umar[12].

---

1. Rāhurmuzī, 37a.
2. *Ma'rifah,* 164.
3. Bājī, 48a.
4. *Tahd.,* iii, 73.
5. Rāzī, iii, i, 154.
6. Khazrajī, 16.
7. Rāzī, i, i, 112; *Tahd.,* i, 138.
8. Khazarajī, 14.
9. *Thiqāt,* 133.
10. *Tahd.,* i, 164.
11. *Kāmil,* i, 72b; *Mīzān,* i 66; *Tahd.,* i, 165.
12. *Tahd.,* i, 165.

37. Isḥāq b. 'Abd Allāh b. Abū Farwah (c. 50 - 144)[1].
He saw Mu'āwiyah b. Abū Sufyān.
Al-Laith b. Sa'd transmitted a large *Nuskhah* from him[2].

38. Iyās b. Mu'āwiya (d. 122)[3].
'Umar b. 'Abdul 'Azīz wrote down *aḥādīth* from him[4].

39. Jamīl b. Zaid al-Tā'ī al-Baṣrī (c. 50 - 120).
He saw Ibn 'Umar, while on the pilgrimage[5]. After the death of Ibn 'Umar, he went to al-Madīnah and wrote down his *aḥādīth*[6]. He had no opportunity to hear them from Ibn 'Umar.

40. Jawwāb b. 'Ubaid Allāh al-A'war al-Taimī (c. 50 - c. 120).
He transmitted from al-Ḥārith b. Suwaid al-Taimī (d. 71)[7] and others. Sufyān al-Thaurī found him in Jurjān, but did not write from him, and later he wrote Jawwāb's *aḥādīth* from one of his students[8].

41. Khālid b. Abū 'Imrān al-Tujībī (c. 60 - 129)[9].
The following derived *aḥādīth* from him in written form:
Al-Laith b. Sa'd, Khalid sent *aḥādīth* to him in writing[10].
Yaḥya b. Sa'īd. Khālid sent some *aḥādīth* to him in writing[11].
Anonymous. He had a book from Khālid[12].

42. Maimūn b. Mihrān, Abū Ayyū al-Raqqī (17 - 117)[13].
Ja'far b. Burqān transmitted a *Nuskhah* from him[14].

---

1. *Tahd.*, i, 240-2.
2. *Kāmil*, i, 118a.
3. *Taqrib*, i, 87.
4. Baihaqi, *Sunan*, x, 194-5.
5. *Tahd.*, ii, 114.
6. *'Ilal*, i, 168; 237; BTK, i, ii, 215; *Ta'jīl*, 73; *Tahd.*, ii, 114.
7. *Tahd.*, ii, 121.
8. Rāzī, *introd.*, 80-81; i, i, 536; see also, *Mīzān*, i, 426.
9. *Tahd.*, iii, 111.
10. *Annales*, iii, 2374.
11. Rāmhurmuzī, 48b.
12. *'Ilal*, i, 232.
13. *Tahd.*, x, 392.
14. *Kāmil*, i, 213b.

43. MAKḤŪL AL-SHĀMĪ (c. 55 - 118)[1].

According to Ibn al-Nadīm, he compiled *Kīb al-Sunan* and *Kitāb al-Masā'il fi Al-Fiqh*[2]. There is another reference to one of his works — *Kitāb al-Ḥajj*[3].

The following transcribed *aḥādīth* from him:

'Abd al-'Azīz b. Abū al-Sā'ib[4].

'Amr b. Abū al-Walīd[5].

Rukn b. 'Abd Allāh al-Shāmī[6]. He transmitted a *Nuskhah* from him which was mostly false.

'Ubaid Allāh b. 'Ubaid al-Kalā'ī[7].

Al-'Alā' b. al-Ḥārith[8].

Al-'Alā' b. Kathīr[9].

44. MANṢŪR B. AL-MU'TAMAR (c. 50 - 132)[10].

It was understood that he was against the writing down of *aḥādīth*[11]. During his early education he depended on memory only, but later on he regretted it[12]. A collection of 800 *aḥādīth* in his class is mentioned[13].

The following wrote *aḥādīth* from him:

'Abīdah b. Ḥumaid and his fellows. They had a book from Manṣūr containging 800 *aḥādīth*[14].

Jarīr B. 'Abd al-Ḥamīd[15].

---

1. *Tahd.,* x. 291.
2. *Fihrist,* 227.
3. Zur'ah, 56b; *Sharḥ 'Ilal,* 104b; *Tahd.*, viii, 178.
4. *Jāmi'*, 58b. - 59a.
5. *Kifāyah,* 265.
6. *Majrūḥīn,* 102b.
7. *Kifāyah,* 320.
8. Zur'ah, 56b; *Sharḥ 'Ilal,* 104b; *Tahd.*, viii, 178.
9. *Tahd.*, viii, 191.
10. *Tahd.*, x, 315. It is said that he fasted 60 years, so he must have lived more than 70 years.
11. *Taqyīd,* 48.
12. Fasawī, iii, 189b.
13. *'Ilal,* i, 361.
14. *'Ilal,* i, 361.
15. *'Ilal,* i, 362; Fasawī, ii, 213b.

Sa'īd b. Maslamah b. Hishām al-Umawī[1].

Shu'bah. He wrote from Manṣūr[2] and Manṣūr also sent him *aḥādīth* in writing[3]. He was doubtful whether or not to transmit them. Shu'bah expressed his doubts to Manṣūr when he met him. Manṣūr replied: "When I wrote to you, I imparted *aḥādīth* to you"[4].

Warqā' b. 'Umar[5].

45. Manṣūr b. Zādhān al-Wāsiṭī (c. 65 - 128)[6].

Hushaim says: "We used to write from him after *'Ishā* prayer[7].

Muḥammad b. 'Alī b. Ḥasan (56 - 114)[8]. He had many books[9].

46. Muḥammad b. Abū Bakr al-Anṣārī (60 - 132)[10].

Mūsā b. 'Isā asked him to write down some of his *aḥādīth*[11].

47. Muḥammad b. al-Munkadir (54 - 130)[12].

The following wrote *aḥādīth* from him:

Nūḥ b. Abū Maryam[13].

Ṣadaqah b. 'Abd Allāh al-Samīn transmitted a forged *Nuskhah* from him[14].

Sa'īd b. Muḥammad[15].

48. Muḥammad b. Muslim b. Shihāb al-Zuhrī (51 - 124).

Al-Zuhrī had a number of pupils who made collections of his *aḥādīth*, either copying his books or writing down his lectures.

---

1. Rāzī, ii, i, 67; *Tahd.*, iv, 83.
2. *'Ilal*, i, 266; Khaithamah, iii, 49b; *Kifāyah*, 233.
3. *'Ilal*, 148b; i, 281; Ḥanbal, i, 438; ii, 461; 498; iv, 60; Ibn Mājah, *Iqāmat Ṣalāt.* Trad. No. 1211; Nas, i, 184; 230; *Kifāyah*. 164.
4. *'Ilal*, 148b; i, 281.
5. *Mīzān*, iv, 332.
6. *Tahd.*, x, 307.
7. *Jāmi'*, 115a.
8. *Tahd.*, ix, 351.
9. See *Tahd.*, ii, 104.
10. *Tahd.*, ix, 80.
11. *Annales*, i, 1086.
12. *Tahd.*, ix, 474.
13. *Ma'rifah*, 164.
14. *Majrūḥīn*, 124b.
15. *Majrūḥīn*, 109b.

The following derived *aḥādīth* from him in writing:

'Abbās b. Ḥasan transmitted a *Nuskhah* from al-Zuhrī[1].

'Abd al-Malik b. 'Abd al-'Azīz b. Juraij. Al-Zurhrī gave him a *Juz'*[2].

'Abd al-Raḥmān b. 'Amr al-Auzā'ī. Al-Zuhrī gave him a *Ṣaḥīfah*, permitting him to transmit it on his authority[3].

'Abd al-Raḥmān b. Khālid b. Musāfir. According to Ibn Ma'īn's statement he had a book from al-Zuhrī[4].

'Abd al-Raḥmān b. Namirah al-Yaḥṣubī. He was the scribe who came with Ibn Hishām, and al-Zhurī dictated to them. He had a *Nuskhah* from al-Zuhrī[5].

'Abd al-Raḥmān b. Yazīd al-Dimashqī. He had a large book from al-Zuhrī[6].

'Abd al-Razzāq b. 'Umar. He wrote from al-Zuhrī, and later lost the book; then he gathered *aḥādīth* of al-Zuhrī from various sources. Therefore he is a weak narrator of al-Zuhrī[7].

Āl-Abī 'Atīq. Wāqidī saw a *Ṣaḥīfah* from al-Zuhrī in the family of Āl-Abī 'Atīq[8].

Ayyūb b. Mūsā had a book from al-Zuhrī[9].

Ayyūb al-Sakhtiyānī had a book from him[10].

Al-Ḥārith b. Jārūd had a book from al-Zuhrī[11].

Ḥumaid b. Qais al-Makkī had a book from al-Zuhrī[12].

Hushaim b. Bashīr al-Sulamī. He wrote a *Ṣaḥīfah* from al-Zuhrī in Makkah[13].

---

1. *Thiqāt*, 571.
2. Ja'd, 192; *Kifāyah*, 319; Rāzī, ii, ii, 357-8; *Tahd.*, ii, 465.
3. Zur'ah, 62a; 150a; *Tahd.*, vi, 241.
4. *Tahd.*, vi, 165.
5. *Tahd.*, vi, 287-8.
6. *Tahd.*, vi, 295; see also Fasawī, iii, 124b.
7. Fasawī, iii, 275b; Zur'ah, 53b; Rāzī, iii, i, 39.
8. Dāraquṭnī, 61.
9. BU. *Faḍā'il Aṣḥāb al-Nabī*, 18.
10. Khaithamah, iii, 127a.
11. Al-Azdī, *Tārīkh al-Mauṣil*, 174.
12. Khaithamah, iii, 37a.
13. *Kāmil*, i, 31b; *Mīzān*, iv, 308. *Tahd;* xi, 60. It contained 300 traditions.

Ibrāhīm b. al-Walīd al-Umawī. He brought a *Ṣaḥīfah* to al-Zuhrī and read it to him عرض عليه so al-Zuhrī permitted him to transmit the *Ṣaḥīfa*[1].

Isḥāq b. Rāshid al-Jazarī. He found the book of al-Zuhrī in Jerusalem, but did not see him personally[2].

Ismā'īl b. Rāfi' b. 'Uwaimir, died between 110-120. He lost his books from al-Zuhrī[3].

Ja'far b. Rabī'ah. Al-Zuhrī sent him *aḥādīth* in writing[4].

Ja'far b. Burqān al-Kilābī had a *Nuskhah* from al-Zuhrī[5].

Al-Laith B. Sa'd. He wrote a great many *aḥādīth* of al-Zuhrī[6].

Mālik b. Anas. He had the book of al-Zuhrī. He and 'Ubaid Allāh both went to al-Zuhrī with the book and there they heard *aḥādīth* from him[7].

Ma'mar b. Rāshid wrote *aḥādīth* from Al-Zuhrī. Even in the lifetime of al-Zuhrī, 'Ubaid Allāh wrote from Ma'mar from al-Zuhrī[8].

Maslamah b. 'Amr al-Qāḍī. He found a book in al-Zuhrī's office, written in his own hand[9].

Mu'āwiyah b. Yaḥyā al-Ṣadafī. He bought the book of al-Zuhrī[10].

Muḥammad b. 'Abd Allah, Ibn Akhī al-Zuhrī, had the books of his uncle al-Zuhrī[11].

Muḥammad b. 'Abd al-'Azīz. His son Aḥmad says, "Among my father's books I found a book of al-Zuhrī..."[12].

---

1. *Kifāyah,* 266.
2. Ibn Ḥajar, *Ṭabaqāt al-Mudallisīn,* 4; see also Ṭkabīr, iv, 198.
3. *Tahd.,* i, 296.
4. *Tahd.,* ix, 447; BU, *Adhān,* 157; A.D. *ḥadīth,* No. 2084.
5. *Kāmil,* i, 213a.
6. Fasawī, ii, 18b; iii, 138a.
7. Fasawī, iii, 308a-b.
8. *'Ilal,* i, 305; Fasawī, iii, 264a; 308b; Zur'ah, 68b; Rāzī *introd.* 205.
9. *Ṭawsat,* i, 46.
10. *Tahd.,* x, 220; Bukhārī, *Du'afā' Saghīr,* 33.
11. Rāzī, *introd.* 260; *Kāmil,* i, 360b; iii, 57a.
12. Dāraquṭnī, 442.

Muḥammad b. 'Abd al-Raḥmān, Ibn Abī Dh'īb. Al-Zuhrī wrote some *aḥādīth* and sent them to him who in turn transmitted them[1].

Muḥammad b. Isḥaq.

Muḥammad b. al-Walīd al-Zubaidi[2].

Mūsa b. 'Ubaidah al-Rabzī. Yaḥyā b. Ma'īn said that his transmission from al-Zhurī is by *Munāwalah*[3].

Mūsā b. 'Uqbah. Ibn Ma'īn used to say, "The book of Mūsā b. 'Uqbah from al-Zuhrī is the most correct book of all"[4].

Rabī'ah al-Ra'ī. He had *aḥādīth* of al-Zuhrī in writing[5].

Ruzaiq b. Ḥukaim. Al-Zuhrī wrote down some *aḥādīth* and sent them to him[6].

Ṣāliḥ b. Abū al-Akhḍar al-Yammanī[7].

Shu'aib b. Abū Ḥamzah. He was the scribe of al-Zuhrī, and wrote for the Caliph as well. Ibn Ḥanbal saw his books and praised them highly[8].

Sufyān b. Ḥusain al-Wāsiṭī. Ibn Ḥibbān said that he mixed up the pages of al-Zuhrī's book and hence he was a weak transmitter[9].

Sufyān b. 'Uyaynah. He wrote from al-Zuhrī while he was quite a young man[10].

---

1. *'Ilal,* 125a; Bājī, 72a; *Kifāyah,* 321; Ibn Ḥajar, *Hady al-Sārī,* ii, 209; *Tahd.*, ix, 305; 307.
2. Sa'd, vii, ii, 169; *Sharḥ 'Ilal,* 101a; see also *Thiqāt,* 596.
3. *Tahd.*, x, 360.
4. *Tahd.*, x, 361-2.
5. *Kāmil,* i, 387b.
6. BU. *Jum'ah,* 11.
7. *'Ilal,* i, 23; Rāzī, ii, i, 394; *Majrūḥīn,* 122b; *Mīzān,* ii, 288.
8. *Tahd.*, iv, 351-2; see also Bājī, 163a.
9. *Majrūḥīn,* 120a, *Mīzān,* ii, 166; *Tahd.*, iv, 108.
10. Rāmhurmuzī, 18; *'Ilal,* I, 123; see also Khaithamah, iii, 39a; Fasawī, iii, 227b.

Sufyān b. Sa'īd al-Thaurī. Al-Zuhrī gave him a book but he did not transmit it because he did not hear it from al-Zuhrī[1].

Sulaimān b. Kathīr al-'Abdī. He had a *Ṣaḥīfah* from al-Zuhrī. but according to Ibn Ḥibbān, his *Ṣaḥīfah* was not in correct order[2].

Sulaimān b. Mūsā al-Asdī. He had a book from al-Zuhrī[3].

'Ubaid Allāh b. Abū Ziyād al-Ruṣāfī. When al-Zuhrī went to al-Ruṣāfah, he followed him and there he heard his *aḥādīth* and wrote them down[4].

'Ubaid Allāh b. 'Umar. He borrowed the book of al-Zuhrī from Mālik b. Anas, and went with him to read it to al-Zuhrī[5]; al-Zuhrī also handed him a *Nuskhah* to copy it and to transmit it[6].

'Uqail b. Khālid al-Ailī. He used to accompany al-Zuhrī wherever he went. He wrote the book from al-Zuhrī and later on the book was in the possession of his nephew[7].

Al-Walīd b. Muḥammad al-Mūqirī. 'Alī b. al-Madīnī says, "I think his books of al-Zuhrī are copies from al-Zuhrī's office"[8].

Yaḥyā b. Abū Unaisah. Students used to read from his book in al-Zuhrī's lecture[9].

Yazīd b. Abū Ḥabīb. Al-Zuhrī wrote down *aḥādīth* and sent them to him who in turn transmitted them[10].

---

1. *Islām,* v, 149.
2. *Tahd.*, iv, 216.
3. *'Ilal,* 148B; *Thiqāt,* 479-80.
4. Sa'd, vii, ii, 175; *Mīzān,* iii, 8, *Tahd.*, ii, 207; vii, 13.
5. Fasawī, iii, 308a-b; see *Ṭawsat,* i, 124; Tirmidhī, *'Ilal,* ii, 239.
6. *Kifāyah,* 326.
7. Rāzī, iii, ii, 43; Bājī, 141a; *Tahd.*, iv, 289, vii, 256; see also *Tahd.*, vii, 42; A.D. *Sunan;* No. 4488.
8. Rāzī, iv, ii, 15.
9. *Mīzān,* iv, 365.
10. *'Ilal,* i,. 193; 142b; BU. iii, 478; *Tahd.*, ix, 447; *Ta'jīl,* 127.

Yūnus b. Yazīd. He wrote down everything from al-Zuhrī[1].

Ziyād b. Sa'd. Sufyān asked him for his book from al-Zuhrī, but he refused to give it, saying, "al-Zuhrī is here and you are a *Ḥāfiẓ*; after reading my book you might go to him and ask him without my knowledge"[2].

Yazīd b. Yazīd b. Jabir. Sa'īd saw him reading the book to al-Zuhrī[3].

Anonymous. Al-Zuhrī gave him a book[4].

A son of Hisham. Al-Zuhrī dictated 400 *aḥādīth* to him[5].

49. MUḤAMMAD B. MUSLIM B. TADRUS (c. 50 - 126)[6].

He transmitted *aḥādīth* from Jābir (d. 73) etc. He memorized Jābir's *aḥādīth* well[7]. He had two books from Jābir, only one of which he had heard from him[8].

The following wrote *aḥādīth* from him:

'Abd al-Malik b. Abū Sulaimān[9].

Hushaim[10].

Ibn Juraij[11].

Al-Laith b. Sa'd[12].

Nūḥ b. Abū Maryam[13].

---

1. *'Ilal*, i, 23; Bājī, 15a; *Tahd.*, vii, 256; iv, 307; xi, 450; 451; see also *Kāmil*, i, 130b; ii, 83b.
2. Rāzī, *Introd.* 39.
3. Fasawī, iii, 263b; *Jāmi'*, 58b.
4. *Kifāyah*, 319.
5. Fasawī, iii, 214a; *Ḥuffāẓ*, i, 97.
6. *Tahd.*, ix, 442.
7. Khaithamah, iii, 35b; *Tahd.*, ix, 441.
8. *Kāmil*, iii, 38a.
9. *Kifāyah*, 265.
10. Rāzī, introd. 151; iv, i, 75; *Mīzān*, iv, 38; *Tahd.*, ix, 441.
11. *Kāmil*, iii, 39a.
12. *Kāmil*, iii, 38a; *Jāmi'*, 162b; *Tahd.*, ix, 442.
13. *Ma'rifah*, 164.

50. MUḤAMMAD B. SĪRĪN (33 - 110)[1].

It is reported that he was against the writing down of *ḥadīth*[2] and did not allow books to be kept in his house[3]. On the other hand, we find that Ibn 'Aun – who reported Ibn Sīrīn's dislike of books – himself related that he used to read books to Ibn Sīrīn[4]. Furthermore, he reported that once Ibn Sīrīn informed him of a certain *Kitāb* which was in the possession of Ibn Jubair's family and asked him to go to Ziyād b. Jubair and read it[5]. Apart from this, Ibn Sīrīn used to attend the lecture of 'Abīdah with *Aṭrāf*[6] – the partly written *aḥādīth* –. There are other reports concerning his agreement with the writing of *aḥādīth* for the sake of memorizing only[7]. In another report he is described as dictating *aḥādīth* to Hishām, who wiped them out after memorizing them[8].

A book has been reported in the possession of his brother Yaḥyā b. Sīrīn. According to the available descriptions, it appears that the book was written by Ibn Sīrīn himself[9]. Either in his early age he agreed to the writing down of *aḥādīth* and abandoned this practice in later days, or his statement was misunderstood, or both. In his later days, it looks as if he disliked mixing with people or having any kind of social contacts. When Al-Zuzā'ī went to see him, he did not allow him to sit down, and asked him to depart after the salute[10]. So it is quite possible that he gave up his books and cut off his relationships with people. One of his statements quoted by al-Khaṭib in *Kifāyah,* was that one should not read any book, except from one's own teacher[11]. The same idea is maintained by Wakī' who said that students should not look in other people's books lest they remember some *aḥādīth* from the book before receiving it through proper channels and later relate it as if they had heard them from the authority[12].

---

1. *Tahd.*, ix, 216.
2. Rāmhurmuzī, 36b; *Taqyīd,* 46, 48.
3. *'Ilal,* i, 255; 154b; see also Sa'd vii, i, 141.
4. Ibn Wahb; *Jāmi'*, 76.
5. *Amwāl,* 99.
6. *'Ilal,* i, 387.
7. Sa'd, vii, i, 141; Rāmhurmuzī, 36b.
8. Rāmhurmuzī, 36b; 36b-37a; *Mīzān,* iv, 297.
9. Fasawī, iii, 14b; *Jāmi'*, 56b; *Imlā,* 173.
10. *Tahd.*, vi, 240.
11. *Kifāyah,* 353.
12. *Kifāyah,* 353.

These kinds of mistakes had already been committed by the scholars[1]. This statement of Ibn Sīrīn perhaps was partly reported and it was thought that he was against the writing and keeping of books.

The following transcribed *aḥādīth* from him:

Al-Auzā'ī transmitted a *Nuskhah* from him, though he did not read it to Ibn Sīrīn[2].

Hishām b. Ḥassān[3].

Sālim b. 'Abd Allāh al-Baṣrī transmitted a *Nuskhah* from him[4].

Yaḥyā b. Sīrīn had the book of his brother, Muḥammad[5].

50. Muḥammad b. Ziyād al-Qurashī (c. 35 - c. 120).

He transmitted from Abū Hurairah, 'Ā'ishah (d. 58) etc...[6].

Ibrāhīm b. Ṭahmān had a *Nuskhah* from him[7].

52. Makhāriq b. Khalīfah (c. 65 - c. 130).

He transmitted *aḥādīth* from Ṭāriq b. Shihāb (d. 83)[8].

'Abīdah b. Ḥumaid had a *Nuskhah* from him[9].

53. Mūsā b. 'Uqbah (c. 60 - 141)[10].

He compiled a book on *al-Maghāzī*[11] which was very trustworthy and famous among scholars[12]. An extract from the work has been published[13] and a small chapter is still preserved in

---

1. *Sharḥ 'Ilal,* 63a.
2. *Thiqāt,* 519; *Tahd.,* vi, 240.
3. Rāmhurmuzī, 36b; *Kāmil,* i, 8a; *Mīzāan,* iv, 297.
4. *Kāmil,* ii, 30b; There were two students who transmitted from it Sālim; 1 - Al-Walīd and 2 - Zuhair b. Muḥammad *ibid* 30b.
5. Fasawī, iii, 24b; *Jāmi',* 56b; *Imlā,* 173.
6. *Tahd.,* ix, 169.
7. *Ma'rifah,* 164.
8. *Tahd.,* x, 67.
9. *'Ilal,* i, 384.
10. *Tahd.,* x, 362; he saw Ibn 'Umar (d. 74).
11. *Ḥuffāẓ,* i, 133.
12. Rāzī, iv, I, 154; 155; *Tahd.,* x, 361; 362.
13. Sachau, *Das Berliner Fragment des Mūsā Ibn 'Ukba,* in *Sitzunger Preuss. Akad. Weiss,* 1904, pp. 445-470.

Amālī of Ibn al-Ṣā'id[1]. He mostly depended on al-Zuhrī, but added new materials from other sources[2]. This book was transmitted at least by two persons: — 1) His nephew Ismā'īl b. Ibrāhīm b. 'Uqbah[3], — 2) Muḥammad b. Fulaiḥ[4].

The following derived *aḥādīth* from him in written form:

Fuḍail b. Sulaimān[5].

Ibn Lahī'ah[6].

Ibrāhīm b. Ṭahmān[7].

Ismā'īl b. Ibrāhīm b. 'Uqbah[8].

Muḥammad b. Fulaiḥ[9].

Yūsuf b. Khālid[10].

54. MUṬARRIF B. ṬARĪF AL-ḤĀRITHĪ (c. 60 - 133)[11].

He transmitted from 'Abd al-Raḥmān Ibn Abū Lailā.

His book was perfect[12].

55. NĀFI', THE FREED MAN OF IBN 'UMAR (c. 30 - 117)[13].

He served Ibn 'Umar (d. 74) for more than 30 years[14] and was an authority on the *aḥādīth* of Ibn 'Umar. He had *aḥādīth* of Ibn 'Umar in writing[15], and used to dictate to students[16] and asked them to bring their notes for correction[17]. Even scholars

---

1. Ẓāhiriyah Library Mss., Damascus.
2. For example see, *Annales* i, 2981; 2998; 3073; 3103; 3137; ii, 1231.
3. Sachau, *op. cit.*
4. Ṭkabīr, i, 82a; 89a; quoting the work.
5. Fasawī, iii, 275b.
6. Ḥanbal, v, 185.
7. Ẓāhirīyah Lib. Mss of Ibn Ṭahmān. Folio 250a.
8. Sachau, *op. cit.*
9. Ṭkabīr, i, 82a; 89a; 95b.
10. Fasawī, iii, 275b.
11. *Tahd.*, x, 173.
12. *Tahd.*, x, 173.
13. *Tahd.*, x, 414.
14. *Ḥuffāz*, i, 88.
15. Ḥanbal, ii, 29; *Islām*, v, 11; see also *Bagh.*, x, 406.
16. Zur'ah, 50a; Khaithamah, iii, 115a; see also Fasawī, iii, 220b; Rāmhurmuzī, 76a; *Imlā*, 13.
17. *Imlā*, 78.

wrote to him asking for *aḥādīth*[1] and in turn he sent them *aḥādīth* in writing[2]. If he did not know the answer, he responded that he did not know[3]. Scholars unanimously agree on his trustworthiness[4].

The following wrote *aḥādīth* from him:

'Abd Allāh b. 'Aun[5].

'Abd Allāh b. 'Umar[6].

'Abd Al-'Azīz b. Abū Ruwād transmitted a forged *Nuskhah* from Nāfi'[7].

Ayyūb al-Sakhtiyānī[8].

Ibn Juraij[9].

Khālid b. Abū 'Imrān[10].

Khālid b. Ziyād[11].

Al-Laith b. Sa'd[12].

Mālik b. Anas[13].

Muḥammad b. 'Abd al-Raḥmān[14].

Mūsā b. 'Uqbah[15].

Ṣaklır[16].

Shu'aib b. Abū Ḥamzah[17].

'Ubaid Allāh b. 'Umar[18].

---

1. See for example Ḥanbal, ii, 31; Ja'd 139.
2. See for example Ḥanbal, ii, 32; BU. *'Itq*, 13.
3. See for example Fasawī, ii, 217a.
4. See any book dealing with his biography, e.g. *Tahd.*, x, 412;415.
5. *Amwāl*, 119; Ḥanbal, ii, 31; 32; BTK, iii, i, 3; BU. *'Itq*, 13; MU, *Jihād*, i; 37; Balādhurī, *Ansāb*, i, 342; *Mustadrak*, i, 15.
6. Khaithamah, iii, 150a.
7. *Majrūḥīn*, 166a.
8. Ja'd, 139; Fasawī, II, 217a; Rāmhurmuzī, 48b; *Kifāyah*, 342-3.
9. Khaithamah, iii, 40a; Fasawī, iii, 220b; Rāzī, ii, ii, 357; Rāmhurmuzī, 76a; *Imlā*, 13; *Kifāyah*, 302.
10. *Mustadrak*, i, 117.
11. *Thiqāt*, 451; *Tahd.*, iii, 90.
12. *Kifāyah*, 279.
13. *Mashāhir*, 190.
14. *Tahd.*, ix, 300.
15. *Kāmil*, i, 104a; *Bagh.*, vi, 223; *Kifāyah*, 267.
16. *Fasawī, iii, 41a.*
17. *Zur'ah, 67a; 67b; see also Kifāyah*, 214.
18. *Mashāhīr*, 190; see also *Kifāyah*, 267.

56. AL-QĀSIM B. 'ABD AL-RAḤMĀN AL-SHĀMĪ (c. 40 - 112)[1].

The following wrote *aḥādīth* from him:

'Alī b. Yazīd b. Abū Hilāl transmitted a large book – *Nuskhah Kabīrah* – from him[2].

Bishr b. Numair al-Qushairī transmitted an untrustworthy *Nuskhah* from him[3].

57. QATĀDAH B. DI'ĀMAH AL-SADDŪSĪ (61 - 117)[4].

He transcribed *aḥādīth* and compiled a commentary on the *Qur'ān*[5]. When he was asked about the writing of *aḥādīth,* he gave his full support; he even quoted a verse from the *Qur'ān* to this effect[6].

The following derived *aḥādīth* from him in writing:

Abū 'Awānah[7].

Abū Hilāl al-Rāsibī[8].

Al-Auza'ī[9].

Ḥammād b. Anū al-Ja'd[10].

Ḥammād b. Salamah[11].

Hammām b. Yaḥyā[12].

Al-Ḥārith b. Jarūd [13].

Hishām al-Dastawā'ī. It is said that he had 10,000 *aḥādīth* from Qatādah[14].

---

1. *Tahd.,* viii, 324.
2. *Tahd.,* vii, 396.
3. *Mīzān,* i, 326.
4. Qaisarānī, 422-3.
5. *Fihrist,* 34, where Ibn Nadīm mentions 2 persons who transmitted this work. See also Sa'd, vii, ii, 33.
6. Sa'd, vii, ii, 2.
7. *Kifāyah,* 216; *Tahd.,* xi, 119; Ibn Ḥajar, *Hady al-Sārī,* ii, 220.
8. *Kāmil,* iii, 78a; see also Sa'd, vii, ii, 2.
9. Ḥanbal, iii, 223; MU, *Ṣalāt,* 13; Rāmhurmuzī, 48b.
10. *Majrūḥīn,* 86b; Rāzī, i, ii, 134; *Tahd.,* iii, 5.
11. Rāmhurmuzī, 61a; *Kifāyah,* 196.
12. Sa'd, vii, ii, 33; *'Ilal,* 166b; Ḥanbal, ii, 127; 306; BU, *Buyū',* 46; Fasawī, iii, 40b; Bājī, 167a; *Kifāyah,* 220; *Jāmi',* 100a.
13. Al-Azdī, *Tārīkh al-Mauṣil,* 177.
14. *'Ilal,* i, 353; Ṭkabīr, i, 202b; see also, *Mīzān,* i, 57; *Tahd.,* i, 156.

Jarīr[1].

Ma'mar b. Rāshid[2].

Sa'īd b. Anū 'Arūbah[3].

Sa'īd b. Bashīr[4].

Sallām b. Miskīn[5].

Shainān al-Naḥwī[6].

Shu'ba'.[7].

58. RABI'AH B. FARRUKH AL-TAIMI (c. 65 - 136)[8].

He transmitted from Ibn Abū Lailā (86) etc. and wrote *aḥādīth* which he sent to Al-Laith[9].

59. RAJA' B. ḤAIWAH (c. 20 - 112)[10].

He transmitted from Abū al-Dardā'(d. 34), and had *aḥādīth* in writing[11].

60. RUQBAH B. MISQALAH AL-'ABDI AL-KUFĪ (c. 65 - 129)[12].

It is said that he transmitted from Anas b. Mālik (d. 93).

Abū Ḥamzah al-Sukkarī transmitted a *Nuskhah* from him[13].

---

1. Fasawī, iii, 24a.
2. *Fihrist*, 34. See also Ḥanbal, iv, 225.
3. Ḥanbal, iv, 225; Fasawī, iii, 24a; 83a; Rāzī, ii, i, 65; *Kifāyah*, 216; see also Sa'd, vii, ii, 33. It is reported that he stated that he did not write from Qatādah. Sa'd, vii, ii, 33.
4. *Fihrist*, 34.
5. *Tahd.*, viii, 319.
6. Rāzī, iv, i, 168.
7. Ja'd, 118; *Madkhal* 21; Bājī, 6a; *Kifāyah*, 164.
8. *Tahd.*, iii, 258.
9. A.D. Tr. No 1217.
10. *Tahd.*, iii, 266.
11. Zur'ah, 50a; *Taqyīd*, 108.
12. *Tahd.*, iii, 287.
13. Rāzī, i, i, 130; 216; iii, i, 285-6 *Ma'rifah*, 164.

61. Sa'īd b. Iyās al-Jurairī[1] (c. 60 - 144)[2].

He transmitted from 'Abd al-Raḥmān b. Abū Bakrah (d. after 80) and others.

The following derived *aḥādīth* from him in writing:

Ibn Abū 'Adī[3].

Ibn 'Ulayyah[4].

Sālim b. Nūḥ[5].

62. Sa'd b. Ibrāhīm b. 'Abd al-Raḥmān (54 - 126)[6].

The following transcribed *aḥādīth* from him:

Shu'bah.

Sufyān al-Thaurī.

Many Iraqians[7].

63. Ṣāliḥ b. Nabhān, Maulā al-Tau'amah (c. 40 - 125)[8].

He transmitted from Abū Hurairah (d. 59) etc.

Aḥmad b. Khāzim sl-Mu'āfarī transmitted a *Nuskhah* from Sālih[9].

64. Shu'bah b. Dīnār al-Hāshimī (c. 50 - c. 115).

A client of Ibn 'Abbās, he died in the reign of Hishām, b. 'Abd al-Malik (105 - 125)[10].

He had a book.[11].

1. *Mushtabih,* 149.
2. *Tahd.,* iv, 6.
3. Bājī, 146b.
4. Rāzī, i, i, 154.
5. *Kifāyah,* 236; *Mizān,* ii, 113; *Tahd.,* III, 443, where it is printed erroneously al-Jazrī.
6. *Tahd.,* iii, 464.
7. *Mashāhīr,* 136; *Tahd.,*III, 464; see also Rāzī, ii, i, 79.
8. Khaithamah, iii, 117b; *Tahd.,* iv, 406.
9. Al-Ḥumaidi, *Jadhwat al-Mutqtabis,* 112.
10. *Tahd.,* iv, 347.
11. Fasawī, iii, 275a.

65. SIMĀK B. ḤARB AL-KŪFĪ (c. 55 - 123)[1].

He transmitted from Jābir b. Samurah (d. 73). Muḥammad b. Sawār wrote down Simāk's *aḥādīth* from Ḥammād b. Salamah[2].

66. SIMĀK B. AL-WALĪD, ABŪ ZUMAIL (c. 50 - c. 120)[3].

He transmitted from Ibn 'Abbās (d. 68) etc.

Many Iraqians wrote *aḥādīth* from him[4].

67. SALAMAH B. KUḤAIL (47 - 121)[5].

Ḥammad b. Salamah wrote from him[6].

68. SULAIMĀN B. MIHRĀN AL-A'MASH (61 - 147)[7].

He wrote *aḥādīth*[8]. Even his *Shaikh* Ibrāhīm (d. 96) copied from him[9]. He used to dictate *aḥādīth* to students[10].

The following derived *aḥādīth* from him in writing:

Abū 'Awānah[11].

Abū Bakr b. 'Ayyāsh and others[12].

Abū Mu'āwiyah. He was a blind man and memorized A'mash's *aḥādīth,* so that he used to dictate after finishing the lesson[13].

Ḥafṣ b. Ghayāth[14].

Hushaim[15].

---

1. *Tahd., iv, 234.*
2. Ja'd 439.
3. *Tahd.,* iv, 235.
4. *Mashāhīr,* 123.
5. *Tahd.,* iv, 156-7.
6. *'Ilal,* i, 344; Fasawī, ii, 243b.
7. *Tahd.,* iv, 223-4.
8. Ja'd, 80; *'Ilal.,* i, 140.
9. *Ilal,* i, 140.
10. *Bagh.,* ix, 11; Rāmhurmuzī, 17.
11. *Sharḥ al-'Ilal,* 63a.
12. Rāmhurmuzī, 17; see also *Bagh.,* ix, 11.
13. Ja'd 83; *'Ilal,* i, 51.
14. *Kāmil,* i, 275b; *Tahd.,* ii, 416.
15. *'Ilal,* i, 353-4.

Ibn Idrīs[1].

Isḥāq b. Tāshid[2].

Jarīr b. 'Abd al-Ḥamīd[3].

Khālid b. 'Abd Allāh wrote down A'mash's *aḥādīth* but they were not read to him[4].

Ma'mar[5].

Nūḥ b. Abū Maryam[6].

Sufyan[7].

Wakī[8].

Anonymous[9].

69. Sulaimān b. Mūsā al-Ashdaq (c. 60 - 115)[10].

He transmitted from Wāthilah b. Asqa' (d. 81) and had a *Ṣaḥīfah*[11].

70. Sulaiman b. Ṭarkhan al-Baṣri (46 - 143)[12].

He lost his book[13] which earlier Ibn 'Uyaynah saw him carrying[14]. The following derived *aḥādīth* from him:

Haudhah[15].

Mu'tamar b. Sulaimān[16].

---

1. Rāmhurmuzī, 37a.
2. Fasawī, iii, 270b; Sa'd, vi, 239; *Bagh.*, ix, 11.
3. Fasawī, iii, 264b; Rāzī, i, i, 506; Rāmhurmuzī, 55b; *Kifāyah*, 71; *Bagh.*, ix, 10.
4. BTK, i, i, 74.
5. Fasawī, iii, 274a.
6. *Ma'rifah*, 164.
7. Madkhal 36.
8. *Bagh.*, xiii, 468; 469.
9. *Islām*, vi, 77.
10. *Thiqāt*, 479-80; *Tahd.*, iv, 226-7.
11. *Mīzān*, ii, 225.
12. *Tahd.*, iv, 202.
13. *Tahd.*, iv, 202.
14. *Islām*, vi, 73.
15. Sa'd, vii, ii, 80.
16. *'Ilal*, 158a; see also Rāmhurmuzī, 35b.

71. S'LAIMĀN B. YASĀR (34-107)[1].

He had a book which was transmitted by Bukair. Later, this book was in the possession of his son Makhrimah[2].

72. ṬALḤAH B. NĀFI', ABŪ SUFYĀN (c. 50 - c. 110).

He transmitted from Ibn 'Abbās (68)[3].

Al-A'mash transmitted a *Ṣaḥīfah* from him which contained 100 *aḥādīth*[4].

73. THĀBIT B. ASLAM AL-BUNĀNĪ (c. 40 - 127)[5].

According to his statement he followed Anas b. Mālik (d. 93) for 40 years. He wrote *aḥādīth* from the authorities and trustworthy *Shuyūkh*[6].

Ja'far b.. Sulaimā wrote *aḥādīth* from him[7].

74. THĀBIT B. 'AJLĀN (c. 65 - c. 130).

He transmitted from Abū Umāmah (d. 81) etc.[8].

Baqiyah had Thābit's *aḥādīth* in written form[9] as did Ḥammād b. Salama.[10].

75. THUWAIR B. ABŪ FĀKHTAH (c. 50 - c. 120)[11].

He transmitted from Zaid b. Arqan (d. 65) etc.[12].

The following derived *aḥādīth* from him in writing:

'Abīdah b. Ḥumaid had a *Nuskhah* from him[13].

Isra'īl[14].

---

1. *Tahd.*, iv, 229.
2. *Tahd.*, x, 70; 71; *Mīzān*, iv, 81; see also *'Ilal*, 171a.
3. *Tahd.*, v, 26.
4. *Tahd.*, iv, 224.
5. *Tahd.*, ii, 3.
6. *Kāmil*, i, 196b.
7. *Tahd.*, ii, 96.
8. *Tahd.*, ii, 10.
9. Rāzī, intro. 271; i, i, 455; *Tahd.*, ii, 10.
10. *Hady as-Sārī*, i, 23.
11. *Tahd.*, ii, 36.
12. *Thad.*, ii, 36.
13. *'Ilal*, i, 198b.
14. *Kāmil*, i, 198b.

76. 'Ubaid Allāh b. Abū Ja'far al-Miṣrī (60-135)[1].

He wrote a book and sent it to Al-Laith b. Sa'd, who transmitted it, though he did not read the book to 'Ubaid Allāh[2].

77. 'Umārah b. Juwain, Abū Hārūn (c. 55 - 134)[3].

He transmitted from Ibn 'Umar (d. 74) etc. but was an untrustworthy narrator. He had a book[4].

78. 'Uthmān b. 'Āsim al-Asdī (128)[5].

He transmitted from Anas b. Mālik (d. 93) etc.
Abū Bakr b. 'Ayyāsh had a *Nuskhah* from him[6].

79. 'Uthmān b. Ḥāḍir al-Ḥimyarī (c. 45 - c. 110).

He transmitted from Ibn 'Abbās (d. 68) etc.[7].
Students in Al-Ḥijāz wrote from him[8].

80. Wahb b. Munabbih (34-114)[9].

He compiled many books.

The following are mentioned as his works:

The Biography of the Prophet. Al-Tabārānī has preserved a portion of this work in his book, *Mu'jam al-Kabīr*[10].
Qiṣaṣ al-Anbiyā'[11].
Qiṣaṣ al-Akhyār[12].

---

1. *Ṭahd.*, vii, 6.
2. Khaithamah, iii, 39a; *Kifāyah,* 321; *Tahd.*, viii, 462.
3. *Tahd.*, vii, 413.
4. Rāzī, introd. 149; iii, i, 363; 364.
5. *Tahd.*, vii, 127-8; Khazarajī, 220.
6. *Kāmil,* i, 21a.
7. *Tahd.*, vii, 109.
8. *Mashāhīr, 124.*
9. Ziriklī, ix, 150.
10. *Tkabir,* i, 174a-176a, over 4 pages.
11. Ḥājī Khalīfah, *Kashf al-Ẓunūn,* 1328; see also, Brockalmann, *G.A.L.* Translated by al-Najjār, i, 252.
12. Ḥājī Khalīfah, *op. cit.,* 1328.

Kitāb al-Mubtada', which was transmitted by Abū Ja'far b. Bariyah[1].

81. Yazīd b. Abān al-Raqqāshī (c. 50 between 110-120)[2].

'Umar b. 'Abd al-'Azīz wrote some *aḥādīth* from him[3].

82. Yazīd b. 'Abdal-Raḥmān b. Abū Mālik (60-130)[4].

He was the *Faqīh* of Damascus, and had books[5].

His son Khālid transmitted a book—*Kitāb al-Masā'il*—from him[6].

83. Yazīd b. Abū Ḥabīb (53-128)[7].

He wrote *aḥādīth*, even from his own students[8].

The following wrote *aḥādīth* from him:

Ibn Lahī'ah wrote some of his *aḥādīth*[9].
Al-Laith b. Sa'd had a *Nuskhah* from him, which was transmitted by Yaḥyā b. Bukair, Qutaibah, Zaghbah and Yazīd b. Wahb etc.[10].

84. Yazīd b. Sufyān Abū al-Muhazzim (c. 40 - c. 110).
He transmitted from Abū Hurairah (d. 59).
Shu'bah wrote 100 *aḥādīth* from him[11].

---

1. *Bagh.*, i, 416.
2. *Tahd.*, xi, 311.
3. Rāmhurmuzī, 35b.
4. *Tahd.*, xi, 346.
5. *Kāmil,* I, 309a.
6. Zur'ah, 150a; see also *Tahd.*, xi, 346, where the book is mentioned with the interpretation of it, but Abū Zur'ah does not explain this way, and as his book was transmitted by his son, here it must mean book in its ordinary sense.
7. *Tahd.*, xi, 319.
8. Fischer, 82-83; see also *'Ilal,* 142b.
9. *Istī'āb,* No. 1439.
10. *Kāmil,* i, 315a; *Mīzān,* i, 636; see also *Tahd.*, iii, 110.
11. Rāzī, iv, ii, 269.

85. ZAID B. ASLAM. CLIENT OF IBN 'UMAR (c. 40-136)[1].

He transmitted from Abū Hurairah, 'Ā'ishah etc.[2].

The following derived *aḥādīth* from him in writing:
'Abd al-Raḥmān b. Zaid transmitted a *Tafsīr* from him[3].
Ḥafṣ b. Maisarah al-'Uqailī[4] read a book to Zaid.
Sa'īd b. Abū Ayyūb had a book from him[5].

86. ZAID B. RUFAI' (c. 60 - c. 125.).

He transmitted from Abū 'Ubaidallāh b. 'Abd Allāh b. Mas'ūd (d. 82)[6].
The following derived *aḥādīth* from him writing:
'Abd al-Ḥāmīd b. Yūsuf[7].

Ḥammād b. 'Amr al-Naṣībī. It is said that he took the book from 'Abd al-Ḥāmīd, and transmitted it on the authority of Zaid[8].

87. ZUBAID B. AL-ḤĀRITH AL-AYĀMĪ (c. 60 - 122)[9].

'Isā b. Yūnus had Zubaid's book[10].

IV. WRITINGS OF AND FROM THE EARLY SECOND CENTURY SCHOLARS

1. ABAN B. ABŪ 'AYYĀSH (c. 70 - 138)[11].

He transmitted *aḥādīth* from Anas b. Mālik (d. 93) and others.
Salm al-'Alawī saw him writing from Anas[12], so he advised

---

1. *Tahd.*, iii, 396.
2. *Tahd.*, iii, 395.
3. *Ḥuffāẓ*, i, 119; see also *Fihrist*, 33.
4. Rāzī, i, ii, 187.
5. *Tahd.*, iv, 8.
6. *Mīzān*, ii, 103.
7. *Bagh.*, viii, 154; *Mīzān*, i, 598.
8. *Bagh.*, viii, 154; *Mīzān*, i, 598.
9. *Tahd.*, iii, 311.
10. *Kifāyah*. 142-3; see also Rāmhurmuzī, 67b.
11. *Tahd.*, i, 99.
12. *Kāmil*, ii, 24b; *Mīzān*, i, 10; *Taqyīd*, 109.

Ḥammād b. Zaid to attend Abān's lectures[1], but Sh'ubbah discredited Abān[2].

The following derived *aḥādīth* from him in writing:

Abū 'Awānah. He brought a book to Abān, which contained his *aḥādīth* and those of others. Abān did not notice this and read them all[3].

'Alī bin Mushir wrote about 500 *aḥādīth* from him[4].

Ghālib b. 'Ubaid Allāh[5].

Ḥamzah al-Zayyāt wrote about 500 *aḥādīth* from him[6].

Ibn Juraij[7].

Ibrāhīm b. Ṭahmān had a collection of *aḥādīth* from him[8].

Ma'mar had a collection, which was in the possession of 'Abd al-Razzāq. Later, Yaḥyā b. Ma'īn copied it, although he knew it was unauthenticated, in order to be aware of these false *aḥādith*[9].

2. Abān b. Taghlab al-Kūfī (c. 80-141)[10].

He transmitted from 'Ikrimah (d. 105) and others and had many books (Nusakh)[11].

3. Abān b. Yazīd al-'Aṭṭār (c. 90 - c. 165)

He transmitted from Ḥasan (d. 110) and Qatādah, etc. Mūsā b. Ismā'īl and others transmitted from him. Many students assembled at the lectures of Mūsā, and everyone of them had

1. *Kāmil*, i, 137; ii, 24b, *Mīzān*, i, 10.
2. *Kāmil*, i, 137; *Mīzān*, i, 11-12.
3. Rāzī, i, i, 295.
4. *Mīzān*, i, 12; *Tahd.*, i, 100.
5. MU., *Introduction*, p. 18.
6. *Mīzān*, i, 12; *Tahd.*, i, 100.
7. *Kifāyah*, 320.
8. *Kāmil*, i, 138b.
9. *Tahd.*, i, 101; Bājī, 5b.
10. Khazrajī, 13.
11. *Kāmil*, i, 141a; *Tahd.*, i, 93. (In *Tahd.*, his death is printed 241, instead of 141 which is wrong).

aḥādīth of Abān and wanted to hear them from Mūsā who, perhaps, had a copy from his teacher Abān[1].

4. 'Abbas b. al-Faḍl al-Anṣari (105-186)[2].

He had a book[3] and compiled a large book on the recitation of the *Qur'ān,* which contained a large number of *aḥādīth* [4].

5. 'Abd al-A'la b. Abu al-Musāwir (c. 80 - after 160)[5].

He transmitted from Abū Burdah al-Ash'arī (d. 103) etc. He came to Baghdād where students wrote from him[6].

6. 'Abd al-'aziz b. 'Abd Allah b. Abu Salamah al-Māshun (c.100-164)[7].

Many students of Baghdād had *aḥādīth* from him in writing[8]. He compiled many books[9], one of them entitled *Muwaṭṭa'*. Mālik, perhaps, compiled his work after going through *al-Muwaṭṭa',* of 'Abd al-'Azīz[10].

The students in Baghdād wrote *aḥādīth* from him[11].

7. 'Abd al-'Aziz b. al-Ḥusain (c. 100 - c. 160)[12].

He transmitted from al-Zuhrī (d. 124) etc. He had a *Nuskhah* which was transmitted by Khālid b. Makhlad al-Kūfī[13].

8. 'Abd al-'Aziz b. Ṣuhaib al-Bunānī (c. 70 - 130)[14].

He transmitted from Anas b. Mālik (d. 93) etc.

Mubārak b. Suḥaim transmitted a *Nuskhah* from him[15].

---

1. Fasawī, iii, 281b.
2. *Mīzān,* ii, 385.
3. *Tahd.,* v, 127.
4. *Mīzān,* ii, 385; *Tahd.,* v, 127.
5. *Tahd.,* vi, 98.
6. *Bagh.,* xi, 69.
7. *Tahd.,* vi, 344.
8. *Bagh.,* x, 438.
9. *Bagh.,* x, 439; *Ḥuffāẓ,* i, 201; *Tahd.,* vi, 344; see also Rāzī iii, i, 53.
10. Suyūṭī, *Tanwīr, al-Ḥawālik,* i, 6.
11. *Tahd.,* vi, 344.
12. *Mīzān,* ii, 627.
13. *Kāmil,* i, 316b.
14. *Tahd.,* vi, 342.
15. *Mīzān,* iii, 430.

9. ʻAbd al-Jabbar b. al-Ward al-Makhzumi (c. 95 - c. 160).

He transmitted from ʻAṭā' b. Abū Rabāḥ (d. 117) etc.[1].
ʻUbaid b. Abū Qurrah had a book from him[2].

10. ʻAbd Allāh b. ʻAbd Allāh b. Uwais (c. 100-169)[3].

His book was perfect[4].
Students in Baghdād had *aḥādīth* from him in writing[5].

11. ʻAbd Allāh b. ʻAbd al-Raḥmān b. Abū Ḥusain (c. 75-c. 140).

He transmitted from Nāfi' b. Jubair (d. 97) and others[6].
Shuʻaib b. Abū Ḥamzah had his *aḥādīth* in written form.
This book came into the hands of Abū al-Yamān[7].

12. ʻAbd Allāh b. Abū Labīd (c. 140)[8].

He transmitted from Abū Salamah b. ʻAbd al-Raḥmān etc.
Al-Thaurī and many students in al-Kūfah wrote *aḥādīth* from him[9].

13. ʻAbd Allāh b. al-ʻAlā b. Zabr al-Dimashqī (75-165)[10].

Many students wrote *adādīth* from him in Baghdād[11].

1. *Tahd.*, vi, 106.
2. *Bagh.*, xi, 96.
3. *Tahd.*, v, 281.
4. *Tahd.*, v, 281.
5. *Bagh.*, x, 7.
6. *Tahd.*, v, 293.
7. *Tahd.*, ii, 442. See also *Al-Mustadrak*, i, 68.
8. *Tahd.*, v, 372.
9. *Thiqāt*, 244.
10. *Bagh.*, x, 18; see also *Tahd.*, v, 351.
11. *Bagh.*, x, 16.

14. ʻAbd Allāh b. Shubrumah (72-144).

He transmitted *aḥādī th* from Anas.

He had a book[1].

15. ʻAbd Allāh b. al-Ḥusain, Abū Ḥarīz (c. 70 - c. 130)[2].

He transmitted from Ibrāhīm al-Nakhaʻī (d. 96) and others.

The following derived *aḥādīth* from him in writing:

Anonymous[3].

Fuḍail b. Maisarah[4].

People of Baṣrah wrote from him[5].

16. ʻAbd Allāh b. Idrīs (110-192)[6].

He used to write *aḥādīth* after memorizing them[7].

He was a close friend of Mālik who utilized ʻAbd Allāh's sources in his *Muwaṭṭa'*[8].

Al-Ḥasan b. Rabīʻ[9] and Yaḥyā b. Ādam wrote from him[10].

17. ʻAbd Allāh b. Jaʻfar b. Nujaiḥ al-Saʻdī (c. 105-178)[11].

He transmitted from ʻAbd Allāh b. Dīnār (d. 127).

Bahz had a *Kurrāsah* from him[12].

---

1. Ibn ʻAbd al-Barr, *Bayān,* i, 76.
2. *Tahd.*, v, 187.
3. *Kāmil,* ii, 124a; *Tahd.*, viii, 300.
4. *Kāmil,* ii, 124a; *Tahd.*, viii, 300; see also Ḥanbal, iv, 193; 399; *Mīzān,* ii, 407; *Kifāyah,* 236.
5. *Mashāhīr,* 198.
6. *Tahd.*, v, 145.
7. *ʻIlal,* 177b.
8. *Bagh.*, ix, 420.
9. *Jāmiʻ*, 85b.
10. Ḥanbal, i, 418.
11. *Tahd.*, v, 175.
12. Tah., v, 174; 176.

18. 'ABD ALLĀH B. LAHĪ'AH (96-174)[1].

It is said that his books were burnt[2].

The following wrote *aḥādīth* from him:

Abū al-Aswad b. 'Abd al-Jabbār al-Murādī[3].

Anonymous — a number of students[4].

Ibn Mahdī[5].

Ibn Ma'īn[6].

Ibn al-Mubārak[7].

Ibn Wahb[8].

Lahī'ah b. 'Isā[9].

Qutaibah b. Sa'īd[10].

Uthmān b. Ṣāliḥ[11].

Yaḥyā b. Bukair[12].

19. 'ABD ALLAH B. AL-QĀSIM RUZAIN (c. 70 - c. 130).

He transmitted from Ibn al-Musayyab (d. 93) etc.[13] and Mu'tamar had his *aḥādīth* in writing[14].

20. 'ABD ALLĀH B. RAJĀ' AL-MAKKĪ (c. 110 - after 187)[15].

He transmitted from Ayyūb al-Sikhtayānī (d. 131) but lost his books[16].

---

1. *Mīzān*, ii, 477-82; see also *Tahd.*, v, 377.
2. Rāzī, ii, ii, 146; *Mīzān*, ii, 477; *Tahd.*, v, 376.
3. Fasawī, iii, 136b; *Tahd.*,v, 376.
4. Fasawī, iii, 136b; *Tahd.*, v, 376.
5. *Tahd.*, v, 377.
6. *Tahd.*, v, 377.
7. Rāzī, ii, ii, 146; 147-8; *Tahd.*,v, 374.
8. Rāzī, ii, ii, 147-8; *Tahd.*, v. 376.
9. *Tahd.*,v, 375-6.
10. *Tahd.*, v, 375-6.
11. *Tahd.*, v, 376.
12. Qāḍī 'Ayāḍ, Iadārik, i, 529.
13. *Tahd.*, v, 359.
14. *'Ilal*, 158a.
15. *Tahd.*, v, 211.
16. *Mīzān*, ii, 421; *Tahd.*, v, 211.

21. ʻAbd Allāh b. Sālim al-Ashʻarī (c. 110-179)[1].

ʻAbd al-Ḥamīd b. Ibrāhīm had his books which were lost[2]. Abū Dāwūd saw his book in Ḥimṣ[3].

22. ʻAbd Allāh b. Shaudhab al-Khurāsānī (86-144)[4].

He wrote *aḥādīth*[5]

23. ʻAbd Allāh b. ʻUmar al-Umarī (c. 95-172)[6].

He transmitted *aḥādīth* from Nāfiʻ (d. 117) etc.

The following derived *aḥādith* from him in writing:

Al-Ḥusain b. al-Walīd al-Nīsābūrī had a *Nuskhah* from him[7].

Al-Laith b. Saʻd had a book from him[8].

24. ʻAbd Allāh b. ʻUthmān b. Khuthaim (c. 70-132)[9].

He transmitted from Saʻīd b. Jubair (d. 95) etc.

Yaḥyā b. Salīm had a perfect book from him[10].

25. ʻAbd Allāh b. Yazīd al-Makhzūmī (C. 75-148)[11]

He transmitted from ʻUrwah (d. 93) etc.

According to Ibn Ḥibbān, he wrote a large number of *aḥādīth*[12].

---

1. *Tahd.*, v, 228.
2. *Tahd.*, vi, 109.
3. A.D. *Ḥadīth* no. 1582.
4. *Tahd.*, v, 255-6.
5. *Tahd.*, v, 255.
6. *Tahd.*, v, 327.
7. *Maʻrifah*, 165.
8. *Kifāyah*, 344.
9. *Tahd.*, v, 315; Khazrajī, 174.
10. *ʻIlal*, 150b; *Thad.*, xi, 226.
11. *Mashāhīr*, 137; *Tahd.*, vi, 82.
12. *Mashāhīr*, 137.

26. 'Abd Allāh b. Ziyād b. Sulaimān al-Makhzūmī (c. 100 - c. 160).

He transmitted from al-Zuhrī (d. 124) etc.[1]. He is accused of collecting books from here and there, and transmitting them without the permission of their authors[2]. According to Sa'id b. 'Abd al-'Azīz, in Iraq, students added additional material to 'Abd Allāh's books and handed them to him. When he read them they proclaimed him a liar[3].

Al-Walīd b. Muslim wrote a book from him[4].

27. 'Abd al-Malik b. 'Abd al-'Azīz b. Juraij (80-150)[5].

In the very beginning of his studentship, he went to 'Aṭā' b. Abū Ribāḥ to learn *Ḥadīth*; in turn he was directed to learn the *Qur'ān* and *al-Farā'id*[6]. After possessing himself of these requirements he joined the circle of 'Aṭā' and accompanied him for 17 years[7].

His memory was somewhat weak[8], but his books were highly esteemed[9].

He worked hard to collect the *aḥādīth* of Ibn 'Abbās, and claimed that no one had worked like him[10].

He used to show his book to other scholars to hear their advice and to gain additional material[11].

It seems that he used to write drafts before making final copies[12].

---

1. *Tahd.*, v, 219.
2. Rāzi, ii, ii, 61; *Bagh.*, ix, 456; *Tahd.*, v, 220.
3. Rāzī, ii, ii, 61; *Bagh.*, ix, 458; *Mīzān*, ii, 423; *Tahd.*, v, 220.
4. *Mīzān*, ii, 423.
5. *Tahd.*, vi, 405.
6. *Bagh.*, x, 401-2.
7. *Bagh.*, x, 402.
8. *Bagh.*, x, 405.
9. *'Ilal*, 154a; *Bagh.*, x, 404.
10. *'Ilal*, i, 348-9; 154a; *Bagh.*, x, 404.
11. Khaithamah, iii,39b.
12. Fasawī, iii, 6b, where it is mentioned, that he compiled on the leaves of *'Ushr* trees, which has according to *Lisān al-'Arab* art, " *'Ashr*". Vol. iv, 574, very wide leaves, then copied it on the white.

It is also said that he was one of the first to compile books[1]. According to Ibn Nadīm, he compiled *Kitāb al-Sunan*[2]; the other sources give the names of *Kitāb al-Manāsik*[3] and *Kitāb al-Tafsīr*[4] as well. There may have been some other books whose titles are not mentioned.

The following derived *aḥādīth* from him in written form:

'Abd Allāh b. al-Ḥārith al-Makhzūmī[5].

'Abd al-Majīd b. 'Abd al-'Azīz[6].

Ḥajjāj b. Muḥammad al-A'war[7].

Haudhah b. Khalīfah[8].

Hishām b. Yūsuf[9].

Ibn Lahī'ah[10].

Ibn al-Mubārak[11].

Khālid b. Nazār al-Ailī. He went to Ibn Juraij with his books, and found him dead[12].

Mu'ādh b. Mu'ādh[13].

Mūsā b. Ṭāriq[14].

Muslim b. Khālid[15].

Nūḥ b. Abū Maryam[16].

1. *Bagh.*, x, 400; *Ḥuffāẓ*, i, 153.
2. *Fihrist*, 226.
3. Khaithamah, iii, 39b; *Kāmil*, i, 38a.
4. *Bagh.*, viii, 237.
5. Aḥmad Shākir, *intro.* to *Al-Risālah*, p. 7.
6. Rāzī, iii, i, 64; *Kāmil*, i, 392b; *al-Mustadrak*, ii, 169; Bājī, 20a; *Mīzān*, ii, 649; Aḥmad Shakir, *Introd. Al-Risālah*, p. 7.
7. *'Ilal*, i, 237; 349; *Bagh.*, viii, 237; *Kifāyah*, 251; 290; *Jāmi'*, 109a; *Tahd.*, ii, 205; iv, 244.
8. Sa'd, vii, ii, 80.
9. Ḥanbal, v, 119; Khaithamah, iii, 56b; *Majrūḥīn*, 24a: *Al-Madkhal*, 39; *Tahd.*, xi, 57.
10. Rāmhurmuzī, 49a.
11. Rāzī, *introd.* 264.
12. *Huffāẓ*, i, 153; *Islām*, vi, 97.
13. *'Ilal*, i, 370.
14. Nas., ii, 42.
15. Aḥmad Shākir, *introd.* to *Risālah*, p. 7.
16. *Ma'rifah*, 164.

Rauḥ b. 'Ubādah[1].

Ṣadaqah b. 'Abd Allāh[2].

Sa'īd b. Sālim[3].

Sulaimān b. Mijālid[4].

Sufyān[5].

28. 'ABD AL-MALIK B. ABŪ NAḌRAH AL-'ABDĪ (c. 75 - c. 140).

He transmitted from his father (d. 108) etc.[6].

'Uthmān al-Marwazī transmitted a *Nuskhah* from him[7].

29. 'ABD AL-QUDDŪS B. ḤABĪB AL-SHĀMĪ (c. 80 - c. 140).

He transmitted from Mujāhid etc.[8]. He had a book, and made a mistake in reading it, so he transmitted *ḥadīth* erroneously and then explained it incorrectly, also[9].

30. 'ABD AL-RAḤMĀN B. 'ABD ALLĀH B. 'UTBAH AL-MAS'ŪDĪ (c. 90-160)[10].

He transmitted from al-Qāsim b. 'Abd al-Raḥmān b. Mas'ūd (d. 110) and had books[11].

The following derived *aḥādīth* from him in writing:

Abū Dāwūd[12].

Abū Qutaibah[13].

Bishr b. al-Mufaḍḍal[14].

---

1. Rāzī, i, ii, 498.
2. *Mīzān,* ii, 310.
3. Aḥmad Shākir, *introd.* to *Risālah,* p. 7.
4. *'Ilal,* i, 349.
5. Ḥanbal, i, 347.
6. *Tahd.,* vi, 437.
7. *Ma'rifah,* 164.
8. *Bagh.,* xi, 126.
9. *Bagh.,* xi, 127.
10. *Mīzān,* ii, 575; *Tahd.,* vi, 211.
11. Rāzī, introduction 145; see also Rāmhurmuzī, 40a; *Bagh.* x, 219; *Islām,* vi, 224; *Tahd,* vi, 211.
11. *Bagh.,* xi, 281- *Islām,* vi, 224.
12. *Majrūḥīn,* 142a; *Bagh.,* x, 219; *Islām,* vi, 224.
13. *Bagh.,* xi, 281.

Khālid b. al-Ḥārith[1].

Mu'ādh and many students of Baghdad[2].

Shu'bah[3].

'Uthmān b. 'Umar[4].

31. 'Abd al-Raḥmān b. Abū al-Zinād (100-174)[5].

He compiled many books. Ibn al-Nadīm mentioned *Kitāb al-Farā'iḍ* and *Ra'y al-Fuqahā' al-Sab'ah*[6].

The students used to read to him and write down *aḥādīth* from him[7].

32. 'Abd al-Raḥmān b. 'Amr al-Auzā'ī (88-158)[8].

He is one of the masters of the school of law in the history of Muslim Jurisprudence. His school of law flourished for many centuries before it became extinct.

He compiled many books[9] which have perished.

The following derived *aḥādīth* from him in writing:

'Amr b. Hāshim. He was quite young when he wrote from al-Auzā'ī and so was a weak authority in al-Auzā'ī's *aḥādīth*[10].

Anonymous[11].

Ismā'il b. Samā'ah. Abū Mishar copied 13 books of al-Auzā'ī from him.[12].

1. *Bagh.*, xi, 281.
2. Ja'd 250; *Bagh.*, x, 219.
3. Rāzī, *introduction,* 145.
4. *Bagh.*, xi, 281.
5. Sa'd, v, 307-8; *Tahd.*, vi, 172.
6. *Fihrist,* 225; the book *Ra'ī al-Fuqahā' al-Sab'ah* is not his work, but according to his own statement, his father's work. Therefore, Mālik objected to it. See *Tahd.*, vi 172.
7. Sa'd v, 308.
8. *Tahd.*, vi, 240.
9. Rāzī, introd. 217; see also *Kifāyah,* 255; for quotation from his books, see *Al-Radd, 'Alā Siyar al-Auzā'ī,* see also *Fihrist,* 227.
10. Rāzī, iii, i, 268; *Mīzān*, iii, 290; *Tahd.*, viii, 112.
11. *Tahd.*, vi, 242. Al-Auzā'ī's books were burnt. This man brought his books to him which were corrected but not read by Auzā'ī himself.
12. Rāzi, iii, i, 29. See also *Madkhal*, 34.

Muḥammad b. Kathīr al-Miṣṣīṣī[1].

Muḥammad b. Shu'aib b. Shābūr. Al-Auzā'ī corrected his book[2].

Ṣadaqah b. 'Abd Allāh al-Samīn. He wrote 1500 *aḥādīth* from al-Auzā'ī[3].

'Umar b. 'Abd al-Wāḥid[4].

Al-Walīd b. Mazīd[5].

Al-Walīd b. Muslim al-Dimashqī[6].

33. 'ABD AL-RAḤMĀN B. ḤARMALAH (c. 80-145)[7].

He wrote *aḥādīth*[8] and had a book[9].

Yaḥyā b. Sa'īd had a book from him[10].

34. 'ABD AL-RAḤMĀN B. THĀBIT B. THAUBĀN (75-165)[11].

He went to Baghdād, where students wrote *aḥādīth* from him[12].

35. 'ABD AL-RAḤMĀN B. YAZĪD B. AL-JĀBIR AL-AZDĪ (c. 70 - 153)[13].

He had two books; only one of them was read to the authority[14].

---

1. Rāzī, iv, i, 69-70; *Mīzān*, iv, 19.
2. *Kifāyah*, 322; Sakhāwī, *Mughīth*, 218.
3. *Mīzān*, ii, 310.
4. Zur'ah, 150a; Rāzim iiim im 122; *Tahd.*, vii, 479;
5. Rāzī, introd. 205; iii, i, 29; iv, ii, 18; *Kifāyah*, 302.; *Tahd.*, xi, 151.
6. Rāzī, iv, ii, 17.
7. *Tahd.*, vi, 161.
8. Khaithamah, iii, 141b; *Tahd.*, vi, 161.
9. Khaithamah, iii, 141b.
10. Dūlābī - *Kunā*, i, 190-1.
11. *Tahd.*, vi, 151.
12. *Bagh.*, x, 223.
13. *Tahd.*, vi, 298; see also *Mīzān*, ii, 599.
14. BTK, iii, i, 365; BTS, 179; *Mīzān*, ii, 599.

36. ʻAbd al-Razzāq b. ʻUmar al-Thaqafī (c. 100 - c. 160).

He transmitted *aḥādīth* from al-Zuhrī (d. 124)[4] but lost his books[5].

37. ʻAbd al-Wārith b. Saʻīd (102-180)[6].

He transmitted *aḥādīth* from ʻAbd al-ʻAzīz b. Ṣuhaib (d. 130). His book was perfect, and was the final authority if scholars differed about some *aḥādīth* of his teachers[7].

The following derived *aḥādīth* from him in written form:

ʻAbd al-Ṣamad,

ʻAbd Allāh b. ʻAmr - Abū Maʻmar[8].

38. ʻAbīdah b. Ḥumaid al-Taimī (107-190)[9].

He had a book[10].

Many students wrote *aḥādīth* from him[11].

39. Abū Bakr b. ʻAbd al-Raḥmān b. al-Miswar b. Makhrimah (c. 75 - c. 135).

He transmitted from Muḥammad b. Jubair etc.

He had a book which contained *aḥādīth* from Muḥammad b. Jubair b. Muṭʻim (d. 100) and papers from other scholars, relating

1. *Tahd.*, vi, 175. There are other dates given about his birth and death; see *Majrūḥīn*, 142b.
2. *Bagh.*, x, 215; *Tahd*, vi, 175.
3. Rāzī, ii, ii, 234; *Bagh.* X, 216.
4. *Tahd.*, vi, 309.
5. *Tahd.*, vi, 310.
6. *Tahd.*, vi, 443.
7. Muslim - *Tamyīz*, 5b.
8. *Bagh.*, x, 25.
9. *Tahd.*, vii, 82.
10. *Tahd.*, vii, 82.
11. *Tahd.*, vii, 82.

to the History of Makkah and the ka'bah[1]. It appears that al-Miswar b. Makhrimah had compiled some works on the *Sīrah* and the early history, and perhaps later his work was transmitted by his daughter Umm Baḳr. Ibn Sa'd quotes the work through her nephew[2]. 'Abd al-Raḥmān son of Miswar also transmits it[3].

40. ABŪ BAKR B. ABŪ SABRAH (c. 100-162)[4].

The following derived *aḥādīth* from him in writing:

Ibn Juraij. According to al-Wāqidi, Abū Bakr sent Ibn Juraij 1,000 *aḥādith* in writing.[5]

41. ABŪ BAKR B. 'AYYĀSH (96 - 194)[7].

He lived for a long time, so that the younger generations wrote from him[7]. His books were perfect[8].

Yaḥyā b. Yaḥyā derived *aḥādīth* from him in writing:

42. AḤMAD B. KHĀZIM AL-MIṢRĪ (c. 85 - c. 150)[10].

He transmitted from 'Aṭā' b. Abū Rabāḥ, etc.

He had a book which was known to scholars and was even read to al-Dhahabī[11].

43. 'ALI B. 'ĀṢIM B. ṢUHAIB AL-WĀSIṬĪ (105-201)[12].

He was a rich man, hence he was able to employ many scribes who wrote *aḥādīth* for him. In the copying of the

1. Sa'd ,i, i, 39. Ibn Sa'd transmitted from this source more than one page, concerning Makkah and Ka'bah, etc.
2. Sa'd, i, i, 58.
3. Sa'd, i, i, 51.
4. *Tahd.*, xii, 28.
5. Sa'd, v, 361; Ibn Qutaibah, *Ma'ārif*, 489, see also Dūlābī, i, 121.
6. *Tahd.*, xii, 36.
7. Sa'd vi, 269.
8. Rāzī, iv, ii, 350; *Mīzān*, iv, 500; *Tahd.*, xii, 35.
9. *Kifāyah*, 340.
10. *Islām*, vi, 36.
11. *Islām*, vi, 36.
12. *Bagh.*, xi, 447.

original books many errors were made, and for this reason he was discredited[1]. He had three *Mustamly* in his lectures[2], and the number of students was enormous[3].

44. 'ALĪ B. MUBĀRAK AL-HUNĀ'Ī (c. 105 - c. 165).

He transmitted from Yaḥyā b. Abū Kathīr (d. 129) etc.[4].

Hārūn b. Ismā'īl had a book from him[5].

45. 'ALĪ B. MUSHIR AL-QURASHĪ (c. 85 - 189)[6].

He transmitted from Abū Burdah.b. Abū Mūsā (d. 104) etc.[7].

He buried his books, which were perfect[8].

46. 'ALĪ B. ZAID B. JUD'ĀN (c. 70 - 131)[9].

Ibn 'Uyaynah wrote a large book from him, and then gave it away to someone[10].

47. 'AMMĀR B. MU'ĀWIYAH AL-DUHNĪ (c. 70-133)[11].

'Abīdah b. Ḥumaid b. Ṣuhaib had a *Ṣaḥīfah* from him[12].

48. 'AMR B. 'AMR. ABŪ AL-ZZ'RĀ' (c. 70 - c. 130)[13].

'Abīdah b. Ḥumaid had a *Nuskhah* from him[14].

---

1. *Bagh.*, xi, 447-8; *Tahd.*, vii, 345; see also *Mīzān*, iii, 135.
2. *Bagh.*, xi, 454.
3. *Bagh.*, xi, 454; where 30,000 are mentioned; see also *Mīzān* iii, 135.
4. *Tahd.*, vii, 375.
5. Rāzī, iv, ii, 87.
6. *Tahd.*, vii, 383.
7. *Tahd.*, vii, 383.
8. *Tahd.*, vii, 384.
9. *Mīzān*, iii, 129; *Tahd.*, vii, 324.
10. *Mīzān*, iii, 129; *Tahd.*, vii, 323-4; see also Rāzī, iii, i, 186.
11. *Tahd.*, vii, 407; Ibn Khaṭīb al-Dahshah, *Tuḥfah*, 156.
12. *Bagh.*, xi, 122.
13. *Tahd.*, viii, 82. He died after Abū Isḥāq (d. 127).
14. *'Ilal*, i, 384.

49. 'Amr b. al-Ḥārith al-Anṣārī (90-149)[1].

Ibn Wahb had a book from him[2], and wrote some of his *aḥādīth* for Ibn Mahdī[3].

50. 'Amr b. Thābit b. Hurmuz (c. 105-172)[4].

He transmitted from al-Sabī'ī etc.

Hannād wrote down *aḥādīth* from him in quantity[5].

51. 'Amr b. 'Ubaid b. Bāb al-Tamīmī (c. 80-142)[6].

Ibn 'Uyaynah wrote a book from him[7].

52. Anas b. 'Ayāḍ, Abū Ḍamrah (104-185)[8].

Mālik b. Anas used to praise him. He said that Anas had heard *aḥādīth* and had transcribed them, but that the only weakness he had was that he had presented his books to Iraqians[9].

53. Arṭāt b. al-Mundhir (c. 70-162)[10].

He saw Abū Umāmah al-Bāhilī (d. 81) [11].

Al-Jarrāḥ b. Mulaih al-Bahrānī had a *Nuskhah* from him, containing some 20 *aḥādīth*[12].

54. Ash'ath b. 'Abd al-Malik, Abū Hābī al-Baṣrī (c. 85-142)[13].

He transmitted from Ibn Sīrīn and others and had a book[14].

---

1. *Tahd.*, viii, 16.
2. Fasawī, iii, 52a; see also Bājī, 106a; *Kifāyah,* 152.
3. *Tahd.*, viii, 15.
4. *Tahd.*, viii, 10.
5. *Mīzān,* iii, 249.
6. *Tahd.*, viii, 72.
7. Rāzī, *introd.* 47; iii, i, 247; *Tahd,* viii, 71.
8. *Tahd.*, i, 376.
9. *Tahd.*, i, 376.
10. *Tahd.*, i, 198.
11. *Tahd.*, i, 198.
12. *Kāmil,* i, 223b.
13. *Tahd.*, i, 358.
14. Rāzī, i, i, 275.

The following derived *aḥādīth* from him in writing:

Al-Anṣārī[1].
Haudhah b. Khlīfah[2].
Muḥammad b. Maisarah, Abū Salamah[3].

55. Ash'ath b. Sawwār al-Kindī (c. 80-136)[4].

He transmitted from al-Sha'bī and others.

The following wrote *aḥādīth* from him:

Jarīr b. 'Abd al-Ḥamīd[5].

Ḥafṣ b. Yhayāth [6].

56. 'Aṣim v. Kulaib al-Kūfī(c. 70-137)[7].

'Abd Allāh b. Idrīs had his *aḥādīth* in writing[8].

57. 'Aṣim b. Muḥammad v. Zaid al-'Umarī (c. 100 - c. 160).

He transmitted from Muḥammad b. Ka'b al-Quraẓī (d. 120) etc.[9].

Ibrāhīm b. Sa'īd had a book from him[10].

58. 'Asim b. Rajā' b. Ḥaiwah al-Kindī (c. 90 - c. 150).

He transmitted from his father (d. 112)[11].

Many Iraqians wrote from him[12].

59. 'Aṣim b. Sulaimān al-Aḥwal (c. 70-142)[13].

He transmitted from Anas (d. 93) etc.

---

1. *Kāmil,* i, 132a.
2. Sa'd, vii, ii, 80.
3. Bājī, 68b; *Tahd.,* ix, 124.
4. *Tahd.,* i, 353.
5. *'Ilal,* i, 195; Rāzī, i, i, 431; Bājī 36b.
6. *Tahd.,* v, 56.
7. Ḥanbal, i, 418.
8. *Tahd.,* v, 57.
9. *Bagh.,* ix, 123-4.
10. *Tahd.,* v, 41.
11. *Mashāhīr,* 183.
12. *Tahd.,* v, 43.
13. Ibn Ma'in, *Tārīkh,* 82b.

The following transcribed *aḥādīth* from him:

Jarīr[1].

Sufyān[2].

Shu'ba[3].

60. 'ĀṢIM B. 'UMAR AL-'UMARĪ (c. 105 - c. 170).

He transmitted from 'Abd Allāh b. Dīnār (d. 127) etc.[4].

He had a book, titled *al-Nāsikh wa al-Mansūkh*[5].

62. AL-ASWAD B. SHAIBĀN (c. 90-165)[6].

He transmitted from al-Ḥasan al-Baṣrī (d. 110) and others[7].

'Abd al-Raḥmān b. Mahdī had *ḥādīth* from him, in writing[8].

62. 'AṬṬĀF B. KHĀLID (91 - c. 150)[9].

His book was perfect[10].

Mukhallad b. Mālik had a book from him.[11].

---

1. *'Ilal,* i, 195; Rāzī, i, i, 431; Bājī, 36b.
2. Ḥanbal, iii, 111.
3. Baihaqī, Sunan, ii, 56.
4. *Tahd.*, v, 51.
5. Rāzī, iii, i, 347.
6. *Tahd.*, i, 339.
7. *Tahd.*, i, 339.
8. *'Ilal,* 179b.
9. *Tahd.*, vii, 223.
10. *Kāmil,* ii, 335b.
11. *Kāmil,* ii, 336b; *Mīzān,* iii, 69; *Tahd.*, x, 77.

63. AYYUB B. KHALŪṬ (c. 90 - c. 150)[1].

He transmitted from Qatādah, etc. His book was imperfect[2].

Ḥusain b. Wāqid wrote *aḥādith* from him[3].

64. AYYŪB B. MUSA B. 'AMR B. SA'ID B. AL-'AṢ (c. 75 - 132)[4].

He transmitted from Nāfi'and others.

'Ubaid Allāh b. 'Umar took a book from him. This book was read to al-Zuhrī, "Aṭā' and Makḥūll. It contained regulations for blood money[5].

65. AYYUB B. 'UTABAH AL-YAMANI (c. 100-160)[6].

He transmitted from Yaḥyā b. Abū Kathir (d. 129) and others. He went to Baghdād without his books, and there he imparted *aḥādith* from memory, hence he made many mistakes[7]. His books were, however, perfect[8].

66. BAḤI B. SA'D AL-SAḤIMSI (c. 80-160)[9].

He transmitted from Khālid b. Ma'dān (d. 103) and others.

Baqiyah b. al-Walīd[10] read the book of Baḥīr to Shu'bah who was very pleased [11].

67. BAḤR B. KUNAIZ (c. 90-160)[12].

He transmitted from al-Ḥasan al-Baṣrī (d. 110) etc.

1. *Tahd.*, i, 402.
2. *Tahd.*, i, 402.
3. *Thiqat*, 438.
4. *Tahd.*, i, 413.
5. BTK ,i, i, 422-3.
6. *Tahd.*,i, 410.
7. Rāzi, i, i, 253; *Bagh.*, vii, 3; *Tahd.*, i, 409.
8. *Bagh.*, vii, 4; *Mizān*, i, 290.
9. Khazraji, 46.
10. Rāzī, i, i, 412.
11. *Kāmil*, i, 168b; *Mīzān*, i, 332.
12. *Tahd.*, i, 419; *Mizān* i, 298.

The following transmitted his books:

Ḥārith b. Muslim[1].

Muḥammad b. Muṣ'ab al-Qarqasānī[2].

'Umar b. Sahl[3].

Yazīd b. Zurai'[4].

68. Bahz b. Ḥakīm al-Qushairī (c. 80 after 140)[5].

He transmitted a *Nuskhah* from his father, who in turn transmitted from the grandfather of Bahz[6].

The following had his books:

Al-Anṣārī[7].
Makkī b. Ibrāhīm al-Balkhī[8].

69. Bakr b. Wā'il b. Dāwūd (c. 90 - c. 130).

He died earlier than his father[9] who had a book from him[10].

70. Baqiyah b. al-Walīd al-Kalā'ī (110-196)[11].

He wrote from everyone without discrimination[12], and Ibn Thaubān wrote *aḥādīth* from him[14].

---

1. *Mīzān,* i, 298.
2. *Mīzān,* i, 298.
3. *Mīzān,* i, 298.
4. *Mīzān,* i, 298.
5. *Islām,* vi, 43.
6. *Islām,* vi, 42.
7. *Islām* vi, 43.
8. *Ma'rifah,* 165.
9. *Tahd.,* i, 488.
10. *Kifāyah,* 354.
11. *Mīzān,* i, 331-9.
12. *Bagh.,* vii, 125; *Tahd.,* i, 474.
13. *Taqyīd,* 110.
14. *Jāmi',* 155a.

71. BUKAIR B. 'ABD ALLĀH B. AL-ASHAJJ (c. 70-127)[1].

He transmitted from Ibn al-Musayyab and others.

The following had his books:

Makhrimah b. Bukhair. He did not read these books to his father[2].

Al-Laith b. Sa'd[3].

72. DĀWŪD B. ABŪ HIND (c. 75-139)[4].

He had books[5],and wrote a commentary on the *Qur'ān*[6].

The following wrote *aḥādīth* from him:

Adī b. 'Abd al-Raḥmān transmitted a *Nuskhah* from him[7].

Al-Anṣārī had written a large number of *aḥādīth*[8].

73. DĀWŪD B. AL-ḤUṢAIN AL-UMAWĪ (c. 70-135)[9].

Ibrāhim b. Abū Yaḥyā had a large *Nuskhah* (book) from him[10].

74. DĀWŪD B. NUṢAIR AL-ṬĀ'Ī (c. 100-160)[11].

He buried his books[12], probably about 140A.H.

75. DĀWŪD B. SHĀBŪR AL-MAKKĪ (c. 80 c. 140).

He transmitted from Mujāhid[13].

Shu'bah wrote his *aḥādīth*[14].

---

1. *Annales.*, iii, 2501.
2. *'Ilal,* i, 91; 282; Fasawī, iii, 318a; Khaithamah, iii, 145a; *Thiqāt,* 609; Rāzī, iv, i, 363; 364. (There is a single quotation that he heard from his father, see Rāzi, iv, i, 364); *Mīzān,* iv, 81; *Tahd.,* x, 70.
3. *Tahd.*, viii, 465; *Mīzān,* iii, 423; see also Bājī, 33b; *Tahd.,* i, 493.
4. *Tahd.*, iii, 204.
5. *Thiqāt,* 455; *Tahd.*, iii, 204.
6. *Fihrist,* 33.
7. *Thiqāt,* 575; Rāzī, iii, ii, 3.
8. *Kifāyah,* 235.
9. *Tahd.*, iii, 182.
10. *Kāmil* i, 335a.
11. *Tahd.*, iii, 203.
12. *Thiqāt,* 456; *Tahd.*, iii, 203.
13. *Tahd.*, iii, 187.
14. *Wāsit,* 162.

76. Ḍimā b. Ismā'īl (97-185)[1].

The following derived *aḥādīth* from him in writing:

Abū Mūsā had his book[2].

Muḥammad al-Iskandarānī[3].

77. Ḍirār b. Murrah al-Kūfī (c. 70-132)[4].

His book was in possession of Tamīm b. Nāṣiḥ[5].

78. Al-Fuḍail b. Maisarah (c. 85 - c. 145).

He transmitted from al-Sha'bi etc.[6].

Mu'tamar b. Sulaimān had a book from him[7].

79. Ghailān b. Jāmi' (c. 80 - 132)[8].

He had a book[9].

80. Ḥabīb b. Abū Ḥabīb al-Ḥarmī (c. 90-162)[10].

He transmitted from Ibn Sīrīn (d. 110) and others[11].

The following wrote *aḥādīth* from him:

Dāwūd b. Shabīb[12].

Yaḥyā b. Sa'īd[13].

---

1. *Tahd.*, iv, 459; *Taqrīb*, i, 374.
2. *Madkhal*, 44; *Kifāyah*, 153.
3. *Madkhal*, 44; *Kifāyah*, 153.
4. *Tahd.*, iv, 457.
5. *Bagh.*, vii, 138-9.
6. *Tahd.*, viii, 300.
7. *'Ilal*, 158a.
8. *Tahd.*, viii, 253.
9. *'Ilal*, i, 342.
10. *Tahd.*, ii, 180.
11. *Tahd.*, ii, 180.
12. Rāzī, i, ii, 99.
13. Rāzī, i, ii, 99; *Mīzān*, I, 453.

81. Ḥafṣ b. Ghailān al-Dimashqī (c. 90 - c. 150).

He transmitted from Makḥūl (d. 112) and others[1].

Each of Ḥafṣ's students transmitted a book from him[2].

82. Ḥafṣ b. Sulaimān al-Asadī (90-180)[3].

He copied other scholars' books and put their material in his own. He borrowed a book from Shu'bah, but did not return it[4].

83. Ḥaiwah b. Shuraiḥ (c. 95-158)[5].

He had books[6].

84. Al-Ḥajjāj al-Bāhilī (c. 80-131)[7].

Ibrāhīm b. Ṭahmān transmitted a lengthy book from him[8].

85. Al-Ḥakam b. 'Aṭīyah al-'Aishī (c. 90 - c. 160).

He transmitted from Ibn Sīrīn (d. 110) and others[9].

Sulaimān b. Ḥarb wrote his *aḥādīth* and then wiped them out[10].

86. Ḥammād b. Salamah (c. 87-167)[11].

It is said that he was one of the first to compile books[12].

---

1. *Tahd.*, ii, 418.
2. *Kāmil,* i, 284a; *Tahd.*, ii, 419.
3. *Tahd.*, ii, 401.
4. Rāzī, i, ii, 173; *Mīzān,* i, 558.
5. *Tahd.*, iii, 70.
6. *Tahd.*, v, 375; See also about his book, Rāmhurmuzī, 48a-b; *Kifāyah,* 315.
7. *Tahd.*, ii, 100.
8. *Ma'rifah,* 164; *Tahd.*, ii, 200.
9. *Tahd.*, ii, 435.
10. Rāzī, i, ii, 126; *Tahd.*, ii, 435.
11. *Ḥuffāẓ,* i, 183.
12. *Ḥuffāẓ,* i, 182. See also about his books *Tahd.*, iii, 13.

The following scholars transmitted his books or wrote down his *aḥādīth*:

'Abd al-Wāḥid b. Ghayāth al-Baṣrī[1].

'Affān. Ḥammād dictated to him[2].

'Amr b. 'Āṣim al-Kilābī wrote more than 10,000 *aḥādīth* from him[3].

Anonymous, a large number. Yahyā b. Ma'in heard Ḥammād's book from 18 of the latter students in order to separate the mistakes of Ḥammād from those of his students[4].

Anonymous person[5].

Ḥajjāj b. al-Minhāl transmitted *Musnad* of Ḥammād[6].

Hudbah b. Khālid b. al-Aswad had two copies of his books[7].

Ibn al-Mubārak[8].

Muḥammad b. al-Faḍl[9].

Mūsā b. Ismā'īl al-Tabūdhakī's grandfather[10].

Al-Shāmī[11].

Sulaimān b. Ḥarb[12].

Wahb[13].

Yaḥyā b. Ḍurrais had 10,000 *aḥādīth* from Ḥammād[14].

Yaḥyā al-Qaṭṭān[15].

Zaid b. 'Auf[16].

---

1. Rāzī, *introd.* 329.
2. *Imlā,* 11.
3. *Mīzān,* iii, 269; *Ḥuffāz,* i, 183; *Tahd.,* viii, 59.
4. *Majrūḥīn,* 10a.
5. Fasawī, iii, 205b.
6. Ḥumaidī, *Jadhwat al-Muqtabis,* 235.
7. *Tahd.,* xi, 25; Bājī, 168b.
8. Rāzī, i, ii, 570-1.
9. Tirmidhī, *Shamā'il,* 6.
10. Abū Nu'aim, *Tārīkh Iṣbahān,* i, 100.
11. Ja'd, 441.
12. Fasawī, iii, 205b.
13. Fasawī, iii, 205b.
14. Rāzī, i, ii, 141-2; *Ḥuffāz,* i, 182.
15. Ja'd, 442.
16. Rāzī, i, ii, 570-1.

87. Ḥammās v. Zaid b. Dirham al-Azdī (98-179)[1].

Yaḥyā said, "Nobody used to write in the lectures of Ayyūb (d. 131) save Ḥammād"[2]. It is said that he was illiterate, but 'Ubaid Allāh b. 'Umar saw him writing[3]. It is also maintained that he had only one book of Yaḥyā[4].

The following wrote *aḥādīth* from him:

'Abd al-Raḥmān b. Mahdi[5].

'Abd al-Raḥmān b. Mubārak[6].

Aḥmad[7].

'Alī b. Madīnī was young when he wrote from Ḥammād; hence, he is a weak transmitter[8].

Khalf b. Hishām al-Baghadādī copied out many books of Ḥammād[9].

Sufyān al-Thaurī[10].

Sulaimān b. Ḥarb[11].

88. Hammām b. Yaḥyā al-Baṣrī (c. 90-163)[12].

He transmitted from al-Ḥasan (d. 110) etc.,[13] and had books which were perfect[14].

The following derived *aḥādīth* from him in writing:

'Affān[15].

Hudbah transmitted a *Nuskhah* from him[16].

---

1. *Tahd.*, iii, 11.
2. *Tahd.*, iii, 11.
3. *Tahd.*, iii, 11.
4. Rāzī, i, ii, 138; *Ḥuffāz*, i, 207.
5. *Kifāyah*, 235.
6. *Kifāyah*, 235.
7. *Tahd.*, I, 51.
8. *Mīzān*, iii, 82.
9. *Tahd.*, iii, 156.
10. *Imlā*, 86-7.
11. *Kifāyah*, 241.
12. *Tahd.*, xi, 70.
13. *Khazṛalī*, 353.
14. *'Ilal*, i, 111; Rāzī, iv, II, 108; 109; *Mīzān*, iv, 309; *Tahd.*, xi, 68; 69; *Kifāyah*, 223.
15. *Jāmi'*, 113b.
16. *Kāmil*, i, 266b.

89. ḤANẒALAH B. ABŪ SUFYĀN AL-JUMAḤĪ (c. 85 - after 151)[1].

He transmitted from Sālim b. 'Abd Allāh (d. 106) and had a book[2].

90. ḤARĪZ B. 'UTHMĀN B. JABR (80-163)[3].

'Alī b. 'Ayyāsh wrote *aḥādīth* from him[4].

91. HĀRŪN B. SA'D AL-'IJLĪ (c. 100 - before 150)[5].

He transmitted from Abū Isḥāq al-Sabī'ī (d. 127) etc. Many students of Wāsiṭ wrote from Hārūn[6].

92. AL-ḤASAN B. DĪNĀR, ABŪ SA'ĪD AL-TAMĪMĪ (c. 90 - c. 150).

He transmitted from Ibn Sīrīn (d. 110) etc.[7] He had books and used to take them to other people's houses to read them[8].

93. ḤASSĀN B. IBRĀHĪM, ABŪ HISHĀM AL-KŪFĪ (86-186)[9].

Scholars wrote *aḥādīth* from him in Baghdad[10].

94. AL-ḤASAN B. ṢĀLIḤ B. ḤAY (100-169)[11].

The following had *aḥādīth* from him in writing:

Abū Nu'aim[12].

Many unnamed scholars transmitted books from him[13].

---

1. *Tahd.*, iii, 61.
2. Khaithamah, iii, 40b; Rāzī, i, ii, 241; *Tahd.*, iii, 61.
3. *Tahd.*, ii, 240.
4. *Bagh.*, viii, 266; *Tahd.*, ii, 238.
5. *Islām*, vi, 143.
6. Rāzī, iv, ii, 91; *Islām*, vi, 143; *Tahd.*, xi, 6.
7. *Tahd.*, ii, 275.
8. *Mīzān*, i, 489.
9. *Tahd.*, ii, 245.
10. *Bagh.*, viii, 260.
11. *Tahd.*, ii, 288.
12. *Ḥuffāẓ*, i, 195; *Tahd.*, ii, 287; *Kāmil*, i, 256b-57a.
13. *Tahd.*, ii, 287.

Mālik b. Ismā'īl[1], Salamah b. 'Abd al-Malik[2], and Yaḥyā b. Fudhail each had a *Nuskhah* from him[3].

95. Al-Ḥasan b. 'Umārah al-Kūfī (c. 90-153)[4].

The following transcribed *aḥādīth* from him :

Anonymous[5].

Muṣ'ab b. Sallām[6].

Wakī[7].

96. Al-Haitham b. Ḥumaid al-Ghassānī (c. 110 - c. 170).

He transmitted from al-Nu'mān b. al-Mundhir al-Ghassānī (d. 133) etc.[8] and had books[9].

Muḥammad b. Ā'idh had a book from him[10].

97. Ḥaushab b. 'Aqīl al-'Abdī (c. 90 - c. 150).

He transmitted from Ḥasan al-Baṣrī (d. 110), 'Aṭā' and others[11].

The following derived *aḥādīth* from him in writing:

Hishām b. Ḥassān. It was assumed that Hishām b. Ḥassān took Haushab's book[12].

Sulaim al-Taimī. Ziyād b. al-Rabī' saw him writing from Ḥaushab[13].

---

1. *Kāmil,* i, 258b.
2. *Kāmil,* i, 258b.
3. *Kāmil,* i, 258b.
4. *Tahd.,* ii, 306.
5. Fischer, 11; *Mīzān,* i, 514.
6. *'Ilal,* 163b.
7. *Mīzān,* i, 515.
8. *Tahd.,* xi, 92.
9. *Tahd.,* xi, 93.
10. Rāzī, introd. 343.
11. *Tahd.,* iii, 65.
12. *Tahd.,* xi, 37.
13. *Kāmil,* i, 301b.

98. HISHĀM B. ḤASSĀN AL-QURDŪSĪ (c. 90-148)[1].

He transmitted from Ibn Sīrīn (d. 110) etc.

The following derived *aḥādīth* from him in writing:

Abū 'Awānah[2].

Abū Juzai al-Qaṣṣāb[3].

Hārūn b. Abū 'Īsā[4].

Ismā'īl b. 'Ulayyah[5].

Rauḥ b. 'Ubādah[6].

Sallām b. Abū Muṭī'[7].

'Uthmān b. 'Umar borrowed his book from Rauḥ[8].

Yazīd b. Zurai'[9].

99. HISHĀM B. SAMBAR AL-DASTAWĀ'Ī (74-152)[10].

He wrote a large number of *aḥādīth*, about 10,000 of them from Qatādah alone[11].

The following wrote *aḥādīth* from him:

'Abd al-Wahhāb b. 'Aṭā' al-Khaffāf[12].

Ismā'īl b. 'Ulayyah[13].

100. ḤUMAID B. ZIYĀD, ABŪ SAKHR (c. 80-189)[14].

He transmitted from Abū Ṣāliḥ al-Sammān (d. 101).

---

1. *Tahd.*, xi, 36.
2. *Majrūḥīn*, 115b.
3. *Majrūḥīn*, 115b.
4. *Majrūḥīn*, 115b.
5. *Majrūḥīn*, 115b.
6. *'Ilal*, i, 109; *Bagh.*, viii, 404.
7. *Majrūḥīn*, 115b.
8. *'Ilal*, i, 109; *Bagh.*, viii, 404.
9. *Majrūḥīn*, 115b.
10. *Tahd.*, xi, 45.
11. *Tahd.*, x, 197.
12. *Mīzān*, ii, 681-2.
13. *'Ilal*, i, 367.
14. *Tahd.*, iii, 42.

The following derived *aḥādīth* from him in writing:

Ibn Lahī'ah[1] and Ibn Wahb[2] transmitted a *Nuskhah* each from him.

101. Ḥasan b. Abū Ja'far al-Jufrī (c. 95-161)[3].

He transmitted from Nāfi' (d. 117) etc.[4].

Ibn Mahdī had Ḥasan's *aḥādīth* in writing[5].

102. Al-Ḥusain b. Qais al-Rahbī (c. 85 - c. 150).

He transmitted from 'Ikrimah (d. 105) etc.[6].

'Alī b. 'Āṣim had a book containing al-Raḥabī's *aḥādīth*. Later on Abū 'Awānah borrowed this book from 'Alī b. 'Āṣim[7].

103. Al-Ḥusain b. Wāqid al-Marwazī (c. 90-159)[8].

He transmitted from 'Abd Allāh b. Buraidah (d. 115) and compiled a commentary on the *Qur'ān*[9].

104. Hushaim b. Bashīr al-Wāsiṭī (104-183)[10].

He compiled many books[11]. Ibn al-Nadīm gives us the names of three of them; — 1) *Kitāb al-Sunan* — 2) *Kitāb al-Tafsīr* — 3) *Kitāb al-Qirā'āt*[12].

The following wrote *aḥādīth* from him:

'Abd Allāh b. Mūsā[13].

---

1. *Kāmil*, i, 240b.
2. *Kāmil*, i, 240b.
3. *Tahd.*, ii, 260.
4. *Mīzān*, i, 483.
5. *Majrūḥīn*, 81b.
6. *Tahd.*, ii, 364.
7. *Kāmil*, i, 270b.
8. *Tahd.*, ii, 374.
9. *Fihrist*, 34.
10. *Tahd.*, xi, 62.
11. *Mashāhīr*, 177.
12. *Fahrist*, 228.
13. *Bagh.*, vi, 195.

Abū Ṣāliḥ[1].

Anonymous[2].

Ḥajjāj b. Muḥammad[3].

Ḥayyān b. Bishr[4].

Ibn Ḥanbal[5].

Al-Laith b. Sa'd[6].

Shujā' b. Makhlad[7].

105. IBRĀHĪM B. 'AQĪ L B. MA'QAL B. MUNABBIH (c. 95 - 180).

He transmitted from Wahb b. Munabbih[8]. Yaḥyā b. Ma'īn saw him, and described him as a good transmitter, but added that he must have a *Ṣaḥīfah*[9].

106. IBRĀHĪM B. DHĪ ḤIMĀYAH (c. 100 - 160).

Al-Jarrāḥ b. Mulaiḥ transmitted a *Nuskhah* from him[10].

107. IBRĀHĪM B. MAIMŪN AL-ṢĀ'IGH (c. 90 - 131)[11].

He transmitted from 'Aṭā' b. Abū Rahāḥ (d. 117) and others. He was killed by Abū Muslim al-Khurāsānī[12].

The following derived *aḥādīth* from him in writing:

Al-Sakan. He says: "I asked Ibrāhīm b. Muslim al-Sā'igh to lend me a book and when he demanded a mortgage, I handed him a copy of the Holy *Qur'ān* as mortgage[13].

1. *Bagh.*, ix, 479.
2. Rāzī, i, i, 68.
3. *'Ilal,* i, 381.
4. Abū Nū'aim, *Tārikh Isfahān,* i, 118.
5. *'Ilal,* 141b; i, 366.
6. *Bagh.*, ix, 479.
7. Sa'd, vii, ii, 90.
8. *Tahd.*, i, 146.
9. Rāzī, i, i, 121.
10. *Kāmil,* i, 223b.
11. *Tahd.*, i, 172.
12. *Tahd.*, i, 173.
13. *Imlā,* 178.

108. Ibrāhīm b. Muḥammad b. al-Ḥārith al-Fazārī (c. 100 - 188)[1].

He transmitted from Abū Isḥāq al-Sabī'ī (d. 124) and others. He began to write *aḥādīth* when he was 28 years old[2]. Al-Shāfi'ī saw his book and then compiled his own following al-Fazārī's methods[3].

One of his books, *Kitāb al-Siyar,* is still preserved in the al-Qarawiyyīn Library at Fez[4]. This was transmitted by:

Maḥbūb b. Mūsā[5].

Mu'āwiyah b. 'Amr al-Azdī[6].

Al-Musayyab b. Wāḍiḥ[7].

According to Ibn al-Nadīm, as quoted by Ibn Ḥajar, Ibrāhīm was the first to make an *Astrolabe* in Islam, and he compiled a book on this subject[8].

109. Ibrāhīm b. Muḥammad b. Abū Yaḥyā al-Aslamī (c. 105 - 184)[9].

He transmitted from al-Zuhrī (d. 124) and others. In order to prevent his *aḥādīth* from being transcribed, Ibn Ḥanbal stated that he used to enter other scholar's *aḥādīth* in hiw own books[10].

He compiled *al-Muwaṭṭa'* which was much larger than that of Mālik b. Anas[11].

---

1. *Tahd.*, i, 152.
2. *Tahd.*, i, 153.
3. *Tahd.*, i, 152.
4. Airiklī, x, 8. I saw this book on my visit to al-Qarawiyyīn. See also, *Liste de manuscrits arabes précieux, exposés a la Bibliotheque de l'Université Quaraouyine a Fés,* p. 33, MSS. NL.
5. Rāzī, iv, i, 386.
6. Sa'd, vii, ii, 82; Rāzī, iv, i, 386.
7. Rāzi, iv, i, 386.
8. *Tahd.*, i, 153, quoting *al-Fihrist,* but Ibn al-Nadim gives the nameof Ibrāhim b. Ḥabīb. According to al-Ziriklī's research, it was Muḥammad b. Ibrāhim al-Fazārī (c. 180) who made Astrolabe see, Ziriklī, vi, 181.
9. *Tahd.*, i, 159.
10. Rāzi, i, , 126.
11. *Ḥuffāz,* i, 224; *Tahd.*, i, 159; *Kāmil,* i, 78a.

He had many *Nuskhahs*[1]. Nu'aim b. Ḥammād spent 50 dinars on his books. One day Ibrāhīm gave him a book containing the opinion of Jahm, etc., and as a result Nu'aim abandoned the book[2].

110. IBRĀHĪM B. SA'D (108 - 184)[3].

He transmitted from his father, al-Zuhrī, etc. and had 17,000 *aḥādīth* from Ibn Isḥāq, excluding *al-Maghāzī*[4]. Shu'bah encouraged people to copy from Ibrāhīm[5].

The following derived *aḥādīth* from him in writing:

Aḥmad b. Ḥanbal[6].

Aḥmad b. Muḥammad b. Ayyūb had his book on *al-Maghāzī*[7].

Al-Faḍal b. Yaḥyā. Ibrāhīm sent him his book on *al-Maghāzī*[8].

Ibn Isḥāq had a book from him[9].

Nūḥ b. Yazīd[10].

Sa'd B. Ibrāhīm had his books and transmitted them[11].

Ya'qūb b. Ibrāhīm transmitted *al-Maghāzī* from his father[12].

It is not clear whether this book *al-Maghāzī* was Ibrāhīm's father's work, or the work of Ibn Isḥāq. He transmitted other books as well from his father[13].

---

1. *Kāmil,* i, 78a; *Mīzān,* i, 59.
2. *Kāmil,* i, 75a; *Tahd.,* I, 158-9.
3. *Tahd.,* i, 122.
4. *Bagh.,* vi, 83; *Mīzān,* i, 35; *Tahd.,* i, 122.
5. *Kāmil,* i, 88a.
6. *Mīzān,* iii, 82.
7. Sa'd, vii, ii, 91.
8. Rāzī, i, i, 70.
9. *Bagh.,* i, 230.
10. *Tahd.,* x, 489.
11. Sa'd, vii, ii, 83.
12. Sa'd vii, ii, 84.
13. Sa'd, vii, ii, 84; see also for books of Ibrāhīm *Mīzān,* i, 34; *Tahd.,* i, 123.

111. Ibrāhīm b. Ṭahmān, Abū Sa'īd al-Khurāsānī (c. 100 - 163)[1].

Isḥāq b. Rāhwaih said that no one had more *aḥādīth* than Ibrāhīm in Khurāsān[2]. He was not only a transmitter of his teachers' traditions, but was also a compiler of many books[3]. According to Ibn al-Nadīm he compiled:

Kitāb al-Sunan.

Kitāb al-Manāqib.

Kitāb al-'Īdain.

Kitāb al-Tafsīr[4].

Ibn al-Mubārak says, "His books were perfect"[5].

The following derived *aḥādīth* from him in writing:

Abū Ḥanīfah, al-Imām. He copied from Ibrāhīm what he had transcribed from Mālik b. Anas in al-Madīnah[6].

Ḥafṣ b. 'Abd Allāh b. Rāshid al-Sulamī. He was the scribe of Ibrāhīm b. Ṭahmān[7] and transmitted a book from him[8]. This book was transmitted later on by his son Aḥmad[9] and is still preserved in Ẓāhiriyah Library, Damascus.

Khālid b. Nazār transmitted a *Nuskhah* from him[10].

Muḥammad b. Sābiq. He wrote from Ibrāhīm in Baghdād[11].

1. *Tahd.*, i, 129.
2. *Tahd.*, i, 129.
3. *Tahd.*, i, 130; See also Rāzī, *introd.* 270; i, i, 108; *Bagh.*, vi, 107; Bājī, 68b.
4. *Fihrist*, 228.
5. Bājī, 17a.
6. Rāzī, *introd.* 3-4.
7. Rāzī, i, ii, 175.
8. *Tahd.*, ii, 403; see also *Tawsat*, i, 273a; for a part of this work.
9. Rāzī, i, i, 48.
10. *Tahd.*, iii, 123.
11. *Bagh.*, vi, 106.

112. IBRAHĪM B. 'UTHMĀN, ABŪ SHAIBAH (c. 105 - 169)[1].
He transmitted from al-Sābī'ī (d. 127) etc.
The following derived *aḥādīth* from him in writing:
'Alī b. Ja'd wrote from him when he came to Baghdād[2].
Yazīd b. Zurai' had a book from him[3].

113. 'IKRIMAH B. 'AMMĀR AL-'IJLĪ (c. 80 - 159)[4].
He transmitted from Hirmās, whom he met in 102 A.H.[5], and had a book[6].
The following wrote *aḥādīth* from him:
Bishr b. al-Sarrī[7].
Faḍl b. al-Rabī'[8].
Sufyān al-Thaurī[9].
Yaḥyā b. Sa'īd al-Qaṭṭān saw him dictating *aḥādīth* to al-Faḍl b. Rabī', but Yaḥyā did not have writing materials so he missed the lecture. Later he and his son Muḥammad wrote down 'Ikrimah's *aḥādīth* from the dictation of Bishr[10].

114. 'IMRAN B. ABU QUDĀMAH AL-'AMMĪ (c. 70 - c. 140).
He transmitted from Anas b. Mālik (d. 93) etc.[11] and Yaḥyā b. Qaṭṭān wrote from him[12].

---

1. *Tahd.*, i, 145.
2. *Bagh.*, vi, 111.
3. Rāzī, i, i, 115.
4. *Bagh.*, xii, 262.
5. *Tahd.*, xi, 28.
6. Fasawī, ii, 242a; iii, 48b; see also *Thiqāt*, 292.
7. Khaithamah, iii, 32b; 49b; *Imlā*, 14-15; *Bagh.* xii, 258.
8. Khaithamah, iii, 32b; *Bagh.*, 285; *Imlā*, 14-15.
9. *Bagh.*, xii, 258; see also Rāzī, *introd.* 117.
10. Khaithamah, iii, 49b; *Imlā*, 14-15.
11. *Mīzān*, iii, 241.
12. *Mīzān*, iii, 241.

115. 'Imrān b. Ḥudair al-Saddūsī (c. 75 - 149)[1].

He transmitted from Abū 'Uthmān al-Nahdī (d. 95).

Rauḥ b. 'Ubādah had a book from him, which was borrowed by 'Uthmān b. 'Umar[2].

116. 'Isa b. Abū 'Isā, Abū Ja'far al-Tamīmī (c. 100 - c. 160)[3].

Hāshim b. al-Qāsim wrote from him[4].

117. 'Isma'īl b. Abū Khālid al-Aḥmasī (c. 70 - 146)[5].

He transmitted from 'Abd Allāh b. Abū Awfā (d. 86) etc. According to al-'Ijlī he had 500 *aḥādīth*[6].

The following derived *aḥādīth* from him in writing:

Ismā'īl b. 'Ayyāsh. Wakī' says: "Ismā'īl took from me the *Aṭrāf* of Ibn Abū Khālid, but I found him imperfect in the reading of it"[7].

Wakī[8].

Yaḥyā b. Sa'īd, and from him Ibn Ḥanbal[9].

118. Ismā'īl b. 'Ayyāsh (102 - 181)[10].

He wrote a large number of *aḥādīth*. He was a weak transmitter as far as Ḥijāzit were concerned because he lost the book he had from his Ḥijāzit *Shuyūkh*[11].

He compiled many books, e.g., *Muṣannaf*[12], *Kitāb al-Fitan*[13] etc.

---

1. *Tahd.*, vii, 125.
2. *Bagh.*, vii, 405.
3. Khazrajī, 384.
4. *Bagh.*, xi, 144.
5. *Tahd.*, i, 291.
6. *Tadh.*, i, 291.
7. *Tahd.*, i, 292.
8. *Tahd.*, i, 324.
9. *'Ilal*, i, 183; 151b.
10. *Tahd.*, i, 325.
11. Ṭṣaghīr, 42; *Bagh.*, vi, 226; *Tahd.*, i, 323.
12. Rāzī, i, i, 192; *Tahd.*, i, 324; see also *Ḥuffāẓ*, i, 230.
13. Rāzī, iii, ii, 211.

The following wrote *aḥādīth* from him:

'Abd Allāh b. al-Mubārak[1].

Al-Ḥakam b. Nāfi', Abū al-Yamān. He wrote down all the books of Ismā'īl twice and sold the first copy for 30 *dinars*[2].

A large number of other students who are unnamed in Yaḥyā b. Ma'īn's statement. Yaḥyā saw Ismā'īl sitting on a roof, reading about 500 *aḥādīth* from his book every day. After reading, students would take the book and copy from it every day until night[3].

Yaḥyā b. Ma'īn[4].

119. Ismā'īl b. Ibrāhīm al-Asdī, Ibn 'Ulayyah (110 - 193)[5].

He transmitted from Ayyūb, Yaḥyā al-Anṣārī and others. Ziyād b. Ayyūb says: "I never say Ibn 'Ulayyah with a book"[6]. But according to Ibn al-Nadīm, he compiled *Kitāb al-Tafsīr, Kitāb al-Ṭahārah, Kitāb al-Ṣalāt* and *Kitāb al-Manāsik*[7].

'Alī b. Abū Hāshim, the scribe of Ibn 'Ulayyah wrote *aḥādīth* from him. He had the books from Ibn 'Ulayyah. Abū Zakariyā saw these books in 'Alī's possession a long time before the death of Ibn 'Ulayyah[8].

120. Ismā'īl b. Muslim al-Makkī (c. 80 - c. 145).

He transmitted from 'Āmir b. Wāthilah (d. 100) and others[9]. Muḥammad b. 'Abd Allāh al-Anṣārī wrote *aḥādīth* from him[10].

1. *Bagh.*, vi, 223.
2. Fasawī, iii, 133a; *Bagh.*, vi, 224.
3. Ja'd, 451; *Kāmil,* i, 104a; *Bagh.*, vi, 222.
4. *Mīzān,* i, 244.
5. Khazrajī, 27; *Tahd.*, i, 276-7.
6. *Mīzān,* i, 217; *Ḥuffāẓ,* i, 295; *Tahd.*, i, 276; see about his book from Ayyūb, *Zur'ah,* 76a.
7. *Fihrist,* 227.
8. *Bagh.*, xii, 10.
9. *Tahd.*, i, 331.
10. Sa'd, vii, ii, 34; *Tahd.*, i, 333.

121. ISMĀ'ĪL B. SĀLIM ABŪ YAḤYĀ AL-ASDĪ (c. 70 - c. 135).

He transmitted from Ibn al-Masayyab (d. 93) and others[1] and had books which were seen by Shu'bah[2].

122. ISMĀ'ĪL B. SUMAI' AL-ḤANAFĪ (c. 75 - c. 140).

He transmitted from Anas b. Mālik (d. 93) and others[3].

Jarīr b. 'Abd al-Ḥamīd derived *aḥādīth* from him in writing, then abandoned him because Ismā'īl was described as a *Khārijī*[4].

123. ISRĀ'ĪL B. YŪNUS B. ABŪ ISḤĀQ AL-SABĪ'Ī (100 - 160)[5].

He transmitted from his grandfather and others. He memorized the *aḥādīth* of his grandfather and was as perfect in them as if they were a *Sūrah* of the holy *Qur'ān*[6]. Abū Isḥāq al-Sabī'ī dictated *aḥādīth* to his grandson Isrā'īl[7]. He complained that his grandson Isrā'īl filled the house with books[8].

Ibn Ḥanbal says that Isrā'īl had a book[9].

The following wrote *aḥādīth* from him:

Ḥujain b. al-Muthannā and very many other students in Baghdād[10].

Yaḥyā b. Ādam. He says: "We used to write from his memory"[11]. It means that when he dictated to Yaḥyā, he did not use the book for dictation, but dictated from memory. At the same time, we find him using the book when he dictated to Ḥujain and his colleagues.

---

1. *Tahd.*, i, 301.
2. *Bagh.*, vi, 214; *Tahd.*, i, 302.
3. *Tahd.*, i, 305.
4. Dūlābī, ii, 93; *Kāmil,* i, 101b; *Tahd.*, i, 305.
5. *Tahd.*, i, 263.
6. Rāzī, i, i, 330; *Bagh.*, vii, 21; *Tahd.*, i, 261.
7. Rāzī, i, i, 330; *Tahd.*, i, 262; Bājī, 27b.
8. *Bagh.*, vii, 22.
9. *Bagh.*, vii, 23; Bāji, 27b; *Tahd.*, i, 262.
10. *Bagh.*, vii, 21, *Mīzān,* i, 209-10.
11. *Bagh.*, vii, 21.

124. JĀBIR B. YAZĪD B. AL-ḤĀRITH AL-JU'FĪ (c. 70 - 128)[1].
Zuhair had a collection of Jābir's *aḥādīth*[2].

125. AL-JA'D B. 'ABD AL-RAḤMĀN B. AUS (c. 70 - after 144)[3].
He transmitted from the Companion Ṣā'ib b. Yazīd (d. 91) and others.
Yaḥyā b. Sa'īd al-Qaṭṭān had a book from him[4].

126. JA'FAR B. BURQĀN AL-KILABĪ (c. 90 - 150)[5].
He transmitted from Nāfi' (d. 117) etc.
Miskīn b. Bukair wrote *aḥādīth* from him[6].

127. JA'FAR B. AL-ḤĀRITH AL-WĀSIṬĪ (c. 110 - c. 170).
He transmitted from Manṣūr b. Zādhān (d. 129) etc.[7].
Muḥammad b. Yazīd al-Wāsiṭī transmitted a *Nuskhah* from him[8].

128. JA'FAR B. MAIMŪN AL-TAMĪMĪ (c. 75 - c. 140).
He transmitted from 'Abd al-Raḥmān b. Abū Bakrah (d. 96) etc.[9].
Ibn Mahdī shared his book with another man[10].

129. JA'FAR B. MUḤAMMAD B. 'ALĪ B. ḤUSAIN (80 - 148)[11].
He had many books[12].

1. *Tahd.*, ii, 48.
2. *Tahd.*, ii, 50.
3. *Tahd.*, ii, 80.
4. Rāzī, i, ii, 208.
5. *Tahd.*, ii, 86.
6. *Kāmil,* i, 213a.
7. *Tahd.*, ii, 88.
8. *Kāmil,* i, 212b.
9. *Tahd.*, ii, 108.
10. *'Ilal,* 135a.
11. Khazrajī, 54; *Tahd.*, ii, 104.
12. *Kāmil,* i, 210b; *Tahd.*, ii, 104.

Al-Afṭas and Yaḥyā al-Qaṭṭān[1] wrote *aḥādīth* from him.

130. Ka'far b. Sulaimān al-Ḍuba'ī (c. 100 - 178)[2].

He transmitted fromm Thābit al-Bunānī (d. 127) etc.

'Abd al-Razzāq al-Ṣanānī wrote from him[3].

131. Jarīr b. 'Abd al-Ḥamīd, Abū 'Abd Allā al-Ḍabbī (110 - 188)[4].

He wrote *aḥādīth* from al-Ash'ath[5], Manṣūr, Mughīrah and very many others[6]. His books were perfect[7].

The following derived *aḥādīth* from him in writing:

'Abd al-Raḥmān[8].

Ibrāhīm b. Hāshim wrote 1500 *aḥādīth* from him[9].

Muḥammad b. 'Īsā's brother[10].

Shādhān[11].

Sulaimān b. Ḥarb[12].

132. Jarīr b. Ḥāzim (90 - 175)[13].

He had a book[14] and Al-Laith b. Sa'd transmitted a lengthy book[15] from him.

---

1. Rāzī, ii, ii, 69-70.
2. *Tahd.*, ii, 97.
3. Ḥanbal, vi, 337.
4. *Tahd.*, ii, 76.
5. *Tahd.*, ii, 76.
6. *Bagh.*, vii, 256-7.
7. *Tahd.*, ii, 75; see also Rāzī, i, i, 431; *Mīzān*, i, 394.
8. *Bagh.*, vii, 257; *Mīzān*, i, 395.
9. *Mīzān*, i, 395.
10. Rāzī, iv, i, 39.
11. *Bagh.*, vii, 257; *Mīzān*, i, 395.
12. *Bagh.*, vii, 257; *Mīzān*, i, 395.
13. *Tahd.*, ii, 71.
14. Ja'd, 418; Rāzī, i, i, 505; *Tahd.*, ii, 70.
15. *Kāmil*, i, 207b.

133. Juwairīyah b. Asmā' (c. 95 - 173)[1].

He transmitted from Nāfi' (d. 117) and others[2] and dictated *aḥādīth* to 'Affān b. Muslim[3].

His book which was derived from Nāfi' was transmitted by his nephew 'Abd Allāh, and is still preserved[4].

134. Kahmas b. al-Ḥasan al-Tamīmī (c. 85 - 149)[5].

Mu'tamar b. Sulaimān had a book from him[6].

135. Kathīr b. 'Abd Allā b. 'Amr b. 'Awf (c. 85 - c. 155)[7].

He transmitted a *Nuskhah* on the authority of his father from his grandfather. This *Nuskhah* contains many faulty *aḥādīth*[8]. He wrote some *aḥādīth* and sent them to *Mālik*[9].

136. Kathīr b. Zaid al-Aslamī (c. 80 - 158)[10].

He transmitted from 'Umar b. Abd al-'Azīz (101) etc. and many books were transmitted from him[11].

137. Khalf b. Khalīfah al-Ashja'ī (c. 90 - 181)[12].

Many students wrote *aḥādīth* from him[13].

138. Khālid b. Abū Nauf al-Sijistānī (c. 80 - 140).

He transmitted from al-Daḥḥāk (d. 105) etc.[14].

Many Iraqians and Khurusanites wrote from him[15].

---

1. *Tahd.*, ii, 125.
2. *Ḥuffāz*, i, 209.
3. Sa'd, vii, ii, 38-9.
4. Sehid Ali, *Ms. Istanbul.*
5. *Tahd.*, viii, 450.
6. *'Ilal*, 158a.
7. *Tahd.*, viii, 423.
8. *Tahd.*, viii, 423.
9. *Kifāyah*, 343.
10. *Tahd.*, viii, 414.
11. *Tahd.*, vii, 414.
12. *Tahd.*, iii, 151.
13. *Bagh.*, vii, 319.
14. *Tahd.*, iii, 123.
15. *Mashāhīr*, 198.

139. KHĀLID B. MIHRĀN AL-ḤADHDHĀ (c. 80 - 141)[1].

He wrote only lengthy *aḥādīth* and wiped them out after he had memorized them[2].

140. KHĀLID B. YAZĪD AL-DIMASHQĪ (105 - 185)[3].

He compiled a book, called *Kitāb al-Diyāt*[4].

141. KHĀLID B. YAZĪD AL-JUMAḤĪ (c. 80 - 139)[5].

Al-Laith b. Sa'd had books from him, which he transmitted without reading them to Khālid[6].

142. KHĀRIJAH B. MUṢ'AB AL-SARAKHSĪ (70 - 168)[7].

He transmitted many books from scholars[8] and had a large number of books[9]. He was perhaps the compiler of some of them[10].

143. KHUṢAIF B. 'ABD AL-RAḤMĀN AL-JAZARĪ (c. 70 - 137)[11].

He had many books (*Nuskhahs*)[12].

Yaḥyā b. Sa'id wrote from him[13].

144. LAITH B. ABŪ SULAIM (c. 80 - 143)[14].

Ḥammād b. Ja'd had a *Ṣaḥīfah* from him[15].

Ibn Idrīs wrote his *aḥādīth*[16].

---

1. *Tahd.*, iii, 121.
2. Ja'd, 149; Rāmhurmuzī, 37a; *Mīzān*, i, 643.
3. *Tahd.*, iii, 127.
4. *Tahd.*, iii, 127.
5. *Tahd.*, iii, 129.
6. Fasawī, iii, 263b; *Kifāyah*, 344.
7. *Tahd.*, iii, 78.
8. *Ma'rifah*, 165.
9. *Tahd.*, iii, 78.
10. *Tahd.*, iii, 78.
11. *Tahd.*, iii, 144.
12. *Kāmil*, i, 329a; *Tahd.*, iii, 144.
13. Rāzī, i, ii, 403.
14. *Tahd.*, vii, 468.
15. Rāzī, i, ii, 134; *Majrūḥin*, 86b; *Tahd.*, iii, 5.
16. Rāmhurmuzī, 37a; see also *'Ilal*, 177b.

145. AL-LAITH B. SA'D AL-FAHMĪ (94 - 175)[1].

He had books in a good number[2].

The following transcribed *aḥādīth* from him:

Abū Qatādah, 'Abd Allāh b. Wāqid[3].

Abū Ṣāliḥ, the scribe of al-Laith[4].

Khālid al-Madā'inī[5].

Qutaibah b. Sa'īd[6].

Yaḥyā b. Bukair[7].

146. MAIMŪN B. MŪSĀ AL-MAR'Ī (c. 90 - c. 150).

He transmitted from Ḥasan al-Baṣrī (d. 110) etc.[8] and had a book[9].

147. MĀLIK B. ANAS (93 - 179)[10].

He is one of the authorities on *aḥādīth*. He began to learn *aḥādīth* by writing. It seems that he wrote from all his teachers and did not depend on mere memorizing. Ibn 'Uyaynah said that the scholars followe Mālik in testifying the narrator. If Mālik had written from him, they would write from him[11]. Once a student asked Mālik about a certain scholar, and he asked the student whether he found this man's name in his book. He replied: "No". Then Mālik said:"Had he been trustworthy, you would have found his name"[12]. Almost all his wordings and decisions were recorded by his keen pupils[13].

---

1. *Tahd.*, viii, 464.
2. *Tahd.*, viii, 465.
3. *Mīzān*, ii, 518.
4. See Ibn Abū Dh'ib, in this chapter.
5. *Tahd.*, viii, 360.
6. *Tahd.*, viii, 360.
7. *Kāmil*, i, 222a.
8. *Tahd.*, x, 392.
9. *Tahd.*, x, 393.
10. Daraquṭnī, *Aḥādīth Muwaṭṭa'* 7; see also *Tahd.*, x, 8.
11. *Tahd.*, x, 9.
12. Rāzī, *introd.* 24; *Tahd.*, x, 6-7.
13. Rāzī, *introd.* 26; see also Ḥumaidī, *Jadhwat al-Muqtabis*, p. 232, where it is mentioned that Mālik forbade people to write everything they heard from him.

He used to correct the books of his students. Ibn Wahb says: —"Mālik used to read my book, and whenever he found a mistake, he erased it and rewrote it correctly"[1].

His book *al-Muwaṭṭa'* has been published time after time, and hundreds of students read it. The book has some 15 versions. Later on, al-Dāraquṭnī compiled a book, giving all the different versions of the book[2]. It was thought that this was the first book compiled in *Ḥadīth* or *Fiqh,* but now, fortunately, we have some of Mālik's sources at our disposal.

148. MA'MAR B. RĀSHĪD (96 - 153)[3].

He wrote *aḥādīth* and, according to Ibn Nadīm, he compiled a book on *al-Maghāzī*[4], but, perhaps it was the work of al-Zuhrī with some of his contributions. He is said to be one of the earliest compilers of *aḥādīth*[5] and compiled *al-Jāmi'* which is still preserved[6]. A book of *Tafsīr* is also mentioned[7]; it is not clear whether it was his own work or that of Qatādah, his teacher; most likely the latter.

The following transcribed *aḥādīth* from him:

'Abd al-Razzāq wrote 10,000 *aḥādīth* from him[8].

Hishām b. Yūsuf[9].

Ibn al-Mubārak[10].

---

1. Ibn Wahb, *Jāmi', introd.*, xv.
2. Dāraquṭnī, *Aḥādīth Muwaṭṭa.* According to Ibn Nāṣir al-Dīn 83, students transmitted *Muwaṭṭa',* see al-Kauthari, introduction to *Aḥādīth Muwaṭṭa'* by Dāraquṭnī, p. 5.
3. *Ḥuffāẓ,* i, 171-2; *Mīzān,* iv, 154; *Tahd.,* x, 245. He was older than al-Thaurī (b. 97) only one year. See Rāzī, iv, i, 256.
4. *Fihrist,* 94.
5. *Ḥuffāẓ,* i, 172.
6. Al-Kattānī, *al-Risālah al-Mustaṭrafah,* 41; for its manuscript, see Faiḍ Allāh Affendi, Istanbul MSS, No. 541; as a portion of *Muṣannaf,* 'Abd al-Razzāq. Murād, Mulla, 591; also in Ismā'īl Ṣā'ib, collection No. 2164, Ankarah, as cited by Ḥamidullah, in *Ṣaḥīfah Hammām,* footnote 43. See also Ibn al-Khair, *Fihrist,* 129. Dr. Fuad Sazgin has edited it and perhaps it is under print.
7. *'Ilal,* i, 377.
8. *Mīzān,* iv, 154; *Ḥuffāẓ,* i, 171.
9. *Majrūḥīn,* 24a.
10. *'Ilal,* i, 377.

Muṭarrif b. Māzin[1].

Rabāḥ[2].

Yaḥyā b. al-Yamān[3].

149. Ma'qil b. 'Ubaid Allāh al-Jazarī (c. 95 - 166)[4].

He transmitted from 'Aṭā' (d. 117) etc.

The following wrote *aḥādīth* from him:

Abū Ja'far[5].

Al-Ḥasan b. Muḥammad transmitted a *Nuskhah* from him[6].

150. Mis'ar b. Kidām (c. 90 - 155)[7].

The following copied *aḥādīth* from him:

Abū Nu'aim[8].

Muḥammad b. Bishr[9].

Muḥammad b. 'Ubaid[10].

Ḥafṣ b. Ghayāth[11].

151. Mu'āwiyah b. Sallām al-Ḥabashī (c. 95 - 170)[12].

He transmitted from Nāfi' (d. 117) etc. and had books[13].

Many Egyptians wrote from him[14].

1. *Majrūḥīn,* 24a.
2. BTK, iii, i, 253.
3. Rāmhurmuzī, 35b.
4. *Tahd.,* x, 234.
5. *Tawsat,* 57b-58a. Dāraquṭnī, 77.
6. Qaisarānī, 513.
7. *Tahd.,* x, 115.
8. Rāzī, ii, ii, 192.
9. *Ḥuffāẓ,* i, 169.
10. *'Ilal,* 169a.
11. Rāzī, iv, i, 8.
12. *Tahd.,* x, 209.
13. *Tahd.,* x, 209.
14. *Mashāhīr,* 184.

Ibn Ma'īn said that one who did not write every *Ḥadīth* from Sallām could not be a scholar[1].

152. Mu'āwiyah b. Ṣāliḥ al-Ḥimṣī (c. 95-158)[2].

He transmitted from Makḥūl al-Shāmī (d. 118) and had books[3].

The following derived *aḥādīth* from him in writing:

'Abd Allāh b. Ṣāliḥ transmitted a large *Nuskhah* from him[4].

Ibn Wahb handed Ibn Ma'īn two books of Mu'āwiyah containing more than 500 *aḥādīth*[5].

Al-Laith b. Sa'd ordered his scribe Abū Ṣāliḥ to write Mu'āwiyah's *aḥādīth*[6].

Many students of Egypt and Mecca wrote from him[7].

Many students of Iraq wrote from him[8].

153. Mu'āwiyah b. Yaḥyā al-Dimashqī (c. 90 - c. 150).

He transmitted from Makḥūl (d. 112 or 118) etc.[9].

He would buy books from the market and impart *aḥādīth* from them[10].

The following derived *aḥādīth* from him in writing:

Haql b. Ziyād had a book from him[11].

Isḥāq had *aḥādīth* from him in writing[12].

Shu'aib had a *Nuskhah* from him[13].

---

1. Rāzī, iv, i, 383.
2. *Tahd.*, x, 211; according to some other historians, he died in 172. See *Tahd.*, x, 212.
3. *Tahd.*, x, 211; see also al-Khushanī, *Quḍāt Qurṭubah*, p. 30.
4. *Kāmil*, ii, 142a.
5. *Jāmi'*, 146a.
6. Zur'ah, 57b; al-Azadī, *Tārīkh al-'Ulamā*, ii, 137.
7. *Tahd.*, x, 210; see also Rāzī, iv, i, 382.
8. Al-Khushanī, *Quḍāt Qurṭubah*, 30.
9. *Tahd.*, x, 219.
10. *Mīzān*, iv, 138; *Tahd.*, x, 220.
11. Rāzī, iv, I, 384; *Tahd.*, x, 220.
12. *Tahd.*, x, 220.
13. *Tahd.*, x, 220.

154. AL-MUGHĪRAH B. MIQSAM AL-ḌABBĪ (c. 70-136)[1].

It is reported that he was born blind[2].

According to Ibn al-Naīm, he compiled a book on inheritance[3].

The following wrote *aḥādīth* from him:

Ibn Fuḍil[4].

Jarīr[5].

Sulaimān[6].

155. MUḤAMMAD B. ʻABD ALLĀH B. ʻULĀTHAH (c. 100-163)[7].

He wrote *aḥādīth*[8].

156. MUḤAMMAD B. ʻABD AL-RAḤMĀN B. ABŪ LAILĀ (c. 75; 148)[9].

He compiled a book, titled *Muṣannaf Ibn Abū Lailā*, which was transmitted by ʻIsā b. al-Mukhtār[10].

He had many *Nuskhahs*[11].

157. MUḤAMMAD B. ʻABD AL-RAḤMĀN AL-BAILAMĀNĪ (c. 80 - c. 140).

He transmitted a semi-forged *Nuskhah* from his father[12] and sent *aḥādīth* in writing to al-Thaurī who transmitted them[13].

---

1. *Tahd.*, x, 270.
2. *Tahd.*, x, 269.
3. *Fihrist*, 226.
4. Jaʻd, 68; *Tahd.*, x, 269.
5. *Tahd.*, x, 270; see also Rāzī, i, i, 507.
6. Rāzī, iv, i, 228; see also *ʻIlal*, 158a.
7. *Tahd.*, ix, 270.
8. *Bagh.*, v, 389.
9. *Tahd.*, ix, 302.
10. Saʻd, vi, 264; *Tahd.*, viii, 229.
11. *Kāmil*, iii, 66a.
12. *Tahd.*, ix, 294.
13. Rāzī, iii, ii, 311.

158. MUḤAMMAD B. ʻABD AL-RAḤMĀN, IBN ABŪ DHI'B (80-158)[1].

He compiled a book called *al-Muwaṭṭa'* before Mālik[2]. Ibn al-Nadīm records that he compiled a book called *Kitāb al-Sunan,* which contained the books of the sacred laws, e.g. prayer, fasting, pilgrimage, etc.[3]. It is not clear whether it was the same *al-Muwaṭṭa'* or another work. It seems that the work existed until a few centuries later. Yūsuf b. Muḥammad transmitted this book from Abū Ṭāhir in the fifth century[4]. He used to read his book to students[5].

The following transcribed *aḥādīth* from him:

ʻAbd Allāh b. Nāfiʻ[6].

ʻAbd Allāh b. Salamah al-Afṭas. He used to copy these *aḥādīth* after the lecture from Yaḥyā's book[7].

ʻAbd al-Wahhāb al-Khaffāf[8].

Al-Laith b. Saʻd[9].

Rauḥ[10].

Yaḥyā b. Saʻīd[11].

159. MUḤAMMAD B. ʻAMR B. WAQQĀṢ AL-LAITHĪ (c. 80-144)[12].

He would not transmit *aḥādīth* until he was sure the students would write them, saying that they might make mistakes[13]. Most of his students transmitted *Nuskhahs* from him[14].

The following derived *aḥādīth* from him in writing:

Ḥammād b. Jaʻd al-Baṣrī[15].

---

1. Fasawī, ii, 11b; *Tahd.*, ix, 306.
2. *Jāmiʻ*, *188a.*
3. *Fihrist,* 225, But al-Dhahabī says that he has no book, *Ḥuffāẓ,* i, 173.
4. Ḥumaidī, *Jadhwat al-Muqtabis,* 344.
5. *Kifāyah,* 239.
6. A.D. *Hadīth* No. 2042.
7. Rāzī, *introduction,* 248.
8. *'Ilal,* i, 109.
9. Rāzī, ii, ii, 86-7.
10. *'Ilal,* i, 109; *Bagh.*, viii, 404.
11. Jaʻd, 376; Rāzī, *introduction,* 248.
12. *Tahd.*, ix, 376.
13. Rāmhurmuzī, 38a; *Jāmiʻ*, 102a.
14. *Kāmil,* iii, 83a; *Tahd.*, ix, 376.
15. Rāzī, i, ii, 134; *Majrūḥīn,* 86b; *Tahd.*, iii, 5.

Ibn Abū 'Adī[1].

Yazīd b. Zurai'[2].

160. MUḤAMMAD B. ISḤĀQ B. YASĀR (c. 80-151)[3].

He transmitted from Abū Salamah b. 'Abd al-Raḥmān (d. 100) and met Ibn al-Musayyab (d. 93) and Anas b. Mālik (d. 93). He had a number of books[4]. Utilizing the extensive available material he compiled a voluminous biography of the Prophet[5]. Once the original text of this book existed in at least 15 versions[6]. The book survived in the verions of Ibn Hishām. Of late, original copies have been discovered[7]. Although these manuscripts are incomplete, they provide sufficient material for research and perhaps would lead to changes in many theories.—

The following derived *aḥādīth* from him in writing:

Bakr b. Sulaimān[8].

Ibrāhīm b. Sa'd had 17,000 *aḥādīth* from Ibn Isḥāq besides al-Maghāzī[9].

Jarīr[10].

Salamah b. al-Mufaḍḍal[11].

Yaḥyā by. Sa'īd[12].

Yazīd b. Abū Ḥabīb[13].

Ziyād b. 'Abd Allāh al-Bakkā'ī[14].

Abū Uwais[15].

---

1. Nas. i, 45.
2. *'Ilal,* 103a.
3. *Bagh.*, i, 233.
4. *Bagh.*, i, 231; *Ḥuffāẓ,* I, 229; *Tahd.*, ix, 42; 43.
5. See for his method of compiling, Khaithamah, iii, 144a; see for his sources, 'Alī Jawād, *Majallah al-Majma' al-'Ilmī al-'Irāqī,* vol. iii, 37-8.
6. Guillaume, *The life of Muḥammad,* p. xxx.
7. Al-Ẓāhirīyah Library MSS; Rabāṭ MSS, 2 copies.
8. Tṣaghīr, 82.
9. *Ḥuffāẓ,* i, 229.
10. Rāzī, iii, ii, 193.
11. Rāzī, i, i, 139; ii, i, 169; *Kāmil,* ii, 27a; *Bagh.*, vi, 179; *Mīzān,* ii, 192; *Tahd.*, iv, 153-4; ix, 129; see also Rāzī, iv, i, 42; Manuscript in al-Ẓahirīyah, Library Damascus.
12. Sa'd, vii, ii, 81.
13. *'Ilal,* 142b.
14. *Bagh.*, viii, 477; *Mīzān,* ii, 91; *Tahd.*, iii, 376.
15. Bukhārī, *Qirāt,* 33.

161. MUḤAMMAD B. JĀBIR B. SAYYĀR AL-ḤANAFĪ (c. 100 - after 168)[1].

He transmitted from Simāk b. Ḥarb (d. 123) etc.

He had many books which were originally correct, but later many erroneous additions were made[2].

The following wrote *aḥādīth* from him:

Isḥāq b. Inrāhīm[3].

Many students in al-Yamāmah and Makkah[4].

162. MUḤAMMAD B. JUḤĀDAH AL-KŪFĪ (c. 70-131)[5].

He transmitted from Anas (d. 93) etc.

The following wrote *aḥādīth* from him:

'Abd al-Wārith[6].

Al-Ḥasan b. Abū Ja'far[7].

163. MUḤAMMAD B. MAIMŪN, ABŪ ḤAMZAH AL-SUKKARĪ (c. 100-166)[8].

He transmitted from al-Sabī'ī (d. 127) and others.

The following wrote *aḥādīth* from him:

'Alī b. Ḥasan b. Shaqīq. He heard *Kitāb al-Ṣalāt* from Abū Ḥamzah[9].

Ibn al-Mubārak says that his books were perfect[10].

---

1. *'Ilal,* i, 369; *Kāmil,* iii, 48 a-b.
2. *'Ilal,* i, 369; Rāzī, iii, ii, 219; *Kāmil,* iii, 48 a-b; *Mīzān,* iii, 496; *Tahd.,* ix, 89.
3. Sa'd, vii, ii, 91; *Kāmil,* iii, 51 a.
4. Rāzī, iii, ii, 220; *Tahd.,* ix, 89.
5. *Tahd.,* ix, 92.
6. *'Ilal,* i, 144.
7. *Kāmil,* i, 256b; *Tahd.,* ii, 260.
8. *Tahd.,* ix, 487.
9. *Tahd.,* vii, 299; *Kifāyah,* 234.
10. Rāzī, *introd.* 270; Bājī, 68 b; *Tahd.,* ix, 487.

164. Muḥammad b. Maisarah (c. 90 - c. 150).

He transmitted from Qatādah (d. 117) etc.[1].

Mu'ādh b. Mu'ādh[2] and Yaḥyā b. Sa'īd[3] derived *aḥādīth* from him in writing.

165. Muḥammad b. Muslim al-Ṭā'ifī (c. 105-177)[4].

He transmitted from 'Amr b. Dīnār (d. 126).

His books were perfect[5].

Al-Thaurī wrote from him[6].

166. Muḥammad b. Rāshid al-Makḥūlī (c. 90 - after 160)[7].

He transmitted from Makḥūl al-Shāmī (d. 112 or 118).

Al-Walīd b. Muslim had a book from him[8].

167. Muḥammad b. Sālim al-Hamdānī (c. 80 - 140).

He compiled a book on interitance[10] and had books which, according to Ḥafṣ, belonged to his brother[11].

The following wrote *aḥādīth* from him:

Yazīd b. Hārūn[12].

---

1. *Tahd.*, ix, 123.
2. *Kāmil,* iii, 98a; Bājī, 68b; *Tahd.*, ix, 124.
3. *Kāmil,* iii, 98a; Bājī, 68a-b; *Tahd.*, ix, 123.
4. Khazrajī, 306.
5. *Mīzān,* iv, 40; *Tahd.*, ix, 444.
6. *Mīzān,* iv, 40.
7. *Tahd.*, ix, 160.
8. Rāzī, i, i, 221.
9. *Tahd.*, ix, 176.
10. Rāzī, iii, ii, 272; *Tahd.*, ix, 176. See also *Kāmil*, iii, 52a; *Tahd.*, ix, 177.
11. *'Ilal,* i, 81; Dūlābī, i, 198; *Kāmil,* iii, 51b; *Tahd.*, ix, 176.
12. Dāraquṭnī, footnote p. 464.

168. MUḤAMMAD B. SŪQAH AL-GHANAWĪ (c. 70 - c. 135).

He transmitted from Sa'īd b. Jubair etc.[1].

Sufyān al-Thaurī had a book from him[2].

169. MUḤAMMAD B. 'UBAID ALLĀH AL-'ARZAMĪ (c. 90-155)[3].

He had many books[4] which were lost.

His son[5] and his nephew[6] each transmitted a *Nuskhah* from him.

170. MUḤAMMAD B. 'UBAID ALLĀH B. ABŪ RAFI' (c. 70 - c. 130).

He transmitted from his father who was a scribe of 'Alī (d. 40)[7]. His son transmitted a *Nuskhah* from him[8].

171. MUḤAMMAD B. AL-WALĪD AL-ZUBAIDĪ (76-146)[9].

'Abd Allāh b. Sālim al-Ash'arī had his books[10].

Muḥammad b. Ḥarb had a *Nuskhah* from him[11].

172. MUJĀLID B. SA'ĪD B. 'UMAIR (c. 80-144)[12].

He had a book on the biography of the Prophet[13]. The book possibly belonged originally to al-Sha'bī, with some contributions from Mujālid.

The following wrote *aḥādīth* from him:

Ismā'īl b. Mujālid[14].

---

1. *Tahd.*, ix, 209.
2. Rāzī, *Introd.* 75; ii, ii, 281; *Tahd.*, ix, 210.
3. *Tahd.*, ix, 323.
4. *Majrūḥīn*, 198a; *Sharḥ al-'Ilal*, 73a; *Mīzān*, iii, 636; *Tahd.*, ix, 323.
5. *Kāmil*, iii, 28a.
6. *Kāmil*, 28a.
7. *Tahd.*, vii, 101
8. *Mīzān*, iv, 157.
9. *Tahd.*, ix, 503.
10. Rāzī, iii, i, 8.
11. *Tahd.*, iv, 188.
12. *Tahd.*, x, 40.
13. Rāzī, iv, i, 361; *Tahd.*, x, 40,
14. *Tahd.*, vii, 427.

Sufyān b. ʻUyaynah[1].

Wahb b. Jarīr[2].

173. Muqātil b. Sulaiman (c. 90-150)[3].

He transmitted from Nafiʻ (d. 117) etc.

He compiled many books and a commentary on the *Qur'ān*[4].

174. Muqātil (c. 70 - c. 130).

He transmitted from Anas B. Mālik.

Saʻīd b. Abū ʻArūbah transcribed from him[5].

175. Muʻtamar b. Sulaiman b. Ṭarkhan (100-187)[6].

He had a book[7].

176. Nafī b. ʻUmar al-Makkī (c. 100-169)[8].

His book was perfect[9].

177. Nafī b. Yazīd al-Kalaʻī (c. 100-168)[10].

Abū al-Aswad, al-Naḍr b. ʻAbd al-Jabbār[11] derived *aḥādīth* from him in writing:

---

1. *ʻIlal,* i, 233.
2. Rāzī, iv, i, 3611.
3. *Tahd.*, x, 284.
4. Rāzī, iv, i, 354; *Tahd.*, x, 279. See also al-Sahmī, *Tārīkh Jurjān*, p. 127, for commentary on 500 verses only, for his other works on the Quranic Science, see Ziriklī, viii, 206.
5. *Mīzān,* iv, 175.
6. *Tahd.*, x, 227.
7. *Mīzān,* iv, 142; Ibn Ḥajar, *Hady al-Sārī,* ii, 236; *Tahd.*, x, 228.
8. *Tahd.*, x, 409.
9. *Tahd.*, x, 409.
10. *Tahd.*, x, 412.
11. Rāzī, iv, i, 480; *Tahd.*, x, 441.

178. AL-NAḤḤĀS B. QAHM AL-QAISĪ (c. 70 - c. 140).

He transmitted from Anas b. Malik (d. 93) etc.[1].

Yaḥyā b. Sa'īd wrote from him[2].

179. NAJĪḤ B. 'ABD AL-RAḤMĀN AL-SINDĪ (c. 90-170)[3].

He was As'ad b. Sahl b. Ḥunaif (d. 100).

He compiled a book on *Al-Maghāzī*[4] and his book was one of the sources of Ibn Sa'd[5].

The following transmitted this book:

Ḥajjāj[6].

Ḥusain b. Muḥammad[7].

Muḥammad b. Najīḥ[8].

180. NU'AIM B. MAISARAH (c. 105-175)[9].

He transmitted from Abū Isḥāq al-Sabī'ī (d. 127).

The following derived *aḥādīth* from him in writing:

Ibn al-Mubārak[10].

Students in Ray and Marw wrote down from him[11].

181. NU'MĀN B. THĀBIT, AL-IMĀM ABŪ ḤANĪFAH (80-150)[12].

He used to write *aḥādīth* and imparted only what he remembered by heart[13].

---

1. *Tahd.*, x, 478.
2. Rāzī, iv, i, 511; *Tahd.*, x, 478.
3. *Tahd.*, ix, 421.
4. Fasawī, iii, 325a; *Tahd.*, x, 422; see also *Ḥuffāz*, i, 212.
5. Sa'd, II, I, 1.
6. *Tahd.*, ix, 488.
7. Sa'd, vii, ii, 79.
8. *Tahd.*, ix, 488; see also *Bagh.*, viii, 376.
9. *Tahd.*, x, 467.
10. *Tahd.*, x, 467.
11. *Thiqāt*, 616.
12. *Tahd.*, x, 449-451.
13. *Tahd.*, x, 450.

The following wrote *aḥādīth* from him:

Abū Yūsuf and al-Shaibānī[1].

Ibn al-Mubārak[2].

182. Qais b. al-Rabī al-Asadī (c. 100-167)[3].

He had many books[4].

Abū-al-Walīd wrote 6,000 *aḥādīth* from him[5].

183. Qaid b. Sa'd (c. 70-119)[6].

He transmitted from Ibn Jubair (d. 95) et.

The following derived *aḥādīth* from him in writing:

Ḥammād b. Salamah[7].

'Aqbah[8].

184. Qurrah b. Khālid al-Saddūsī (c. 90-155)[9].

'Alī Abū Naṣr had his *aḥādīth* in writing[10].

185. Al-Rabī' b. Ṣabīḥ al-Sa'dī(c. 90-160)[11].

He transmitted from Al-Ḥasan (d. 110) etc.

It is said that he was the first who compiled books in Al-Baṣrah[12].

186. Sa'd b. Sa'īd b. Qais al-Anṣ ārī (c. 75-141).

He transmitted from Anas (d. 93) etc. and made mistakes when he transmitted from memory[13].

1.See Abū Yūsuf, *Kitāb al-Ā thār;* al-Shaibānī, *K. al-Ā thār.*
2. *'Ilal,* 158b.
3. *Tahd.*, viii, 394.
4. BTS, 192; *Majrūḥīn,* 25b; *al-Madkhal,* 42; *Bagh.*, xii, 460; *Mīzān,* iii, 394; see also *Ḥuffāz,* i, 205; *Tahd.*, viii, 393; 394.
5. *Bagh.*, xii, 458; *Mīzān,* iii, 396; *Tahd.*, viii, 395.
6. *Mīzān,* iii, 397; *Tahd.*, viii, 397.
7. *'Ilal,* 139b; Fasawī, iii, 44a; 274 a-b; *Mīzān,* i, 592; *Tahd.*, iii, 15.
8. *Tahd.*, vii, 244..
9. *Tahd.*, viii, 372.
10. *Al-Mustadrak, I, 161.*
11. *Tahd.*, iii, 248.
12. *Tahd.*, iii, 248; Rāmhurmuzī, 78b; *Mīzān,* ii, 41.
13. *Mashāhīr,* 136.

187. SA'ĪD B. 'ABD ALLĀH B. JURAIJ (c. 95 - c. 160)[1].

He transmitted from Nāfi' (d. 117) etc.

He gave Ḥaushab b. 'Aqîl a book[2].

188. SA'ĪD B. ABŪ 'ARŪBAH (c. 80-156)[3].

It is said that he had no books[4]; but we know from several sources that he wrote *aḥādīth* of Qatādah[5]. However, he is one of the earliest compilers and wrote many books[6] e.g.:

A Commentary on the *Qur'ān*.[7].

Kitāb al-Sunan[8].

Kitāb al-Manāsik[9].

The following wrote *aḥādīth* from him:

'Abd al-A'lā al-Shāmī[10].

'Abd al-Wahhāb b. 'Aṭā' al-Khaffāf[11].

Ghundar[12]

Ibn Abū 'Adī[13].

Ibrāhīm b. Ṣadaqah[14].

'Imrān al-Qaṣir[15].

Ismā'il b. Ibrāhīm[16].

---

1. *Tahd.*, iv, 52.
2. *Kāmil*, 1, 301b.
3. *Tahd.*, iv, 65.
4. Rāzī, ii, i, 65; *Mīzān*, ii, 153; *Ḥuffāz*, i, 160; *Tahd.*, iv, 63.
5. See *supra* Qatādah.
6. *Kāmil*, ii, 49b; *Mīzān*, ii, 151.
7. *'Ilal*, 166 a.
8. *Fihrist*, 227.
9. Ẓahiriyah Library, Mss.
10. *Kāmil*, i, 227a-b; ii, 49b; see also Manuscript of *Kitāb al-Manāsik;* al-Ẓāhiriyah Lib. Damascus.
11. Sa'd, vii, ii, 76; Hanbal, iii, 232-3; *Bagh.*, xi, 22; *Kāmil*, ii, 49b; *Tahd.*, vi, 451.
12. *Kāmil*, ii, 48b; *Tahd.*, iv, 65; see also *'Ilal*, 147a.
13. *'Ilal*, i, 412; 97b.
14. *'Ilal*, i, 92.
15. *Taqyīd*, 113; *Jāmi'* 44b.
16. *'Ilal*, i, 412; 97b.

Mughīrah b. Mūsā al-Baṣrī[1].

Muslim b. Ibrāhīm[2].

Rauḥ[3].

Ṣadaqah b. 'Abd Allāh al-Samīn[4].

'Umar b. Ḥammād[5].

189. SA'ĪD B. BASHĪR AL-AZDĪ (79-168)[6].

He was the author of many books, and compiled a commentary on the *Qur'ān* as well[7].

190. AL-ṢAKAN B. ABŪ KHĀLID (c. 90 - c. 175).

He transmitted from Ḥasan (d. 110) and lived so long that Qutaibah b. Sa'īd wrote from him[8]. Qutaibah first started writing in 172.

191. SALM B. ABŪ DHAYYĀL AL-BAṢRĪ (c. 70 - 135).

He transmitted from Sa'īd b. Jubair (d. 95) etc.[9].

Mu'tamar had his *aḥādīth* in written form[10].

192. SALAMAH B. DĪNĀR, ABŪ ḤĀZIM AL-ASHJA'Ī (c. 70-140)[11].

He transmitted from Sahl b. Sa'd (d. 91).

He wrote *aḥādīth*, and after his death these books were in the possession of his son 'Abd al-'Azīz.

The following transcribed *aḥādīth* from him:

'Abd al-'Azīz b. Abū Ḥāzim[12].

---

1. Rāzī, iv, i, 230; *Mīzān*, iv, 166.
2. *Kāmil*, ii, 48b; *Mīzān*, ii, 152.
3. Ḥanbal, v, 10; *'Ilal*, 166a.
4. Rāzī, ii, i, 429.
5. *Majrūḥīn*, 153b.
6. *Tahd.*, iv, 10.
7. *Kāmil*, ii, 42a; *Mīzān*, ii, 130; *Tahd.*, iv, 10.
8. *Thiqāt*, 490.
9. *Tahd.*, iv, 129.
10. *'Ilal*, 158a.
11. Khaithamah, iii, 136a; see also *Tahd.*, iv, 144.
12. *'Ilal*, i, 289; 306; Rāzī, ii, ii, 382; Ibn Ḥajar, *Hady al-Sārī*, ii, 185; *Tahd.*, vi, 333.

Ismā'īl b. Qais[1].

Mūsā b. 'Ubaidah[2].

Nūḥ b. Abū Maryam[3].

Sa'īd b. Abū Ayyūb[4].

193. SALIM B. 'ABD ALLAH AL-KHAYYAṬ (c. 85 - 150).

He transmitted from Ḥasan (d. 110) etc.[5].

Walīd transmitted a *Nuskhah* from him[6].

Zuhair b. Muḥammad al-Khurāsānī transmitted a *Nuskhah* from him[7].

194. ṢADAQAH B. 'ABD ALLĀH AL-SAMĪN (c. 100-166)[8].

He wrote down *aḥādīth* from Ibn Abū 'Arūba etc. and compiled many books[9].

'Abd Allāh b. Yazīd had his books[10].

195. ṢADAQAH B. KHĀLID (108-180)[11].

He used to write *aḥādīth* during lectures[12].

196. ṢAKHR B. JUWAIRIYAH (c. 95 - c. 160).

He transmitted from Nāfi' (d. 117) etc.[13].

---

1. BTS, 4; Rāzī, i, i, 193; *Kāmil*, i, 107b.
2. *Tahd.*, x, 360.
3. *Ma'rifah*, 164.
4. *Tahd.*, iv, 8.
5. *Tahd.*, iii, 439.
6. *Kāmil*, ii, 30b.
7. *Kāmil*, ii, 30b. See also *Tawsat*, i, Folio 54-55, where a part of this work is still preserved.
8. Khazrajī, 146.
9. Rāzī, ii, i, 429; *Mīzān*, ii, 310.
10. Fasawī, iii, 137b. Rāzī, ii, i, 429; *Mīzān*, ii, 310.
11. Khazrajī 146; see also, *Tahd.*, iv, 415.
12. Dūlābī, ii, 25.
13. *Tahd.*, iv, 410.

He lost his book; later a copy of the work was brought to him from al-Madīnah[1].

Gundar had a copy of his book[2]

197. Sālim b. 'Ajlān al-Afṭas (c. 70-132)[3].

He had a commentary on the *Qur'ān*. Scholars praised his work[4].

198. Shaibān b. 'Abd al-Raḥmān al-Tamīmī (c. 90-164)[5].

He transmitted from Ḥasan al-Baṣrī (d. 110) and had a commentary on the *Qur'ān*[6]. It is not clear whether it was his own work, or of one of his teachers' of which he was only a transmitter.

His book was a perfect one[7].

Al-Ḥasan b. Mūsā wrote his *aḥādīth*[8].

199. Shaqīq b. Ibrāhīm al-Balkhī (c. 90-153)[9].

He compiled a book on asceticism[10].

200. Sharīk b. 'Abd Allāh al-Kūfī (90-177)[11].

He was a milkman. In his early days he used to write *aḥādīth*[12] and thus collected a great deal of them, and later compiled many books [13]. His books were perfect [14].

---

1. Ja'd, 402; Fasawī, iii, 41a; *Tahd.*, iv, 411.
2. *'Ilal,* 144a.
3. *Tahd.*, iii, 442.
4. Al-Azdī, *Tārīkh al-Mauṣil,* 120-1.
5. *Tahd.*, iv, 374.
6. Sa'd vii, ii, 79; see also Rāzī, i, ii, 64.
7. Rāzī, ii, i, 356; *Bagh,* ix, 272; *Mīzān,* ii, 285; Ibn Ḥajar, *Hady al-Sārī,* ii, 174; *Tahd.*, iv, 373; 374.
8. Al-Azdī, *Tārīkh al-Mausil,* ~~306-7~~.
9. Ibn Khallikān, *Wafayāt,* I, 226.
10. Rāzī, iv, i, 188.
11. *Tahd.*, iv, 335.
12. *Bagh.*, ix, 280.
13. Rāzī, i, ii, 417—where about 30 parts of volumes of his works are mentioned.
14. *Bagh.*, ix, 284; see also *Mashāhīr,* 170; *Kifāyah,* 223; *Mīzān,* ii, 274.

He committed mistakes when he transmitted *aḥādīth* from memory[1].

The following transmitted *aḥādīth* from him:

'Abd Allāh b. 'Amr al-Mauṣilī[2].

'Abdullah b. Mubārak[3].

Abū Bakr b. Abū Shaibah[4].

Ḥajjāj b. Muḥammad[5].

Al-Ḥakam b. Ayyūb[6].

Isḥāq[7].

Al-Marzūqi[8].

Many students of Wāsiṭ[9].

Yazīd[10].

Ḥātim b. Ismā'īl[11].

201. Shu'aib b. Abū Ḥamzah (c. 90-162)[12].

He wrote *aḥādīth* for the Caliph Hishām from the dictation of al-Zuhrī[13]. His books were perfect and were in a very good hand writing[14]. He did not allow anyone to utilize his books[15], but on his death-bed he gave permission to:

Bishr and al-Ḥakam b. Nāfi' to transmit these books on his authority[16].

---

1. *Mashāhīr,* 170; *Bagh.,* ix, 284.
2. al-Azadī, *Tārī kh al-Maus il,* 306.
3. *'Ilal,* 126 a.
4. *Mīzān,*iii, 82.
5. *'Ilal,* 113b.
6. Abū Nu'aim, *Tārīkh Iṣbahān,* i, 298.
7. *Wāsiṭ,* 34.
8. *'Ilal,* 127a.
9. *Wāsiṭ,* 34.
10. *Wāsiṭ,* 34.
11. Rāzī, i, ii, 417.
12. *Tahd.,* iv, 352. When he died he was over 70.
13. Rāzī, ii, i, 345; *Huffāz,* i, 200; *Tahd.,* iv, 351.
14. Rāzī, ii, i, 345; *Huffāz,* i, 200, *Tahd.,* iv, 351.
15. Zur'ah 67 b; see also, *Tahd.,* ii, 442; *'Ilal,* 107 a-b.
16. *'Ilal,* 107 a-b; Rāzī, i, i, 359; *Kifāyah* 322; 330; *Mīzān,* i, 581-2.

202. SHU'BAH B. AL-ḤAJJĀJ AL-AZDĪ (83-160)[1].

He studied poetry in his early life, and afterwards turned his attention to *aḥādīth*[2]. He was a very keen learner and was not content to learn *aḥādīth* only once[3]. He himself wrote *aḥādīth*[4]. He used to watch Qatadah's mouth, when he said , he wrote it, otherwise not[5]. His masters wrote for him as well[6], but according to Ibn Ḥanbal, the number of his writings was not great. Shu'bah usually memorized *aḥādīth*[7]. He was believed to be the first who criticized the *Isnād* and narrators in Iraq[8]. It seems that he even compiled books[9].

The following derived *aḥādīth* from him in writing:

'Abbād b. Ḥabib [10].

'Abd Allāh b. 'Uthmān[11]. He used to dictate *aḥādīth* of Shu'bah to Abū Nūh. It is not clear whether he dictated from memory or from a book.

Abū Dāwūd al-Ṭayālisī[12].

Abū al-Walīd al-Tayālisī[13].

Adam b. Abū Iyās[14].

'Alī b. Ja'd[15].

'Alī al-Nasā'ī[16].

1. *Tahd.*, iv, 345.
2. *Bagh.*, ix, 257.
3. Rāzī, introd. 161.
4. See for his writing Ja'd, 6; *Kifāyah.* 220; Ḥanbal, i, 107; *Bagh.*, ix, 260.
5. Ja'd, 118-119; Bājī, 6a; *Madkhal*, 21; *Kifāyah*, 164.
6. Ja'd, 97; see supra under Manṣ ūr.
7. *Sharḥ 'Ilal.* 38b; *Bagh.*, ix, 259.
8. *Thiqāt*, 494.
9. Rāzī, *Introd.* 129.
10 *Bagh.*, xi, 102.
11. *'Ilal.* i, 64; *Bagh.*, 264-5.
12. *Bagh.*. ix, 25; *Mīzān*, ii, 204. In some manuscript of *Mizan*; he dictated Shu'bah's *aḥādīth* from memory.
13. *'Ilal.* i, 383; *Jāmi'*. 53a; see slso *Kifāyah.* 241.
14. Rāzi, i, i, 268; *Tahd.*. i, 196.
15. *Bagh.*. ix, 256; *Ḥuffāẓ*. i, 176; see also his Musnad which covers about one hundred pages for the *aḥādīth* of Shu'bah.
16. Rāzi, i, i, 268.

'Amr b. Marzūq al-Bāhilī[1].

Bahz b. Asad[2].

Baqiyah b. al-Walīd al-Ḥimṣī[3].

Dāwūd b. Ibrāhīm[4].

Ghassān[5].

Ghundar. He accompanied Shu'bah for 20 years, copied most of his *aḥādīth* and read them to him[6].

Ḥajjāj b. Muḥammad al-Miṣṣīṣī[7].

Hāshim b. al-Qāsim[8].

Al-Ḥusain b. al-Walīd al-Nīsābūrī[9].

Ibn Bazī[10].

Ibn Mahdī[11].

Ismā'īl or Wuhaib[12].

Khālid b. Ḥārith al-Baṣrī[13].

Mālik b. Sulaimān al-Harawī[14].

Mu'ādh[15].

Al-Naḍr b. Shumail al-Māzinī[16].

Qurrād Abū Nūḥ[17].

Sa'd b. Ibrāhīm[18].

Yaḥyā al-Qaṭṭān[19].

---

1. Rāzī, iii, i, 264.
2. *Tahd.*, i, 497.
3. *Kāmil*, i, 188a.
4. Rāzī, i, ii, 407.
5. *Lisān*, iv, 409.
6. BTK, i, i, 57; BTS, 218; Fasawī, iii, 58b; *'Ilal*, i, 285; *Mīzān*, iii, 502; *Ḥuffāẓ*. i, 275; *Tahd*, ix, 97; see also Ḥanbal, ii, 166; iv, 378-9; v, 140.
7. *Bagh.*,viii, 238; *Tahd*, ii, 206.
8. Bājī, 167b.
9. *Ma'rifah*, 165.
10. *'Ilal*, i, 122.
11. *Kāmil*, i, 36 b.
12. Rāzī, *introd*, 242.
13. Rāzī. *introd.* 248; i, ii, 325.
14. *Ma'rifa*, 165.
15. Rāzī, *introd.* 248; i, ii, 325.
16. *Tahd.*, x, 438.
17. *'Ilal*, i, 64; *Bagh.*,ix, 264-5.
18. Ja'd, 192; *Wāsiṭ*. 88; *Bagh.*, ix, 260.
19. Rāzī, *introd.* 248.

203. Sufyān b. Sa'īd al-Thaurī al-Kūfī (97-161)[1].

His studies began in early childhood[2]. Al-Shamī has preserved the advice of Sufyān's mother regarding the writing down of *aḥādīth* and the effect of knowledge on personal morals and behaviour[3].

According to some statements, he transmitted less than ten percent of what he had collected[4]. He was very frank and even blunt with rulers. He did not accept any kind of assistance or money from others[5] and led a life of poverty. Sometimes he had to sleep without food[6].

When orders for his arrest were given by the Caliph Al-Mahdī, he fled from Mecca to Baṣ rah and the last few years of his life (115-161) were spent in hiding[7]. He was such a keen learner that even in the days of his hiding, he contacted scholars and learnt from them[8], while teaching others[9]. He used to go through his books to refresh his memory[10]. He imparted *aḥādīth* from memory. If he had any doubt about his memory he asked students not to write them[11], and sometimes said that as he had not seen the books for years, he should not be asked that sort of *aḥādīth*[12]. He asked his pupil Yaḥyā to fetch his book from Al-Kūfah. Yaḥyā replied that he was afraid for his life, so how could he dare to go and fetch the books[13]. Once, being afraid of some trouble, he hid his books in a cell. Later, when they were brought out, it was found that there were nine heaps of them each reaching in height to the chest of the man[14]. He asked his students to bring

1. Sa'd, vi, 258.
2. *Ḥuffāẓ*, i, 186.
3. Al-Sahmī *Tārīkh Jurjān*. 449.
4. *Bagh.*,ix, 165.
5. *Bagh.*,ix, 161.
6. Sa'd, vi, 259.
7. *Bagh.*, ix, 160; see also Zur'ah 32a.
8. Rāzī, *introduction*, 117.
9. Sa'd, vi, 259; *Bagh.*.ix, 160.
10. *Sharḥ al-'Ilal*, 39b; *Kifāyah*, 164.
11. Rāzī, *introduction*, 67.
12. Fasawī, ii, 241b.
13. *Bagh.*, ix, 160.
14. Ja'd, 248; Rāzī, *Introduction*. 115; *Bagh.* ix, 161.

their books to revise and correct them[1]. It is reported that he asked someone to erase his books[2]. Ibn al-Nadīm mentioned some of his works:

Al-Jāmi' al-Kabīr.

Al-Jāmi' al-Ṣaghīr.

Al-Farā'iḍ.

Risālah ilā 'Abbād b. 'Abbād.

Kitāb Risālah[3].

The following wrote *aḥādīth* from him:

'Abd Allāh b. 'Amr[4].

'Abd Allāh b. al-Walīd[5].

'Abd al-Raḥmān b. Mahdī[6].

'Abd al-Razzāq al-Ṣan'ānī[7].

Abū Mihrān[8].

Abū Nū'aim[9].

Al-Firyābī[10].

Ghassān b. 'Ubaid al-Azdī[11].

Hayyāj b. Bustām al-Burjumī[12].

Hishām b. Yūsuf al-Ṣan'ānī[13].

Al-Ḥuṣain b. al-Walīd al-Nīsābūrī[14].

Ibn Abū 'Uthmān[15].

Ibn al-Mubārak[16].

---

1. Ja'd, 245; 246; Rāzī, *introduction*, 80.
2. *Thiqāt*, 484; Rāzī, *introduction*, 116.
3. *Fihrist*, 225.
4. Al-Azdī, *Tārīkh Mauṣil*, 306.
5. *Tahd.*, vi, 70.
6. Sa'd, vi, 259.
7. Fasawī, ii, 243a.
8. *Ma'rifah*, 165.
9. Fasawī, ii, 241a.
10. Rāzī, iv, i, 120; al-Sam'ānī, *Ansāb* 427.
11. *Bagh.*, xii, 327.
12. *Ma'rifah*, 165.
13. *'Ilal*, I, 371; Fasawī, ii, 241a; *Tahd.* xi, 57; Rāzī, iv, ii, 71.
14. *Ma'rifah*, 165.
15. Rāzī, *Introd.* 225; ii, ii, 389.
16. *Bagh.*, ix, 156; *Ḥuffāẓ*. i, 184; *Tahd.*, iv, 113.

Khalf b. Tamīm[1].
Muḥammad b. 'Abd Allāh b. al-Zubair[2].
Mu'āfā b. 'Imrān[3].
Mūsā b. Mas'ūd[4].
Muṣ'ab b. Māhān al-Marwazī[5].
Nūḥ b. Maimūn al-Marwazī[6].
Qabīṣah[7].
Al-Rabī' b. Yaḥyā[8].
Rawwād b. al-Jarrāḥ[9].
'Ubaid Allāh b. 'Ubaid al-Raḥmān al-Ashja'ī[10].
Wakī'[11].
Al-Walīd al-Qaṭṭān[13].
Zā'idah[14].

204. SUFYAN B. 'UYAYNAH (107-198)[15].

He began to write *aḥādīth* when he was fifteen[16]. He wrote many *aḥādīth* for Ayyūb al-Sakhtiyānī[17]. It is said that his *aḥādīth* amounted to 7000, and yet he had no books[18]. But we know that he wrote *aḥādīth* from al-Zuhrī, 'Amr b. Dīnār, etc. Moreover, he

1. Rāmhurmuzī, 37a; 76a; *Kifāyah*, 70.
2. *Bagh.*, v, 403; 405; *Mīzān*, iii, 595; *Tahd*, ix, 255.
3. *Tahd.*, x, 164.
4. Rāzī, iv, i, 164.
5. *Tahd.*, x, 164.
6. *'Ilal*, 116b; *Ma'rifah*, 165.
7. Rāzī, iv, i, 120; Sam'ānī, *Ansāb*, 427.
8. *Kifāyah*, 241.
9. *Tahd.*, x, 164.
10. Sa'd, vii, ii, 72; *'Ilal*, 117a; Fasawī, ii, 241a; *Bagh.*, x, 312; *Ḥuffāẓ*, I, 284; *Tahd.*, vii, 35.
11. Fasawī, ii, 231a.
12. Rāzī, *Introd.* 66.
13. Ja'd, 245; *'Ilal*, i, 54; Rāzī, *introd.* 67; 246-8; Sa'd, vi, 259.
14. Ja'd, 246; Rāzī, *introd.* 80.
15. *Tahd.*, iv, 119-120.
16. Khaithama, iii, 42a.
17. Rāzī. *Introd.* 50.
18. *Bagh.*, ix, 179.

dictated from a *Ṣaḥīfah* in the year 160[1]. He delivered his first lecture on *aḥādīth* in 42 A.H.[2].

The following derived *aḥādīth* from him in written form:

'Alī b. Ja'd[3].

Ghundar[4].

Ḥumaidī[5].

Wakī'[6].

205. SUHAIL B. ABŪ ṢĀLIḤ (c. 70-138)[7].

He transmitted from Ibn al-Musayyab (d. 93) etc.[8].

He had many books: *Lahū Nusakh*[9] including a Nuskhah from his father[10].

He sent traditions of Abū Ṣālih to Wuhaib in writing[11].

Mālik b. Anas wrote from him[12].

206. SULAIMĀN B. ABŪ SULAYMĀN, ABŪ ISḤĀQ AL-SHAIBĀNĪ (c. 75-138)[13].

Abū Mu'āwiyah had his *aḥādīth* in writing[14].

207. SULAIMĀN B. BILĀL AL-TAIMĪ (c. 100-172)[15].

He transmitted from 'Abd Allāh b. Dīnār (d. 127) etc.

The following wrote *aḥādīth* from him:

'Abd Allāh b. 'Abd al-Raḥmān al-Samarqandī[16].

---

1. *Bagh.*, xi, 362.
2. *Bagh.*, ix, 175.
3. Rāmhurmuzī 32a; *Bagh.* xi, 362.
4. *'Ilal*, i, 87.
5. See al-Ḥumaidī, Musnad which draws mostly on the traditions of Ibn 'Uyaynah.
6. Fasawī, ii, 7a; Rāzī, *Introd.* 50.
7. *Tahd.*, iv, 264 (according to Ibn Qāni').
8. *Tahd.*, iv, 263.
9. *Kāmil*, ii, 67b; *Mīzān*, ii, 243-4.
10. Suyūṭī, *Tadrīb al-Rāwī*, 42; See also *Jāmi'*, 194a.
11. Rāmhurmuzī, 49 a-b.
12. Khaithamah, iii, 141b.
13. *Tahd.*, iv, 198. There are many other dates ranging from 129 to 142.
14. *Kifāyah*, 228.
15. *Tahd.*, iv, 176.
16. Rāzī, iv, ii, 169.

'Abd al-'Azīz b. Abū Ḥāzim was entrusted with Sulaimān's books which were in his possession after the compiler's death[1].

'Abd al-Ḥamīd transmitted a large *Nuskhah* from him[2].

Ibn Abū Uwais[3].

'Ubaid b. Abū Qurrah[4].

Yaḥyā b. Yaḥyā[5].

208. SULAIMĀN B. AL-MUGHĪRAH AL-QAISĪ (c. 90-165)[6].

He transmitted from al-Ḥasan (d. 110) etc.

Abū Dāwūd al-Ṭayālisī wrote *aḥādīth* from him, and Ibn Ḥanbal had this book[7].

209. SULAIMĀN B. QARM AL-TAIMĪ (c. 100 - c. 160).

He transmitted from al-Sabi'ī (d. 127) etc.[8] and had books[9].

210. THAUR B. YAZĪD AL-KINDĪ (85-155)[10].

The following wrote *aḥādīth* from him:

Sufyān al-Thaurī[11].

Yaḥyā b. Sa'īd al-Qaṭṭān[12].

Many Iraqian scholars[13].

---

1. Khaithamah, iii, 151a; Fasawī, ii, 127a; Rāzī, ii, ii, 382; Bājī, 115b; *Mīzān*, ii, 626; *Tahd.*, vi, 334; Qaisarānī, 316; *Huffāz*, i, 244.
2. *Mīzān*, i, 287; Khazrajī 37.
3. *Tahd.*, iv, 176.
4. *Bagh.*, xi, 96.
5. Qaisarānī, 316.
6. *Tahd.*, iv, 220; Khazrajī, 131.
7. *'Ilal*, i, 45.
8. *Tahd.*, iv, 213.
9. *Tahd.*, iv, 213.
10. *Thiqāt*, 420.
11. *Thiqāt*, 420.
12. *Kāmil*, i, 197a.
13. *Mashāhīr*, 181.

211. 'UBAID ALLĀH B. ABŪ ZIYĀD AL-SHĀMĪ (c. 75-158).

He had books, which were transmitted by:
Abū Manī', son of 'Ubaid Allāh and
Ḥajjāj the grandson of 'Ubaid Allāh[1].

212. 'UBAID ALLĀH B. 'AMR, ABŪ AL-RAQQĪ(101-180)[2].

'Amr b. Qusaiṭ al-Raqqī[3] and Zakariyā b. 'Adī al-Kūfī[4] wrote *aḥādīth* from him.

213. 'UBAID ALLĀH B. AYĀD AL-SADDŪSĪ(c. 100-169)[5].

He had a *Ṣaḥīfah*[6].

214. 'UBAID ALLĀH B. 'UMAR B. ḤAFṢ AL-'UMARĪ (c. 80-145)[7].

He had many books[8].
The following transcribed *aḥādīth* from him:
'Ubaid Allāh[9].
'Abd Allāh b. 'Umar b. Ḥafṣ al-'Umarī[10].
'Aqbah b. Khālid[11].
Ḥātim b. Ismā'īl[12].
Nūḥ b. Abū Maryam[13].

---

1. *Islām*, vi, 246.
2. *Tahd.*, vii, 43.
3. Rāzī, iii, i, 256; *Tahd.*, viii, 91.
4. Rāzī, i, ii, 600.
5. *Tahd.*, vii, 4.
6. *Tahd.*, vii, 4.
7. *Tahd.*, vii, 40.
8. *Tahd.*, v, 328.
9. *Ma'rifah*, 164.
10. *Tahd.*, v, 328.
11. Rāzī, *Introd.* 68; see also Rāzī, iii, i, 310; Ja'd, 234.
12. *Kifāyah*, 235.
13. *Ma'rifah*, 164.

Al-Qāsim b. 'Abd Allāh al-'Umarī[1].

Yaḥyā b. Sa'īd al-Qaṭṭān[2].

215. 'UMAR B. ABŪ SALAMAH (C. 70-132)[3].

The following wrote *aḥādīth* from him:

Abū 'Awānah[4].

Hushaim[5].

Many Students of Wāsiṭ[6].

216. 'UMAR B. DHAR AL-HAMDĀNĪ (c. 70-153)[7].

He transmitted from Sa'id b. Jubair (d. 95) etc.

Ma'rūf b. Ḥassān transmitted a lengthy book from him which was unreliable[8].

Sufyān al-Thaurī wrote from him[9].

217. 'UMAR B. IBRĀHĪM AL-'ABDĪ (95 - c. 155).

He transmitted from Qatādah (d. 114)[10].

He had writing on a piece of wood[11].

'Abbād b. Al-'Awwām had his *aḥādīth* in writing[12].

218. 'UMAR B. MUḤAMMAD B. ZAID (c. 80-145)[13].

Many Iraqian students wrote from him[14].

---

1. *Kāmil,* iii, 2a.
2. Rāmhurmuzī 37b; *Kifāyah,* 220; see also *Mīzān,* i, 504.
3. *Thiqāt,* 544.
4. *Thiqāt,* 544.
5. *Thiqāt,* 544; *Mashāhīr,* 133.
6. *Mashāhīr,* 133.
7. *Tahd.,* vii, 445.
8. *Mīzān,* iv, 143.
9. Ja'd, 233-4.
10. *Tahd.,* vii, 425.
11. *Tahd.,* vii, 426.
12. I. M. Ṣalāt 7.
13. *Tahd.,* vii, 496.
14. *Thiqāt,* 544.

219. 'UMAR B. QAIS AL-MAKKĪ (c. 95 - c. 160).

He transmitted from Nāfi' (d. 117) etc.[1].

Khālid b. Nazār transmitted a *Nuskhah* from him[2].

220. 'UMAR B. SA'ĪD (c. 100 - c. 160)[3].

Ibn Ṭahmān had his *aḥādīth* in writing[4].

221. 'UMĀRAH B. GHAZIYAH (C. 75-140)[5].

Ibn Lahī'ah had a book from him[6].

222. 'UQAIL B. KHĀLID AL-AILĪ (c. 75-141)[7].

He had a book[8].

223. USĀMAH B. ZAID AL-LAITHĪ (c. 75-153)[9].

When he died, he was between 70 and 80 years old.

According to al-Ḥākim, his book was perfect[10].

The following derived *aḥādīth* from him in written form:

Ibn Wahb transmitted a correct book (*Nuskhah Ṣāliḥah*) from him[12].

Yaḥyā b. Sa'īd al-Qaṭṭān wrote from him[13].

'Uthmān b. 'Umar[14].

---

1. *Tahd.*, vii, 490.
2. *Tahd.*, vii, 492.
3. *Tahd.*, vii, 454.
4. Ibn Ṭahmān, *Nuskhah*, 252a.
5. Khazrajī, 138; *Tahd.*, vii, 423.
6. *Mīzān*, ii, 476; *Ḥuffāz*, i, 216; *Tahd.*, v, 376.
7. *Tahd.*, vii, 256.
8. *Mīzān*, iii, 89; *Islaa¯m*, vi, 101.
9. *Thiqāt*, 407; *Tahd.*, i, 210.
10. *Tahd.*, i, 210.
11. *Tahd.*, i, 210.
12. *Kāmil*, i, 143a; *Tahd.*, 209.
13. *Thiqāt*, 407.
14. Bukhari in his *Tarikh*, see Hanbal, ii, 248 (Shakir's edition) footnote 1098

224. 'UTBAH B. ḤUMAID AL-ḌABBĪ (c. 85 - c. 105).

He transmitted from 'Ikrimah (D. 105) etc. [1] and wrote *aḥādīth* in a very good number[2].

225. 'UTHMĀN B. MIQSAM AL-BURRĪ (c. 95 - after 160)[3].

He transmitted from Qatādah (c. 114) and had a book[4].

'Abd Allāh b. Mukhallad wrote from him[5].

226. AL-WADDAH B. 'ABD ALLĀH, ABŪ 'AWĀNAH (92-176)[6].

He was a slave of 'Atā', who bought him to carry the books and ink for his son Yazīd[7].

It is said that he knew how to read, but did not know how to write, so he employed someone to write *aḥādīth* for him[8]. He read *aḥādīth* from the book[9], and sometimes, when he related them memory he committed mistakes[10], but his books were perfect[11].

The following derived *aḥādīth* from him in written form:

Hishām b. 'Abd al-Malik[12].

Yaḥyā b. Ḥammād[13].

---

1. *Tahd.*, vii, 96.
2. Rāzī, iii, i, 370; *Yahd.*, vii, 96.
3. *Mīzān*, iii, 58.
4. *Mīzān*, iii, 57.
4. *Mīzān*, iii, 57.
6. *Mashāhīr*, 160. See also *Tahd.*, xi, 118.
7. *Wāsiṭ*, 135; Bājī, 171a-b.
8. *'Ilal*, i, 155; Rāzī, iv, ii, 41; *Ḥuffaāẓ*, i, 213.
9. Sa'd, vii, ii, 43.
10. *Mashāhīr*, 160; see also Sa'd, vii, ii, 43.
11. Fasawī, iii, 48a; Rāzī, iv, ii, 40; Rāmhurmuzī, 40a; Bājī, 171a; *Mīzān*, iv, 334; *Ḥuffāz*, i, 213; 214; Tahd., xi, 117; 118; Khazrajī 360.
12. *'Ilal*, i, 351.
13. *'Ilal*, i, 351.

227. AL-WALĪ B. MUḤAMMAD AL-MUWAQQARĪ (c. 100 - c. 160).

He transmitted from al-Zuhrī (d. 124) etc.[1] and had books[2].

228. WĀSIL B. 'ABD AL-RAḤMĀN, ABŪ ḤURRAH (c. 90-152)[3].

He transmitted from al-Ḥasan (d. 110) etc.

Yaḥyā b. Sa'īd wrote from him[4].

229. WĀSIṬ B. AL-ḤĀRITH (c. 90 - c. 150).

'Abd Allāh b. Kharāsh transmitted a *Nuskhah* from him[5].

230. WUHAIB B. KHĀLID AL-BĀHILĪ (107-165)[6].

'Affan had 4,000 *aḥādīth* from him in writing[7].

231. YAḤĀ B. ABŪ KATHĪR (c. 70-129)[8].

He used to transmit *aḥādīth,* even from the books which he had not read to their authors[9]. He used to write *aḥādīth* and send them to inquirers[10].

He was aware of the importance of revising after copying[11].

The following derived *aḥādīth* from him in writing:

'Alī b. Mubārak al-Hunā'ī had two books from him[12].

---

1. *Tahd.*, xi, 149.
2. *Tahd.*, xi, 149; see also BTS, 197. He did not read from his own book.
3. *Tahd.*, xi, 105.
4. *'Ilal,* 153a.
5. *Thiqāt,* 623-4.
6. *Tahd.*, xi, 170.
7. *Jāmi',* 148 b.
8. *Tahd.*, xi, 269.
9. Ibn Ḥajar, *Hady al-Sārī,* 223.
10. See e.g. Ḥanbal, v, 309; MU, *Nikāḥ,* 37.
11. *Imlā,* 78.
12. *'Ilal,* i, 189; Fasawī, iii, 318b; Rāzī, iii, 203; Bājī, 126; *Tahd.*, vii, 376; Ibn Ḥajar, *Hady al-Sārī,* ii, 197; Khazrajī, 134.

Al-Auzā'ī wrote thirteen books from him[1].

Ayyūb b. 'Utbah[2].

Dahtham b. Qurrah al-Yamāmī[3].

Hishām al-Dastawā'ī[4].

Khalīl b. Qurran[5].

Ma'mar[6].

Mu'āwiyah b. Sallām[7].

Shaibān b. 'Abd al-Raḥmān[8].

232. Yaḥyā b. Ayyūb al-Ghāfiqī (c. 110-168)[9].

His book was perfect, but his memory was weak[10].

233. Yaḥyā b. Ḥamzah al-Dimashqī (103-183)[11].

The following wrote *aḥādīth* from him:

Anonymous[12].

Muḥammad b. 'Ā'idh[13].

234. Yaḥyā b. Sa'īd al-Anṣārī (c. 70 - 144)[14].

He transmitted from Anas b. Mālik (d. 93) etc.

In his early life he did not write *aḥādīth,* but depended on memory[15]. When his students collected his *aḥādīth* and brought

---

1. Fasawī, iii, 128b; see also, Zur'ah, 150a; Rāzī, *introd.* 186; Rāmhurmuzī, 47b; *Kifāyah,* 321; *Tahd.*, vi, 241.
2. Rāzī, i, i, 253; *Tahs.*, i, 409.
3. *'Ilal,* i, 106b; *Mīzā,* ii, 29; *Tahd.*, iii, 213.
4. Ḥanbal, i, 225; v, 309; BU, *Adhān,* 22; MU, *Nikāḥ,* 37.; Khaithamah, iii, 59a; Nas, ii, 283; *Kāmil,* i, 291a; Dāraquṭnī, 442.
5. *Majrūḥīn,* 96a.
6. Fasawī, iii, 269b; Khaithamah, iii, 58b; see also *Taqyīd,* 110; 111.
7. *Tahd.*, x, 209.
8. Rāzī, ii, i, 356.
9. *Tahd.*, xi, 187.
10. Ibn Ḥajar, *Hady al-Sārī,* ii, 221; *Tahd.*, xi, 187.
11. *Tahd.*, xi, 210.
12. Rāzī, *introd.* 343.
13. Rāzī, *introd.* 343.
14. *Tahd.*, xi, 223.
15. Fasawī, ii, 217b.

them back to him in written form, he disapproved of them looking at the volume. Later, they read to him, and he confirmed that those were his *aḥādīth*[1].

Later, he wrote *aḥādīth* and sent them to his students[2].

The following wrote *aḥādīth* from him:

'Abd al-Waḥhāb b. 'Abd al-Majīd al-Thaqafī[3].

Ḥammād b. Zaid[4].

Ibn Lahī'ah[5].

Ibn 'Uyaynah[6].

Ismā'īl b. 'Ayyāsh[7].

Ismā'īl b. Qais[8].

Jā'far b. Muḥammad[9].

Jarīr b. Ḥāzim and his companions[10].

Al-Laith b. Sa'd[11].

Rabī'ah[12].

Yazīd b. 'Abd Allāh b. Usāmah[13].

235. Ya'lā b. Ḥakīm (c. 70 - before 130)[14].

He transmitted from Ibn Jubair (d. 95), etc.

He wrote down some *aḥādīth* and sent them to Ayyūb[15].

Yaḥyā b. Abū Kathīr wrote down his *aḥādīth* and sent them to Hishām[16].

---

1. Fasawī, ii, 217b; *Tahd.*, xi, 222.
2. See e.g. *Amwāl,* 393; 395.
3. Fasawī, ii, 218a; *Bagh.*, xi, 20; *Ḥuffāẓ,* i, 293; *Mīzān,* ii, 681; *Tahd.*, vi, 450.
4. Rāzī, *introd.* 178; i, ii, 138, *Sharḥ 'Ilal,* 42a; see also *Ḥuffāẓ,* i, 207.
5. *Amwāl*, 393; 395.
6. *'Ilal,* i, 20.
7. *'Ilal,* 129b; Rāzī, i, i, 192; *Tahd.*, i, 324.
8. BTS, 4; Rāzī, i, i, 193; *Kāmil,* i, 107b.
9. Rāzī, *introd.* 38-9; *Kāmil,* i, 213a.
10. *Taqyīd,* 111.
11. *Tahd.*, v, 257.
12. *Tahd.*, xi, 222.
13. *Kāmil,* i, 89a.
14. *Tahd.*, xi, 401.
15. MU, *Buyū',* 113.
16. Ḥanbal, i, 225; Dāraquṭnī, 442.

236. YAZĪD B. 'AṬĀ' B. YAZĪD AL-YASHKURĪ (c. 95-177)[4].

He transmitted from Nafi (d. 117), etc.[5].

He had books. Abū 'Awānah used to carry the books and an ink-pot for Yazīd[6].

237. YAZĪD B. AL-HĀD (c. 75-139)[7].

Ibrāhīm al-Anṣārī had a disorderly *Nuskhah* from him[8].

238. YŪNUS B. ABŪ ISḤĀQ (c. 70-159)[9].

He transmitted from Anas b. Mālik (d. 93), and had books[10].

239. YŪNUS B. 'UBAID AL-'ABDĪ (c. 80-140)[11].

He saw Anas b. Mālik (d. 93).

He is reported as saying: "I did not write anything"[12], but it is also reported that he said that he wrote what was for others' benefit and missed what was useful to him[13].

The following dervied *aḥādīth* from him in writing:

Sālim b. Nūḥ[14].

Yazīd b. Zurai'[15].

---

1. *Tahd.*, xi, 391.
2. *'Ilal,* 139b.
3 Rāzī, iii, ii, 232; *Tahd.*, ix, 129.
4. *Tahd.*, xi, 351; Khazrajī, 372-3.
5. Khazrajī, 372-3.
6. Bājī, 171a-b.
7. *Tahd.*, xi, 340.
8. *Lisān*, i, 69.
9. *Tahd.*, xi 434.
10. Rāzī, iv, ii, 244; *Tahd.*, xi, 434.
11. *Tahd.*, xi, 442.
12. *Tahd.*, xi, 442.
13. *Tahd.*, xi, 444.
14. *Kāmil,* ii, 31a; *Kifāyah,* 236; *Mīzān,* ii, 113; *Tahd.*, iii, 443.
15. *Tahd.*, xi, 445.

240. YŪNUS B. YAZĪD AL–AILĪ (c. 95-159)[1].

He transmitted from Nāfi' (d. 117), etc.

His books were perfect[2].

The following wrote *aḥādīth* from him:

'Anbasah b. Khālid[3].

Ibn al-Mubārak[4].

Shabīb b. Sa'īd[5].

241. YŪSUF B. ṢUHAIB AL-KŪFĪ (c. 85 - c. 150).

He transmitted from al-Sha'bī (d. 104), etc.[6].

Muṣ'ab b. Sallām had his *aḥādīth* in disorderly form[7].

242. ZAID B. 'ALĪ B. ḤUSAIN (80-122)[8].

'Amr b. Khālid al-Qurashī transmitted a book from Zaid[9].

243. ZAID B. ABŪ SALLĀM, MAMṬŪR AL-ḤABASHĪ (c. 80 - c. 140).

He transmitted from 'Adī b. Arṭāt (d. 102)[10].

Mu'āwiyah b. Sallām derived *aḥādīth* from him in writing.

He handed the book of Zaid to Yāḥya b. Abū Kathīr (d. 124)[11].

---

1. *Tahd.*, xi, 452.
2. Bājī, 178b; Rāzī, iv, ii, 248; *Tahd.*, xi, 450; Khazrajī, 380; see also *Kāmil,* i, 33b.
3. *Tahd.*, viii, 154.
4. *Kāmil,* i, 33 b.
5. Rāzī, ii, i, 359; *Tahd.*, iv, 307.
6. *Tahd.*, xi, 415.
7. *'Ilal,* 162b; *Tahd.*, x, 161.
8. *Tahd.*, iii, 419.
9. *Tahd.*, viii, 26.
10. *Tahd.*, iii, 415.
11. Zur'ah, 52a; Fasawī, iii, 268b; *Tahd.*, iii, 415; *Kifāyah*, 347; see also *Mīzān*, iv, 403.

244. Zā'idah b. Abū Ruqād (c. 105 - c. 170).

He transmitted from Thābit al-Bunānī (d. 127), etc. [1].

'Ubaid Allāh b. 'Umar al-Qawārīrī wrote down all his *aḥādīth*[2].

245. Zā'idah b. Qudāmah (c. 100-160)[3].

He was the compiler of many books, e.g.:

Kitāb al-Sunan.

Kitāb al-Qirā'āt.

Kitāb al-Tafsīr.

Kitāb al-Zuhd.

Kitāb al-Manāqib[4].

Mu'āwiyah b. 'Amr al-Azdī transmitted his books[5].

246. Zakariyā b. Isḥāq al-Makkī (c. 105 - c. 170).

He transmitted from 'Amr b. Dīnār, etc.[6] and had a book[7].

The following derived *aḥādīth* from him in writing:

Rauḥ. Zakariyā dictated to him from the book[8].

Sa'īd b. Sallām b. Sa'īd al-Baṣrī had a book from him[9].

247. Ziyād b. Abū Ziyād al-Jaṣṣāṣ (c. 75 - c. 140).

He transmitted from Anas b. Mālik (d. 93) etc.[10].

Muḥammad b. Khālid al-Duhnī[11] and Yazīd b. Hārūn[12] each transmitted a *Nuskhah* from him.

---

1. *Tahd.*, iii, 305.
2. Rāzī, i, ii, 613; al-Sahmī, *Tārīkh Jurjān,* 513; *Tahd.* iii, 305.
3. *Tahd.*, iii, 307.
4. *Fihrist,* 226.
5. Sa'd, vii, ii, 82.
6. *Tahd.*, iii, 328.
7. Sa'd, v, 362; Khaithamah, iii, 40 b; Bājī, 58a; *Tahd.*, iii, 329.
8. Ḥanbal, iv, 390.
9. *Bagh.*, ix, 80.
10. *Tahd.*, iii, 368.
11. *Kāmil,* i, 366a.
12. *Kāmil,* i, 366a.

248. ZIYĀD B. SA'D AL-KHURĀSĀNĪ (c. 90 - c. 150).

He transmitted from al-Zuhrī (d. 124) and others.

Mālik, Ibn Juraij and Ḥammām, etc. transmitted from him[1].

He did not learn from any teacher,except in the form of dictation[2].

Zam'ah had a book from him[3].

249. AL-ZUBAIR B. 'ADĪ (c. 70-131)[4].

He transmitted from Anas b. Mālik (d. 93)[5].

Bishr b. Ḥusain al-Isbahānī transmitted a *Nuskhah* from him which contained about 150 *aḥādīth* and were wrongly attributed to him[6].

Sufyān al-Thaurī wrote 50 *aḥādīth* from him[7].

250. ZUHAIR B. MU'ĀWIYAH (100-174)[8].

When he heard a *ḥadīth* twice, he used to make a sign meaning that the work was finished[9].

He had a book[10].

251. ZUFAR B. AL-HUDHAIL (110-158)[11].

Muḥammad b. Muzāḥim al-Marwazī transmitted a *Nuskhah* from him[12].

Shaddād b. Ḥakīm al-Balkhī also transmitted a *Nuskhah* from him[13].

1. *Tahd.*, iii, 369.
2. Dūlābī, i, 7.
3. Fasawi, ii, 217 a.
4. *Thiqāt,* 193.
5. Qaisarānī, 150.
6. *Kāmil,* i, 161a; Rāzī, i, i, 366; *Mīzān,* i, 316,
7. Rāzī, *Introd.* 80-81.
8. *Tahd.*, iii, 352.
9. Ja'd, 351; *Imlā,* 9; *Ḥuffāẓ,* i, 211.
10. Rāzī, i, ii, 589.
11. *Mīzān,* ii, 71.
12. *Ma'rifah,* 164.
13. *Ma'rifah,* 164.

CHAPTER IV

TAḤAMMUL AL-'ILM

THE LEARNING AND THE TRANSMITTING OF ḤADĪTH IN THE FIRST AND THE SECOND CENTURIES OF ISLAM.

According to the *Qur'ān,* a group should remain behind even in the time of war, to gain sound knowledge in religion so that they may preach to their folk when they return[1].

Learning at least a portion of the *Qur'ān* and the *aḥādīth* of the Prophet is obligatory for every Muslim. In response to this requirement, there was an outburst of educational activities in the entire Islamic world. For many centuries, in the educational history of Islam, the word Knowledge – *'Ilm* – was applied only to the learning of *aḥādīth* and related subjects[2].

In this chapter a sketch of the educational method of the early centuries of Islam will be drawn. It should be clear that this is only a sketch. As there were no organized universities and colleges with fixed curricula and definite methods of instruction, all activities could take any shape the tutors preferred. The manner, even of a single teacher and a single student, would differ from time to time and from place to place. Therefore, any kind of generalization of the method, and any restriction to a certain practice would be dangerous and misleading.

The Teachers.

The Prophet called himself a teacher[3], and used to sit with the Companions in a circle to teach them[4]. His words and deeds

---

1. *Al-Qur'ān,* ix, 122.
2. See for example: The titles of Abū Khaithamah's book, *Kitāb al-'Ilm,* and al-Khaṭīb's book, *"Taqyīd al-'Ilm"* which deal with the problem of the recording of *aḥādīth,* also, Ibn 'Abd al-Barr, *"Jāmi', Bayāyan al-'Ilm".*
3. Ibn Mājah, *introduction,* 17. *Ḥadīth* No. 229.
4. BU, *'Ilm,* 8; *Muwaṭṭa', Salām,* 4; Ḥanbal, v, 219.

were carefully watched by his Companions and were recited by them with the help of each other till they memorized them[1].

As it was not possible for every Companion to be with the Prophet on every occasion, they came to an agreement between themselves to attend his circle in shifts[2]. It was a common practice among them to inform absentees about the Prophet's sayings and deeds[3]. This was not only the agreement among them but was also the command of the Prophet. The Companion Sulaiṭ was so embarrassed by his absence which was due to his residence on a far off piece of land given to him by the Prophet, that he requested him to take the land back from him[4].

Memorizing the aḥādīth of the Prophet in early days.

Some Companions made their memoranda of *aḥādīth* in the life of the Prophet and some others made their collections later on[5]. However, it was a common practice among them to recollect the *aḥādīth* of the Prophet either individually or with each other's help[6]. The same practice continued in the time of the Successors[7].

---

1. *Faqīh,* 132a.
2. See for example, 'Umar's agreement with an Ansarite, Sa'd, viii, 136.
3. *'Ilal,* 96b; Khaithamah, iii, 53b; Rāmhurmuzī, 15b; *Mustadrak,* i, 95; 127; where it is mentioned that the attendants used to inform absentees about the Prophet's *Ḥadīth.* The Prophet specifically told the Companions to do so. See, *Sharaf,* 11a; 11b.
4. *Amwāl,* 272-3; Zanjuwaih, 100a.
5. For details of the Companions' writings see supra, chapter iii.
6. For personal recollections, e.g., see;
   Abū Hurairah, *Jāmi',* 181b-182a;
   For group recollections, e.g., see;
   Abū Mūsā and 'Umar, *Faqīh,* 132a; see also *Jāmi',* 46b as cited by 'Ajjāj, *Sunnah Qabl al-Tadwīn,* 160.
   For Companions' advice to recollect *aḥādīth,* see;
   1. Abū Sa'īd al-Khudrī, Zur'ah, 95; *Mustadrak,* i, 94; *Sharaf,* 56a;
   2. 'Alī b. Abū Ṭālib, *Mustadrak,* i, 95; *Sharaf,* 55a;
   3. Ibn 'Abbās, *Sharaf,* 56a;
   4. Ibn Mas'ūd, *Mustadrak,* 1, 95; *Sharaf,* 55b.
7. See as example:
   1. 'Alqamah, *'Ilm,* 7a; *Sharaf,* 57a;
   2. Abū al-'Āliyah, *Sharaf,* 57a;
   3. Ibn Abī Lailā, Sa'd, vi, 76; *Sharaf,* 57a;
   4. Ibn Sīrīn, *'Ilm,* 9a;
   5. Ibrāhīm, *Jāmi',* 109a;
   6. 'Urwah b. al-Zubair, Fischer, 45-6.

The appearance of the books.

In the middle of the first century of the *Hijrah,* books of *aḥādith* compiled from the teachers' lectures began to appear, of which one of the earliest mentioned was the book of Bashīr b. Nahīk and Hammām, the pupils of Abū Hurairah[1]. The books of Ibn 'Abbās and Jābir b. 'Abd Allāh, etc., belong to the same period.

The Aṭrāf system and its effect.

According to the sources now available, in the third quarter of the first century of the *Hijraḥ* a new technique was employed in the learning of *ḥadīth,* which was called *Aṭrāf,* which meant copying only a part of *aḥādīth.*

The earliest recorded usage of this method —so far as I know —was that of Ibn Sīrīn in the lecture of his teacher 'Abīdah al-Salmānī (d. 72 A.H.)[2]. The practice continued in the traditionists' circles[3]. Later on many books were compiled according to this technique and were used as a concordance by the early scholars[4].

The *Aṭrāf* method was a very important step towards the writing of *aḥādīth.* It contained three main issues:

A student's knowledge of a *ḥadīth,* gained by some source before attending the lecture.

The writing down of *aḥādīth* in part before attending the lectures.

The effort to gain *ḥadīth* from a higher narrator in the chain of transmitters and non-satisfaction with the material gained from the lower source.

---

1. *Supra,* Abū Hurairah, in the third chapter.
2. *'Ilal,* i, 387.
3. See for example:
   1. Ḥammād b. Abū Sulaimān, Fasawī, iii, 83a;
   2. Ismā'īl b. 'Ayyāsh, *Tahd.,* i, 324;
   3. Mālik b. Anas and 'Ubaid Allāh b. 'Umar, *'Ilal,* 154a;
   4. Sufyān al-Thaurī, *Jāmi',* 43b;
   5. Yazīd b. Zurai', *Majrūḥīn,* 115b.
4. See for details, al-Kattānī, *al-Risālah al-Mustaṭrafah,* 167-70.

Until the end of the third quarter of the first century of the *Hijrah,* a pattern was almost fixed for the learning and teaching of *hādīth* which flourished in the second and third centuries.

The curricula of education in the first century.

It looks as though, in the very early days, there were only two methods of learning *aḥādīth*: either to associate oneself with one of the scholars, or to attend the lectures which were regularly held. The Companions of the Prophet used oral transmission, dictation, and even reading from a book[1], yet it is not clear whether or not they used to impart *aḥādīth* according to subjects, or only narrated on their personal choice, or whether the discussion was conducted on a certain topic which was raised by someone.

Perhaps the earliest record of a classified diffusion of *aḥādīth* is the method of Ibn 'Abbās and 'Urwah[2]. It appears that these scholars used to revise *hādīth* among themselves according to subjects[3]; hence, it was not an open lecture. So, in the above two instances, they did not transmit *aḥādīth* completely, nor its proper wording; they only referred to it by mentioning its essential aspects. Therefore, they forbade students to learn traditions by this method[4].

Teaching of aḥādīth according to Shuyūkh.

The common practice of the second century was the teaching of *aḥādīth* according to *shuyūkh* they came from. Once Yaḥyā asked Al-Fallās whence he was coming. He replied, "From the lecture of Mu'ādh". Then he asked whose *Ḥadīth* was he transmitting? al-Fallās replied that he was imparting the *Ḥadīth* of 'Awn...[5]. It is understood from this conversation that the teacher used to impart *aḥādīth* according to their teachers. This method seems to be easy and natural. As the early scholars made their memoranda or books from the lectures of the Companions and the first generation of the Successors, naturally they might have kept the notes of every teacher separately.

1. See for detail *supra,* p. 41; 50.
2. *Supra* Ibn 'Abbās, and 'Urwah, in the third chapter.
3. See the revising of Shu'bah and Ibn Idrīs, Rāzī, ii, i, 112.
4. See for example: Abū Zur'ah, *Jāmi',* 109a; Ibn Mahdī, *Jāmi',* 108b; Ibn al-Mubārak, *Jāmi',* 109a.
5. *Tahd.,* i, 358.

The description of books available to us at present makes the matter quite clear. Here are a few examples:

Mujāhid says, "I went to Ḥammād b. 'Amr and requested him to bring the book of Khuṣaif. Then he brought the book of Ḥuṣain"[1].

Al-Qawārīrī says that he went to 'Abd al-Wārith, accompanied by 'Affān. 'Abd al-Wārith enquired of them what they wanted. Then they asked him to bring the book of Ibn Juḥādah[2].

Once al-Thaurī said that he would bring the book of the best man of al-Kūfah. The students thought that he meant the book of Manṣūr, but he produced the book of Muḥammad b. Sūqah[3].

Ibn Ḥanbal discussed a *ḥadīth* which was transmitted on the authority of Ibrāhīm from Hushaim from Ya'lā b. 'Aṭā', so he asked al-Athram to go to 'Abd Allāh b. Mūsā and to look up in his book this particular *ḥadīth* as he had heard that it was noted there. Al-Athram said that he went to the house of 'Abd Allāh b. Mūsā, and his books from Hushaim were brought to him. He then searched the books of Hushaim, in particular for the *ḥadīth of* Ya'lā, but did not find it. He further said that he found the *aḥādīth* of Ya'lā in the books of Hushaim in one place, and in that there was no reference to the *ḥadīth*[4] for which he was looking.

There are a good many references which give sufficient ground to maintain that the general practice of the teaching of *ḥadīth* was to impart *aḥādīth* of one *Shaikh* at one time, and to keep *aḥādīth* of every *Shaikh* separately[5].

---

1. *Bagh.*, viii, 154.
2. *'Ilal,* i, 144.
3. Rāzī, iii, ii, 281.
4. *Bagh.*, vi, 195.
5. See for examples:
   1. *Kitāb Ṣafwān, Tahd.*, i, 475;
   2. *Nuskhah of Abū Ḥusain, Kāmil,* 1, 21a;
   3. Book of 'Abd Allāh b. Ja'far al-Madīnī, *Tahd.*, v, 174;
   4. al-Ḥakam and the book containing Yaḥyā's *aḥādīth, Kifāyah,* 112; *Tahd.*, ii, 305-6;
   5. Ibn Ma'īn and the book of Nāfi' b. Yazīd; Rāzī, iv, i, 480, *Tahd.*, x, 441.

The Method of Teaching.

For the teaching of *aḥādīth,* the following systems were generally employed:

Oral recitation,

reading from books,

questions and answers,

dictation.

A. *Oral recitation of aḥādīth by the teacher.* This practice began to decline from the second half of the second century, though it persisted to a much lesser extent for a long period. Mostly students were attached to a certain teacher for a very long time, until they were believed to be authorities on his *aḍādīth.* Sometimes they were called *Rāwī* or *Sāḥib* of so and so[1]. Even if regular meetings were held for the teaching, only a few *aḥādīth* were taught in one lesson, say about three or four[2].

---

1. See for *Rāwīs:*
   1. 'Abd al-Wahhāb b. 'Aṭ ā', Rāwī of Ibn Abī 'Arūbah, *Mīzān,* 11,681;
   2. 'Alī b. Mubārak. Rāwī of Yaḥyā b. Abū Kathīr, *Thiqāt,* 556;
   3. Harmalah b. Yaḥyā of Ibn Wahb, *Mīzān,* i, 472;
   4. Ḥumaid of Sufyān b. Ḥabīb, *Tahd.,* iv, 107;
   5. Qais b. 'Abd al-Raḥmān of Sa'd b. Ibrāhīm, *Thiqāt,* 584
   6. Yaḥyā b. Mutawakkil of Ibn Juraij, *Thiqāt,* 633.
2. For a very limited number of students for teaching, see:
   1. Abū al-'Āliyah had no more than 3 students at one time, *'Ilm,* 5;
   2. 'Abd Allāh al-Ṣunābaḥī had only 2 students at a time, Fassawī, iii, 112b.
3. For the quantity of *aḥādīth* in one lecture, see:
   1. Abū Qilābah only 3 *aḥādīth. Jāmi',* 37b;
   2. Abū al-Walīd only 3 *aḥādīth. Jāmi',* 37b;
   3. A'mash about 3 or 4 *aḥādīth. Jāmi'* 37b; 45a;
   4. Ayyūb, about 5. *Jāmi',* 45a;
   5. Ma'mar: "We used to learn one or two *aḥādīth; Jāmi',* 45a;
   6. Manṣūr about 5 *aḥādīth; 'Ilal,* i, 362; Fasawī, iii, 213b;
   7. Qatādah, 1 or 2, sometimes even half; *Jāmi',* 45a: 46a;
   8. Shu'bah learnt only 100 *aḥādīth* from 'Amr b. Dīnār in 500 meetings; *Jāmi',* 37b;
   9. Ṣulaimān al-Taimī. He taught only 5 *aḥādīth* ; Bājī, 155a;
   10. al-Zuhrī. He advised students to learn 1 or 2 *aḥādīth* daily and said that those who learnt a lot forgot a lot. *Jāmi',* 45a.

B. *Reading from books.*

1. *Reading by the teacher, from his own book*[1], which was much more preferred.

2. *Reading by the teacher from the student's book,* which was either a copy[2] or a selection from his own work[3]. This method had a great many pitfalls for the teachers who did not memorize their *aḥādīth.* Many students and scholars played tricks, inserting *aḥādīth* here and there into the teacher's *aḥādīth* and handing the book to the teacher for reading, to examine the soundness of his knowledge and memory. Failing to recognise the additional material, they were denounced and were declared untrustworthy[4].

3. *Reading to the teacher.* Another method was that the book was read by the students[5] or by a certain man called

---

1. See for example:
'Abd Allāh b. al-Mubārak. *Tahd.*, v, 384; *Jāmi'*, 100a;
Ibn Ḥanbal. *Imlā*, 47;
Mālik b. Anas. He read al-Muwaṭṭa' to Yaḥyā. *Imlā*, 8-9;
Shu'aib b. Abū Ḥamzah, Zur'ah, 67a;
Zuhair b. Muḥammad, Rāzī, 1, ii, 590; Bājī, 59a.

2. See for the examples of the reading from students's books:
Abān b. A. 'Ayyāsh, see *supra;* 107;
'Abd al-'Azīz al-Darāwardī. Rāzī, ii, ii, 396; *Tahd.*, vi, 354;
'Aṭā' b. 'Ajlān, *Bagh.*, xii, 325;
'Abd al-A'lā al-Shāmī, Mu'tamar b. Sulaimān, Jarīr and 'Abd al-Wahhāb al-Thaqafī. *Kāmil*, i, 37b; *Bagh.*, xi, 19;
Ibn Juraij. *Kifāyah*, 258;
Rishdain b. Sa'd. *Tahd.*, iii, 279;
Suwaid b. 'Abd al-'Azīz. Rāzī, ii, i, 238.

3. 'Alī b. al-Madīnī and his selection. *Tahd.*, v, 174. Abū Zur'ah and his selection, Rāzī, *introduction*, 333.
Sulaimān b. Ḥarb and selection from Ḥammād b. Salamah. Fasawī, iii, 205b.

4. See for inserting materials, e.g.:
'Abd Allāh b. Ziyād b. Sam'ān. Rāzī, ii, ii, 61;
Abū 'Awānah's trick with Abān. See *supra* Abān, p. 107.
Shu'bah's trick with Abān b. 'Ayyāsh. *Jāmi'*, 18a;
Ḥarith al-Naqqal with Ibn Mahdī. *Jāmi'*, 18a;
B. Mis'ar and Ghiyāth with Ibn 'Ajlān. *Bagh.*, xii, 325;
Yaḥyā b. Ma'īn with Abū Nu'aim. *Jāmi'*, 18 a.

5. See e.g., reading of:
'Āṣim al-Aḥwal to al-Sha'bī. *'Ilal*, 153b; Rāmhurmazī, 44a; *Kifāyah*, 264;
Ibn al-Mubārak to Ma'mar. *'Ilal*, i, 377;
Ibn Mahdī to Mālik b. Anas, *'Ilal*, i, 354;

"*Qārī*"[1], and other students compared these *aḥādīth* with their books or only listened attentively. Later they copied the books.

It seems that this was the most common practice from the beginning of the second century. In this case copies were provided by the teachers themselves[2] as many of them had their own scribes, *Kātib* or *Warrāq*[3], or students had their own books, copied earlier from the original or from another copy of the same work[4].

Jarīr to Ayyūb. *Kāmil,* i, 208b;
Ma'mar to al-Zuhrī, Fasawī, iii, 264a.

1. Ḥabīb b. Ruzaiq, *Qārī* (reader) to Mālik b. Anas. *Majrūḥīn* 90b.

2. For copies provided by teachers, Ibn Ḥibbān says that when Ḥabīb used to read to Mālik, he caught the chapter in his own hand and, "did not give them its copies", then used to read some of them, omitting some *aḥādīth* here and there. *Majrūḥīn,* 90b. Therefore it seems that it was a common practice of the time to provide copies, otherwise he would not have made this remark against Ḥabīb. It looks as if they had spare copies of their works, see, e.g.:
Hishām b. 'Urwah, *Kifāyah,* 321;
Mūsā b. 'Uqbāh and spare copies, Fasawī, iii, 275b;
Yaḥyā b. Abū Kathīr handed a book to Mu'āwiyah b. Sallām to transmit it. *Tahd.,* x, 209, and another copy to al-Auzā'ī. Zur'ah, 150a; Rāmhurmuzī, 47b; *Kifāyah,* 321; Most probably these were not the original works, as it was hard to offer the original manuscript;
Makḥūl handed a book to 'Abd Allāh al-Kalā'ī. *Kifāyah,* 320.

3. For Scribe, Kātib or Warrāq, see e.g.:
'Abd al-Ḥamīd scribe of al-Auzā'ī. Fasawī, iii, 144b; *Mīzān,* ii, 539;
'Abd al-Ḥakīm al-Baṣrī of Ibn Abī 'Arūbah. *Mīzān,* ii, 537;
Abū Ṣāliḥ of al-Laith b. Sa'd, *Tahd.* xii, 131.
Ḥabīb b. Abū Ḥabīb of Mālik b. Anas. Rāzī, i, ii, 100; *Majrūḥīn,* 90b;
Ḥafṣ b. 'Abd Allāh of Ibrāhīm b. Ṭahmān. Rāzī, i, ii, 175;
al-Ḥakam b. Nāfi', of Ismā'īl b. 'Ayyāsh, *Mīzān,* i, 582;
al-Naḍr b. 'Abd al-Jabbār of Ibn Lahī'ah. Fasawī, ii, 136b;
Ṣadaqah b. Khālid of Shu'aib b. Isḥāq. *Tahd.* iv, 415;
Shu'aib b. A. Ḥamzah of al-Zuhrī, *Tahd.* iv, 352.
Ṣubaiḥ, client of Ibn Rabāḥ, scribe of Ibn 'Umar, *Thiqāt,* 225;
Warrāq of Ibn Waki'. Rāzī, ii, i, 231;
Warrāq of al-Ḥumaidī. Dāraquṭnī, 302, (name of warrāq is Muḥd. b. Idrīs).

4. See for examples of having books before reading to teachers:
'Abd al-Raḥmān b. Abū Ḥātim al-Rāzī and al-Raqqī's *aḥādīth.* Rāzī, ii, ii, 176;
Abū Dāwūd and *aḥādīth* of Shaibān. A.D. Tradition No. 4564;
Abū 'Awānah and *aḥādīth* of Abān. Rāzī, i, i, 295;
Abū Zur'ah and *aḥādīth* of Yaḥyā b. Ḥamzah. Rāzī, *introd.* 343;

Sometimes they read the same book more than once[1].

C. *Questions and answers.* In this way students read a part of the tradition and the teacher read it in full[2].

'Ayyūb and *aḥādīth* of 'Amr. *'Ilal,* i, 20;
'Ayyūb and *aḥādīth* of Yaḥyā al-Anṣārī, *'Ilal,* i, 20;
Ḥumaid al-A'raj and al-Zuhrī. Khaithamah, iii, 37a;
Ibrāhīm b. Sa'd and *aḥādīth* for al-Faḍl. Rāzī, i, i, 70;
Ibn Abū Khaithamah and book of Ḥabīb b. Abū Ḥabīb. Rāzī, i, ii, 99;
Ibn Ḥanbal and *aḥādīth* of 'Abd al-Ṣamad, Ḥanbal, ii, 184;
Ibn Ḥanbal and Yaḥyā al-Qaṭṭān. *'Ilal,* 112b; i, 183;
Ibn Ḥanbal and Wakī'. *Mīzān,* i, 515;
Ibn Ḥanbal and Ghundar. *'Ilal,* 147a;
Ibn Ḥanbal and Mu'ādh b. Hishām. *Kifāyah,* 272;
Ibn Juraij and Hishām b. 'Urwah. Fasawī, ii, 263b; *Kifāyah,* 320;
Ibn Lahī'ah and his students. Fasawī, iii, 136b;
Jarīr and Qatādah. Fasawī, iii, 24a;
Kkālid b. 'Abd Allāh and *aḥādīth* of al-A'mash. BTK, i, i, 74;
Mūsā b. Ismā'il and *aḥādīth* of Abān al-'Aṭṭār. Fasawī, ii, 281b;
Mūsā b. 'Uqbah and *aḥādīth* of Nāfi'. *Kifāyah,* 267;
Mālik b. Anas and al-Zuhrī. Fasawī, iii, 308a-b; *Imlā.* 94;
Qurrād, Abū Nūḥ and Shu'bah. *'Ilal,* i, 64;
al-Laith b. Sa'd and al-Zuhrī's *aḥādīth.* Fasawī, iii, 139a;
Sulaimān b. Ḥarb and Ḥammād b. Salamah. Fasawī, iii, 205b;
Yaḥyā b. Ma'īn and *aḥādīth* of 'Ubaid Allāh. *Kifāyah,* 235;
Zā'idah b. Qudāmah and his books. *Majrūḥīn,* 9b;
Zuhair b. Mu'āwiyah and his books. Ja'd, 351; *Jāmi',* 56b; *Imlā,* 9.

1. See for examples:
Ghundar and his books from Shu'bah. *Jāmi',* 56b;
Ibn Ḥanbal and his books with dots and circles. *Jāmi',* 56b. Every dot or circle denoted the times of the reading of the books. *Jāmi',* 56b;
Ibrāhīm al-Ḥarbī and al-Tabarī's books. *Jāmi',* 56b;
Yaḥyā b. Ma'īn and books of Ḥammād b. Salamah. They were read 17 times at least. *Majrūḥīn,* 10a;
Zā'idah b. Qudāmah and description of his books. *Majrūḥīn,* 9b;
Zuhair b. Mu'āwiyah and description of his books. Ja'd, 351, *Imlā,* 9.

2. See e.g.:
Ḥammād and Ibrāhīm. Fasawī, iii, 83a;
Ibn Sīrīn and 'Abīdah. *'Ilal,* i, 387;
Ismā'īl b. 'Ayyāsh and Ismā'īl b. Abū Khālid. *Tahd.,* i, 324;
Mālik and al-Zuhrī. *'Ilal,* 154a.

D. *Dictating the aḥādīth.* Apart from the Prophet's dictations[1] and his early Companions' infrequent dictations of *aḥādīth*[2], perhaps Wāthilah b. Asqa' (d. 83) was the first who held classes for dictation[3]. This method was not encouraged in the early days, because in this way a man was able to gather much knowledge in a very short time without much effort. It seems that al-Zuhrī was the first to depart from this attitude. About the end of the first century we find him dictating *aḥādīth,* a method which he followed during the rest of his life[4].

There were certain extremists who disliked dictating or did not allow writing down[5], and there were others who did not transmit *aḥādīth* until the students wrote them down[6]. Some of them even refused to dictate *aḥādīth* if the students used wooden boards for writing, because they could erase it[7]. There were some others who wrote down *aḥādīth* and after memorizing, wiped them out[8]. Others used to learn by heart and after memorizing wrote them down[9]. It seems, after comparing with the other methods of the teaching of *aḥādīth*, that these were rare and uncommon practices. From the second century onwards, besides the usual method of

1. Rāmhurmuzī, 76a; *Imlā*, 12; see also *al-Wathā'iq al-Siyāsiyah* by Ḥamīdullāh.
2. *Nubalā*, ii, 333; Rāmhurmuzī, 35a; *Kāmil*, ii, 113b.
3. *Imlā*, 13; *Jāmi'*, 113b; *Mīzān*, iv, 145.
4. Rāmhurmuzi, 39b; Fischer, 69; Ibn Kathīr, *Bidāyah*, ix, 342; 345.
5. See Sulaimān b. Ṭarkhān, Bājī, 155a.
6. Muḥammad b. 'Amr, *Jāmi'*, 102a.
7. Abū Jamīlah, *Jāmi'*, 102a.
8. See for examples:
   Khālid al-Hadhdhā'. Ja'd, 149; *Mīzān*, i, 643;
   Ayyūb. Fasawī, iii, 67a;
   Masrūq. Khaithamah, iii, 183b; *'Ilal*, i, 43.
9. See for examples:
   A'mash. Rāmhurmuzī, 37a; *Taqyīd*, 112; see also, *'Ilal*, i, 104; 360
   'Abd Allāh b. Idrīs. Rāmhurmuzī, 37a; 77a-b; see also *'Ilal*, 177b;
   'Abd al-Wārith. Fasawī, iii, 37b;
   Ḥammād b. Salamah. He wrote down Qais' book from memory. Fasawī, iii, 44a;
   Hushaim. *'Ilal*, i, 353; Rāmhurmuzī, 37a;
   Khālid, Mu'ādh and Qaṭṭān and Shu'bah's traditions. Rāzī, i, ii, 325;
   Sulaimān b. Ḥarb. *Kifāyah*, 241;
   Wakī' and al-Thaurī's traditions. Fasawī, ii, 23a;
   Yaḥyā al-Qaṭṭān. Rāmhurmuzī, 77a;
   al-Thaurī and 'Umar b. Dhar's traditions. Ja'd, 233-4.

reading books, the custom of dictations was most usual[1]. Regular classes were held for this purpose[2].

The method of dictation.

For dictations, two methods were employed; either from a book[3],

---

1. See as examples of dictating:
'Abdah b. Sulaimān al-Kilābī and his dictation. *'Ilal,* i, 239;
'Abbād b. 'Abbād and his dictation. *'Ilal,* i, 376;
Abū Bakr b. 'Ayyāsh. *Kifāyah,* 340.;
Abū Bakr b. Abū Sabrah. Dūlābī, i, 121;
'Affān says, "We did not agree from anyone without dictation save Sharīk". Ramhurmuzi 67a.
Al-Hasan al-Baṣrī, Rāmhurmuzī, 76b;
Ḥammād b. Salamah, Ja'd, 442;
Hishām b. Ḥassān al-Qurdūsī. *Majrūḥīn,* 115b;
Hushaim. *'Ilal,* 141b; i, 366;
Ibn Juraij. *'Ilal,* i, 370;
'Ikrimah b. 'Ammār. Khaithamah, iii, 49b; Rāzī, *Introd.* 117; Rāmhurmuzī, 76b; *Bagh.,* xii, 258; *Imlā,* 14-15;
Ismā'īl b. 'Ayyāsh. *Mīzān,* i, 244;
Juwairiyah b. Asmā', Sa'd, vii, ii, 38-39;
al-Mas'ūdī. *Bagh.,* x, 219;
Muḥammad b. Isḥāq. *Bagh.,* viii, 477; *Tahd.,* iii, 376;
Nāfi', Fasawī, iii, 220b; Rāmhurmuzī, 76a; *Imlā,* 13; see also, Rāzī, ii, ii, 357;
Shahr b. Ḥaushab. *Bagh.,* xi, 59;
Ṭa'ūs, *'Ilal,* i, 63;
Wāthilah b. Asqa'. *Imlā,* 13; *Mīzān,* iv, 145;
al-Zuhrī, see *supra,* p. 164.
2. See for example:
Shu'bah and his dictation. *Jāmi',* 113b.
Yazīd b. Ḥassān. *Jāmi',* 113b.
3. See for examples of dictation from a book:
'Abd Allāh b. Idrīs. Ḥanbal, i, 418;
'Abd al-Wārith. *'Ilal,* i, 144;
Abū 'Awānah. Sa'd, vii, ii, 43;
Abū 'Āṣim. *Jāmi',* 100a;
Ghālib b. 'Ubaid Allāh. MU, *Introd.* 18;
Ḥajjāj b. Muḥammad. Rāzī, ii, i, 326;
Hammām b. Yaḥyā. *Jāmi',* 113b;
Ibn Abī 'Adī. Dāraquṭnī, 76;
Ibn Lahī'ah. Fasawī, iii, 136b;
Mālik b. Ismā'īl. Rāzī, iv, i, 206;
Rauḥ b. 'Ubādah. Ḥanbal, iv, 390;
'Uthmān b. al-Aswad. *Jāmi',* 100a;
Zakariyā b. A. Zā'idah. *'Ilal,* 153a.

or from memory[1]. In some cases the students refused to write *aḥādīth* while being dictated from memory[2], yet it seems that it was the fashion of the time to rely on memory in transmitting or dictating *aḥādīth*[3]. Perhaps it was a matter of prestige and reputation. This practice resulted in many mistakes owing to the inherent deficiencies of memory[4]. They had to go through their books to refresh their memories, and in many cases when they were uncertain they did not dictate[5].

The Mustamlīs.

The dictation method, due to large audiences, gave rise to a new type of work for certain people who were called *Mustamlīs*. They used to repeat the words of the *Shaikh* in a loud voice to the audience[6].

---

1. See for examples of dictating from memory:
Abū Mu'āwiyah. *Bagh.*, v, 245;
Baqiyah. Rāzī, *Introd.* 271;
Ḥafṣ b. Ghiyāth. *Bagh.*, viii, 195;
al-Ḥasan b. Mūsā. *Tārīkh Mauṣil*, 361;
Ibn Juraij. *Bagh.*, viii, 237;
Isrā'īl. *Tahd.*, i, 262;
Ṭalḥah b. 'Amr. *Kāmil*, ii, 107b; *Mīzān*, ii, 341;
Wuhaib b. Khālid. *Ḥuffāẓ*, i, 213;
Zakariyā b. 'Adī, *Tahd.*, iii, 331.
2. e.g., Yaḥyā b. Ma'īn. *'Ilal*, 122a; 124a.
3. See for examples:
Ayyūb b. 'Uthbah. Rāzī, i, i, 253; *Tahd.*, i, 409;
Ḥajjāj, *'Ilal*, i, 103; *Jāmi'*, 109a;
Hammām b. Yaḥyā, *Kifāyah*, 23;
al-Mu'mil. Qaisarānī, 216;
Sufyān al-Thaurī. *Kifāyah*, 164.
4. Yaḥyā b. Sa'īd. Rāmhurmuzī, 37b;
Hammām. *Kifāyah*, 223;
Al-Mu'mil. Qaisarānī, 216;
Ayyūb b. 'Utbah. Rāzī, i, i, 253; *Tahd.*, i, 409.
5. See for examples:
Ibn al-Mahdī and Sufyān al-Thaurī. *Jāmi'*, 101b.
6. See for examples:
'Abd al-Wahhāb b. 'Aṭā' of Ibn Abū 'Arūbah. *Jāmi'*, 117b; *Bagh.*, xi, 22; *Imlā*, 86;
Ādam b. Abū Iyās of Shu'bah. *Jāmi'*, 117b; *Bagh.*, vii, 28;
'Alī b. Āṣim. He had 3 Mustamlīs. *Bagh.*, xi, 454;
Barbakh, of Yazīd b. Hārūn. *Jāmi'*, 117b; *Imlā*, 90;
al-Jammāz of Khālid b. al-Ḥārith. *Jāmi'*, 117b; *Imlā*, 90;
Ismā'īl b. 'Ulayyah of Mālik. *Jāmi'*, 117b; *Imlā*, 89;
Sibwaih of Ḥammād b. Salamah. *Jāmi'*, 118a; *Imlā*, 105.

Selection of a Writer.

As all the students could not write rapidly, sometimes a fast writer was chosen to take down *aḥādīth*[1], while others watched him writing, lest he should make any mistake[2]. Later, either they borrowed the books or copied them in the presence of the owner[3]. In the literary circle a class of scribes or *Warrāqūn* was found for the purpose of copying, which gave rise to the trade in books[4].

---

1. See examples of selection of a fast scribe:
   Ādam b. Abū Iyās. *Tahd.*, i, 196;
   al-Anṣārī. *Kifāyah*, 235;
   Hishām b. Yūsuf. *'Ilal*, i, 371; *Kifāyah*, 238-9;
   Shu'bah. *Kāmil*, ii, 107b; *Mīzān*, ii, 341;
   Sufyān al-Thaurī. *Jāmi'*, 142a;
   Yaḥyā al-Qaṭṭān. Rāzī, ii, ii, 69.
2. For the watching the writing of the scribe, see:
   'Abd al-Razzāq and Hishām b. Yūsuf. *Kifāyah*, 239;
   Ma'mar, Ibn Juraij, al-Thaurī and their watching of Shu'bah's writing. *Kāmil*, ii, 107b; *Imlā*, 14; *Mīzān*, ii, 341;
   Yazīd b. Ismā'īl and his colleagues. *Majrūḥīn*, 115b.
3. See for borrowing, e.g.:
   Abū 'Awānah from 'Alī b. 'Āṣim. *Kāmil*, i, 270b;
   Ḥafṣ b. Sulaimān from Shu'bah. Sa'd, vii, ii, 21; Rāzī, i, ii, 173;
   Ḥammād b. Salamah from Ḥajjāj. Fasawī, iii, 274 a-b;
   Ḥumaid al-Ṭawīl from Ḥasan al-Baṣrī, *'Ilal*, 1, 15; *Kifāyah*, 236;
   Laith from Ibn al-Ḥasan; Ja'd, 64; *'Ilal*, 143a;
   Rauḥ from 'Abd al-Wahhāb. *'Ilal*, i, 109;
   al-Sakan from Ibrāhīm al-Ṣā'igh. *Imlā*, 178;
   'Uthmān b. 'Umar from Rauḥ. *Bagh.*, viii, 405;
   Anonymous from al-Anṣārī. *Kifāyah*, 235;
   Al-Zuhrī encouraged the lending of the book. *Imlā*, 176.
   – See for those who did not lend books:
   Abū Qaṭṭan. Dūlābī, ii, 87; *Bagh.*, xii, 199; *Tahd.*, viii, 114;
   Hammām and Ibn Abū 'Arūbah. Sa'd, vii, ii, 33;
   Muḥammad al-Sukkarī. He had the advice of al-Thaurīnot to lend. Ja'd, 240;
   Abū Uṣāmah. *Tahd.*, iii, 3.
   – For those who asked mortgage for lending, see, e.g.:
   Ibrāhīm b. Maimūn al-Ṣā'igh. *Imlā*, 178;
   Yaḥyā b. Sulaim. *'Ilal*, 105b; *Mīzān*, iv, 384. See also *Tahd.*, xi, 226.
4. For bookselling and buying see:
   Anonymous Shaikh, see Ḥajjāj b. Muḥammad. *Majrūḥīn*, 24a;
   Abū al-Yamān sold his books. *Bagh.*, vi, 224;
   Aḥmad b. 'Isā and books of Ibn Wahb. Rāzī, i, i, 64;
   Ibrāhīm b. Abū al-Laith. *Bagh.*, vi, 194;
   Mu'āwiyah b. Yaḥyā. *Mīzān*, iv, 138; *Tahd.*, x, 220;
   Yaḥyā b. Aktham, *Tahd.*, xi, 180.

It is mentioned that Hammām b. Munabbih used to buy books for his brother Wahb[1], but, perhaps, these books were non-Arabic.

The employment of scribes for writing aḥādīth.

The early record of employment of people to write down or to sell a book on *aḥādīth*, goes back to the later days of the Umayyad dynasty[2].

The correction of written copies.

It seems that the scholars were aware of the importance of revision after copying[3].

After copying or dictating, the copies were corrected either by the students with each other's[4] or under the supervision of their masters[5].

---

1. *Tahd.*, xi, 67.
2. For copying of the traditions see:
   Abū Zakariyā. *Bagh.*, viii, 302;
   'Abdur Razzāq b. Hammām al-Ṣan'ānī. Khaithamah, iii, 574a;
   'Alī b. 'Āṣim. *Bagh.*, xi, 448; *Tahd.*, vii, 345;
   Abū Mu'āwiyah, the blind, Rāzī, iii, ii, 247;
   'Aṭā' b. Yazīd. He had a slave to carry the books, ink, etc. of his son to the Shuyūkh. *Wāsiṭ*, 135; Bājī, 171b.
   There were scribes of the *Qur'ān* even in the time of 'Alī. See Dūlābī, i, 155-6;
3. See for examples:
   Akhfash and his sayings. *Kifāyah*, 237-8;
   'Urwah and his sayings; *'Ilal*, 102b. *Wāsiṭ*, 168; Rāmhurmuzī, 64b; *Kifāyah* 237; *Imlā*, 79;
   Yaḥyā b. Abū Kathīr and his sayings. Rāmhurmuzī, 64b; *Kifāyah*, 237; *Imlā*, 79.
4. See for examples:
   Ḥammād and his fellows. *Kifāyah*, 71;
   Ibn 'Uyaynah and his fellows in al-Zuhrī's dictation. Rāmhurmuzī, 8a;
   Jarīr and his fellow. Fasawī, iii, 264b; Rāzī, i, i, 506.
5. See for examples:
   Ayyūb. *'Ilal* i, 24; Fasawī, iii, 69b; *Kifāyah*, 240;
   'Azrah correcting in the presence of Ibn Jubair (d. 95); Khaithamah, iii, 178b;
   Mālik b. Anas. *Jāmi'* of Ibn Wahb. *Introduction*, by D. Weill, p. xv.
   Ḥajjāj b. Muḥammad. *'Ilal*, i, 381;
   Nāfi' asked his students to bring the books for correction; *Jāmi'*, 138b; *Imlā*, 78;

The writing materials.

Wooden boards seem to have been used mostly for writing dictations and taking notes, and fair copies were made later[1]. Sometimes abridged words were used to save time and space[2].

Students: their ages.

First, they learned the *Qur'ān,* mostly by heart. Many scholars used to examine new students in the *Qur'ān*[3]. They also learned some other subjects such as Islamic Law, religious practices, grammar, etc. Usually they joined *Muḥaddithīn's* circles around the age of twenty[4].

Shu'bah and Ghundar. Fasawī, iii, 85b; *Tahd.*, ix, 97;
Sufyān al-Thaurī corrected books of Zā'idah. Ja'd, 246; Rāzī, *Introduction,* 80. He asked Yaḥyā al-Qaṭṭān to bring his books for correction but Yaḥyā disagreed, Ja'd, 245; Rāzī, *Introduction,* 80;
'Urwah. *Imlā,* 78;
al-Qāsim b. Muḥammad (d. 105) asked his son to watch Ṭalḥah who was writing al-Qāsim's traditions. Ṭalḥah said that if he wanted to lie, he would not have come there. Al-Qāsim said that he had not implied thus, but to help him if he omitted by mistake. Rāmhurmuzī, 63b.

1. For writing on wooden boards and other materials and making fair copies later on, see:
'Abd al-Ṣamad and his book from Ayyūb. Fasāwī, iii, 37b;
Abū al-Walīd al-Ṭayālisī's book of Shu'bah, *Jāmi',* 53a;
Aḥmad b. Ṣāliḥ and his method of making fair copies, Fasawī, iii, 136b;
Ibn Juraij and his method. *Jāmi',* 188a;
Sa'īd b. Jubair and his copying. Rāmhurmuzī, 77b; *Taqyīd,* 103;
Sulaimān b. 'Abd al-Raḥmān and his errors due to his fair copy making. Fasawī, iii, 127b; Ibn Ḥajar, *Hady al-Sārī,* ii, 171;
Ḥasan al-Baṣrī says, "One who joins the learning circle without a wooden board is like the one who joins battle without a weapon". *Jāmi',* 155a.
2. Abū al-Walīd al-Ṭayālisī and his method of abridgment, *Jāmi',* 53a.
3. See for examining new students in the *Qur'ān* who wanted to join traditionists' circles:
A'mash examines, Rāmhurmuzī, 9a; see also, *Jāmi',* 105 a-b;
'Aṭā' b. Abū Rabāḥ, *Bagh.*, x, 401-2;
Auzā'ī examines. *Jāmi',* 9b;
Ibn al-Mubārak examines. Rāmhurmuzī, 9b;
Yaḥyā b. al-Yamān examines. *Jāmi',* 9b;
al-Zuhrī examines Ibn 'Uyaynah. *Ḥuffāz,* I, 99.
4. Students in the time of the Successors were about twenty years of age

Education in *aḥādīth* was free. Only a few scholars charged some money but they were denounced for this practice.

The students' relations with their teachers were based on reverence and respect. Some of them used to help or serve their tutors[1], but there were tutors who did not accept any kind of service, lest it might be taken as service in return for teaching[2].

In many cases the teachers helped their students financially[3], and it was quite common to offer meals to them[4]. An odd phenomenon of the education in *ḥadīth* was the continuous traveling of students and scholars to collect *aḥādīth*. Perhaps journeying was an essential part of studentship. Al-Khaṭīb al-Baghdādī wrote

---

when they started learning traditions; Rāmhurmuzī, 6a.

Zuhrī said about Ibn 'Uyaynah that he was the youngest student he had ever seen, and was fifteen years old. Rāmhurmuzī, 6a;

Mūsā b. Isḥāq says the Kufans sent their sons to learn traditions when they were twenty. Rāmhurmuzī, 6a;

al-Thaurī and Abū al-Aḥwaṣ, give 20 years to begin tradition study. Rāmhurmuzī, 6b;

The Syrians began to write at 30. *Kifāyah,* 55;

The Basrites began to learn when they were only 10; *Kifāyah,* 55;

Ibn Ḥanbal started when he was only 16. *'Ilal,* 141b. However in later periods it was not observed. Al-Dabarī transmitted 'Abd al-Razzāq's book, and when 'Abd al-Razzāq died he was not more than 7 years old (*Kifāyah,* 64). It was said that if a child could discriminate between a cow and a donkey he could start learning traditions (*Kifāyah,* 65). It was at the time when the texts were fixed, and learning meant transmission of a book through *Isnād 'Alī.* On the other hand, especially in the second century, many scholars were weakened in their traditions from certain teachers on the grounds of their youth at the time when they wrote down from them; e.g. 'Amr al-Bairūtī is weak in the traditions of al-Auzā'ī as he was young when he wrote down from him (Rāzī, iii, i, 268; *Mīzān,* iii, 290). See for similar charges against Ibn al-Madīnī in *Mīzān,* iii, 82.; against Ibn Abū Shaibah, *Mīzān,* iii, 82; and against Hishām b. Ḥassān, *Kifāyah,* 54.

1. For serving a teacher, al-Zuhrī, *infra,* chapter viii.
2. For refusing any service, Ibn Idrīs, *Jāmi',* 85b.
3. For offering money; al-Zuhrī, *Islām,* v, 137.
   Ḥasan b. 'Amārah, *Mīzān,* i, 514; Abū Ḥanīfah, offered money to Abū Yūsuf.
4. For offering meals, e.g.:
   A'mash, *Bagh.,* ix, 11;
   'Alī b. Ja'd, *Bagh.,* xi, 361;
   Anas b. Mālik, Ḥanbal, iii, 250;
   Ismā'īl b. 'Ayyāsh, *Ḥuffāẓ,* i, 230;
   al-Zuhrī, *infra,* chapter viii.

a book on this subject, and the biographies of *Muḥaddithīn* are full of the stories of their journeys, but this subject is not a part of the present study.

The Number of Students.

There are references to hundreds of teachers from whom al-Thaurī, Ibn al-Mubārak, al-Zuhrī, etc. had written down *aḥādīth.* In the works of biographers we find a long list of teachers and students of eminent scholars. As an example, let us take only one scholar, al-Zuhrī. We do not know precisely how many students wrote from him, and how many attended his lectures. However, we have at least fifty references to his students who made their written collections from him[1]. The growing number of transmitters resulted in the tremendous growth of *aḥādīth.* The books grew so voluminous that it was difficult to handle them.

Therefore, to avoid chaos and discrepancies, Shu'bah advised writing the famous *aḥādīth* through a reference to the famous scholars[2]. Nevertheless, the numbers of a few thousand *aḥādīth* reached about three quarters of a million in the mid third century.

Many modern scholars — being unaware of the nature of this material — were perplexed by their immense number, and thus reached very strange conclusions. In Appendix No. II, there is a detailed discussion to clarify this issue.

School buildings.

From the very days of the Prophet, mosques were used as schools[3], a practice which still persists in the Muslim world. There are references occasionally to *Kuttāb* or *Maktab*, or to the houses which were used as schools[4], yet it does not seem that separate buildings were built for this purpose in the early days.

The classes were usually held in mosques, sometimes in teacher's houses and sometimes, if the numbers of the audiences were very great, in a public place[5].

---

1. *Supra,* al-Zuhrī, in the third chapter, pp. 89-93.
2. *Imlā,* 58.
3. See *supra* p. 4; also Ernest Diez, art., *Masjid.* The Mosque as an Educational Centre, *E.I.,* iii, i, 352.
4. For the early reference to the *Kuttāb* see: *'Ilm,* 7a; Sa'd, iv, i, 59;— Ḥanbal, i, 389; Ibn Ḥabīb, *al-Muḥabbar,* 477; Khaithamah, iii, 98b; *Thiqāt,* 296-7; Rāmhurmuzī, 7b; al-Qaisarānī, 27; *Tahd.,* vii, 276; viii, 337.
5. See for lectures in open places: Isma'īl b. 'Ayyāsh, *Bagh.,* vi, 222.

CHAPTER V

THE BOOK

Material for Writing.

At first the *Qur'ān* was recorded on scraps of parchment, leather, tablets of stone, ribs of palm branches, camel ribs and shoulder-blades and pieces of wooden board[1]. *Qirṭās,* papyrus, was known to Arabs even before Islam. The word *Qirṭās* is used in the *Qur'ān*[2] and even in pre-Islamic poetry[3]. It is not clear whether or not this material was utilized in the very early days for the recording of the *Qur'ān* or *ḥadīth.* There are, however, references to papyri which came into use after the conquest of Egypt. As early as 35 A.H., there is a reference to *Bait al-Qirṭās* as an annexe to the house of Caliph 'Uthmān[4].

Leather and papyrus were usually used in the early days and gradually paper replaced them to a large extent. Whether or not paper was known to the Arabs in the early days of Islam is disputable. According to the Encyclopaedia Brittanica, paper was introduced for the first time into the Islamic world after the conquest of Samarqand through Chinese slaves[5]. Ibn al-Nadīm, however, mentions that he himself saw a book written on Khurāsānī paper belonging to a very early period of Islam[6]. Yet he is not sure and gives a contradictory statement later in his book[7]. According to Shaikh 'Ināyatullah, "The Chinese paper was imported by the Arab traders engaged in maritime trade with the Far East; but

1. Arberry, *The Qur'ān Interpreted, introd.,* ix.
2. *The Qur'ān,* vi, 7; 91.
3. Nāṣir al-Asad, *Maṣādir al-Shi'r al-Jāhilī,* 91-92.
4. Baladhurī, *Ansāb,* i, 22.
5. *Encyclopaedia Brittanica,* art. paper, vol. xvii, 229.
6. *Fihrist,* 61, as cited by Nāṣir al-Asad, *op. cit.,* 89.
7. *Fihrist,* 21.

the introduction of the art of paper-making itself into the Muslim world is due to an accident of war''[1]. Unfortunately he does not give any reference in support of his statement. However, at the end of the second century, paper was used even in Egypt, the homeland of papyrus, for writing purposes[2].

It looks as if loose sheets of papyrus were used for writing in early days. The Companion Shamghūn is reported to be the first who wrote on both sides of papyrus, and pressed them and sewed them together[3]. It does not mean that the practice of loose sheets came to an end. There are many references, even in later periods, where unsewn sheets are mentioned[4].

As for the shape of the book, we find, besides the words *Kitāb* and *Ṣuḥuf,* the words *Daftar*[5], *Kurrāsah*[6] and *Dīwān*[7]. Words like *Daftar, Dīwān, Kurrāsah, Ṣaḥīfah, Kitāb,* express, perhaps, the flat shape of the written material something like a book in its form, while words like *Ṭūmār*[8] and *Darj*[9], which are also found in references, express the form of scrolls.

Qalqashandī says that *Darj* المراد بالدرج في العرف العام الورق المستطيل in the general usage المركب من عدة اوصال ... عشرين وصلا متلاصقة لاغير . means a rectangular paper consisting of joined pieces[10]. In his own time it contained twenty pieces of paper stuck together. Therefore, most probably, it was kept in the form of a scroll.

The Method of Writing on Paper.

In early days, the scholars had every teacher's *aḥādīth* in separate books or sheets or whatever it might be. In this case they

1. Sh. Inayatullāh, *Bibliophilism in Mediaeval Islam, I.C.,* 1938, p. 158.
2. For example see *Risālah* of al-Shāfa'ī. Introduction by Aḥmad Shākir, pp. 17-22.
3. *Iṣābah,* No. 3921.
4. See e.g., the book of Ya'qūb al-Qummī and Ibn Ḥanbal, Rāzī, iii, ii, 232; *Tahd.,* ix, 129.
5. *Daftar:* of Hishām b. 'Urwah. Fasawī, iii, 263, *Kifāyah,* 321; of Makḥūl, *Kifāyah,* 320.
6. Kurrāsah of Hishām b. Ḥassān, Fasawī, iii, 274b; see also, *Tahd.,* v, 174; *'Ilal,* i, 44.
7. e.g., *Tawsaṭ,* i, 4b, in the *Dīwān* of Zuhrī, in his own handwriting.
8. *'Ilal,* i, 340.
9. Rāzī, i, ii, 364, ii, ii, 87.
10. Qalqashandī, *Subḥ al-A'shā,* i, 138.

used to note some information about the narrator. Once Abū Zur'ah said that the books of Ibn Ḥanbal did not contain information about the scholars from whom he had heard on the first pages, while Abū Zur'ah himself, could not manage without such information[1].

It seems that the complete *isnād* was introduced only in the very beginning of the book. In the following part of the book every *ḥadīth* was written with only higher part of *isnād,* or the *isnāds* were eliminated altogether leaving only the material. By this method they economized time, space and labour. There is, however, an example of quite a different type. Muḥammad b. Kathīr al-Miṣṣīṣī had a book from al-Auza'i in which he wrote the complete *isnād* with every *ḥadīth*, even including his own name. Al-Dhahabī described this method as foolish[2]. The description of Ismā'īl b. Abū Khālid's books which was in the hands of Ibn Ḥanbal shows that they mostly used only the earlier authorities of the *isnāds* in the middle of the book[3]. This saved the scholars space and time, but it had some disadvantages. The full *isnād* was given on the top of the page or scroll, and every transmission of the book from one transmitter to another demanded an extra entry, not at the bottom but right on the top. As the papers or papyri were brittle, the upper portion easily wore out, so that students in many cases were unable to know whose *aḥādīth* those were. Likewise, one often finds references to the mixing of *aḥādīth,* e.g., Jarīr b. 'Abd al-Ḥamīd mixed up books of 'Āṣim and Ash'ath[4]. The same was the case in the books which were set in order by Ibn 'Uyaynah[5]. Abū Ṣāliḥ, the scribe of al-Laith, brought a *Darj* - tell from whom those *aḥādīth* were related. He was told that those were the *aḥādīth* of Ibn Abū Dhi'b[6]. An incident of this nature is also reported about Khālid al-'Abd where the name of the final authority was erased[7].

1. Rāzī, *introd.* 296.
2. *Mīzān,* iv, 19.
3. For a detailed description of this book, see *'Ilal,* i, 183; see for another example, *Madkhal,* 34.
4. *'Ilal,* i, 195.
5. *Tahd.,* i, 165.
6. Rāzī, ii, ii, 87.
7. Rāzī, i, ii, 364.

Al-Khaṭīb al-Baghdādī says that the scholars have many famous *Nusakh,* each of which contains a number of *aḥādīth.* The students could transmit a single *ḥadīth* from anywhere in the book giving a complete *isnād* as it was mentioned in the first *ḥadīth*[1]. Ibn Ma'in was asked whether or not it was allowed to write down the complete *isnād* with every *ḥadīth,* with reference to the *aḥādīth* of Warqā' from Ibn Abū Najīḥ from Mujāhid, where the complete *isnād* was given in the beginning of the book. Yaḥyā replied, "It is right"[2]. Wakī' was asked a similar question: a teacher said at the beginning of the book "Sufyān from Manṣūr," and later he only said "from Manṣūr"; now, is it right to say the complete *isnād* with each *ḥadīth.* He replied it was correct to do so[3].

Diacritical signs, dotting and other kinds of punctuation.

Some students were said to be perfect in the copying of books. Their books were quite clear, full of dots and other necessary notes of clarification[4], while some others were careless in dotting and other signs. Such imperfections in copying caused many mistakes (*Taṣḥīf*) in reading.

Once Ibn Ḥanbal was asked whether Abū al-Walīd was a perfect narrator. Ibn Ḥanbal replied, "No, his book had neither dots nor diacritical signs, but he was skilled in the *aḥādīth* of Shu'bah"[5].

This is a very important statement. It shows that in judging a man, at least sometimes, they used to notice his writing as well.

Other Signs.

To separate one *ḥadīth* from the other, they made a small circle instead of a full stop. This kind of inscription is found at the beginning of the second century, e.g., the book of Abū al-Zinād from al-A'raj[6]. In the book of Ibn Sīrīn we find a circle after every

1. *Kifāyah,* 214.
2. *Kifāyah,* 215.
3. *Kifāyah,* 215.
4. e.g., books of Abū 'Awānah, Fasawī, iii, 48a, Rāzī, iv, ii, 40, *Tahd.,* xi, 117.
5. *'Ilal,* i, 383. See also *Kifāyah,* 241.
6. Rāmhurmazī, 77b; *Jāmi',* 56b; *Imlā,* 173.

ten *aḥādīth*[1]. Students used to copy books before attending the lecture of their teachers[2]. Therefore, when a *ḥadīth* was read to them in class they put an "okay" mark on it. In many cases they listened to certain *aḥādīth* more than once, hence they put different signs and various numbers of dots to show the number of times the traditions were read[3]. Khālid b. 'Abd Allāh al-Ṭaḥḥān wrote *aḥādīth* and could not read them to the authority. Later, when his son began to impart them he was told, "Even your father did not hear these *aḥādīth*"[4].

Theft of Material.

Since in those days there was no system of copyright, material from any book could be utilized in composing a book or imparting *aḥādīth*, but it was against the literary custom of the period.

Every student, before utilizing any verbal or written material, had to obtain it through proper channel - *isnād* - otherwise it was thought to be forgery or theft of material. There are many references to men said to be *Sāriq al-Ḥadīth*[5].

Adding External Material in the Body of a Book.

Most of the people who listened to *aḥādīth* and copied them out had their own books. Students felt at liberty to include additional material even in a fixed text to clarify some obscure word, or their own opinion or some such thing. As any additional material would have a completely different *isnād* or the name of the inserter, there was no danger of spoiling the text. In Appendix IV of this book there appears a very explicit and clear example of this sort[6], wherein the copyist added two lines even before completing the sentences. There is another example of Abū Sa'īd, the transmitter of the book *Al-Muḥabbar,* where he adds two lines[7].

1. Fasawī, iii, 14b; *Imlā,* 173; *Jāmi',* 56b.
2. *Supra,* p. 190.
3. See *supra,* p. 191.
4. *Kifāyah,* 148.
5. See for example:
Muḥammad b. Jābir b. Sayyār, *Majrūḥīn,* 203b;
Muḥammad b. Yazīd, Rāzī, iv, i, 129;
Sufyān b. Wakī', Rāzī, ii, i, 231-2.
6. Appendix No. iv.
7. Ibn Ḥabīb, *Muḥabbar,* 122.

There is clear evidence of this nature in *Ṣaḥīḥ* of al-Bukhārī, where al-Firabrī adds extraneous material, giving his *isnād*[1].

Books and the Problems of Authorship.

The problem of the authorship of works compiled in the early days is common to all literature. This phenomenon is found in Jewish and Christian literatures as well[2]. But Islamic literature gives a definite ascription to all the documents, in contrast with many other scriptures, where it is difficult to find the reference to the source[3].

Muslim writers, as a matter of preference and style, referred to the author, rather than to the works[4], a practice which persisted for centuries. A close examination of *Muwaṭṭa'* of Mālik b. Anas and his material incorporated in later books reveals this method. The method was not confined to *ḥadīth* literature; it was applied even to history and other Arabic literatures in general. In short, all literature used the same pattern of Muḥaddithīn in transmitting knowledge. For example, we take one statement from *Ṭabaqāṭ* Khalīfah b. Khayyāṭ (240) from which al-Khaṭīb al-Baghdādī frequently quotes[5]. We find him quoting from the book, and referring to the author, giving full *isnād* going back to Khalīfah, but not mentioning the name of the work. We can trace this system in the entire product of Muslim literature. In the early days, it appears that if they utilized some material without receiving it through proper *isnād,* they referred to the book without giving the *isnād*[6].

In many cases even when they referred to a title, they were not so precise in giving the authorship. For instance *Maghāzī* of Ibn

1. BU, i, 407; ii, 107. For other examples see A.D. Tr. No. 2386; MU, *Ṣalāt,* 63, p. 304.
2. See for example: Hoskyns, *The Riddle of the New Testament,* p. 183. Aland Kurt, *The Problem of anonymity and Pseudonymity in Christian Literature of the First Two Centuries,* p. 5. Russell, D. S. *The Method and Message of Jewish Apocalyptic,* pp. 127-139.
3. Robson, *Ibn Isḥāq's use of isnād, Bulletin of the John Ryl. Lib.,* Vol. 38, No. 2, p. 465.
4. Sprenger, *J.A.S.B.* 1850, p. 109; it seems that it was the trend of early Christian literature as well; see B. Gerhardsson, *Memory and Manuscript,* p. 198.
5. *Bagh.,* x, 401. Compare with Ṭabaqāt Khalīfah, Folio 19.
6. Al-Azdī, *Tārīkh al-Mauṣil,* 174; 177; Khaithamah, iii, 147a.

Isḥāq is a well-known work. The book was transmitted by a number of transmitters. One of the transmitters was Salamah b. al-Faḍl al-Abrash. In many cases the work was attributed to him, as he was the transmitter of the work. Yaḥyā b. Ma'īn says, "There is a man in Baghdād called Ibrāhīm b. Mus'ab who transmits *Kitāb* of Salamah from Ibn Isḥāq"[1]. يحدث بكتاب سلمة عن محمد بن اسحاق The same scholar Yaḥyā in another statement describes Salamah b. al-Faḍl as a trustworthy man. Yaḥyā himself had written on his authority, and his books on the Maghāzī were most complete and there was no book more complete than his[2].

It would be useful to add one more statement in this connection, as it concerns the same man, Ibrāhīm b. Muṣ'ab. It reads thus "Ibrāhīm b. Muṣ'ab transmitted the book of Ibn Isḥāq from Salamah b. al-Faḍl"[3].

Now it is clear that the work actually belongs to Ibn Isḥāq. At some time it was attributed to Salamah as he was his transmitter, and at another time to the real author.

The commentary of Mujāhid on the *Qur'ān* is a well-known work[4]. Ibn Abī Najīḥ was one of the transmitters of this book[5] from whom Warqā' transmitted it[6].

Once when Yaḥyā was asked whether he preferred the commentary ofd Warqā' or of Shaibān, he replied that he preferred the commentary of Warqā' because it was transmitted from Ibn Abī Najīḥ from Mujāhid[7].

The same book was attributed to Ibn Abū Najīḥ in the statement of Ibn Ḥanbal[8]. Thus it becomes clear in this statement that the work belonged to Mujāhid, but it was attributed to Ibn Abū Najīḥ as he was the transmitter of the works and sometimes was even attributed to the Warqā' as he was the second man in the chain of transmitters.

Here is the last, but not least important example of this kind. *Sharḥ al-Mufaḍḍaliyāt* belongs to al-Qāsim b. Muḥammad al-

1. *Bagh.*, vi, 179.
2. Rāzī, ii, i, 169.
3. *Bagh.*, vi, 179. See also Rāzī, i, i, 139.
4. See for detail, *supra,* Mujāhid in Chapter iii.
5. *Thiqāt,* 506; *Mashāhīr,* 146; Rāzī, ii, ii, 203.
6. Rāzī, iv, ii, 51; Khaithamah, iii, 36b; *Tahd.*, xi, 114.
7. *Bagh.*, xiii, 486.
8. *Tahd.*, xi, 114.

Anbārī and was erroneously attributed to his son. — C. J. Lyall states in the introduction to *Sharḥ al-Mufaḍḍaliyāt,* "The preface to our edition states clearly that the commentary is to be regarded as the work of Abū Muḥammad al-Qāsim (b. Muḥammad b. Bashshār) al-Anbārī; and this is placed beyond doubt by the colophon of the Leipzig fragment, which is reproduced at the end of the text, p. 884. Notwithstanding this, the commentary is generally cited under the name of the son, Abū Bakr Muḥammad, commonly known as Ibn al-Anbārī (so in the *Fihrist,* p. 75, the *Khizānah,* Ḥajjī Kalīfah, the *Lisān al-'Arab* and the *Tāj al-'Arūs*). The preface shows that this is a mistake. The son's function was merely to publish what had been compiled by his father, occasionally adding a note by his own hand"[1].

Summing up, it was the style of the period that they mostly referred to the author, and not to the work. In many cases one work was attributed to more than one person: to the real author, to the first transmitter of the book, and even to the second transmitter.

In this connection, L. Zolondek's approach is very sound where he says, "I strongly suspect that a work of Ibn Ḥabīb which has an almost identical title, *Kitāb man summiya bi Baytain qālahū* (F. 106, 28-29) was nothing else than a second of Ibn al-Kalbī's works . . . It would seem that the works listed for these transmitters with identical titles are not really independent works, but mere editions of the earlier works of their teachers"[2]. In the present research, not a single reference has been made where the book is attributed to one of the teachers of the real compiler, or any higher authority.

Schacht and the Authenticity of Mūsā b. 'Uqbah's authorship of Maghāzī.

At this stage, it is worthwhile looking at the *Kitāb al-Maghāzī* by Mūsā b. 'Uqbah. We do not know at the moment of any independent copy of Mūsā's work. It is either in the form of quotations in the works of historians like Ṭabarī, Balādhurī[3], etc., or in the form of extracts which were published by Sachau[4] or in the Amālī of Ibn al-Ṣā'id.

---

1. Lyall, *Introd.* xiv.
2. L. Zolondek, *The Sources of the Kitāb al-Aġānī,* Arabica, 1961, Vol. viii, p. 302 footnote.
3. See *supra,* Mūsā b. 'Uqbah, p. 96; *Infra,* 209.
4. *Das Berl. Fragment des Mūsā Ibn 'Ukba, Sitzung. der Phil. Hist. Classe,* Feb. 1904, pp. 465-470.

In his article on Mūsā b. 'Uqbah's *Kitāb al-Maghāzī,* J. Schacht discusses the authorship of the work[1]. In his words, "Mūsā claimed that he derived his information from Zuhrī . . . Yaḥyā b. Ma'īn (d. 233) regarded the work of Mūsā b. 'Uqbā which is derived from Zuhrī, as one of the most correct of these books on *Maghāzī* . . . It is therefore unlikely that the *Kitāb al-Maghāzī* in its original form contained traditions from authorities other than Zuhrī" . . . [but it has additional material Nos. 8, 9, 10 and 19, and so it seems] to be additions made to the original work . . .[2]" About the remaining material he says, "Mūsā himself had ascribed to Zuhrī traditions which he could not possibly have received from him . . .[3]" "These additions may have been made either by Ismā'īl b. Ibrāhīm b. 'Uqba, or by the next transmitter of the text . . .[4]", . . . "Ismā'īl, and it is safe to assume that Ismā'īl was its only transmitter[5]". Bukhārī's transmission of Nos. 5 and 6 through Muḥammad b. Fulaiḥ does not prove that the Maghāzī was transmitted from Mūsā to Bukhārī in this way, but only two stories from *K. al-Maghāzī* were transmitted to him[6]. The names of Mūsā's teachers and students grew in number as the number of spurious *isnāds* and traditions grew[7]. Therefore, the whole standard biography of Mūsā in the later works is without documentary value[8]. In this respect he advises us to compare the standard biographies of Mūsā with the relevant entries in Ibn Sa'd and Bukhārī's Tārīkh[9].

It appears, therefore, that we are not on solid ground about the authorship of the *Maghāzī* of Mūsā. What is necessary to discuss at the moment is not the authenticity and trustworthiness of Mūsā, but the authorship of the *Maghāzī.* It seems that all the difficulties about the relevant document come from Schacht's adherence to only one statement of Ibn Ma'īn with his arbitrary comments, while he ignores or overlooks all the other statements. Let us see the references to Mūsā's *Maghāzī.* Mālik b. Anas, who died

1. J. Schacht, *on Mūsā* b. *'Uqba's Kitāb al-Maghāzī, Acta Orientalia,* Vol. xxi, pp. 288-300.
2. Schacht, *op. cit.,* 291.
3. Schacht, *op. cit.,* 300.
4. Schacht, *op. cit.,* 292.
5. Schacht, *op. cit.,* 293.
6. Schacht, *op. cit.,* 297-8.
7. Schacht, *op. cit.,* 299.
8. Schacht, *op. cit.,* 299.
9. Schacht, *op. cit.,* 299, footnote.

some fifty-five years earlier than Yaḥyā b. Ma'īn, refers to the *Maghāzī* without mentioning al-Zuhrī[1]. Ibn Ma'īn refers to Mūsā's adaptation of al-Zuhrī[2] which means that Mūsā depended to a large extent on al-Zuhrī. The wording of Ibn Ma'īn does not confine his sources to al-Zuhrī. Therefore, any material in this book coming from sources other than al-Zuhrī belongs entirely to Mūsā. Schacht thinks that when Mūsā relates from Nāfi' or Sālim or others, al-Zuhrī is invariably the intermediary between Mūsā and these persons[3]. But why should it be so? If we accept the statement that Mūsā saw Ibn 'Umar (d. 74) — and we have no reason to reject it — still giving him a normal life of sixty-five years, he must have been born about 75-80, since he died about 140[4].

Sālim (d. 106), Nāfi' (d. 117) and Mūsā all belong to Madīnah and at the time of the deaths of Sālim and Nāfi', Mūsā should have been at least between 26 and 37 years, and, according to the biographers, he was 40-55 years old. What sound reason, then, do we have to think that he could not get direct information from these authorities and must have obtained it from al-Zuhrī? Was there any custom that restricted learning to one teacher, to the exclusion of all others, or were Nāfi' and Sālim worthy of less respect than al-Zuhrī, so that Mūsā ignored them? In the circumstances, the claim that Mūsā was not the author of the work appears baseless. It is worthwhile noting that Mūsā had Nāfi''s traditions in writing to which Ibn al-Mubārak was witness[5]. The statement that the work was transmitted only through his nephew is a mere assumption and contrary to the fact.

When Bukhārī transmits through Muḥammad b. Fuliaḥ, it could be suggested — as Schacht did — that he transmitted only two stories. Unfortunately for Schacht's theory, al-Ṭabarānī has preserved quotations from the book explicitly through Muḥammad b. Fulaiḥ[6]. Other quotations are preserved by Balādhurī in *Ansāb al-Ashrāf*[7] where immediate narrators from Mūsā are Wuhaib, al-Darāwardī and al-Mundhir b. 'Abd Allāh. Some further quota-

1. Rāzī, iv, i, 154; *Tahd.*, x, 361.
2. *Tahd.*, x, 361-2.
3. Schacht, *op. cit.*, 292-3.
4. *Mashāhīr*, 80, where Ibn Ḥibbān says that Mūsādied in 135 A.H.
5. *Kāmil*, i, 104a; *Bagh.*, vi, 223; see also, *Kifāyah*, 267.
6. *Tkabir*, iii, 38b; 40a.
7. Balādhurī, *Ansāb*, i, 98; 224, 469, 569.

tions could be provided from the *Annales* of al-Ṭabarī. Therefore, on what reasonable grounds can one suggest that Ismā'īl was the only narrator! One makes no sense by trying to cast doubt on the names of Mūsā's authorities or his students provided by his standard biographer on the basis of al-Bukhārī's *Tārīkh* and Ibn Sa'd's work. Have these two authors taken any responsibility to record all the names? In spite of the value of these books, they have their own limitations, e.g., Ibn Sa'd describes *Maghāzī* of Abān b. 'Uthmān, not in the biography of Abān but somewhere else[1]. Ibn Sa'd utilized the History of Abū Ma'shar, but did not mention the work in Abū Ma'shar's biography and devoted only three lines to him[2].

Here are other examples from Ibn Sa'd and Bukhārī's works pertaining to the *aḥādīth* of earlier scholars.

Two eminent scholars of the mid-second century of the Hijrah, Shu'bah (d. 160) and Sufyān al-Thaurī (d. 161) are described in both the works.

Ibn Sa'd (d. 230) gives only nine lines — in the printed edition — for the biography of Shu'bah[3] and over two pages for Sufyān al-Thaurī[4], omitting all the references to the earlier's teachers and students and providing only two names of the latter's teachers and about ten names of his students; while Bukhārī (d. 256), describing Shu'bah as امير المؤمنين في الحديث devoted only eight lines[5], giving three or four names of his teachers and about the same number for his students. For Sufyān he has devoted almost one page[6] — in the printed edition — naming four or five persons each as his teachers and students.

Ibn Ḥanbal (d. 241), on the other hand, gives about 150 names as teachers of Shu'bah. Furthermore, he gives forty-five names from whom Shu'bah alone transmitted and ninety-seven names for Sufyān as such[7].

---

1. See biography of Abān. Sa'd, v, 112-3 while the book is mentioned in v, 156.
2. Sa'd, v, 309.
3. Sa'd, vii, 11, 38.
4. Sa'd, vi, 257-60.
5. BTK, ii, ii, 245-6.
6. BTK, ii, ii, 93-4.
7. *'Ilal,* i, 160-165.

Between the deaths of Ibn Sa'd and Ibn Ḥanbal on the one hand, and the deaths of Ibn Sa'd and al-Bukhārī on the other, there are respectively 11 and 15 years. According to Schacht's theory the names of Mūsā's teachers and students grew in number as the number of spurious *isnāds* and traditions grew[1]. If the spurious *isnāds* and traditions grew so quickly in a span of eleven years that the number of Shu'bah's teachers increased from one or zero to 150, then what process was utilized by Bukhārī to check the growth and to reduce the numbers of the spurious authorities to four only? Therefore, the theory of forgery basing itself on the entries of Bukhārī and Ibn Sa'd is without justification.

It would be sufficient to look only at the 'prologue' of al-Sakhāwī's Historiography to know that every city had its book or books of biographies[2], beginning with a small volume and rising to eighty volumes. The later writers were able to utilize all these materials and were capable of producing more comprehensive biographies. None of them intended or claimed to furnish all the information available to them.

1. Schacht, *op. cit.,* 299.
2. Al-Sakhāwī, *Al-Taubīkh li-man dhamm al-Tārīkh.*

CHAPTER VI

ISNĀD

The Beginning of Isnād.

Isnād seems to have been used casually in some literatures in the Pre-Islamic period, in a vague manner, without attaching any importance to it[1]. The *isnād* system was also used — to some extent — in transmitting pre-Islamic poetry[2]. But it was in the *Ḥadīth* literature that its importance culminated till it was counted a part of the religion[3]. The advantage of the system was utilized to the full, and in some cases to extravagent limits, for documenting the *Ḥadīth* literature, the storehouse of the *Sunnah.* The *Sunnah* of the Prophet being a basic legal source, it was natural to deal with these documents with utmost care. Thus with the introduction of *isnād,* a unique science, *'Ilm al-Jarḥ wa al-Ta'dīl* — the knowledge of invalidating and declaring reliable — came into existence for the valuation of *isnād* and *aḥādīth.*

The Beginning of Isnād in Ḥadīth Literature.

We have seen in the fourth chapter that it was the common practice among Companions — even during the life of the Prophet — to transmit the traditions of the Prophet. Some of them had made special arrangements to attend the Prophet's circle by turns and to inform each other of what they had heard and seen in the presence of the Prophet[4].

---

1. *Mishna, the fathers,* 446.
2. Nāṣir al-Asad, *Maṣādir al-Shi'r al-Jāhilī,* 255-267.
3. MU, *introduction,* pp. 14-16.
4. *Supra,* pp. 183-4.

In informing their fellows they would have naturally used sentences like 'the Prophet did so and so' or 'the Prophet said so and so'. It is also natural that one of them who had gained knowledge at second hand, while reporting the incident to a third man, might have disclosed his sources of information and might have given the full account of the incident. There are ample references of this kind in the *Ḥadīth* literature.

These methods, which were used in the early days for the diffusion of the *Sunnah* of the Prophet, gave birth to *isnād*, and were the rudimentary beginning of this system.

An important early statement about Isnād.

Ibn Sīrīn (d. 110) says, "They did not ask about the *isnād*, but when civil war – *Fitnah* – broke they said 'Name to us your men'; those who belong to *Ahl al-Sunnah*, their traditions were accepted and those who were innovators their traditions were neglected"[1].

This statement gives the impression that the *isnād* were used even before the *Fitnah*, but the narrators were not so particular in applying it. Sometimes they employed it and, at others, neglected it; but, after civil war, they became more cautious and began to enquire about the sources of information and scrutinize them. At the end of the first century the science of the *isnād* was fully developed. Shu'bah used to watch the lips of Qatādah, in the lecture, to discriminate between his first and second-hand information[2]. There are ample references to asking and enquiring about the *isnād* in the first century of the *Hijrah*[3].

Orientalists and Isnād.

Among the orientalists there have been differences of opinion about the beginning of *isnād*. According to Caetani, 'Urwah (d. 94), the oldest systematic collector of traditions, as quoted by Ṭabarī, used no *isnāds* and quoted no authority but the *Qur'ān*. Caetani, therefore, holds that in the time of 'Abd al-Malik (c. 70-80), more than sixty years after the Prophet's death, the practice of

1. MU, *Introduction*, 15; Rāmhurmuzi, 10a.
2. See *supra*, Qatādah and Shu'bah in the third chapter.
3. Fasawī, iii, 182b.

giving *isnād* did not exist. So, he concludes that the beginning of the *isnād* system may be placed in the period between 'Urwah and Ibn Isḥāq (d. 151). In his opinion the greater part of the *isnād* was put together and created by traditionists belonging to the end of the second century, and perhaps also by those belonging to the third[1].

Sprenger has also pointed out that the writing of 'Urwah to 'Abd al-Malik does not contain *isnād* and it was only later that he was credited with it[2].

The quotations from the writing of 'Urwah to 'Abd al-Malik are preserved not only in Ṭbarī but in many classical collections of *Ḥadīth* as well[3] which are earlier than Ṭabarī. In one of the quotations, through the same *isnād* which is utilized by Ṭabarī, we find 'Urwah quoting his authority 'Ā'ishah[4]. The main difficulty which arises in searching for the sources of 'Urwah is the lack of original work existing in a separate form. The available material is only in the form of quotations. It was left to later scholars to quote certain lines from the work as they were wanted. 'Urwah had personal contact with most of the Companions so his authority must have been a single name or the very person who was present at the incident. Hence, the *isnād* consisted of a single name. And it is easy to omit or overlook a single man's name in quoting. The other versions of his work, especially the one transmitted by Zuhrī, have *isnāds*. 'Urwah even uses composite *isnāds*[5] in the writing, as well as the single one.

Horovitz, who has studied the problem of *isnād,* has answered the arguments of Caetani and other scholars thoroughly in his article *Alter und Ursprung des Isnād*[6]. He points out that those who denied the use of *isnād* by 'Urwah did not notice all his *isnāds.* Furthermore he argues that there is a difference between what one writes when one is asked questions and what one does

1. J. Robson, *The Isnād in Muslim Traditions, Glasgow Univ. Oriental Society Transaction,* vol. xv, 1955, p. 18; quoting *Annali dell Islam.*
2. Robson, *op. cit.,* 19.
3. See for example Ḥanbal, iv, 323-6; 328-331.
4. Ḥanbal, vi, 212.
5. *Annales,* i, 1529; 1534; 1549. Ḥanbal, iv, 323-6.
6. *Der Islam,* vol. viii, 1918, pp. 39-47.

within learned circles. His conclusion is that the first entry of the *isnād* into the literature of tradition was in the last third of the first century[1]. But as 'Urwah also uses composite *isnāds,* the use of single *isnād* in writing must have been earlier than this period and the use of the single *isnād* in oral transmission of traditions much earlier than that.

A Scottish scholar, J. Robson, who has studied the subject at some length, says, "It is during the middle years of the first century of Islam that one would first expect anything like an *isnād.* By then many of the Companions were dead, and people who had not seen the Prophet would be telling stories about him. It might therefore naturally occur to some to ask these men for their authority. The growth of a hard and fast system must have been very gradual"[2]. He concludes, "We know that Ibn Isḥāq, in the first half of the second century, could give much of his information without an *isnād,* and much of the remainder without a perfect one. His predecessors would almost certainly be even less particular than he in documenting their information. But we are not justified in assuming that the *isnād* is a development of Zuhrī's period and was unknown to 'Urwah. While the developed system had a slow growth, some element of *isnād* would be present from as early a period as people could demand it"[3].

Professor Schacht and Isnād.

Recently Schacht has dealt with the legal traditions and their development. In his opinions *isnāds* are the most arbitrary part of traditions. They were developed within certain groups who traced back their doctrines to early authorities[4]. Commenting on Schacht's criticism, Professor Robson says, "The criticism levelled at the *isnāds* is very thoroughgoing, and some strong arguments are brought forward to suggest that the use of *isnāds* is a late development: but one hesitates to accept it to the full extent... Schacht is dealing primarily with legal traditions, a sphere where his argument may apply more closely than elsewhere, as changing conditions and the development of legal thought must have demanded new regulations; but one wonders whether the argument is not too sweeping"[5].

---

1. *Der Islam,* vol. viii, 1918, pp. 39-47.
2. Robson, *op. cit.,* 21.
3. Robson, *op. cit.,* 21.
4. This is a well summarised theory of Schacht by Robson, *op. cit.,* 20.
5. Robson, *op. cit.,* 20.

Schacht's approach to the subject and its weakness will be discussed later on. At the moment only one of his statements requires immediate attention. He says, "It is stated on the authority of the Successor Ibn Sīrīn that the demand for and the interest in *isnāds* started from the civil war *(Fitna),* when people could no longer be presumed to be reliable without scrutiny; we shall see later that the civil war which began with the killing of the Umaiyad Caliph Walīd b. Yazīd (A. H. 126), towards the end of the Umaiyad dynasty, was a conventional date for the end of the good old time during which the *Sunna* of the Prophet was still prevailing; as the usual date for the death of Ibn Sīrīn is A. H. 110, we must conclude that the attribution of this statement to him is spurious. In any case, there is no reason to suppose that the regular practice of using *isnāds* is older than the beginning of the second century A.H.[1]" But his whole argument is based on his arbitrary interpretation of the word *Fitnah.* The assassination date of Walīd b. Yazīd has never been a conventional date in Islamic history and was never reckoned as the end of the "good old time". This title is given only to the Period of four righteous Caliphs.

Furthermore, there were many *Fitnahs* before this date. There was the civil war between Ibn al-Zubair and 'Abd al-Mālik b. Marwān about 70 A.H. But the biggest of all was the civil war between 'Alī and Mu'āwiyah, which produced a breach among Muslims which exists to the present day. Ṭāhā Ḥusain has described it rightly as the most fierce quarrel known in Islamic History[2]. «وحين إختصم المسلمون حولها اعنف خصومة عرفها تاريخها»

So, on what grounds does the word *Fitnah* need to be interpreted in the sense of the civil war after the killing of Walīd b. Yazīd? To take the word arbitrarily in this sense is equal to interpreting it as the *Fitnah* of Tartar and Halaku. Schacht takes this word in the sense which suits him, without any historical justification, to prove his own theory. This, of course, is logically absurd.

Professor Robson inclines to take the word in the sense of the *Fitnah* of Ibn al-Zubair, considering the birth date of Ibn Sīrīn, as well as the occurrence of the word *Fitnah,* in the text of *Muwaṭṭa'* Mālik which refers to this period[3]. The present research indicates

1. *Origin.* 36-37.
2. Ṭāhā Ḥusain, *'Uthmān,* 5. See also Nicholson, *Lit. Hist.,* 193.
3. Robson, *isnād in Muslim Tradition, Glas. Univ. Or. Soc.,* xv, 22.

that it should be taken back to the first and the most dangerous civil war in the history of Islam. For this suggestion, there are the following reasons:

1. Professor Robson has pointed out that at the middle of the first century, when many of the Companions were dead and people who had not seen the Prophet would be telling the story of the Prophet, someone would naturally ask them to name the authority. If we accept the status of the Prophet as it is shown in Robson's statement — which is quite unfair — this is possibly what might have occurred.

Yet before reaching this stage, there was a great upheaval in the fourth decade. Most likely, the first fabrication of traditions began in the political sphere, crediting and discrediting the parties concerned. In the well-known work of Al-Shaukānī, concerning spurious and similar traditions we find:

42 spurious traditions about the Prophet
38 spurious traditions about the first three Caliphs
96 spurious traditions about 'Alī and his wife Fāṭimah
14 spurious traditions about Mu'āwiyah[1]

Therefore, it looks as if the spurious traditions began to originate for political purposes at and about the period of the war between 'Alī and Mu'āwiyah, and continued later on as a counter-attack on the Umayyad dynasty. The traditionists and other scholars found it necessary from that time onwards to be more cautious in selecting their authorities.

2. The second reason for this assumption is the statement of Ibn Sīrīn itself[2]. There is no reason whatsoever to discredit it and challenge its authenticity. Ibn Sīrīn's wording suggests that he relates a practice earlier than his own period. He uses the words "They did not ask", "they said 'Name to us your men', "were accepted", etc. He does not use the first person of the personal pronoun in a period when its usage was common. So it seems that he points to a practice in very early days. Furthermore, he says 'they did not ask', which implies that the practice of *isnād* was in existence, but people did not usually inquire, and it was left to the transmitter whether or not to disclose his sources.

---

1. Al-Shaukānī, *Al-Fawā'id al-Majmū'ah,* pp. 320-408.
2. As quoted on page 213 of this book.

Material for the study of Isnād.

Perhaps a lot of confusion in the study of *isnād* is due to the selection of the material for research of this kind. Professor Robson says: "Horovitz has reminded us that there are three sources for the sayings and doings of the Prophet, viz. *Ḥadīth* (Tradition), *Sīra* (Biography of the Prophet), and *Tafsīr (Qur'ān* commentary), the ground-element in all being a pronouncement introduced by a chain of witness; and Lammens has rightly insisted the *Sīra* and *Ḥadīth* are not distinct sources, as did Horovitz"[1]. So, Professor Robson inclines to accept the view of Lammens, while Horovitz wants to draw a line between *Sīrah* and *Ḥadīth.* Horovitz's approach seems to be much more natural in this context. There is a difference in the very nature of *Sīrah* (Biography) and the documentation of *Ḥadīth.*

In *Ḥadīth* any single statement can be put together with any other statement of quite a different subject without causing much perplexity. But *Sīrah,* being a biography, requires a flow and continuance of episode. Therefore compilers of biography put together their different sources to knit a complete story[2], while the same authors and the same authorities, when transmitting traditions of other than biographical nature, do not put into practice the biographical method. Therefore, from this angle, there is a difference between *Ḥadīth* and *Sīrah* literature, and so *Sīrah* is not a proper subject for the study of the system of *isnād.* Until now most of the research on *isnād* has been carried out in the biographical literature.

Schacht and the study of Isnād in legal literature.

Schacht has studied the *Muwaṭṭa'* of Mālik, Al-Umm of al-Shāfi'ī, *Muwaṭṭa'* of al-Shaibānī, etc., works which belong to legal science. He has imposed the results of his study on the entire *Ḥadīth* literature, as if the *Ḥadīth* literature does not exist at all and as if it does not have an independent footing of its own.

It seems quite clear that he has not paid much attention to the nature of a legal work. A lawyer, a judge or a *Muftī,* whenever

1. Robson, *Ibn Isḥāq's Use of Isnād. Bull. John Ryland, Library,* vol. 38, No. 2, p. 451.

2. For early practice of this sort see *'Urwah* and his Composite *Isnād,* Ḥanbal, iv, 323-26.

he gave his verdict, was not bound to give the full documents to support his verdict. When a scholar writes to a certain scholar, he may make only slight allusions to his references, so his colleague can recall the necessary items to his mind.

These were the methods used by the prominent lawyers of the early centuries of Islam. Though most of the writings of that period are not available in separate form, yet we still have a few legal books which belong to the second century A.H. A glance at their methods of quoting traditions would reveal this very fact. Shāfʿī has utilized the material from *Muwaṭṭa'* of Mālik, and Abū Yūsuf has utilized the work of Ibn Isḥāq and others. Here are a few examples which show their method in quoting traditions.

Methods of quoting traditions by early lawyers.*

1. A.Y. – 1.1. . . . . U.S.[1]
   1.1 . . . A.H. . . . S.M. . . . M . . . A.U. . . . U.S.[2]

2. A.Y. – 1.1 . . . . the Prophet[3]
   1.1. . . . . S.Y. . . . . A.J. . . . . the Prophet[4]

3. A.Y.. . . . . the Prophet[5]
   A.Y. . . . Q.R. . . . M.A. . . . I.A. . . . A.H. . . . A.D. . . . the Prophet[6]

4. A.Y. . . . M . . . S + Z . . . U . . . S.A.W.[7]
   A.Y. . . . M . . . S . . . U . . . S.A.W.[8]

5. A.Y. . . . 1.1. . . Z. . . Y. . . H. . . N wrote to Ibn ʿAbbās[9]
   A.Y. . . . 1.1 + I.b.U . . . Y.b.H . . . N wrote to Ibn ʿAbbās[10]

* In these quotations of *isnāds* abbreviations are used.

1. Abū Yūsuf, 7.
2. Ibn Isḥāq, *Sīrah,* 456.
3. Abū Yūsuf, 90.
4. Abū al-Wafā al-Afghānī, footnote, *Al-Radd ʿalā al-Auzāʿī,* p. 90, quoting *Sīrah of Ibn Isḥāq*.
5. Abū Yūsuf, 21.
6. *Kharāj,* 22.
7. Abū Yūsuf, 35.
8. Abū Yūsuf, 5-6.
9. *Kharāj,* 235.
10. Abū Yūsuf, 38.

A.Y. . . . .1.1+I.b.U. . . . .Anonymous. . .Ibn 'Abbās wrote to N.[1]
A.Y. . . . .1.1 . . . . Z. . . . . .N wrote to Ibn 'Abbās[2]
A.Y. . . . .H. . . .A.D.. . . . . .N wrote to Ibn 'Abbās[3]

6. Arguing with Auzā'ī, Abū Yūsuf says that had he not been afraid of the volume of the book he would have given *Ḥadīth* with *isnād*[4].

7. Shāfi'ī says, "And the tradition of Anas reporting the statement of the Prophet, 'If the *Imām* prays sitting, you should pray sitting' is abrogated by the tradition of 'Ā'ishah'"[5]. But in this tradition he did not give any *isnād*. In another place he gives only a part of *isnād*;

Ibrāhīm al-Nakha'ī — Al-Aswad b. Yazīd — 'Ā'ishah[6] and at another place gives the complete *isnād* by another channel.

Yaḥyā — Ḥammād — Hishām — 'Urwah — 'Ā'ishah[7].

8. He says in the *Risālah*, p. 67: وسن رسول الله ان لا قطع في ثمر ولا كثر He gives here a legal maxim without mentioning any *isnād*, but he gives the complete *isnād* at another place. It reads:

Mālik — Yaḥyā — Muḥammad — Rāfi' b. Khadīj — The Prophet[8].

and in the *Muwaṭṭa'*:

Mālik — Yaḥyā — Muḥammad — Rāfi' b. Khadīj with the full detail of an incident with Marwān, etc.[9].

9. In the *Risālah* he gives his deduction from the action of the Prophet, referring to the tradition without giving any details.

---

1. Abū Yūsuf, 43.
2. *Kharāj*, 24.
3. *Kharāj*, 208.
4. Abū Yūsuf, 31.
5. Shāfi'ī, *Umm*, i, 151.
6. Shāfi'ī, *Risālah*, 253.
7. Shāfi'ī, *Ikhtilāf*, 100.
8. Shāfi'i, *Umm*, vi, 118.
9. Mālik, *Muwaṭṭa'*, *Ḥudūd* 3?

It reads[1]: ... فلما اعطى رسول الله السلبَ القاتلَ في الاقبال دلت سنة النبي على ان الغنيمة ... But we find a complete *isnād* in *al-Umm* and in his immediate source *Muwatta'* Mālik:

Mālik — Yaḥyā — 'Umar b. Kathīr — Abū Muḥammad — Abū Qatādah — The Prophet[2].

Mālik — Yaḥyā — 'Amr — Abū Muḥammad — Abū Qatādah — The Prophet[3].

10. Shāfi'ī says, "And Ibn 'Umar transmitted *Ṣalāt al-Khauf* from the Prophet" without mentioning any *isnād*[4]. But we find a complete *isnād* in *al-Umm* and his immediate authority the *Muwaṭṭa'*:

    Mālik — Nāfi' — Ibn 'Umar — the Prophet[5]
    Mālik — Nāfi' — Ibn 'Umar — the Prophet[6]

11. He mentions in the *Risālah* the Ṭawāf performance of 'Umar after the morning prayer and some other ritual activities without giving any *isnād*, saying only[7].

    وقد ذهب بعض اصحابنا الى ان عمر بن الخطاب طاف بعد الصبح

    But in his immediate authority Mālik there is a complete *isnād*: Mālik — Ibn Shihāb — Ḥumaid — 'Abd al-Raḥmān, who performed *Ṭawāf* accompanying 'Umar[8].

12. In another place, Shāfi'ī says explicitly, "Every *Ḥadīth* I have copied out (meaning in his books) with *Munqaṭi' isnād,* I have heard it with complete *isnād* or transmitted by well-known authorities relating from well-known authorities. But I disliked quoting a *Ḥadīth* which I did not memorize well. I lost some of my books but have verified what I have remembered from what is known to scholars; I have made it brief, being afraid of its volume, and have given only what will be sufficient, without exhausting all that can be known about the subject"[9]

---

1. Shāfi'ī, *Risālah,* 70-71.
2. Shāfi'ī, *Umm,* iv, 66.
3. Mālik, *Muwaṭṭa', Jihād,* 18.
4. Shāfi'ī - *Risālah,* 126.
5. Shāfi'ī - *Umm,* i, 197.
6. Mālik - *op. cit., Ṣalāt al-Khauf* 3.
7. Shāfi'ī - *Risālah,* 326-7.
8. Mālik, *Muwaṭṭa', Ḥajj* 117.
9. Shāfi'ī, *Risālah,* 431.

The above evidence and its implications.

In the writings of early Scholars, mostly in non-tradition literature, the following features are very common:

The cutting of *isnāds* and their confining to the least possible quotations to serve the purpose, as the complete *isnād* and ample references would make the work bulky[1].

The omission of the complete *isnād* and quotation direct from the highest authority[2].

The use of *isnād* by Abū Yūsuf reveals that he uses the complete *isnād,* cuts it off, puts the anonymous word رجل , while he himself has mentioned the exact name a few pages earlier[3].

The use of the word *Al-Sunnah* and other words derived from it to mention the practice of the Prophet, without giving the text or *isnād,* as the *Ḥadīth* in question was well-known to the scholars[4].

The conclusion.

Summing up the argument, the literature of legal science or the *Sīrah* work is inadequate for the study of the traditions and *isnāds* and their 'growth'.

Ḥadīth is a complete subject by itself with a good many subsidiary branches. It is totally wrong, even unscientific, to study *Ḥadīth* as a subject in the legal books. Therefore, any conclusion about the traditions, their transmission, or the *isnād* system, etc., based on the study of legal literature would be faulty and unreliable.

Flourishing of Isnāds in the later period.

It is the common phenomenon of *isnād* system that as we go further the number of transmitters increases. Sometimes a tradition transmitted by one companion acquires ten students in the

1. Exm. No. 6; 8-12.
2. Ex. 1-3.
3. Ex. 5.
4. Ex. 8, 9.

next generation, in the class of Successors and, in their turn, these ten students have in some cases twenty or thirty students belonging to different countries and provinces.

Here are a few examples:

Tradition No. 3 ([1]).

This tradition is transmitted by at least ten Companions. Available sources at the moment provide some details about the chains of transmission for seven Companions out of ten. These seven Companions belong to three different places:

4 out of 7 Companions who transmitted this *Hadīth* belong to Madīnah.

1 belongs to Syria.

2 belong to Iraq.

The Companion Abū Hurairah has at least 7 students who transmit this tradition from him.

4 students out of 7 belong to Madīnah.
2 students belong to Egypt.
1 student belongs to Yemen.

The students who transmitted from these seven students of Abū Hurairah are at least twelve in number.

Their localities are as below:

1 out of 12 belongs to Syria.

5 belong to Madīnah.

1 belongs to Kūfah.

1 to Makkah.

1 to Ṭā'if.

1 to Egypt.

1 to Yemen.

---

1. All the numbers of traditions and the numbers of transmitters refer to the edited work of Suhail which forms Part Two of this dissertation.

If we take other Companions and their students who transmitted this tradition into account, then the number in the second generation goes up to at least sixteen and in the third generation up to at least twenty-six, and their localities are as below:

The Transmitters from the Companions.

9 out of 16 belong to Madīnah.

1 belongs to Makkah.

2 belong to Egypt.

2 to Baṣrah.

1 to Ḥimṣ.

1 to Yemen.

Those who transmitted in turn from these authorities are twenty-six.

9 out of 26 belong to Madīnah.

4 belong to Makkah.

2 belong to Egypt.

1 to Baṣrah.

1 to Ḥimṣ.

1 to Yemen.

2 to Kūfah.

3 to Syria.

1 to Wāsiṭ.

1 to Ṭā'if.

1 is of a locality unknown to me.

3 of the 26 scholars transmitted from more than one source.

This tradition is quoted by Ibn Ḥanbal nine times on the authority of Abū Hurairah and thirteen times on the authorities of six other Companions.

Tradition No. 4.

This tradition is transmitted by seven other Companions. These traditions agree with Abū Hurairah's tradition in general.

9 students transmitted this tradition from Abū Hurairah.

5 out of 9 belong to Madīnah.

2 belong to Egypt.

1 to Yemen

One I have been unable to trace

There are ten students who transmitted this tradition from the students of Abū Hurairah.

4 out of 10 belong to Madīnah.

1 belongs to Egypt.

1 to Yemen.

2 to Kūfah.

1 to Makkah.

1 to Ṭā'if.

The number of transmitters of similar tradition from the different Companions would increase to fourteen and the number of their students to fifteen.

There is only one narrator, Abū Ṣāliḥ, who transmitted from two Companions, 'Ā'ishah and Abū Hurairah. No other student of 'Ā'ishah is known to me who transmitted this tradition from her.

There is only one transmitter, al-Zuhrī, amongst ten who transmitted from two authorties.

Ibn Ḥanbal has quoted this tradition eight times on the authority of Abū Hurairah.

Tradition No. 7.

At least thirteen students of Abū Hurairah transmitted this tradition from him.

8 out of 13 belong to Madīnah.

1 belongs to Kūfah.

2 belong to Baṣrah.

1 to Yemen.

1 to Syria.

There are sixteen scholars who transmitted this tradition from the students of Abū Hurairah.

6 out of 16 belong to Madīnah.

4 belong to Baṣrah.

2 to Kūfah

1 to Makkah.

1 to Yemen.

1 to Khurāsān.

1 to Ḥimṣ.

Two of these transmitters narrate this tradition from more than one authority. They are al-Zuhrī and al-A'mash. The same tradition is transmitted by four other Companions, namely Ibn 'Umar, Jābir, 'Ā'ishah and 'Alī, and taking into account their students, the numbers of the second generation of transmitters increase from thirteen to sixteen and in the third generation from sixteen to eighteen. Some of the students of Abū Hurairah also transmitted the same tradition from other sources than Abū Hurairah.

There is quite a different channel for this tradition in Shi'ite sources.

Ibn Ḥanbal has endorsed this tradition at least fifteen times on the authority of Abū Hurairah.

Tradition No. 8.

This tradition is a lengthy one. A good many scholars have transmitted it in parts. Ibn Ḥanbal has endorsed it at least twenty-four times. It world be tedious to study the complete *isnāds* and their final shapes in the period of the classical authors. Confining the discussion only to the third generation of narrators of this tradition, who mostly belong to the first half of the second century of the *Hijrah,* the following feature appears:

Abū Hurairah has at least eleven students who transmitted this tradition, one part or another of it.

The analysis of their homes is as below:

9 out of 11 belong to Madīnah.

1 to Baṣ rah.

1 to Kūfah.

They in turn have twenty-two students.

9 out of 22 belong to Madīnah.

1 belongs to Makkah.

4 to Kūfah.

5 to Baṣrah.

1 to Wāsiṭ.

1 to the Ḥijāz.

1 to Khurāsān.

The other feature is that not all the Medinites or Basrites or Kufis are the students of one single man.

Nine Medinites have obtained their knowledge from seven different Medinites.

3 out of 5 Basrites have transmitted from one Basrite.

1 Basrite has transmitted from a Madnite.

1 Basrite has transmitted from another Medinite.

Five of the students of Abū Hurairah have more than one student. The localities of their students are as follows:

1. 1 Abū Ṣāliḥ al-Madanī has five students.

 2 out of 5 belong to Madīnah.

 1 to Makkah.

 2 to Kūfah.

2. Ibn al-Musayyab al-Madanī has four students.

 2 out of 4 belong to Madīnah.

 1 toKūfah

 1 to Baṣrah.

3. Al-Maqburī has two students:

 One from Madīnah and the other from the Ḥijāz. His precise city is unknown to me.

4. Muḥammad b. Ziyād al-Madanī has three students.

 one each from Baṣrah, Wāsiṭ, and Khurāsān.

5. Ibn Sīrīn al-Baṣrī has three students.

 All of them from Baṣrah.

In later parts of the *isnād* the localities of the narrators would appear more and more mixed and from different provinces.

There are at least seven other Companions who have transmitted this tradition from the Prophet. If their transmitters are added to Abū Hurairah's transmitters, the number would increase.

This single tradition of Abū Hurairah is endorsed by Ibn Ḥanbal at least twenty-four times.

Furthermore, the tradition is preserved in the collections of A'mash (d. 148), Ibn Juraij (d. 150), and Ibrāhīm b. Ṭahmān (d. 168), who are transmitters of this tradition from the students of Abū Hurairah.

The same tradition is found in Shi'ite, Zaidī, and Ibāḍī sources.

Tradition No. 10.

This tradition is transmitted by only two students of Abū Hurairah and each of them has only one student. There are eight other Companions who transmit this tradition from the Prophet. The number of the students of all these Companions reaches twenty and they in turn have twenty-five students of different provinces. This tradition is endorsed by Ibn Ḥanbal only once on the authority of Abū Hurairah.

Tradition No. 11.

This tradition is transmitted by only one student of Abū Hurairah. He is Abū Ṣāliḥ, who has only one student, his son Suhail who in turn has four students. This tradition is endorsed by Ibn Ḥanbal three times on the authority of Abū Hurairah.

No other transmitter of this tradition is traceable. Perhaps, Abū Hurairah is the only one who transmitted this tradition from the Prophet.

Tradition No. 27.

There are nine students who transmitted this tradition from Abū Hurairah.

6 out of 9 belong to Madīnah.

1 to Baṣrah.

1 to Makkah.

1 to Syria.

Their students in turn reach twelve.

6 out of 12 belong to Madīnah.

1 belongs to Yamāmah.

1 to Tustar.

1 to Baṣrah.

1 to Syria.

1 is untraceable.

This tradition is endorsed eight times by Ibn Ḥanbal, on the authority of Abū Hurairah.

The same tradition is transmitted by twenty-one Companions.

10 out of 21 belong to Madīnah.

6 belong to Baṣrah.

2 belong to Kūfah.

1 to Khurāsān.

1 to Ḥimṣ.

1 to the tribe of 'Abd al-Qais.

Their students reach fifty-eight in number.

11 out of 58 belong to Madīnah.

13 belong to Baṣrah.

13 belong to Kūfah.

1 to Syria.

3 to Makkah.

1 to Egypt.

2 to Marw.

1 to Bahrān.

1 to Yemen.

12 are unknown to me.

If we go one step further towards these scholars' students, we find the number increases to seventy-four.

12 out of 74 belong to Madīnah.

18 belong to Baṣrah.

1 to Yamāmah.

5 to Makkah.

1 to Tūstar.
1 to Syria.
15 to Kūfah.
1 to Wāsiṭ.
2 to Yemen.
1 to Ṭā'if.
1 to Egypt.
1 to Jazīrah.
1 to Khurāsān.
14 are unknown to me.

One of them, Shu'bah, has transmitted from seven authorities; Zuhair, Salamah, Ḥammād, and Qatādah, each from three authorities, and Qurrah from two authorities.

Shi'ite, Zaidī and Ibāḍī sources quote this tradition through their own channels.

The common feature of a good many traditions in the early part of the second century A.H. is the great number of transmitters who belong to different provinces and countries. We have for example seen in tradition No. 27 some seventy-four students belonging to a dozen different places. It was hardly possible for all these persons to consult each other so as to give a similar form and sense in transmitting a particular tradition. So if a particular tradition is transmitted by so many persons with a similar form and sense, then its genuineness cannot be questioned, as the trust worthiness of the individuals has been vouched for by their contemporaries. It is a general practice that if a man's honesty is proved by his dealing with the people, then his words are accepted as a true statement unless it is proved otherwise by facts. For the past generation with whom personal contact is impossible one needs to rely to a large extent on the testimony of contemporary sources. The standard fixed by the traditionists from the very early days was that if someone tells a lie in his personal life, though he was honest in the transmitting of traditions, his traditions would not be accepted[1]. They criticised their fathers, brothers, friends and close relatives[2]. And, perhaps, it was the highest possible

1. Rāzī, i, i, 289-90. See also Suyūṭī, *Tadrīb,* 220-21.
2. *Mīzān,* iv, 364.

standard that could be set for documentation of any source. Therefore, there is no good reason to reject the testimony of the contemporaries.

Ḥadīth literature offers an opportunity for further satisfactions. The other method to test their trustworthiness and honesty is by cross-references to the statements of scholars. The method was employed by traditionists in early days. Ayyūb (d. 131) says that if one wants to know the mistake of his teacher he ought to frequent other teachers as well[1]. Ibn al-Mubārak (d. 181) says that to reach an authentic statement one needs to compare the words of scholars with each other[2]. When Ibn 'Uyaynah delivered his lectures on traditions, he was questioned by students whenever he differed from his colleague Mālik[3]. Ḥammād b. Salamah committed some mistakes. His pupils, transmitting his books, committed some more. Yaḥyā b. Ma'īn collected the records from eighteen students of Ḥammād to discriminate between the errors of Ḥammād and his students[4].

The same method can be utilized to compare the statements of later authorities; then going one step back to compare their teachers' statements till we reach the Prophet. If in a number of cases this method works and gives satisfactory results, it will provide confidence as a whole in the traditionists' literature. The present research provides sufficient grounds to accept this literature as a whole. The study also indicates the early beginning of the *isnād* system in *Ḥadīth*. Abū Hurairah died in 58 or thereabouts, but there are other Companions who died earlier than Abū Hurairah and their traditions are also transmitted through an *isnād*. As it is found in many cases that 5, 6, 10, or more students belonging to different countries transmit a tradition from one Companion and they provide an *isnād* going back to the Prophet, their statement should be accepted as authentic. We even find that some early companions, e.g., 'Umar and 'Uthmān, etc., transmitting traditions gave as their immediate authorities not the Prophet but some other Companions. Had the system of *isnād* not existed, it would not have been possible for them to transmit this way.

---

1. Dārimī, i, 153.
2. *Jāmi'*, 193a.
3. See for examples, Ḥumaidī, 226, 238, 281, 934.
4. *Supra*, 129.

Refutation of Schacht's theory of the spread of Isnāds.

Professor Schacht has formulated a theory to detect the date for the forgery of *Ḥadīth.* Professor Robson has commented on the method and conclusions of Schacht, paying him very high tribute for his achievements. It reads,... "This is a very valuable contribution to the study of the development of Tradition, for it not merely suggests a date when certain traditions became attributed to the Prophet, but gives a ceratin value to the chain of authorities, suggesting that the latter part of the chain is genuine, whereas the earlier part which goes back to the Prophet is fictitious"[1].

Schacht describes his method as follows:

> "These results regarding the growth if *isnāds* enable us to envisage the case in which a tradition was put into circulation by a traditionist whom we may call N.N., or by a person who used his name, at a certain time. The tradition would normally be taken over by one or several transmitters, and the lower, real part of the *isnād* would branch out into several strands . . . But N.N. would remain the (lowest) common link in the several strands of *isnāds* (or at least in most of them, allowing for his being passed by and eliminated in additional strands of *isnāds* (or at least in most of them, allowing for his being passed by and eliminated in additional strands of *isnāds* which might have been introduced later) . . .
>
> "The case discussed in the preceding paragraph is not hypothetical but of common occurrence. It was observed, though of course not recognized in its implications, by the Muhammadan scholars themselves... .
>
> "A typical example of the phenomenon of the common transmitter occurs in *Ikh.* 294, where a tradition has the following *isnāds:*

1. Robson, *Muslim Tradition...* Manchester Memoirs, vol. xciii, (1951-2), No. 7, pp. 98-9.

Prophet	Prophet	Prophet
Jābir	Jābir	Jābir
a man of Banū Salama	Muṭṭalib	Muṭṭalib
	ʻAmr b. Abī ʻAmr the freedman of Muṭṭalib	
ʻAbd al-ʻazīz b. Muḥammad	Ibrāhīm b. Muḥammad	Sulaimān b. Bilāl
		Anonymous
Shāfiʻī	Shāfiʻī	Shāfiʻī

ʻAmr b. Abī ʻAmr is the common link in these *isnāds*. He would hardly have hesitated between his own patron and an anonymous transmitter for his immediate authority"[1].

In support of his statement, Schacht produces only one example, which gives a false impression. At first, his diagram, as we have seen, gives an impression that there were three authorities from whom ʻAmr had transmitted this tradition. As a matter of fact, the name of his teacher, Muṭṭalib, occurs twice in the diagram. Hence, it should be drawn as follows:

1. Origins 171-2. For the cases of anonymity in *isnād* see, *supra*, p. 222.

Prophet

Jābir

a man of Banū Salam   Muṭṭalib

'Amr

'Abd al- 'Azīz   Ibrāhīm   Sulaimān

Besides this, it seems that Professor Schacht either over-looked the text of *Ikh.* 294 or did not understand it. Shāfi'ī, comparing between three students of 'Amr, makes it clear that 'Abd al-'Azīz was wrong in naming the authority of 'Amr as a man of Banū Salama, that Ibrāhīm was a stronger transmitter than 'Abd al-'Azīz and his statement is attested to by Sulaimān as well. Hence, it appears, that there is only one channel through which 'Amr has received his information. Accordingly, the diagram would appear as follows:

Prophet

Jābir

Muṭṭalib

'Amr

'Abd al-'Azīz   Ibrāhīm   Sulaimān

Thus all the conclusions of Schacht and that of Robson are irrelevent and baseless.

Furthermore, even if we accept Schacht's explanation that 'Amr claimed that he received the information through different lines, we have to remember that this is a single case. It does not appear that Professor Schacht has made any thorough investigation of *isnāds* of a considerable part of legal traditions necessary to put forward a theory of this nature, let alone his investigation of all of them or most of them. A theory of such common application is unacceptable on such a meager evidence. It seems that he has two kinds of measurements for research. To formulate a theory, he uses the term 'common occurrence'[1], basing his research on a few examples that suit his theory; and if there are cases which cover 99% of the subject that refute his theory, then he uses the word 'occasionally'[2] to minimize their effect. This dual standard of argument shows his prejudice and bias and consequently jeopardizes the conclusions of his whole research.

Moreover, even if it happens that there are some cases where a tradition is transmitted through a variety of lines of authorities and has a common transmitter at a certain age, the conclusion of Schacht would still be invalid. Because the edited work of Suhail makes it clear that dozens of scholars, belonging to different countries, transmitted a single tradition from one source while a few of them such as al-Zuhrī, Shu'bah etc., transmitted it from more than one. If we find a scholar like al-Zuhrī who is the only narrator from one source or more, in some cases, his trustworthiness has been established, there is no reason to suspect someone, even to charge him with forgery, on the basis that he is the sole authority who has transmitted a tradition and no other source for the same tradition is traceable, as is done by Schacht, is nonsense. For this kind of charge one should have some solid positive ground. It is doubtful if we apply the same standard to any other literature of the world, we would be able to prove its authenticity. However, traditionists themselves were aware of this kind of problem and its implications and they have given the proper place to everything according to its merits. Here is an example. Dhahabī says[3]:

« ... فانظر اول شيء الى اصحاب رسول الله صلى الله عليه وسلم الكبار والصغار ،
احد إلا وقد انفرد بسنة . فيقال له : هذا الحديث لا يتابع عليه . وكذلك التابعون،

1. *Origin.* 172
2. *Origin.* 28.
3. *Mīzān,* iii, 140-1.

كل واحد عنده ما ليس عند الآخر من العلم ، وما الغرض ؛ فان هذا مقرر على ما ينبغي فى علم الحديث . وان تفرد الثقة المتقن يعد صحيحاً غريباً ، وان تفرد الصدوق ومن دونه يعد منكراً . وان اكثار الراوى من الأحاديث التى لا يوافق عليها لفظا او اسنادا يصيره متروك الحديث»

There remains one more point. A scholar had material on a single topic by different authorities and had collected many traditions to this effect. Later scholars have utilized all these materials in such a way that he appears to be the common link in all *isnāds.* This does not provide a proof of fabrication of material by this certain person. It means, most probably, that the later authorities were quoting from his work referring to the author instead of the work, as was the fashion of the time.

General conclusion about the the growth of Isnāds with special reference to Suhail's Work.

If we analyse the traditions regarding the growth of their *isnāds* with special reference to Suhail's work, we may put them in three categories:

1. Traditions transmitted by only one Companion, who has only one student, who in turn has only one transmitter from him. The following traditions of Suhail come under this category:— 11; 28; 35; 43; 44 = 5 traditions.

2. Traditions transmitted by a certain Companion, who has only one student but the traditions have been attested to by other Companions. The following traditions of Suhail come under this category: 1; 2; 13; 14; 29; 31; 34; 37; 38; 39; 42 = 11 traditions.

3. Traditions transmitted by a certain Companion having more than one student; meanwhile the traditions in the same sense are transmitted by other Companions with a fair number of students. The following traditions of Suhail come under this category: 3; 4; 5; 6; 7; 8; 9; 10; 12; 15; 16; 17; 18; 19; 20; 21; 22; 23; 24; 25; 26; 27; 30; 32; 33; 36; 40; 41; 45; 46; 47; 48 = 32 traditions.

4. Besides these there may be traditions transmitted from more than one Companion, but in the later period a single transmitter is the only transmitter from all the higher authorities. This is rare and there is no example of this sort in Suhail's work.

Schacht and the authenticity of Isnāds.

"... The *isnāds* constitute the most arbitrary part of the traditions ... [And] it is common knowledge that the *isnād* started from rudimentary beginnings and reached perfection in the classical collections of traditions in the second half of the third century A.H. ... The *isnāds* were often put together very carelessly. Any typical representative of the group whose doctrine was to be projected back on to an ancient authority, could be chosen at random and put into the *isnād* ... The following are further examples of the general uncertainty and arbitrary character of *isnāds*"[1].

The present study shows quite different phenomena of the *isnāds.* Now, it is beyond doubt that the system of *isnād* began from the time of the Prophet. The scholars differed from one to another in utilizing the system. At the end of the century it had reached almost its peak. The numbers of transmitters of one tradition and their different localities make it difficult to imagine the theory of "projecting back". It was not that perfection extended into the time of classical collection, as maintained by Schacht[2], but in the words of Fouad Sezgin, who studied Bukhārī in this context, "He [Bukhārī] can, in fact, be regarded as the first person to seriously shake the authority of the *isnād*"[3].

In the thousands of traditions transmitted by Mālik or other scholars, Professor Schacht picks out the faulty cases to formulate a theory. This is the main feature of his research. Even the references provided by him tend to refute his theory. For example[4], where he points out Mālik's mistakes, referring to Zurqānī, he does not quote the complete paragraph. For Zurqānī has also pointed out that even Mālik's student, Shāfi'ī, checked his fault[5]. The scholars, comparing Mālik's *Ḥadīth* with several of his colleagues, found him faulty. And as seven out of eight scholars were almost agreed and unanimous in their actual *Ḥadīth* against Mālik, thus the mistake was checked[6]. If it were a common practice to attach

1. *Origin.* 163-4.
2. *Origin.* 163.
3. Sezgin, F., *Buharinin Kaynaklari,* preface xiv.
4. He says, "The *isnāds* were often put together carelessly" (Origin. 163) and says in the footnote see: significant examples above, p. 53f and below, p. 263. This example is given by Schacht in *Origin,* p. 263.
5. Zurqānī, I, 70.
6. Suyūṭī, *Tanwīr al-Ḥawālik,* i, 44, quoting Daraquṭnī.

isnāds to forged *Aḥādīth* it would have been impossible to check and remove the discrepancy. The fact that checking was and could be done shows that a fictitious *isnād* was very rare and almost impossible to remain undetected. It cannot be denied that every scholar commits mistakes in copying at one time or another[1], but these cases cannot be accepted as the only relevant material for research.

Argument concerning Schacht's examples of the arbitrary character of Isnāds.

1. He refers to 'Umar's prostration after the recitation of a certain chapter from the *Qur'ān* which is related by 'Urwah, and which has a *"Munqaṭi' isnād"*. He says, "Bukhārī has a different, uninterrupted *isnād.* But old copies of the *Muwaṭṭa'* have 'and we did it together with him', which is impossible in the mouth of 'Urwa. This, of course is the original text of the *Muwaṭṭa'* . . . This shows that the formulation of the text of the tradition came first, the *isnād* was added arbitrarily and improved and extended backwards later"[2]. It does not appear on what authority Professor Schacht thinks that this "of course" is the original text of the *Muwaṭṭa'*. The most famous commentator on the *Muwaṭṭa',* Ibn 'Abd al-Barr (d. 463 A.H.) has not seen anything of this sort. Here is the text:

ان عمر بن الخطاب قرأ سجدة وهو على المنبر فنزل فسجد وسجد الناس معه . هكذا الرواية الصحيحة وهى التى عند ابى عمرو ، ويقع فى نسخ وسجدنا معه ... ثم قرأها يوم الجمعة الاخرى فتهيأ الناس للسجود ، فقال على رسلكم ... فلم يسجدوا ومنعهم ان يسجدوا.

Zurqānī says that this is the correct version and in some copies *'wa sajadnā ma'ahā',* but there is no reference to the 'old copies'. After all every Arabist would reach the conclusion in this case that this was due to the scribe's mistake who dropped a single letter *sīn* س from وسجد الناس معه which was sufficient to make all these versions. Moreover, if it had been the original text as it is assumed

1. Schacht himself has committed mistakes in his book, for example when he mentions that Ibrāhīm confirms certain things by pointing out the absence of any information on the matter from the Prophet (Origin. 60), and refers to A.Y. 349-52. But A.Y. 349-50 have explicit statements contrary to this claim.

2. *Origin.* 164.

by Schacht, and 'Urwah had used the first person personal pronoun plural number, most likely he would have changed the structure of the whole of the next sentence and it would have been فتهيأ للسجود .. فلم نسجد .. ومنعنا ان نسجد .

Furthermore, as Mālik transmits this tradition on the authority of Hishām, if it were a case of forgery, they would not have been so foolish as to make such a blunder because both of them were clever scholars. Therefore to cast doubt on the *isnād* of Bukhārī, basing it on a discrepancy of the text which occurred in later centuries is wrong and unacceptable.

2. *Another Example.*

"A significant example of the arbitrary creation of *Isnāds* occurs in TR. II 6 (a) and (b). Here we have first three versions of an Iraqian tradition that 'Alī said, or gave orders to say prayers over the tomb of Sahl b. Ḥunaif. [He is mistaken here[1]; there is only one version to this effect.]. The prayer over the tomb was an Iraqian invention, but did not become prevalent in Iraq... Nor did it become prevalent in Medina, although a tradition from the Prophet in its favour found currency there. The *isnād* of this tradition uses the son of Sahl... It is *Mursal;* the *isnād* was later completed by inserting Sahl himself and by creating new *isnāds* through other companions"[2]. If the prayer over the tomb was an Iraqian invention, as assumed by Schacht, and later on the traditions were fabricated, both in Medinite and Iraqian circles, going back to the Prophet, then why did it not become prevalent either in Iraq or in Medīnah? How did the Iraqians convince their opponents, Medinites, to invent a tradition in their favour? What impossibility is there if the Prophet had prayed on the tomb once or twice in his life, and this was taken by 'Alī?

Schacht did not quote Zurqānī completely. Zurqānī says that all the transmitters of the *Muwaṭṭa'* agree unanimously that it is a *Mursal* tradition but Mūsā b. Muḥammad transmitted from Mālik with full *isnād.* Mūsā is *Matrūk* — abandoned —. Sufyān b. Ḥusain, transmitting this tradition through al-Zuhrī, provides a complete *isnād,* and the scholars unanimously held that Sufyān is

1. The wordings in the brackets are the notes of the present writer.
2. *Origin.* 165.

a weak narrator from al-Zuhrī. Thus the correct conclusion is that this is a *Mursal* tradition[1]. It means that the scholars have checked this mistake and did not accept it, yet Zurqānī adds that the tradition itself is authentic and transmitted by many Companions with authentic *isnāds*. It proves that they judge everything on its own merits; even if the text is correct, it is not accepted with a false *isnād*.

Example 3.

Schacht notices that the editor of *Āthār* Abū Yūsuf "has collected in the commentary the parallels in the classical and other collections; a comparsion shows the extent of the progressive completion, improvement, and backward growth is *isnāds*"[2].

A few examples already collected from Abū Yūsuf and Shāfi'ī's writings show the method of handling their documents. They were more content with the subject matter referred to it in the easiest way[3], but it was the duty of traditionist as specialists in the subject to guard it by every means. So, it is fundamentally unscientific to carry a research in *isnād* through law books as it has been clear from Abū Yūsuf's own writings[4].

Example 4.

Professor Schacht gives another example, where he thinks a *Mursal* tradition was awarded a full *isnād*, and quotes, "But Ṭaḥāwī remarks that the most reliable of Mālik's companions, including Qa'nabī and Ibn Wahb, relate it with an imperfect *isnād*, that is, *mursal*"[5]. The learned Professor misunderstood here, the text of Ṭaḥāwī. Ṭaḥāwī speaks only of the tradition transmitted by the students of Mālik. Some students of Mālik transmitted it with full *isnāds*, but his famous students transmitted it as *Munqaṭi*[6]. He does not speak about the traditions coming through different channels other than Mālik.

---

1. Zurqānī, ii, 11.
2. *Origin.* 165.
3. *Supra,* 219-22.
4. *Supra,* 219-20.
5. *Origin.* 166.
6. Ṭaḥāwī, *Ma'ānī al-Āthār,* ii, 265.

Example 5.

"The first tradition from the Prophet in favour of the Medinese doctrine, and the only one known to Mālik, in *Mursal*... In Mecca, the tradition was provided with an uninterrupted *isnād* of Meccan authorities... This was the only additional version which Shāfi'ī knew when he wrote TR. III, 15 [in the same paragraph the document of Sa'd (d. 15) is mentioned, see *Umm* vii 112, and Schacht has overlooked it]. When he wrote *Ikh.* 346, he knew a further version with a Medinese *isnād,* relating it from the Prophet on the authority of two Companions. In *Umm* vi, 273 ff. he quotes the following additional versions"[1]. Professor Schacht, afterwards, gives those other versions[2]. Two of them are transmitted through Darāwardī, and so Schacht thinks that either Darāwardī or someone who utilized his name was responsible for this.

We cannot say that Mālik knew about this case. Even without discussing it in detail, the case of Shāf'ī is much clear. He gives nine versions in *Umm*, vol. vi, 273, in vol. vii (Tr. III, 15). Therefore it is incorrect to say that when he wrote Tr. III, 15, he knew only one additional version, because Tr. III, 15, has two versions and because it makes a part of vol. vii, while Shāfi'ī has given in vol. vi, nine versions. Naturally he would have composed vol. vi, earlier than vol. vii. Furthermore, Shāfi'ī says that he has lost some of his books and aimed at conciseness, so has given only what would be sufficient, without exhausting all that can be known on the subject[3].

To conclude the discussion on the 'arbitrary character' of *isnāds,* only one more case is examined.

Example 6.

Schacht says, "We sometimes find that *isnāds* which consist of a rigid and formal chain of representatives of a school of law and project its doctrine back to some ancient authority, are duplicated by others which go back to the same authority by another way. This was intended as a confirmation of the doctrine of the school by seemingly independent evidence. A Medinese example is:

---

1. *Origin.* 168.
2. *Origin.* 168.
3. Shāfi'ī, *Risālah,* 431. This is well-known to Prof. Schacht, see *Origin. Preface,* vii.

I.U.—A.Q.—his father—the opinion of ʿUthmān, Zaid and Marwān (Tr. III, 89(a)).

The interruption in the *isnād* above Qāsim was remedied, and A.Q. eliminated, in: Mālik—Yaḥyā—Qāsim—Furāfiṣa—ʿUthmān (*Muw.* ii, 151 [see 152]); finally there appeared: Mālik—Ibn Abū Bakr—b. ʿĀmir—ʿUthmān, with a composite anecdote (*Muw.* ii, 192)"[1].

Professor Schacht reverses the case. He says that the interruption of the above-mentioned *isnād* was remedied and A.Q. was eliminated in Mālik. But *Mursal isnād* occurs in Shāfiʿī's book *al-Umm,* VII, 224. Mālik had compiled his work some forty or fifty years earlier than Shāfiʿī's work. If we accept Schacht's statement, then we would have to wait till after the death of Shāfiʿī for the compilation of *Muwaṭṭa*'!!! which actually existed some fifty years before Shāfiʿī's work. So, according to Professor Schacht, the mistake was remedied before it was ever committed. The whole problem which is described in these two *Ḥadīth* is that they report the act of the Caliph ʿUthmān, that he covered his face in the time of pilgrimage to save himself from the scorching heat. What impossibility do we face, if two men have seen him in the pilgrimage doing this!!!

Difficulties in the 'Projecting Back' theory of Schacht.

All scholars, even of one city, differ in their fame. Every student wants to attach himself to the most respectable authority of his time. In the second century a good deal of literature was available about الجرح والتعديل . The mastery of many scholars had been accepted, while others had been denounced. Why did not all the students choose the most respected personality and put their traditions in his mouth and link them with the most reliable *isnād*? Why did they choose weak and *Matrūk* personalities so often?

The other difficult problem we face is the existence of quite a number of traditions common in form and sense in the traditionist literature of different Muslim sects, e.g., *Sunnī, Zaidī,* Shiʿīte and Khārijite, etc.[2], who had split off only thirty years after the death

1. *Origin.* 169 (some abbreviations are used in copying the names in this passage).
2. This phenomenon has been noticed by Nallino.

of the Prophet. Had all the legal traditions been fabricated in the second and third century A.H., there could not be a single tradition common to sources of these different sects. Schacht's explanation is historically unacceptable. He says, "for a considerable period, and during the second and the third centuries A.H. in particular, the ancient sects remained in a sufficiently close contact with the *Sunnī* community, for them to adopt Muhammadan law as it was being developed in the orthodox schools of Law, introducing only such superficial modifications as required by their own political and dogmatic tenets"[1]. How can one accept this theory while the pages of history are full of war? The continually fought each other with the sword, condemning their opponents as out of Islam, rejecting their beliefs and ideas and abusing each other from the pulpits of mosques. All these circumstances make it hard even to suggest a close relation with the *Sunnī* community only for borrowing legal ideas!

His claim that the *isnāds* were duplicated by others which go back to the same authority by another way providing independent evidence to confirm the doctrine, is absurd. As it has been shown earlier, the transmitters of a single tradition, in so many cases, belong to a dozen different countries and thus their meetings and agreement on this sort of fabrication was almost impossible.

Professor Robson, commenting on Schacht's theory of the improvement of *isnād,* points out that, "Traditionist themselves have drawn attention to certain men who have a reputation for taking traditions which go back only to Followers or Companions and giving them a complete *isnād* back to the Prophet... But we have seen that there is reason to believe that the same thing has been done with traditions which are accepted everywhere. Why were some men blamed for acting dishonestly while others were allowed to do the same thing without any attention being drawn to the fact? I feel sure that is was not because they were cleverer and more able to conceal their handiwork. It was rather that they were working within schools which had certain principles to establish"[2].

Professor Robson may be sure, but he does not provide any basis for his hypothesis. If he had taken a few names who are ac-

---

1. *Origin.* 260; see also Schacht, *Foreign Element, J.C.L.I. Law,* 1950, 13 also *Law.* 16.

2. Robson, *Muslim Tradition, op. cit.,* 100.

cused of this kind of practice, had examined their traditions which are supposed to have been improved in this way and had found some common fact of scholastic dispute, then it could be a tenable theory. Otherwise there can be no value in maintaining a theory without any base. There is a very famous tradition كلكم راع وكلكم مسئول عن رعيته with full *isnāds* and transmitted by many Companions. Ibn 'Uyaynah used to transmit this tradition *Mursal*. All of his students transmitted it *Mursal*, while Ibrāhīm b. Bashshār transmitted it with full *isnād* and on this basis the scholars "weakened" him, saying: ليس بالمتقن [1]. The tradition in question does not have any political or religious basis but an ethical one. What scholastic feeling can one find in it?

There is another tradition concerning *zakāt:* that it is not due till the year ends. It is transmitted as an *athar* of Ibn 'Umar[2] and is accepted among all lawyers. Someone has transmitted it as going back to the Prophet, which was rejected, and it is accepted as the words of Ibn 'Umar and as a basis for *Zakāt* taxation. The scholars charged someone of this practice after making comparisons between the notes of different students of one teacher and then tracing them back and comparing their materials. Sometimes they collected fifteen and twenty versions of one work to compare for mistakes and discrepancies[3].

Schacht and the Isnād of Mālik and Nāfi'.

Professor Schacht has cast suspicion on the *isnād* of Mālik – Nāfi' – Ibn 'Umar and has challenged its authenticity on two grounds:

On the age of Mālik.

Relation of Nāfi' with Ibn 'Umar as he was the client. In his own words: "But as Nāfi' died in A.H. 117 or thereabouts, and Mālik in A.H. 179, their association can have taken place, even at the most generous estimate, only when Mālik was little more than a boy. It may even be questioned whether Mālik, whom Shāfi'ī

---

1. *Mīzān*, I, 23. ابراهيم بن بشار... ليس بالمتقن، وله مناكير قال ابن عدى: لا اعلم انكر عليه الا هذا (اي رفعه كلكم راع...).
2. Dārāquṭnī, 198, foot-note.
3. *Supra*, Ḥammād b. Salamah and Yaḥyā b. Ma'īn, p. 129.

charged elsewhere with concealing imperfections in his *isnāds,* did not take over in written form traditions alleged to come from Nāfi'"[1]. He says in the footnote that, "Nothing authentic is known of Mālik's date of birth"[2].

Professor Schacht treats the case in reverse. Instead of giving the birth date of Mālik to show how old he was when Nāfi' died, he gives the death date of Mālik claiming nothing authentic is known of his date of birth and gives the impression, even in writing, that he was little more than a boy. Had he consulted any bibliographical work he would have found that most of the scholars, even those who were born a little earlier than Mālik, state that he was born in 93 A.H.; a few put it in the early months of 94 A.H., a few in 90 A.H. and a few in 97[3]. But there is no one who maintains any date later than this. So, Mālik was at least twenty years old, if not twenty-four or twenty-seven, when Nāfi' died. He transmitted in the *Muwaṭṭa'* from Nāfi' only eighty traditions of the Prophet, which covers about fifteen pages[4] in the printed text of Ibn 'Abd al-Barr. Other *āthār* transmitted by Mālik on the authority of Nāfi', are not taken into account; if we give an equal number to those from the Prophet, then it would be some thirty pages. The teacher Nāfi' and the student Mālik both lived in one city till Mālik was twenty-four years old, which makes it difficult to say that he might not have learned these thirty pages from his teacher. Schacht's omission of Mālik's birth date in this argument can lead only to erroneous conclusions.

The other point raised by Schacht is that Nāfi' was a client of Ibn 'Umar. But if a man is being accepted amongst his contemporaries and among the later authorities as most trustworthy, then why should he be dishonest? If a statement of a father about his son or vice versa, or a wife about her husband or a friend about a friend or a colleague about a colleague is always unacceptable, then on what sources could a biography possibly be written? Nāfi' was not the only scholar who transmitted from Ibn 'Umar, but there were students in great numbers, and the scholars always

1. *Origin.* 176-7.
2. *Origin.* 176 footnote.
3. Ibn 'Abd al-Barr, *Intiqā'* 10; Mashāhīr, 140; Zurqānī, *commentary on Muwaṭṭa',* i, 5.
4. Ibn 'Abd al-Barr, *Tajrīd al-Tamhīd,* pp. 170-184.

tried to cross-check each other's statements[1]. If there had been falsification of the sort suggested by Schacht, it would have been impossible that all the other scholars should have kept quiet about him. To claim that hundreds of thousands of scholars spent their lives making forgeries in collusion and produced this vast literature with all biographical details is to show an utter disregard for human nature.

Professor Robson has said in this context, "Was the family *isnād* invented to supply apparent evidence for spurious traditions, or did genuine family *isnāds* exist which later served as models? It seems better to recognise that they are a genuine feature of the documentation, but to realize that people often copied this type of *isnād* to support spurious traditions. Therefore, while holding that family *isnāds* do genuinely exist, one will not take them all at face value"[2].

It is always the case that the genuine thing exists first, and forgery follows. It is quite right that all the family *isnāds* should not be taken as genuine ones. The traditionists, as is obvious from their biographical works, were aware of this fact, and there is no lack of references where they denounce this sort of *isnād*; e.g. (1) Ma'mar b. Muḥammad and his transmission from his father[3], (2) 'Isā b. 'Abd Allāh from his father, (3) Kathīr b. Abd Allāh from his father, (4) Mūsā b. Maṭīr from his father, (5) Yaḥyā b. 'Abd Allāh from his father, etc.

FINAL CONCLUSION.

Summing up the discussion one reaches the following conclusions.

The *isnād* system began in the lifetime of the Prophet and was used by Companions in transmitting the traditions of the Prophet.

Political upheavals in the fourth decade gave birth to the forgery of traditions in the political sphere, to credit or discredit certain parties. So, scholars became more cautious and began to

---

1. *Supra*, p. 231.

2. Robson, *Isnād in Muslim Tradition, Glas. Univ. Orient. Society Tran.*, xv, 1955, p. 23.

3. *Majrūḥīn* 228b; for other people see in *Majrūḥīn* under their names or *Mīzān al-I'tidāl* by Dhahabī, for these sort of remarks.

scrutinize, criticize and search for the sources of information. The use of *isnād,* therefore, became more and more important.

Orientalists have not chosen the right field for the study of *isnād.* The writings of Abū Yūsuf and Shāfi'ī clearly show the inadequacy of law books for the study of *isnāds.*

The nature of *Sīrah* work is far from being merely documentary; for this reason the study of *isnād* or *Ḥadīth* ought to be carried out in its own literature.

The examples supplied by Schacht tend to refute his own theory. The phenomena of *isnād,* the numbers of transmitters belonging to scores of provinces, thoroughly invalidate the theory of "projecting back", "artificial creations" and similar statements.

There does not seem to be "any sort of improvement in *isnād*". Traditionists themselves have checked for this sort of fault. To maintain that they were criticized when they served opponents' scholastic interests is only an assumption without historical evidence. The documents positively refute this theory.

There is no reason whatsoever to discredit the *isnād* of Mālik—Nāfi'—Ibn 'Umar.

All the "family *isnāds*" are not genuine, and all the "family *isnāds*" are not spurious.

According to traditionists, a correct document was wrong and unacceptable unless it came through a proper channel.

There is no reason to reject the *isnād* system. It is proved that it has every element which can command the acceptance of the system as a whole.

Traditionists have taken the utmost care to check errors and discrepancies with sincerity.

The literature still provides sufficient ground for research, and all reasonable methods may be applied to test it.

CHAPTER VII

AḤĀDĪTH

The Authenticity of Ḥadīth.

It has already been shown that the great number of transmitters of traditions, belonging to different provinces and countries, and the constant checking of discrepancies at every stage, leaves very little room for forgery in *isnād*.

The second part of this work contains the text of three early manuscripts which were the primary sources of Mālik for his *Muwaṭṭa'*. The primary sources of Bukhārī viz. 'Abd al-Razzāq, Ḥumaidī and others are in our hands. Even the earliest sources of *Shuyūkh,* viz. Al-Thaurī, Ibn Juraij and al-A'mash are at our disposal. Cross-checking of traditions in these sources in various stages gives us sufficient basis to accept them as genuine, especially when we bear in mind the literary activity of scholars of the pre-Classical period, which has been described in the third chapter of this work. It gives us more confidence when we find that the students used to check their teachers in the class-room, referring to the teachers' colleagues and their documents.

Schacht and the authenticity of Ḥadīth.

The result of Professor Schacht's study contradicts the conclusion of the present study. In Chapter VI, it has been explained that the study of *Ḥadīth* and *isnād* in legal or *Sīrah* books would lead to wrong conclusions. Schacht has outlined the sketches of the early legal activities of the first and second centuries of the *Hijrah,* and has provided some examples of "forged traditions". In this chapter we shall at first examine the picture drawn by him of early legal activities, and then we shall look into his illustrations.

An Outline of Early Legal Activities of the First and Second Centuries A.H. as given by Professor Schacht.

The Prophet, in Madīnah, "Became a 'Prophet-Lawgiver' ... his authority was not legal but, for the belivers, religious and, for the lukewarm, political"[1].

The Caliphs (632-62) "were the political leaders of the Islamic Community... but they do not seem to have acted as its supreme arbitrators... the caliphs acted to a great extent as the lawgivers of the community"[2].

"The first caliphs did not appoint *Kāḍīs*[3]... The Umayyads... took the important step of appointing Islamic judges or *Kāḍīs*"[4]. "...From the turn of the century onwards (c. A.D. 715-20) appointments [of *Kāḍīs]* as a rule went to 'specialist'... the specialists from whom the *Kāḍīs* came increasingly to be recruited were found among those pious persons whose interest in religion caused them to elaborate, and individual reasoning, an Islamic way of life"[5]. "As the groups of pious specialists grew in numbers and in cohesion, they developed, in the first few decades of the second century of Islam, into the ancient schools of Law"[6].

"The ancient schools of law shared... the essentials of legal theory... The central idea of this theory was that of the 'living tradition of the school' as represented by the constant doctrine of its authoritative representatives... It presents itself under two aspects. retrospective and synchronous. Retrospectively it appears as *Sunna* or "Practice" (*'Amal*)[7]...

"Nevertheless, the idea of continuity inherent in the concept of *sunna,* the idealized practice, together with the need to create

1. *Law.,* 11.
2. *Ibid.,* 15.
3. *Ibid.,* 16
4. *Ibid.,* 24.
5. *Ibid.,* 26.
6. *Ibid.,* 28.
6. *Ibid.,* 28
7. *Ibid.,* 29-30. It is wrong to say, as described by Schacht, *Origin.* 58, that the old concept of *Sunnah* was the customary of generally agreed practice and the place was filled in later systems by the *Sunnah* of the Prophet. The word *Sunnah* of the Prophet is used by the Prophet, Abū Bakr, 'Umar, 'Uthmān and 'Ali See Wensinck, *Concordance,* vol. ii, 555-8, Yaqūbī, *History,* ii, 104. For the usage of the word in the first century Mu'tazilah writings see al-Murtaḍā, *Ṭabaqāt al-Mu'azilh,* 19. See also Ṭabarī, *Annales,* i, 3166, 3299, 3044.

some kind of theoretical justification for what so far had been an instinctive reliance on the opinions of the majority, led, from the first decades of the second century onwards, to the living tradition being projected backwards and to its being ascribed to some of the great figures of the past. The Kufians were the first in attributing the doctrine of their school to Ibrāhīm al-Nakh'ī... The Medinese followed suit..."[1].

"The process of going backwards for a theoretical foundation of Islamic religious law... did not stop at these relatively late authorities..., [but was taken back to and] directly connected with the very beginnings of Islam in Kūfa, beginnings associated with Ibn Mas'ūd[2] ...".

"The movement of the Traditionists... in the second century of the *Hijrah,* was the natural outcome and continuation of a movement of religiously and ethically inspired opposition to the ancient schools of law"[3]. "The main thesis of the Traditionists... was the formal "traditions"... deriving from the Prophet superseded the living tradition of the school... The Traditionists produced detailed statements or 'traditions' which claimed to be the reports of ear-or eye-witnesses on the words or acts of the Prophet, handed down orally by an uninterrupted chain (*Isnād*) of trustworthy persons. Hardly any of these traditions, as far as matters of religious law are concerned, can be considered authentic"[4]. All "the ancient schools of law, ... offered strong resistance to the disturbing element represented by the traditions which claimed to go back to the Prophet"[5]. And, "Traditions from the Prophet had to overcome a strong opposition on the part of the ancient schools of law..."[6].

1. *Law.* 31.
2. *Ibid.,* 32.
3. *Ibid.,* 34.
4. *Law.* 34.
5. *Ibid.,* 35.
6. *Origin.* 57. This conception is entirely wrong. The over-ruling authority of the *Sunnah* of the Prophet and as the basic source of law is a rule accepted by all from the earliest days of Islam. See for details, Shāfi'ī, *Umm,* vii, 250; Sibā'ī, *Sunnah,* 160; al-Baṣrī al-Mu'tazilī, *al-Mu'tamad,* 377-387; Kayyāṭ, *Intiṣār,* 89, 98; 135-6, 137; Ibn 'Umar's saying, Ḥanbal, ii, 95; for the sayings of Abū Ḥanīfah see Ibn 'Abd al-Barr, *Intiqā',* 145; and for Auzā'ī, Abū Yūsuf, 37, 46.

The main reason for this wrong conclusion of Schacht is his unscientific method of research. He utilizes the polemic writings of scholars, mainly Shāfi'ī's accusation of his opponent, to define the legal doctrines of Shāfi'ī's

"It is safe to assume that Muhammadan law hardly existed in the time of the historical Sha'bī", (d. 110)[1]. "Ibrāhīm al-Nakha'ī of Kūfa (d. 95 or 96 A.H...) did no more than give opinions on questions of ritual, and perhaps on kindred problems of directly religious importance... but not on technical points of law"[2].

Schacht's Conception of the Nature of Law in Islām.

It seems as if Schacht is fundamentally wrong in the conception of the function of the Prophet Muḥammad as a legislator. To say that the Prophet in Madīnah became a "prophet-lawgiver" and simultaneously claim that his authority was not legal is a statement with misleading implications. He ignored the *Qur'ān* totally in this context. Had he gone through it, he would have found the clear divine legislative authority of the Prophet[3]. Furthermore, the earliest written document of "the Constitution of Medina" gives him the supreme authority in all their disputes and his decision was the final one[4]. He has the highest judicial authority according to the *Qur'ān*[5]. Law in Islam has a divine origin[6]. Kharijites parted from 'Alī, on his setting up of a human tribunal as they believed it was against the divine word, loudly protesting that "judgment belongs to God alone"[7]. All the community was and is bound to judge according to the law revealed by God, otherwise they would no longer remain Muslims[8]. Therefore it was the prime duty of the Prophet as well as the Caliphs to promulgate the law and administer justice according to it. As law in Islam has a divine origin, so is the administration of justice a

---

while ignoring the writings of those scholars and their own expression of their attitudes towards the *Sunnah* of the Prophet. See, *Origin,* 11, 28, 35, 88, 259.

1. *Origin.* 230 footnote 1; for the date of his death, see *Origin.* General Index, 347.
2. *Law.* 27.
3. *The Qur'ān,* vii, 157; lix, 7.
4. Ḥamidullāh, *al-Wathā'iq al-Siyāsīyah,* No. I, pp. 18-20. See for the authenticity of the document, Serjeant, *Islamic Quarterly,* viii, 1-16.
5. See for example; *Al-Qur'ān,* iv, 59, 65, 105; xxiv, 51; xlii, 15.
6. See for example: Fitzgerald, *The Alleged Debt of Islamic to Roman Law. The Law Quarterly Review,* vol. 67; p. 82.
7. G. Levi Della Vida, Art. *Kharidjites, E.I.,* vol. ii, 905; see also Aḥmad Amīn, *Fajr al-Islām,* 256.
8. *The Qur'ān,* v, 44-9; xii, 40; xxxiii, 36.

Divine ordinance and a practice of the Prophet which ought to be followed[1]. There are references to the Companions who were sent as *Qāḍīs* by the Prophet[2]. Meanwhile, the governors of the Prophet were ordered to administer justice and were given clear instructions to dispense justice impartially[3]. A very good list of the early *Qāḍīs* appointed by 'Umar and the other early Caliphs could be provided, even now, from the available sources[4]. Therefore Schacht's claim that the Prophet's authority was not legal and that the first Caliphs did not appoint *Qāḍīs* and that the conception of Islamic way of life is the production of pious persons' individual reasoning, is absurd and contrary to facts. The Caliph 'Uthmān even built a separate building for the Court of Justice with the name *Dār al-Qaḍā'*[5]. Professor Schacht does not give us any reason as to what compelled early scholars of the first century to confine themselves to ritual decisions. Did no dispute occur among them for 100 years? Did they not buy or sell[6], which could cause some misunderstanding, so that they had to go to the court?

Schacht's 'ancient schools of law' and the birth of an opposition party in their chronological setting.

Abū Ḥanīfah died in 150. His clear statement about the over-ruling authority of the *Sunnah* of the Prophet goes back to about 140 A.H.[7]. We have been told that in the life of Sha'bī, d. 110, Islamic law did not exist. Between 110 and 140, there remain only thirty years for the following activities:

Birth of ancient schools of law.

Growth of the schools and ideas of consensus.

---

1. The letter of Caliph 'Umar to Abū Mūsā, *J.R.A.S.*, 1910, as quoted by Ḥamīdullāh, *Administration of Justice in Early Islam. Islamic Culture,* 1937, p. 169.
2. Sa'd, iii, ii, 121.
3. Ḥamīdullāh, *Administration of Justice, I.C.*, 1937; 166-7.
4. See for details about 'Umar's Qāḍīs, *Shiblī Nu'mānī*, 304-15.
5. Al-Kattānī, *Tarātīb idārīyah,* i, 271-2, quoting Ibn 'Asākir.
6. See also Coulson, *A History of Islamic Law*, 64-5.
7. Dhahabī says that in 143 A.H. Abū Ḥanīfah and others compiled the book. For the doctrine of Abū Ḥanīfah regarding the over-ruling authority of *Sunnah,* see Ibn 'Abd al-Barr, *al-Intiqā,* 142, 143, 144; Nu'mānī, *Sīrat al-Nu'mān,* 124; Shaibānī, *'Athār* almost every page; Abū Zahrah, *Abū Ḥanīfah,* 275-7; *Bagh.* xiii, 368; see also, *Origin.* 28.

Projecting back of ideas, for example by Iraqian, to the higher authority, Al-Nakha'ī.

Further projecting to an older authority than Al-Nakha'ī such as Masrūq.

Further projecting to the oldest authority such as Ibn Mas'ūd.

Projecting back to the Prophet as a last resort.

Birth of opposition group, (traditionists).

Their fabrications of *Ḥadīth* with full details of the life and decisions of the Prophet as well as of the Companions.

The opposition's fight with the ancient schools, and the loss of ground by ancient schools and the establishment of the overruling authority of the *Sunnah.*

Meanwhile one must bear in mind that an opposition party comes into existence after a considerable time from the birth of the opposed party, especially if this is quite a new thing. A mere thirty years for all these activities is inconceivable, and thus Schacht falls back on the theory of living traditions.

Now, it is obvious that the legal activities of the first centuries and the birth of the opposition party is unacceptable in their chronological setting as described by Schacht.

Schacht and "The Growth of Legal Traditions in the Literary Period".

According to Schacht "...The best way of proving that a tradition did not exist at a certain time is to show that it was not used as a legal argument in a discussion which would have made reference to it imperative, if it had existed"[1].

There are many problems which need to be solved before accepting this theory.

1. *Contradictory Statement.*

First of all one has to observe the contradictory statements of Schacht. He says that two generations before Shāfi'ī, reference to the tradition of the Prophet was the exception[2]. Furthermore,

1. *Origin.* 140.
2. *Ibid.*, 3.

according to him, all these ancient schools of law offered strong resistence to the traditions of the Prophet[1]. In view of the above statements what would have made reference to traditions of the Prophet imperative even if they existed. Either his two earlier statements are wrong, or his whole chapter is irrelevant for the purpose.

2. *The theory against human nature.*

The other fundamental objection to this theory is that this is against human nature. Who can claim that he has all the knowledge of the subject and nothing is missing. Therefore, if a tradition is not quoted by a certain scholar, how does it prove that it did not exist?[2].

3. *Chaos in Terminology.*

Moverover Schacht gives the title of 'The Growth of Legal Tradition', yet he fills it up mostly with a number of ritual traditions. The other drawback is that he has put the *Āthār* of Successors and Companions under the name of Traditions. When he speaks about the *'Sunnah'* he translates it as "the living tradition of ancient schools" and when he speaks about the legal decision of the scholars, then he puts them under the aegis of tradition, which causes more chaos and does not give a fair picture of the subject.

Argument about Schacht's examples of the growth of legal traditions.

Example 1.

Let us examine a few of his examples in this chapter. He says: "The evidence collected in the present chapter has been chosen with particular regard to this last point, and in a number of cases one or the other of the opponents himself states that he has no evidence other than that quoted by him, which does not include the tradition in question. This kind of conclusion *e silentio* is furthermore made safe by Tr. VIII, 11, where Shaibānī says: '[this is so] unless the Medinese can produce a tradition in support of their doctrine, but they have none, or they would have produced it". Commenting on this statement, Schacht says: "We may safely assume that the legal traditions with which we are concerned were quoted as arguments by those whose doctrine they

1. *Ibid.*, 57.

2. Professor Schacht denies the existence of certain traditions, and they are on the same page referred to by him. See *Origin.* 60. Compare with *A.Y.*, 349-52.

were intended to support, as soon as they were put into circulation"[1].

Here is the original text: «قال ابو حنيفة كل شىء يصاب به العبد من يد او رجل . ... فهو من قيمته على مقدار ذلك .... وقال اهل المدينة فى موضحة العبد نصف عشر ثمنه ... فوافقوا ابا حنيفة فى هذه الخصال الاربعة وقالوا فيما سوى ذلك ما نقص من ثمنه . قال محمد بن الحسن كيف جاز لأهل المدينة ان يتحكموا فى هذا فيختاروا هذه الخصال الاربعة من بين الخصال ... فينبغى ان ينصف الناس ولا يتحكم فيقول قولوا بقولى ما قلت من شىء إلا ان يأتى أهل المدينة فيما قالوا من هذا باثر فننقاد له . وليس عندهم فى هذا اثر يفرقون به بين هذه الاشياء . فلو كان عندهم جاءوا به فيما سمعنا من آثارهم فاذا لم يكن هذا فينبغى الانصاف فاما ان يكون هذا على ما قال ابو حنيفة....»

The first striking fact in the whole discussion is that there is neither a reference to the tradition from the Prophet nor to any other authority. The whole discussions concerns the decision of Abū Ḥanīfah about certain kinds of injuries to slaves and their compensations. The Medinite scholars agree with Abū Ḥanifah in some cases and disagree in others. Al-Shaibānī, arguing with the Medinites, asks what is the reason for their discrimination in certain matters. Why do they follow Abū Ḥanīfah's decision only halfway? Have they any *Athār* to this effect? Let them bring it out; then the Iraqians would follow them in their discrimination. But they have nothing of this sort, so people need to be just...

It is astonishing how Professor Schacht was able to involve the tradition and its forgery in this context.

Example 2.

He says:

Traditions later than "Ḥasan Baṣrī"[2].

There is no tradition in the treatise ascribed to Ḥasan Baṣrī.

His statement would be valid if it could be proved that:

Ḥasan Basrī was the actual author of the work.

He cannot be ignorant of any tradition.

---

1. *Origin.* 140-1
2. *Origin.* 141.

But when the authenticity of the work is challenged, and Schacht himself does not accept it as the work of Ḥasan, then what reason does he have for his hypothesis? It might have been written by a member of *Ahl al-Kalām* or by any heretic or by anyone, but how would the consequences involve Ḥasan Baṣrī and forgery of *Ḥadīth.*

Example 3.

"Tradition originating between "Ibrāhīm Nakha'ī" and Ḥammad".

"...Ibn Mas'ūd did not follow a certain practice... But there is a tradition in favour of the Practice polemically directed against the other opinion. The same tradition with another Iraqian *isnād* occurs in *Tr. II,* 19 (t)"[1].

The tradition concerns the prostration after the reciting of certain verses from *Sūrah Ṣād.* It is reported that Ibn Mas'ūd did not prostrate, but another tradition transmitted by Abū Ḥanīfah—Ḥammād — 'Abd al-Karīm — says the Prophet prostrated after reciting the verses from the *Sūrah Ṣād*[2], and also Ibn 'Uyaynah — Ayyūb — 'Ikrimah — Ibn 'Abbās — the Prophet did[3]. 'Umar — his father — Ibn Jubair — Ibn 'Abbās — the Prophet did[4]. These statements go quite contrary to Professor Schacht's assumption.

It is not a legal tradition but a purely ritual tradition.

Nobody can claim that Ibn Mas'ūd knew all the traditions and missed nothing.

There is no contradiction between these two traditions; one of them is a personal practice of a Companion who did not know the Prophet prostrated. The practice of the Prophet is reported by three different channels. How could the Iraqians persuade the Makkan, Ibn 'Uyaynah to fabricate and transmit traditions to this extent?

This tradition and similar ones shake the theory of Schacht. He says, "The name of Ibn Mas'ūd is usually an indication

---

1. *Origin.* 141.
2. *A.Y.* 207.
3. Shāfi'ī, *Umm,* vii, 174.
4. Shaibānī, *Āthār,* 72.

of the prevailing doctrine of the school of Kūfa''[1]. And ''Ibn Sa'd (vi, 232) identified Ḥammād's own doctrine with what Ḥammād put under the aegis of Ibrāhīm...''[2].

And ''Judging from *Āthār A.Y.* and *Āthār Shaib.* which are the main sources of Ibrāhīm's doctrine...traditions transmitted by Ibrāhīm occur mostly in the legal chapters... and hardly at all in those devoted to purely religious... matters''[3].

If Ibrāhīm and Ibn Mas'ūd were the source for the doctrine of the Kūfan school, as claimed by Schacht, then what was the necessity of attributing statements and practices to them which the Kūfans rejected themselves? Why did they not put their positive doctrine in their sponsor's mouth? If the Kūfans were unscrupulous and exploiting the names of these scholars, then why did they not keep quiet and erase the traditions, instead of weakening the personalities and damaging the prestige of their sponsors to the extent that those scholars were ignorant of certain traditions from the Prophet?

Professor Schacht points out that hardly any tradition from Ibrāhīm relates to purely religious matters. This is quite wrong. For example, the first chapter of A.Y. – *Al-Wuḍū'* is counted, and 29 Āthār out of 53 belong to Ibrāhīm.

Schacht has misreported the wording of Ibn Sa'd to blame Ḥammād. Ibn Sa'd reports Ibn Shaddād saying that he saw Ḥammād writing in the (lecture) of Ibrāhīm. He further reports on the authority of Al-Battī that when Ḥammād decided according to his opinion he was right and when he reported from an authority other than Ibrāhīm, he made a mistake[4].

It means he was a good *Muftī,* and had sufficient knowledge of Ibrāhīm's doctrine and had even written from him, but when he transmitted from authorities other than Ibrāhīm, he made a mistake[4]. There is no mention of forgery.

It is suggested by Schacht–''Ḥammād transmitted traditions which had recently come into circulation, from the Prophet and from various Companions of the Prophet. These outside traditions, which did not belong to the 'Living Tradition' of the school and

1. *Origin.* 232.
2. *Ibid.,* 238-9.
3. *Ibid.,* 234.
4. Sa'd, vi, 232.

often contradicted it and Ḥammād's own doctrine, were the result of the rising pressure of the traditionists on the ancient school of law''[1].

But the problem is much more complicated than this statement suggests.

When late Kufan scholars Ḥammād etc. related *Āthār* from Ibrāhīm and Ibn Mas'ūd either they were really transmitted by them or were ascribed to them falsely as suggested by Schacht. In the second hypothesis, if the Kufans attributed certain traditions to their patrons and acted against them as they often did, it would mean that they themselves weakened the personalities of their sponsors by showing their ignorance. Consequently, it would mean that they cut the very branch on which they rested, and perhaps Ḥammād and Kufan scholars were wiser than this.

Therefore, what their scholars ascribed to certain authorities must have been taken from them.

According to Schacht, until 110 A.H. there was hardly any "Muḥammadan law". Ten or twenty years, which Ḥammād had at the beginning of the second century, was not sufficient even to lay the foundation of the ancient schools of law. Hence the existence of any traditionist movement against recently born or perhaps unborn schools, in such an early stage, is almost impossible. The theory of the rising pressure of the traditionist on the ancient schools of law is totally imaginary and, therefore, unacceptable.

Example 4.

"Tradition Originating between Mālik and the Classical Collections".

"Mālik adds to the text of a tradition from the Prophet his own definition of the aleatory contract *mulāmasa*... [and] the same definition appears as a statement of Mālik... But this interpretation has become part of the words of the Prophet in Bukhārī and Muslim"[2].

The early traditionists were quite aware of this kind of discrepancy. In every *Uṣūl al-Ḥadīth* work one finds a chapter on *Mudraj,* where problems of this sort are discussed. As far as this particular tradition is concerned, Bukhārī has given the exact

---

1. *Origin.* 239.
2. *Origin.* 144.

tradition transmitted by Mālik without any additional materials from Mālik's commentary. The additional material similar to Mālik's statement occurs in a tradition transmitted by 'Uqail—Ibn Shihāb—'Āmir b. Sa'd—Abū Sa'īd al-Khudrī.

The commentators of the book have discussed this sentence, collecting all the material relative to this tradition. Some scholars describe it as the wording of Ibn 'Uyaynah, but Ibn Ḥajar has argued this point and says that this is the commentary of Abū Sa'īd al-Khudrī[1]. Hence, Mālik himself might have taken this definition.

Example 5.

Here is another example of forgery and falsification provided by Professor Schacht.

He makes the startling statement, "That the 'Practice' existed first and traditions from the Prophet and from Companions appeared later, is clearly stated in *Mud.* iv, 28, where Ibn Qāsim gives a theoretical justification of the Medinese point of view. He says: 'This tradition has come down to us, and if it were accompanied by a practice passed to those from whom we have taken it over by their own predecessors, it would be right to follow it. But in fact it is like those other traditions which are not accompanied by practice. [Here Ibn Qāsim gives examples of traditions from the Prophet and from the Companions]. But these things could not assert themselves and take root..."

"The practice was different, and the whole community and the Companions themselves acted on other rules. So the traditions remained neither discredited [in principle] nor adopted in practice, ... and actions were ruled by other traditions which were accompanied by Practice"... "The Medinese thus oppose 'practice' to traditions"[2]. An unwarranted remark! Ibn Qāsim's whole discussion is based on the point that there are two sorts of traditions: one group which is accompanied by the practices of the Companions and the Successors, and another group which is not accompanied by any sort of practice. So, if there were a conflict between these two groups, then the one accompanied by the prac-

1. Ibn Ḥajar, *Fatḥ al-Bārī*, vol. iv, 358-60, edited by Fuwād 'Abd al-Bāqī.

2. *Origin.* 63.

tice would be preferred. Where does he indicate that the practice came first and the tradition later?

Example 6.

Schacht says: "Ibrāhīm is aware that the imprecation against political enemies during the ritual prayer is an innovation introduced only under 'Alī and Mu'āwiyah some considerable time after the Prophet. He confirms this by pointing out the absence of any information on the matter from the Prophet, Abū Bakr and 'Umar". [*Āthār A.Y.* 349-52, etc]. "It follows that the tradition, which claims the Prophet's example for this addition to the ritual and which Shāfi'ī of course accepts, must be later than Ibrāhīm"[1].

Here are the quotations from *A.Y.* 349-52:

آثار أبي يوسف. ‎/٣٤٩ ابو حنيفة—حماد—ابراهيم—ان النبي لم يقنت فى الفجر الا شهرا واحدا

‎/٣٥٠ ابو حنيفة—حماد—ابراهيم—علقمة—عبدالله— عن النبي مثله

‎/٣٥١ ابو حنيفة—حماد—ابراهيم— ان ابا بكر لم يقنت

‎/٣٥٢ ابو حنيفة—حماد—ابراهيم— ان عليّا قنت يدعو على معاويه حين حاربه....

There is one tradition with complete *Isnād* and another one with *Mursal isnād,* both narrated by Ibrāhīm, describing the practice of the Prophet. After this clear reference, it is astonishing how Professor Schacht can make his abovementioned statement while he refers to the same *Āthār!*

The criticism of tradition as carried out by Schacht in this context is entirely irrelevant and quite unacceptable.

Schacht as the Critic of Ḥadīth on Material Grounds.

Mūsā b. 'Uqbah died in about 140 A.H. His book *Kitāb al-Maghāzī* has been incorporated in later works[2], and a few pages in extract form have survived. E. Sachau edited the extract and published it in 1904[3]. After half a century, Schacht wrote an

---

1. *Origin.* 60, where he refers to *A.Y.* 349-52...
2. *Supra.* See Mūsā b. 'Uqbah in the third chapter, pp. 95-6.
3. *Sitzungsber. Preuss. Akad d. Wiss.* 1904, pp. 445-470.

article[1] contradicting the opinion of the earlier scholar Sachau. He describes it thus: "The contents of the extracts are the kind of traditions we should expect about the middle of the second century...[Tradition] No. 6 tries to mitigate, in favour of the ruling dynasty, the episode in which its ancestor 'Abbās, fighting against the Prophet, was captured by the Muslims and had to be ransomed; No. 9, which denies privileges in penal law to the descendants of the Prophet, is anti-Alid; No. 10 praises the Anṣār and, by implication, the pro-Abbasid party in Medina"[2].

"Abbāsid traces are unmistakable; the strong anti-Alid tendency and, particularly, the favourable attitude to the Caliphate of Abū Bakr even point to a period somewhat later than the very first years of 'Abbāsid rule. It would hardly be possible to consider Mūsā himself the author..."[3].

Before the discussion it is better to note the Arabic text for easy reference[4].

Tr. No. 6.

قال ابن شهاب ثنا انس بن مالك ان رجالا من الانصار استأذنوا رسول الله صلى الله عليه وسلم فقالوا ائذن لنا يا رسول الله فلنترك لابن اختنا عباس فداءه . فقال « لا والله ولا تذروا درهماً »

Tr. No. 8.

ثنا اسماعيل بن ابراهيم بن عقبة قال قال سالم بن عبدالله قال عبدالله بن عمر فطعن بعض الناس فى امارة اسامة فقام رسول الله صلعم فقال « ان تطعنوا فى امارة اسامة فقد كنتم تطعنون فى امارة ابيه من قبله . وايم الله ان كان لخليقا لامارة وان كان لمن احب الناس كلهم الى وان هذا لمن احب الناس الى بعده فاستوصوا به خيرا من بعدى فانه من خياركم . »

Tr. No. 9.

قال موسى قال سالم بن عبدالله قال عبدالله بن عمر ما كان رسول الله يستثنى فاطمة رضى الله عنها .

Tr. No. 10.

قال موسى بن عقبة حدثنى عبدالله بن الفضل انه سمع انس بن مالك يقول حزنت

1. Schacht, *On Mūsā b. 'Uqbah, Acta Orientalia*, xxi, 1953, pp. 288-300.
2. Schacht, *On Mūsā, op. cit.*, pp. 289-90.
3. *Ibid.*, 290.
4. Sachau, *op. cit.*, 467-8.

على من اصيب بالحرة من قومى فكتب الى زيد بن ارقم وبلغه شدة حزنى يذكر انه سمع رسول الله صلعم يقول « اللهم اغفر للانصار ولابناء الانصار ونسأل الفضل فى ابناء ابناء الانصار »

1. Guillaume has remarked on the fragment of Mūsā, saying, "Clearly Mūsā's sympathies lay with the family of al-Zubayr and the Anṣār. They alone emerge with credit. The 'Alids on the other hand, are no better than anyone else. The Umayyads are implicitly condemned for the slaughter at al-Harra, and al-'Abbās is shown to have been a rebel against the Prophet who was forced to pay for his opposition to him to the uttermost farthing"[1].

Now it is obvious that Guillaume takes the incident of 'Abbās, (Tr. No. 6) as a sign of anti-'Abbāsid feeling, while Schacht finds in it pro-'Abbāsid elements!! 'Abbās was the uncle of the Prophet. According to Eastern custom, uncles are given rank near to the father. It is quite natural that the man was the brother of the Prophet's father; people wanted to honour him for the sake of the Prophet. Had the Prophet pardoned him, it would have been natural, but the Prophet strongly rejected this recommendation and he had to pay to 'the uttermost farthing'. So, the Prophet did not show any kind of mercy, and did not adopt any lenient policy towards him. Therefore, Schacht's claim that it is in favour of the Abbasids is unacceptable.

Furthermore, if it were fabricated in the 'Abbāsid period and moulded to serve the ruling party, then why was not the whole story changed? Why did the 'Abbāsids not try to clear their forefathers? It was possible at least to drop the last sentence of the Prophet's wording and he would not have been shown paying the uttermost farthing! Moreover, if it were fabricated against 'Alids, so why not in the first century? Were there no wars between 'Alids and the Umayyads in the first century, and was not Zuhrī working in Umayyad courts?

Therefore, on what grounds can one accept that this tradition or episode came into existence in the mid-second century and did not exist earlier? Moreover the same episode is accepted by Shi'ites as a fact[2].

---

1. Guillaume, *Sīrah Ibn Isḥāq, Introduction,* xlvii.
2. Al-Majlisī, *Biḥār,* ixx, 273-4.

2. No. 10. Praises the Anṣār and by implication the pro-'Abbāsid party in Medina, and then would be anti-'Alid as well. But the same tradition is repeated by Shi'ite theologians, traditionists and commentators, time after time[1]. It is doubtful that the Shi'ites, who denounced all the Companions of the Prophet except a few and expelled them from Islam, were so unaware that they quoted this tradition time after time and only Professor Schacht was able to notice this anti-Alid element.

Guillaume found it anti-Umayyad, as they are condemned for the slaughter at al-Harrah. But who would praise any army or government in the world who slaughtered the population in this way?

Moreover, the Anṣār gave the Prophet shelter when his own tribe tried to kill him and he was forced to migrate from his birthplace, Mecca. The Anṣār defended him, fought with him, offered sacrifices of lives and wealth for his mission. So, if he would not have praised them, he would have been ungrateful. Why do we have to wait until the mid-second century for this tradition to be born, particularly when there are verses in the *Qur'ān*[2]. in praise of them?

Furthermore, one does not find sentences in praise of Anṣār in this tradition. The Prophet asks God for the pardon of these people. It is a very simple matter. The Prophet was commanded —according to the *Qur'ān*[3]— to ask pardon of God for the people.

3. No. 9 is anti-'Alid as it denies the privilege in penal law to the descendants of the Prophet. But where has the Prophet himself acquired a privilege in penal law, and where has he said that he was above the law? We find that he offered himself for the *Qiṣāṣ*. What sources have we, where the Prophet or his descendants are described as being above the law? Is it not the superiority of the law and the equality of subjects that is the right thing? So where is the anti-'Alid element in it? 'Alī himself never claimed that he was above the law.

Furthermore, as a matter of fact it is not a separate tradition but a part of No. 8. Sachau was misled, due to the occurrence of

---

1. Al-Majlisī, *Biḥār* xxi, 159-60; Ṭabrasī, *Majma' al-Bayān* v, 18-20; see also Ibn Abū Ḥadīd, *Nahaj al-Balāghah,* ii, 252.
2. *The Qur'ān,* ix, 100, 117.
3. *The Qur'ān,* iii, 159.

the *isnād* twice as well as the word Rasūl Allāh, and so he split one tradition into two. Professor Schacht follows him without proper attention. In this case Tradition No. 9 does not refer to any penal law's privilege or its condemnation. It refers simply to the case of Usāmah: when the Prophet said that Usāmah was the dearest of all he did not exempt from it even his own daughter Fāṭimah. Ṭayālisī transmits a tradition from Ḥammād from Mūsa b. 'Uqbah. It reads:

كان رسول الله يقول « اسامة احب الناس إلى ولم يستثن فاطمة ولا غيرها » طس /١٨١٢

This is another question of love, whether he loved Usāmah more than his daughter or vice-versa, because the relation of love has many aspects. So it could not be taken as an anti-'Alid sentiment.

Professor Schacht has later on discussed this 'fictitious *isnād*' of Tr. No. 8 and some other relative problems. To him, error is not human nature and everything is 'projected back'!

This extract is not an original work, but a work copied and recopied and just an extract. At the time of editing no other copy was available, so any discrepancy occurring in one copy in due course would remain in other copies. Even the great scholar Sachau has made a blunder in copying the text and has changed the complete tradition from a positive to a negative sense. In No. 12 he has copied: ... ان الله لا يؤيد الدين بالرجل الفاجر
while it is quite clear in the manuscript[1] ان الله ليؤيد الدين بالرجل الفاجر
So there is always a possibility of miscopying, and it becomes more likely when the same word such as 'Uqbah occurs with the name of two narrators. The later part of No. 9 is a part of No. 8, and No. 9 has complete *isnād;* such is the case of No. 8 where the scribe committed an error. Hence, in this case Schacht's remarks are rendered irrelevant.

To say that no one has transmitted the work of Mūsā except his nephew[2] has been proved wrong historically[3]. Now, there are two documents still existing which have Traditions No. 8 and 9 as one complete incident. One of them is as old as Ismā'īl b. Ibrāhīm. It is transmitted by Ibrāhīm b. Ṭahmān directly and

1. Sachau, *op. cit.*, p. 467 and the Fragment supplied by him.
2. Schacht, *on Mūsā, op. cit.*, 293.
3. See *supra*, pp. 95-6.

is a part of Ibrāhīm's collection[1] and another is Al-Ṭabarānī (d. 360 A.H.) who has preserved this tradition transmitting through 'Abd al-'Azīz b. Mukhtār from Mūsā b. 'Uqbah[2].

Therefore, in criticizing the earlier scholars we must be more cautious, as most of the early sources are unavailable. The arguments of Schacht and the discussion in this chapter make it clear that the method, mood and generalization from a single incident serve, in the long run, neither research nor scholars.

Some further examples.

Schacht, in his article "Foreign elements in ancient Islamic law", says that "There is a maxim in Islamic law that 'the child belongs to the [marriage] bed'. This maxim, which was intended to decide disputes about paternity, has been regarded, on insufficient evidence, as an authentic rule of pre-Islamic Arab practice, but Goldziher has shown that it had not yet prevailed in the middle Umaiyad period, say about A.H. 75. In the middle of the second century, it had been put into the mouth of the Prophet, but it is, strictly speaking, incompatible with the Koranic rulings regarding paternity, and in Islamic law as it exists the maxim, though often quoted, is never taken at its face value... It is likely that the maxim, which agrees neither with old Arab custom nor with the *Koran,* but has its parallel in the Roman legal maxim... penetrated from outside into Islamic discussions, though it did not succeed in modifying positive law"[3].

The statement is based on misunderstanding of the tradition and on eliminating half of it. This tradition is transmitted by more than twenty Companions, the number of their students and localities and growth of *isnāds* being tremendous. Their agreement to forge this tradition and put it in the mouth of the Prophet is impossible[4]. The tradition is also transmitted by Zuhrī (d. 124) and is part of the manuscript edited with the present work.

The wording of the tradition is الولد للفراش وللعاهر الحجر. It is not

1. *Juz' Ibrāhīm b. Ṭahmān,* Ẓāhirīyah Library Ms. Folio 250a.
2. *Tkabīr,* v, 286a.
3. Schacht, *Foreign Elements in Ancient Islamic Law.* - *J. Com. Law. Int. Law,* xxxii, 14.
4. For detail of transmitters see *infra,* Arabic Section, *Aḥādīth Abū al-Yamān* notes on Tr. No. 2.

clear why Schacht did not mention the complete *Ḥadīth*. It is hardly possible that Roman law punishes the adulterer with stoning to death—the penalty which is mentioned in this *Ḥadīth*.

The tradition has unanimously been accepted amongst all the Muslim sects[1]. Mu'āwiyah was denounced on the basis on this tradition when he accepted Ziyād b. Abīh[2].

To say that it is against Qura'nic law—as claimed by Schacht—means that such an expounder has neither a clear idea of the Qura'nic Law of *'Iddah,* nor of the tradition, nor of its meaning, nor yet of the time when this tradition was announced by the Prophet.

The Prophet announced this tradition in 8 A.H. at Makkah after the victory. There arose a case of paternity, and two people differed about a child. Then to put an end to the old custom, and to uproot it and to promulgate the new law, this maxim was announced[3].

As for Goldziher's showing that it had not yet prevailed about 75 A.H., examination shows that Goldziher was misunderstanding the text. He refers to Arṭāt b. Zufar who was born on the bed of Zufar and it was assumed that his real father was Ḍarār, and so there was some trouble about his paternity. When he grew up his father wanted to take him back but did not succeed. It means that the boy was given the *Nasab* of the man upon whose bed he was born.

Furthermore, this incident most probably occurred in the early days of the Prophet, as Arṭāt was born at that time. It is clear from his discussion with 'Abd al-Malik b. Marwān where it is stated that he was too old وكان قد اسن, and had lost interest in everything, even in life itself[4]. Therefore this man was neither born about 75 A.H., nor did the case of paternity arise at that time, but this date is when he was awaiting death, after a long life of 80 or 90 years.

Another example: "Mutilation as a punishment for coin-clippers and counterfeiters is advocated by spurious "traditions" quoted in Balādhurī, ibid 470. R.S. Lopez, in *Byzantion,* xvi,

---

1. *Ibid.*
2. Al-Murtaḍā, *Ṭabaqāt al-Mu'tazilah,* 23-4, quoting Ḥasan al-Baṣrī.
3. Ya'qūbi, *History,* ii, 61.
4. *Agh.* xi, 140 - Būlaq edition.

445 ff, has suggested a Byzantine origin. If this is correct, it would be a case of proposed adoption of a judicial practice which existed in the conquered territories"[1].

In Balādhurī, there are references to the practice of Marwān and Abān b. 'Uthmān who punished coin-clippers by flogging or chopping off the hand. But there is no tradition: neither spurious nor authentic. Thus his statement is wrong. Furthermore, if they punished, and Romans also used to punish this crime, then to claim that it might have been taken from them is ridiculous. It is doubtful whether any government would reward the coin-clippers for their "fine-art" and "handskill". It is natural that every government would punish them.

Wensinck as the critic of tradition of five pillars of Islam on material ground — a refutation.

The standard of criticism of *Ḥadīth* on material grounds, as is shown, is very poor, unreasonable and based on sheer ignorance. The same standard is demonstrated by Wensinck, in his work *'Muslim Creed'*. He discusses the authenticity of the tradition of Five Pillars of Islam. In his imagination it must be the work of Companions many decades later, after the death of the Prophet, when the Muslims felt the need to make a formula of their creed, i.e., *Shahādah*. As the tradition of five pillars contains *Shahādah* it cannot be an authentic saying of the Prophet. Wensinck knew quite well that this *Shahādah* is the part of *Tashahhud* which every worshipper has to recite after every two Rak'ah[2]. Instead of modifying his theory in the light of this knowledge he produced another theory that the *Ṣalāt* was also standardized after the death of the Prophet[3].

The command for prayer occurs about 99 times in the

---

1. Schacht, *"Foreign Elements", op. cit.* 14, footnote, 27. But it is almost certain that Islamic Law was free from the influence of Roman Law; see: Bousquet, G.H., *Le mystère de la formation et des origines du Fiqh.* Translated by Ḥamīdullāh, *Ma'ārif,* 1958, pp. 165-184, 245-261. Also, *The Alleged Debt of Islamic to Roman Law, The Law Quarterly Review,* Vol. 67, Jan. 1951, pp. 81-102, by S. V. Fitzgerald. — Also, Dawālībī, *Ḥuqūq Rumāniya,* pp. 58-85.

2. Wensinck, *Muslim Creed,* 32. See also p. 19. He says, "Theory and practice, as they were developed during some decades after Muhammad's death, allowed the leading powers in spiritual matters to express the essentials of Islam in traditions of which the confession of faith (*Shahāda*) and the enumeration of the five pillars of Islam are the most important".

3. Wensinck, *op. cit.,* 32.

Qur'ān[1], and in traditions it amounts to thousands. So it is inconceivable that the Prophet only ordered them and did not teach the prayer and left it to Companions to standardize it. But the trouble does not end here. The prayer in Islam is collective, five times a day. The passages in the *Qur'ān* refer to and command the collective prayers, and even show the actual practice. So, in 1 or 2 A.H. *Adhān* was introduced[2], and there is no reason whatsoever to reject the very early existence of this system. The *Qur'ān* itself refers to *Adhān*[3]. This very *Shahādah* forms the part of *Adhān* and the part of *Iqāmah* which is recited before the commencing of actual prayers. It is not clear at what date Professor Wensinck would like to introduce this system into Islam. If it is accepted that *Adhān* was introduced in the lifetime of the Prophet, as it actually was, the entire hair-splitting argument about forgery of the tradition of five pillars becomes nonsense, and all the deductions and theories based on that theory need to be radically revised. revised.

1. *The Qur'ān*, lxii: 9.
2. Fuwād, A. Bāqī, *Mu'jam*, 413, 4.
3. *E.I.*, Article *Adhān*.

CHAPTER VIII

DESCRIPTION OF THE EDITED TEXTS

THE MANUSCRIPTS AND THEIR AUTHORS.

At the beginning of my research I had photocopies of the following invaluable manuscripts:

A'mash (d. 148), his traditions transmitted by Wakī'.

Ibn Abū 'Arūbah (d. 156), *Kitāb al-Manāsik,* Part I.

Ibn Isḥāq (d. 151) a portion of *al-Maghāzī.*

Ibn Juraij (d. 150), his traditions.

Ibn Ṭahmān (d. 168), first part of his traditions.

Nāfi', client of Ibn 'Umar (d. 117), his traditions.

Suhail b. Abū Ṣāliḥ (d. 138), his *Nuskhah.*

Al-Thaurī (d. 161), Part I of his traditions.

Yazīd b. Abū Ḥabīb (d. 128), his traditions transmitted. by al-Laith.

Zubair b. 'Adī (d. 135), a forged copy.

Al-Zuhrī (d. 124), his traditions transmitted by Shu'aib.

These fragments contain more than 1,000 traditions. I intended to edit all of them. As time passed I realized that it would be almost impossible to edit all these traditions on the standard which was set for the work. Therefore the smallest was chosen, which contained only 48 traditions, which were derived from Abū Hurairah. All the traditions of this *Nuskhah* have the same *isnād.*

Suhail — his father Abū Ṣāliḥ — Abū Hurairah.

The Method of Editing.

In editing the work of Suhail the following method has been adopted for every tradition:

To trace the different students of Abū Hurairah who transmitted this particular tradition.

To trace the different students of Abū Ṣāliḥ who transmitted the same tradition from him.

To trace the different students of Suhail who transmitted the same tradition from him.

Later on, it is attempted to discover whether or not some other Companions of the Prophet transmitted *aḥadīth* on the subject.

If there were other Companions who transmitted traditions on the subject, then the channels of the narrations are traced down mostly to the third rank in *isnād.*

A comparison between the wording of the different students of Abū Hurairah – in general terms – has been made.

Finally, the evidence of other Companions is added to compare – in wider issues – with the traditions of Abū Hurairah.

The names of the narrators of the traditions are mostly given to the third rank in the *isnāds.*

An attempt has been made to find those people who transmitted particular traditions from more than one *source.*

I have also attempted to find out how many times Ibn Ḥanbal has endorsed this particular tradition in his *Musnad* on the authority of Abū Hurairah and how many times on the authority of others.

Notes on the references. For the most part, the method of Wensinck in the *Concordance* has been followed except where the volume numbers and pages, or the numbers of the tradition, are given. Not all the books adopt the method of the *Concordance,* so, in some cases, there are certain discrepancies in numbering the chapters.

The reasons for confining the names of transmitters to the third rank of *isnāds* are:

It would add to the volume of material very much if we go any further.

Most of these people belong to the early half of the second century of the *Hijrah.* Therefore, it would be useful to find out how a certain tradition flourished and the numbers of narrators with their localities, to see whether it was practically possible – at that time – to fabricate a tradition and attribute it to the Prophet or a certain authority.

Other Manuscripts.

Besides the *Nuskhah* of Suhail, there are two other manuscripts which have been added to the second part of the work. One of them belongs to Nāfi' and the other to Al-Zuhrī.

Nāfi' and al-Zuhrī were both the most important sources of of Mālik for his book, *Muwaṭṭa'*. Therefore, only the references to *Muwaṭṭa'* are given to check the method of narration and transmission. The text, thus, would provide valuable material for the further study of the subject by comparing different narrators of Nāfi''s and al-Zuhrī's students.

The study reveals the degree of scrupulousness and adherence to the original text.

The third manuscript in this series has the traditions of al-Zubair b. 'Adī. According to Ibn Ḥibbān it is a forged *Nuskhah*[1] نسخة موضوعة and therefore its traditions cannot be taken as genuine. A photocopy of the manuscript is attached, with footnotes showing several *Aḥadīth* of this *Nuskhah* which occur in the classical collections of al-Bukhārī and Muslim. This reveals the fact that when the traditionists described certain traditions as forged, it did not necessarily mean that the materials were spurious. It only implies that the method of receiving the documents was improper according to their standards. The subject matter may or may not be false.

NUSKHAH OF SUHAIL.

Authorship.

It is entitled on the first page.

جزء فيه نسخة عبد العزيز بن المختار البصري عن سهيل بن ابى صالح عن أبيه

1. See *supra,* p. 182; *Mizān,* 1,316.

But at the end of the *Juz'* is written: آخر نسخة سهيل بن أبي صالح

The early writers were not so precise in describing the authorship[1].

The work belongs to Suhail, because:

None of the biographers has mentioned 'Abd al-'Azīz as author of any book.

Al-Dhahabī, quoting Ibn 'Adī, has described Suhail as having many *Nuskhah*[2].

He had a *Nuskhah* from his father[3].

Suhail sent the traditions of his father in writing to Wuhaib[4].

Comparison of the wordings of Suhail's students shows that the wording of this manuscript tally with that of Wuhaib. There are a few other features common to Wuhaib's *Nuskhah* and that of 'Abd al-'Azīz, e.g.

1. Tr. No. 9 Wuhaib and 'Abd al-'Azīz transmitted: من ادرك ركعتين من العصر but most of the narrators transmitted من ادرك ركعة. The other students of Suhail who transmitted this tradition sometimes transmitted من ادرك ركعة من العصر and at others من ادرك ركعتين من العصر.

2. Tr. No. 17. Suhail was informed by 'Ubaid Allāh that Abū Ṣāliḥ added one more sentence in this particular tradition. Two students of Suhail, namely Ḥammād and al-Zuhrī, did not mention this incident. Two other students of Suhail, Jarīr and Khālid, mentioned it with a difference in the wording of conversation, but the wording of Wuhaib and 'Abd al-'Azīz b. al-Mukhtār are the same.

3. Tr. No 18. Three students of Suhail, namely Ḥammād, Jarīr and al-Thaurī who transmitted this tradition, inserted the name of 'Abd Allāh b. Dīnār, between Suhail and his father, and only Wuhaib and 'Abd al-'Azīz did not insert the name. In the same tradition there is the word شكّ and this is not found in

1. See *supra,* Chapter iv, pp. 205-7.
2. See *supra;* Suhail b. Abū Ṣāliḥ in the third chapter, p. 170.
3. *Ibid.*
4. *Ibid.*

Wuhaib's work. This word شك even suggests the late reading of 'Abd al-'Azīz to Suhail because Suhail became mentally weak and thus, perhaps, he doubted. So, the word شك was used by 'Abd al-'Azīz.

4. There are traditions transmitted from Suhail only by his two students, Wuhaib and 'Abd al-'Azīz, e.g., 6, 10, 13.

A part of the *Nuskhah* of Wuhaib is preserved by Ibn Ḥanbal in *Musnad* ii, 388-9, who transmitted it on the authority of 'Affān.

Summing up, the early scholars have mentioned books —*Nuskhah*— in possession of Suhail, and as he had the *Nuskhah* from his father and as he wrote down his father's traditions and sent them to Wuhaib and as the wording of these two *Nuskhahs* and some very uncommon features are found only in these two *Nuskhahs,* and as at the end of the manuscript is given نسخة سهيل بن أبي صالح, so it is almost certain that the work was compiled by Suhail, and 'Abd al-'Azīz was no more than a narrator. Most probably these two *Nuskhahs* were either copied from the original of Suhail, or the *Nuskhah* of 'Abd al-'Azīz was copied from the *Nuskhah* of Wuhaib.

Authenticity of the Work.

All of its traditions have been transmitted through different channels and have been quoted time after time in all the works on traditions.

The Chain of Transmitters of the Nuskhah.

The *Nuskhah* was copied out at the end of the sixth century of the *Hijrah,* as it is obvious from the first line of the manuscript. The chain of the transmitters from the author to the last transmitter is as follows:

Abū al-Futūḥ Yūsuf b. al-Mubārak (527-601)[1].
Abū Bakr Muḥammad b. 'Abd al-Bāqī al-Bazzāz (442-535)[2].
Abū al-Ḥusain Muḥammad b. Aḥmad al-Narsī (367-456)[3].

---

1. *Nubalā,* xvii, 157, Photo-copy, Ẓāhirīyah Library.

2. *Lisān,* v, 241-2; Ibn 'Asākir, *Tārīkh Dimashq,* xv, 293b; *Nubalā* xii, 150-1.

3. *Bagh.* i, 356; Sam'ānī, *Ansāb,* 558; *Nubalā,* xi, 162.

Abū al-Ḥasan 'Alī b. 'Umar al-Ḥarbī (296-386)[1].
Abū 'Ubaid Allāh Muḥammad b. 'Abdah b. Ḥarb (218-313)[2].
Ibrāhīm b. al-Ḥajjāj (c. 155-233)[3].
'Abd al-'Azīz b. al-Mukhtār (c. 110 - c. 170)[4].
Suhail[5].
Abū Ṣāliḥ[6]
Abū Hurairah

The *Nuskhah* has an uninterrupted chain, and the narrators are trustworthy, except Muḥammad b. 'Abdah b. Ḥarb (d. 313) who was a *Ḥanafī* and Chief Justice of Egypt, and a great patron of the *Ḥanafī* scholar, Abū Ja'far al-Ṭaḥāwī. His character has been criticized. Ḥanafī sources are not available to examine the charges. There are scholars who have explained that the charges were unfair[7].

He is a very late narrator and the work has been absorbed in much earlier collections, he does not create any difficulty in its acceptance, though the traditionists may not agree.

The Location of the Manuscript.

The original manuscript belongs to al-Ẓāhirīyah Library, Damascus, no. Majmū' 107, Folio 155-160. It was dedicated to al-Madrasah al-Ḍiyā'iyah. The fragment is a part of a big volume which contains many other works.

The size of the original book is 18 cm. X 13 cm., and the writing covers a space of about 15 cm. X 10½ cm. It looks as if the manuscript was copied out in 598 A.H. as the date appears in the beginning of the *Nuskhah.* The date is confirmed from the reading certificate written in 598 A.H. The copy was made from an older manuscript which had the reading certificates in 455 A.H. as well as 535 A.H.

The work contains several readings and autographs of the

---

1. *Bagh.* xii, 41, Sam'ānī, *Ansāb,* 162a; *Nubalā,* x, 281.
2. *Mīzān,* iii, 634; Ibn Ḥajar, *Raf' al-Iṣr,* 514-8; Printed with el-Kindī; *Bagh.* ii, 379; *Nubalā,* ix, 246-7; *Lisān,* v, 272-3.
3. Rāzī, i, i, 93; *Tahdhīb,* i, 113; *Taqrīb,* i, 33.
4. *BTK,* iii, ii, 24; *Tahdhīb,* vi, 355; *Taqrīb,* i, 512.
5. See *supra,* p. 170.
6. See *supra,* p. 65.
7. Ibn Ḥajar, *Raf' al-Iṣr,* 515, Printed with Kindi's *Governors of Egypt.*

eminent scholars of the 7th and 8th century of the *Hijrah,* and has the reading date in 677 A.H. and 687 A.H.

THE SECOND MANUSCRIPT.

الجزء من حديث عبيد الله بن عمر

Al-Juz' min Ḥadīth 'Ubaid Allāh b. 'Umar.

The Authorship of the Work.

According to Ibn Ḥibbān, 'Ubaid Allāh b. 'Umar had a *Nuskhah* from Nāfi'. It is not clear how it was written. The sources describe how Nāfi' had the traditions of Ibn 'Umar in written form. Nāfi' dictated traditions to his students and also sent them in writing. It is not clear whether 'Ubaid Allāh copied it himself or wrote in dictation, or whether or not he showed it to Nāfi' to correct it, as Nāfi' asked students to bring their copies for corrections[1].

'Ubaid Allāh was a very great authority on the traditions of Nāfi'; and Mūsā b. 'Uqbah, the famous historian, brought the book containing Nāfi''s traditions to 'Ubaid Allāh to read, as he had not read those traditions to Nāfi'[2].

Authenticity of the Work.

It has not been edited thoroughly and only references to Mālik's *Muwaṭṭa'* are provided, yet it is almost certain that all its contents would be found in classical literature.

The Transmission of the Nuskhah.

This *Nuskhah* has reached us through the following channels:

Aḥmad b. Muḥammad al-Silafī (472-576)[3].

Murshid b. Yaḥyā, Abū Ṣādiq (c. 430-517)[4].

'Alī b. Muḥammad, Abū al-Qāsim (350-443)[5].

---

1. For details see *supra,* Nāfi' in the third Chapter, pp. 96-7.
2. Kifāyah, 267.
3. *Ḥuffāz,* iv, 93-99; Ibn Khallikān, *Wafayāt,* i, 31-32; Ibn 'Imād, *Shadharāt,* iv, 255.
4. Ibn 'Imād, *Shadharāt,* iv, 57.
5. *Nubalā,* xi, 137.

'Abd Allāh b. Muḥammad - Ibn al-Mufassir (c. 275-365)[1].

Abū Sa'īd b. Abū Zur'ah (c. 215 - c. 290)[2].

Sulaimān b. 'Abd al-Raḥmān (153-233)[3].

Shu'aib b. Isḥāq al-Qurashī (118-189)[4].

'Ubaid Allāh b. 'Umar b. Ḥafṣ (c. 80-145)[5].

Nāfi'[6].

The original manuscript belongs to al-Ẓāhiriyah Library, Damascus, which bears the number Majmū' 105, Folio 135 to 149. This is part of a big volume which contains many other small works.

The size of the original volume is 17.5 cm. X 13 cm. and the writing space is about 14.5 cm. X 10 cm. Its heading reads *Al-Juz' min Ḥadīth 'Ubaid Allāh b. 'Umar.*

The manuscript was copied by 'Abd al-Ghanī b. Muḥammad al-Muqrī on Saturday, 29th of Rabī' al-Awwal, 576 A.H.

After copying, it was compared with another copy as is mentioned on Folio 149 b. The last tradition does not belong to this collection, so the last of al-'Umarī's tradition is written on Folio 149a.

The second folio (136b-137a) of this manuscript was lost and supplied by another hand. The difference between the two scripts is quite clear. It is mentioned even in the reading certificate. The first reading certificate, dated 24 Rabī' al-Awwal, 596, has no reference to this missing page but another reading certificate which has the date 12 Jumādā al-ūlā, 732, states explicitly at the beginning of the reading that the second *Warqah* is missing. Another reading note which is dated 735 does not mention this missing portion and most probably this missing page was copied from another manuscript still existing at that time and perhaps it was supplied before 735 A.H. There are some other reading certificates dated 637 and 739 A.H.

---

1. *Nubalā,* x, 217.
2. Ibn 'Asākir *Tārīkh Dimashq,* xiii, 280b; nothing known about his birth date or death.
3. *BTK.* ii, ii, 25; Rāzī, ii, i, 129; *Tahdīb.*iv, 207-8; *Taqrīb,* i, 327.
4. Sa'd, vii, ii, 173; *BTK,* ii, ii, 224; Rāzī, ii, i, 341; *Tahdīb,* iv, 347-8; *Taqrīb,* i, 351.
5. *Supra,* p. 172.
6. *Supra,* p. 96-7.

THE THIRD MANUSCRIPT.

Aḥādīth Abū al-Yamān...

جزء فيه احاديث ابى اليمان الحكم بن نافع و..

The Authorship of the Work.

The work undoubtedly belongs to al-Zuhrī, though it is entitled *Juz' Fīh Aḥādīth Abū al-Yamān.*

Abū al-Yamān did not even read these traditions to his teacher Shu'aib, who gave him permission to transmit on his authority when he was on his death-bed.

Shu'aib was the scribe of al-Zuhrī, who was sent by the Caliph Hishām to write traditions for him from al-Zuhrī. Al-Zuhrī dictated traditions to him and thus he wrote them for Hishām, and most probably made a copy of them for himself. Abū al-Yamān borrowed these books from the son of Shu'aib[1].

Ibn Ḥanbal had seen Shu'aib's books and was very much impressed by their neatness and the beautiful handwriting.

The Authenticity of the Work.

Shu'aib has a very good reputation among traditionists. Most of the traditions of the *Nuskhah* are found in the *Ṣaḥīḥ* work of al-Bukhārī.

As the source of these traditions is al-Zuhrī, who has been gravely accused by some modern scholars, his life and character need thorough investigation, which will be carried out after the description of the *Nuskhah.*

The Transmission of the Nuskhah.

This *Nuskhah* was copied out in 519 A.H., and through the following channel it reaches its compiler:

'Abd al-Raḥmān b. Muḥammad, Abū Manṣūr[2].

Muḥammad b. al-Ḥasan al-Ṣaffār[3].

1. For details, see *supra,* Shu'aib b. Abī Ḥamzah in the third Chapter.
2. Untraceable.
3. Untraceable.

Muḥammad b. 'Abd Allāh al-Karābīsī[1].

'Alī b. Muḥammad al-Ḥakkānī (c. 200-292)[2].

Al-Ḥakam b. Nāfi' - Abū al-Yamān (138-222)[3].

Shu'aib b. Abū Ḥamzah (c. 85-162)[4].

Al-Zuhrī[5].

The original manuscript belongs to al-Ẓāhiriyah Library, Damascus, which bears No. Majmū' 120, Folio 68-87. This small portion is a part of a big volume.

Its heading reads: *Juz' fīh Aḥādīth Abū al-Yamān al-Ḥakam b. Nāfi' wa Aḥādīth Abū Dhūwālah wa Aḥādīth Yaḥyā b. Ma'īn wa ghairihi.*

Aḥādīth Abū al-Yamān begins from Folio 70a and ends at Folio 80a.

The size of the volume is 16.5 cm by 10.5 c. and the writing space approximately 15 cm by 9 cm.

The manuscript was copied in 519 A.H., and was read to 'Abd al-Raḥīm b. Muḥammad al-Shīrāzī in the same year. The manuscript was read to him again in the same year in the Public Library of Shīrāz. It has more than twenty reading certificates and perhaps the last certificate is dated 732. A.H.

It was dedicated by the famous traditionist al-Ḥāfiẓ 'Abd al-Ghanī to — perhaps at Madrasah — al-Ḍīyā'iyah at Qāsiyūn.

LIFE AND WORKS OF MUḤAMMAD B. MUSLIM B. 'UBAID ALLĀH B. SHIHĀB AL-ZUHRĪ (51-124)[6].

He was one of the most celebrated traditionists and one of the early writers in the history of Islamic literature.

It is reported that his grandfather, 'Abd Allāh b. Shihāb,

---

1. *Nubalā,* x, 225.
2. *Nubalā,* ix, 107.
3. *BTK,* i, ii, 342; Rāzī, i, ii, 129; *Tahd.,* ii, 441-3; *Taqrīb,* i, 193.
4. Sa'd, vii, ii, 171; *BTK,* ii, ii, 223; Rāzī, ii, i, 344-5; *Tahd.,* iv, 351-2; *Taqrīb,* i, 352; *supra* 164.
5. *Infra,* 279-293.
6. Ibn Qutaibah, *Ma'ārif,* 472; Ibn Kathīr, *Bidāyah,* ix, 341; *Islām,* v, 136; Fischer, 73-4. The historians differ about his birth and given dates are 50, 51, 56; and 58 but most probably it was in 50 or 51.

fought on the side of the polytheists against the Prophet at Badr and Uḥud[1].

His father, Muslim b. 'Ubaid Allāh, was on the side of Ibn al-Zubair against the Umayyad dynasty[2]. He transmitted traditions from Abū Hurairah[3].

His Education.

It seems that al-Zuhrī was very poor in his early days and his family was dependent upon him[4]. He was a gifted child; poverty could not prevent him from learning. His memory was excellent, so that he was able to memorize the whole *Qur'ān* within three months[5]. Later, he devoted his time to the study of poetry and genealogy, favourite subjects of Arabs. He memorized a great deal of the poetry[6] and was himself a poet[7]. Probably he was in his twenties when, due to a certain incident, he turned to the study of the traditions[8]. He transmitted only two traditions[9] directly from Ibn 'Umar while he lived with him in the same city for twenty-four years. Had he been interested in the subject a little earlier or had he been a liar, he would have related many more than two traditions from Ibn 'Umar. He was a very keen learner and active student. He used to serve his teacher 'Ubaid Allāh so that he was thought to be his servant[10]. He also accompanied Ibn al-Musayyab for a long period of at least seven years. In his early life he was very selective regarding his teachers. He studied mostly under the famous scholars of *Muhājirīn* families, e.g., 'Urwah, 'Ubaid Allāh, 'Abd Allāh b. Tha'libah, etc.

Historians have preserved many interesting testimonies of his colleagues about him. Abū Zinād says, "I used to go about with al-Ẓuhrī, who had tablets and sheets of paper with him, for

1. Ibn Qutaibah, *op. cit.,* 472; Ibn Khallikān, *Wafayāt,* i, 451.
2. Ibn Qutaibah, *op. cit.,* 472.
3. *Thiqāt,* 333.
4. Abū Nu'aim, *Ḥilyah,* iii, 367; *Islām,* v, 139.
5. Khaithamah, iii, 125b; *BTK* , i, i, 220; *Islām,* v, 137; Ibn Kathīr, *op. cit.,* ix, 341.
6. *Aghānī,* iv, 248.
7. Marzubānī, *Mu'jam al-Shu'rā',* 413.
8. Sa'd, ii, i, 131; *Islām,* v, 138.
9. *Islām,* 136.
10. Abū Nu'aim, *op. cit.,* iii, 362; *Islām,* v, 137.

which we laughed at him, but he used to write down all he heard"[1]. Ṣāliḥ b. Kaisān and al-Zuhrī learnt together. Al-Zuhrī suggested that they write traditions. So they wrote all that come from the Prophet. Ibn Kaisān adds, "Furthermore, he (al-Zuhrī) suggested that we should write down what had come from the Companions, because it was also *Sunnah.* I said, 'It was not *Sunnah',* so he wrote down and I did not. Eventually he succeeded and I failed"[2]. Ma'mar reports of his teacher, al-Zuhrī, that he sometimes even wrote on the soles of his shoes[3]. It appears that he collected books in quantity and used to spend his time with them. His wife used to say, "I swear by God, these books are harder for me to bear than three co-wives"[4].

His Reputation and Place in the Traditionists' Circle.

'Umar b. 'Abd al-'Azīz admired him, and advised people to attend his study circle and make use of his knowledge[5]. The traditionists agree unanimously that he was an authority on *Sunnah* and a most trustworthy scholar[6].

His Literary Career.

1. *The Maghāzī of the Prophet.*

Undoubtedly he compiled a book on the *Maghāzī.* However, it is difficult to say whether the method he employed in compiling the work was originated by him or he followed someone else. If we compare him with 'Urwah, we fine that al-Zuhrī uses a somewhat different style. Al-Zuhrī collected information about incidents from various sources, then instead of passing on the material in the form of separate statements with the name of their transmitters, he wove them all into a full, complete and comprehensive statement of incidents. Here is a quotation. "Al-Zuhrī related to me on the authority of 'Alqamah b. Waqqāṣ..., Sa'īd, 'Urwah b. al-Zubair and 'Ubaid Allāh b. 'Abd Allāh b. 'Utbah.

---

1. Zur'ah, 61b; *Jāmi',* 155a; *Ḥuffāẓ,* i, 96.
2. Sa'd, ii, i, 135; Zur'ah, 61b; Khaithamah, 125b; Bājī, 94a; *Taqyīd,* 107; *Jāmi',* 156a; Fischer, 67-8; Ibn Kathīr, *op. cit.,* ix, 344.
3. Taqyīd, 107. See for further information about his zeal of learning; Khaithamah, 125b; Razī, iv, i, 73; Ranhurmuzī, 32b; *Jāmi',* 183a; *Islām,* v, 148; Fischer, 67, 69; Ibn Kathīr, *op. cit.,* ix, 341.
4. Ibn Khallikan, *op. cit.,* i, 451; Abū al-Fida, *Tārīkh,* i, 204.
5. *Islām,* v, 136, 144.
6. *Mashāhīr,* 66; and any biography dealing with the Traditionists.

Al-Zuhrī said, every one of them related a portion of this *Ḥadīth,* and some of them had more information than others. I have collected for you all that has been related to me by them"[1]. On the other hand the work of 'Urwah transmitted by al-Zuhrī has a composite *isnād* of two men, Marwān and Miswar. As none of these works is available in its original form, it is difficult, even dangerous, to make any definite comment on their method of compilation. 'Urwah, perhaps, originated this style and later on it was developed by al-Zuhrī.

It looks as if the work of al-Zuhrī was mainly planned on the scheme of 'Urwah. Some quotations, as well as headings of the chapters of both works, have been preserved by al-Ṭabaranī in his *Mu'jam Kabīr,* and mostly they are placed side by side. It is quite clear from the quotations that the work of al-Zuhrī was very extensive. The headings, for example, read as below:

Names of the persons who attended *'Uqbah Bai'at*[2].

Names of the persons who were killed in the battle of Badr[3], and of Uḥud[4], and of Khandaq[5], and of Ajnādīn[6].

He gives full details of different tribes who joined the war. The work has been preserved in quotation form in several sources[7]. In his work, Mūsā b. 'Uqbah has included almost the whole work of al-Zuhrī, so that Yaḥyā b. Ma'īn said that the best on *al-Maghāzī* was the book of Mūsā from al-Zuhrī[8].

There are a few pages published with *Jāmi'* of Ibn Wahb, which appear to be a part of al-Zuhrī's work on the *Maghāzī*[9].

2. *The Sīrah.*

Al-Iṣfahānī reports that Khālid al-Qasrī asked al-Zuhrī to compile a book on the *Sīrah*[10]. It is not clear whether the request

1. *Annales,* i, 1518.
2. *Tkabīr,* i, 38b, 45a, 118a.
3. *Ibid.,* i, 40b.
4. *Ibid.,* i, 45a.
5. *Ibid.,* i, 52a.
6. *Ibid.,* i, 89b.
7. See for example, al-Balādhurī, *Ansāb al-Ashrāf,* i, 286, 445, 454, 545, 549, 550, 552; *Futūḥ,* 24, 28, 31; Ḥanbal, vi, 194-197.
8. *Tahd.,* x, 362.
9. Ibn Wahb, *al-Djāma,* i, 96-98.
10. *Agh.,* xix, 59 (Būlāq edition 1285 A.H.).

was fulfilled and whether the book referred to, which has just been mentioned, was in response to al-Qasrī's request or an independent work.

3. *Memoranda about the Umayyad Caliphs.*

He compiled some historical memoranda about the Umayyad Caliphs; a chronological list of the births, deaths, and extents of their reigns. Al-Ṭabarī has preserved two quotations from this work[1].

4. *A Book on Genealogy.*

He also compiled a book on the genealogy of his tribe[2].

5. *The Book on Nāsikh and Mansūkh.*

From the statement of al-Ḥāzimī, it seems as if al-Zuhrī compiled a work on the subject of *Nāsikh and Mansūkh Ḥadīth* as well[3].

6. *The Collection of Traditions.*

He was asked by 'Umar b. 'Abd al-'Azīz to write traditions[4]. After being copied out, these books were sent to different cities[5]. A lengthy quotation from the work on the subject of taxation is preserved by Abū 'Ubaid al-Qāsim b. Sallām. It is obvious from the quotation that these three pages are a small portion of a lengthy book[6].

7. *His Other Literary Activities.*

He dictated, twice, four hundred traditions to one of Hishām's sons[7].

---

1. Annales, ii, 428, 1269.
2. Fischer, 68; *Islām,* v, 143; see also, Ibn 'Abd al-Barr, *Al-Inbāh 'alā qabā'il al-Ruwāt,* 44; *Agh.*, xix, 59. Būlaq edition.
3. Al-Ḥāzimī, *Al-I'tibār,* 3.
4. Khaithamah, iii, 126a;
5. 'Ajjāj, *Sunnah,* p. 494.
6. *Amwāl,* 578-581.
7. Rāmhurmuzī, 39b; Fischer 69; Ibn Kathīr, *op. cit.*, ix, 342.

8. Hishām b. 'Abd al-Malik sent two scribes to him who accompanied him for one year to write from him[1].

9. More than fifty of his students had his traditions in writing[2].

Further he had 'ready-made collections of *Ḥadīth*' which were given by him to many scholars and students[3].

10. In the later period, it looks as if the collections of Ḥadīth on the authority of al-Zuhrī were made for most of the nobles of the Caliph's palace. Shu'aib b. Abū Ḥamzah was employed for this purpose[4]. There is a statement of Ma'mar which confirms this. According to his report, the books of al-Zuhrī were brought on ponies after the assassination of al-Walīd[5].

Al-Zuhrī's Relations with his Students.

He was very generous to the needy. Having been very poor in his early life, he knew what poverty meant. So when he had some income, he did not accumulate the money and always tried to help the poor. Al-Laith b. Sa'd, a very generous man himself, describes al-Zuhrī's generosity saying: "I have not seen a man more generous than Ibn Shihāb. He used to help everyone who came to him, and if he had nothing left, he used to borrow"[6].

Al-Zuhrī and the Equality of Students.

Though he had been very selective in his teachers, yet he was himself fair to all his students. He did not make any kind of discrimination between the rich and the poor. When he dictated traditions to Hishām's son, he related at once the same traditions to other students[7].

1. Abū Nu'aim, *op. cit.*, iii, 361; *Islām,* v, 143.
2. See *supra,* 88-93.
3. *Kifāyah,* 319; *Islām,* v, 149.
4. *Tahd.*, iv, 351-2; *Islām,* v, 151.
5. Fasawī, ii, 146a; see also *Kāmil,* i, 18a; *Islām,* v, 141.
6. Fischer 70. For more details see *Islām,* v. 138; 141, 150; Fischer 73.
7. *Islām,* v, 148.

Al-Zuhrī and the Diffusion of Knowledge.

It was the general attitude of that time that the teachers could hardly be brought to speak. The students had to accompany them and when their teachers spoke they wrote it down or memorized it. Al-Zuhrī says: "People used to sit with Ibn 'Umar, but none dare call upon him till someone came and asked him. We sat with Ibn al-Musayyab without questioning him, till someone came and questioned him; the question roused him to impart *Ḥadīth* to us or he began to impart at his own will"[1].

Quite contrary to the pattern of the time, al-Zuhrī was very approachable as a teacher. It looks as if he followed, in his early days, the method of his teachers. He did not want to communicate his knowledge very freely, but later flexibility appeared in his attitude. Walīd b. Muslim informs us that when al-Zuhrī came out of 'Abd al-Mālik's meeting, he sat near by the pillar and called the traditionists, "O people, we forbade you something which we delivered to those (*Amīrs*). Come here, I will relate to you"[2].

His Attitude towards the Writing of Ḥadīth.

He, like other Successors, wrote down the traditions for his own use, but was not in favour of making them public. One who wants to learn must strive, and the students should not be given any 'ready-made' knowledge in the shape of books or regular dictations[3].

The first change in his attitude came when he was asked by 'Umar b. 'Abd al-'Azīz to write the traditions, and later on he was persuaded by Hishām.

Abū al-Mulaiḥ says, "We could not strive to write in the meetings (lectures) of al-Zuhrī, til Hishām compelled him, then he wrote for Hishām's sons and then the people wrote tradition..."[4]. This incident as well as al-Zuhrī's reaction is found in the following statement of al-Zuhrī: معمر عن الزهري قال : كنا نكره كتاب العلم حتى اكرهنا عليه هؤلاء الامراء فرأينا ان لا نمنعه احدا من المسلمين "We had an aversion to recording knowledge, till these *Amirs*

1. Fischer, 69.
2. *Islām,* v, 148.
3. See Mālik's statement. Mālik dislikes *Ijāzah,* because a student would gain much knowledge in a short time without much effort, *Kifāyah,* 316.
4. Abū Nu'aim, *op. cit.,* iii, 363.

forced us to do it; then we were of the opinion that we should not withhold it from any of the Muslims"[1].

Dr. A. Sprenger translates this statement as follows: "Zohry said according to Ma'mar: "We disapproved of writing down hadythes to such an extent, that we induced also those chiefs (who are not mentioned) to disapprove of it, but at last we saw that no Moslem forbids writing"[2]. The translation is not clear, and it gives a different interpretation. Guillaume's conclusion is rather strange. He says, "If any external proof were needed of the forgery of tradition in the Umayyad period, it may be found in the express statement of Al-Zuhrī: 'These princes have compelled us to write Ḥadīth'[3]." The text makes it quite clear that the statement has nothing to do with forgery.

There is another statement of Ma'mar regarding al-Zuhrī's permission to Ibrāhīm b. al-Walīd al-'Umawī to transmit a book on his authority[4].

This statement of Ma'mar and the previous statement of al-Zuhrī about pressure from the *Amīrs* to write down traditions, led Goldziher to deduce that, though al-Zuhrī was a scrupulous man, yet he sometimes came under Umayyad pressure to such an extent that he gave permission to transmit books on his authority, without having read them; thus the Umayyad succeeded in circulating the traditions in their favour on the authority of al-Zuhrī[5]!

This whole story is based on misunderstanding of the term *'Araḍ*. In the term of traditionists when a student reads to his teacher it is called *'Araḍ* عرض and when a teacher reads to students it is called حدّث *Ḥaddatha*[6].

There is the statement of 'Ubaid Allāh b. 'Umar who describes how the people brought books to al-Zuhrī who, after looking into them, turning the pages, used to say, "This is my tradition... accept them from me"[7].

---

1. Sa'd, ii, ii, 135; Khaithamah, iii, 126b; 127a relating by Sufyān. Taqyīd, 107; the text of Ibn Sa'd is misprinted. Quotation from *Taqyīd*.
2. Sprenger, *On the Origin of Writing...J.A.S.B.*, xxv, 1856, p 322.
3. Guillaume, 50.
4. Khaithamah, iii, 127a; *Kifāyah*, 266.
5. Goldziher, *Muh. Stud.*, ii, 38.
6. Subḥī Ṣāliḥ, *'Ulūm al-Ḥadīth*, 93 or any work in *Uṣūl al-Ḥadīth* in the Chapter of Taḥammul al-'Ilm.
7. Khaithamāh, iii, 39a; *Kifāyah*, 318.

Therefore, it is not the case, as understood by Goldziher, that the Umayyads exploited al-Zuhrī in this way. Was it not possible for them to add traditions to their books after reading to al-Zuhrī? Had they been eager to do this, they might have done something to al-Zuhrī's dictations, expecially when it was written by their own employed scribes, without bringing the book to him for his permission. Therefore, to examine this kind of forgery there should be some other methods, and the permission of al-Zuhrī does not provide a new instance of forgery. It is also strange that not a single tradition is transmitted in Ibrāhīm's name.

As a matter of fact, these statements concerning the transmission of books, without being read or being read by students, have their own problems of a quite different nature.

In early days, the traditionists preferred to listen to their teachers, and it was the best method for learning and transmitting traditions. To read to the teachers was a second-class method for learning the traditions and the word *Ḥaddathanā* may not be used in this case. The idea prevailed to such an extent that al-Ṭaḥāwī had to write a book in the fourth century *Hijrah* to refute this and to prove that both methods were equally valid.[1].

There was also the problem of receiving the books without reading. If a teacher gave a book to his students, without its being read in his presence, or someone brought the book to his teacher, asking his permission to transmit it without its being read, would this kind of transmission be lawful and should it be permitted? Some professors rejected this sort of permission while others approved of it and al-Zuhrī belongs to the second group[2]. It is called *Munāwalah.* 'Ubaid Allāh describes the practice of al-Zuhrī that he used to look into books and turning the pages here and there used to permit them to transmit the traditions on his authority.

Al-Zuhrī's Educational Activities in His Last Days.

In the last days he became tired and it affected his activities. He gave books to some students and did not read to them nor did

1. Chester Beaty, MSS. No 3415.

2. Khaithamah, iii, 39a; *Kifāyah,* 326, 329; see also The Practice of Mālik Fasawī, iii, 263a; *Kifāyah,* 327; and sometimes Mālik disliked it. *Kifāyah,* 316.

he allow them to be read[1]. Afterwards he retired from teaching[2]. This was perhaps only a year or so before his death.

Al-Zuhrī and his Critics.

He has been accused of three things by some traditionists.

Irsāl or Tadlīs.

It is reported, as the saying of Yaḥyā al-Qaṭṭān, that al-Zhurī's *Mursals* were like wind. As he was *ḥāfiz,* he could have given the name of his authority if he had wished, but sometimes he did not name his authorities[3]. Therefore, there must have been some defect in the *isnād.* This charge requires a thorough study of his *Mursalāt,* because sometimes he transmitted only the *Matn* and at another meeting he mentioned *isnāds* when the students asked him[4]. Perhaps the charge was based on deduction instead of an actual enquiry into the materials. Therefore, Aḥmad sharply refutes this charge[5].

Not Transmitting from Mawālī.

He was told that people blamed him for not transmitting traditions from *Mawālī.* He replied that he did transmit traditions from them, but when he found the same traditions in the families of *Muhājirīn* and *Anṣār* he did not transmit from other sources[6]. Nāfi', client of Ibn 'Umar, also complained that al-Zuhrī learnt traditions from him, then went to Sālim and confirmed whether or not he had heard those traditions from his father. Later, he related them on the authority of Sālim[7].

He is also accused of using black colour for dyeing his hair, so one of the scholars did not write from him.

---

1. Fischer, 69-70; *Islām,* v, 149; see also Fasawī, iii, 308a-b.
2. *Islām,* v, 149.
3. *Islām,* v, 149.
4. *'Ilal,* i, 82; Khaithamah, iii, 126a.
5. Fasawī, ii, 231b.
6. Zur'ah, 61b; Rāhurmuzī, 41b; *Jāmi',* 15a. Muslim has given a list of Mawālī scholars from whom al-Zuhrī transmitted traditions. See Muslim, *Rijāl 'Urwah,* p. 11, where more than twenty Mawālies are named as his teacher.
7. Fasawī, ii, 216a; *Jāmi',* 15a; *Ḥuffāz,* i, 88. See also *Kāmil,* i, 292a.

3. The gravest charge against him is his co-operation with the ruling family[1]. There were many great scholars who cooperated with the government and held offices, e.g., al-Sha'bī, Ḥasan al-Baṣrī, Qabīṣah and others. Therefore, it cannot be a charge against someone that he accepted an office in the government, provided that his conduct was right.

Goldziher and some other modern scholars charged him with falsification of traditions for the benefit of the Umayyads. Therefore his relation with the Umayyads needs investigation.

AL-ZUHRĪ AND THE UMAYYADS.

Al-Zuhrī and Marwān.

It is said, "When still quite a youth, he had paid his respects to Marwān"[2]. This statement is refuted by an early historian, Yaḥyā b. Bukair[3]. Historical circumstances did not provide a chance for this kind of visit.

Marwān became Caliph in 64 A.H., reigning only for nine to ten months[4]. In such a short period, he had to fight three battles and had to send many expeditions. Meanwhile al-Zuhrī's father was against Marwān, on the side of Ibn al-Zubair[5] who was at the climax of his power at that time. Al-Zuhrī was then between seven and fifteen years of age. He could not have been independent of his father at such an early age; also it was not easy to take a journey from al-Madīnah to Damascus, especially in those days. Had he been there he could not have achieved anything. Therefore, all the historical facts are against this hypothesis.

Al-Zuhrī and 'Abd al-Mālik.

Undoubtedly he was attached to the Caliph's court from the time of 'Abd al-Mālik to Hishām's[6]. It is also true that he had

1. Fischer, 72; Goldziher, *Muh. Stud.* ii, 35 sq; Guillaume, 48.
2. Horovitz, *Art. al-Zuhrī,* in *E.I.*; also 'Ajjāj, *Sunnah qabl al-Tadwīn,* p. 489.
3. *Islām,* v, 147.
4. Abulfidā, *Tārīkh* i, 194; *Annales,* ii, 578; Mas'ūdī, *Murūj alu-Dhahab,* v, 207.
5. Ibn Qutaibah, *Ma'ārif,* 472.
6. *Islām,* v, 140.

been heavily in debt several times, that was paid off by Caliphs[1], yet his relation with the Caliphs was not always smooth. It was impossible for him to make a false statement or to remain quiet on certain occasions. Walīd asked him about a saying, in circulation at that time in Syria, "God writes down only the good deeds of *Amīrs* and does not record any bad deed". He replied that this was (*Bāṭil*) a false statement, and proved it quite wrong. Walīd said, "these people mislead us..."[2].

Once Hishām asked a certain question concerning the name of a person mentioned in the *Qur'ān* but who was not named precisely. Al-Zuhrī said, "It was 'Abd Allāh b. Ubai b. Salūl". The answer was against the wish of Hishām. He told al-Zuhrī, "You lie, it was 'Alī". On this occasion al-Zuhrī became so furious that he rebuked Hishām and even his father. He said, "By Allāh, if a voice from Heaven proclaimed that Allāh had permitted lying, still I would not lie..."[3].

Not only this, but Hishām had to listen calmly to al-Zuhrī. He used to denounce al-Walīd for his bad character, and asked Hishām to dismiss al-Walīd from *Wilāyat al-'Ahd.* Al-Walīd swore that if he had a chance, he would kill al-Zuhrī[4]. Al-Zuhrī himself was aware of this danger, and was ready to flee to the Byzantine Empire, in the event of al-Walīd's inheriting the Caliphate[5]. He did not give any special privileges to his princely student while teaching him traditions[6]. Therefore, it would be unfair to history, to deduce from al-Zuhrī's relation with the Umayyad dynasty, that he was a tool in their hands, and that they exploited his name, fame and knowledge to circulate false traditions in their favour.

Did Al-Zuhrī Provide a Substitute for the Pilgrimage? Refutation of Al-Ya'qūbī and Goldziher.

The most crucial point is the statement of the Shi'ite historian, al-Ya'qūbī who said that 'Abd al-Malik, for certain political reasons, prevented the Syrians from *al-Ḥajj,* because Ibn

1. *Ibid.*, 141.
2. Ibn 'Abd Rabbih, *'Iqd,* 1, 70-71.
3. Fischer, 72; *Islām,* v. 149-50.
4. *Islām,* v, 140.
5. *Agh.*, ii, 103, as cited by Horovitz, *The Earliest Biographies, I.C.*, 1928, p. 42.
6. Khaithamah, iii, 128b.

al-Zubair was imposing his *Bai'at* upon them. 'Abd al-Malik quoting a tradition from al-Zuhrī, gave them a substitute for *al-Ḥajj;* the pilgrimage to Jerusalem, and *al-Tawāf* around the Rock. So he built the Dome, and *ṭawāf* continued in the Umayyad dynasty[1]. According to Goldziher, it was left to the theologian al-Zuhrī to legalize and justify this action[2].

Goldziher reached this conclusion relying, for the most part, on al-Ya'qūbī's statement, but it needs much more careful study, because its implications and consequences are far-reaching. Many other scholars, depending upon al-Ya'qūbī, have established misleading opinions about Al-Zuhrī[3].

Apart from al-Zuhrī's meeting with 'Abd al-Malik which did not take place earlier than 81 A.H.[4], it is better to judge this statement on its own merits.

Palestine in 67 A.H. was out of 'Abd al-Malik's control[5]. The Umayyad had been in Mecca on the occasion of the pilgrimage in the year 68 A.H.[6]. Therefore if 'Abd al-Malik had prevented the people from *al-Ḥajj* it would have been after 68 A.H., when he might have thought about a substitute for *al-Ḥajj* and declared that the Rock and Jerusalem were as sacred as Mecca. As he began to build the Dome on the Rock in 69 A.H.[7], he might have announced his decree on the substitute for *al-Ḥajj* on the authority of al-Zuhrī in the beginning of the year 69 A.H.

At this time al-Zuhrī was somewhere between ten and eighteen years of age. It is inconceivable that a mere child of ten or a boy of eighteen had already achieved such a great fame and respect — not in his native land al-Madinah, but far away in the anti-al-Madīnah region, Syria — that he was able to cancel the

1. Ya'qūbī, *History,* ii, 311.
2. Goldziher, *Muh. Stud.,* ii, 35; Guillaume says: 'the inventor is Al-Zuhrī, Guillaume, 48.
3. For example, apart from Goldziher and Guillaume, see J. Walker, "*Kubbat al-Sakhra*" in *E.I.,* Ruth, *Arabic Books and Libraries in the Umaiyad Period, A.J.S.L.,* vol. lii, p. 252, F. Buhl, *Art al-Kuds* in *E.I.*
4. *B T S,* 93 read with *Annales* ii, 1052.
5. Ya'qūbī, *History,* ii, 321; Caetani, *chron., Islamica* 786; Mas'ūdī, *Murūjal-Dhahab,* v, 225.
6. Ya'qūbī, *History,* ii, 320.
7. Sibṭ ibn al-Jauzī, as quoted by al-Maqedesi, *Muthīr* (no mention of the Rock) *J.R.A.S.,* xix, 1887, p. 300.

divine obligatory order of *al-Ḥajj* and was in a position to command a substitute[1]. Moreover there were many Companions of the Prophet at that time in Syria. Why did 'Abd al-Malik not exploit them? Their authority and the respect they commanded were far greater than that of al-Zuhrī, a boy of ten to eighteen years, and the Syrians would have heard them with more reverence. If these Syrian scholars were anti-Umayyads, then their sayings and protests must have come to us through their pupils or Abbasid historians, but there seems to be no record of such protests. If they were pro-Umayyad and worldly people who would not have protested for the sake of the Prophet, then they would have protested at being slighted, because this 'honour' of fabrication was given to someone else, their authorities were challenged, and they were not given full respect.

Further, how could those religious-minded people who agitated against 'Abd al-Malik's prevention of *al-Ḥajj* agree on such a false deed and accept it? Was the whole population of Syria so foolish that they were mocked by 'Abd al-Malik and al-Zuhrī so easily? According to al-Ya'qūbī, this practice as a substitute for *al-Ḥajj* continued during the Umayyad period, but he himself describes how from 72 A.H. onwards *al-Ḥajj* ceremony was performed under the governorship of the Umayyad. So this 'Anti-Meccan' Caliph, 'Abd al-Malik, went to Mecca for *al-Ḥajj* in 75 A.H. as did other Umayyad Caliphs[2].

Apart from this, the building of the Rock was completed in 72 A.H., and at that time Mecca was under al-Ḥajjāj's control, who was nothing more than 'Abd al-Malik's governor. According to al-Ya'qūbī himself, *al-Ḥajj* was performed in 72 A.H., under the governorship of al-Ḥajjāj[3]. Thus there would have been no necessity to make a substitute for *al-Ḥajj*, and there would have been no need to continue this practice during the Umayyad dynasty, which was as good as putting an effective weapon in the hands of anti-Ummayyad elements.

Moreover, the wording of al-Zuhrī, quoted by 'Abd al-Malik and given by al-Ya'qūbī, does not mention, or even suggest the

---

1. Ya'qūbī gives a list of distinguished scholars in the reign of 'Abd al-Malik. He mentions about 30 names, yet does not mention al-Zuhrī *History* ii, pp. 337-8.
2. Ya'qūbī, *History*, ii, 336.
3. *Ibid.*, ii, 336.

sacredness of the Rock and its *Tawāf* and so on[1]. The statement of al-Zuhrī only gives the mosque of Jerusalem as a special privilege. This mosque has been given a special place even in the holy *Qur'ān*[2]. Besides all this, this tradition is not transmitted only by al-Zuhrī, but by many others such as:

Hishām – Nāfi' – Ibn 'Umar[3].

Salamah b. Kuhail – Ḥajiyah b. 'Adī – 'Alī b. Abū Ṭālib[4].

Quṣaim – Qaz'ah – Abū Sa'īd al-Khudrī[5].

Abān b. Tha'labah – 'Aṭiyah Abū Sa'īd al-Khudrī[6].

Muḥd b. Ibrāhīm – Abū Salamān – Abū Huraira[7].

Zaid b. Sālim – Sa'īd b. Abū Sa'īd – Abū Huraira[8].

Yazīd b. Abū Maryam – Qaz'ah – 'Abd Allāh b. 'Amr[9], and so on.

Therefore, how did the credit for this "fabrication" and theological enterprise go to al-Zuhrī alone, who did not see 'Abd al-Malik earlier than 81 A.H.? It is better to quote here J. Horovitz's conclusion about this *Ḥadīth*. He says: "Whatever one may think about the authenticity of the *Ḥadīth*. there is no ground whatever to doubt but that al-Zuhrī really had heard the *Ḥadīth* from the mouth of Sa'īd ibn al-Musaiyab..."[10].

---

1. *Ibid.*, ii, 311.
2. *The Qur'ān*, Sūrah xvii, Isrā'. All the commentators and historians unanimously agree that the Sūrah is Meccan. Even if it could be proved that the mosque *al-aqṣā* was in al-Yi'rana, according to Guillaume in his article in *al-Andalus* xviii, 323-36, yet Jerusalem, being first *qiblah*, has its holiness.
3. *Ṭawsaṭ*, ii, 305a.
4. *Ibid.*, i, 210a; *Ṭsaghīr*, 97-8.
5. *Ibid.*, i, 261a, Fasawī, iii, 89a.
6. *Ṭawsaṭ*, ii, 3a.
7. Fasawī, iii, 89a.
8. *Ibid.*
9. *Ibid.*, 89a-b.; for further reference in the classical literature see Wensinck, Concordance.
10. Horovitz, *op. cit.*, 36. See also Ruth, *A.S.J.L.*, vol. liii, 243; she agrees with Horovitz, saying, "One would rather agree with Horovitz that whereas at the behest of the Caliphs he departed from his former reticence and dictated traditions, this innovation does not prove that he invented traditions in their interests".

APPENDIX I

THE MEANING OF THE WORDS ḤADDATHANĀ, ETC.

Do the words *Ḥaddathanā, Akhbaranā* and *'An* etc. in the chains of transmitters necessarily mean only an oral recitation?

Professor Margoliouth, discussing the letter of the second Caliph 'Umar to Abū Mūsā al-Ash'arī and its *isnād,* says, "It is no surprise to the student of Moslem history that even for a letter oral tradition should be preferred to written documents"[1]. There are other scholars who generally assume that the traditions collected in the classical collections were recorded for the first time by their compilers[2].

The main reason for this assumption is misunderstanding of the term *Ḥaddathanā.* Among the orientalists, perhaps, Sprenger was the first scholar who made it clear that this word usually did not mean an oral recitation, and in those days it was the fashion to refer to authors instead of works[3].

The word *Ḥaddathanā* was used in a very wide sense. If a man read a book of traditions to his teacher, he could use this word. If the teacher read to his students from a book or from memory, the same word was used to describe the channel of knowledge. Some scholars applied different terms to these two different methods of learning. If the teacher read to his students, then the students could use the word *Ḥaddathanā* whenever they transmit-

---

1. Margoliouth, *Omar's instruction to the Kadi, J.R.A.S.* 1910, p. 308.

2. See Justice M. Shafi' as cited in the *Tarjumān, Risālat Number* Lahore 1961 p. 267. Mingana has more far-fetched ideas. In his opinion the terms *Rawā* and *Ḥaddathanā,* etc., mean only oral transmission. He says, "But to my knowledge neither expression has ever referred to a written document lying before the narrator". See Mingana, *An important manuscript of Bukhārī,* p. 21. Therefore when Ibn Khallikān writes about Abū Zaid al-Marwazī , Mingana translates it "And he taught orally", *op. cit.,* 24. He thinks, depending upon this peculiar meaning of the term Ḥaddatha, etc. that the text of Bukhārī was written down, very late at the end of the fourth century, *op. cit.,* 22-3.

3. Sprenger, *J.A.S.B.,* 1850, p. 109.

ted that particular tradition, but if the student read to his teacher then he would use the term *Akhbaranā.* In general this difference was not strictly observed[1].

Here are some examples collected from the classical books to investigate the meaning of this word which will explain the word and its usage in the science of traditions.

حدّثنا عمرو بن عباس حدثنا محمد بن جعفر حدثنا شعبه ... قال عمرو فى كتاب محمد بن جعفر بياض

1. Bukhārī relates a tradition from ʻAmr who in turn relates from Muḥammad b. Jaʻfar from Shuʻbah. Bukhārī does not give the complete *Ḥadīth* and leaves a blank space in the book, quoting his teacher ʻAmr, saying, "In the book of Muḥammad was a blank space"[2]. Yet the word *Ḥaddathanā* is used throughout the chains (*isnād*) without any reference to the book.

١ — اسماعيل عن ايوب عن يعلى بن حكيم عن سليمان بن يسار
٢ — حماد بن زيد عن ايوب قال كتب إلىّ يعلى بن حكيم قال سمعت سليمان بن يسار

2. The two above-mentioned channels are given by Muslim one after the other on one page[3]. In the *isnād* of the first *Ḥadīth* there is no mention of writing, while the second one explicitly admits a written record. In this case even the word *ʻan,* instead of *Ḥaddathanā,* is used which is much inferior to the latter one.

3. ʻUmar wrote a *Waqf* testimony for his Khaibar land. The testimony was transmitted as a written document, but the word *ʻan* is used for its transmission[4].

4. Al-Mughīrah wrote traditions and sent them to Muʻāwiyah. These traditions were related by Manṣūr *ʻan* al-Shaʻbī *ʻan* Warrād — he was the scribe who wrote down the traditions — *ʻan* Al-Mughīrah, without giving any hint of what they recorded. The same traditions were related by Ibn Ashwaʻ *ʻan* al-Shaʻbī with details of the incidents[5].

عبدالله حدثنى أبى ثنا عبّاد بن العوّام ثنا سفيان بن حسين.... قال أبى ثم اصابتنى

1. See for details, Qāsimī, *Qawāʻid al-Taḥdīth,* 207-8; or any similar work.
2. BU, *Adab,* 14 (vol. iv, 112-3).
3. MU. *Buyūʻ,* (pp. 1181).
4. MU. *Waṣiyah,* (pp. 1255).
5. MU. *Aqḍiyah,* (pp. 1341).

علة فى مجلس عباد بن العوام فكتبت تمام الحديث فاحسبنى لم افهم بعضه فشككت فى بقية الحديث فتركته

5. 'Abd Allāh b. Aḥmad b. Ḥanbal describes this *Ḥadīth,* saying, "My father said, 'then I suffered from something in the lecture of 'Abbād; then I wrote *Tamām al-Ḥadīth'* ..."[1]. Here is an example of taking traditions by dictation, yet the word *Ḥaddathanā* is used throughout the *isnād.*

ثنا ابى ثنا عبد الصمد ثنا همام ثنا عباس الجزرى ثنا عمرو بن شعيب عن ابيه عن جده... قال عبد الصمد : عباس الجزرى . كان فى النسخة عباس الجويرى فاصلحه أبى كما قال عبد الصمد : الجزرى :

6. Here is a very interesting remark. It shows that Ibn Ḥanbal had a copy of al-Jazarī's traditions and went to read them to his teacher 'Abd al-Ṣamad who asked him to correct the name and so he did[2]. 'Amr b. Shu'aib, the earlier transmitter of this tradition, imparted it from books[3]. Now it appears that in every stage of the transmission of this tradition, a book was employed, yet for the narration the word *Ḥaddathanā* is used without referring to the book.

يزيد بن هارون انا حميد الطويل عن ثابت البنانى قال بلغنا ان النبىّ ... قال يزيد وكان فى الكتاب الذى معى « عن انس » . فلم يقل عن أنس فأنكره واثبت ثابتا.

7. Yazīd says that this tradition was written in his book from Thābit al-Bunānī from Anas; then Ḥumaid rejected the word Anas and approved of Thābit only[4]. Here is a written source, copied before it was read to the teacher, transmitted with the usual word *Akhbaranā.*

... ثنا همام ثنا قتاده عن بشير بن نهيك عن ابى هريرة ... قال همام وجدت فى كتابى عن بشير بن نهيك ولا اظنه إلا عن النضر بن انس .

8. Ḥammām says, "I found [a tradition] in my book from Bashīr b. Nahīk and I do not think it is from him but from al-Naḍr b. Anas"; the same *Isnād* is repeated by Ibn Ḥanbal only

1. Ḥanbal, ii, 14.
2. Ḥanbal, ii, 184.
3. See *supra,* 'Amr b. Shu'aib, p. 44.
4. Ḥanbal, iii, 243.

after three lines with the same expression of doubt, but without mentioning the book[1].

9. 'Abd al-Razzāq asked Yaḥyā b. Ma'īn to write only a single tradition, while he dictated to him from memory – without any book – Yaḥyā replied, "Never, not a single word"[2]. The method of imparting the traditions is dictation from the *book*, but it is not mentioned in Yaḥyā's traditions when he imparted them.

عبدالله حدثني أبي ثنا روح من كتابه ثنا سعيد بن ابي عروبة

10. Here the word *Ḥaddathanā* is used for the reading of the teacher from the book to his students[3].

قال أبي في حديثه ثنا به وكيع في المصنف عن سفيان ...

11. Ibn Ḥanbal is quoting the tradition of Wakī' from his book *al-Muṣannaf*, which is a lengthy one. He took many traditions from this book, but perhaps only once he did refer to this work, otherwise always referring to the author[4].

يحى بن آدم ثنا عبدالله بن ادريس املاه عليّ من كتابه عن عاصم بن كليب

12. Yaḥyā informs us that 'Abd Allāh b. Idrīs dictated to him from his book[5]. Here the book is employed for transmitting the traditions in dictating, yet the word *Ḥaddathanā* is used for this purpose.

... قتيبة ثنا الليث عن ابن عجلان عن عمرو بن شعيب عن ابيه عن جده ...

13. Tirmidhī says that some scholars criticized 'Amr b. Shu'aib's traditions because he related them— in their opinion — from his grandfather's book without being read in his presence[6]. Here a book is used but the word employed for its transmission is '*an*.

قال ابن أبي عمر فوجدت في موضع آخر في كتابي عن سفيان عن عبدالله عن نافع

14. Here the book is employed for imparting the traditions with the use of the usual term *Ḥaddathanā*[7].

1. Ḥanbal, ii, 306.
2. Ḥanbal, iii, 297.
3. Ḥanbal, v, 10.
4. Ḥanbal, i, 308.
5. Ḥanbal, i, 418.
6. Tirmidhī, i, 43.
7. Ibn Majah, p. 801, Tr., No. 2397.

مسدد بن مسرهد حدثنا عبدالله بن داود عن الاعمش ... « يكرهون العادة » ...
قال مسدد قلت لعبدالله بن داود « يكرهونه للعادة » فقال هكذا هو ولكن وجدته فى كتابى هكذا .

15. In this tradition we find a minor mistake of the copyist, who copied العادة instead of للعادة . The teacher read it as it was written. When a student wanted to correct him, he was assured by his teacher that the remark was right but the teacher read it according to what was written in the book [1]. Here is a use of the book with the usual term *Ḥaddathanā*.

16. Abū Dāwūd transmitted a portion of the booklet of Samurah, in different chapters of his *Sunan* without mentioning the book and employing the usual term *Ḥaddathanā* [2].

اخبرنا محمد بن المثنى قال حدثنا ابن ابى عدى هذا من كتابه ... وحدثنا ابن ابى عدى من حفظه ...

17. In this statement al-Nasa'ī gives an example of a *Ḥadīth* which was read to students twice by the teacher, once from memory and once from the book [3]. Had there been no variation, perhaps he would not have mentioned this practice.

شعبه عن قتاده عن الحسن عن سمرة قال قال رسول الله .... قال ابو عبد الرحمن الحسن عن سمرة كتاب

18. The term *'an* is employed to transmit the traditions, while according to the author these traditions were handed down to al-Ḥasan in the form of a book [4].

محمد بن منصور عن سفيان عن بيان بن بشر .... قال ابو عبد الرحمن هذا خطأ ، ليس من حديث بيان ولعل سفيان قال حدثنا اثنان فسقط الألف فصار بيان .

19. A tradition was transmitted on the authority of Muḥammad b. Manṣūr — Sufyān — Bayān b. Bishr. Al-Nasā'ī says that this tradition does not belong to Bayān, and perhaps Sufyān said, "*Ḥaddathanā Ithnān* [it was reported to me by two persons]", and the letter *Alif* was dropped from the book, eventually becoming *Bayān* [5]. He supported his argument by another tradition which

1. A.D., i, 106.
2. A.D., i, 182; 353; ii, 128.
3. Nas. i, 45.
4. Nas., i, 205.
5. Nas., i, 329.

reads, *"Ḥaddathanā Rajulān"*[1]. This error could only take place if the book was used for copying and reading and was without dots and other diacritical signs, yet there is no mention of the book and the usual method *'an* is used for imparting.

20. There is another example of discrepancy in the text explained by al-Nasa'ī. A tradition is transmitted by three channels and their ultimate source is ابن الحوتكية عن ابي ذر Abī Dharr, but one of the narrators related it on the authority of Ubai أبي . al-Nasa'ī says, "The correct reading is Abī Dharr أبي ذر and it seems that the word Dhar was dropped from the book and was read أبي Ubai"[2].

21. Aḥmad b. Ḥanbal, speaking about Ibn al-Mubārak, says that he used to transmit traditions from the book[3], but if we go through the traditions transmitted on his authority we may never find a reference to the book.

22. Ibn Ḥanbal says that Shu'bah used to read in Baghdād. There were four students who used to write in the lectures. One of them was Ādam b. 'Abd al-Raḥmān. When Ādam was asked, he affirmed the statement and said that he had a very high speed of writing. He further added, "I used to write and the people used to copy from me. Shu'bah came to Baghdād. He imparted traditions in forty lectures... I attended twenty of them. I *heard* two thousand traditions and missed twenty lectures"[4]. In this statement Ādam uses the word *heard*, though he took these traditions by means of dictation and wrote them down. So the word *Ḥaddathanā* gives half of the picture.

23. Whenever Zuhair b. Mu'āwiyah *heard* a tradition twice from his teacher he wrote down 'finished the task' كتب عليه فرغت[5].

Now here are two further examples of this kind.

24. The *Muwaṭṭa'* of Mālik b. Anas is a well-known book. The book was entitled by the author himself, not like most of the

1. Nas., i, 329.
2. Nas., i, 329.
3. *Tahd.*, v, 384.
4. Rāzī, i, i, 268.
5. Ja'd, 351; *Imlā*. 9.

the early books which did not have any titles save the names of their compilers, e.g., the book of 'Urwah, the book of Qatādah, etc.

The authors of the classical books utilized the material of the *Muwaṭṭa'* freely, referring to Mālik without mentioning the book. Here is an example of one tradition regarding ablution with sea-water, taken from the *Muwaṭṭa'* with its quotations in the classical books.

1.	Ḥaddathanī Yaḥyā	'An Mālik	'An Ṣafwān...[1]	
2.	Ḥaddathanā b. Maslamah	'An Mālik	'An	[2]
3.	Akhbaranā Qutaibah	'An	'An	[3]
4.	M. b. al-Mubārak	'An	'An	[4]
5.	Ḥaddathanā Hishām	Thanā	Ḥaddathanī	[5]
6.	Qutaibah	'An		
7.	Ma'n Ḥaddathanā		'An	[6]
8.	Abū Salamah		'An	[7]

In all the above cases the traditions were transmitted, not orally, but through the book, yet referring to the author only.

25. *Al-Maghāzī* of Ibn Isḥāq is a well-known book. The text was established and the book was titled by the author himself. The book was transmitted by several pupils of Ibn Isḥāq[8].

Now we may compare the version of Ibn Hishām with that of Muḥammad b. Salamah[9] (see Appendix No. iv). There are very minor differences here and there as are usually found between two manuscripts of the same work, except for one main variation only in *isnād* which is quite different and reads as follows: 'Abd Allāh b. al-Ḥasan al-Ḥarrānī – al-Nufailī – Muḥammad b.

1. Mālik, *Ṭahārah,* 12.
2. A.D., *Ṭahārah,* 41.
3. Nas, *Ṭahārah,* 47.
4. Dārimī, i, 186.
5. Ibn Majah, i, 136.
6. Tirmidhī, *Ṭahārah,* 52.
7. Ḥanbal, ii, 361.
8. There were at least 15 versions of this work. See Guillaume, *The Life of Muḥammad, intro.*, p. xxx.
9. For the version of Ibn Salamah see Rāzī, ii, i, 169; *Kāmil,* ii, 27a; *Mīzān,* ii, 192; *Bagh.*, vi, 179; *Tahd.*, iv, 153-4; ix, 129.

Salamah – Ibn Isḥāq. The date goes back to 454 A.H. when the manuscript was read to al-Khaṭīb al-Baghdādī.

It is inconceivable that such a large book should have been transmitted orally for five centuries and that students had to memorize the whole book instead of writing it down.

Therefore, if any *isnād* bears the usual term *Ḥaddathanā, Akhbaranā, 'An,* etc., it does not necessarily mean that the traditions were transmitted orally and no books were used. In fact it indicates only the current methods of that time for the handling of documents: by means of copying from a book or dictation from a written source, etc.

Summing up the discussion, the terms *Ḥaddathanā, Akhbaranā, 'An,* etc., were employed to indicate only the current methods of documentation, which took several forms, e.g.,

Copying from a written document.

Writing from a written source through dictation.

Reading of a written document by the teacher.

Reading of a written document by a student.

Transmitting a document orally and recording by students.

Transmitting a document orally and its being received by students aurally.

The only common key point between all these methods is the permission of the *Shaikh* to students to utilize the information. Those who utilized the material without permission were called *'Sāriq al-Ḥadīth'*.

APPENDIX II

The Problem of Enormous Numbers of Ḥadīth.

In Chapter III, we have already seen a sketch of the educational activities on the subject of *ḥadīth.*

There are references to hundreds of teachers from whom al-Taurī, Ibn al-Mubārak, al-Zuhrī, etc. had written *aḥādīth.* In the works of biographers we find a long list of teachers and students of eminent scholars. There are at least fifty students of al-Zuhrī who made their written collections from him[1]. If, on an average, every one of them had written only five hundred traditions from him, then this number would have been 25,000. If we go one step further and assume for example that every student of al-Zuhrī had only two or three students, then this number of traditions might have increased at the end of the second century to some 75,000, and in the time of Bukhārī and his contemporaries they would have been in hundreds of thousands.

Thus, the numbers of a few thousand *aḥādīth* reached about three quarters of a million in the mid third century.

According to Ibn Ḥanbal's statement, over 7,000,000 traditions were sound, of which 6,000,000 were memorized by Abū Zur'ah[2].

Al-Bukhārī claimed that he made his collection of traditions out of six hundred thousand[3]. His book contains only 7,397 *Ḥadīth* with repetition, and only 2,602 *Ḥadīth* without repetition[4].

1. *Supra,* al-Zuhrī, in the third chapter.
2. *Madkhal,* 13.
3. *Bagh.,* ii, 8, 14. Other traditionists also gave an enormous number which they memorized or wrote down. I discuss only one case of al-Bukhārī to clarify the problem.
4. Ibn Ḥajar, *Hady al-Sārī,* as quoted by al-Sibā'i in *Sunnah,* 501.

The actual number of traditions preserved in the *Ṣiḥāḥ* and the other collections is only a small fraction of the body of the traditions described above. This is a puzzling problem. Many scholars have been perplexed, and so have reached very strange conclusions. Guillaume says "Bukhārī's biographer says that he selected his material from no less than 600,000 *Ḥadīth.* If we allow for repetitions which occur under different heads, he reduced this vast number of forgeries or dubious reports to less than 3,000 *Ḥadīth*. In other words, less than one in every 200 traditions which circulated in his day could pass his test"[1].

The problem consists of (a) *Ḥadīth* and (b) enormous numbers and their implications.

(a) *Ḥadīth* in the terms of some traditionists, means utterances, deeds and tacit approval of the Prophet[2], while in definitions of other scholars it covers utterances, deeds, legal decisions and tacit approval of the Prophet as well as those of Companions and the Successors[3].

(b) As for the problem of enormous numbers, every channel of transmission is counted as a separate *Ḥadīth*. 'Abd al-Raḥmān b. Mahdī (d. 198) says, "I have thirteen traditions from al-Mughīrah transmitting from the Prophet, concerning *"al-masḥ 'ala al-Khuffain"*[4]. It is quite obvious that al-Mughīrah is reporting a single action or habit of the Prophet. It does not matter how many times this action was repeated. It would be reported as a single action. As this single action is reported to 'Abd al-Raḥman b. Mahdī from thirteen channels, he counts them as thirteen traditions.

The first four centuries of the *Hijrah* were the golden age for the science of tradition, and the number of transmitters grew tremendously. Ibn Khuzaimah (d. 311) gives some thirty *isnāds* for

---

1. Guillaume, *Islam,* 91; a similar idea is maintained by Aḥmad Amīn, *Fajr al-Islām,* 211-12; Muir, *Mahomet,* xxxvii; see also J. Robson, *Tradition in Islam, M.W.*, vol. xli, pp. 101-1; Nicholson, *A Literary History of the Arabs,* p. 146; Gibb, *Mohammedanism* 79, Haikal, *Ḥayāt Muḥammad,* p. 49.

2. Tahānwī, *Kashshāf,* 279; Qāsimī, *al-Taḥdīth* 61; Suyūṭī, *Alfiyah* 3; Ṣubḥī, *Muṣṭalaḥāt* 3; Sakhāwī, *Mughīth* 4.

3. Jurjānī, *Risālah,* 1; see Tahānwī, Kashshāf, 279; Suyūṭī, *Tadrīb,* quoting al-Ṭībī, 6; Sakhāwī, *Mughīth,* 12 "predecessors called them *Ḥadīth*"; Gīlānī, *Tadwīn* 62; for early usage of this word for the sayings other than the Prophet see Ḥasan b. 'Imārah's discussion with al-Zuhrī, *Islām,* v, 149.

4. Rāzī, *Introd.* 261.

one *Ḥadīth* in one chapter, concerning the single act of 'Ā'ishah, for cleansing the cloth[1]. Meanwhile it is obvious that there might have been many other channels of transmission which were unknown to him. Muslim b. al-Ḥajjāj (d. 261) cites the names of a great number of transmitters, when he argues about certain points, especially when there is a mistake committed by some transmitters. For example, he gives thirteen traditions concerning the single incident of Ibn 'Abbās and his *tahajjud* prayer. In the prayer, he stood on the left of the Prophet and then the Prophet pulled him to his right side. Yazīd b. Abū Ziyād related on the authority of Kuraib, that Ibn 'Abbās stood on the right side of the Prophet, but he was placed on the left. On this occasion Muslim gives thirteen *isnāds* — making thirteen *Ḥadīth* — contradicting Yazīd's statement[2]. Further, he does not give the complete *isnād* and their full growth until his time. He mostly gives the details of channels until about 130 A.H. Had he given the complete comprehensive *isnād* flourishing in his own time, they might have grown to fifty traditions at least.

Growth and development of isnād in the third century.

There have been some traditionists who claim that they had every *Ḥadīth* from one hundred channels[3], and many others who have written every *Ḥadīth* from twenty or thirty channels[4]. So we may now infer what the real numbers of the traditions were which were described as 600,000. Another point is that they were not purely traditions of the Prophet, but the sayings of the Companions and the Successors and their legal decisions as well; the word '*Ḥadīth*' covers all these subjects and matters in some scholars' terms.

---

1. See Appendix No. V, photocopy of the MSS. of *Ṣaḥīḥ* of Ibn Khuzaimah, page related to this subject.
2. Muslim, *Tamyīz,* fol. 6b-7a; for more examples see fol. 10a; 11 channels; fol. 11b; 17 channels; these *isnadās* are shown in the mid-second century as they flourished, not at the time of Muslim, who was a century later.
3. Sibā'ī, *Sunnah,* 224, quoting sayings of Ibrāhīm b. Sa'īd al-Jauharī from Tānīb al-Khaṭīb.
4. *Madkhal,* 9; and it is quite possible, at least 50 students transmitted al-Zuhrī's book, so within 25 years' time his traditions might have grown 30 or 40 times, see also *Majrūḥīn,* 10a; *Jāmi'* 165a; *Mizān,* i, 35.

The True Numbers of the Traditions.

What is the real number of authentic traditions? The exact number is unknown, but according to Sufyān al-Thaurī, Shu'bah, Yaḥyā al-Qaṭṭān, 'Abd al-Raḥmān b. Mahdī and Ibn Ḥanbal 4,000 *Ḥadīth* only[1]. The statement is incomprehensible. Gīlānī is inclined to a number of less than 10,000 *Ḥadīth,* based in his statement, on the quotation from Ṭāhir al-Jazā'irī, who in turn was quoting al-Ḥākim al-Nishābūrī[2]. This is apparently a misinterpretation of al-Ḥākim's attitude. He gives an estimate of less than 10,000 *Ḥadīth* for the first-class authentic traditions which are transmitted according to al-Bukhārī and Muslim b. al-Ḥajjāj's stipulation. Furthermore he himself objects to this number, saying, "How can it be said that his [Prophet] traditions do not reach 10,000 traditions when 4,000 Companions... have transmitted traditions from him, who associated with him for more than twenty years..."[3].

It is said that the *Musnad* of Ibn Ḥanbal consists of some 40,000 Traditions, and without repetition it would be about 30,000[4], but there has not been any research so far.

Al-Bukhārī, his Ṣaḥīḥ, and other Traditions.

Al-Bukhārī did not claim that what he left out were the spurious, nor that there were no authentic traditions outside his collection. On the contrary he said, "I only included in my book *al-Jāmi'* those that were authentic, and I left out many more authentic traditions than this to avoid unnecessary length"[5]. He had no intention of collecting all the authentic traditions. He only wanted to compile a manual of *Ḥadīth,* according to the wishes of his *Shaikh* Isḥāq b. Rāhwaih[6], and his function is quite clear from the title of his book *"Al-Jāmi', al-Musnad, al-Ṣaḥīḥ, al-Mukhtaṣar, min umūr Rasūl al-Allāh wa Sunanihi, wa ayyāmih"*[7]. The

---

1. Rashīd, *Ibn Mājah,* 164, quoting al-Amīr al-Ṣan'ānī.
2. Gīlānī, *Tadwīn,* 66-67.
3. *Madkhal,* 11-12.
4. Shākir, Commentary on Suyūṭī's *alfīyah,* pp. 218-222, Shākir gives the estimate of the early scholars of 30,000 to 40,000; perhaps the first number indicates traditions without repetition. For the average of repetitions see, *infra,* Arabic Section.
5. Bājī, 9b; also Ibn Ḥajar, *Hady al-Sārī,* i, 18; also *Bagh.,* ii, 8-9.
6. Ibn Ḥajar, *op. cit.,* 18; *Bagh.* ii, 8.
7. Ibn al-Ṣalāḥ, *'Ulum al-Ḥadīth,* 24-5.

word *al-Mukhtaṣar,* 'epitome', itself explains that al-Bukhārī did not make any attempt at a comprehensive collection.

Now it is clear that when traditionists give enormous numbers for the traditions, they mean channels and sources of their transmission, and do not mean real numbers of *Ḥadīth.* But when they give small figures, saying: "Al-Zuhrī has 1,000 *Ḥadīth,* or al-Qāsim has 200 *Ḥadīth*" they most probably mean *Ḥadīth* as a subject matter not counted according to its *isnād.*

Does 'Unauthentic' Mean a False Statement?

Traditionists, at first, look into the *isnād* and if it is defective, they call the *Ḥadīth* defective, without scrutinizing the subject matter[1]; because a *Ḥadīth,* according to their criteria, cannot be authentic unless both its parts are perfect.

Authentic matter with false *isnād* is a false statement. This will be clear from Appendix III. This appendix — which is a collection of traditions, transmitted by Bishr b. al-Ḥusain on the authority of Zakariyā b. 'Adī from Anas b. Mālik from the Prophet — is called spurious, though about one quarter of the traditions of this collection are found in Bukhārī and Muslim's *Ṣaḥīḥ* collections, and are called authentic. The only reason for discarding them is that it is maintained that Zakariyā did not hear all these traditions from Anas, and they are falsely attributed to him.

Therefore, if the scholars say that 200,000 *Ḥadīth* were not authentic, it does not mean that they were spurious. It only means that their *isnāds* are questioned while the subject itself may or may not be false.

1. See for the priority of *isnād* criticism, Robson, *Materials of Tradition, M.W.*, vol. xli, p. 166; Guillaume, 55.

APPENDIX III

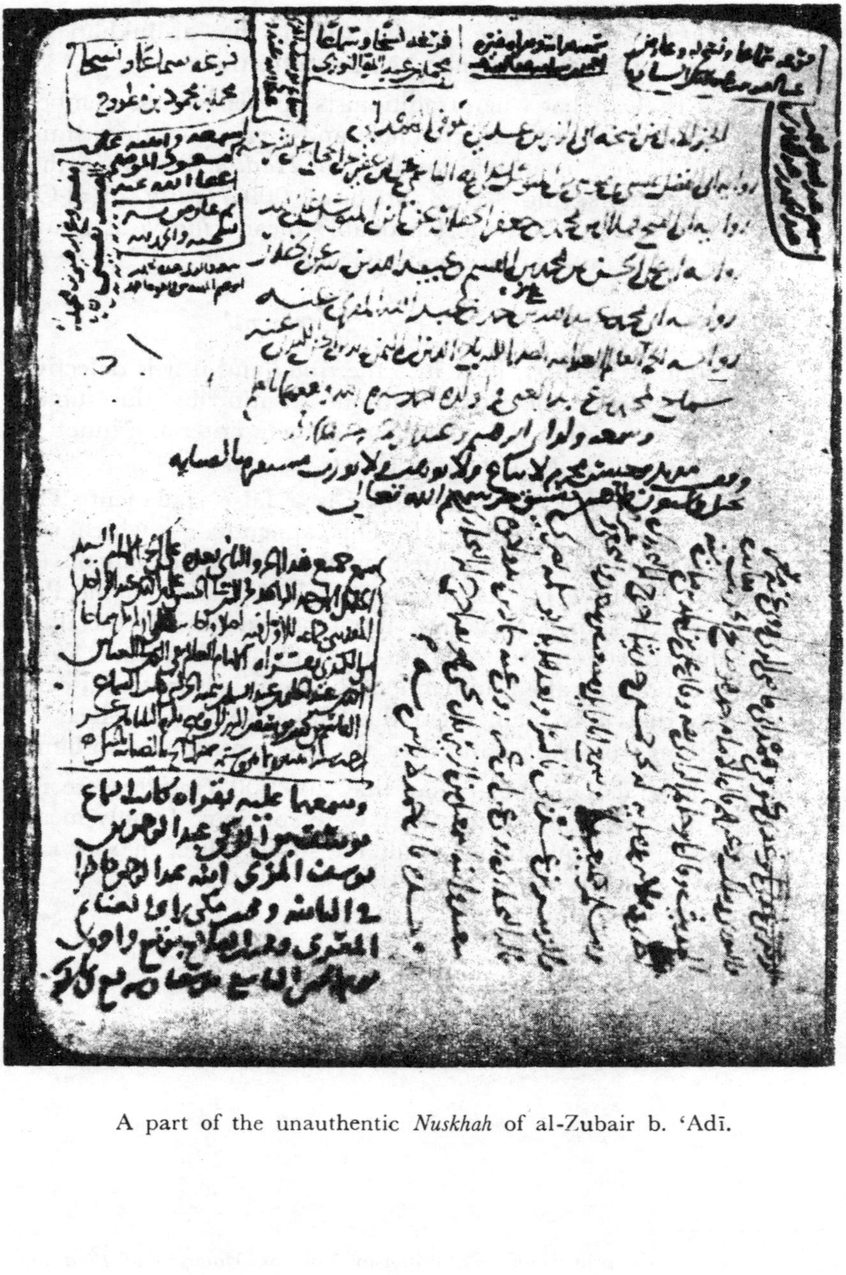

A part of the unauthentic *Nuskhah* of al-Zubair b. ʿAdī.

١٦٥

السلاح ثم تنطلقوا فيتجهوا اليه فاجتمعوا عند رسول الله صلى
الله عليه و اخبرنا عبد الله بن الحسن الحراني قال نا النفيلي قال نا محمد
بن سلمه عن محمد بن اسحق قال حدثني ثور عن عكرمه مولى ابن عباس عن
ابن عباس قال مشا معهم رسول الله صلى الله عليه الى بقيع الغرقد
ثم وجههم وقال انطلقوا على اسم الله اللهم اعنهم ثم رجع الى بيته
في ليلة مقمره فانتهوا الى حصنه فهتف به ابو نايله وكان
حديث عهد بعرس فوثب في ملحفته فاخذت امراته بناحيتها وقالت
انك رجل محارب وان صاحب الحرب لا ينزل في مثل هذه الساعه
قال ابو نايله لو وجدني نايما ما ايقظني فقالت فو الله اني لاعرف في صوته
الشر قال يقول لها لو دعا الفتى لطعنه لاجاب قال فنزل فتحدث
قال ابو شعيب حدثنا التوزي ابو محمد قال قال الاصمعي ما تكلم بهذه
الكلمه لو وجدني نايما ما ايقظني احد في جاهليه ولا اسلام الا فتك
معهم ساعه وتحدثوا معه ثم قال هل لك يا ابن الاشرف ان نتماشا
الى شعب العجوز فنتحدث بقيه ليلتنا هذه قال ان شيتم فخرجوا
يتماشون ساعه ثم ان ابا نايله شام يده في فودي راسه ثم شم يده
ثم قال ما رايت كالليله طيبا اعطر قط ثم مشا ساعه ثم عاد لمثلها
حتى اطمان ثم مشا ساعه ثم عاد لمثلها فاخذ بفودي راسه ثم
قال اضربوا عدو الله فضربوه فاختلفت عليه اسيافهم فلم يغن
شيا قال محمد بن مسلمه فذكرت معولا في سيفي حين رايت اسيافنا
لم تغن شيا فاخذته وقد صاح عدو الله صيحه لم يبق حولنا حصن الا
اوقدت عليه النار فوضعته في ثنته ثم تحاملت عليه حتى بلغت

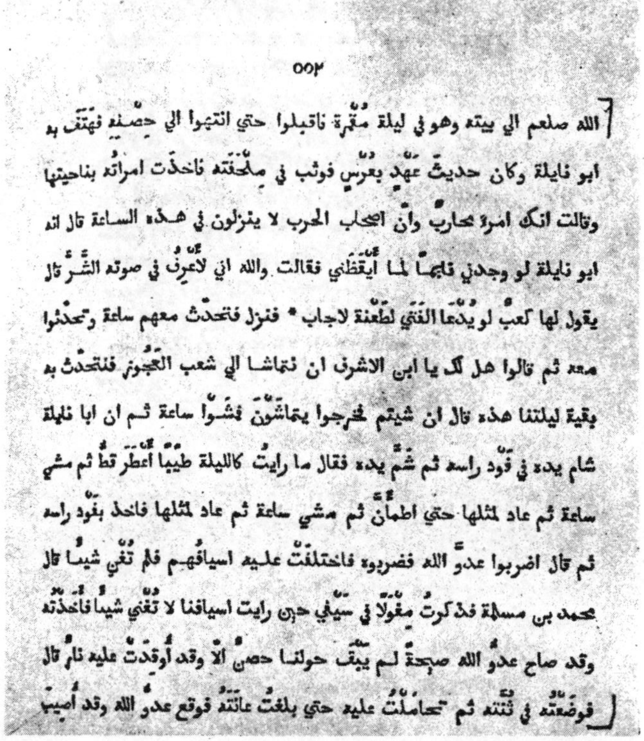

٥٥٢

الله صلعم الي بيته وهو في ليلة مُقْمِرة فاقبلوا حتي انتهوا الي حِصْنه فهتَف به
ابو نايلة وكان حديثَ عَهْدٍ بعُرْسٍ فوثب في مِلْحَفته فاخذَت امراتُه بناحيتها
وقالت انك امرؤٌ محاربٌ وانّ اصحاب الحرب لا ينزلون في هذه الساعة قال انه
ابو نايلة لو وجدني نايمـًا لما أيْقَظَني فقالت والله اني لأعرِفُ في صوته الشَّرَّ قال
يقول لها كعبٌ لو يُدْعَا الفَتَي لطَعْنة لاجاب * فنزل فتحدّث معهم ساعة وتحدّثوا
معه ثم قالوا هل لك يا ابن الاشرف ان نتماشا الي شعب العَجُوز فنتحدّث به
بقية ليلتنا هذه قال ان شيتم فخرجوا يتماشَوْنَ فمَشَوْا ساعة ثم ان ابا نايلة
شام يده في فَوْد راسه ثم شَمّ يده فقال ما رايتُ كالليلة طيبًا أعطَرَ قطُّ ثم مشي
ساعة ثم عاد لمثلها حتي اطمانّ ثم مشي ساعة ثم عاد لمثلها فاخذ بفَوْد راسه
ثم قال اضربوا عدوَّ الله فضربوه فاختلفَتْ عليه اسيافُهم فلم تُغْنِ شيئًا قال
محمد بن مسلمة فذكرتُ مِغْوَلًا في سَيْفي حين رايت اسيافنا لا تُغني شيئا فاخذته
وقد صاح عدوُّ الله صيحةً لم يَبْقَ حولنا حصنٌ الا وقد أُوقِدَتْ عليه نارٌ قال
فوضَعْتُه في ثُنَّته ثم تحامَلْتُ عليه حتي بلغَتْ عانَتَه فوقع عدوُّ الله وقد أُصيبَ

A page from *al-Maghāzī* of Ibn Isḥāq with the corresponding printed text in the *Sīrat* of Ibn Hishām.

APPENDIX V

Folio 42 from the Ms. of *Ṣaḥīḥ* Ibn Khuzaimah.

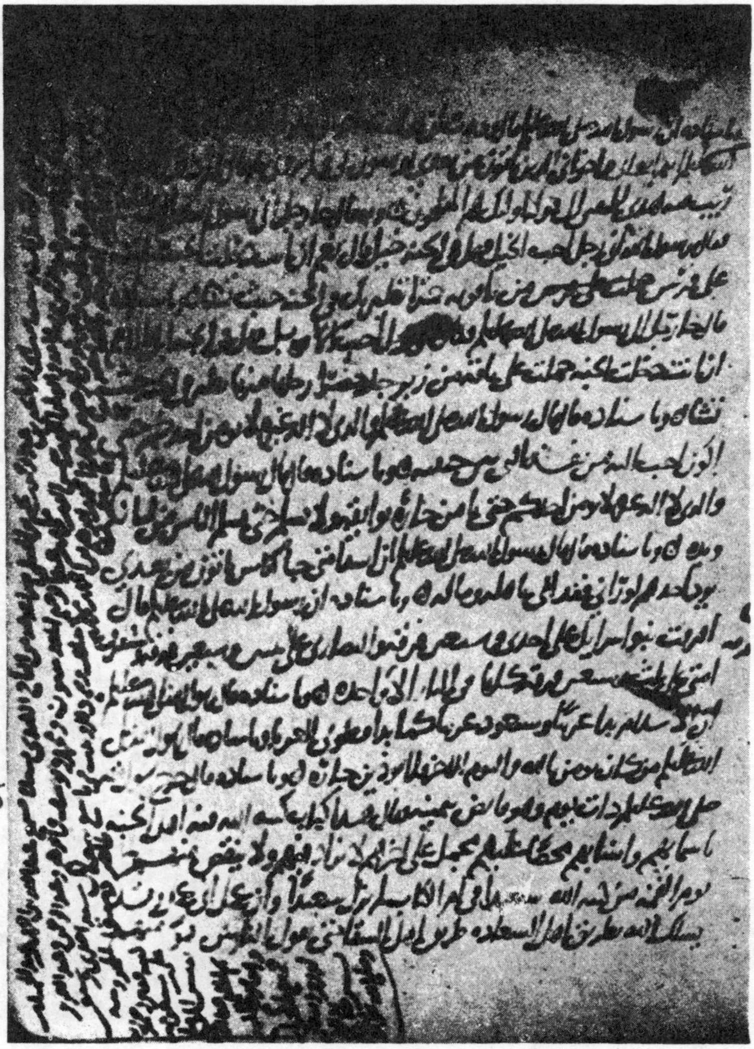

التخريجات : (٥٦) – نحوه م طهارة ٣٩ (٥٧) – نحوه مم ٥ /٣٥٢ (٥٨) – نحوه مم ٥ /٣٥٢ (٥٩) – خ ايمان ٨ ؛ م ايمان ٦٩ (٦٠) – خ ادب ٢٩ ؛ م ايمان ٦٤ ؛ ٦٥ ؛ ٧٣ (٦٢) – نحوه مم ٣ /١٢٠ ؛ ١٤٥ (٦٣) – م ايمان ٢٢٢ (٦٤) – نحوه م ايمان ٧٣ (٦٥) – نحوه خ قدره ؛ ومم ٥ /٣٣٥ مختصراً

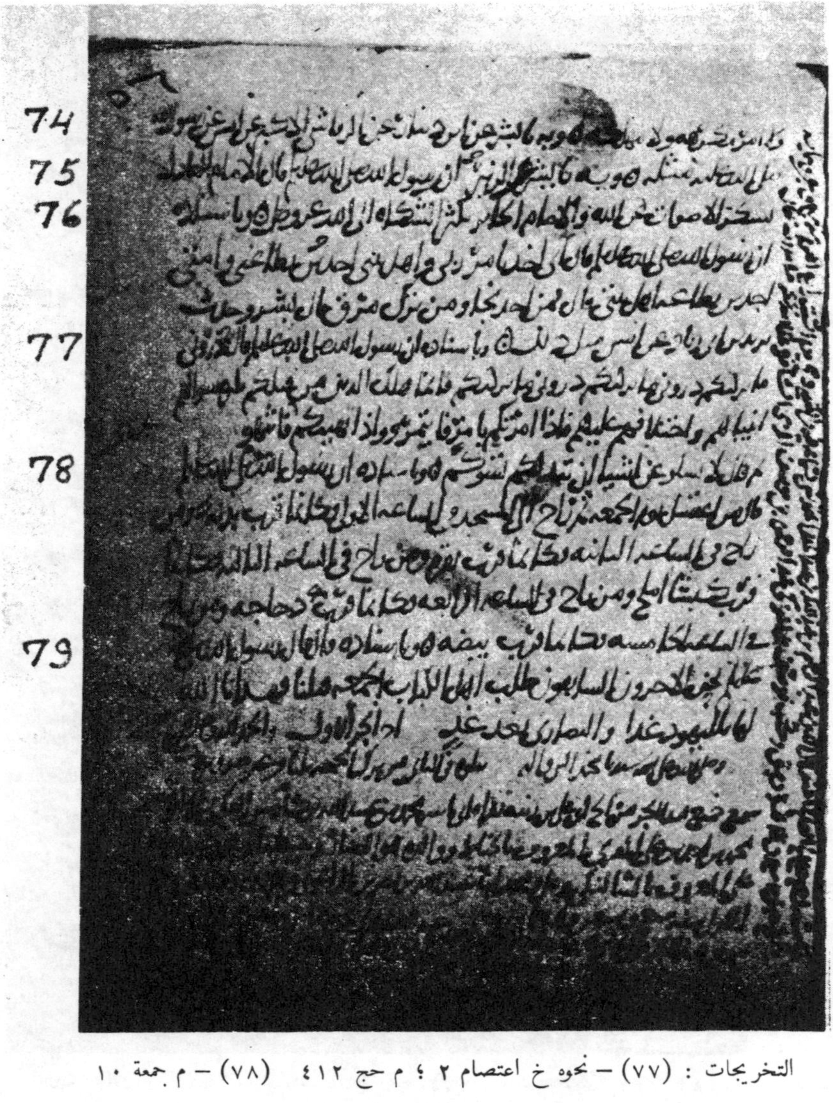

التخريجات : (٧٧) – نحوه خ اعتصام ٢ ؛ م حج ٤١٢ (٧٨) – م جمعة ١٠

BIBLIOGRAPHY

A. LIST OF MANUSCRIPTS

Abū Ja'far al-Ṭaḥāwī, Muḥammad b. Aḥmad b. Salāmah: *al-Taswīyah bain Ḥaddathanā wa Akhbaranā*. Chester Beatty Library, Dublin, MS. No. 3415.

Abū Khaithamah, Zuhair b. Ḥarb: *Al-'Ilm*, Chester Beatty Library, MS. No. 3491.

Abū Ya'lā al-Tamīmī, Aḥmad b. 'Alī b. al-Muthannā: *Musanad*. Photocopy› Public Library, Doha, Original, Sehid Ali Pasa, MS. No. 564. Istanbul·

Abū al-Yamān, Al-Ḥakam b. Nāfi': *Aḥādīth*, Ẓāhiriyah Library, MS. Majmū', 120, fol. 68-87, Damascus.

Abū Zur'ah, 'Abd al-Raḥmān b. 'Amr b. 'Abd Allāh al-Dimashqī.: *Tārīkh*, Fatih, MS. No. 4210, Istanbul.

Al-'Alā'ī, Khalīl b. Kaikaladī: *Jāmi' al-Taḥṣīl fi Aḥkām al-Marāsīl*. Ẓāhiriyah Library, MS. No. Ḥadīth, 405, Damascus.

'Alī b. al-Ja'd, Abū al-Ḥasan, 'Alī b. al-Ja'd: *Musnad*. Collected by 'Abd Allāh b. Muḥammad al-Baghawī, Egyptian Library, MS. No. 2240. Cairo.

Al-Azdī: *Tārīkh Mauṣil*, edited by A.H.M. Abū Ḥabība, The University of Cambridge, Thesis No. Ph. D. 5147.

Al-Bājī, Sulaimān b. Khalaf: *Al-Ta'dīl wa al-Tajrīḥ li man Kharraja 'Anhu al-Bukhārī fī al-Jāmi' al-Ṣaḥīḥ*, Nuruosmaniye MS. No. 766. Istanbul.

Al-Dhahabī, Muḥammad b. Aḥmad: *Siyar A'lām al-Nubalā'*, Photocopy, Ẓāhirīyah Library, Damascus.

Al-Fasawī, Ya'qūb b. Sufyān:*Tārīkh*, 2nd vol. Revan, MS. No. 1554, Istanbul. 3rd vol. Esad Efendi, MS. No. 2391. Istanbul.

Ibn Abū Khaithamah, Aḥmad b. Zuhair b. Ḥarb: *Tārīkh*, vol. iii, Qarawiyyīn, MS. No. 244/40, Fez.

Ibn Abū Ṣaliḥ, Suhail b. Abū Ṣāliḥ: *Nuskhah*, photocopy Public Library, Doha, Original, Ẓāhiriyah Library, MS. No. Majmū', 107, fol. 155-160. Damascus.

Ibn Abū Shaibah, 'Abd Allāh b. Muḥammad: *Muṣannaf*. Madinah, MS. No. 333-4. Istanbul.

Ibn 'Adī, 'Abd Allāh b. 'Abd Allāh al-Jurjānī.: *Al-Kāmil*, 3 volumes. Photocopy, Public Library, Doha, Original, Aḥmad iii, MS. No. 2943. Istanbul.

Ibn 'Asākir, 'Alī b. al-Ḥasan: Tārīkh Dīmashq, Ẓāhiriyyah Library, Vol. xiii.

Ibn Ḥanbal, Aḥmad b. Muḥammad b. Ḥanbal: *Al-'Ilal wa Ma'rifat al-Rijāl*, Ayasofya, MS. No. 3380. Istanbul.

Ibn Ḥibbān, Muḥammad b. Ḥibbān al-Bustī: a) *Al-Majrūḥīn min al-Muḥaddithīn*, Aya Sofya, MS. N°. 496. Istanbul.
b) *Al-Thiqāt*, Photocopy, Public Library, Doha, Original in Egyptian Library, Cairo.

Ibn Isḥāq, Muhammad b. Isḥāq: *Al-Maghāzī*, Ẓāhiriyah Library, Damascus.

Ibn Juraij, 'Abd al-Mālik b. 'Abd al-'Azīz.: *Aḥādīth Ibn Juraij*, transmitted by Rauḥ, photocopy, Public Library, Doha, Original in Ẓāhiriyah Library, MS. N°. Majmū' 24.

Ibn Khuzaimah, Muḥammad b. Isḥāq al-Nisābūrī: *Ṣaḥīḥ Ibn Khuzaimah*, photocopy, Public Library, Doha.

Ibn Rāhawaih, Isḥāq b. Rāhwaih: *Musnad*. Egyptian Library, MS. No. Ḥadîth 776.

Ibn Rajab, 'Abd al-Raḥmān b. Aḥmad al-Ḥanbalī: *Sharḥ 'Ilal al-Tirmidhī*, photocopy, Public Library, Doha, original, Ẓāhiriyah Library, Damascus.

Ibn Zanjuwaih, Ḥumaid b. Makhlad al-Azdī: *Kitāb al-Amwāl*, Burdur Umumi Kutuphanesi, No. MS. No. 183, Turkey.

Ibrāhīm b. Ṭahmān al-Khurāsānī: *Nuskhah*. Photocopy, Public Library, Doha, original Ẓāhiriyah Library, Damascus.

Al-Iṣbahānī, Bashīr b. al-Huṣain: *Nuskhah Zubair b. 'Adī*. Photocopy, Public Library, Doha, original in Ẓāhiriyah Library, MS. No. Majmū', 90, fol. 50-58, Damascus.

Juwairīyah b. Asmā': *Ṣaḥīfah*, photocopy, Public Library, Doha, original Sehid Ali pasa, MS. No. 539, Istanbul.

Al-Khaṭīb al-Baghdādī, Aḥmad b. 'Alī b. Thābit: a) *Al-Faqīh wa al-Mutafaqqih*, Koprulu, MS. No. 392. Istanbul.
b) *Al-Jāmī' li Akhlāq al-Rāwī wa Ādāb al-Sāmi'*, photocopy in Egyptian Library, original in Alexandria.
c) *Sharaf Aṣḥāb al-Ḥadīth*. Atif Effandi, MS. N°. 601, Istanbul.

Al-Kushshī, 'Abd b. Ḥumaid: *Al-Muntakhab min Musnad 'Abd b. Ḥumaid*, photocopy, Public Library, Doha, original Koprulu, MS. N°. 456. Istanbul.

Al-Laith b. Sa'd: *Ḥadīth al-Laith 'an Yazīd b. Abū Ḥabīb*, photocophy, Public Library, Doha, original MS. in Ẓāhiriyah Library, Damascus.

Al-Qushairī, al-Nisābūrī, Muslim b. al-Ḥajjāj: a) *Rijāl 'Urwah b. al-Zubair wa Jamā'ah min al-Tābi'īn wa Ghairihim*, Ẓāhiriyah Library, MS. N°. Majmū', 55.
b) *Al-Tamyīz wa al-Ifrād*, Ẓāhiriyah Library, MS. Majmū', 19, photocopy in Public Library, Doha.

Al-Rāmhurmuzī, Al-Ḥasan b. 'Abd al-Raḥmān: *Al-Muḥaddith al-Fāṣil bain al-Rāwī wa al-Wā'ī*, Köprûlû, MSS. N°. 397. Istanbul.

Al-Ruwāsī, Wakī' b. Al-Jarrāḥ: *Nuskhah Wakī'*, photocopy, Public Library, Doha, original, Faizullah Effandi, Istanbul.

Shabāb, Khalīfah b. Khayyāṭ: *Ṭabaqāt*, Ẓāhiriyah Library, Damascus.

Al-Ṭabarānī, Sulaimān b. Aḥmad b. Ayyūb: a) *Al-Mu'jam al-Awsaṭ* 1-2 vol. Corra Chebil Zade, MSS. Nos. 72, 73.
b) *Al-Mu'jam al-Kabīr*,
vol. 1-2 Aḥmad iii, MS. No. 465/1-2.

vol. 3-4. Fatih, MSS. No. 1198.
vol. 5-6. Aḥmad iii, MS. No. 465/5-6.
vol. 9-10. Aḥmad iii, MS. No. 465/9-10. Istanbul.

Al-Thaurī, Sufyān b. Sa'īd: *Al-Juz'al-Awwal Mimmā Asnad al-Thaurī*, photocopy Public Library, Doha, original in Ẓāhiriyah Library, fol. 40-47, Damascus.

Al-'Umarī, 'Ubaid Allāh b. 'Umar: *Nuskhah*, Ẓāhiriyah Library, MS. No. Majmū', 105. (Min Ḥadīth 'Ubaid Allāh)

Al-Wāsiṭī, Aslam b. Sahl b. Aslam: *Tārīkh Wāsiṭ*. Iraq Museum Library, Baghdad.

B. LIST OF ARTICLES

'Alī, Jawād: *Mawārid Tārīkh al-Ṭabarī*, Majallah Majma' al-'Ilmī al-'Irāqī, 1954, p. 16-56.

Bousquet, G.H.: *Le mystère de la formation et des origines du Fiqh*. Translated by Ḥamīdullāh, Ma'ārif, 1958, pp. 165-184; 245-261.

Fitzgerald, S.V.: *The Alleged Debt of Islamic to Roman Law*, The Law Quaterly Review, Vol. 67, Jan. 1951, p. 81-102.

Guillaume, A.: *Where was al-Masyid al-Aqṣa*, Al-Andalus, Madrid, 1953, pp. 323-336.

Ḥamīdullāh, Muḥammad: a) *Administration of Justice in Early Islam*, I.C. 1937, pp. 163-171.
b) *Educational System in the Time of the Prophet*, I. C., 1939, pp. 48-59.
c) *Review on 'An Introduction to Islamic Law'* by J. Schacht, M.E.J., Vol. IX, 238-9.

Horovitz, J.: a) *Alter und Ursprung des Isnad*, Der Islam, Vol. VIII, 1918, pp. 39-47.
b) *The Earliest Biographies of the Prophet and their Authors*, I.C., Vol. I, pp. 535-559, Vol. II, pp. 22-50; 164-182; 495-526.

Inayatullah, Shaikh: *Bibliophilism in Mediaeval Islam*, I.C., 1938, 154-169.

Miles, G.C.: *Early Islamic Inscriptions near Tā'f in the Ḥijāz*, J.N.E.S., Chicago, Vol. VII, 1948, pp. 236-242.

Rashīd Riḍā: Notes on Al-Tadwīn fī al-Islām, *Al-Manār*, Vol. X, 1907, pp. 752-769.

Robson, J.: a) *Ibn Isḥāq's Use of the Isnād*, Bulletin of the John Rylands Library, Vol. 38, No. 2, March 1956, p. 449-465.
b) *The Isnād in Muslim Tradition*, Glasgow University Oriental Society Transactions, Vol. XV, 1955, p. 15-26.
c) *The Material of Tradition*, M.W. Vol. XLI, p. 166-180.
d) *Muslim Traditions, the Question of Authenticity*, Memoirs & Proc., Manchester Lit. Philosophical Society, Vol. XCIII, (1951-52) No. 7, pp. 84-102.

Ruth, S. Mackensen: *Arabic Books and Libraries in the Umaiyad Period*, A.J.S.L. Chicago, Vol. LII, pp. 245-53; Vol. LIII, 239-250, Vol. LIV, pp. 41-61.

Sachau: *Das Berliner Fragment des Mūsā Ibn 'Ukba,* Sitzung. der Phil. Hist. Classe, Feb. 1904, pp. 465-470.

Schacht, J.: a) *Foreign Elements in Ancient Islamic Law,* Journal of Comparative Legislation and International Law, 3rd series, Vol. XXXII (1950), parts III, IV, pp. 9-17.

b) *On Mūsā b. 'Uqba's Kitāb al-Maghāzī* Acta Orientalia, Vol. XXI, 1953, pp. 288-300.

c) *A Revaluation of Islamic Traditions,* J.R.A.S., 1949, pp. 143-154.

Serjeant, R.B.: *The 'Constitution of Medina',* The Islamic Quarterly, Vol. VIII, Number 1-2, p. 1-16.

Sprenger, A.: *On the Origin and Progress of Writing Down Historical Facts among the Musalmans,* J.A.S.B., Vol. 25, 1856, pp. 303-29.

Strange, G.L.: *The Noble Sanctuary of Jerusalem,* J.R.A.S. XIX, 1887, pp. 247-305.

Zolondek, Leon: *The Sources of the Kitāb al-Agānī,* Arabica, Tome VIII, Anne 1961, pp. 294-308.

C. LIST OF PUBLISHED BOOKS

'Abd al-Rāziq, Muṣṭafā: *Tamhīd Li Tārīkh al-Falsafah al-Islāmiyah,* 2nd ed. Cairo, 1959.

'Adid b. Sharyah: *Akhbār 'Abīd,* 1st ed. Hydrabad, 1347.

Abū 'Awāna: *Musnad,* Hydrabad, India.

Abū Dāwūd: *Sunan,* 4 vols. ed by M.M. 'Abd al-Ḥamīd, 2nd emp. Cairo, 1369/1950.

Abū al-Faraj al-Iṣfahānī 'Alī b. al-Ḥusain: *Al-Aghānī,* Dār al-Kutub al-Miṣriyah, Cairo, 1345-/1927- except where stated Būlāq edition Cairo, 1285.

Abū al-Fidā', Ismā'īl: *Al-Mukhtaṣar fī Akhbār al-Bashar,* 4 vols., Constantinople, 1286.

Abū Nu'aim, Aḥmad b. 'Abd Allāh al-Iṣbahānī: a) *Gescichte Iṣbahans,* ed. Dr. Seven Dedering, Leiden, 1931.

b) *Ḥilyat al-Awliyā',* 10 vols., Khānjī, Cairo, 1932.

Abū Rayyah, Maḥmūd: *Aḍwā' 'Alā al-Sunnah al-Muḥammadiyah,* 2nd ed. New Ṣūr Press, Lebanon, 1383/1964.

Abū Ṭālib al-Makkī: *Qūt al-Qulūb,* Al-Maimaniyah Press, Cairo, 1310/1893.

Abū Yūsuf, Ya'qūb b. Ibrāhīm: a) *Al-Athār,* ed. by Abū al-Wafā' al-Afghānī, Cairo, 1355/1937.

b) Al-Kharāj, Cairo, 1346/1927.

c) *Al-Rad 'Alā Siyar al-Auzā'ī,* ed. by Abū al-Wafā' al-Afghānī, Cairo, 1357/1938.

Abū Zahrah, Muḥammad: a) *Abū Ḥanīfah,* 2nd emp., Cairo, 1955.

b) *Mālik,* 2nd imp. Cairo, 1952.

c) *Al-Shāfi'ī,* 'Ulūm Press, Cairo, 1364/1945.

Abū Zahw, Muḥammad Muḥammad: *Al-Ḥadīth wa al-Muḥaddithūn,* 1st ed. Cairo, 1958.

Aḥmad Amīn: *Fajr al-Islām,* sixth imp. Al-Nahḍah al-Miṣriyah, Cairo, 1370/1950.

'Ajjāj al-Khaṭīb Muḥammad: *Al-Sunnah Qabl al-Tadwīn,* Cairo, 1383/1963.

Aland, Kurt: *The Problem of anonymity and Pseudonymity in Christian Literature of the First Two Centuries,* S.P.C.K. Theological Collection Series No. 4, London, 1965.

'Alī Ḥasan 'Abd al-Qādir: *Naẓrah 'Āmmah fī Tārīkh al-Fiqh al-Islāmī,* 'Ulūm Press, Cairo, 1361/1942.

'Alī b. Mūsā b. Ja'far al-Ṣādiq: *Musnad,* Beirut, 1966.

Arberry, A.J.: *The Koran Interpreted,* Oxford University Press, 1964.

Al-Azadī, 'Abd Allāh b. Muḥammad: *Tārīkh al-'Ulamā wa al-Ruwāt lil 'Ilm bil al-Andalus,* 2 vols., Cairo, 1954.

Al-'Aẓīmābādī, Muḥammad: *Al-Ta'līq al-Mughnī,* Commentary on Sunan al-Daraquṭnī, Anṣarī Press, Delhi, 1310.

Al-Balādhurī, Aḥmad b. Yaḥyā: a) *Ansāb al-Ashrāf,* 1st vol. ed. by Ḥamīdullāh, Cairo, 1959.

b) *Futūḥ al-Buldān,* ed. by al-Munajjid, Cairo, 1956.

c) *Liber Expugnationis Regionum,* ed. by M.J. de Goeje, Leiden, 1866.

Al-Baṣrī, Muḥammad b. 'Alī: *Al-Mu'tamad Fī Uṣūl al-Fiqh,* 2 vols. ed. by Ḥamīdullāh and others, Damascus, 1384-5/1964-5.

Brockelman, K.: *Geschichte der Arabischen Literatur* translated by al-Najjār, under the title, *Tārīkh al-Adab al-'Arabī,* 3 parts, Cairo, 1959.

Al-Bukhārī, Muḥammad b. Ismā'īl: a) *Al-Ḍu'fā',* Allahabad, 1325.

b) *Al-Jāmi' al-Saḥīḥ,* 4 vols., ed. by Juynboll, and others Leyde, Paris 1862-1908.

c) *Al-Tārīkh al-Kabīr,* 4 vols., Hydrabad, 1361.

d) *Al-Tārīkh al-Ṣaghīr,* Allahabad, 1325.

Caetani, Leone: *Chronographia Islamica,* Roma, 1912.

Coulson, N.J.: *A History of Islamic Law, Edinburgh,* 1964.

Cowan, J. Milton: *A Dictionary of Modern Written Arabic,* Wiesbaden, 1961.

Dāraquṭnī, 'Alīb. 'Umar: *Aḥādīth al-Muwaṭṭa' wa Ittifāq al- Ruwāt 'an Mālik wa Ikhtilāfihim fihā ziyadatan wa Naqṣan,* ed. by al-Kautharī, Ist ed. Cairo, 1365/1946.

Sunan al-Daraquṭnī, Anṣarī Press, Delhi, 1310.

Danby, Herbert: (Translated) *Mishna,* 1st ed. London, 1933.

Al-Dawālībī, Muḥammad Ma'rūf: *Al-Ḥuqūq al-Rumānīyah wa Tārīkhuhā.* 5th ed. Allepo, 1383/1963.

De Goeje, M.J.: *Quotations from the Bible in the Qoran and the Tradition,* pp. 179-185 in Semitic Studies in Memory of Rev. Dr. Alexander Kohut, ed. by G. A. Kohut, Berlin 1897.

Al-Dhahabī, Muḥammad b. Aḥmad: a) *Biographien von Gewährsmannern des Ibn Isḥāq hauptsächlich aus al-Dahabī,* ed. by Fischer August, Leiden, 1890.

b) *Mīzān al-I'tidāl,* 4 vols. ed. by Al-Bijāwī, Cairo, 1382/1963.

c) *Al-Mushtabih.* ed. by al-Bijāwī, Cairo, 1962.

d) *Siyar al-A'lām al-Nubalā',* 1-3 vols. ed. Al-Munajjid and others Cairo, 1956.

e) *Tadhkirat al-Ḥuffāẓ,* 4 vols, Hydrabad, N.D.

f) *Tārīkh* al-Islām, Vol. I-VI, Cairo, 1367-/1948-.

Al-Dhahabī, Muḥammad Ḥusain: *Al-Tafsīr wa al-Mafassirūn,* 3 vols. Cairo, 1381/1961.

Al-Dūlābī, Muḥammad b. Aḥmad: *Al-Kunā wa al-Asmā',* 2 vols., Hydrabad, 1322.

Al-Farrā', Yaḥyā b. Ziyād: *Ma'ānī al-Qur'ān,* Cairo, 1955.

Dārimī, 'Abd Allāh b. 'Abd al-Raḥmān: *Sunan al-Dārimī,* 2 vols., ed., by M. A. Dahmān, Damascus, 1349.

Fischer, see p. 282 footnote.

Fuwād 'Abd al-Bāqī: a) *Miftāḥ Kunūz al-Sunnah,* 1st ed. Cairo, 1352/1933.

b) *Mu'jam al-Mufahras li Alfāẓ al-Qur'ān,* 2nd imp. Cairo.

c) *Taysīr al-Manfa'ah,* Cairo, 1935-9.

Gérhardsson, Birger: *Memory and Manuscript,* Upsala 1961.

Gibb, H.A.R.: *Mohammedanism,* 2nd ed. London, 1964.

Gīlānī, Manāẓir Aḥsan: *Tadwīn Ḥadīth,* 1st ed. Karachi, 1375/1956.

Goldziher, Ignaz: a) *History of Classical Arabic Literature,* trans. by J. Desomogyi, Hildesheim, 1966.

b) *Muhammedanische Studien,* 2nd imp. Hildesheim, 1961. French translation by Leon Bercher, Paris, 1952.

Grohmann, A.: *From the World of Arabic Papyri,* Cairo, 1952.

Guillaume, A.: a) *Islam,* Penguin Ser. 66.

b) *The Life of Muḥammad,* the translation of Sīrah of ibn Isḥāq, Oxford University Press, 1955.

c) *The Traditions of Islam,* Oxford, 1924.

Haikal, Muḥammad Ḥusain: *Ḥayāt Muḥammad,* 3rd ed. Cairo, 1358.

Al-Haithamī, 'Alī b. Abū Bakr: a) *Majma' al-Zawāyid wa manba' al-Fawāyid,* Maktabah Al-Qudsī, 1352.

b) *Mawārid al-Ẓam'ān ilā Zawā'id Ibn Hibbān,* 1st ed. Cairo, N.D.

Ḥājī Khalīfah, Musṭafā b. 'Abd Allāh: *Kashf al-Ẓunūn 'an Asāmī al-Kutub wa al-Funūn,* Turkey, 1941.

Al-Ḥākim, Muḥammad b. 'Abd Allāh: a) *Ma'rifat 'Ulūm al-Ḥadīth,* ed. by Mu'aẓẓam Ḥusain, Cairo, 1937.

b) *Al-Madkhal Fī 'Ilm al-Ḥādīth,* ed. and translated by J. Robson, Luzac, 1953.

c) *Al-Mustadrak,* 4 vols. Hydrabad.

Ḥamīdullāh, Muḥammad.: a) *Imām Abū Ḥanīfah Kī Tadwīn Qānūn Islāmī,* Hydrābād, 1361.

b) *Al-Wathā'iq al-Siyāsiyah,* 2nd ed. Cairo, 1956.

Hammām b. Munabbih: a) *Ṣaḥīfah,* ed. by Muḥammad Ḥamīdullāh, 1st ed. Damascus, 1372/1953.

b) *Ṣaḥīfah,* English Translation, 5th edition, Hydrabad, 1380/1961.

Al-Ḥarrānī, Al-Ḥasan b. 'Alī: *Tuḥaf al-'Uqūl 'an Āl al-Rasūl,* Tehran, 1376.

Al-Ḥāzimī, Muḥammad b. Mūsā: *Al-I'tibār fī al-Nāsikh wa al-Mansūkh min al-Āthār*. Aleppo, 1346/1927.

Al-Hindī, 'Alī al-Muttaqī: *Kanz al-'Ummāl*, 8 vols., 1st ed., Hydrabad, 1312-14.

Hoskyns, Edwyn, Sir: *The Riddle of the New Testament*, Faber, London, MCMLXIII.

Al-Ḥumaidī, 'Abd Allāh b. Zubair: *Musnad al-Ḥumaidī*, 2 vols. ed. by Ḥabīb al-Raḥmān al-A'ẓamī, published by al-Majlis al-'Ilmī, Karachi, 1963.

Al-Ḥumaidī, Muḥammad b. Fatūḥ: *Jadhwat al-Muqtabas fī Dhikr Wulāt al-Andalus*, Cairo, 1953.

Ibn 'Abd al-Barr, Yūsuf b. 'Abd Allāh: a) *Al-Intiqā' fī Faḍā'il al-Thalāthah al-fuqahā'*, Cairo, 1350.
b) *Al-Istī'āb fī Ma'rifat al-Aṣḥāb*, 4 vols. ed. M. Al-Bijāwī, Cairo.
c) *Mukhtaṣar Jāmi' Bayān al-'Ilm*, ed. by Beirutī.
d) *Jāmi' Bayān al-'Ilm*, 2 vols., Al-Muniriyah, Cairo.
e) *Al-Qaṣd wa al-Umam*, Cairo, 1350.
f) *Tajrīd al-Tamhīd Limā fī Muwaṭṭa' min al-Asānīd*, Cairo, 1350.

Ibn 'Abd al-Ḥakam: a) *Sīrat 'Umar b. 'Abd al-'Azīz*, ed. by Aḥmad 'Ubaid, Cairo, 1927.
b) *Le Livre de la Conquete de l'Egypte du Magreb et de l'Espagne*, ed. M. Henri Massé, Cairo, 1914.

Ibn 'Abd Rabbih, Aḥmad b. Muḥammad: *Al-'Iqd al-Farīd*, ed. Aḥmad Amīn and others, Cairo, 1359-/1940-.

Ibn Abū Ḥātim al-Rāzī, 'Abd al-Raḥmān: *Al-Jahrḥ wa al-Ta'dīl*, Introduction, 8 volumes, Hydrabad, 1360-1373.

Ibn Abū Uṣaibi'ah: *'Uyūn al-Anbā' fī Ṭabaqāt al-Aṭibbā'*, ed. by Mûeller, A., Konigsberg, 1882-4.

Ibn al-Athīr, 'Alī b. Muḥammad: *Usd al-Ghābah*, 5 vols., Cairo, 1285-7.

Ibn al-Athīr, Mubārak b. Muḥammad: *Al-Nihāyah fī Gharīb al-Ḥadīth*, 4 vols., Cairo, 1311/1893.

Ibn Bābwaih, Muḥammad b. 'Alī: *'Ilal al-Sharā'i'*, 2 vols., Tehran, 1377/1957-8.

Ibn Bashkuwāl, Khalaf b. 'Abd al-Mālik: *Al-Ṣilah*, 2 vols., Cairo, 1374/1955.

Ibn Farḥūn, Ibrāhīm b. 'Alī: *Al-Dībāj al-Mudhahhab fī Ma'rifat A'yān 'Ulamā' al-Madhhab*, Cairo, 1329.

Ibn Ḥabīb, Muḥammad al-Baghdādī: *Al-Muḥabbar*, Hydrabad, 1361/1942.

Ibn Ḥajar, Aḥmad b. 'Alī: a) *Fatḥ al-Bārī, Sharh Saḥīḥ al-Bukhārī*. Al-Ḥalabī Press, 1959.
b) *Fatḥ al-Bārī, Sharh Ṣaḥīḥ al-Bukhārī*, edited by M.F.A. Bāqī, Cairo.
c) *Haḍy al-Sārī*, 2 vols., Cairo, 1383/1964.
d) *Al-Iṣābah fī Tamyiz al-Ṣaḥābah*, 4 vols., Cairo, 1358/1939.
e) *Lisān al-Mīzān*, 6 vols., Hydrabad.
f) *Raf' al-Iṣr 'an Quḍāt Miṣr*, ed. by H. 'Abd al-Majīd, Cairo, 1957.
g) *Ṭabaqāt al-Mudallisīn*, Cairo, 1322.
h) *Tahdhīb al-Tahdhīb*, 12 vols., Hydrabad, 1325-7.

i) *Ta'jīl al-Manfa'ah*, Hydrabad, 1324.
j) *Taqrīb al-Tahdhīb*, 2 vols., ed. 'Abd al-Wahhāb, 'A. Laṭīf, Cairo, 1960.
Ibn Ḥanbal, Aḥmad b. Muḥammad: a) *Al-'Ilal wa Ma'rifat al-Rijāl*, ed. by Talat Kocyigit, Ankara, 1963.
b) *Al-Musnad*, 6 vols., Cairo, 1313.
c) *Al-Musnad*, ed. by Aḥmad Shākir, 15 vols., Cairo, 1949-
Ibn Ḥazm: a) *Jawāmī' al-Sīrah*, ed. by Nāṣir al-Dīn al-Asad, Cairo, 1956.
b) *Djamharat ansab*, ed. by Lévi Provençal, Cairo, 1948.
Ibn Ḥibbān, Muḥammad b. Ḥibbān al-Bustī: a) *Ṣaḥīḥ Ibn Ḥibbān*, 1st vol., ed. Aḥmad Shākir, Cairo, 1952.
b) *Die Beruhmten Traditionarie: Der Islamischen Länder*, ed., by M. Fleischhammer, Wiesbaden, 1959.
Ibn Hishām: a) *Das leben Muhammed's Nach Muhammad Ibn Ishak*, ed. by F. Wustenfeld, Gottingen, 1859.
b) *Al-Tijān*, Hydrabad, 1347.
Ibn al-Humām, Muḥammad b. 'Abd al-Wāḥid al-Siwāsī: *Fatḥ al-Qadīr*, 8 vols., Cairo, 1356.
Ibn al-'Imād, 'Abd al-Ḥa'ī: *Shadharāt al-Dhahab Fī Akhbār man Dhahab*, Cairo, 1350.
Ibn al-Jārūd al-Nīsābūrī, 'Abd Allāh b. 'Alī: *Al-Muntaqā min al-Sunan al-Musnadah 'an Rasūl Allāh*, ed. by 'Abd Allāh Hāshim al-Yamānī, Cairo, 1382/1963.
Ibn Juljul: *Les Generations des Medecins et des Sages*, ed. Fuad Sayyid, Cairo, 1955.
Ibn Kathīr, Ismā'īl b. 'Umar: *Al-Bidāyah wa al-Nihāyah*, 14 vols., 1st ed. Cairo, 1932-
Ibn Khair, Muḥammad b. Khair al-Ashbīlī: *Fihrist*, Baghdād, 1963.
Ibn Khallikān, Aḥmad b. Muḥammad: a) *Wafyāt al-A'yān*, Cairo, 1310.
b) *Wafyāt al-A'yān*, ed. by F. Wustenfeld, Gottingen, 1835.
Ibn Ḥatīb al-Dahša: *Tuḥfa Dawi-l-Arbāb*, ed. by T. Mann, Brill, 1905.
Ibn Mājah, Muḥammad b. Yazīd: *Sunan*, 2 vols., ed. by M.F.A. Bāqī, Cairo, 1373/1954.
Ibn Manẓūr al-Afrīqī, Muḥammad b. Mukarram: *Lisān al-'Arab*, Beirut, 1375/1955.
Ibn Miskawayh: *Tajārib al-Umam*, ed. by L. Caetani, Luzack, 1909.
Ibn al-Muqaffa': *Risālah fi al-Ṣaḥābah*, ed. by M. Kurd 'Alī, 3rd imp. Cairo, 1365/1946.
Ibn al-Murtaḍā, Aḥmad b. Yaḥyā: *Die Klassen Der Mu'taziliten*, ed. Susanna Diwald-Wilzer, Wiesbaden, 1961.
Ibn al-Nadīm: *Al-Fihrist*, ed. G. Flugel, Leipsig, 1871.
Ibn al-Qayyim: *Tahdhīb Sunan Abū Dāwād*, 8 vols. ed. by M. H. Alfiqī, Cairo, 1948-9.
Ibn al-Qaisarānī, Muḥammad b. Ṭāhir: *Al-Jam' bain Rijāl al-Ṣaḥīḥain*, Hydrabad, 1323.
Ibn al-Qifṭī, 'Alī b. Yūsuf: *Tariḥ Al-Ḥukamā*, ed. by J. Lippert, Leipzig, 1903.
Ibn Qutaibah, 'Abd Allāh b. Muslim: a) *Ma'ārif*, ed. by 'Ukāshah, Cairo, 1960.

b) *Tāwīl Mukhtalif al-Ḥadīth*, Cairo, 1326-
c) *'Uyūn al-Akhbār*, Cairo, 1925-30. 4 vols.

Ibn Sa'd: *Al-Ṭabaqāt al-Kabīr*, 9 vols. ed. by E. Sachau, Leiden, 1904-1940.

Ibn al-Ṣalāḥ: 'Ulūm al-Ḥadīth, ed. by al-Ṭabbākh, Ḥalab, 1350.

Ibn Sallām, Al-Qāsim b. Sallām: *Al-Amwāl*, ed. by M. Ḥāmid al-Fiqī, Cairo, 1353.

Ibn Ṭūlūn: *I'lām al-Sā'ilīn 'an Kutub Sayyid al-Mursalīn*, Al-Qudsi, Damascus.

Ibn Wahb, 'Abd Allāh: *Le Djami d'Ibn Wahb*, ed. by S. David-Weill, Cairo, 1939.

Al-Jahshayārī, Muḥammad b. 'Abdūs: *Al-Wuzarā' wa al-Kuttāb*, ed. by Ibrāhīm al-Abyārī and others, 1st ed. Cairo, 1357/1938.

Jurjānī, Al-Sharīf 'Alī: *Risālah fi Fann Uṣūl al-Ḥadīth*, printed with Jāmi' Tirmidhī, Delhi, N.D.

Al-Kattānī, 'Abd al-Ḥa'ī b. 'Abd al-Kabīr: *Al-Tarātīb al-Idāriyah*, 2 vols., Rabāṭ, 1346-9.

Al-Kattānī, Muḥammad b. Ja'far: *Al-Risālah al-Mustāṭrafah*, 3rd ed. Damascus, 1964.

Al-Khatīb al-Baghdādī, Aḥmad b. 'Alī: a) *Al-Kifāyah fī 'Ilm al-Riwāyah*, Hydrabad, 1357.
b) *Taqyid al-'Ilm*, ed. Y. Eche, Damascus, 1949.
c) *Tārīkh Baghdād*, 14 volumes, Cairo, 1931.

Al-Khaṭṭābī: *Ma'ālim al-Sunan*, 8 vols. ed. M. H. Alfiqī, Cairo, 1948-9. Printed with Tahdhīb al-Sunan of Ibn al-Qayyim.

Al-Khawalānī, 'Abd al-Jabbār: *Tārīkh Dāriyā*, Arab Academy, Damascus, 1950.

Al-Khayyāṭ, 'Abderraḥīm Ibn Moḥammed: *Le Livre du Triomphe et de la Refutation d'Ibn Er.-Rawendi L'Heretique*, ed. by H.S. Nyberg, Cairo, 1925.

Al-Khazrajī, Aḥmad b. 'Abd Allāh: *Khulāṣat Tadhhīb al-Kamāl*, 1st ed. Cairo, 1322.

Al-Khushanī, Muḥammad b. Ḥārith: *Quḍāt Qurṭubah wa 'Ulamā' Afrīqiyah*, Cairo, 1372.

Kilgour, The Rev. R.: *The Gospel in Many Years*, 2nd ed., British and Foreign Bible Society, London, 1929.

El-Kindī, Muḥammad b. Yūsuf: *The Governors and Judges of Egypt*, ed. by Rhuvon Guest, Leiden, 1912.

Krenkow: *The Use of Writing for the Preservation of Ancient Arabic Poetry*, a volume of Oriental Studies presented to Professor E.G. Browne, pp. 261-268, Cambridge, 1922.

Al-Kulainī, Muḥammad b. Ya'qūb: *Al-Kāfī*, 8 vols., Tehrān, 1381.

Lammens, P.H.: *La Mecque a la Veille de L'Hegire*, Beyrouth, 1924.

Lane, E.W.: *Arabic English Lexicon*, 8 vols., Edinburgh, 1867.

Lyall, C.J. (editor): *The Mufaḍḍaliyāt... with the Commentary of... al-Qāsim b. Muḥammad Al-Anbārī*, 2 vols., 1st ed. Oxford, 1918-20.

Macoudi: a) *Les Prairies D'Or*, ed. by C. B. De Menard, Paris, MDCCCLXI-LXXVII, 9 vols.
b) *Al-Tanbīh wa al-Ishrāf*, Leiden, 1894.

Al-Maidānī, Aḥmad b. Muḥammad al-Nīsābūrī: *Majma' al-Amthāl*, Cairo, 1310.

Al-Majlisī, Muḥammad Bāqir: *Biḥār al-Anwār*, 58 vols., 1st ed. Tehran, 1376.

Mālik b. Anas: *Muwaṭṭā*, 2 vols. ed. by M. F. A. Bāqī, Cairo, 1370/1951.

Maqrīzī: *Khiṭāṭ*, 2 vols, Būlāq, 1270.

Margoliouth, D.S.: *The Early Development of Muhammedanism*, London, 1914.

Maroc: Royaume du Maroc. Ministère de l'Éducation Nationale, Liste des Manuscrits Arabes, précieux, exposés à la Bibliothèque de l'Université Quaraouyin à Fes, à l'Occasion du Onzième Centenaire de la Fondation de cette Université. Rabat, 1960.

Al-Marzubānī, Muhammad b. 'Imrān: *Mu'jam al-Shu'arā'*, Cairo, 1379/1960.

Maudūdī, A.: *Tarjumān al-Qur'ān*, Risālat Number, September 1961, Lahore, Vol. 56, Part VI.

Mingana, A.: *An Important Manuscript of the Traditions of Bukhārī*, Cambridge, 1936.

Ministry of Auqāf, Egyptian Government: *Al-Fiqh 'Alā al-Maḏāhib al-Araba'ah*, 5th imp. Cairo, 1369/1950.

Muir, Sir William: *The Life of Mahomet*, 3rd, ed., London, 1894.

Al-Mundharī, 'Abd al-'Aẓīm b. 'Abd al-Qawī: *Mukhtaṣar Sunan Abū Dāwūd*, ed. by M. H. Alfiqī. 8 vols. Cairo, 1948-printed with *Tahdhīb al-Sunan*

Muslim b. Al-Ḥajjāj al-Qushairī: *Ṣaḥīḥ*, 5 vols. ed. by M.F.A. Bāqī, 1st ed. Cairo, 1374/1955.

Nasa'ī, Aḥmad b. Shu'aib: *Al-Sunan*, 2 vols., Delhi, 1959.

Nāṣir al-Dīn al-Asad: *Maṣādir al-Shi'r al-Jāhilī*, 2nd ed. Dar al-Ma'ārif Press, Cairo, 1962.

Nicholson, R.A.: *A Literary History of the Arabs*, Cambridge, 1962.

Nu'mānī, Muhammad 'Abd al-Rashīd: *Ibn Mājah aur 'Ilm Ḥadīth*, Karachi, N.D.

Pearson, J.D.: *Index Islamicus*, Cambridge, 1958.

Pickthal, Mohammed Marmaduke: *The Meaning of the Glorious Koran*, 10th imp. New American Library, 1963.

Al-Qalqashandī, Aḥmad: *Subḥ al-A'shā*, 14 vols., Cairo, 1922-

Al-Qāsimī, Muḥammad Jamāl al-Dīn: *Qawā'id al-Taḥdīth*, ed. by M.B. Al-Baiṭār, 2nd Ed. Cairo, 1380/1961.

Al-Qasṭalānī, Aḥmad b. Muḥammad: *Irshād al-Sārī, Sharḥ Ṣaḥīḥ al- Bukhārī*, 10 vols., Cairo, 1285.

Al-Rabī' b. Ḥabīb: *Musnad*, 3rd imp. Quds, 1381.

Rāghib al-Isfahānī, Ḥusain b. Muḥammad: *Mufradāt Gharīb al-Qur'ān*, Cairo, 1324.

Russell, D.S.: *The Method and Message of Jewish Apocalyptic*, S.C.M. Press, London 1964, 127-139.

Saḥnūn:*Al-Mudawwanah al-Kubrā*, 16 vols., Cairo, 1323-4.

Al-Sakhāwī, Muḥammad: *Fatḥ al-Mughīth Sharḥ Alfīyat al-Ḥadīth*. Lucknow, N.D.

Al-Ṣāliḥ Ṣubḥī: *'Ulūm al-Ḥadīth*, 3rd ed. Beirut, 1384/1965.

Sahmī, Ḥamzah b. Yūsuf: *Tārikh Jurjān*, 1st ed. Hydrabad, 1369/1950.

Al-Sālimī, 'Abd Allāh b. Ḥumaid: *Sharḥ Musnad al-Rabī'*, 3rd vol., Damascus, 1383/1963.

Al-Sam'ānī, 'Abd al-Karīm b. Muḥammad: a) *Die Methodik des Diktatkollegs*, ed. Max Weisweiber, Leiden, 1952.

b) *Al-Ansāb*, Luzac, 1912.

Al-Ṣan'ānī, Muḥammad b. Ismā'īl Al-Amīr: *Tauḍīh Al-Afkār*, 2 vols. ed. by M. M. 'Abd al-Ḥamīd, Cairo, 1366.

Sarakhsī: *Mabsūṭ*, 30 vols., Cairo, 1324-31.

Schacht, J.: a) *An Introduction to Islamic Law*, Oxford, 1964.

b) *The Origins of Muhammadan Jurisprudence*, 2nd edition, Oxford, 1959.

Sezgin, M. Fuad: *Buharinin Kaynaklari*, Istanbul, 1956.

Al-Shāfi'ī, Muḥammad b. Idrīs: a) *Al-Risālah*, edited by Aḥmad Shākir, 1st ed. Cairo, 1358/1940.

b) *Al-Umm*, 7 vols., 1st ed., Cairo, 1321-5.

c) *Ikhtilaf al-Ḥadīth*, on the margin of Kitāb al-Umm, vol. VII.

Al-Shaibānī, Muḥammad b. al-Ḥasan: *Kitāb al-Āthār* with Urdu Commentary, Faiḍ al-Sattār by 'Abd al-'Azīz, Lahore, 1347.

Shākir, Aḥmad Muḥammad: a) *Al-Bā'ith al-Ḥathīth Sharḥ Ikhtiṣār 'Ulūm al-Ḥadīth*, 2nd imp. Cairo, 1951.

b) *Sharḥ alfiyat al-Suyūṭī*, Cairo N.D.

Al-Shaukānī, Muḥammad b. 'Alī: *Al-Fawa'id al-Majmū'ah fi al-Aḥādīth al-Mauḍū'ah*, ed. by Al-Yamānī, 1st ed. Cairo, 1380/1960.

Shiblī Nu'mānī: a) *Al-Fārūq*, 2 vol. in one, Lahore, N.D.

b) *Sīrat al-Nu'mān*

Sibā'ī, Musṭafā: *Al-Sunnah wa Makānatuhā fī al-Tashrī' al-Islāmī*, 1st ed. Cairo, 1380/1961.

Al-Sijistānī, Ibn Abū Dāwūd: *Al-Maṣāḥif*, ed. by Jeffery, A., 1st ed. Brill, 1937.

Al-Ṣūlī, Muḥammad b. Yaḥyā: *Adab al-Kuttāb*, ed. Bahjat al-Atharī, Cairo, 1341.

Al-Suyūṭī: a) *Tadrīb al-Rāwī Sharh Taqrīb al-Nawāwī*, ed. by A. A. Laṭīf, 1st ed. Cairo, 1379/1959.

b) *Tanwīr al-Ḥawālik Sharh Muwaṭṭa' Mālik*, 2 vols., Cairo, 1348.

Al-Ṭabarānī, Sulaimān b. Aḥmad: *Al-Jāmi' al-Ṣaghīr*, Delhi, 1311.

Al-Ṭabarī, Moḥammed Ibn Djarir: *Annales*, ed. De Goeje, 1st ed., Brill, 1879-1901.

Ṭāhā Ḥusain: *Al-Fitnah al-Kubrā* I — *Uthmān* Cairo, 1951.

Al-Tahānwī, Muḥammad 'Alī: *A Dictionary of the Technical Terms*, Calcutta, 1862.

Ṭaḥāwī: *Sharḥ Ma'ānī al-Āthār*, 2 vols. Lucknow, 1301-2

Tibrīzī: *Commentary on the Ḥamāsah of Abū Tammām*, 4 vols., Būlāq, 1296.

Tirmidhī, Muḥammad b. 'Isā: a) *Al-'Ilal*, printed with Jāmi', Delhi, N.D.

b) *Al-Jāmi'*, 2 vols., Delhi, N.D.

c) *Shamā'il*, printed with Jami', N.D.

Ṭūsī: *Fihrist*, ed. by Sprenger, Calcutta, 1853.

Wensinck, A.J.: a) *Concordance et indices de la Tradition Musulmane*, 5 vols., Leiden, 1936 —
b) *A Handbook of Early Muhammadan Tradition*, Leiden, 1927.
c) *The Muslim Creed*, Cambridge, 1932.

Al-Yamānī, 'Abd al-Raḥmān b. Yaḥyā: *Al-Anwār al-Kāshifah*, Cairo, 1378.

Al-Ja'qubī, Aḥmad b. Abū Yā'qūb:*Historiae*, 2 vols., ed. M. Houtsma, Brill, 1883.

Yūsuf b. Taghrī Bardī: *Al-Nujūm al-Ẓāhirah*, 1st ed. vols. 1-8, Cairo, 1348-1929-

Al-Zabīdī, Muḥammad Murtuḍā al-Ḥusainī: *Taj al-'Arūs*, 10 vols., Cairo, 1306.

Zaid b. 'Alī b. Al-Ḥusain b. 'Alī b. Abū Ṭālib: *Musnad*, Beirut, 1966.

Al-Zaila'ī: *Naṣb al-Rāyah*, 4 vols., Cairo, 1357/1938.

Zakarīyā 'Alī Yūsuf: *Difā' 'an al-Ḥadīth al-Nabawī*, Cairo, N.D.

Al-Ziriklī, Khair al-Dīn: *Al-A'lām*, 10 vols, 2nd ed., Cairo, 1373-8/1954-9.

Al-Zurqānī, Muḥammad b. 'Abd al-Bāqī: *Sharḥ Muwaṭṭa'*, 4 vols., Būlāq 1280/1863.

INDEX

Abān b. Abū 'Ayyāsh 50, 106-7
Abān b. Sa'īd 35
Abān b. Tha'labah 292
Abān b. Taghlab al-Kūfī 107
Abān b. 'Uthmān 60, 138, 210, 267
Abān b. Yazīd al-'Aṭṭār 107, 108
'Abbād 81, 295
'Abbād b. Ḥabīb 165
'Abbās b. al-Faḍl al-Anṣārī 108
'Abbās b. Ḥasan 89
'Abdah b. Abū Lubābah al-Ghāḍirī 74
'Abd al-A'lā b. Abū al-Musāwir 108
'Abd al-'Alā al-Shāmī 160
'Abd al-A'lā b. 'Āmir al-Tha'labī 65, 69
'Abd Allāh b. 'Abbās 10, 21, 28, 36, 39, 40, 42, 48, 66, 70, 113, 185, 186, 219, 220, 256, 303
'Abd Allāh b. 'Abd Allāh b. Uwais 109
'Abd Allāh b. 'Abd al-Raḥmān b. Abū Ḥusain 109
'Abd Allāh b. 'Abd al-Raḥmān al-Samarqandī 170
'Abd Allāh b. Abū Awfā 42, 43
'Abd Allāh b. Abū Bakr b. Ḥazm 74
'Abd Allāh b. Abū Labīd 109
'Abd Allah b. Aḥmad b. Ḥanbal 295
'Abd Allāh b. al-'Alā' al-Dimashqī 109
'Abd Allāh b. 'Amr b. al-'Āṣ 7, 28, 43, 44, 30, 292
'Abd Allāh b. 'Amr, Abū Ma'mar 118
'Abd Allāh b. 'Amr al-Mauṣilī 164, 168
'Abd Allāh b. 'Aun al-Baṣrī 21, 75, 94, 97
'Abd Allāh b. Bishr al-Kātib 75
'Abd Allāh b. Buraidah al-Aslamī 75
'Abd Allāh b. Dhakwān, Abū al-Zinād 76, 77, 203, 279
'Abd Allāh b. Dīnār 49, 272
'Abd Allāh b. al-Ḥarith 114
'Abd Allāh b. Ḥasan al-Ḥarrāni 299
'Abd Allāh b. Hurmuz 60
'Abd Allāh b. al-Ḥusain, Abū Ḥarīz 110
'Abd Allāh b. Idrīs 85, 102, 110, 122, 146, 296
'Abd Allāh b. 'Isā b. Abū Lailā al-Anṣārī 76
'Abd Allāh b. Ja'far b. Nujaiḥ al-Sa'dī 110
'Abd Allāh b. Jarrāḥ 172
'Abd Allāh b. Kharāsh 176
'Abd Allāh b. Lahī'ah 29, 85, 96, 105, 111, 114, 134, 174, 178
'Abd Allāh b. Mas'ūd 21, 44, 58, 61, 63, 250, 253, 256-8
'Abd Allāh b. Mughaffal 13
'Abd Allāh b. Muḥammad b. 'Alī 60, 69
'Abd Allāh b. Muḥammad b. 'Aqīl 52, 76

‘Abd Allāh b. Muḥammad, Ibn al-Mufassir 276
‘Abd Allāh b. Mukhallad 175
‘Abd Allāh b. Mūsā 134, 187
‘Abd Allāh b. Nāfi‘ 152
‘Abd Allāh b. al-Qāsim, Ruzain 111
‘Abd Allāh b. Rabāḥ al-Anṣārī 61
‘Abd Allāh b. Sakhbarah al-Azdī 61
‘Abd Allāh b. Rajā’ al-Makkī 111
‘Abd Allāh b. Sa‘īd b. al-‘Āṣ 4
‘Abd Allāh b. Salamah 152
‘Abd Allāh b. Sālim al-Ash‘arī 112, 156
‘Abd Allāh b. Shaudhab al-Khurāsānī 112
‘Abd Allāh b. Shihāb 278
‘Abd Allāh b. Shubrumah 110
‘Abd Allāh b. Tha‘libah 279
‘Abd Allāh b. Ubai b. Salūl 289
‘Abd Allāh b. ‘Umar 21, 45, 46, 57, 58, 70, 96, 138, 209, 221, 226, 244-5, 247, 274-5, 279, 284, 292
‘Abd Allāh b. ‘Umar al-‘Umarī 97, 112, 172
‘Abd Allāh b. ‘Utbah 46
‘Abd Allāh b. ‘Uthmān 112, 165
‘Abd Allāh b. al-Walīd 168
‘Abd Allāh b. Yazīd al-Makhzūmī 112, 162
‘Abd Allāh b. Ziyād b. Sulaimān al-Makhzūmī 113
‘Abd Allāh b. al-Zubair 12, 46, 216, 279, 288-9
‘Abd al-‘Azīz b. ‘Abd Allāh 108
‘Abd al-‘Azīz b. Abū Ruwād 97
‘Abd al-‘Azīz b. al-Ḥuṣain 108
‘Abd al-‘Azīz b. Abū al-Sā’ib 87
‘Abd al-‘Azīz b. Marwān 37, 46, 67
‘Abd al-‘Azīz b. Muḥammad 233-4
‘Abd al-‘Azīz b. al-Mukhtār 265, 272 *ff*
‘Abd al-‘Azīz b. Sa‘īd b. Sa‘d b. ‘Ubādah 74
‘Abd al-‘Azīz b. Salamah 161, 171
‘Abd al-‘Azīz b. Ṣuhaib al-Bunānī 108
‘Abd al-Ghafūr b. ‘Abd al-‘Azīz al-Wāsiṭī 74
‘Abd al-Ghaffār b. al-Qāsim 78
‘Abd al-Ghanī b. Muḥammad 276
‘Abd al-Ḥakam b. ‘Amr al-Jumaḥī 16
‘Abd al-Ḥamīd 171
‘Abd al-Ḥamīd b. Bahrām 71
‘Abd al-Ḥamīd b. Ibrāhīm 112
‘Abd al-Ḥamīd b. Yūsuf 106
‘Abd al-Jabbār b. al-Ward 109
‘Abd al-Kabīr b. Dīnār 78
‘Abd al-Karīm 61, 109, 256
‘Abd al-Majīd b. ‘Abd al-‘Azīz 114
‘Abd al-Malik b. ‘Abd al-‘Azīz b. Juraij 32, 66, 69, 74, 80, 84, 89, 93, 97, 107, 113-4, 119, 228, 248, 269
‘Abd al-Malik b. Abū Naḍrah al-‘Abdī 115
‘Abd al-Malik b. Abū Sulaimān 93
‘Abd al-Malik b. Ḥabīb al-Azdī 61
‘Abd al-Malik b. Marwān 12, 46, 70, 74, 213-4, 216, 266, 284, 288-92
‘Abd al-Malik b. Ṭufail al-Jazarī 72
‘Abd al-Malik b. Muḥammad 74
‘Abd al-Malik b. ‘Umair 49
‘Abd al-Quddūs b. Ḥabīb al-Shāmī 115
‘Abd al-Raḥmān 221
‘Abd al-Raḥmān b. ‘Abd Allāh b. Mas‘ūd 61
‘Abd al-Raḥmān b. ‘Abd Allāh b. ‘Utbah al-Mas‘ūdī 115
‘Abd al-Raḥmān b. Abū al-Zinād 76, 116
‘Abd al-Raḥmān b. ‘Āidh 61
‘Abd al-Raḥmān b. ‘Amr al-Auzā‘ī 32, 89, 94-5, 98, 116-7, 177, 202, 220
‘Abd al-Raḥmān b. Ghanm 62

'Abd al-Raḥmān b. Ḥarmalah 117
'Abd al-Raḥmān b. Hurmuz al-A'raj 76, 203
'Abd al-Raḥmān b. Khālid 89
'Abd al-Raḥmān b. Mahdī. See Ibn Mahdī
'Abd al-Raḥmān b. Mubārak 130
'Abd al-Raḥmān b. Muḥammad 29
'Abd al-Raḥmān b. Muḥammad, Abū Manṣūr 277
'Abd al-Raḥmān b. Namirah 89
'Abd al-Raḥmān b. Mull, Abū 'Uthman al-Nahdī 62
'Abd al-Raḥmān b. Sābiṭ 77
'Abd al-Raḥmān b. Thābit b. Thaubān 117
'Abd al-Raḥmān b. Yazīd al-Dimashqī 89
'Abd al-Raḥmān b. Yazīd b. al-Jābir al-Azdī 117
'Abd al-Raḥmān b. Zaid 22, 106
'Abd al-Raḥmān b. Ziyād b. An'ūm al-Ifrīqī 118
'Abd al-Razzāq al-Ṣan'ānī 57, 107, 144, 148, 168, 248, 296
'Abd al-Razzāq b. 'Umar al-Thaqafī 89, 118
'Abd al-Ṣamad 81, 118, 295
'Abd al-Wahhāb b. 'Abd al-Majīd 178
'Abd al-Wahhāb b. 'Aṭā' 133, 152, 160
'Abd al-Wāḥid b. Ghayāth 129
'Abd al-Wārith b. Sa'īd 81, 118, 154
'Abīd b. Sharyah 8, 53
'Abīdah b. 'Amr al-Salmānī 21, 27, 62, 94, 185
'Abīdah b. Ḥumaid al-Taimī 79, 87, 95, 103, 118, 120
Abū al-'Āliyah. See Rufai'
Abū 'Amr b. al-'Alā' 79
Abū al-Aswad 73, 111, 157
Abū Ayyūb al-Anṣārī 34
Abū Bakr b. 'Abd al-Raḥmān b. Hishām 39
Abū Bakr b. 'Abd al-Raḥmān b. al-Miswar b. Makhrimah 118
Abū Bakr b. Abū Sabrah 119
Abū Bakr b. Abū Shaibah 164
Abū Bakr b. 'Ayyāsh 101, 104, 119
Abū Bakr b. Muḥammad b. 'Amr b. Ḥazm al-Anṣārī 18, 69, 77
Abū Bakr al-Ṣiddīq 34, 35, 43, 44, 260 *f*
Abū Bakrah al-Thaqafī 35
Abū al-Dardā' 55, 58
Abū Dāwūd 112, 115, 165, 171, 297
Abū Dharr 58, 298
Abū Ḥamzah al-Sukkarī. See Muḥammad b. Maimun
Abū Ḥanīfah 252, 255-6
Abū Ḥarīz. See 'Abd Allāh b. Ḥusain
Abū Hilāl al-Rāsibī 98
Abū Hurairah 21, 22, 29, 35-38, 185, 223-9, 231, 269, 270, 274, 279, 292
Abū Idrīs 21
Abū 'Imrān 61
Abū Isḥāq al-Sabī'ī. See 'Amr b 'Abd Allāh
Abū Ja'far 29, 149, 274
Abū Juḥaifah 47
Abū Juraij 133
Abū Khaladah 70
Abū al-Malīḥ b. Usāmah al-Hudhalī 62
Abū Manī' 172
Abū Ma'shar 210
Abū Mihrān 168
Abū Mishar 116
Abū Mu'āwiyah 101, 170
Abū Muḥammad 221
Abū al-Mulaiḥ 284
Abū Mūsā al-Ash'arī 13, 21, 39, 293

Abū Mūsā 127
Abū Nu'aim 22, 131, 149, 168
Abū Nūḥ 165
Abū Qatādah 147, 221
Abū Qilābah 60, 63
Abū Qutaibah 115
Abū al-Rabī' 179
Abū Sa'īd b. Abū Zur'ah 276
Abū Rāfi' 13, 39
Abū Sa'īd 204
Abū Sa'īd al-Khudrī 21, 22, 23, 25, 39, 259, 292
Abū Salamah 292, 299
Abū Salamah b. 'Abd al-Raḥmān 51, 63
Abū Ṣāliḥ 37, 38, 65, 135, 147, 150, 202, 225, 227-8, 269, 270, 272, 274
Abū Shāh 40
Abū Ṭāhir 152
Abū al-Ṭufail 47
Abū Umāmah 40
Abū al-Walīd 159, 165, 203
Abū al-Yamān 57, 109, 141, 277-8
Abū Yaḥyā al-Kunāsī 69
Abū Yūsuf 27, 159, 219-20, 222, 240, 247
Abū Zinād. See 'Abd Allāh b. Dhakwān
Abū Zur'ah 202, 301
Ādam b. Abū Iyās 165, 298
'Adī b. 'Abd al-Raḥmān 126
'Affān 129, 130, 145, 176
Aḥmad b. Ḥanbal. See Ibn Ḥanbal
Aḥmad b. Khāzim al-Miṣrī 100, 119
Aḥmad b. Muḥammad 137
Aḥmad b. Muḥammad al-Silfī 275
Aḥmad Shākir 37
'Āishah, Umm al-Mu'minīn 46, 47, 53, 72, 214, 219, 225-6, 303
Ajnādīn 73, 281
Āl-Abī 'Atīq 89
Al-'Alā' b. 'Abd al-Raḥmān 77
'Alā' al-Ḥaḍramī 35, 36
Al-'Alā' b. al-Ḥārith 87
Al-'Alā' b. Kathīr 87
Al-'Alā' b. Zaid 50
'Alī b. 'Abd Allāh b. 'Abbās 78
'Alī b. 'Abd Allāh b. Rāshid 109
'Alī b. Abū Hāshim 141
'Alī b. Abū Ṭālib 8, 11, 15, 36, 41, 47, 48, 51, 71, 216-7, 226, 239, 260, 263, 289, 292
'Alī b. 'Āṣim b. Ṣuhaib al-Wāsiṭī 84, 119, 134
'Alī Abū Naṣr 159
'Alī b. 'Ayyāsh 131
'Alī b. Ḥasan b. Shaqīq 154
'Alī b. Ja'd 139, 165, 170
'Alī b. Madīnī 130
'Alī b. Mubārak al-Hunā'ī 120, 176
'Alī b. Muḥammad 275
'Alī b. Muḥammad al-Ḥakkānī 278
'Alī b. Mushir al-Qurashī 107, 120
'Alī al-Nasā'ī 165
'Alī b. 'Umar al-Ḥarbī 274
'Alī b. Yazīd al-Alhānī 78
'Alī b. Yazīd b. Abū Hilāl 98
'Alī b. Zaid b. Jud'ān 120
'Alqamah b. Waqqāṣ 280
Amālī of Ibn al-Ṣā'id 95-6
Al-A'mash. See Sulaimān b. Mihrān
'Āmir b. 'Abd Allāh b. Mas'ūd 63
'Āmir b. Sa'd 53, 259
'Āmir b. Sharāḥil b. al-Sha'bī 26, 48, 52, 59, 63
'Ammār b. Mu'āwiyah al-Duhnī 120
'Amr 221
'Amr b. 'Abbās 294
'Amr b. 'Abd Allāh, Abū Isḥāq al-Sabī'ī 65, 66, 78
'Amr b. Abū 'Amr 233-4
'Amr b. Abū al-Walīd 87
'Amr b. 'Amr, Abū al-Za'rā' 120

'Amr b. al-'Āṣ 35
'Amr b. 'Āṣim 129
'Amr b. Dīnār al-Makkī 21, 42, 79, 169
'Amr b. al-Ḥārith al-Anṣārī 121
'Amr b. Ḥazm 48
'Amr b. Hāshim 116
'Amr b. Khālid 180
'Amr b. Marzūq 166
'Amr b. Qusaiṭ 172
'Amr b. Sa'd 2
'Amr b. Sa'īd al-Ashdak 2, 16
'Amr b. Shu'aib 7, 44, 295, 296
'Amr b. Thābit b. Hurmuz 121
'Amr b. 'Ubaid b. Bāb al-Tamīmī 121
'Amr b. 'Utbah 55, 56
'Amrah bint 'Abd al-Raḥmān 77
Anas b. 'Ayāḍ, Abū Ḍamrah 121
Anas b. Mālik 13, 35, 49, 52, 59, 295, 305
Anas b. Sīrīn 49
Anbār 1
Ansarite, anonymous (comp.) 50
Al-Anṣārī 122, 125, 126, 141
'Anbasah b. Khālid 180
'Aqbah b. Abū al-Ḥasnā' 38, 159
'Aqbah b. Khālid 172
Arabia 1
Arṭāt b. al-Mundhir 121, 125
Arṭāt b. Zufar 266
Asad b. Mūsā 8, 9
Ash'ath b. 'Abd al-Malik, Abū Hānī al-Baṣrī 82, 121, 202
Ash'ath b. Sawwār al-Kindī 122
Al-Ashtar 47
'Āṣim b. Kulaib al-Kūfī 122
'Āṣim b. Muḥammad b. Zaid al-'Umarī 122
'Āṣim b. Rajā' b. Ḥaiwah al-Kindī 122
'Āṣim b. Sulaimān al-Aḥwal 122, 202
'Āṣim b. 'Umar b. Qatādah 79
'Āṣim b. 'Umar al-'Umarī 123
Asmā' bint 'Umais 50
Al-Aswad b. Qais al-Bajalī 79
Al-Aswad b. Shaibān 123
Al-Aswad b. Yazīd 220
'Aṭā' b. Abū Muslim al-Khurāsānī 80
'Atā' b. Abū Rabāḥ 48, 80, 113
'Atā' b. Dīnār 70
'Aṭā' b. Sā'ib 123
'Atā' b. Yasār al-Hilālī 64
Āthār Abī Yūsuf 240
Al-Athram
'Aṭiyah 292
The Aṭrāf system and its effect 185
'Aṭṭāf b. Khālid 123
'Auf b. Abū Jamīlah 81
'Aun b. 'Abd Allāh b. 'Utbah 81
Al-Auzā'ī. See 'Abd al-Raḥmān b. 'Amr
'Awānah 14
Ayyūb b. Abū Tamīmah al-Sakhtiyānī 63, 66, 79, 81, 89, 97, 169, 178, 231, 256
Ayyūb b. Khauṭ 124
Ayyūb b. Khālid b. Ayyūb 34
Ayyūb b. Mūsā b. 'Amr b. Sa'īd b. Al'āṣ 89, 124
Ayyūb b. 'Utbah al-Yamānī 124, 177
'Azrah 70

Badr 41, 73, 279, 281
Baghdād 108, 124, 298
Baḥīr b. Sa'īd al-Saḥūlī al-Ḥimṣī 67, 124
Baḥr b. Kunaiz 124
Baḥrain 35, 36
Bahz b. Asad 166
Bahz b. Ḥakīm al-Qushairī 110, 125
Bait al-Qarātīs 16

Balādhurī 207, 209, 266, 267
Bakr b. Sulaimān 153
Bakr b. Wā'il b. Dāwūd 125
Banū 'Abd Ashhal 10, 13
Banū Salamah 233-4
Baqiyah b. al-Walīd al-Kalā'ī 103, 124, 125, 164, 166
Al-Barā' b. 'Āzib 50
Barhebraeus 2
Baṣrah 61, 110, 167, 224-29
Bashīr b. Nahīk 37, 38, 185, 295
Al-Battī 257
Bayān b. Bishr 297
The Bible, its translation 2, 3
Biography of the Prophet 104
Bishr 164
Bīr Ma'ūnah 5, 73
Bishr b. Ḥusain 182, 305
Bishr b. Mufaḍḍal 115
Bishr b. Numair 98
Bishr b. al-Sarrī 139
Books, writing material 200 — The method of writing 201-3 — adding external material in the body of a book 204 — Problem of authorship in Jewish and Christian literature 205 — in Islamic literature 205-7
Book of Daniel 2
Bukhair b. 'Abd Allāh b. al-Ashajj 103, 126
al-Bukhārī 23, 25, 32, 205, 208-11, 238-9, 248, 258, 271, 277, 294, 301 *ff*
Bundār 81

Caetani 213-4
Churchill 19

Al-Daḥḥāk 21, 70
Al-Daḥḥāq b. Muzāḥim 64
Al-Daḥḥāk b. Qais b. Khālid 51
Al-Daḥḥāk b. Sufyān al-Kilābī 51
Dahtham b. Qurrah 177
Damascus 8, 138, 288
The *Daniel* 2
Dāraquṭnī 148
Ḍarār 266
al-Darāwardī 209, 241
Darj, its meaning and shape 201
Dāwūd b. Abū Hind 126
Dāwūd b. al-Ḥuṣain al-Umawī 126
Dāwūd b. Ibrāhīm 166
Dāwūd b. Nuṣair al-Ṭā'ī 126
Dāwūd b. Shabīb 127
Dāwūd b. Shābūr al-Makkī 126
al-Dhahabī 19, 29, 34, 38, 119, 235, 272
Dhakwān. See Abū Ṣāliḥ
Dimām b. Ismā'īl 127
Dīnār b. 'Abd Allāh al-Ahwāzī 50
Dirār b. Murrah al-Kūfī 127
Dumat al-Jandal 1

Egypt 150, 223-5, 229-30
Egyptians 149
Europe 11

Faḍl b. Rabī' 139
Al-Faḍl b. Yaḥyā 137
Fallās 186
Fātimah daughter of the Prophet 51, 217, 264
Fātimah daughter of Qais[2] 51
Fāṭimah bint Sharīk 16
al-Firabrī 205
Al-Firyābī 57, 168
Fitnah 216
Al-Fuḍail b. Maisarah 110, 127
Fuḍail b. Sulaimān 96
Furāfiṣah 242
Fuwād Sezgin

Ghailān b. Jāmi' 127
Ghālib b. 'Ubaid Allāh 107
Ghassān 168

Ghīlānī 304

Goldziher 265-6, 285-6

Goldziher's conception of early Islamic literature 8, his conception of early Muslim community 9-11, an analysis of his deductions 12-15, see also 17 and 27; approval and disapproval of the recording of *Aḥādīth* and his deduction 18, his accusation of Al-Zuhrī and its absurdity 285 *ff*

Guillaume 18, 262-3, 285, 288-90, 302

Ghundar 160, 163, 166, 170

The Gospels 2

Ḥabīb b. Abū Ḥabīb al-Ḥarmī 127

Ḥabīb b. Abū Thābit 82

Ḥabīb b. Sālim al-Anṣārī 54, 82

Ḥaddāthanā, its meaning 293 *ff*

Ḥadīth, its recording and the Prophet 22 *ff;* and Rashīd Riḍā 24 *ff;* and Goldziher's deduction 27, and mis-interpretation of early scholars' statements about recording of *Ḥadīth*, writings of Companions 34 *ff;* of first century Successors 60 *ff;* of scholars covering late first and early second century 74 *ff;* of early second century scholars 106 *ff.* Its memorising in early days 184. Its teaching according to *Shuyūkh* 186; its teaching orally 188; by reading from books 189; by questions and answers 191; by dictation 192 *ff.* Method of its counting 302 *ff;* Schacht and its authenticity 248. Its criticism on material ground 260 *ff;* stealing of *Ḥadīth* 204.

Ḥāfiẓ Abd al-Ghanī 278

Ḥafṣ b. 'Abd Allāh 138

Ḥafṣ b. Ghailān al-Dimashqī 128

Ḥafṣ b. Ghayāth 101, 149

Ḥafṣ b. Maisarah 106

Ḥafṣ b. Sulaimān al-Asadī 128

Ḥafṣ b. Sulaimān al-Tamīmī al-Minqarī 82, 83

Al-Haitham b. Ḥumaid al-Ghassānī 132

Ḥaiwah b. Shuraiḥ 128

Ḥajiyah b. 'Adī 292

Al-Ḥajjāj 45, 172, 291

Al-Ḥajjāj b. al-Ḥajjāj al-Bāhilī 128

Ḥajjāj b. al-Minhāl 129

Ḥajjāj b. Muḥammad 114, 135, 158, 164, 166

Ḥajjāj b. Yūsuf 182

Al-Ḥakam b. 'Aṭīyah al-'Aishī 128

Al-Ḥakam b. Ayyūb 164

Al-Ḥakam b. 'Utaibah b. al-Kindī 68, 69, 74, 82

al-Ḥākim 22, 174

al-Ḥākim al-Nisabūrī 304

Halaku 216

Ḥammād 220, 230, 257-258, 264, 272

Ḥammād b. Abū al-Ja'd 98

Ḥammād b. Abū Sulaimān 27, 66, 82

Ḥammād b. 'Amr 106, 187

Ḥammād b. Ja'd 146, 152

Ḥammād b. Salamah 82, 101, 128, 129, 159, 231

Ḥammād b. Zaid b. Dirham al-Azdī 79, 81, 106-7, 178

Hammām b. Munabbih 29, 30, 38, 185, 196

Hammām b. Yaḥyā al-Baṣrī 130, 295

Ḥamzah al-Zayyāt 107

Hannād 121

Ḥanẓalah b. Abū Sufyān al-Jumaḥī 131

Haql b. Ziyād 150

Ḥārith b. 'Abd Allāh al-A'war 48, 65

Al-Ḥārith b. Jārūd 89, 98

Ḥārith b. Muslim 125

Al-Ḥārith b. Suwaid 47

Ḥarīz b. 'Uthmān 131
Ḥarrah 262
Hārūn b. Abū 'Isā 133
Hārūn b. Ismā'īl 120
Hārūn b. Sa'd al-'Ijlī 131
Ḥasan b. Abū Ja'far al-Jafrī 134, 154
Ḥasan b. 'Alī 48, 51
Ḥasan b. 'Amr al-Ḍamarī 37
Al-Ḥasan b. Dīnār al-Tamīmī 131
Al-Ḥasan b. Jābir 40
Al-Ḥasan b. Muḥammad 149
Al-Ḥasan b. Mūsā 163
Al-Ḥasan b. Rabī' 110
Al-Ḥasan b. Ṣāliḥ b. Ḥay 131
Al-Ḥasan b. 'Umārah al-Kūfī 132
Al-Ḥasan b. Yasār al-Baṣrī 13, 52, 55, 83, 255, 288, 297
Hāshim b. al-Qāsim 140, 166
Ḥassān b. Ibrāhīm, al-Kūfī 131
Hātim b. Ismā'īl 164, 172
Haudhah b. Khalīfah 75, 81, 102, 114, 122
Ḥaushab b. 'Aqīl al-'Abdī 80, 83, 132
Hayyāj b. Bustām 168
Ḥayyān b. Bishr 135
Al-Ḥāzimī 282
Ḥibbān b. Jaz' al-Sulamī 65
Ḥijāz 104, 207
Ḥimṣ 224, 226, 229
Hīrah 1
Hishām 83, 299
Hishām b. 'Abd al-Malik 175, 277, 283-4, 288, 289
Hishām b. Ḥassān al-Qurdūsī 80, 83, 94-5, 132-3
Hishām b. Sambar al-Dastawā'ī 98, 133, 177
Hishām b. 'Urwah 73-4, 84, 220, 239, 292
Hishām b. Yūsuf 114, 148, 168
Horovitz 214, 218, 292
Hubairah b. 'Abd al-Raḥmān 49
Hudbah b. Khālid 129, 130
Ḥujain b. al-Muthannā 142
Ḥujr b. 'Adī 48
Ḥumaid 49, 83, 221, 295
Ḥumaid b. Qais 89
Ḥumaid b. Ziyād, Abū Sakhr 133
Ḥumaidī 170, 248
Ḥumrān b. Abān 65
Ḥunain 73
Ḥuṣain 187
Ḥuṣain b. 'Abd al-Raḥmān al-Sulamī 84
Ḥuṣain b. 'Aqīl 64
Ḥuṣain al-Mu'allim 75
Ḥuṣain b. Muḥammad 158
Al-Ḥusain b. Qais al-Raḥbī 66, 134
Al-Ḥusain b. al-Walīd 112, 168
Al-Ḥusain b. Wāqid al-Marwazī 76, 81, 124, 134
Ḥusain Abū Sufyān b. Ḥusain al-Wāsiṭī 83
Hushaim b. Bashīr al-Wāsiṭī 81, 84, 88, 89, 93, 101, 134, 173, 187
Ḥuyay b. Hānī, Abū Qabīl 85

Ibn 'Abbās. See 'Abd Allāh
Ibn 'Abd al-Barr 238, 245
Ibn Abū 'Adī 100, 153, 160
Ibn Abū 'Arūbah. See Sa'īd
Ibn Abū Bakr 242
Ibn Abū Ḥātim 29
Ibn Abū Lailā 16
Ibn Abū Mulaikah 42
Ibn Abū Najīḥ 69, 203, 206
Ibn Abū 'Uthmān 168
Ibn Abū Uwais 171
Ibn 'Adī 272
Ibn 'Ā'idh 53
Ibn Akhī al-Zuhrī 90
Ibn 'Āmir 242
Ibn al-Anbārī 207

Ibn Ashwa'
Ibn 'Aun. See 'Abd Allāh
Ibn Bashkuwāl 29
Ibn Bazīl 166
Ibn Fuḍail 151
Ibn Ḥabīb 207
Ibn Ḥajar 19, 136, 259
Ibn al-Ḥanafiyah. See Muḥammad b. 'Alī
Ibn Ḥanbal 135, 137, 140, 142, 165, 171, 187, 202, 203, 206, 210-211, 224-6, 228-9, 273, 277, 287, 295-6, 298, 301, 304
Ibn Ḥibbān 22, 112, 174, 271, 275
Ibn Hishām 153, 299
Ibn Idrīs. See 'Abd Allāh
Ibn Isḥāq. See Muḥammad
Ibn al-Jauzī 37
Ibn Jubair. See Sa'īd
Ibn Juraij. See 'Abd al-Malik b. 'Abd al-'Azīz
Ibn al-Kalbī 14, 207
Ibn Khuzaimah 302
Ibn Lahī'ah. See 'Abd Allāh
Ibn Mahdī 111, 121, 123, 130, 134, 143, 144, 166, 168, 302, 304
Ibn Ma'īn 111, 129, 135, 141, 150, 203, 206, 208-9, 231, 281, 296
Ibn Mas'ūd. See 'Abd Allāh
Ibn al-Mubārak 29, 111, 114, 129, 138, 141, 148, 154, 158, 159, 168, 180, 203, 209, 231, 301
Ibn al-Musayyab 83, 227, 279, 284, 292
Ibn al-Nadīm 87, 114, 116, 134, 136, 138, 141, 148, 151, 152, 168, 181, 200
Ibn Qāsim 259
Ibn al-Ṣā'id 207
Ibn Ṭahmān. See Ibrāhīm
Ibn Ṭūlūn 48
Ibn 'Umar. See 'Abd Allāh
Ibn Umm Maktūm 4
Ibn 'Uyaynah. See Sufyān
Ibn Sa'd 13, 81, 119, 210-11, 257
Ibn al-Ṣā'id 96
Ibn Shaddād 257
Ibn Shihāb. See Muḥammad b. Muslim
Ibn Sīrīn. See Muḥammad
Ibn Thaubān 125
Ibn 'Ulayyah. See Ismā'īl b. Ibrāhīm
Ibn 'Uyaynah. See Sufyān
Ibn Wahb 29, 57, 111, 121, 134, 148, 150, 174, 240, 281
Ibn al-Zubair. See 'Abd Allāh
Ibrāhīm 187
Ibrāhīm b. 'Abd al-A'lā al-Ju'fī 85
Ibrāhīm b. Abū Yaḥyā 126
Ibrāhīm al-Ansārī 179
Ibrāhīm b. 'Aqīl b. Ma'qal b. Munabbih.
Ibrāhīm b. Bashshār 244
Ibrāhīm b. Dhī Ḥimāyah 135
Ibrāhīm b. al-Ḥajjāj 274
Ibrāhīm b. Hāshim 144
Ibrāhīm b. Hudbah 49
Ibrāhīm b. Jarīr b. 'Abd Allāh al-Bajalī 85
Ibāhīm b. Maimūn al-Ṣā'igh 135
Ibrāhīm b. Muḥammad 233-4
Ibrāhīm b. Muḥammad b. Abū Yaḥyā 136, 137
Ibrāhīm b. Muḥammad al-Fazārī 136
Ibrāhīm b. Mus'ab 206
Ibāhīm b. Muslim 85
Ibrāhīm b. Sa'd 137, 153
Ibāhīm b. Ṣadaqah 160
Ibrāhīm b. Sa'īd 122
Ibrāhīm b. Ṭahmān 95, 96, 107, 128, 138, 174, 228, 264-5, 269
Ibrāhīm b. 'Umar 138
Ibrāhīm b. 'Uthmān 139
Ibrāhīm b. al-Walīd al-Umawī 90, 285-6

Ibrāhīm b. Yazīd al-Nakha' al-A'war 21, 26, 27, 65, 66, 37, 62, 101, 220, 250, 253, 257, 260
Ibrāhīm b. Yazīd 82
'Ikrimah b. 'Ammār 139
'Ikrimah Client of Ibn 'Abbās 42, 66, 77, 256
'Imrān b. Abū Qudāmah 139
'Imrān 56
'Imrān b. Ḥudair 140
'Imrān al-Qaṣīr 160
Iraq 223
Iraqians 145, 239
'Isā b. 'Abd Allāh 246
'Isā b. Abū 'Isā al-Tamīmī 140
'Isā b. Mukhtār 151
'Isā b. Yūnus 106
al-Isfahānī 281
Isḥāq 164
Isḥāq b. 'Abd Allāh 86
Isḥāq b. Ibrāhīm 154
Isḥāq b. Rāhwaih 304
Isḥāq b. Rāshid 90, 102
Isḥāq b. Sulaimān 150
Ismā'īl 75
Ismā'īl b. Abū Khālid al-Aḥmasī 42, 140, 202.
Ismā'īl b. 'Ayyāsh 140, 178
Ismā'īl b. Ibrāhīm al-Asdī, Ibn 'Ulayyah 81, 100, 123, 133, 141, 160
Ismā'īl b. Ibrāhīm b. 'Uqbah 96, 208, 210, 264
Ismā'īl b. Mujāhid 156
Ismā'īl b. Muslim al-Makkī 141
Ismā'īl b. Qais 162, 178
Ismā'īl b. Rāfi' 90
Ismā'īl b. Sālim al-Asdī 142
Ismā'īl b. Samā'ah 116
Ismā'īl b. Sumai' al-Ḥanafī 142
Isnād. *Isnād 'Ālī* 33; family *isnād* 246; Mālik and Nāfi''s *isnād* 237; Mūsā and Nāfi''s 209 *f*. Its beginning in *Ḥadīth* literature 212; Ibn Sīrīn's statements about it 213; its beginning and Caetani 213 *f;* and Sprenger 214; and Horovitz 214 *f;* and Robson 215; and Schacht 215 *f;* Material employed for the study of *isnād* 218. Schacht and study of *isnād* in legal literature and its inadequateness for the research 218; its flourishing in later part 222 *ff;* Refutation of Schacht's theory of flourishing of *isnād* 232 *ff.*
Isrā'īl b. Yūnus b. Abū Isḥāq al-Sabī'ī 78, 85, 103, 142.
'Itbān b. Mālik 52

Jābir b. 'Abd Allāh b. 'Amr 28, 52, 53, 93, 226, 233-4
Jābir b. 'Abd al-Ḥamīd al-Ḍabbī 144
Jābir b. Samurah 53
Jābir b. Yazīd al-Ju'fī 143
Jābir b. Zaid al-Azdī 66, 67, 77
al-Ja'd b. 'Abd al-Raḥmān 143
Ja'far b. Burqān 86, 90, 143
Ja'far b. al-Ḥārith 143
Ja'far b. Maimūn al-Tamīmī 143
Ja'far b. Muḥammad 143, 148
Ja'far b. Rabī'ah 84, 90
Ja'far b. Sulaimān al-Duba'ī 103, 144
al-Jāmi' 281
al-Jāmi' al-Kabīr 168
al-Jāmi' al-Ṣaghīr 168
Jamīl b. Zaid al-Ṭā'ī 45, 86
Jarīr 123, 151, 153, 272
Jarīr b. 'Abd Allāh 53, 185
Jarīr b. 'Abd al-Ḥamīd 87, 102, 122, 142, 144, 202
Jarīr b. Ḥāzim 99, 144, 178
Jariyah b. Qudāmah 47
Jarrāḥ b. Mulaiḥ 121, 135
Jawwāb b. 'Ubaid Allāh 86

al-Jazarī 295
Jazīrah 230
Jerusalem 290, 292
John I. 1, 2
Jumai' b. Thaub al-Shāmī 67
Juwairīyah b. Asmā' 145

Kahmas b. al-Ḥasan 145
Kathīr b. 'Abd Allāh 145, 246
Kathīr b. Aflaḥ I 60
Kathīr b. Murrah 67
Kathīr b. Salīm 50
Kathīr b. Ṣalt 60
Kathīr b. Zaid al-Aslamī 145
Khaibar 35, 36, 73, 294
Khalf b. Hishām 130
Khalf b. Khalīfah al-Ashja'ī 145
Khalf b. Tamīm 169
Khālid 105
Khālid al-'Abd 83, 202
Khālid b. 'Abd Allāh 102, 272
Khālid b. 'Abd Allāh al-Ṭaḥḥān 204
Khālid b. Abū 'Imrān al-Tujībī 86, 97
Khālid b. Abū Nauf al-Sijistānī 145
Khālid b. Ḥārith 75, 84, 116, 166
Khālid b. Ma'dān 67
Khālid al-Madā'inī 147
Khālid b. Makhlad 108
Khālid b. Mihrān al-Ḥadhdhā' 146
Khālid b. Nazār 114, 138, 174
Khālid al-Qasrī 281-2
Khalid b. 'Ubaid al-Baṣrī 51
Khālid b. Yazīd al-Dimashqī 146
Khālid b. Yazīd al-Jumaḥī 146
Khālid b. Yazīd b. Mu'āwiyah 16
Khālid b. Ziyād 97
Khalīfah b. Khayyāṭ 205
Khalīl b. Qurrah 177
Kharāsh b. 'Abd Allāh 50
Khārijah b. Muṣ'ab 146
Khārijah b. Zaid 60
al-Khaṭīb al-Baghdādī 20, 26, 27, 198, 203, 205, 300
Khilās b. 'Amr al-Ḥajarī 48
Khurāsān 226-7, 229-30
Khurasanites 145
Khuṣaif b. 'Abd al-Raḥmān 146, 187
Kifāyah 94
K. al-Diyāt 146
K. al-Farā'iḍ 64, 116, 168
K. Al-Ḥajj 73
K. al-'Īdain 138
K. Al-Jāmi' 148
K. Jarāḥat 64
K. al-Maghāzī : of Mūsā b. 'Uqbā, 260
and the authenticity of authorship 201-109
of Ibn Isḥāq 299 *ff*
K. Man Summiyya bi baitain qālahū 207
K. al-Manāsik 114, 141, 160
K. al-Manāqib 138, 181
K. al-Masā'il 104
K. al-Masā'il fil Fiqh 73
K. al-Mubtada' 104
K. al-Qirā'āt 134, 181
K. Risālah 168
K. Al-Ṣalāt 141
K. al-Siyar 136
K. Al-Sunan 87, 114, 134, 138, 152, 160, 181
K. al-Tafsīr 114, 134, 138, 141, 181
K. al-Ṭahārah 141
K. Ṭalāq 64
K. Al-Umm
K. Al-Zuhd 8, 9, 181
Krenkow 16
Kūfah 14, 51, 61, 75, 109, 167, 223-7, 229-30
Kuraib 41, 42, 303

Kurdūs b. 'Abbās 67

Lahī'ah b. 'Isā 111.
Lāḥiq b. Ḥumaid - Abū Mijlaz 67
Laith b. Abū Sulaim 69, 146
Al-Laith b. Sa'd al-Fahmī 84, 86, 90, 93, 97, 99, 104, 105, 112, 126, 135, 144, 146, 147, 150, 152, 178, 202, 269, 283
Lammens 218
Libraries in Umayyad Period 16-17
Lisān al-'Arab 207
Lopez, R.S. 266
Lyall, C.J. 207

Madā'in 73
al-Madīnah 1, 3, 4, 13, 36, 45, 49, 52, 77, 86, 209, 223-9, 288, 290
al-Madrasah al-Ḍiyā'iyah 274, 278
Maḥbūb b. Mūsā 136
al-Mahdī, the Caliph 167
Maimūn b. Mihrān al-Raqqī 86
Maimūn b. Mūsā al-Mar'ī 147
Maisarah 62
Makhāriq b. Khalīfah 95
Makhrimah 103, 126.
Makhūl al-Shāmī 87
Makkah 1, 12, 36, 40, 119, 150, 154, 167, 223-9, 241, 263, 266, 290-1
Makkī b. Ibrāhīm 125
Mālik b. Anas 27, 76, 82, 90, 92, 97, 108, 110, 121, 136, 138, 145, 147-8, 152, 170, 205, 208, 220-1, 231, 239 *ff*, 244 *ff*, 247 *ff*, 258 *ff*, 271, 299
Mālik b. al-Ḥuwairīth 13
Mālik b. Ismā'īl 132
Ma'mar b. Muḥammad 246
Ma'mar b. Rāshīd 32, 57, 84, 90, 99, 102, 107, 148, 177, 280, 283, 285
Mālik b. Sulaimān 166
Mamṭūr al-Ḥabashī, Abū Sallām 68
Ma'n 61, 299
Manṣūr 21, 203, 294, 297
Manṣūr b. al-Mu'tamar 87, 88
Manṣūr b. Zadhān al-Wāsiṭī 88
Ma'qil b. 'Ubaid-Allāh al-Jazarī 149
Al-Maqbutī 227
Margoliouth 293
Ma'rūf b. Ḥassān 173
Marw
Marwān b. Ḥakam 16, 38, 53, 59, 242, 267, 281, 288
Marwān b. Ja'far b. Sa'd 55
al-Mazrūqī 164
Maslamah b. 'Amr 90
Masrūq 56
Maṭar al-Warrāq 75
Mayyāḥ b. Sarī'
Mecca. See Makkah
Miqsam b. Bujrah 68
Mirzā Kazem Beg, 19
Mis'ar b. Kidām 149
Miskīn b. Bukair 143
al-Miswar b. Makhrimah 119, 281
Mu'ādh 116, 186
Mu'ādh b. Jabal 53
Mu'ādh b. Mu'ādh 75, 114, 155, 166
Mu'ādhah al-'Adwiyah 68
Mu'āfā
Mughīth b. Sumai 68
Mu'āwiyah b. 'Abd al-Karīm al-Thaqafī 80, 84
Mu'āwiyah b. Abū Sufyān 8, 11, 14, 15, 36, 47, 53, 65, 71, 216-7, 260, 266, 294
Mu'āwiyah b. 'Amr 136, 181
Mu'āwiyah b. Ṣāliḥ al-Ḥimṣī 150
Mu'āwiyah b. Sallām al-Ḥabashī 149, 177, 180
Mu'āwiyah b. Yaḥyā al-Dimashqī 90, 150

Mubārak b. Suḥaim 108
Mughīrah 21, 294, 302
al-Mughīrah b. 'Abd al-Raḥmān, 60, 76
al-Mughīrah b. Miqsam al-Ḍabbī 151
Mughīrah b. Mūsā 161
al-Mughīrah b. Shu'bah 11, 14, 53, 54
Muḥammad 220
Muḥammad b. 'Abdah b. Ḥarb 274
Muḥammad b. 'Abd al-Bāqī 273
Muḥammad b. 'Abd Allāh al-Karābīsī 278
Muḥammad b. 'Abd Allāh b. 'Ulāthah 151
Muḥammad b. 'Abd Allāh b. Zubair 169
Muḥammad b. 'Abd al-'Azīz 90
Muḥammad b. 'Abd al-Raḥmān b. Abū Lailā 151
Muḥammad b. 'Abd al-Raḥmān al-Bailamānī 151
Muḥammad b. 'Abd al-Raḥmān 97
Muḥammad b. 'Abd al-Raḥmān, Ibn Abū Dhīb 91, 152
Muḥammad b. Abū Bakr al-Anṣārī 88
Muḥammad b. Aḥmad al-Narsī 273
Muḥammad b. 'Ā'idh 132
Muḥammad b. 'Ajlān 38
Muḥammad b. 'Alī 52
Muḥammad b. 'Alī b. 'Abd Allāh b. 'Abbās 61
Muḥammad b. 'Alī b. Abū Ṭālib - Ibn al-Ḥanafiyah 52, 68
Muḥammad b. 'Amr b. Waqqāṣ 152
Muḥammad b. Bishr 149
Muḥammad b. Ḥarb
Muḥammad b. al-Ḥasan al-Ṣaffār 277
Muḥammad b. Ḥumaid 179
Muḥammad b. al-Faḍl 129
Muḥammad b. Fulaiḥ 96, 208-9
Muḥammad b. Ibrāhīm 292
Muḥammad b. Isḥāq b. Yasār 8, 32, 91, 137, 153, 203-6, 214-5, 219, 269, 299, 300
Muḥammad al-Iskandarānī 127
Muḥammad b. Jābir b. Sayyār 83, 154
Muḥammad b. Ja'far 294
Muḥammad b. Jubair 118
Muḥammad b. Juḥādah al-Kūfī 154
Muḥammad b. Kathīr 117, 202
Muḥammad b. Khālid 181
Muḥammad b. Maimūn, Abū Ḥamzah al-Sukkarī 99, 154
Muḥammad b. Maisarah 122, 155
Muḥammad b. Maslamah al-Anṣārī 54
Muḥammad b. al-Mubārak
Muḥammad b. al-Munkadir 88
Muḥammad b. Muṣ'ab 125
Muḥammad b. Muslim b. Tadrus 52, 93
Muḥammad b. Muslim b. Shihāb al-Zuhrī 8, 18, 20, 27, 32, 57, 72-3, 77, 88-93, 96, 148, 169, 192, 203, 208-9, 214-5, 221, 225-6, 235, 239-40, 259, 262, 265, 269, 271, 272, 277 *ff*, 301, 305
Muḥammad b. Muslim al-Ṭā'ifī 155
Muḥammad b. Muzāḥim 182
Muḥammad b. Najīḥ 158
Muḥammad b. Rāshid al-Makḥūlī 155
Muḥammad b. Sābiq 138
Muḥammad b. Salamah 299 *f*
Muḥammad b. Sālim al-Hamdānī 155
Muḥammad b. Sawār 101
Muḥammad b. Shu'aib 117
Muḥammad b. Sīrīn 21, 27, 30, 38, 55, 62, 94-5, 185, 213, 216 *ff*, 227

Muh. Stud. 8, 19
Muḥammad b. Sūqah 156
Muḥammad b. 'Ubaid 149
Muḥammad b. 'Ubaid Allāh b. Abū Rāfi' 156
Muḥammad b. 'Ubaid Allāh al-'Arzamī 156
Muḥammad b. al-Walīd al-Zubaidī 91, 156
Muḥammad b. Yazīd 143
Muḥammad b. Ziyād al-Qurashī 95, 227
Muir 18
Mujāhid 187
Mujāhid b. Jabr al-Makkī 42, 48, 52, 69, 203, 206
Mujāhid b. Sa'īd 156
Al-Mu'jam al-Kabīr 73, 281
Mukhallad b. Mālik 123
al-Mundhir b. 'Abd Allāh 209
Muqātil b. Sulaimān 157
Muqātil 157
Murshid b. Yaḥyā 275
Mūsā b. 'Abd Allāh al-Ṭawīl 50
Mūsā b. 'Isā 88
Mūsā b. Mas'ūd 169
Mūsā b. Maṭīr 246
Mūsā b. Muḥammad 239
Mūsā b. Ṭalḥah 53
Mūsā b. Ṭāriq 114
Mūsā b. 'Ubaid Allāh 162
Mūsā b. 'Uqbah 8, 41, 91, 95, 97 207-11, 260 *ff*, 264 *ff*, 275, 281
Muṣ'ab b. Māhān 169
Muṣ'ab b. Sallām 132, 180
Muṣ'ab b. 'Umair 3-4
Muṣannaf 140, 296
al-Musayyab b. Wāḍiḥ 136
Muslim b. al-Ḥajjāj 32, 258, 271, 294, 303 *ff*
Muslim b. Ibrāhīm 161
Muslim b. Khālid 114
Muslim b. 'Ubaid Allāh 279
Musnad of: Baqī 37
Ibn Ḥanbal 37, 51
Mu'tamar b. Sulaymān 102, 111, 127, 145, 157, 161
Muṭarrif b. Māzin 149
Muṭarrif b. 'Abd al-Raḥmān 65
Muṭarrif b. Ṭarīf al-Ḥārithī 96
Al-Muṭṭalib 233 *f*
al-Muṭṭalib b. 'Abd Allāh 22
al-Muṭṭalib b. Ḥanṭab 59
Muwaṭṭa' of: Ibn Abū Dhi'b 32, 152
— Ibrāhīm b. Muḥammad 136
— Mālik b. Anas 32, 108, 110, 136, 148, 216, 218-21, 238-9, 242, 245, 248, 271, 275, 298-9
— Al-Shaibānī 218

al-Naḍr b. Anas 295
al-Naḍr b. Shumail 166
Nāfi', The Freed Man of Ibn 'Umar 33, 45, 58, 75, 96, 209, 221, 244-5, 247, 269, 271, 275-6, 287, 292
Nāfi' al-Qārī 77
Nāfi' b, 'Umar al-Makkī 157
Nāfi' b. Yazīd al-Kala'ī 157
al-Naḥḥās b. Qahm al-Qaisī 153
Najdah 42
Najīḥ b. 'Abd al-Raḥmān al-Sindī 158
Najrān 5, 48
al-Nasa'ī 297 *ff*
Nephew of 'Amr 79
Nicholson 8
Nu'aim b. Ḥammād 137
Nu'aim b. Maisarah 158
al-Nufailī 299
Nūḥ b. Abū Maryam 78, 84, 85, 88, 93, 102, 114, 162, 172
Nūḥ b. Maimūn 169
Nūḥ b. Yazīd 137
al-Nu'mān b. Bashīr 54
Nu'mān b. Thābit, al-Imām Abū Ḥanīfah 27, 82, 138, 158

The Prophet 3, 4, 5, 6, 7, 8, 9, 13, 14, 15, 16, 20, 21, 22, 23, 24, 25, 26, 34, 35, 39, 40, 43, 44, 45, 46, 47, 48, 49, 50, 51, 56, 59, 63, 72, 183, 184, 212-222, 228, 231-4, 239, 241, 243-6, 249-68, 279, 302

Qabīṣah 57, 60, 169, 288
Qabīṣah b. al-Mukhāriq 13
Qais b. 'Abbād 47
Qais b. al-Haitham 51, 54.
Qais b. al-Rabī al-Asadi 159
Qais b. Sa'd 80, 159
Qalqashandī 201
Qa'nabī 240
Qāsim 242, 305
al-Qāsim b. 'Abd Allāh 173
al-Qāsim b. 'Abd al-Raḥmān 98
al-Qāsim b. Abū Bazzah 69
al-Qāsim b. Muḥammad 21, 57, 69, 77
al-Qāsim b. Muḥammad al-Anbārī 206, 207
al-Qāsim b. Sallām 282
Qatādah b. Diāmah al-Saddūsī 52, 63, 66, 70, 74, 82, 98, 133, 148, 160, 165, 213, 230, 299
Qaz'ah 292
Qiṣaṣ al-Akhyār 104
Qiṣaṣ al-Anbiyā' 104
al-Qur'ān 5, 11, 14, 16, 21, 22, 23, 24, 25, 26, 30, 41, 44, 56, 57, 64, 66, 69, 70, 80, 83, 98, 113, 135, 142, 157, 160, 161, 163, 183, 197, 200, 213, 238, 263, 265, 267, 268, 279, 289, 292
Qurrād Abū Nūḥ 166
Qurrah b. Khālid al-Saddūsī 159, 230
Quṣaim 292
Qutaibah b. Sa'īd 111, 147, 161, 299

Rabāḥ 149
al-Rabī' b. Ṣabīḥ al-Sa'dī 159
al-Rabī' b. Yaḥyā 169
Rabī'ah b. Farrūkh al-Taimī 91, 99, 178
Rāfi' b. Khadīj 54, 220
Rajā' b. Ḥaiwah 99
Rashīd Riḍā 24, 25
Rauḥ b. 'Ubādah 115, 133, 140, 152, 161, 181
Rawwād b. al-Jarrāḥ 169
Ra'y al-Fuqahā' al-Sab'ah 116
Risālah ilā Abbād b. Abbād 168
Risālah of al-Shāfi'ī 30, 220-1
Robson, J. 215 *ff*, 232, 234, 243, 246
Rufai' b. Mihrān, Abū al-'Āliyah al-Riyāḥī 21, 56, 70
Rukn b. 'Abd Allāh al-Shāmī 87
Ruqbah b. Misqalah 99
Ruth 2, 18, 40
Ruzaiq b. Ḥakīm 91

Sachau 207, 260-1, 263-4
Sa'd b. Ibrāhīm 137
Sa'd b. Ibrāhīm b. 'Abd al-Raḥmān 100, 166
Sa'd b. Mu'adh 13
Sa'd b. Sa'īd 159
Sa'd b. 'Ubādah 54, 241
Ṣadaqah b. 'Abd Allāh al-Samīn 88, 115, 117, 161, 162
Ṣadaqah b. Khālid 162
Ṣafwān 299
Ṣaḥīfat Hammām 38
al-Ṣaḥīfah al-Ṣādīqah 30
Ṣaḥīḥ al-Bukhārī 205
Sahl b. Ḥunaif 239
Sahl b. Ḥusain b. Muslim 84
Sahl b. Sa'd al-Sa'dī 55
al-Sahmī 167
Sa'īd 280
Sa'īd b. 'Abd Allāh b. Juraij 160
Sa'īd b. Abū 'Arūbah 32, 99, 157, 160, 269
Sa'īd b. Abū Ayyūb 106, 162

Sa'īd b. Abū Maryam 157
Sa'īd b. Abū Sa'īd 292
Sa'īd b. Bashīr al-Azdī 99, 161
Sa'īd b. Fairūz al-Ṭā'ī 70
Sa'īd b. Iyās al-Jurairī 100
Sa'īd b. Jubair al-Asdī 42, 46, 70, 94, 256
Sa'īd b. Maslimah 88
Sa'īd al-Maqburī 38
Sa'īd b. Muḥammad 88
Sa'īd b. Sālim 115
Sa'īd b. Sallām 181
al-Ṣakan b. Abū Khālid 135, 161
Sakhr b. Juwairiyah 97, 162
Salam al-'Alawī 106
Salamah 230
Salamah b. 'Abd al-Malik 132
Salamah b. Dīnār; Abū Ḥāzim al-Ashja'ī 55, 161
Salamah b. al-Faḍl 206
Salamah b. Kuhail 101, 292
Salamah b. al-Mufaḍḍal 153
Ṣāliḥ b. Abū al-Akhḍar 91
Ṣāliḥ b. Kaisān 280
Ṣāliḥ b. Nabhān 100
Sālim 209, 287
Sālim b. 'Abd Allāh al-Khayyāt 162
Sālim b. 'Abd Allāh al-Baṣrī 95
Sālim b. Abū al-Ja'd 71
Sālim b. 'Ajlān al-Afṭas 144, 163
Sālim, the scribe of 'Abd Allāh 42
Salīm b. Akhḍar 75
Sālim b. Nūḥ 100, 179
Sallām b. Miskīn 99
Sallām b. Abū Muṭī' 133
Sālim b. Dhayyāl al-Baṣrī 161
Salmān al-Fārisī 55
Samurah b. Jundub 55, 56, 297
Sarij of al-Yarmūk 43
Schacht, J. 8, 9, 18, 19, 208-9, 211, 215, 218, 232-5, 238-45, 247-9, 251-60, 262, 264-6
Schacht and 'Umar b. 'Abd al-'Azīz's order for recording of Ḥadīth, 'a spurious tradition' 18-19; and the authenticity of Mūsā b. 'Uqbā's authorship of al-Maghāzī 207-208; and standard biographies and their values 208; refutation of his statements 209-11. Isnād of Mālik and Nāfi' 244; and of Mūsā and Nāfi' 209. Schacht and isnād 215 and flourishing of isnād 232 *ff;* refutation of his theory 236; argument about his examples of arbitrary character of isnād 238; refutation of his 'projecting back theory' 242; his unscientific method of research 250 F. n. 6; false quotation 260, 267; his conception of the nature of Law in Islam 251 *f;* 'ancient schools of Law', absurdity of his theory 252 *f;* argument about his examples and condumnation 253 *ff;* refutation of his criticism of Ḥadīth on material ground 260 *ff.*
Schools in Pre-Islamic Arabia 1, in early Islam 4, School buildings 199
Secretaries of the Prophet and their duties 5-6
al-Sha'bī, see 'Āmir b. Sharāḥīl
Shabīb b. Sa'īd 180
Shaddād b. Aus b. Thābit 56
Shaddād b. Ḥakīm 182
Shādhān 144
al-Shāfi'ī 30, 136, 219-21, 233-4, 240-2, 247, 253, 260
Shahr b. Ḥaushab 71
Shaibān b. 'Abd al-Raḥmān 163, 177, 206
Shaibān al-Naḥwī 99,
Shaibānī 159, 255
Shaikh 'Ināyatullāh 200
Shamghūn al-Azdī 56, 201
al-Shāmī 129

Shaqīq b. Ibrāhīm al-Balkhī 163
Shaqīq b. Salamah al-Asdī 71
Sharḥ al-Mufaḍḍalīyāt 206-7
Sharāḥīl b. Shuraḥbīl 71
Sharīk b. 'Abd Allāh al-Kūfī 85, 163
al-Shaukānī 217
Shīrāz 278
Shu'aib 150
Shu'aib b. Isḥāq 276
Shu'aib b. Abū Ḥamzah 57, 76, 91, 97, 109, 277-8, 283
Shu'bah b. Dīnār al-Hāshimī 100
Shu'bah b. al-Ḥajjāj al-Azdī 68, 75, 78, 82, 83, 88, 99, 100, 105, 107, 116, 124, 126, 128, 142, 203, 210-11, 213, 230, 235, 294, 298, 304
Shuraiḥ 62
Simāk b. Ḥarb al-Kūfī 101
Simāk b. al-Walīd 101
Son of Hishām 93, 282-3
Sprenger 214, 285, 293
Stanley Adams 19
Students, examination before admission 197, their ages 197, their numbers 199
Subai'ah al-Aslāmiyyah 55
Sufyān 76, 297
Sufyān b. Ḥusain al-Wāsiṭī 91, 239-40
Sufyān b. Sa'īd al-Thaurī al-Kūfī 27, 32, 57, 71, 86, 92, 100, 109, 123, 130, 139, 151, 155, 156, 167, 171, 173, 182, 203, 210, 248, 269, 272, 301, 304
Sufyān b. 'Uyaynah 69, 79, 85, 91, 121, 157, 169, 178, 202, 231, 244, 256 259
Suhail b. Abū Ṣāliḥ 38, 65, 170, 235-6, 269, 270-4
Sulaimān 151
Sulaimān b. 'Abd al-Raḥmān 276
Sulaimān b. Abū Sulaymān 170, 171
Sulaimān b. Bilāl al-Taimī 170, 233-4
Sulaimān b. Ḥarb 128, 129, 130, 144
Sulaimān b. Kathīr al-'Abdī 92
Sulaimān b. Mihrān al-A'mash 21, 27, 37, 65, 78, 101-3, 226, 228, 248, 269
Sulaimān b. al-Mughīrah al-Qaisī 171
Sulaimān b. Muḥammad 115
Sulaimān b. Mujālid 115
Sulaimān b. Mūsā al-Ashdaq 92, 102
Sulaimān b. Qais al-Yashkurī 52, 71
Sulaimān b. Qarm al-Taimī 62, 171
Sulaimān b. Samurah 55
Sulaimān b. Tarkhān al-Baṣrī 102
Sulaimān b. Yasār 103
Sulaimān b. Zaitūn 72
Sulaiṭ 184
Syria 223-5, 228-30, 289-91
al-Ṭabarānī 30, 55, 60, 72-3, 104, 209, 265, 281

Ṭabarī 14, 73, 207, 210
Tābūt 16
Ṭāhā Ḥusain 216
Ṭaḥāwī 240, 274, 286
Ṭāhir al-Jazā'irī 304
Tāj al-'Arūs 20, 207
al-Taimī 50
Ṭā'if 1, 223-5, 230
Ṭalḥah b. 'Abd al-Malik 69
Ṭalḥah b. Nāfi', Abū Sufyān 52, 103
Tamīm al-Jaishānī 60
Taqyīd 20, 27
Tārīkh of al-Bukhārī 210
Ṭāriq b. Shihāb 47
Ṭayālisī 264
Teachers, sending them outside Madīnah 4-5

Thābit b. 'Ajlān 103
Thābit b. Aslam al-Bunānī 103, 295
Thaur b. Yazīd al-Kindī 171
al-Thaurī, su Sufyān b. Sa'īd
Thuwair b. Abū Fākhtah 103
Tirmidhī 296
Tustar 229-30

Ubai b. Ka'b 56, 298
'Ubaid b. Abū Qurrah 109, 171
'Ubaid b. al-Qāsim 84
'Ubaid Allāh b. 'Abd Allāh b. Mauhab 38
'Ubaid Allāh b. 'Abd Allāh 21, 279, 281
'Ubaid Allāh b. Abū Rāfi' 71
'Ubaid Allāh b. Abū Ja'far al-Miṣrī 104
'Ubaid Allāh b. Abū Ziyād 92, 172
'Ubaid Allāh b. 'Amr al-Raqqī 76, 172
'Ubaid Allāh b. Ayād al-Saddūsī 172
'Ubaid Allāh b. 'Ubaid al-Kalā'ī 87
'Ubaid Allāh b. 'Ubaid al-Raḥmān 169
'Ubaid Allāh b. 'Umar b. Ḥafṣ al-'Umarī 90, 92, 97, 124, 172, 272, 275 *f*, 285 *f*
'Ubaid Allāh b. 'Umar al-Qawarīrī 181
'Ubaid Allāh b. Zahr 78
Uḥud 279, 281
Um al-Dardā', Hujaimah 72
'Umar b. 'Abd al-'Azīz 18, 19, 25, 72, 77, 105, 282, 284
'Umar b. 'Abd al-Wāhid 117
'Umar b. Abū Salamah 173
'Umar b. Dhar al-Hamdānī 173
'Umar b. Ḥammād 161
'Umar b. Ibrāhīm al-'Abdī 173
'Umar b. Isḥāq b. Yasār 64
'Umar b. Kathīr 221
'Umar b. al-Khaṭṭāb 2, 14, 16, 21, 35, 36, 45, 51, 56, 57, 59, 85, 221, 231, 238, 252, 293, 294
'Umar b. Muḥammad b. Zaid 173
'Umar b. Qais al-Makkī 174
'Umar b. Sahl 125
'Umar b. Sa'īd 174
'Umar b. 'Ubaidullāh 42, 43, 46
'Umārah b. Ghaziyah 174
'Umārah b. Juwain 104
Al-Umm 218, 221, 241 *ff*
'Uqail b. Khālid al-Ailī 92, 174, 259
'Urwah b. al-Zubair 47, 56, 57, 72, 73, 186, 213 *ff*, 220, 238 *ff*, 279 *ff*, 299
Usaid b. Ẓahīr 59
Usāmah 264
Usāmah b. Zaid al-Laithī 174
'Utaibah bin al-Naḥḥās al-'Ijlī 14
'Utbah b. Ḥumaid al-Ḍabbī 175
'Uthmān 11, 14, 15, 16, 25, 200, 231, 242, 252
'Uthmān b. Abū Shaibah 75
'Uthmān b. 'Āṣim al-Asdī 104
'Uthmān b. Ghiyāth 66
'Uthmān b. Ḥāḍir al-Ḥimyarī 104
'Uthmān al-Marwazī 115
'Uthmān b. Miqsam al-Burrī 175
'Uthmān al-Mushāhid 68
'Uthmān b. Ṣāliḥ 111
'Uthmān b. 'Umar 116, 133, 140
Al-'Uyūn wa al-Ḥadā'iq 11

Al-Waḍḍah b. 'Abd Allāh, Abū 'Awānah 98, 101, 107, 133, 134, 173, 175
Wahb 129
Wahb b. Jarīr 157
Wahb b. Munabbih 8, 53, 104, 196
Wakī' 102, 132, 140, 169, 170, 203, 269, 296
Al-Walīd 283, 289

Al-Walīd b. Mazīd 117
Walīd 162
Al-Walīd b. Muḥammad al-Muwaqqarī 92, 176
Al-Walīd b. Muslim 113, 117, 155, 284
Al-Walīd al-Shaibānī 169
Al-Walīd b. Al-Walīd 79
Walīd b. Yazīd 216
Warqa' 76, 88, 203, 206
Waraqah b. Naufal 2
Warrād 294
Warrāq 190, 195
Wāṣil b. 'Abd al-Raḥmān, Abū Ḥurrah 176
Wāsiṭ 131, 224, 227, 230
Wāsiṭ b. al-Ḥārith 176
Wāthilah b. al-Asqa' 59, 192
Wensink 267-8
Wuhaib b. Khālid al-Bāhilī 166, 170, 176, 209, 272-3

Yaḥyā 220-1, 242, 299
Yaḥyā b. 'Abd Allāh 246
Yaḥyā b. Abū Kathīr 63, 68, 176, 178, 180
Yaḥyā b. Abū Unaisah 92
Yaḥyā b. Ādam 110, 142
Yaḥyā b. Ayyūb al-Ghāfiqī 66, 177
Yaḥyā b. Bukair 147, 288
Yaḥyā b. Durrais 129
Yaḥyā b. Fudhail 132
Yaḥyā b. Ḥammād 175
Yaḥyā b. Ḥamzah al-Dimashqī 177
Yaḥyā b. Ja'dah 57
Yaḥyā b. al-Jazzār al-'Uranī 74
Yaḥyā b. Ma'īn. See Ibn Ma'īn
Yaḥyā b. Sa'īd b. Abān 153
Yaḥyā b. Sa'īd al-Anṣārī 86, 177
Yaḥyā b. Sālim 112
Yaḥyā al-Qaṭṭān 67, 75, 84, 117, 118, 127, 129, 139, 140, 143, 144, 146, 152, 155, 158, 166, 169, 171, 173, 174, 176, 186, 287, 304
Yaḥyā b. Sīrīn 38, 94-5
Yaḥyā b. 'Urwah 73
Yaḥyā b. Yaḥyā 119, 171
Yaḥyā b. al-Yamān 149
Ya'lā b. 'Aṭā' 187
Ya'lā b. Ḥakīm 178
Yamāmah 73, 154, 229
Ya'qūb al-Ashajj 81
Ya'qūb b. 'Abd Allāh al-Qummī 179
Ya'qūb b. 'Aṭā' 80
Ya'qūb b. Ibrāhīm 137
Al-Ya'qūbī 289 *ff*
Al-Yarmūk 43
Yazīd 164
Yazīd b. Abān al-Raqqāshī 105
Yazīd b. Abū Maryam 292
Yazīd b. 'Abd Allāh 178
Yazīd b. 'Abdal-Raḥmān b. Abū, Mālik 105
Yazīd b. Abū Ḥabīb 80, 92, 105 153, 269
Yazīd b. Abū Ziyād 303
Yazīd b. 'Aṭā' b. Yazīd al-Yashkurī 179
Yazīd b. al-Hād 179
Yazīd b. Hārūn 155, 181, 295
Yazīd b. Nu'mān 54, 82
Yazīd al-Rashk 68
Yazīd b. Sufyān Abū al-Muhazzim 105
Yazīd b. Yazīd b. Jabir 93
Yazīd b. Zurai' 125, 133, 139, 153, 179
Yemen 5, 223-6, 229-30
Yūnus b. Abū Isḥāq 78, 179
Yūnus b. 'Ubaid al-'Abdī 179
Yūnus b. Yazīd al-Ailī 57, 93, 180
Yūsuf b. 'Abd al-Raḥmān 78
Yūsuf b. Khālid 96
Yūsuf b. al-Mubārak 273
Yūsuf b. Muḥammad 152

Yūsuf b. Ṣuhaib al-Kūfī 180

Ẓāhiriya Library 138, 274, 276
Zā'idah 169
Zā'idah b. Abū Ruqād 181
Zā'idah b. Qudāmah 181
Zaid b. Abū Sallām, Mamṭūr al-Ḥabashī 180
Zaid b. 'Alī b. Ḥusain 76, 180
Zaid b. Arqam 59
Zaid b. Aslam, client of Ibn 'Umar 106
Zaid b. 'Auf 129
Zaid b. Rufai' 106
Zaid b. Sālim 292
Zaid b. Thābit 59, 60, 242
Zakariyā b. 'Adī 172, 305
Zakariyā b. Isḥāq al-Makkī 80, 181
Zam'ah 182
Ziyād b. 'Abd Allāh 153
Ziyād b. Abīh 266
Ziyād b. Abū Sufyān 47
Ziyād b. Abū Ziyād al-Jaṣṣāṣ 181
Ziyād b. Ayyūb 141
Ziyād b. Jubair 94
Ziyād b. Sa'd al-Khurāsānī 93, 182
Zolondek 207
Zubaid b. al-Ḥārith 106
Al-Zubair b. 'Adī 182, 269, 271
Zuhair b. Mu'āwiyah 143, 182, 298
Zufar b. al-Hudhail 182
Zuhair b. Muḥammad al-Tamīmī 162, 230
Al-Zuhrī. See Muḥammad b. Muslim
Zurqānī 238-40

PART TWO

The Edited Texts

بسم الله الرحمن الرحيم

دراسات في الحديث النبوي

وتاريخ تدوينه

الدكتور محمد مصطفى الأعظمي

الطبعة الاولى
بيروت ١٣٨٨ هـ - ١٩٦٨ م

بسم الله الرحمن الرحيم

أجمع المسلمون – منذ ثلاثة عشر قرناً حتى الآن – على أن لشريعة الاسلام مصدرين اساسيين هما القرآن الكريم والسنة المطهرة، فالقرآن هو الأساس، والسنة شارحته ومبينته؛ بقول الرسول ﷺ، وفعله، وتقريره. قال تعالى: « وأنزلنا إليك الذكر لتبين للناس ما نزل إليهم ولعلهم يتفكرون ».

ولهذا كان ما يجيء به الرسول من شرع، واجب الطاعة والامتثال، كالقرآن، وكلاهما وحي من الله عز وجل: «وما ينطق عن الهوى. إن هو إلا وحي يوحى» و: «من يطع الرسول فقد أطاع الله».

وما زال الامر كذلك حتى زحف الاستعمار على بلاد الاسلام فاستذل أهلها علمياً وأدبياً واقتصادياً ونشط الناس في الغرب لمعرفة الشرق والمسلمين، وفتحت الاقسام بالجامعات والكليات للدراسات الشرقية والاسلامية. والتحق بها أناس من أنواع عديدين.

فكان بعضهم – وهم قلة قليلة – مخلصاً للبحث، وان لم يصادفهم التوفيق في كثير من الاحيان وذلك لبعدهم عن روح الشرق وجوه ودياره. وكان هناك آخرون همهم «تبشير المسلمين» بمعتقدات وآراء مغايرة، وكانت طريقتهم الطعن في الاسلام مباشرة وتشويه جماله. لكنها لم تأت بثمرة مرجوة، لذلك اعتمد الآخرون على أسلوب خفي: هدفه التشكيك الدائب في أصول الاسلام. وقد نال هؤلاء الحديث النبوي بنصيب كبير من هذا الهجوم، فكتبوا في الحديث بحوثاً مشحونة بكثير من الاخطاء والتهم والتحريفات نتيجة سوء الفهم أو سوء القصد أو هما معاً.

لقد شككوا في جمع السنة ، وزعموا أنها كانت تنقل شفاها لقرون عديدة ، لهذا لا يمكن الاعتماد عليها . وجاء مستشرق شهير مثل البروفسور جوزيف شاخت فادعى أن مجموعة الاحاديث النبوية — وخاصة الفقهية منها — عبارة عن أقاويل ملفقة اخترعها العلماء المسلمون في القرن الثاني والثالث الهجريين . وما الأسانيد التي اعتمد عليها المحدثون فيما بعد الا بعض مخترعات القرنين المذكورين .

ولعل أخطر ما في هذه الاتهامات الباطلة والدعاوى الهدامة ، انها اتخذت صورة البحث العلمي وموهت على قليلي المعرفة بالاسلام ، بشبهات وتخيلات وتلفيقات ، لا تثبت على النقد والتمحيص .

ولكنها تروج عند السطحيين والفارغين ، وعند المعجبين المفتونين بكل ما جاء من الغرب والغربيين . فلا غرو إن وجد بيننا — نحن المسلمين — من يردد دعاوى المستشرقين ذاتها ترديد الببغاء . ومنهم من يتبناها وينسبها لنفسه على أنها من بنات أفكاره . وما هو في الواقع الا مقلد محض ، لا أصالة له ولا ابتكـــار .

لهذا كانت الحاجة ماسة الى البحث في أمور السنة ، وتجلية ما غمض من تاريخها ، ورد الأمور الى نصابها الصحيح . ولا شك ان الموضوع واسع ومتشعب ولا يستطيع كتاب واحد لفرد واحد ، أن يوفيه حقه ، لهذا آثرت أن أتخذ جانباً واحداً من جوانب الموضوع المتعددة ، فرأيت أن أبحث في تاريخ تدوين الحديث وبداية الأسانيد وما يتصل بها من الموضوعات الفرعية الأخرى ، لأبين قيمة ما أنتجه علماء المسلمين في الماضي ، وبطلان دعوى المتهجمين في الحاضر ، متبعاً في ذلك أسلوب البحث العلمي ، بعيداً عن روح الانشاء .

وكان من توفيق الله لي أني اكتشفت في دنيا المخطوطات الفسيحة المجهولة — للأسف — نسخاً حديثية ألفها العلماء في بداية القرن الثاني منها نسخة سهيل ابن أبي صالح ، ونسخة عبيد الله بن عمر وغيرهما . وقد أدى هذا الاكتشاف

الى نتائج هامة في دراسة الحديث .

وقد عكفت على دراسة الفترة من عهد الرسول صلى الله عليه وسلم الى منتصف القرن الثاني على وجه التقريب ، فوجدت بالبحث مراجع تشير الى آلاف من الكتب التي كانت متداولة بين المحدثين ، وأن الأحاديث كانت تدون في عصر النبوة نفسه ، وان الصحابة ألفوا الكتب في الموضوعات العديدة. ثم بحثت في تدريس الحديث ، وكيف كان استعمال الكتاب شائعاً في الدراسة وطريقة الاملاء رائجة منذ عهد مبكر ... وتطرقت الى مشكلة نسبة الكتب الى المؤلفين ، وكيف كان أسلوبهم .. وبعد ذلك انتقلت الى الأسانيد وبدايتها ، والى أي مدى يمكن الاعتماد عليها .

وكانت هناك موضوعات جانبية احتاجت الى مزيد من التوضيح ، كمعنى كلمة « حدثنا » وطريقة عد الاحاديث .. ومفهوم الاحاديث غير الصحيحة والموضوعة الخ ...

وقد كتبت هذا البحث باللغة الانجليزية وقدمته الى جامعة كامبردج في تشرين أول (اكتوبر) ١٩٦٦ م رسالة لنيل الدكتوراة .

وبعد ذلك تجمعت لدي مواد كثيرة ذات صلة بالبحث وكنت أرغب في الاستفادة منها ، لتوسيع بعض فصول الرسالة ، ولكني رأيت – اتباعاً لمشورة بعض الناصحين– أن أطبع الرسالة بشكلها الراهن ، حتى لا تؤدي اضافة المواد الجديدة الى تأخير نشرها ، مع الحاجة اليها الآن . فاكتفيت باجراء بعض تعديلات طفيفة معظمها يتصل بناحية اللغة .

ومهما يكن من أمر فقد كانت طريقتي في الكتابة هي اتباع المنهج العلمي الاستقرائي، باذلاً جهدي وطاقتي ، غير مدع الكمال فالكمال لله وحده . وحسبي أني أمطت اللثام عن كثير من الحقائق ورددت كثيراً من الشبهات والأباطيل وذلك بفضل الله وحده . وأرجو بذلك أن أكون قد خدمت ديني ، وأرضيت ربي ، وأنصفت الحقيقة من ظالميها ، وساهمت مع المخلصين في

الذود عن حرم الاسلام وسنة رسوله عليه الصلاة والسلام .

واني أرحب بكل نقد بناء من طبيعته ان يسهم في خدمة الموضوع والله من وراء القصد .

قطر الدوحة نوفمبر ١٩٦٧م
شعبان ١٣٨٧ هـ

محمد مصطفى الاعظمي

الرموز المستعملة في تحقيق المخطوطات

ابن جريج	روح بن عبادة ، أحاديثه عن ابن جريج
ابن طهمان	ابراهيم بن طهمان . جزء من أحاديثه
الأصـل	سهيل بن ابي صالح « نسخته »
الأعمش	وكيع ـ نسخته عن الأعمش
بغداد	الخطيب البغدادي ، تاريخ بغداد
ت	الترمذي « الجامع »
الثوري،	مما أسند الثوري
جعـد	علي بن الجعد « المسند »
جـه	ابن ماجه « السنن »
جويرية	جويرية بن أسماء « نسخته عن نافع »
حم	مسند ابن حنبل
الحميدي	الحميدي ، المسند
خ	البخاري « الجامع الصحيح »
خزيمة	ابن خزيمة « صحيح ابن خزيمة »
خيثمة	ابن أبي خيثمة « التاريخ »
د	أبو داود « السنن »
الدار قطني	الدار قطني « السنن »
دي	الدارمي « السنن »
راهويه	ابن راهويه « المسند »
سعد	ابن سعد « الطبقات »

ط	مالك « الموطأ »
طس	الطيالسي « المسند »
طص	الطبراني « المعجم الصغير »
طط	الطبراني « المعجم الأوسط »
طك	الطبراني «المعجم الكبير »
عوانة	ابو عوانة « المسند »
الفسوي	الفسوي « التاريخ »
الكشي	عبد بن حميد الكشي « المنتخب من المسند »
الليث	الليث نسخته عن يزيد بن أبي حبيب
م	مسلم بن الحجاج « الصحيح »
المستدرك	الحاكم النيسابوري « المستدرك على الصحيحين »
مسند الربيع	الربيع « المسند »
المنتقى	ابن جارود . المنتقى . الاشارة الى رقم الحديث
ن	النسائي – المجتبى من السنن
يعلى	أبو يعلى الموصلي « المسند »
عنه	ذكرناها في الشواهد بالاسانيد ونعني بها الراوي الاول للحديث وهو غالباً الصحابي

* * *

راموز الصفحة الاولى من مخطوطة نسخة سهيل بن ابي صالح

The Title of the Nuskhah of Suhail

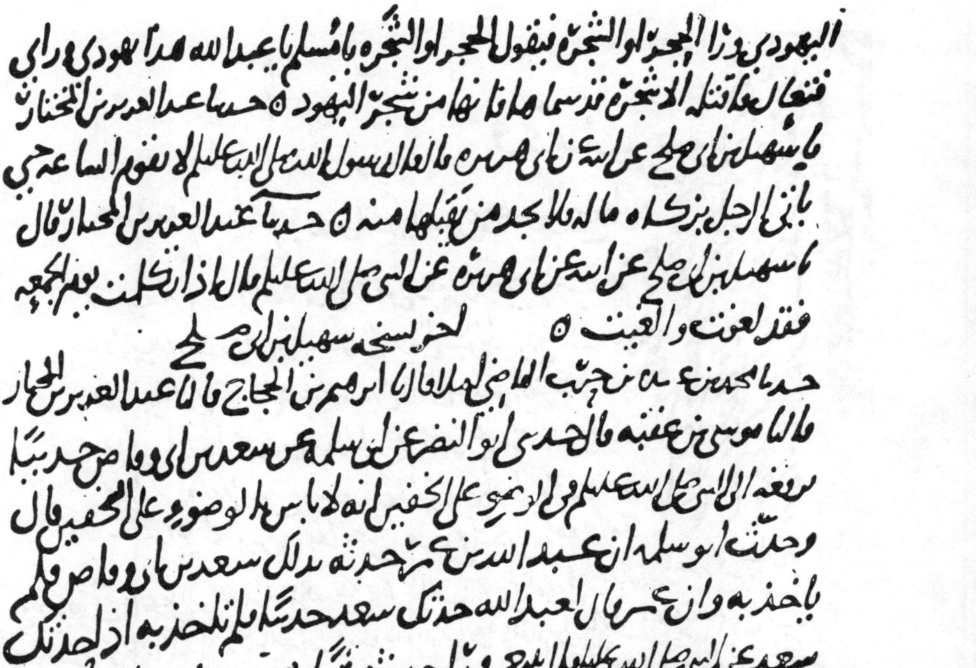
اليهودي وراء الحجر او الشجرة فيقول الحجر او الشجرة يا مسلم يا عبد الله هذا يهودي ورائي
فتعال فاقتله الا شجرة الغرقد فانها من شجر اليهود ٥ حدثنا عبد العزيز بن المختار نا
نا سهيل بن ابي صالح عن ابيه عن ابي هريرة قال قال رسول الله صلى الله عليه وسلم لا تقوم الساعة حتى
ياتي الرجل بزكاة ماله فلا يجد من يقبلها منه ٥ حدثنا عبد العزيز بن المختار قال
نا سهيل بن ابي صالح عن ابيه عن ابي هريرة عن النبي صلى الله عليه وسلم قال اذا تكلمت يوم الجمعة
فقد لغوت والغيت ٥ آخر نسخة سهيل بن ابي صالح
حدثنا محمد بن عيسى بن نجيب القاضي املاء انا ابراهيم بن الحجاج قال نا عبد العزيز بن المختار
قال نا موسى بن عقبة قال حدثني ابو النضر عن ابي سلمة عن سعد بن ابي وقاص حديثا
يرفعه الى النبي صلى الله عليه وسلم في المسح على الخفين انه لا باس بالوضوء على الخفين قال
وحدث ابو سلمة ان عبد الله بن عمر حدثه بذلك سعد بن ابي وقاص فلم
ياخذ به وان عمر قال لعبد الله حدثك سعد حديثا فلم تاخذ به اذا حدثك
سعد عن النبي صلى الله عليه وسلم فلا تبغ وراءه شيئا ٥ حدثنا عبد العزيز بن
المختار نا موسى بن عقبة قال حدثني محمد بن عمرو بن عطاء انه سمع ابن عباس يقول
ان النبي صلى الله عليه وسلم اكل اما ذراعا واما كتفا ثم صلى ولم يتوضا ولم يمس ما
فزعم ان ابن عباس [illegible] ٥ حدثنا عبد العزيز بن
المختار نا موسى بن عقبة قال سمعت ابا النضر يحدث عن بسر بن سعيد
عن زيد بن ثابت ان النبي صلى الله عليه وسلم احتجر حجرة في المسجد حسبت انه
قال بحصير فصلى فيها النبي صلى الله عليه وسلم ليالي حتى اجتمع اليه الناس ففقدوا
صوته ليلة فظنوا انه نائم فجعل بعضهم يتنحنح ليخرج اليهم

راموز الصفحة الاخيرة من مخطوطة نسخة سهيل بن ابي صالح

The End of The Nuskhah of Suhail

بسم الله الرحمن الرحيم

جزء فيه نسخة عبد العزيز بن المختار البصري
عن سهيل بن أبي صالح عن أبيه عن أبي هريرة
رواية أبي عبيد الله محمد بن عبده
عن ابراهيم بن الحجاج عنه
رواية أبي الحسن علي بن عمر بن محمد بن الحسن الحربي عنه
رواية أبي الحسين محمد بن أحمد بن محمد بن حسنون النرسي عنه
رواية أبي بكر محمد بن عبد الباقي بن محمد بن عبد الله البزاز عنه
رواية أبي الفتوح يوسف بن المبارك بن كامل الخفاف عنه
سماع لمحمد بن عبد الغني المقدسي ولاخوته نفعهم الله به .

بسم الله الرحمن الرحيم

أخبرنا الشيخ ابو الفتوح يوسف بن المبارك بن كامل الخفاف بقراءتي عليه في جمادى الاولى سنة ثمان وتسعين وخمسمائة ، قلت له : أخبركم القاضي ابو بكر محمد بن عبد الباقي البزاز ؟ فأقر به .

أنا ابو الحسين محمد بن أحمد بن النرسي سلخ شهر ربيع الآخر من سنة خمس وخمسين وأربعمائة .

قال : أنا ابو الحسن علي بن عمر بن محمد بن الحسن الحربي قراءة عليه .

قال : نا القاضي ابو عبيد الله محمد بن عبدة بن حرب إملاء .

قال : نا ابراهيم بن الحجاج .

قال : نا عبد العزيز بن المختار .

قال : نا سهيل بن ابي صالح عن أبيه .

١ – عن أبي هريرة عن النبي ﷺ قال :

« لأن يجلس أحدكم على جمرة فتحرق ثيابه حتى تخلص اليه خير له من أن يجلس او يطأ على قبر رجل مسلم » .

٢ ـ حدثنا عبد العزيز بن المختار قال : نا سهيل بن أبي صالح عن أبيه عن أبي هريرة ان النبي ﷺ قال :

« اذا سافرتم في الخصب فأعطوا الابل حقها من الأرض ، واذا سافرتم في الجدب او السنة فأسرعوا السير ، واذا أردتم أن تعرسوا فتنحّوا عن الطريق فإنها مأوى الهوام » .

٣ ـ حدثنا عبد العزيز بن المختار قال : نا سهيل بن أبي صالح عن أبيه عن أبي هريرة ان النبي ﷺ قال :

« إنّما الإمام ليؤتمّ به، فاذا كبّر فكبّروا(١)، واذا ركع فاركعوا، واذا قال: سمع الله لمن حمده فقولوا: اللهم ربنا لك الحمد،واذا سجد فاسجدوا ولا تسجدوا حتى يسجد ، واذا رفع فارفعوا ولا ترفعوا حتى يرفع ، واذا صلى قاعداً فصلوا قعوداً أجمعون » .

٤ ـ حدثنا عبد العزيز بن المختار : نا سهيل بن أبي صالح عن أبيه عن أبي هريرة عن النبي ﷺ (١٥٦ ب) قال :

« اذا قال القارىء : ولا الضالين ، قال الذين خلفه : آمين ، فوافق قولهم قول أهل السماء غفر لهم ما تقدم من ذنوبهم ، واذا قالوا: اللهم ربنا لك الحمد فوافق قولهم قول أهل السماء؛ غفر لهم ما تقدم من ذنوبهم » .

٥ ـ حدثنا عبد العزيز بن المختار : قال نا سهيل بن أبي صالح عن أبيه عن أبي هريرة عن النبي ﷺ قال :

« إن الأرواح جنود مجندة ، فما تعارف [منها] ائتلف، وما تناكرمنها اختلف ».

٦ ـ حدثنا عبد العزيز قال : نا سهيل عن أبيه عن أبي هريرة عن النبي ﷺ قال :

« اذا تكلمت يوم الجمعة فقد لغوت وألغأت » .

---

(١) في الاصل « كبروا »

٧ — حدثنا عبد العزيز بن المختار قال : نا سهيل بن أبي صالح عن أبيه عن ابي هريرة عن النبي ﷺ قال :

« إذا استيقظ أحدكم من منامه فليغسل يده ثلاث مرات فإنه لا يدري أين باتت يده » .

٨ — حدثنا عبد العزيز بن المختار نا سهيل بن أبي صالح عن ابيه عن أبي هريرة عن النبي ﷺ قال : قال الله تعالى :

« عمل ابن آدم كله له. والحسنة بعشر أمثالها، الا الصيام؛ فإنه لي ، وأنا أجزي به . يدع الطعام من أجلي ويدع الشراب من أجلي ويذر اللذة من أجلي . فاذا أصبح أحدكم صائماً فلا يرفث ولا يفسق، فإن سُبَّ فليقل: إني صائم . وللصائم فرحتان: فرحة عند إفطاره، وفرحة يوم يلقى ربه . ولخلوفه أطيب عند الله من ريح المسك » .

٩ — حدثنا عبد العزيز بن المختار : نا سهيل بن أبي صالح عن أبيه عن ابي هريرة عن النبي ﷺ قال :

« من أدرك ركعتين من العصر قبل أن تغيب الشمس فقد أدرك ، ومن أدرك ركعة من صلاة الفجر قبل أن تطلع الشمس فقد أدرك ».

١٠ — حدثنا عبد العزيز بن المختار : نا سهيل بن أبي صالح عن ابيه عن ابي هريرة « ان النبي ﷺ أكل كتف شاة فتمضمض وغسل يده وصلى ».

١١ — حدثنا عبد العزيز بن المختار قال : نا سهيل بن أبي صالح عن ابيه عن ابي هريرة عن النبي ﷺ قال :

« من قال هلك (١٥٧—١) الناس فهو أهلكهم » .

١٢ — حدثنا عبد العزيز بن المختار: نا سهيل بن ابي صالح عن ابيه عن ابي هريرة « ان النبي ﷺ أكل اثوار أقط فتوضأ منه وصلى ».

١٣ ـ حدثنا عبد العزيز بن المختار ، نا سهيل بن ابي صالح عن ابيه عن ابي هريرة عن النبي ﷺ قال :

« إذا أكل أحدكم فليلعق أصابعه ، فإنه لا يدري في أيتهن البركة » .

١٤ ـ حدثنا عبد العزيز بن المختار ، نا سهيل بن ابي صالح عن ابيه عن ابي هريرة قال : قال رسول الله ﷺ يوم خيبر :

« لأدفعن الراية الى رجل يحب الله ورسوله » . فقال عمر : « ما أحببت الامارة قبل يومئذ ، فتطاولت لها واستشرفت رجاء ان يدفعها إليّ » .

فلما كان الغد دعا علياً عليه السلام ، فدفعها إليه ، فقال : « قاتل ولا تلتفت حتى يفتح الله عليك » . فسار قريباً ثم نادى : «يا رسول الله» ! ولم يلتفت : « على ما أقاتل الناس ؟ » قال : « حتى يشهدوا أن لا إلـه إلا الله وأن محمداً رسول الله ، فإذا فعلوا ذلك فقد منعوا دماءهم وأموالهم إلا بحقها وحسابهم على الله » .

١٥ ـ حدثنا عبد العزيز بن المختار قال ، نا سهيل بن ابي صالح عن ابيه عن ابي هريرة عن النبي ﷺ قال :

« ويل للأعقاب من النار يوم القيامة » .

١٦ ـ حدثنا عبد العزيز بن المختار ، نا سهيل بن ابي صالح عن ابيه عن ابي هريرة عن النبي ﷺ قال :

« إذا أحب الله عبداً دعا جبريل فقال : إني أحببت فلاناً فأحبه ، فيحبه جبريل ، ثم ينادى في السماء : أن الله قد أحب فلاناً فأحبوه ، ثم يوضع له القبول في الأرض . وإذا أبغض فمثل ذلك » .

١٧ ـ حدثنا عبد العزيز بن المختار ، نا سهيل عن ابيه عن ابي هريرة عن النبي ﷺ قال :

«ما تقولون في الشهيد فيكم ؟» قالوا : القتيل في سبيل الله . قال : « إن

شهداء أمتي إذاً لقليل . من قتل في سبيل الله فهو شهيد . ومن مات في سبيل الله فهو شهيد ، والمبطون شهيد ، والمطعون شهيد » .

قال سهيل : وأخبرني عبيد الله بن (١٥٧ ب) مقسم عن ابي صالح ، وزاد فيه : « والغرق شهيد » .

١٨ — حدثنا عبد العزيز بن المختار ، نا سهيل بن ابي صالح عن ابيه عن ابي هريرة عن النبي ﷺ قال :

« الايمان بضع وسبعون [١] او قال : بضع وثمانون [٢] جزءاً — شك سهيل — عند الله أفضلها قول : لا إله إلا الله ، وأدناها إماطة الأذى عن الطريق . والحياء شعبة من الايمان » .

١٩ — حدثنا عبد العزيز بن المختار ، نا سهيل بن ابي صالح عن ابيه عن ابي هريرة عن النبي ﷺ قال :

« لا تقوم الساعة حتى يحسر الفرات عن جبل من ذهب . يقاتل عليه الناس فيقتل من كل مائة تسعة وتسعون ، كلهم يرى أنه الذي ينجو » .

٢٠ — حدثنا عبد العزيز بن المختار ، نا سهيل بن ابي صالح عن ابيه عن ابي هريرة قال — قلن النساء — يا رسول الله ! لو جعلت لنا يوماً . فواعدهن بيت فلان او قال : بيت فلانة ، فقال : «ما منكن امرأة تموت لها ثلاثة أولاد الا أدخلها الله الجنة » .

قالت امرأة : يا رسول الله او اثنين . فقال : « او اثنين » .

٢١ — حدثنا عبد العزيز بن المختار ، نا سهيل بن ابي صالح عن ابيه عن ابي هريرة قال : « إن الفقراء شكوا الى رسول الله ﷺ فقالوا : ذهب أهل الدثور بالدرجات العلى والنعيم المقيم . صاحبوك كما صاحبناك ، وجاهدوا كما جاهدنا ، ووجدوا مالاً ينفقون » .

---

(١) على هامش الأصل « في الأصل وسبعين ».

(٢) في الأصل « بضع وثمانين ».

فقال : « أدلكم على شيء إذا قلتموه أدركتم به ما فاتكم ولم يدرككم من بعدكم إلا من قال مثل ما قلتم . تسبحون في دبر كل صلاة وتحمدون وتكبرون ثلاثة وثلاثين » ، أحد عشر أحد عشر أحد عشر (١).

فلما سمع ذلك الأغنياء فعلوا مثل ما فعل الفقراء . فقالت الفقراء : يا رسول الله ! لما سمع الاغنياء قالوا مثل ما قلنا .

قال : « ذلك فضل الله يؤتيه من يشاء » .

٢٢ — حدثنا عبد العزيز بن المختار قال : نا سهيل عن ابيه عن ابي هريرة عن النبي ﷺ قال :

« ينزل الله تبارك وتعالى الى السماء الدنيا ، فيقول : أنا الملك من يدعوني فأستجيب له (١٥٨—١) من يسألني فأعطيه ، ومن يستغفرني فأغفر له ، حتى يضيء الفجر » .

٢٣ — حدثنا عبد العزيز بن المختار قال نا سهيل بن ابي صالح عن ابيه عن ابي هريرة عن النبي ﷺ قال :

« من اطلع في بيت قوم من غير إذنهم فقد حل لهم أن يفقؤا عينه » .

٢٤ — حدثنا عبد العزيز بن المختار ، نا سهيل بن ابي صالح عن ابيه عن ابي هريرة ان فاطمة بنت النبي ﷺ أتت النبي ﷺ تستخدمه خادماً ، فقال لها : « ألا أعلمك ما هو خير لك من الخادم ؟ تسبحين ثلاثاً وثلاثين وتكبرين ثلاثاً وثلاثين ، وتحمدين أربعاً وثلاثين ، إذا أويت الى فراشك » .

٢٥ — حدثنا عبد العزيز بن المختار ، نا سهيل عن ابيه عن ابي هريرة عن النبي ﷺ قال :

---

(١) هكذا في الاصل

« خير صفوف الرجال أولها وشرها آخرها ، وخير صفوف النساء آخرها وشرها أولها » .

٢٦ ـ حدثنا عبد العزيز بن المختار ، نا سهيل بن ابي صالح عن ابيه عن ابي هريرة أن النبي ﷺ قال :

« من صلى على جنازة ثم لم يتبعها فله قيراط ، فإن تبعها فله قيراطان ». قيل : وما القيراط ؟ قال : « أصغرهما مثل أحد » .

٢٧ ـ حدثنا عبد العزيز بن المختار ، نا سهيل بن ابي صالح عن ابيه عن ابي هريرة قال : ان النبي ﷺ نهى عن المزفت والحنتم والنقير .

قال : قيل لابي هريرة : ما الحنتم ؟ قال : الجرار الخضر .

٢٨ ـ حدثنا عبد العزيز بن المختار ، نا سهيل بن ابي صالح عن ابيه عن ابي هريرة عن النبي ﷺ قال :

« إذا صليت الجمعة فصل بعدها أربعاً » .

٢٩ ـ حدثنا عبد العزيز بن المختار ، نا سهيل بن ابي صالح عن ابيه عن ابي هريرة عن النبي ﷺ قال :

« إذا لقيتم أهل الكتاب فلا تبدأوهم بالسلام ، واضطروهم الى أضيق الطرق » .

٣٠ ـ حدثنا عبد العزيز بن المختار ، نا سهيل بن ابي صالح عن ابيه عن ابي هريرة عن النبي ﷺ قال :

« لا تباغضوا ولا تدابروا ولا تنافسوا وكونوا عباد الله إخواناً » .

٣١ ـ حدثنا عبد العزيز بن المختار ، نا سهيل بن ابي صالح عن ابيه عن ابي هريرة عن النبي ﷺ (١٥٨ ب) انه كان يقول إذا آوى الى فراشه : «اللهم رب السماوات ورب الأرض ورب كل شيء ، فالق الحب والنوى ، منزل

التوراة والانجيل والقرآن ، أعوذ بك من شر كل ذي شر ، أنت آخذ بناصيتها ، أنت الأول فليس قبلك شيء ، وأنت الآخر فليس بعدك شيء ، وأنت الظاهر فليس فوقك شيء ، وأنت الباطن فليس دونك شيء ، اقض عني الدين واغنني من الفقر » .

٣٢ — حدثنا عبد العزيز بن المختار ، نا سهيل بن ابي صالح عن ابيه عن ابي هريرة عن النبي ﷺ قال :

« ما اجتمع قوم قط فتفرقوا عن غير ذكر الله إلا كأنما تفرقوا عن جيفة حمار ، وكان ذلك المجلس عليهم حسرة » .

٣٣ — حدثنا عبد العزيز بن المختار ، نا سهيل بن ابي صالح عن ابيه عن ابي هريرة عن النبي ﷺ قال :

« إذا نام احدكم وفي يده غمر فلم يغسل يده . فأصابه شيء ، فلا يلومن إلا نفسه » .

٣٤ — حدثنا عبد العزيز بن المختار ، نا سهيل بن ابي صالح عن ابيه عن أبي هريرة عن النبي ﷺ قال :

« إن لله ملائكة سيارة ، يتبعون مجالس الذكر فإذا وجدوا مجلساً فيه ذكر قعدوا معهم ، وحض بعضهم بعضاً او حضر بعضهم بعضاً — بالشك — حتى يملأ ما بينهم وبين السماء ، فاذا تفرقوا عرجوا وصعدوا الى السماء ، فيسألهم الله ، وهو أعلم . من أين جئتم ؟ فيقولون : جئنا من عند عباد لك في الأرض يسبحونك ويكبرونك ويحمدونك ويهللونك ويسألونك .

قال : ماذا يسألوني ؟ قالوا : يسألونك جنتك . قال : وهل رأوا جنتي ؟ قالوا : لا . قالوا : ويستجيرونك . قال : ومما يستجيرونني ؟ قالوا : من نارك . يا رب . قال : هل رأوا ناري ؟ قالوا : لا يا رب . قال : فكيف لو (١٥٩—١) رأوا ناري ؟ قالوا : ويستغفرونك . قال ، فيقول : قد غفرت

لهم وأعطيتهم ما سألوا ، وأجرتهم مما استجاروا .

قال : فيقولون : يا رب فيهم فلان عبدك الخطّاء إنما مر فجلس معهم . فيقول تبارك وتعالى : وله قد غفرت . هم القوم لا يشقى بهم جليسهم » .

٣٥ — حدثنا عبد العزيز بن المختار ، نا سهيل بن ابي صالح عن ابيه عن ابي هريرة عن النبي ﷺ قال :

« لا يجتمعان في النار اجتماعاً يضر أحدهما » . قالوا : من يا رسول الله ؟ قال : « مؤمن قتل كافراً ثم سدد بعده » .

٣٦ — حدثنا عبد العزيز بن المختار ، نا سهيل بن ابي صالح عن ابيه عن ابي هريرة عن النبي ﷺ قال :

« إن أحدكم ليتصدق بالتمرة من الكسب الطيب فيضعها في حقها فيقبضها بيمينه فيربيها كأحسن ما يربي أحدكم فلوّه ، حتى يكون مثل الجبل او أعظم من الجبل » .

٣٧ — حدثنا عبد العزيز بن المختار ، نا سهيل بن ابي صالح عن ابيه عن ابي هريرة عن النبي ﷺ قال :

« إذا قام أحدكم من مجلسه فرجع إليه فهو أحق به » .

٣٨ — حدثنا عبد العزيز بن المختار ، نا سهيل بن ابي صالح عن ابيه عن ابي هريرة عن النبي ﷺ قال :

« لا يستر عبد على عبد في الدنيا الا ستره الله يوم القيامة » .

٣٩ — حدثنا عبد العزيز بن المختار قال : نا سهيل بن ابي صالح عن ابيه عن ابي هريرة عن النبي ﷺ قال :

« تفتح أبواب السماء ، او قال : أبواب الجنة كل يوم اثنين ويوم خميس

فيغفر في ذلك اليوم لكل عبد لا يشرك بالله شيئاً إلا امرءاً كان بينه وبين أخيه شحناء [1] ، فيقول : انظروا هذين حتى يصطلحا » .

٤٠ ـــ حدثنا عبد العزيز بن المختار ، نا سهيل بن ابي صالح عن ابيه عن (١٥٩ ب) ابي هريرة عن النبي ﷺ قال :

« من أخذ شبراً من الأرض بغير حقه طوقه من سبع أرضين » .

٤١ ـــ حدثنا عبد العزيز بن المختار ، نا سهيل بن ابي صالح عن ابيه عن ابي هريرة عن النبي ﷺ قال :

« مر رجل من المسلمين بجزل شوك في الطريق فقال : لأميطن هذا الشوك عن الطريق ، لا يعقر رجلاً ـــ مسلماً يعني ـــ فغفر له » .

٤٢ ـــ حدثنا عبد العزيز بن المختار ، نا سهيل بن ابي صالح عن ابيه عن ابي هريرة عن النبي ﷺ قال :

« لا تجعلوا بيوتكم مقابر ، فإن الشيطان يفر من البيت الذي تقرأ فيه سورة البقرة » .

٤٣ ـــ حدثنا عبد العزيز بن المختار ، قال ، نا سهيل بن ابي صالح عن ابيه عن ابي هريرة قال : قال رسول الله ﷺ :

« ليس السنة ان لا تمطروا ولكن السنة ان تمطروا وتمطروا ولا تنبت الأرض شيئاً » .

٤٤ ـــ حدثنا عبد العزيز بن المختار ، نا سهيل بن ابي صالح عن ابيه عن ابي هريرة قال : قال رسول الله ﷺ :

« لا تقوم الساعة حتى يمطر الناس مطراً لا يكنّ منه بيوت المدر ولا يكنّ منه بيوت الشعر » .

---

(١) في الأصل (شحباء) .

٤٥ ـ حدثنا عبد العزيز بن المختار قال : نا سهيل بن ابي صالح عن ابيه عن ابي هريرة قال : أتى رسول الله ﷺ ناس من أصحابه فقالوا : يا رسول الله إنا نجد في أنفسنا الشيء يتعاظم عند أحدنا أن يتكلم به .

قال : « أوقد وجدتموه » ؟ قالوا : نعم . قال «ذاك صريح الايمان» .

٤٦ ـ حدثنا عبد العزيز بن المختار ، نا سهيل بن ابي صالح عن ابيه عن ابي هريرة قال : قال رسول الله ﷺ :

« لا تصحب الملائكة رفقة فيها جرس ولا كلب » .

٤٧ ـ حدثنا عبد العزيز ، نا سهيل بن ابي صالح عن ابيه عن ابي هريرة قال : قال رسول الله ﷺ :

« لا تقوم الساعة حتى يقاتل المسلمون اليهود فيقتلهم المسلمون حتى يختبىء (١٦٠ـ١) اليهودي وراء الحجر او الشجرة فيقول الحجر او الشجرة : يا مسلم يا عبد الله هذا يهودي ورائي فتعال فاقتله ، الا شجرة قد سماها فإنها من شجر اليهود » .

٤٨ ـ حدثنا عبد العزيز بن المختار ، نا سهيل بن أبي صالح عن أبيه عن أبي هريرة قال : قال رسول الله ﷺ :

« لا تقوم الساعة حتى يأتي الرجل بزكاة ماله فلا يجد من يقبلها منه » .

٤٩ ـ حدثنا عبد العزيز بن المختار ، قال نا سهيل بن أبي صالح عن أبيه عن أبي هريرة عن النبي ﷺ قال :

« اذا تكلمت يوم الجمعة فقد لغوت وألغيت » (١) .

آخر نسخة سهيل بن أبي صالح

---

(١) بهامش الأصل « مكرر » .

التعليقات على نسخة سهيل

الحديث رقم (١)

الرواة عن ابي هريرة أبو صالح :

تلاميذ أبي صالح

سهيل وعنه :

١ – جرير	م جنائز ٩٦
٢ – حماد	حم ٥٢٨/٢
٣ – خالد	دجنائز ٧٣
٤ – سفيان	م جنائز ٩٦ ، حم ٤٤٤/٢ ، ن جنائز ١٠٥
٥ – شريك	حم ٣١١/٢
٦ – عبد العزيز بن أبي حازم	جه جنائز ٤٥
٧ – عبد العزيز الدراوردي	م جنائز ٩٦
٨ – عبد العزيز بن المختار	الأصل/١
٩ – وهيب	حم ٣٨٩/٢

الشواهد :

(١) – أبو مرثد الغنوي : بسر بن عبيد الله – واثلة بن الأسقع – عنه . د جنائز ٧٣ ، ت جنائز ٥٧ ، م جنائز ٩٨ ، ٩٧ ، عوانة ٣٩٨/١ ، الكشي ١/٥٦ ، يعلى ١/٨٧ .

(٢) – جابر : ابن جريج – ابو الزبير – عنه .م جنائز ٩٤ ، الكشي ١٢٠/ب ، ت جنائز ٥٨ ، المستدرك ٣٧٠/١ .

(٣) – عقبة بن عامر : الليث بن سعد – يزيد بن أبي حبيب – مرثد بن عبد الله – عنه جه جنائز ٤٥ .

(٤) – عمرو بن حزم : ابن. أبي هلال – أبو بكر بن حزم– النضر بن عبد الله السلمي عنه ن جنائز ١٠٥ .

مقارنة الروايات :

١ ـ الروايات عن أبي هريرة: لم أجد متابعاً لسهيل في هذه الرواية . وروى عن سهيل عدة أشخاص ، بعضهم يتفق مع البعض تماماً ، وتوجد الفروق أحياناً في رواية الآخرين، مثلا ورد في إحدى الروايات كلمة : « قبر رجل مسلم »، بينما في الأخرى لم ترد كلمة « مسلم » ، وحذف بعض الرواة كلمات مثل : « حتى تخلص إليه » . اتفق الرواة الى حد كبير في كلمات الرواية ، وكذلك اتفقوا في المعنى .

٢ ـ عامة الروايات : الروايات الأخرى عن الصحابة الآخرين تتفق مع رواية أبي هريرة على عدم استحباب الجلوس على القبر ، كما تتفق رواية عقبة بن عامر في التغليظ على الجلوس على القبور .

أسماء الرواة :

الطبقة الاولى :

١ ـ أبو مرثد الغنوي . ٢ ـ أبو هريرة . ٣ ـ جابر .
٤ ـ عقبة بن عامر . ٥ ـ عمرو بن حزم .

الطبقة الثانية :

١ ـ أبو صالح . ٢ ـ أبو الزبير . ٣ ـ مرثد بن عبد الله .
٤ ـ النضر بن عبد الله ٥ ـ واثلة بن الأسقع .

الطبقة الثالثة :

١ ـ أبو بكر بن حزم . ٢ ـ بسر بن عبد الله . ٣ ـ ابن جريج .
٤ ـ سهيل . ٥ ـ يزيد بن حبيب .

الرواية عن أكثر من شيخ: لا يوجد رجل واحد بين رواة هذه الأحاديث يروي عن أكثر من شيخ .

وروده في مسند ابن حنبل : أربع مرات عن طريق أبي هريرة .

الحديث رقم (٢)

الرواية عن ابي هريرة : أبو صالح .

تلاميذ أبي صالح :

سهيل وعنه :

١ ـ جرير	م الامارة ١٧٨ .
٢ ـ حماد بن سلمة	حم ٢/٣٣٧ ، د جهاد ٥٧
٣ ـ عبد العزيز بن محمد	حم ٢/٣٧٨، م الامارة /١٧٨، ت ادب ٧٥ .
٤ ـ عبد العزيز بن المختار	الأصل ٢

الشواهد :

(١) – أنس بن مالك : ليث بن سعد – عقيل – الزهري – عنه
يعلى ١٧١/ ب ، بغداد ٤٢٩/٨ .

(٢) – جابر بن عبد الله : محمد بن سلمة – هشام – الحسن – عنه
حم ٣٠٥/٣ ، دجهاد ٥٧ .

مقارنة الروايات :

١ – الروايات عن أبي هريرة: لم أجد متابعاً لسهيل . وروى عن سهيل عدة أشخاص. ألفاظهم متقاربة ، وهم متفقون في المعنى . لقد حذف بعض الرواة بعض الكلمات أو غير كلمة بأخرى مثل تنحوا / تنكبوا ، حقها / حظها .

٢ – عامة الروايات : بين عامة الروايات تشابه كبير في الكلمات ، وكثير من الكلمات ترد في كل الروايات ، كما يوجد الاتفاق في المعنى العام .

أسماء الرواة :

الطبقة الأولى :

١ – أبو هريرة . ٢ – أنس بن مالك . ٣ – جابر بن عبد الله

الطبقة الثانية :

١ – أبو صالح . ٢ – الحسن . ٣ – الزهري .

الطبقة الثالثة :

١ – سهيل . ٢ – عقيل . ٣ – هشام .

الرواية عن أكثر من شيخ : لا يوجد رجل واحد بين رواة هذه الأحاديث يروي عن أكثر من مصدر .

وروده في مسند ابن حنبل : مرتين عن طريق أبي هريرة ومرة واحدة عن طريق الآخرين .

الحديث رقم (٣)

الرواة عن أبي هريرة :

١ – أبو سلمة . ٢ – أبو صالح . ٣ – أبو علقمة .
٤ – أبو يونس . ٥ – الأعرج . ٦ – عجلان .
٧ – همام بن منبه .

١ – تلاميذ أبي سلمة :

أ – عمرو بن أبي سلمة — يعلى ١/٢٧٢

ب – محمد بن عمرو — حم ٢/٢٣٠، ٤١١، ٤٧٥ دي صلاة ٧١، جه إقامة ١٤٤

٢ – تلاميذ أبي صالح :

أ – الأعمش — حم ٢/٤٤٠ ، م صلاة ٨٧ ، عوانة ٢/١١٠ .

ب – زيد بن أسلم — حم ٢/٤٢٠ ، ن افتتاح ٣٠ ، جه إقامة ١٣ ، د صلاة ٦٨ ، الدارقطني ١٢٤ ، ١٢٥ .

جـ – سهيل بن أبي صالح — الأصل/٣ .

د – مصعب بن شرحبيل — الدارقطني ١٢٥ ، طط ٢/٦٦ ب « وفيه محمد بن شرحبيل » .

هـ – مصعب بن محمد — حم ٢/٣٤١ ، د صلاة ٦٨.

٣ – تلاميذ أبي علقمة : يعلى بن عطاء — حم ٢/٤٦٧ ، عوانة ٢/١٠٩ – ١١٠ ، م صلاة ٨٨ م صلاة ٨٩ .

٤ – تلاميذ أبي يونس : حيوة

٥ – تلاميذ الأعرج : أبو الزناد — م صلاة ٨٦ ، خ أذان ٨٢ ، عوانة ٢/١٠٩، يعلى ٢٨٨ ب .

٦ – تلاميذ عجلان : محمد بن عجلان — حم ٢/٣٧٦ .

٧ – تلاميذ همام بن منبه : معمر — صحيفة همام حديث /٤٣، حم ٢/٣١٤، خ أذان٧٤ .

الشواهد :

(١) أبو أمامة : سليم بن عامر – عفير بن معدان – أبو أمامة طك ١/٢٧٨/٤ .

(٢) أبو موسى الأشعري : يونس بن جبير – حطان الرقاشي – عنه حم٤/٤٠١ ، ٤٠٥ ، ٤٠٩ ، طس ٥١٧ ، ن تطبيق ٢٣ ، الأئمة ٣٨ ، دي صلاة ٧١ ، عوانة ٢/١٢٨ – ١٣٠ .

(٣) أسيد بن حضير : محمد بن صالح –حصين – عنه د صلاة ٦٨ .

(٤) تلاميذ أنس بن مالك : ١ – حميد الطويل . ٢ – الزهري .

١ – تلاميذ حميد الطويل : يزيد بن هارون خ صلاة ١٨ .

٢ – تلاميذ الزهري :

أ – ابراهيم بن أبي عبد — طط ١/٢١٠/الف .

ب – ابن جريج — عوانة ٢/١٠٦ .

جـ – سفيان — حم ٣/١١٠ ، ن أئمة ١٦ ، تطبيق ٢٢ ، الحميدي /١١٨٩ ، جه إقامة ١٤٤ ، م صلاة ٧٧ ، خ أذان ١٢٨ ، عوانة ٢/٦ – ١٠٥ ، يعلى ١٦٨ ب ، ١/١٧٠

د – شعيب   خ أذان ٨٢ ، عوانه ١٠٧/٢ .

هـ – الليث   خ أذان ٨٢ ، م صلاة ٧٨ ، ت صلاة ١٥٠ ، عوانه ١٠٦/٢ .

و – مالك   ط جماعة ١٦ ، خ أذان ٥١ ، م صلاة ٨٠ ، ن أئمة ٤٠ ، د صلاة ٦٨ ، ، عوانة ١٠٦/٢ .

ز – معمر   حم ١٦٢/٣ ، م صلاة ٨١ ، عوانة ١٠٦/٢ ، الكشي ١/١٣٣ .

ح – يونس   م صلاة ٧٩ .

(٥) تلاميذ جابر :

١ – ابراهيم بن عبد الله   ٢ – أبو الزبير   ٣ – أبو سفيان .

١ – تلاميذ ابراهيم بن عبد الله : خالد بن اياس   الكشي ١٣١/ب

٢ – تلاميذ أبي الزبير :

أ – عبد الرحمن الرواسي   م صلاة ٨٥ ، عوانه ١٠٩/٢ .

ب – الليث   حم ٣٣٤/٣ ، د صلاة ٦٨ ، جه إقامة ١٤٤ ، م صلاة ٨٤ ، عوانة ١٠٨/٢ .

٣ – تلاميذ أبي سفيان : الأعمش   حم ٣٠٠/٣ ، يعلى ١/١٠٣ ، خزيمة ١٦٩ ب ، موارد الظمآن ١٠٨ .

(٦) تلاميذ عائشة : عروة

تلاميذ عروة : هشام وعنه :

١ – ابن نمير   حم ٥٨/٦ – ٥٧ ، م صلاة ٨٣ .

٢ – حماد بن زيد   حم ٦٨/٦ .

٣ – عبد الله بن عبد الحكم   عوانة ١٠٧/٢ .

٤ – عبدة بن سليمان   جه إقامة ١٤٤ ، م صلاة ٨٢ .

٥ – مالك   ط جماعة ١٧ ، حم ١٤٨/٦ ، د صلاة ٦٨ ، عوانة ١٠٨/٢ ، خ أذان ٥١ ، تقصير الصلاة ١٧ ، سهو ٩ ، مرض ١٢ .

٦ – يحيى   حم ٥١/٦ ، ١٩٤ ، عوانة ٨/٢ – ١٠٧ .

(٧) عبد الله بن عمر
(٨) قيس بن فهد
(٩) معاوية
} روى هؤلاء أيضاً هذا الحديث .

يوجد هذا الحديث في مصدر إباضي أيضاً

أبو عبيدة – جابر – أنس ، مسند الربيع ٧/١ – ٦٦ .

مقارنة الروايات :

الروايات عن أبي هريرة : الحديث طويل ويختلف الرواة أحياناً في ترتيب الجمل ، ويحذف بعضهم بعض الكلمات التي لا تؤثر في المعنى . وأكثر الروايات تقريباً متحد في الألفاظ مع الاختلاف في ترتيب الجمل . وقطع بعض المؤلفين هذا الحديث فأثبتوه في أمكنة مختلفة . وتوجد في رواية زيد بن أسلم كلمة زائدة « واذا قرأ فأنصتوا » حم ٢/٤٢٠ . وهي مثار جدل عند الفقهاء .

٢ ــ الروايات عن الصحابة الآخرين : كل الرواياتمتفقة في المعنى بعضها يذكرواقعة مرض رسول الله (ص)، والأخرى تذكر حادثة سقوطه عن الفرس ، والبعض الآخر يذكر الأحاديث فقط بدون ذكر الحادثة ورواية أبي هريرة من هذا القبيل .

أسماء الرواة :

الطبقة الأولى :

١ ــ أبو هريرة (المدينة) ٢ ــ أبو أمامة (الشام) ٣ ــ أبوموسى الأشعري (البصرة)
٤ ــ أسيد بن حضير (المدينة) ٥ ــ أنس بن مالك (البصرة) ٦ ــ جابر (المدينة) .
٧ ــ عائشة (المدينة) .

الطبقة الثانية :

١ ــ أبو الزبير (المدينة) ٢ ــ أبو سفيان (مكة) . ٣ ــ أبو سلمة (المدينة)
٤ ــ أبو صالح (المدينة) . ٥ ــ أبو علقمة (مصر) ٦ ــ أبو يونس (مصر) .
٧ ــ ابراهيم بن عبدالله (المدينة) ٨ ــ الأعرج (المدينة) .
٩ ــ حصين من ولد سعد بن معاذ (المدينة) ١٠ ــ حطان الرقاشي (البصرة)
١١ ــ حميد الطويل (البصرة) . ١٢ ــ الزهري (المدينة) .
١٣ ــ عجلان (المدينة) . ١٤ ــ عروة (المدينة) . ١٥ ــ عفير بن معدان (حمص) .
١٦ ــ همام بن منبه (اليمن) .

الطبقة الثالثة :

١ ــ أبو الزناد (المدينة) . ٢ ــ ابراهيم بن أبي عبد . ٣ ــ ابن جريج (مكة) .
٤ ــ الأعمش (الكوفة) . ٥ ــ حيوة (مصر) . ٦ ــ خالد بن أياس (المدينة)
٧ ــ زيد بن أسلم (المدينة) ٨ ــ سفيان بن عيينة (مكة) ٩ ــ سليم بن عامر (الشام)
١٠ ــ سهيل بن أبي صالح (المدينة) ١١ ــ شعيب (حمص) ١٢ ــ عبد الرحمن الرواسي (الكوفة)
١٣ ــ عمرو بن أبي سلمة (دمشق) ١٤ ــ الليث (مصر) ١٥ ــ مالك (المدينة)
١٦ ــ محمد بن صالح (المدينة) ١٧ ــ محمد بن عجلان (المدينة) ١٨ ــ محمدبن عمرو (المدينة)
١٩ ــ مصعب بن شرحبيل (مكة) ٢٠ ــ مصعب بن محمد (مكة) ٢١ ــ معمر (اليمن)

٢٢ – هشام (المدينة) ٢٣ – يزيد بن هارون (واسط) ٢٤ – يعلى بن عطاء (الطائف)
٢٥ – يونس بن جبير (البصرة) ٢٦ – يونس بن يزيد (الشام)

الرواية عن اكثر من شيخ: من ٢٦ (ستة وعشرين) شخصاً الأعمش والليث ومعمر ثلاثة أشخاص فقط يروون عن شيخين ، والبقية كلهم عن شيخ واحد

وروده في مسند ابن حنبل : ٩ (تسع) مرات عن طريق أبي هريرة ، و١٢ (اثنتي عشرة) مرة عن طريق الآخرين .

الحديث رقم (٤)

الرواة عن أبي هريرة :

١ – أبو سلمة . ٢ – أبو صالح . ٣ – أبو علقمة .
٤ – أبو يونس . ٥ – ابن المسيب . ٦ – الأعرج .
٧ – كعب بن زياد . ٨ – نعيم ٩ – همام بن منبه .

١ – تلاميذ أبي سلمة :
أ – الزهري وعنه الزبيدي ن افتتاح ٣٣
ب – محمد بن عمرو خ أذان ١١٣ ، دي صلاة ٣٨ ، حم ٢/٥٠–٤٤٩

٢ – تلاميذ أبي صالح :
أ – الأعمش عوانة ٢/١١٠ ، حم ٢/٤٤٠ .
ب – سمي وعنه مالك ط صلاة ٤٥ ، خ تفسير سورة ١/٢ ، أذان ١١٣ حم ٢/٤٥٩ ، ن افتتاح ٣٤ ، د صلاة ١٦٧ .

جـ – سهيل وعنه :
١ – عبد العزيز بن المختار الأصل ٤
٢ – يعقوب م صلاة ٧٦
٣ – سليمان بن بلال عوانة ٢/٣١ – ١٣٠
٤ – خالد بن عبد الله عوانة ٢/١٣١

٣ – تلاميذ أبي علقمة : يعلى بن عطاء عوانة ٢/١٠ – ١٠٩
٤ – تلاميذ أبي يونس : عمرو م صلاة ٧٤ ، عوانة ٢/١٣١
٥ – تلاميذ ابن المسيب :
الزهري وعنه :
١ – معمر ن افتتاح ٣٣ ، حم ٢/٢٧٠
٢ – سفيان ن افتتاح ٣٣ ، الحميدي ٩٣٣ ، عوانة ٢/١٣٠ جه اقامة ١٤ ، خ دعوات ٦٣ ، حم ٢/٢٣٨ ، يعلى ١/٢٧١ .
٣ – يونس خزيمة ١٦٦ ب .

ابن المسيب وأبي سلمة: الزهري و عنه :

١ – معمر	دي صلاة ٣٨ ، حم ٢٣٣/٢
٢ – يونس	جه اقامة ١٤ ، عوانة ١٣٠/٢
٣ – مالك	ن افتتاح ٣٣ ، ط صلاة ٤٤ ، م صلاة ٧٢ ، ٧٣ ت صلاة ٧١ ، خ أذان ١١١ ، عوانة ١٣٠/٢ ، د صلاة ١٦٧ .

٦ – تلاميذ : الأعرج أبو الزناد وعنه :

١ – مالك	ن افتتاح ٣٥ ، ط صلاة ٤٦ ، خ أذان ١١٢ ، حم ٤٥٩/٢
٢ – المغيرة	م صلاة ٧٥
٧ – تلاميذ كعب بن زياد : ليث بن أبي سليم	راهوية ٤٦ .
٨ – نعيم المجمر	ذكره البخاري معلقاً خ أذان ١١٣
٩ – تلاميذ همام : معمر	م صلاة ٧٥ ، حم ٣١٢/٢ ، عوانة ١٣١/٢ .

الشواهد :

(١) أبو موسى الأشعري: يونس بن جبير – حطان بن عبد الله الرقاشي – عنه حم ٤٠١/٤ ، ٤٠٥ ، ٤٠٩ طس ٥١٧ ، ن تطبيق ٢٣ ، الأئمة ٣٨ ، دي صلاة ٧١ ، عوانة ٣٠/٢ – ١٢٨ خزيمة ١٦٦ ب .

(٢) ابن عباس: طلحة بن عمرو – عطاء – عنه . جه اقامة ١٤ .

(٣) ابن عمر: نافع – عنه . خ أذان ١١١ معلقاً .

(٤) أنس بن مالك: حرمي بن عمارة – زرعي مولى لآل المهلب – عنه . خزيمة ١٦٧/١

(٥) بلال :عاصم – أبو عثمان — عنه كان يقول : يا رسول الله « لا تسبقني بآمين » . د صلاة ١٦٧ ، المستدرك ٢١٩/١

(٦) سمرة بن جندب : قتادة – الحسن – عنه طك ٢١٣/٤

(٧) عائشة : سهيل – أبو صالح – عنه . جه اقامة ١٤ .

مقارنة الروايات :

١ – الروايات عن أبي هريرة : اتفق الرواة على قول المأمومين « آمين » بعد قراءة الامام (ولا الضالين) . ووجود الاختلاف في بعض الكلمات أدى الى الاختلاف بين الفقهاء هل يؤمن مع الامام أو بعد الامام ؟ ؛ اذ ورد في بعض الروايات « اذا أمن الامام فأمنوا »، وروى بعض تلامذة أبي هريرة جزءاً من هذا الحديث الخاص بالتأمين فقط .

٢ ـ مقارنة عامة الروايات عن الصحابة الآخرين : لا توجدالروايات المروية عن الصحابة الآخرين بسياق أبي هريرة ، لكن الروايات المذكورة عن سبعة من الصحابة تتفق مع رواية أبي هريرة على فضيلة التأمين .

أسماء الرواة :

الطبقة الاولى :

١ – أبو هريرة	٢ – أبو موسى الأشعري	٣ – ابن عباس
٤ – ابن عمر	٥ – انس بن مالك	٦ – بلال
٧ – سمرة بن جندب	٨ – عائشة .	

الطبقة الثانية :

١ – أبوسلمة	٢ – أبو صالح	٣ – أبو عثمان
٤ – أبو علقمة	٥ – أبو يونس المصري	٦ – ابن المسيب
٧ – الأعرج	٨ – حسن	٩ – حطان بن عبدالله الرقاشي
١٠ – زرعى	١١ – عطاء	١٢ – كعب بن زياد
١٣ – نعيم بن محمد	١٤ – همام	

الطبقة الثالثة :

١ – أبو الزناد	٢ – الأعمش	٣ – الزهري
٤ – حرمى بن عمارة	٥ – سهيل بن أبي صالح	٦ – سمى
٧ – طلحة بن عمرو	٨ – عاصم	٩ – عمرو
١٠ – قتادة	١١ – الليث بن أبي سليم	١٢ – محمد بن عمرو
١٣ – معمر	١٤ – يعلى	١٥ – يونس

الرواية عن أكثر من شيخ : يوجد راو واحد – أبو صالح – مشترك بين عائشة وأبي هريرة . وكذلك لم يرو عنه عن عائشة الا ابنه سهيل بن أبي صالح.

وروده في مسند ابن حنبل : ٨ (ثماني) مرات عن طريق أبي هريرة ، و ٣ (ثلاث) مرات عن طريق الآخرين .

الحديث رقم (٥)

الرواة عن أبي هريرة :

١ – أبو صالح ٢ – يزيد بن الأصم .

١ – تلاميذ أبي صالح : سهيل وعنه :

١ – حماد بن سلمة حم ٢٩٥/٢ ، ٥٢٧ .
٢ – عبد العزيز بن محمد م البر ١٥٩ .
٣ – عبد العزيز بن المختار الأصل /٥ .

٢ – تلاميذ ابن الأصم : جعفر بن برقان حم ٥٣٩/٢ ، م البر ١٦٠ ، د ادب ١٦ .

الشواهد :

١ – ابن مسعود ٢ – سلمان ٣ – عائشة ٤ – علي بن أبي طالب ٥ – أبو عبدالله .

(١) ابن مسعود : سليمان بن بلال – عمن لا يتهمه – عنه . ابن وهب /٤٠ .

(٢) سلمان :

أ – عيسى بن يونس – الحجاج بن فرافصة – ابن عمر – عنه . طك ١٥٥/٣/ألف

ب – عكرمة – الحارث بن عميرة – عنه . طك ١٥٥/٣/ أ ، ب ، بغداد ٢٠٦/٨

(٣) عائشة : يحيى بن سعيد – عمرة – عنه . خ أنبياء ٢ (معلقا) يعلى ٢٠٢/١

(٤) علي بن أبي طالب : سالم بن عبد الله – عبد الله بن عمر – ان عمر سأل علياً. طط ١٨/٢ ب

(٥) أبو عبد الله : حبيب – عمن رواه – عن أبي عبد الله . علل الشرائع ٨٠/١

مقارنة الروايات :

الروايات كلها متفقة في المعنى وتكاد تكون موحدة الألفاظ .

ملحوظة : الشاهد الخامس مصدر شيعي .

أسماء الرواة :

الطبقة الأولى :

١ – أبو هريرة . ٢ – ابن مسعود . ٣ – سلمان .
٤ – عائشة . ٥ – علي ٦ – أبو عبد الله .

الطبقة الثانية :

١ – أبو صالح . ٢ – ابن عمر . ٣ – الحارث بن عميرة
٤ – عمرة . ٥ – رجلان غير مسميين .

الطبقة الثالثة :

١ – جعفر بن برقان . ٢ – الحجاج بن فرافصة ٣ – سالم بن عبد الله
٤ – سليمان بن بلال . ٤ – سهيل بن أبي صالح ٦ – عكرمة .

وروده في مسند ابن حنبل: ٣ (ثلاث) مرات عن طريق أبي هريرة .

الحديث رقم (٦)

الرواة عن أبي هريرة :

١ – أبو صالح . ٢ – الأعرج . ٣ – سعيد بن المسيب .
٤ – عبد الله بن ابراهيم القارظ ٥ – همام بن منبه .

١ – تلاميذ أبي صالح : سهيل وعنه :

١ – عبد العزيز بن المختار	الأصل ٦
٢ – وهيب	حم ٣٨٨/٢ ، خزيمة ١٨٩ ب – ١/١٩٠

٢ – تلاميذ الأعرج : أبو الزناد وعنه :

١ – سفيان	حميدي ٩٦٦ ، م جمعة ١٢ ، المنتقى ٢٩٩ ، خزيمة ١/١٩٠
٢ – مالك	ط جمعة ٦ ، دي صلاة ١٩٥ .

٣ – تلاميذ سعيد بن المسيب : الزهري وعنه :

١ – ابن جريج	خزيمة ١/١٩٠
٢ – ابن أبي ذئب	جه اقامة ٨٦ ، حم ٣٩٣/٢ ، ٥٣٢ .
٣ – عقيل	خ جمعه ٣٦ ، ت جمعه ٢٢ ، م جمعه ١١ ، خزيمة ١/١٩٠
٤ – مالك	د صلاة ٢٢٧ ، جه اقامة ٨٦ ، دي صلاة ١٩٥ ، حم ٢٨٠/٢ ، ٤٧٤ ، ٥٣٢ .
٥ – معمر	دي صلاة ١٩٥
٦ – يونس	خزيمة ١/١٩٠
٧ – أبو أويس	حم ٣٩٦/٢

٤ – تلاميذ عبد الله بن ابراهيم القارظ : عمر بن عبد العزيز وعنه :

١ – الزهري	م جمعه ١١ ، ن جمعه ٢٢ ، يعلى ١/٢٧٠ ، خزيمة ١/١٩٠

٥ – تلاميذ همام بن منبه : معمر صحيفة همام ١٢٠ ، حم ٢/ ٢٨٠ ، ٣١٨ .

الشواهد :

١ – ابي بن كعب . ٢ – أوس بن أوس . ٣ – جابر . ٤ – سلمان . ٥ – علي . ٦ – عبد الله ابن عمرو . ٧ – أبو عبد الله .

(١) أبي بن كعب : شريك – عطاء بن يسار – عنه . جه اقامة ٨٦ ، ابن خزيمة ١/١٩٠

(٢) أوس بن أوس : عبد الرحمن بن يزيد – أبو الأشعث – عنه . المستدرك ٢١٨/١

(٣) جابر : يعقوب – عيسى بن جارية – عنه . يعلى ١٠٠ ب

(٤) سلمان : علقمة – القرثع الضبي – عنه . ن جمعة ٢٣ ، خ جمعة ٣٦ (معلقا) .
(٥) علي : عطاء الخراساني – عن مولى امرأته – عنه . حم ٩٣/١
(٦) عبد الله بن عمرو : عمرو بن شعيب – أبوه – عنه . د صلاة ٢٢٧
(٧) أبو عبد الله : العلاء – محمد بن مسلم – عن أبي عبد الله . الكافي ٤٢١/٣

مقارنة الروايات :

١ – الروايات عن أبي هريرة: يوجد بعض الاختلاف في الألفاظ ، أما من حيث المعنى فلا .

٢ – الروايات عن الصحابة الآخرين : ذكرت في بعض الروايات القصة مع النهي عن الكلام والوعيد عليه والترغيب في الانصات .

ملحوظة : المصدر رقم /٧ مصدر شيعي .

أسماء الرواة :

الطبقة الأولى :

أبو هريرة	٢ – أبي بن كعب .	٣ – أوس بن أوس .
٤ – جابر .	٥ – سلمان .	٦ – علي بن أبي طالب .
٧ – عبد الله بن عمرو .	٨ – أبو عبد الله .	

الطبقة الثانية :

١ – أبو الأشعث .	٢ – أبو صالح .	٣ – الأعرج .
٤ – رجل غير مسمى .	٥ – سعيد بن المسيب .	٦ – شعيب .
٧ – عبدالله بن ابراهيم القارظ	٨ – عطاء بن يسار .	٩ – عيسى بن جارية .
١٠ – القرثع الضبي	١١ – محمد بن مسلم .	١٢ – همام .

الطبقة الثالثة :

١ – أبو الزناد .	٢ – الزهري.	٣ – سهيل .
٤ – شريك .	٥ – عبد الرحمن بن زيد .	٦ – عطاء الخراساني .
٧ – العلاء .	٨ – علقمة .	٩ – عمر بن عبد العزيز .
١٠ – عمرو بن شعيب .	١١ – معمر .	١٢ – يعقوب .

الرواية عن أكثر من شيخ : الزهري يروي عن كل من ابن المسيب وعمر بن عبد العزيز . ولم أجد لهما راوياً غير الزهري .

وروده في مسند ابن حنبل: ٩ (تسع) مرات عن طريق أبي هريرة ، ومرة واحدة عن طريق الآخرين .

الحديث رقم (٧)

الرواة عن أبي هريرة :

١ – أبو رزين . ٢ – أبو سلمة . ٣ – أبو صالح .
٤ – أبو العلاء . ٥ – أبو مريم . ٦ – ابن المسيب .
٧ – الأعرج . ٨ – ثابت . ٩ – جابر .
١٠ – عبد الله بن شقيق . ١١ – محمد . ١٢ – موسى بن يسار .
١٣ – همام .

١ – تلاميذ أبي رزين : الأعمش طط ١/٢١٤/١

٢ – تلاميذ أبي سلمة :

أ – الزهري م طهارة ٨٧، الحميدي /٩٥١ ، حم ٢٤١/٢ ٢٥٩ عوانة ٢٦٣/١ ، يعلى ١/٢٧٤/١، خزيمة ١٦

ب – محمد بن عمرو حم ٣٨٢/٢ ، يعلى ١/٢٧٤

٣ – تلاميذ أبي صالح :

أ – الأعمش طس ٢٤١٨ ، د طهارة ٤٩ ، حم ٢٥٣/٢ ، عوانة ٢٦٤/١ ، الأعمش ١٠ .

ب – سهيل الأصل ٠٧

جـ – زائدة حم ٢٥٣/٢ .

أبو رزين وأبو صالح وعنهما الأعمش م طهارة ٨٧ ، د طهارة ٤٩ ، حم ٢٥٣/٢ ، ٤٧١ ، الأعمش ١٠، عوانة ٢٦٤/١ .

٤ – تلاميذ أبي العلاء : ابن العلاء م طهارة ٨٨ ، عوانة ٢٦٥/١ .

٥ – تلاميذ أبي مريم : معاوية بن صالح د طهارة ٤٩ ، الدارقطني ١٩ ، حم ١٥ .

٦ – تلاميذ ابن المسيب :

أ – الزهري حم ٢٦٥/٢ ، ٢٨٤ ، م طهارة ٨٧ ، عوانة ٢٦٤/١ ن غسل ٢٩ .

ب – سالم الخياط طط ٢/٥٤/١

ابن المسيب وأبوسلمة وعنهما الزهري وعنه الأوزاعي ت طهارة ١٩ ، جه طهارة ٤٠ .

٧ – تلاميذ الأعرج : أبو الزناد وعنه :

١ – مالك ط طهارة ٩ ، خ وضوء ٢٦ ، حم ٤٦٥/٢ .

٢ – المغيرة م طهارة ٨٨

٣ – سفيان الحميدي ٩٥٢ ، عوانة ٢٦٣/١

٨ – تلاميذ ثابت مولى عبد الرحمن :

زياد م طهارة ٨٨ ، حم ٢٧١/٢ ، عوانة ٥/١ – ٢٦٤

٩ – تلاميذ جابر : أبو الزبير — م طهارة ٨٨ ، حم ٤٠٣/٢ ، عوانة ٤/١ – ٢٦٣ ، يعلى ٢٧٠ ب .

١٠ – تلاميذ عبد الله بن شقيق :
خالد الحذاء — م طهارة ٨٧ ، حم ٤٥٥/٢ ، عوانة ٢٦٣/١ ، خزيمة ١٦ ب ، الدارقطني ١٨ .

١١ – تلاميذ محمد :
أ – هشام — م طهارة ٨٨ .
ب – عوف — حم ٣٩٥/٢ .

١٢ – تلاميذ موسى بن يسار :
محمد بن اسحاق — حم ٥٠٠/٢

١٣ – تلاميذ همام بن منبه : معمر — م طهارة ٨٨ ، عوانة ٢٦٤/١ .

الشواهد :

١ – ابن عمر . ٢ – جابر . – ٣ – عائشة . ٤ – علي .

(١) ابن عمر : الزهري – سالم – عنه . جه طهارة ٤٠ ، خزيمة ٢٣ ب ، الدارقطني ١٨

(٢) جابر : عبد الملك بن أبي سليمان – أبو الزبير – عنه . جه طهارة ، الدارقطني ١٨ . طط ١٩٠/١ ب .

الأرجح أن جابراً سمع هذا الحديث عن أبي هريرة لأنه رواه أحياناً عن أبي هريرة عن النبي صلى الله عليه وسلم، وأحياناً عن النبي صلى الله عليه وسلم مباشرة ، أو لعل الراوي توهم فأسقط اسم أبي هريرة كما يفهم من كلام الطبراني .

(٣) عائشة : ابن أبي ذئب – رجل غير مسمى – أبو سلمة – عنها. ضس ١٤٨٧

(٤) علي : أبو اسحاق – الحارث – عنه . جه طهارة ٤٠

(٥) الامام الصادق : أبو بصير – عبد الكريم بن عتبة قال: سألت الشيخ عن الرجل يستيقظ من نومه ولم يبل : أيدخل يده في الاناء قبل أن يغسلها ؟ قال : لا . لأنه لا يدري اين كانت يده فيغسلها . كافي ١١/٣ ، علل الشرائع ٢٦٧/١ .

مقارنة الروايات :

الروايات كلها متفقة في غسل اليد قبل ادخالها في الاناء . لكن بعضها يذكر الغسل ثلاث مرات بينما الأخرى لا تذكر أي عدد .

ملحوظة :

الشاهد رقم ٥ مصدر شيعي . ويوجد هذا الحديث في مصدر إباضي ايضاً
أبو عبيدة – جابر – أبو هريرة مسند الربيع ٢٨/١ .

أسماء الرواة :

الطبقة الأولى :

١ – أبو هريرة .　٢ – ابن عمر .　٣ – جابر .
٤ – عائشة .　٥ – علي .

الطبقة الثانية :

١ – أبو رزين .　٢ – أبو الزبير .　٣ – أبو سلمة .
٤ – أبو صالح .　٥ – أبو العلاء .　٦ – أبو مريم .
٧ – ابن المسيب .　٨ – الأعرج .　٩ – ثابت .
١٠ – جابر .　١١ – حارث .　١٢ – سالم .
١٣ – عبد الله بن شقيق .　١٤ – محمد .　١٥ – موسى بن يسار .
١٦ – همام .

الطبقة الثالثة :

١ – أبو اسحاق .　٢ – أبو الزناد .　٣ – ابن العلاء .
٤ – الأعمش .　٥ – خالد الحذاء .　٦ – رجل غير مسمى .
٧ – زائدة .　٨ – الزهري .　٩ – زياد .
١٠ – سالم الخياط .　١١ – سهيل .　١٢ – عبد الملك بن أبي سفيان
١٣ – عوف .　١٤ – محمد بن اسحاق .　١٥ – محمد بن عمرو .
١٦ – معاوية بن صالح .　١٧ – معمر .　١٨ – هشام .

الرواية عن أكثر من شيخ : روى الزهري هذا الحديث عن ثلاثة شيوخ والأعمش عن شيخين.

وروده في مسند ابن حنبل : ١٥ (خمس عشرة) مرة عن طريق أبي هريرة .

الحديث رقم (٨)

الرواة عن أبي هريرة :

١ – أبو سلمة .　٢ – أبو صالح .　٣ – ابن المسيب .
٤ – الأعرج .　٥ – داود بن فراهيج .　٦ – سعيد المقبري .
٧ – عجلان .　٨ – قيس بن أبي حازم .　٩ – محمد بن زياد .
١٠ – محمد بن سيرين .　١١ – موسى بن سيار .

١ – تلاميذ أبي سلمة : محمدبن عمرو　دي صوم ٥٠ ، حم ٢/٤٧٥ ، ٥٠١ ، يعلى ١/٢٧٦

٢ – تلاميذ أبي صالح :

أ – المنذر بن عبيد　ن صيام ٤٢

ب – عطاء	خ صيام ٩ ، م صيام ١٦٣ ، ن صيام ٤٢ ، حم ٥١٦/٢ ، خزيمة ١/١٩٨ ، ابن جريج ١٩ ١ب
جـ – الأعمش	الأعمش ١٣ ، خ توحيد ٣٥ ، م صيام ١٦٤ ، ن صيام ٤٢ ، جه صيام ١ ، ادب ٥٨ ، دي صيام ٥٠ ، حم ٢٦٦/٢ ، ٤٤٣ ، ٤٧٧ ، ٤٨٠ .
د – أبوسنان	م صيام ١٦٥ ، حم ٢٣٢/٢ ، ٥/٣ ، الكشي١٠٤/١ يعلى ٦٢ ب ، خزيمة ١٩٨ ب .
هـ – سهيل وعنه :	
١ – الداروردي	حم ٤١٩/٢ ؛ خزيمة ١٩٨ ب .
٢ – عبد العزيز بن المختار	الأصل ٨
٣ – تلاميذ ابن المسيب :	
أ – علي بن زيد	ت صوم ٥٥ ، حم ٤١٤/٢ .
ب – بكير	ن صيام ٤٢
جـ – سليم بن حيان	حم ٥٠٤/٢ ، ٤٦٢
د – الزهري وعنه :	
١ – يونس	م صيام ١٦١ ، ن صيام ٤٢
٢ – معمر	خ لباس ٧٨ ، حم ٢٨١/٢ – ٢٨٢
٤ – تلاميذ الأعرج : أبو الزناد وعنه :	
١ – مالك	ط صيام ٥٨ ، خ صيام ٢ ، حم ٤٦٥/٢ و ٥١٦
٢ – سفيان	الحميدي ١٠١٠ و١٠١٤
٣ – المغيرة	م صيام ١٦٢
٥ – تلاميذ داود بن فراهيج : شعبة	حم ٤٥٨/٢
٦ – تلاميذ سعيد المقبري :	
أ – ابن عجلان	الحميدي ١٠١٥
ب – معن بن محمد	خزيمة ١٩٨
٧ – تلاميذ عجلان : ابن أبي ذئب	الجعد ٣٦٦
٨ – تلاميذ قيس بن أبي حازم :	
اسماعيل بن أبي خالد	راهويه ١/٣٩ – ب
٩ – تلاميذ محمد بن زياد :	
أ – حماد بن سلمة	حم ٤٦٧/٢
ب – شعبة	خ توحيد ، حم ٤٥٧/٢ ، ٥٠٤ ، راهويه ٢٠ الف
جـ – ابراهيم بن طهمان	ابن طهمان ١/٢٤٨

١٠ – تلاميذ محمد بن سيرين :

أ – هشام حم ٢٣٤/٢ ، ١٠ – ٤١١ ، ٥١٦ ، ابن طهمان ٢٤٧ ب

ب – عوف حم ٣٩٥/٢

جـ – سالم الخياط طط ١/٥٤/ب

١١ – تلاميذ موسى بن سيار : داود بنقيس راهويه ٦٥ ب .

الشواهد :

١ – أبو سعيد الخدري . ٢ – ابن مسعود . ٣ – بشير الخصاصية . ٤ – عائشة . ٥ – عبيد ابن عمير . ٦ – عثمان بن أبي العاص . ٧ – علي .

(١) أبو سعيد الخدري :

أ – ضرار بن مرة – أبو صالح – عنه . ن صيام ٤٢

ب – فراس – عطية – عنه حم ٤٠/٣

(٢) ابن مسعود : ابراهيم الهجري – أبو الأحوص – عنه . حم ٤٤٦/١، ن صيام ٤١ ، طك ١/١٠٦/٥ .

(٣) بشير الخصاصية : قتادة – حي بن طيب – عنه . طك ٨٤/١ ب

(٤) عائشة :

أ – جعفر بن برد – أم سالم الراسبية – عنها . حم ٢٤٠/٦

ب – خارجة بن عبد الله–يزيد بن رومان– عنها . طط٢٥٢/١، انظر أيضاً ن صيام٤٣

(٥) عبيد بن عمير : سفيان – عمرو بن دينار – عنه . الحميدي ١٠١١

(٦) عثمان بن أبي العاص :

أ – عنبسه – الحسن – عنه . طك ١/٩/٥

ب – سعيد – مطرف – عنه موارد الظمآن ٢٣٢

(٧) علي بن أبي طالب : ابن اسحاق – عبد الله بن الحارث – عنه . ن صيام ٤١

(٨) أبو عبد الله عليه السلام: ثعلبة – علي بن عبد العزيز– أبو عبد الله والآخرون عن أبي عبد الله الكافي ٣/٤ – ٦٢ ، ٦٥

(٩) زيد بن علي – عن أبيه – عن جده – علي . مسند زيد ٤ – ٢٠٣

(١٠) أبو عبيدة – جابر بن زيد – أبو هريرة . مسند الربيع ٨٧/١

قال الترمذي : وفي الباب عن معاذ بن جبل وسهل بن سعد وكعب بن عجرة وسلامة بن قيصر وبشير بن الخصاصية .

مقارنة الروايات :

لم أجد من خرج هذا الحديث بهذا السياق في محل واحد . وهو في الواقع عبارة عن عدة أحاديث خاصة بالصيام وفضائله جمعت في موضع واحد لوحدة الموضوع وجزأ المؤلفون منه أجزاء وذكروه هنا وهناك . وروى البعض جزءاً من هذا الحديث والبعض الآخر أجزاء أخرى منــه . والروايات كلها متقاربة الألفاظ ومتفقة المعنى . وقد وردت في بعض الروايات زيادة « الحسنة بعشر أمثالها الى سبعمائة ضعف » . كما وردت كلمة « يوم القيامة » ، ولخلوف فم الصائم أطيب عند الله « يوم القيامة » . وهذه الزيادة لا تؤثر في المعنى .

ملحوظة :

الشاهد رقم ٨ مصدر شيعي ، والشاهد رقم ٩ مصــدر زيدي ، والشاهد رقم ١٠ مصدر اباضي .

أسماء الرواة :

الطبقة الأولى :

١ – أبو هريرة .
٢ – أبوسعيد الخدري .
٣ – ابن مسعود .
٤ – بشير الخصاصية .
٥ – عائشة .
٦ – عبيد بن عمير .
٧ – عثمان بن أبي العاص .
٨ – علي بن أبي طالب .

الطبقة الثانية :

١ – أبوالأحوص .
٢ – أبوسلمة .
٣ – أبو صالح .
٤ – ابن المسيب .
٥ – حي بن طيب .
٦ – جابر بن زيد .
٧ – الأعرج .
٨ – داود بن فراهيج .
٩ – الحسن .
١٠ – سعيد المقبري
١١ – عجلان .
١٢ – عطية .
١٣ – عمرو بن دينار .
١٤ – عبد الله بن الحارث .
١٥ – قيس بن أبي حازم .
١٦ – محمد بن زياد .
١٧ – محمد بن سيرين
١٨ – موسى بن يسار .
١٩ – مطرف .
٢٠ – يزيد بن رومان .

الطبقة الثالثة :

١ – أبو الزناد .
٢ – أبو سنان الكوفي
٣ – ابن عجلان المدني
٤ – ابن أبي ذئب .
٥ – ابراهيم بن طهمان الخراساني
٦ – اسماعيل بن خالد الكوفي .
٧ – الأعمش .
٨ – بكير .
٩ – حماد بن سلمة .
١٠ – داود بن قيس المدني .
١١ – الزهري.
١٢ – سالم الخياط البصري .
١٣ – سليم بن حيان الكوفي
١٤ – سهيل .
١٥ – شعبة .
١٦ – عطاء المكي .
١٧ – علي بن زيد البصرى .

١٨ – عوف . ١٩ – ضرار بن مره ٢٠ – فراس .
٢١ – ابراهيم الهجري . ٢٢ – قتاده . ٢٣ – خارجة بن عبد الله
٢٤ – سفيان ٢٥ – عنبسة . ٢٦ – سعيد .
٢٧ – ابن اسحاق . ٢٨ – أبو عبيدة . ٢٩ – محمد بن عمرو .
٣٠ – معن بن محمد الحجازي . ٣١ – المنذر بن عبيد المدني . ٣٢ – هشام .

الرواية عن أكثر من شيخ : فقط شعبة روى عن الشيخين،أما البقية فكل واحد منهم عن شيخ واحد .

وروده في مسند ابن حنبل : ٢٤ (أربع وعشرين) مرة عن طريق أبي هريرة و ٣ (ثلاث) مرات عن طريق الآخرين .

الحديث رقم (٩)

الرواة عن أبي هريرة :

١ – أبو سلمة . ٢ – أبو صالح . ٣ – ابن عباس .
٤ – الأعرج . ٥ – بشر بن سعيد . ٦ – عطاء بن يسار .

١ – تلاميذ أبي سلمة :

أ – الزهري	ن مواقيت ١١ ، خزيمة ١/١٠٩ ، المنتقى /١٥٢
ب – محمد بن عمرو	حم ٣٤٨/٢ ، خزيمة ١/١٠٩
ج – يحيى	خ مواقيت ١٧ ، ن مواقيت ١١ .

٢ – تلاميذ أبي صالح : سهيل ، وعنه :

١ – شعبة	حم ٤٥٩/٢ ، خزيمة ١/١٠٩ ، جعد ٢٠٢
٢ – عبد العزيز	الأصل ٩
٣ – وهيب	طس ٢٤٣١
٤ – أبو حازم	خزيمة ١/١٠٩

٣ – تلاميذ ابن عباس : طاوس	م مساجد ١٦٥ ، د صلاة ٥ ، ن مواقيت ١١ ، يعلى /٢٧١ ب .

٤ – تلاميذ الأعرج :

أ – أبو الزناد	يعلى ١/٢٨٨
ب – زيد بن أسلم	ن مواقيت ١١ ، ت صلاة ٢٣ ، عوانة ٣٥٨/١ ، ط مواقيت ٦ ، م مساجد ١٦٣ ، دي صلاة ٢٢ ، حم ٢٤٦/٢ ، خزيمة ١/١٠٩
ج – عبد الله بن سعيد	حم ٤٧٤/٢

٥ – تلاميذ بشر بن سعيد
٦ – تلاميذ عطاء بن يسار } زيد بن أسلم عوانة ٣٥٨/١
وتلاميذ الأعرج

الشواهد : ١ – عائشة .

(١) عائشة : الزهري – عروة – عنها . حم ٧٨/٦ ، م مساجد ١٦٤

مقارنة الروايات :

اختلف الرواة في كلمة واحدة فقال بعضهم : « من أدرك ركعتين من العصر » ، وقال أكثرهم : « من أدرك ركعة من العصر فقد أدرك » .

هل روى أبو هريرة هكذا . فقال مرة « ركعتين » والأخرى « ركعة » ، أم أخطأ بعض تلاميذه ؟ الأمر غير واضح . ومن الغريب أن مسلماً أخرج عن عبد الأعلى عن معتمر عن معمر فقال : « ركعة » . وأخرج النسائي عن محمد عن معتمر عن معمر – فقال : « من أدرك ركعتين من العصر » .

وكذلك اختلف تلاميذ شعبة فقال علي بن الجعد عن شعبة : « ركعة من العصر » . خزيمة١٠٩/١ ، الجعد ٢٠٢ . وذكر محمد بن جعفر عن شعبة فقال : « ركعتين من العصر » . حم ٤٥٩/٢.

أسماء الرواة :

الطبقة الأولى :

١ – أبو هريرة . ٢ – عائشة .

الطبقة الثانية :

١ – أبو سلمة . ٢ – أبوصالح . ٣ – ابن عباس .
٤ – الأعرج . ٥ – بسر بن سعيد . ٦ – عطاء بن يسار .

الطبقة الثالثة :

١ – أبو الزناد . ٢ – الزهري . ٣ – زيد بن أسلم .
٤ – سهيل . ٥ – طاوس . ٦ – عبد الله بن سعيد .
٧ – محمد بن عمرو. ٨ – يحيى .

الرواية عن أكثر من شيخ: يبدو أن زيد بن أسلم هو الوحيد الذي يروي عن عطاء بن يسار والأعرج . كذلك لم أجد متابعاً للزهري في روايته عن عائشة ، وقد روى الزهري عن أبي سلمة عن أبي هريرة أيضاً .

وروده في مسند بن حنبل: ٤(أربع) مرات عن طريق أبي هريرة، ومرة واحدةعن طريق عائشة .

الحديث رقم (١٠)

الرواة عن أبي هريرة :

١ – أبو سلمة . ٢ – أبو صالح .

١ – تلاميذ أبي سلمة : محمد بن عمرو — يعلى ٢٧٤ ب .

٢ – تلاميذ ابي صالح : سهيل وعنه :

١ – عبد العزيز بن المختار	الأصل ١٠ ؛ جه طهارة ٦٦
٢ – وهيب	حم ٣٨٩/٢ ؛ طس ٢٤١١

الشواهد :

١ – ابن عباس ٢ – أبو رافع ٣ – ام سلمة ٤ – ضباعة بنت الزبير ٥ – جابر بن عبد الله
٦ – عمرو بن أمية ٧ – عمرو بن عبيد الله ٨ – ميمونة

تلاميذ ابن عباس :

١ – أبو سلمة . ٢ – عطاء بن يسار . ٣ – عكرمة
٤ – علي بن عبدالله بن عباس ٥ – محمد بن علي ٦ – محمد بن عمرو
٧ – يحيى بن يعمر .

١ – تلاميذ أبي سلمة : محمدبن ابراهيم	طلك ١٥٠/٥ ب
٢ – تلاميذ عطاء : زيد بن أسلم	خ وضوء ٥٠ ؛ م طهارة ٩١ ؛ ط طهارة ١٩؛ خزيمة ٩ ب ؛ د طهارة ٧٤ ؛ عوانة ٢٦٩/١ ؛ طس ٢٦٦٢
٣ – تلاميذ عكرمة : سماك بن حرب	حم ٣٢٦-٧/١ ؛ جه طهارة ٦٦ ؛ د طهارة ٧٤

٤ – تلاميذ علي بن عبد الله بن عباس :

أ – الحسن بن سعد	طلك ١/١٤٧/٥
ب – الزهري	خزيمة ٩ ب ؛ المنتقى /٢٢
جـ – محمد بن الزبير	طلك ١/١٤٧/٥
د – محمد بن علي بن عبدالله	خزيمة ٩ ب

٥ – تلاميذ محمد بن علي : جابر الجعفى — حم ٢٤١/١

٦ – تلاميذ محمد بن عمرو :

أ – موسى بن عقبة	حم ٢٥٨/١
ب – الوليد بن كثير	عوانة ٢٦٩/١
جـ – وهب بن كيسان	خزيمة ١/٩

٧ – تلاميذ يحيى بن يعمر : قتادة — حم ٢٧٩/١ ب، د طهارة ٧٤ ؛ طلك ١/٢٦٥/٥

(٢) الرواة عن أبي رافع : ١ – أبو غطفان ٢ – شرحبيل بن سعد ٣ – روح .

١ – أبوغطفان وعنه : عبد الله بن عبيد الله — عوانة ٢٧٠/١

٢ – شرحبيل بن سعد وعنه : زيد بن أبي أنيسه طك ١/٦٧/١

٣ – روح وعنه : يزيد بن زريع طط ١/٤٢/١

(٣) الرواة عن ام سلمة : ١ – زينب ٢ – عبد الله بن شداد

١ – زينب وعنها : علي بن الحسين حم ٢٩٢/٦ ؛ جه طهارة ٦٦

٢ – عبد الله بن شداد وعنه : أبو عون حم ٣١٧/٦ ؛ ٣٢٣ ؛ ٣٠٦ ؛ الجعد ٥٩

(٤) ضباعة بنت الزبير

عبد الله بن الحارث – ام حكيم – عنها حم ٤١٩/٦ ؛ راهويه ١/١٦

(٥) الرواة عن جابر : ١ – ابو الزبير ٢ – عبد الله بن محمد بن عقيل ٣ – محمد بن المنكدر .

١ – أبو الزبير وعنه : بكار طس ٨ ٧٠ ؛

٢ – عبد الله بن محمد وعنه : زائدة طس ١٠

٣ – محمد بن المنكدر وعنه :

شعيب بن أبي حمزة د طهارة ٧٤ ؛ خزيمة ٩ ب

(٦) عمرو بن أمية : الزهري–

جعفر بن عمرو – عمرو بن أمية حم١٣٩/٤ ؛ ١٧٩ ؛ خ وضوء ٥٠ ؛ أطعمة ٢٠ ؛ ٢٦ ؛ ٥٨ . م طهارة ٩١ ؛ المنتقى ٢٣ ؛ طس ١٢٥٥ حم ٣٤٧/٤

(٧) عمروبن عبدالله : مكيبن ابراهيم – الجعيد بن الحسن – عنه حم ٣٤٧/٤

(٨) ميمونة : عمر بن بكير – كريب – عنها خ وضوء ٥١ .

مقارنة الروايات :

الروايات كلها متفقة على أن الوضوء لا ينتقض بأكل شيء مطبوخ .

أسماء الرواة :

الطبقة الأولى :

١ – أبو هريرة .	٢ – أبو رافع .	٣ – أم سلمة .
٤ – ابن عباس .	٥ – جابر بن عبد الله .	٦ – ضباعة بنت الزبير .
٧ – عمرو بن أمية .	٨ – عمرو بن عبد الله .	٩ – ميمونة .

الطبقة الثانية :

١ – أبو الزبير .	٢ – أبوسلمة .	٣ – أبو صالح .
٤ – أبوغطفان .	٥ – أم حكيم .	٦ – روح .
٧ – زينب .	٨ – شرحبيل .	٩ – جعفر بن عمرو .

١٠ – الجعيد بن الحسن . ١١ – عبد الله بن شداد . ١٢ – عطاء .
١٣ – عكرمة . ١٤ – علي بن عبد الله . ١٤ – كريب .
١٦ – محمد بن علي . ١٧ – محمد بن عمرو . ١٨ – محمد بن المنكدر .
١٩ – يحيى بن يعمر . ٢٠ – عبد الله بن محمد بن عقيل .

الطبقة الثالثة :

١ – أبو عون . ٢ – بكار . ٣ – جابر الجعفي.
٤ – الحسن بن سعد . ٥ – الزهري . ٦ – زيد بن أسلم .
٧ – زيد بن أبي أنيسة . ٨ – سماك بن حرب . ٩ – شعيب بن أبي حمزة
١٠ – عبد الله بن الحارث . ١١ – عبد الله بن عبيد الله . ١٢ – علي بن الحسين .
١٣ – عمر بن بكير . ١٤ – قتاده . ١٥ – محمد بن ابراهيم .
١٦ – محمد بن الزبير . ١٧ – محمد بن علي . ١٨ – محمد بن عمرو .
١٩ – مكي بن ابراهيم . ٢٠ – موسى بن عقبة . ٢١ – الوليد بن كثير .
٢٢ – وهب بن كيسان ٢٣ – يزيد بن زريع . ٢٤ – سهيل بن أبي صالح .
٢٥ – زائدة .

الرواية عن أكثر من شيخ : في الطبقة الثانية ، أبو سلمة يروي عن أكثر من شيخ
في الطبقة الثالثة ، الزهري يروي عن أكثر من شيخ

وروده في مسند ابن حنبل : عن طريق أبي هريرة مرة واحدة، وعن الطرق الأخرى ١٢ مرة

ملحوظة : يخالف أبو هريرة والزهري هذا الحديث، ومن مذهبهما الوضوء مما مست النار.

الحديث رقم (١١)

الرواة عن أبي هريرة : أبو صالح :

١ – تلاميذ أبي صالح : سهيل وعنه :

١ – حماد بن سلمة	م البر ١٣٩ ؛ حم ٢/٣٤٢ ؛ جعد ٢ – ٤٤١
٢ – عبد العزيز بن المختار	الأصل ١١
٣ – مالك	م البر ١٣٩ ، حم ٢/٤٦٥ ، ٥١٧
٤ – همام	طس ٢٤٣٨

الشواهد :

لم أجد له شاهداً ولا متابعاً .

مقارنة الروايات :

لا يوجد اختلاف في الروايات .

وروده في مسند ابن حنبل : عن طريق أبي هريرة ٣ مرات

الحديث رقم (١٢)

الرواة عن ابي هريرة:

١ – عبد الله بن ابراهيم ٢ – أبو سلمة ٣ – أبو صالح ٤ – سعيد المقبري ٥ – المطلب بن عبد الله ٦ – عبدالله بن عبد .

١ – تلاميذ عبد الله بن ابراهيم القارظ : عمر بن عبد العزيز وعنه :

ا – الزهري — حم ٢/٢٦٥ ، ٢٧١ ، ٤٢٧ ، ٤٧٠ ، ٤٧٩
عوانة ١/٩-٢٦٨ ، م حيض ٩٠ ، ن طهارة ١٢١
طس ٢٣٧٦

٢ – تلاميذ ابي سلمة :

ا – محمد بن عمرو — حم ٢/٥٠٣ ، ت طهارة ٥٨ .

ب – يحيى بن أبي كثير — طط ١/١٢٢/١

٣ – تلاميذ أبي صالح : سهيل وعنه :

١ – عبد العزيز بن المختار — الأصل ١٢

٢ – وهيب — حم ٢/٣٨٩

٤ – تلاميذ سعيد المقبري : أبو معشر — يعلى ٣٠٣/١

٥ – تلاميذ المطلب بن عبد الله : الأوزاعي — ن طهارة ١٢١

٦ – تلاميذ عبدالله بن عبد : يحيى بن جعده — ن طهارة ١٢١

الشواهد :

١ – ابن عمر ٢ – أبو أيوب ٣ – أبو طلحة ٤ – أم حبيبة ٥ – زيد بن ثابت ٦ – عائشة .

(١) ابن عمر : عبيد الله بن عمر – نافع – عنه — طلك ٥/٢٩٧ ب

(٢) أبو أيوب : يحيى بن جعده – عبد الله بن عمرو القارى – عنه — ن طهارة ١٢١

(٣) أبو طلحة :

أ – يعقوب بن عبد الرحمن – عن أبيه – عن جده – عنه — طلك ٣/٣٢/١

ب – يحيى بن جعده – عبد الله بن عمرو القاري – عنه — ن طهارة ١٢١

(٤) أم حبيبة :

أ – الزهري – أبوسلمة – سفيان – عنها — طس ١٥٩٢ ، (مع خطأ فيه) .
ن طهارة١٢١ ، حم ٦/٣٢٧، ٣٢٨

ب – الزهري – عبيد الله بن عبد الله – سفيان – عنها — حم ٦/٣٢٧

جـ – يحيى – ابو سلمة – سفيان – عنها — حم ٦/٣٢٧

(٥) زيدبن ثابت : الزهري – عبد الملك بن أبي بكر – خارجه بن زيد – عنه — م حيض ٩٠ ؛ ن طهارة ١٢١

(٦) عائشة : الزهري – سعيد بن خالد – عروة – عنها — م حيض ٩٠ .

مقارنة الروايات :

اتفق الرواة على الوضوء مما مست النار .

أسماء الرواة :

الطبقة الأولى :

١ – أبو هريرة . ٢ – ابن عمر . ٣ – أبو أيوب .
٤ – أبوطلحة . ٥ – أم حبيبة . ٦ – زيد بن ثابت .
٧ – عائشة .

الطبقة الثانية :

١ – عبد الله بن ابراهيم القارظ . ٢ – أبو سلمة . ٣ – أبو صالح .
٤ – سعيد المقبري. ٥ – المطلب بن عبد الله . ٦ – عبد الله بن عبد .
٧ – أبو طلحة . ٨ – نافع . ٩ – عبد اللهبن عمرو القارى
١٠ – سفيان . ١١ – خارجة بن زيد . ١٢ – عرمة .

الطبقة الثالثة :

١ – عمر بن عبد العزيز . ٢ – محمد بن عمرو ٣ – يحيى بن ابي كثير .
٤ – سهيل . ٥ – أبومعشر . ٦ – الأوزاعي .
٧ – يحيى بن جعده . ٨ – عبد الرحمن . ٩ – عبيدالله بن عبدالله .
١٠ – عبد الملك بن أبي بكر . ١١ – سعيد بن خالد .

الرواية عن أكثر من شيخ: روى الزهري عن عدة أشخاص ولم أجد لهم راوياً غيره وكذلك يحيى بن جعده روى عن أكثر من واحد .

وروده في مسند ابن حنبل: عن طريق أبي هريرة ٧ مرات وعن طريق أم حبيبة ٤ مرات.

الحديث رقم (١٣)

الرواة عن أبي هريرة : أبو صالح .

١ – أبو صالح .

تلاميذ أبي صالح : سهيل وعنه :

١ – عبد العزيز بن المختار الأصل /١٣ ، ت اطعمة ١٠
٢ – وهيب م الاشربه ١٣٧ ، حم ٣٤١/٢ . انظر ايضاً حم ٤١٥/٢

الشواهد :

١ – أبو سعيد الخدري ٢ – ابن عباس ٣ – ابن عمر ٤ – انس بن مالك ٥ – جابر ٦ – كعب بن مالك .

(١) أبو سعيد الخدري : بكير – بسر بن سعيد – عنه . طط ١/٢٩/٢

(٢) ابن عباس :

أ – ابن جريج – عطاء – عنه . ابن جريج ١/١١٨ – ب ، حم ١/٢٩٣ ، م اشربه ١٣٠/

ب – طلحة – عطاء – عنه الكشي ٧١ ب

جـ – عمرو – عطاء – م اشربه ١٢٩ ؛ حميدي /٤٩٠ ، جه اطعمة ٩

(٣) ابن عمر : حصين – مجاهد – عنه حم ٢/٧

(٤) أنس بن مالك :

أ – حماد – ثابت – عنه حم ١٧٧/٣ ، م اشربة ١٣٦ ، جعد ٤٤٠ ، الكشي ١/١٤٠

ب – همام – قتادة – عنه طص ٩٢ ؛ بغداد ٤٦٣/٨

(٥) جابر :

أ – ابن جريج – أبو الزبير – عنه ابن جريج /١/١٢٠ ، الكشي ٧١ ب ، يعلى ١١٦ب

ب – سفيان – ابو الزبير – جابر حم ٣٠١/٣ ، ٣٣٧ ، ٦–٣٦٥ ، ٣٩٣ ، يعلى ١٠١ ب، م أشربة ١٣٣ ، ١٣٤ ، جه اطعمة ٩

جـ – الأعمش – أبوسفيان – جابر م اشربة ١٣٥

(٦) كعب بن مالك :

أ – سعد بن ابراهيم – ابن كعب – عنه م اشربة ١٣١

ب – عبد الرحمن بن سعد – ابن عنه بن مالك – عنه م اشربة ١٣٢

مقارنة الروايات :

لا يوجد اختلاف بين تلاميذ سهيل وهم متفقون لفظاً ومعنى . وكذلك الرواة عن بقية الصحابة . إلاان بعضهم ذكر : « فان آخر الطعام فيه البركة » وقال أكثرهم: « لا يدري في أيتهن البركة ».

أسماء الرواة :

الطبقة الأولى :

١ – أبو هريرة . ٢ – أبو سعيد الخدري . ٣ – ابن عباس .
٤ – ابن عمر . ٥ – أنس بن مالك . ٦ – جابر بن عبد الله .
٧ – كعب بن مالك .

الطبقة الثانية :

١ – أبو صالح	٢ – بسر بن سعيد .	٣ – عطاء بن أبي رباح .
٤ – مجاهد .	٥ – ثابت .	٦ – قتادة .
٧ – أبو الزبير .	٨ – أبو سفيان .	٩ – ابن كعب بن مالك .

الطبقة الثالثة :

١ – سهيل .	٢ – بكير .	٣ – ابن جريج .
٤ – طلحة .	٥ – عمرو .	٦ – حصين .
٧ – حماد .	٨ – همام .	٩ – سفيان .
١٠ – الأعمش .	١١ – سعد بن ابراهيم .	١٢ – عبد الرحمن بن سعد .

الرواية عن أكثر من شيخ : في الطبقة الثالثة : روى ابن جريج عن أكثر من شيخ .

وروده في مسند ابن حنبل : مرتين عن طريق أبي هريرة و٧ مرات عن طريق الآخرين .

الحديث رقم (١٤)

الرواة عن أبي هريرة : أبو صالح :

١ – تلاميذ أبي صالح : سهيل وعنه :

١ – عبد العزيز بن المختار	الأصل /١٤
٢ – وهيب	حم ٢/٥–٣٨٤ ، طس ٢٤٤١ ، سعد ٢/٢/٨٠
٣ – يعقوب بن عبد الرحمن	م الفضائل ٣٣

الشواهد :

١ – أبو ليلى ٢ – سعد بن أبي وقاص ٣ – سلمة بن الاكوع – ٤ – سهل بن سعد

(١) أبو ليلى : أبو فروة – عبد الرحمن بن أبي ليلى – عن أبيه . طك ٣/١١٦ ب

(٢) سعد بن أبي وقاص : بكير – عامر بن أبي وقاص – عن أبيه م فضائل ٣٢ ؛مناقب ١٩

(٣) سلمة بن الأكوع :

أ – محمد بن اسحاق – بريدة بن سفيان – سلمة بن الأكوع .طك ٤/١٦٩/١

ب – عكرمة بن عمار – عطاء مولى السائب – عنه . طك ٤/١٦٩/١

ج – عكرمة – أياس بن سلمة – عنه م الجهاد ١٣٢

د – حاتم بن اسماعيل – يزيد بن أبي عبيد – سلمة بن الأكوع خ جهاد ١٢١ ، فضائل ٩ ، م فضائل ٣٥

(٤) سهل بن سعد :
أ – عبد العزيز بن أبي حازم – أبو حازم – سهل بن سعد خ جهاد ١٠٢ ، مفضائل ٣٤
ب – يعقوب – أبو حازم – عنه خ جهاد ١٤٣ ، فضائل ٩ ، حم ٣٣٣/٥ ، م فضائل ٣٤
جـ – فضيل بن سليمان – أبو حازم – سهل بن سعد يعلى ١/٢٥

مقارنة الروايات :

لم أجد متابعاً لسهيل . والرواة عنه متفقون فيما بينهم لفظاً ومعنى .
والروايات المذكورة أعلاه تتفق مع رواية أبي هريرة إلا في قول عمر «ما احببت الامارة...».
اذ لم أجد هذه الجملة إلا في رواية أبي هريرة، لكن الروايات الأخرى تشير إلى أن الصحابة كلهم كانوا يتطلعون للراية .

أسماء الرواة :

الطبقة الأولى :

١ – أبو هريرة . ٢ – أبو ليلى . ٣ – سعد بن أبي وقاص .
٤ – سلمة بن الاكوع . ٥ – سهل بن سعد .

الطبقة الثانية :

١ – أبو صالح . ٢ – عبد الرحمن بن أبي ليلى . ٣ – عامر بن سعد.
٤ – بريدة بن سفيان . ٥ – عطاء مولى السائب . ٦ – أياس بن سلمة .
٧ – يزيد . ٨ – أبو حازم .

الطبقة الثالثة :

١ – سهيل . ٢ – أبو فروه . ٣ – بكير .
٤ – محمد بن اسحاق . ٥ – عكرمة بن عمار . ٦ – حاتم بن إسماعيل .
٧ – عبد العزيز بن أبي حازم . ٨ – يعقوب بن عبد الرحمن . ٩ – فضيل بن سليمان .

الرواية عن أكثر من شيخ : في الطبقة الثالثة عكرمة ، ويعقوب، يرويان عن أكثر من شيخ .

وروده في مسند ابن حنبل : مرة واحدة عن طريق أبي هريرة، وكذلك مرة عن طريق سهل.

الحديث رقم (١٥)

الرواة عن أبي هريرة :

١ – أبو صالح ٢ – محمد بن زياد .
١ – تلاميذ أبي صالح : سهيل وعنه :
١ – جرير . م طهارة ٣٠

٢ – روح بن القاسم طط ١/١ ٤ ب
٣ – عبد العزيز بن محمد ت ٥٨/١
٤ – عبد العزيز بن المختار الأصل ١٥ ، جه طهارة ٥٥
٥ – معمر حم ٢٨٢/٢
٦ – وهيب حم ٣٨٩/٢

٢ – تلاميذ محمد بن زياد :
أ – حماد حم ٤٠٦/٢ ، ٤٠٧ ، ٤٦٧ ، ٤٨٢ .
ب – الربيع بن مسلم م طهارة ٢٨
ج – شعبة حم ٤٩٨/٢ ، ٤٣٠ ، ٤٠٩ ، خ وضوء ٢٩ ، م طهارة ٢٩ ؛ جعد /١٣١ ، راهويه ١٩ ب ،
د – شعيب حم ٢٢٨/٢
ه – معمر حم ٢٨٤/٢

الشواهد :

١ – أبو امامة ٢ – جابر ٣ – خالد بن الوليد ٤ – شرحبيل ٥ – عائشة ٦ – عبد الله بن الحارث ٧ – عبد الله بن عمرو بن العاص ٨ – عمرو بن العاص ٩ – معيقيب ١٠ – يزيد بن أبي سفيان

(١) أبو امامة : ليث بن أبي سليم – عبد الرحمن بن سابط – عنه . طك ١/٣٠٨/٤ ، الدارقطني /٤٠

(٢) جابر :
أ – الأعمش – أبوسفيان – عنه حم ٣١٦/٣ ؛ طص ١٦١
ب – أبواسحاق – سعيد بن أبي كعب عنه جه طهارة /٥٥ ؛ طس ١٧٩٧ ؛ يعلى ١١٣ ب

(٣) خالد بن الوليد : أبو صالح الأشعري – أبو عبد الله الأشعري – عنه . جه طهارة ٥٥ .

(٤) شرحبيل : أبو صالح الأشعري – عنه جه طهارة ٥٥ .

(٥) الرواة عن عائشة :
١ – ابو سلمة ٢ – سالم ٣ – عروة
١ – أبوسلمة وعنه : سعيد بن أبي سعيد حم ٢/٦–١٩١ ، جه طهارة /٥٥ ، حميدي ١٦١ يعلى ٢٠٣ ب.

٢ – تلاميذ سالم :
أ – بكير م طهارة ٢٥
ب – عمران بن بشير حم ١١٢/٦ ، ٢٥٨ ، طس ١٥٥٢
ج – نعيم بن عبد الله م طهارة ٢٥
د – يحيى بن أبي بكر حم ٨١/٦ ، ٨٤ ، ٩٩

هـ — أبو سلمة م طهارة ٢٥ ؛ انظر ايضاً ط طهارة ٥

و — محمد بن عبد الرحمن م طهارة ٢٥

٣ — تلاميذ عروة :

أ — هشام جه طهارة ٥٥ ؛ طط ١/٢٥٠/١

ب — الزهري الدارقطني ٣٥

(٦) عبد الله بن الحارث : حيوة — عقبة بن سالم — عبد الله بن الحارث . حم ١٩١/٤ ؛ خزيمة ٢٥ب ؛ الدارقطني ٣٥ ؛ الفسوي ١٥٥/٣ ب .

(٧) عبد الله بن عمرو وعنه : ١ — أبو يحيى ٢ — يوسف بن ماهك .

١ — تلاميذ أبي يحيى : هلال بن يساف حم ١٩٣/٢ ، ٢٠١ ؛ م طهارة ٢٦ ، جه طهارة/٥٥ طس ٢٢٩٠ ، خزيمة ٢٥ ب ، دى ١٧٩/١ ، د ٥٨/١

٢ — تلاميذ يوسف بن ماهك : أبو بشر حم ٢١١/٢ ، ٢٢٦ ، خ علم ٣ ، ٣٠ ، وضوء ٢٧ م طهارة ٢٧ ، خزيمة ٢٦/١

(٨) عمرو بن العاص : أبو صالح الأشعري — أبو عبد الله الأشعري — عنه . جه طهارة ٥٥

(٩) معيقب : يحيى بن أبي كثير — أبو سلمة — عنه حم ٤٢٦/٣ ، ٤٢٥/٥

(١٠) يزيد بن أبي سفيان : أبو صالح الأشعري — أبو عبد الله الأشعري — عنه . جه طهارة ٥٥

مقارنة الروايات :

اختلف الرواة في كلمة « الأعقاب » ، فقال بعضهم : « العقب » والآخرون : « الأعقاب » وغيرهم : « العراقيب » . كما ورد في بعض الرواية زيادة يوم « القيامة » كما هو في الأصل .

اسماء الرواة :

الطبقة الأولى :

١ — أبو هريرة .	٢ — أبو أمامة .	٣ — جابر .
٤ — خالد بن الوليد .	٥ — شرحبيل .	٦ — عائشة .
٧ — عبد الله بن الحارث .	٨ — عبد الله بن عمرو .	٩ — عمرو بن العاص .
١٠ — معيقيب .	١١ — يزيد بن أبي سفيان .	

الطبقة الثانية :

١ — أبو صالح .	٢ — محمد بن رياد .	٣ — عبد الرحمن بن سابط
٤ — أبو سفيان .	٥ — سعيد	٦ — أبوعبد الله الأشعري
٧ — أبو سلمة .	٨ — سالم .	٩ — عروة .
١٠ — عقبة بن مسلم .	١١ — أبو يحيى .	١٢ — يوسف بن ماهك .

الطبقة الثالثة :

١ – سهيل .	٢ – حماد .	٣ – الربيع .
٤ – شعبة .	٥ – شعيب .	٦ – معمر .
٧ – ليث بن أبي سليم .	٨ – الأعمش .	٩ – أبو اسحاق .
١٠ – أبو صالح الأشعري .	١١ – سعيد بن أبي سعيد .	١٢ – بكير .
١٣ – عمران بن بشير .	١٤ – نعيم بن عبد الله .	١٥ – يحيى بن أبي كثير .
١٦ – أبو سلمة .	١٧ – محمد بن عبد الرحمن .	١٨ – هشام .
١٩ – الزهري .	٢٠ – حيوة .	٢١ – هلال بن يساف .
٢٢ – أبو بشر .		

الرواية عن أكثر من شيخ : في الطبقة الثانية أبو عبد الله الأشعري هو الوحيد الذي يروي عن خالد بن الوليد وشرحبيل وعمرو بن العاص ومعيقيب ويزيد بن أبي سفيان .

وفي الطبقة الثالثة فقط أبو صالح الأشعري يروي عن أبي عبد الله الأشعري .

وروده في مسند ابن حنبل : ١١ مرة عن طريق أبي هريرة و ١٤ مرة عن طريق أخرى .

الحديث رقم (١٦)

الرواة عن أبي هريرة :

١ – أبو صالح ٢ – نافع .

١ – تلاميذ أبي صالح :

أ – عبد الله بن دينار	خ توحيد ٣٣
ب – سهيل وعنه :	
١ – أبو عوانة	حم ٤١٣/٢
٢ – العلاء بن المسيب	طط ٤/٢ب
٣ – عبد العزيز بن عبد الله	حم ٥٠٩/٢
٤ – عبد العزيز بن المختار	الأصل ١٦
٥ – ليث	حم ٣٤١/٢
٦ – معمر	حم ٢٦٧/٢ ؛ يعلى ٣٠٦ ب
٧ – مالك	ط شعر ١٥
٨ – وهيب	طس ٢٤٣٦

٢ – تلاميذ نافع : موسى بن عقبة   ابن جريج ١٣١ ب ؛ حم ٢/٥١٤ ؛ في بدء الخلق ٦ .

الشواهد :

(١) أبو امامة : محمد بن سعد الواسطي – أبو ظبية – أبو امامة   حم ٥/٢٦٣

ملحوظة : يوجد هذا الحديث في مصدر إباضي أيضاً .

أبو عبيدة – جابر بن زيد – أبوهريرة   مسند الربيع ١/٢٤

مقارنة الروايات :

اتفقت روايات هذا الحديث معنى وإلى حد كبير لفظاً . وذكر بعضهم «وإذا أبغض فثل ذلك» ولم يذكره الآخرون .

أسماء الرواة :

الطبقة الأولى :

١ – أبو هريرة .   ٢ – أبو امامة .

الطبقة الثانية :

١ – أبو صالح .   ٢ – نافع .   ٣ – أبوظبية .

الطبقة الثالثة :

١ – عبد الله بن دينار .   ٢ – سهيل .   ٣ – موسى بن عقبة .

٤ – محمد بن سعد الواسطي .

الرواية عن أكثر من شيخ : لا توجد .

وروده في مسند ابن حنبل : ٥ مرات عن طريق أبي هريرة ومرة واحدة عن طريق أبي امامة.

الحديث رقم (١٧)

الرواة عن أبي هريرة :

١ – أبوصالح ٢ – عطاء بن خليفه ٣ – عمر بن الحكم .

١ – تلاميذ أبي صالح :

أ – سمى   خ أذان ٣٢ ؛ ٧٣ ؛ جهاد ٣٠ ، طب ٣٠ ،
م امارة ١٦٤ ؛ حم ٢/٣٢٥ ، ٥٣٣

ب – سهيل وعنه :

١ – حماد   حم ٢/٥٢٢

٢ – الزهري   حم ٢/٣١٠

٣ – عبد العزيز بن المختار   الأصل ١٧ ، جه . جهاد ١٧ .

٤ – جرير م امارة ١٦٥

٥ – خالد م امارة ١٦٥

٦ – وهيب طس ٢٤٠٧ ، م امارة ١٦٥ .

٢ – تلاميذ عطاء بن خليفة : أبو النضر طط ١٥/١ ب

٣ – تلاميذ عمر بن الحكم : أبو مالك حم ٤٤١/٢

الشواهد :

١ – أبو عبيدة الجراح . ٢ – أنس بن مالك . ٣ – جابر بن عتيك .
٤ – راشد بن حبيش . ٤ – سعد بن أبي وقاص . ٦ – سلمان الفارسي .
٧ – عائشة . ٨ – عبادة بن الصامت . ٩ – عبد الله بن عمرو
١٠ – عنترة . ١١ – عقبة بن عامر .

(١) أبو عبيدة : خالد بن معدان – العرباض بن سارية – أبو عبيدة . سعد ٣٠١/٢/٣

(٢) أنس : عاصم – حفصة بنت سيرين – أنس . خ طب ٣٠ ؛ م امارة ١٦٦ ؛ طس ٢١١٣

(٣) جابر : عبدالله بن عبد الله – عتيك بن الحارث – جابر بن عتيك . حم ٤٤٦/٥ ؛
ط جنائز ٣٦ ؛ دجنائز ١١ ؛ ن جنائز ١٤ ؛ جه جهاد ١٧ ؛ طك ١٢٠/١ .

(٤) راشد : مسلم بن يسار – أبو الأشعث الصنعاني – راشد بن حبيش. حم ٤٨٩/٣

(٥) سعد بن أبي وقاص : حفص بن عمر – عمر بن سعد – سعد . الكشي ١٩ ب

(٦) سلمان : عاصم الأحول – أبو عثمان النهدي – سلمان الصنعاني . طط ٦٨/١ ب

(٧) عائشة : موسى بن تليد – القاسم – عائشة. طس ١٤٢٨

(٨) عبادة بن الصامت :
أ – عبادة بن نسى – الاسود بن ثعلبة – عبادة حم ٣١٧/٥ ؛ أنظر أيضاًحم ٣١٥/٥
ب – أبو سلمان – يعلى بن شداد – عبادة. حم ٩/٥–٣٢٨

(٩) عبد الله بن عمرو : الافريقي – عبد الله بن يزيد – عبد الله بن عمرو . الكشى ١/٤١

(١٠) عنترة : عبد الملك بن هارون – هارون بن عنترة – عنترة . طك ٩٦/٩ب

(١١) عقبة بن عامر : عبد الله بن ثعلبة – عبد الرحمن بن حجيرة – عقبة بن عامر الفسوى١٥٢/٣ب
أبو عبيد – جابر بن زيد – أبو هريرة الربيع ٢١/٢
وشرح مسند الربيع ٣٩١/٣ (مصدر إبا ضى) ؛ وانظر مسند زيد ١٦٧ ؛ ٤–٣٥٣
(مصدر زيدي)

مقارنة الروايات :

أتفق الرواة على أن القتلى في سبيل الله ليسوا هم الشهداء وحدهم، بل يضاف اليهم غيرهم فذكر بعضهم المبطون والمطعون والغرق وزاد البعض الحرق والنفساء وذات الجنب والهدم .

أسماء الرواة :

الطبقة الأولى :

١– أبوهريرة	٢– أبوعبيده	٣– أنس بن مالك
٤– جابر بن عتيك	٥– راشد بن حبيش	٦– سعد بن أبي وقاص
٧– سلمان الفارسي	٨– عائشة	٩– عبادة بن الصامت
١٠ عبد الله بن عمرو	١١– عنترة	١٢–عقبة بن عامر

الطبقة الثانية :

١– أبو صالح	٢– عطاء بن خليفة	٣– عمر بن الحكم
٤– العرباض بن سارية	٥– حفصة بنت سيرين	٦– عتيك بن الحارث
٧– أبوالاشعث الصنعاني	٨– عمر بن سعد	٩– أبو عثمان النهدي
١٠– القاسم	١١– الاسود بن ثعلبة	١٢–يعلى بن شداد
١٣– عبد الله بن يزيد	١٤–هارون بن عنترة	١٥–عبدالرحمن بن حجيرة
١٦– جابر بن زيد .		

الطبقة الثالثة :

١– سمى	٢– سهيل	٣– أبو النضر
٤– أبو مالك	٥– خالد بن مهدان	٦– عاصم
٧– عبد-الله بن عبد الله	٨– مسلم بن يسار	٩–حفص بن عمر
١٠– جابر	١١–موسى بن تليد	١٢–عبادة بن نسى
١٣–أبو سلمان	١٤–الافريقي	١٥–عبدالملك بن هارون
١٦–عبد الله بن ثعلبة		

الرواية عن أكثر من شيخ : لا توجد .

وروده في مسند ابن حنبل : ٥ مرات عن طريق أبي هريرة و ٤ مرات عن طريق الآخرين .

الحديث رقم (١٨)

الرواة عن أبي هريرة :

١– أبوصالح ٢ – يزيد بن الاصم

١– تلاميذ أبي صالح :

أ– عمارة بن غزية حم ٣٧٩/٢ ، ت أيمان ٧

ب عبد الله بن دينار وعنه :

١– أبن عجلان — جه أقامة ٩

٢– سليمان بن بلال — خ أيمان ٢ : ن أيمان ١٦ ؛ م أيمان ٥٧

٣– سهيل وعنه :– الثوري ؛ حم ٤٤٥/٢ ؛ ن ايمان ١٦

« جه مقدمة ٩ ؛ ت أيمان ٦

« جريرم أيمان ٥٨ ؛ جه أقامه ٩

« حماد حم ٤١٤/٢ ؛ د سنة ١٤

ج– سهيل بن أبي صالح بدون واسطة عبدالله بن دينار : الاصل ١٨

١– عبد العزيز بن المختار .

٢– وهيب طس ٢٤٠٢

٢– تلاميذ يزيد الاصم : جعفر بن برقان حم ٤٤٥/٢

الشواهد :

(١) ابن عمر : الزهرى – سالم – بن عمر. حم ٥٦/٢ ؛ ١٤٧ ؛ الحميدي٥٢٦ ؛ ن أيمان ٢٧؛ م ايمان ٥٩ ؛ ط حسن الخلق ١٠ ؛ جه مقدمة ٩

مقارنة الروايات :

لم أجد أحدا من الصحابة من روى هذا الحديث بهذا السياق . وروى ابن عمر جزءا منه « الحياء من الايمان » . وكذلك رواة حديث أبي هريرة : فقد ذكروه أحياناً بكامله ، واحيانا بحذف جملة كما أختلف الرواة بين بضع وستين وبضعسبعين والبعض: « بضع وثمانون » . وروى البخاري: « بضع وستون » وروى مسلم بنفس السند : « بضع وسبعون » .

ثم روى عن سهيل كل من جرير والثوري وحماد فذكروا بين سهيل وابيه واسطة عبد الله بن دينار بينما لم يذكر وهيب ولا عبد العزيز بن المختار هذه الواسطة ؛

أسماء الرواة :

الطبقة الأولى :

١– أبو هريرة — ٢– أبن عمر

الطبقة الثانية :

١ – ابو صالح — ٢ – يزيد بن الاصم — ٣ – سالم

الطبقة الثالثة :

١ – عمارة بن غزية — ٢ – عبد الله بن دينار — ٣ – جعفر بن برقان

٤ – الزهري

الرواية عن أكثر من شيخ : لا توجد .

وروده في مسند ابن حنبل : ٤ مرات عن طريق ابي هريرة ومرتين عن طريق أبن عمر .

الحديث رقم (١٩)

الرواة عن أبي هريرة :

١ – ابو سلمة　　٢ – ابو صالح　　٣ – الأعرج　　٤ – حفص بن عاصم

١ – تلاميذ ابي سلمة : محمد بن عمرو　　حم ٤٦١/٢ ؛ ٣٤٦ ؛ ٤١٥ ؛

٢ – تلاميذ ابي صالح : سهيل وعنه : –

١ – روح	م فتن ٤٩
٢ – زهير	حم ٣٣٢/٢
٣ – عبد الرحمن القارى	م فتن ٢٩
٤ – عبد العزيز بن المختار	الاصل ١٩
٥ – معمر	حم ٣٠٦/٢

٣ – تلاميذ الأعرج : ابو الزناد　　خ فتن ٢٤ ؛ م فتن ٣١ ؛ دملاحم١٣

٤ – تلاميذ حفص بن عاصم : خبيب بن عبد الرحمن　　خ فتن٢٤ ؛ م فتن ٣٠ ؛ دملاحم١٣

الشواهد :

(١) ابي بن بن كعب :

أ – سليمان – عبد اللهبن الحارث – أبي بن كعب　　حم ١٣٩/٥ ؛ ١٤٠ ؛ م فتن ٣٢ الكشى ١/٢٤

ب – اسحاق – المغيرة – أبي بن كعب　　الفسوى ١/١٢٠/٢ – ب ؛ طك ١/٣٧/١

مقارنة الروايات :

الروايات متفقة في معناها ومتجانسة الى حد كبير في الفاظها

اسماء الرواة :

الطبقة الأولى :

١ – ابو هريرة　　٢ – ابي بن كعب

الطبقة الثانية :

١ – ابو سلمة　　٢ – ابو صالح　　٣ – الأعرج
٤ – حفص بن عاصم　　٥ – عبد الله بن الحارث　　٦ – المغيرة

الطبقة الثالثة :

١ - خبيب بن عبد الرحمن　　٢ - ابو الزناد　　٣ - اسحاق
٤ - سليمان　　٥ - محمد بن عمرو　　٦ - سهيل .

الرواية عن أكثر من شيخ : لا توجد .

وروده فيمسند ابن حنبل : ٥ مرات عن أبي هريرة ومرتين عن طريق ابي بن كعب .

الحديث رقم (٢٠)

الرواة عن أبي هريرة :

١ - ابو زرعة　　٢ - ابو صالح　　٣ - ابن المسيب　　٤ - محمد

١ - تلاميذ أبي زرعة : طلق بن معاوية	ن جنائز ٢٥
٢ - تلاميذ أبي صالح	خ جنائز ٦
أ - عبد الرحمن	خ جنائز ٦
ب - سهيل وعنه : -	
١ - سفيان	الحميدي ١٠١٩
٢ - عبد العزيز بن محمد	م البر ١٥١ ؛ حم ٣٧٨/٢
٣ - عبد العزيز بن المختار	الاصل /٢٠
٣ - تلاميذ ابن المسيب : الزهري	خ جنائز ٦ ؛ م البر ١٥٠ ؛ ن جنائز ٢٥
٤ - تلاميذ محمد : عوف	ن جنائز ٢٥

الشواهد :

١ - ابو سعيد الخدري　　٢ - ام سليم　　٣ - أبو ذر
٤ - ابو النضر السلمي　　٥ - ابن مسعود　　٦ - أنس
٧ - رجاء　　٨ - معاذ

(١) ابو سعيد الخدري : عبد الرحمن - ابو صالح - عنه .　　الجعد ٦١ ؛ خ علم ٣٦ ، جنائز ٦ ؛ اعتصام ٩ ؛ م البر ١٥٢ ؛ ١٥٣ ؛ يعلى ٧٤ ب

(٢) ام سليم : عثمان بن حكيم - عمرو بن عامر - عنها　　راهويه ١/١٥

(٣) ابو ذر : الحسن - صعصعة - عنه　　ن جنائز ٢٥

(٤) ابو النضر السلمي : محمد بن أبي بكر بن حزم - عنه　　ط جنائز ٣٩

(٥) ابن مسعود : عاصم بن بهولة - ابو وائل - عنه　　طك ١٢٥/٥ ب

(٦) انس :

أ – حفص بن عبيد الله – عمران – انس ن جنائز ٢٤

ب – ابن علية – عبد العزيز – انس خ جنائز ٩٢

عبد الوارث – عبد العزيز – انس خ جنائز ٦ ؛ ن جنائز ٢٥

(٧) رجاء : هشام – ابن سيرين – .. جاء حم ٥/٥٣

(٨) معاذ : يحيى – عبيد الله بن مسلم – معاذ الكشى ١٦ ب

ملحوظة : يوجد هذا الحديث في مصدر اباضى ايضاً :

ابو عبيدة – جابر بن زيد – ابو هريرة شرح مسند الربيع ٥٣٤/٣

مقارنة الروايات :

الروايات متفقة في شفاعة الاطفال الميتين . ووردت الزيادة في بعض الروايات وهي « لا تدخل النار إلا تحلة قسم . » وذكرت بعض الروايات ثلاثة أطفال بينما اضافت الاخرى او أثنتين ايضاً .

أسماء الرواة :

الطبقة الأولى :

١ – أبو هريرة	٢ – ابو سعيد الخدري	٣ – ام سليم
٤ – ابو ذر	٥ – ابو النضر السلمي	٦ – ابن مسعود
٧ – انس	٨ – رجاء	٩ – معاذ

الطبقة الثانية :

١ – ابو زرعة	٢ – ابو صالح	٣ – ابن المسيب
٤ – محمد	٥ – عمرو بن عامر	٦ – صعصعة
٧ – ابو بكر بن حزم	٨ – ابو وائل	٩ – عمران
١٠ – عبد العزيز	١١ – عبيد الله بن مسلم	١٢ – جابر بن زيد

الطبقة الثالثة :

١ – طلق بن معاوية	٢ – عبد الرحمن	٣ – سهيل
٤ – الزهري	٥ – عوف	٦ – عثمان بن حكيم
٧ – الحسن	٨ – محمد بن أبي بكر	٩ – عاصم بن بهدلة
١٠ – حفص بن عبيد الله	١١ – ابن عليه	١٢ – عبد الوارث
١٣ – هشام	١٤ – يحيى	١٥ – ابو عبيدة .

الرواية عن أكثر من شيخ :

في الطبقة الثانية : ابو صالح يروى عن ابي هريرة وعن أبي سعيد الخدري ولا أعلم احدا روى غيره عن الخدري، كذلك ابن سيرين روى عن أبي هريرة وهو الوحيد الراوي عن رجاء . وفي الطبقة الثالثة عبد الرحمن يروي عن أبي صالح عن ابي سعيد الخدري وأبي هريرة .

وروده في مسند ابن حنبل: مرة واحدة عن طريق أبي هريرة .

الحديث رقم (٢١)

الرواة عن أبي هريرة :

١ – ابو صالح　　٢ – سعيد　　٣ – محمد بن أبي عائشة

١ – تلاميذ ابي صالح :

أ – رجاء بن حيوة	م مساجد ١٤٢ ؛ عوانة ٢٤٩/٢؛ طص ٦ – ١٦٥؛ طط ٢٤/٢ب
ب – سمى	خ اذان ١٥٥ ؛ م مساجد ١٤٢ ؛ عوانه ٩/٢ –٢٤٨ أنظر ايضاً خ دعوات ١٨
ج – سهيل وعنه : –	
١ – روح	م مساجد ١٤٣
٢ – سفيان الثوري	الثوري رقم ١٠٩
٣ – عبد العزيز بن المختار	الاصل ٢١
٢ – تلاميذ سعيد : ابو معشر	يعلى ٣٠١ ب
٣ – تلاميذ محمد بن أبي عائشة : حسان بن عطية	دي صلاة ٩٠ ؛ حم ٢٣٨/٢ ؛ دو تر ٢٤ ؛ طط ١/١٩/٢

الشواهد :

١ – ابو الدرداء :　　٢ – ابوذر

(١) ابو الدرداء

أ – الحكم – ابو عمر الصيني – عنه	حم ٤٤٦/٦
ب – خصيف – مجاهد وعكرمة – عنه	طك ٢٢٠/٥ ب ؛ ن سهو ٩٥
ج – عبد العزيز – ابن عمر – عنه	الثوري ٤٧ ب
د – عبد العزيز – ابو صالح – عنه	حم ١٥٨/٥

(٢) ابو ذر :

أ – عبد الله بن الحارث – ابوه – عنه	حم ١٥٨/٥
ب – بشر بن عاصم – عاصم – عنه	حميدي ١٣٣ ؛ جه اقامه ٣٢

مقارنة الروايات :

اتفقت الروايات على ان مجموع التحميد والتسبيح والتكبير هو ١٠٠ ما عدا رواية سهيل وسمي، ثم اختلف الرواة في العدد على وجه الانفراد فقال بعضهم : « التحميد ٣٤» والبقية «٣٣» وقال الآخرون غير ذلك . وقال سمي: « كل واحد منها ٣٣ » . أما سهيل فكأنه فهم ٣٣ هو مجموع التحميد والتكبير والتسبيح فقال : « احد عشر ، احد عشر ، احد عشر» . م مساجد ١٤٣

أسماء الرواة :

الطبقة الأولى :

١ – ابو هريرة
٢ – ابو الدرداء
٣ – ابو ذر

الطبقة الثانية :

١ – ابو صالح
٢ – سعيد
٣ – محمد بن أبي عائشة
٤ – ابو عمرو الصيني
٥ – مجاهد
٦ – عكرمة
٧ – ابن عمر
٨ – الحارث
٩ – عاصم

الطبقة الثالثة :

١ – رجاء بن حيوة
٢ – سمي
٣ – سهيل
٤ – ابو معشر
٥ – حسان بن عطيه
٦ – الحكم
٧ – خصيف
٨ – عبد العزيز
٩ – عبد الله بن الحارث
١٠ – بشر بن عاصم

الرواية عن أكثر من شيخ : في الطبقة الثانية : ابو صالح يروي عن أكثر من شيخ
في الطبقة الثالثة : عبد العزيز يروي عن أكثر من شيخ

وروده في مسند ابن حنبل : مرة واحدة عن طريق ابي هريرة ومرتين عن طريق الآخرين .

الحديث رقم (٢٢)

تلاميذ أبي هريرة : –

١ – ابو صالح
٢ – ابو سلمة
٣ – عبد الله الاغر
٤ – ابو جعفر
٥ – عطاء
٦ – ابن مرجانة
٧ – سعيد المقبري

١ – تلاميذ أبي صالح : سهيل وعنه : –

١ – معمر	حم ٢٨٢/٢
٢ – يعقوب	حم ٤١٩/٢ ؛ م مسافرين ١٦٩
٣ – عبد العزيز المختار	الاصل ٢٢

٢ – تلاميذ أبي سلمة :

أ – يحيى — م مسافرين ١٧٠

ب – محمد بن عمرو — حم ٢/٥٠٤ ؛ دى صلاة ١٦٨

٣ – تلاميذ عبد الله الاغر :

أ – الزهري — حم ٢/٤٧٨ ؛ خ توحيد ٣٥

ب – ابو اسحاق — م مسافرين ١٧٢

تلاميذ ابي سلمة + الأغر : الزهري — حم ٢/٥–٢٦٤ ؛ ٢٦٧ ؛ خ دعوات ١٤ ؛ تهجد ١٤ ؛ م مسافرين ١٦٨ ؛ جه اقامة ١٨٢ ؛ ط القرآن ٣٠

٤ – تلاميذ أبي جعفر : يحيى — حم ٢/٢٥٨ : ٥٢١

٥ – تلاميذ عطاء : المقبري — دى صلاة ١٦٨

٦ – تلاميذ ابن مرجانة : سعد بن سعيد — م مسافرين ١٧١

٧ – تلاميذ سعيد المقبري

أ – عبيد الله — حم ٢/٤٣٣

ب – يحيى القطان — حم ٢/٤٣٣

الشواهد :

١ – ابو سعيد الخدرى — ٢ – جبير بن مطعم — ٣ – رفاعة

٤ – عثمان بن أبي العاص — ٥ – علي

(١) ابو سعيد : أبو اسحاق – الاغر – عنه . م مسافرين ١٧٢ ؛ يعلى ٧٠ ب

(٢) جبير بن مطعم : عمرو بن دينار – نافع بن جبير – عنه . حم ٤/٨١ ؛ طك ١/١٠٦ب

(٣) رفاعة : هلال – عطاء بن يسار – عنه . حم ٤/١٦ ؛ دى صلاة ١٦٨ ؛ طك ٣/١/١٦

(٤) عثمان بن أبي العاص :

أ – علي بن زيد – الحسن – عنه . حم ٤/٢١٨ ؛ طك ٥/١/١٠

ب – هشام بن حسان – محمد بن سيرين – عنه . طك ٥/١/١١

(٥) علي : عبد الله بن أبي رافع – أبو رافع – عنه . دى صلاة ١٦٨

ملحوظة . ورد هذا الحديث في مصدر شيعي . الكافي ١/١٢٦

وفي مصدر إباضى ايضاً الربيع ٢/٣٦

مقارنة الروايات :

اختلف الرواة في توقيت نزول الله سبحانه وتعالى إلى سماء الدنيا فذكر بعضهم : « اذا مضى ثلث الليل » وقال الباقون : « إذا بقي ثلث الليل » وبعض الروايات لم يذكر التوقيت .

أسماء الرواة :

الطبقة الأولى :

١ – ابو هريرة	٢ – ابو سعيد الخدري	٣ – جبير بن مطعم
٤ – رفاعة	٥ – عثمان بن أبي العاص	٦ – على

الطبقة الثانية :

١ – ابو صالح	٢ – ابو سلمة	٣ – عبد الله الاغر
٤ – ابو جعفر	٥ – عطاء	٦ – ابن مرجانة
٧ – سعيد المقبري	٨ – نافع بن جبير	٩ – الحسن
١٠ – محمد بن سيرين	١١ – ابو رافع	

الطبقة الثالثة :

١ – سهيل	٢ – يحي	٣ – محمد بن عمرو
٤ – الزهري	٥ – ابو اسحاق	٦ – المقبري
٧ – عبيد الله	٨ – عمرو بن دينار	٩ – هلال
١٠ – على بن زيد	١١ – هشام بن حسان	١٢ – عبدالله بن ابي رافع

الرواية عن أكثر من شيخ :

في الطبقة الثانية : عبد الله الأغر وعطاء يرويان عن أكثر من شيخ
في الطبقة الثالثة : الزهري وأبو اسحاق ويحي يروون عن أكثر من شيخ

وروده في مسند ابن حنبل : ١٠ مرات عن طريق ابي هريرة و ٣ مرات عن طريق الآخرين .

الحديث رقم (٢٣)

الرواة عن أبي هريرة :

١ – ابو صالح	٢ – الأعرج	٣ – بشير بن نهيك

تلاميذ ابي صالح : سهيل وعنه : –

١ – جرير	م ادب ٤٣
٢ – حماد	حم ٢/٤١٤
٣ – عبد العزيز بن المختار	الاصل /٢٣
٤ – معمر	حم ٢/٢٦٦
٥ – وهيب	طس ٢٤٢٦

٢ – تلاميذ الأعرج : أبو الزناد حم ٢٤٣/٢ ؛ ٤٢٨ ؛ الحميدي ١٠٧٨ ؛ خ ديات ١٥ ، ٢٣ ؛ م ادب ٤٤ ؛ ن قسامه ٤٨ .

٣ – تلاميذ بشير بن نهيك : النضر بن انس.حم ٣٨٥/٢ ؛ ن قسامه ٤٨ ؛ راهويه ٢٤ ب .

الشواهد :

١ – انس بن مالك ٢ – سهل بن سعد السعدي .

(١) الرواة عن أنس :

أ – أبو النضر – عيسى بن طهمان – عنه حم ١٤٠/٣

ب – سهل – حميد – عنه حم ١٧٨/٣

ج – يحيى – حميد – عنه حم ١٢٥/٣

د – ابن ابي عدي– حميد – عنه حم ١٠٨/٣

هـ – حماد بن سلمة – إسحاق – عنه حم ١٩١/٣

و – حماد بن زيد–عبيد الله بن أبي بكر– عنه حم ٢٣٩/٣ ؛ ٢٤٢ ؛ خديات ٢٣

(٢) الرواة عن سهل بن سعد السعدي : الزهري وعنه :

أ – الليث خ ديات ٢٣

ب – الأوزاعي دي ديات ٢٣

ج – ابن أبي ذئب دى ديات ٢٣ ؛ الكشي ١/٥٣

د – معمر حم ٣٣٥/٥

مقارنة الروايات :

الرواة متفقون في المعنى وإلى حد كبير في الالفاظ .

أسماء الرواة :

الطبقة الأولى :

١ – ابو هريرة . ٢ – أنس بن مالك . ٣ – سهل بن سعد السعدي

الطبقة الثانية :

١ – أبو صالح . ٢ – الأعرج . ٣ – بشير بن نهيك .

٤ – عيسى بن طهمان . ٥ – حميد . ٦ – اسحاق .

٧ – عبيد الله بن أبي بكر. ٨ – الزهري .

الطبقة الثالثة :

١ – سهيل . ٢ – ابو الزناد . ٣ – النضر بن أنس .

٤ – أبو النضر . ٥ – سهل . ٦ – يحيى .

٧ – ابن أبي عدي . ٨ – حماد بن سلمة . ٩ – حماد بن زيد .
١٠ – الليث . ١١ – الاوزاعي . ١٢ – ابن ابي ذئب .
١٣ – معمر .

الرواية عن أكثر من شيخ : في الطبقة الثالثة معمر يروي عن أكثر من شيخ .

وروده في مسند ابن حنبل : ٥ مرات عن طريق ابي هريرة و ٨ مرات عن طريق الآخرين.

الحديث رقم (٢٤)

الرواة عن أبي هريرة :

١ – تلاميذ أبي صالح : سهيل وعنه :

١ – روح بن القاسم	م ذكر ٨١
٢ – عبد العزيز بن المختار	الأصل /٢٤
٣ – وهيب	م ذكر ٨١

الشواهد :

١ – علي ٢ – علي بن الحسين .

(١) الرواة عن علي :

أ – الحكم – ابن أبي ليلى – عنه خ دعوات ١١ ؛ نفقات ٦ ؛ م ذكر ٣٤ ؛ ٨٠

ب – مجاهد – ابن أبي ليلى – عنه خ نفقات ٧ ؛ م ذكر ٨ ؛ حميدي ٤٣ ؛ حم ٨٠/١ ؛راهويه ١/٢٤٧ – ب.

ج – عمرو بن مرة – ابن أبي ليلى – عنه الكشي ٩ ب

د – خالد – ابن سيرين خ دعوات ١١ (موقوفاً) .

ه – عطاء بنأبي السائب–أبو السائب–عنه حم ١٠٦-١/٧ ؛ الحميدي ٤٤ .

و – محمد – عبيده – عنه. حم١٢٣/١.وانظر موقوفاً علىمحمد خ دعوات١١

ز أبو اسحاق – هبيرة – عنه . حم ١٤٦/١

ح – أبوالورد – ابن أعبد – عنه حم ١٥٣/١

و – معمر – الزهري–عنه بن الحسين (مرسلا) راهويه ١/٢٤٧

ملحوظة: يوجد هذا الحديث فيمصدر شيعي أيضاً علل الشرائع ٥٥/٢ ؛ الكافي ٥٣٦/٢ .

مقارنة الروايات :

الروايات متفقة في المعنى وفي الالفاظ الى حد كبير جداً واختلف الرواة في عدد ٣٤ هل هو للتسبيح او للتحميد أوللتكبير .

أسماء الرواة :

الطبقة الأولى :

١ – أبو هريرة . ٢ – علي . ٣ – علي بن الحسين (مرسلا)

الطبقة الثانية :

١ – أبو صالح . ٢ – ابن أبي ليلى . ٣ – أبو السائب .
٤ – عبيده . ٥ – هبيره . ٦ – ابن اعبد .
٧ – الزهري .

الطبقة الثالثة :

١ – سهيل . ٢ – الحكم . ٣ – مجاهد .
٤ – عمرو بن مرة . ٥ – عطاء . ٦ – محمد .
٧ – أبو اسحاق . ٨ – أبو الورد . ٩ – معمر .

الرواية عن أكثر من شيخ : لا توجد .

وروده في مسند ابن حنبل : ٥ مرات عن طريق علي .

الحديث رقم (٢٥)

الرواة عن أبي هريرة :

١ – أبو صالح ٢ – سعيد ٣ – عجلان ٤ – عبد الرحمن .

١ – تلاميذ أبي صالح : سهيل وعنه :

١ – اسماعيل بن زكريا	د صلاة ٩٧
٢ – جرير	م صلاة ١٣٢
٣ – خالد بن عبد الله	حم ٣٦٧/٢ ؛ د صلاة ٩٧
٤ – عبد العزيز بن محمد	م صلاة ١٣٢ ؛ جه اقامة ٥٢
٥ – عبد العزيز بن المختار	الأصل /٢٥ ؛ خزيمة ١٦٤ ب
٦ – عبد العزيز بن مسلم	حم ٣٣٦/٢
٧ – وهيب	طس ٢٤٠٨
٢ – تلاميذ سعيد : ابن عجلان	حم ٢٤٧/٢؛ الحميدي /١٠٠٠
٣ – تلاميذ عجلان : ابن عجلان	حم ٣٤٠/٢ ؛ دى صلاة ٥٢

٤– تلاميذ عبدالرحمن : العلاء بن عبد الرحمن .حم ٤٨٥/٢ ؛ جه اقامة ٥٢ ؛ خزيمة ١٦٤ ب

الشواهد :

١ – عمر ٢ – ابو سعيد الخدرى ٣ – جابر ٤ – ابن عباس .

(١) عمر : نافع – ابن عمر – عنه . طط ١/٣٠ب
(٢) أبو سعيد الخدري :
أ – عبيد الله بن أبي بكر – ابن المسيب – عنه . خزيمة ١٦٤ ب ؛ يعلى ١/٦٧
ب – عبد الله بن محمد بن عقيل – ابن المسيب – عنه . حم ٣/٣ ؛ ١٦
(٣) جابر :
أ – زائدة – عبد الله بن محمد بن عقيل – عنه . حم ٢٩٣/٣
ب – سفيان – عبد الله بن عقيل – عنه . حم ٣٣١/٣ ؛ جه اقامة ٥٢
(٤) ابن عباس . عمارة بن ثوبان – عطاء بن أبي رباح – عنه . طط ١/٣٦/١ ؛ طك ١٩٣/٥/ ب

ملحوظة : يوجد هذا الحديث في مصدر زيدي أيضاً . مسند زيد ٨ – ١١٧
وكذلك في مصدر امامي ما يقارب في معنى هذا الحديث . الكافي ٣/٣ – ٣٧٢

مقارنة الروايات :

الروايات متفقة في المعنى وكذلك في الكلمات .

أسماء الرواة :

الطبقة الأولى :

١ – أبو هريرة . ٢ – عمر . ٣ – ابو سعيد الخدري .
٤ – جابر . ٥ – ابن عباس .

الطبقة الثانية :

١ – أبو صالح . ٢ – سعيد . ٣ – عجلان .
٤ – عبد الرحمن . ٥ – ابن عمر . ٦ – ابن المسيب .
٧ – عبد الله بن محمد بن عقيل . ٨ – عطاء بن أبي رباح .

الطبقة الثالثة :

١ – سهيل . ٢ – ابن عجلان . ٣ – العلاء .
٤ – نافع . ٥ – عبد الله بن أبي بكر ٦– عبدالله بن محمدبن عقيل .
٧ – زائدة . ٨ – سفيان . ٩ – عمارة بن ثوبان .

الرواية عن أكثر من شيخ :

في الطبقة الثانية يوجد راو مشترك ، عبد الله بن محمد بن عقيل . وفي الطبقة الثالثة محمد بن عجلان الراوي الوحيد عن الشيخين المقبري وعجلان .

وروده في مسند ابن حنبل : ٥ مرات عن طريق أبي هريرة و ٤ مرات عن طريق الآخرين.

الحديث رقم (٢٦)

الرواة عن أبي هريرة :

١ – أبو صالح ٢ – أبو حازم ٣ – أبو سلمة ٤ – ابن سيرين
٥ – ابن المسيب ٦ – الأعرج ٧ – سالم البراد ٨ – عامر الشعبي
٩ – المقبري ١٠ – نافع بن جبير ١١ – نافع مولى ابن عمر ١٢ – الوليد بن عبد الرحمن .

١ – تلاميذ أبي صالح :

أ – سمي — حم ٢٤٦/٢ ؛ الحميدي ١٠٢١ ، المنتقى ٥٢٦ ، دجنائز ٤١ ؛ يعلى ٣٠٥ ب .

ب – سهيل وعنه :

١ – روح بن القاسم — طط ١/٤٠/١
٢ – عبد العزيز بن المختار — الأصل /٢٦
٣ – وهيب . — م جنائز ٥٣

٢ – تلاميذ ابي حازم :

أ – عدي بن ثابت — طص ١٢٦ ؛ يعلى ٢٧٣ ب
ب – يزيد بن كيسان — م جنائز ٥٤

٣ – تلاميذ أبي سلمة : محمد بن عمرو — حم ٤٧٠/٢ ؛ ٤٩٨ ؛ ٥٠٣
٤ – تلاميذ ابن سيرين : عوف — حم ٤٣٠/٢ ؛ ن جنائز ٧٩ ؛ ن إيمان ٢٦
٥ – تلاميذ ابن المسيب : الزهري — حم ٢٣٣/٢ ؛ ٢٨٠ ؛ ن جنائز ٧٩ ؛ خ جنائز ٥٩ م جنائز ٥٢ ؛ جه جنائز ٣٤ ،
٦ – تلاميذ الأعرج : الزهري — حم ٤٠١/٢ ؛ ن جنائز ٧٩ ؛ خ جنائز ٥٩ ؛ م جنائز ٥٢
٧ – تلاميذ سالم البراد : عبد الملك بن عمير حم ٤٥٨/٢
٨ – تلاميذ عامر الشعبي : داود بن أبي هند ن جنائز ٧٩ ؛ طط ١/١١٨/١ ؛ يعلى ٣٠٤ ب
٩ – تلاميذ المقبري : سعيد بن ابي سعيد خ جنائز ٥٩ ؛ الجعد ٣٧٢
١٠ – تلاميذ نافع بن جبير : الحارث بن عبد المطلب حم ٢٧٣/٢
١١ – تلاميذ نافع مولى ابن عمر : جرير بن حازم خ جنائز ٥ ؛ ٥٨ ؛ م جنائز ٥٥
١٢ – تلاميذ الوليد بن عبد الرحمن : يعلى بن عطاء حم ٣٨٧/٢

الشواهد :

١ – ابي بن كعب ٢ – ابو سعيد الخدري ٣ – البراء بن عازب ٤ – ثوبان
٥ – عبد الله بن المغفل ٦ – ابن عمر ٧ – عائشة .

(١) ابن أبي كعب : عدي بن ثابت – ذر بن حبيش – عنه . حم ١٣١/٥ ؛ جه جنائز ٣٤

(٢) أبو سعيد الخدري :
أ – فضيل بن مرزوق – عطية العوفي – عنه . حم ٢٠/٣ ؛ الجعد ٢٥٧
ب – عمرو بن يحيى–محمد بن يوسف – عنه . حم ٢٧/٣ ؛ ٩٧
(٣) البراء بن عازب : برد – المسيب بن رافع – عنه . حم ٢٩٤/٤ ؛ ن جنائز ٥٤ ؛ الفسوى ١/٢٩٩/٣
(٤) ثوبان : سالم بن أبي الجعد – معدان بن طلحة – عنه حم ٢٧٦/٥ ؛ ٢٧٧ ؛ ٢٨٣ ؛ ٢٨٤ ؛ م جنائز ٥٧ ؛ جه جنائز ٣٤
(٥) عبد الله بن المغفل :
أ – اشعث – الحسن – عنه . ن جنائز ٥٤
ب – المبارك – الحسن – عنه . حم ٨٦/٤ ؛ الجعد ٤٢٢
(٦) ابن عمر : اسماعيل – سالم – عنه . حم ١٦/٢ ؛ ١٤٤
(٧) عائشة : عامر بن سعد – خباب – عائشة وابن عمر . م جنائز ٥٦
جرير بن حازم – نافع – عائشة وابن‌عمر وابو هريرة . خ جنائز ٥٨
ملحوظة : يوجد معنى هذا الحديث في مصدر امامي ايضاً الكافي ١٧٣/٣

مقارنة الروايات :

الروايات متفقة في المعنى وكذلك في الالفاظ .

أسماء الرواة :

الطبقة الأولى :

١ – أبو هريرة .
٢ – ابي بن كعب .
٣ – ابو سعيد الخدري .
٤ – البراء بن عازب .
٥ – ثوبان .
٦ – عبد الله بن المغفل .
٧ – ابن عمر .
٨ – عائشة .

الطبقة الثانية :

١ – أبو صالح .
٢ – ابو حازم .
٣ – ابو سلمة .
٤ – ابن سيرين .
٥ – ابن المسيب .
٦ – الأعرج .
٧ – سالم البراد .
٨ – عامر الشعبي .
٩ – المقبري .
١٠ – نافع بن جبير .
١١ – نافع مولى ابن عمر .
١٢ – الوليد .
١٣ – زر بن حبيش .
١٤ – عطية العوفي
١٥ – محمد بن يوسف .
١٦ – المسيب بن رافع .
١٧ – معدان بن طلحة .
١٨ – الحسن .
١٩ – خباب

الطبقة الثالثة :

١ – سمي . ٢ – سهيل . ٣ – عدي بن ثابت .
٤ – يزيد بن كيسان . ٥ – محمد بن عمرو . ٦ – عوف .
٧ – الزهري . ٨ – عبد الملك بن عمير . ٩ – داود بن أبي هند .
١٠ – سعيد بن ابي سعيد . ١١ – الحارث بن عبد المطلب . ١٢ – جرير بن حازم .
١٣ – يعلى بن عطاء . ١٤ – فضيل بن مرزوق . ١٥ – عمرو بن يحيى .
١٦ – برد . ١٧ – سالم بن أبي الجعد ١٧ – أشعث .
١٩ – المبارك . ٢٠ – اسماعيل . ٢١ – عامر بن سعد .

الرواية عن أكثر من شيخ :

في الطبقة الثانية سالم ونافع يرويان عن أكثر من شيخ . في الطبقة الثالثة عدي بن ثابت والزهري وجرير بن حازم واسماعيل يروون عن أكثر من شيخ .

وروده في مسند ابن حنبل : ١١ مرة عن طريق ابي هريرة و ١٢ مرة عن طريق الآخرين.

الحديث رقم (٢٧)

الرواة عن أبي هريرة :

١ – أبو سلمة ٢ – أبو صالح ٣ – ابن سيرين ٤ – ابن المسيب
٥ – شهر بن حوشب ٦ – عبد الرحمن ٧ – عراك بن مالك ٨ – مجاهد
٩ – محمد بن زياد .

١ – تلاميذ أبي سلمة :

أ – الزهري	حم ٢٤١/٢ ؛ ٢٧٩ ؛ م اشربه ٣١ ؛ ن اشربه ٣١
ب – محمد بن عمرو	حم ٥٠١/٢ ؛ ن اشربه ٢٥ ؛ جه اشربه ١٣ يعلى ٣٧٣/ ب
ج – يحيى	حم ٥٤٠/٢ ؛ ن اشربه ٣٣

٢ – تلاميذ أبي صالح : سهيل وعنه :

١ – عبد العزيز بن المختار	الأصل /٢٧
٢ – وهيب	طس ٢٤٠٩
٣ – تلاميذ ابن سيرين : عبدالله بن عون	م اشربه ٣٣ ؛ د اشربه ٧ ؛ يعلى ١/٢٧٨
٤ – تلاميذ ابن المسيب : يزيد بن ابراهيم	حم ٤١٤/٢
٥ – تلاميذ شهر بن حوشب : حفص بن خالد	حم ٣٥٥/٢
٦ – تلاميذ عبد الرحمن : العلاء	حم ٥١٤/٢ ؛ ط اشربه ٦
٧ – تلاميذ عراك بن مالك : عبدالله بن ابي سلمة	طط ١٩٩/١ ب

٨ – تلاميذ مجاهد : أبو اسحاق يعلى ١/٢٨٠ – ب

٩ – تلاميذ محمد بن زياد : أ – الحسين ن اشربه ٣٤

ب – هشام ن اشربه ٣٨ ؛ حم ٢/٤٩١

الشواهد :

١ – أبو سعيد الخدري ٢ – ابن عباس ٣ – ابن عمر ٤ – ام سلمة

٥ – أنس ٦ – بريدة ٧ – ثوبان ٨ – جابر

٩ – الحكم الغفاري ١٠ – سمرة ١١ – عائذ ١٢ – عائشة

١٣ – عبد الرحمن بن يعمر ١٤ – عبد الله بن جابر ١٥ – عبد الله بن الزبير ١٦ – عبدالله بن المغفل

١٧ – علي ١٨ – عمران بن حصين ١٩ – ميمونة ٢٠ – وفد عبد القيس .

(١) أبوسعيد الخدري . وروى عنه : ١ – اخو عبد الحكم ٢ – ابو المتوكل ٣ – ابو النضرة ٤ – بشر بن حرب .

١ – تلاميذ اخي عبد الحكم بن عبد الله : عبد الحكم . يعلى ٧٢ ب

٢ – تلاميذ ابي المتوكل : المثنى بن سعيد . م اشربه ٤٥ ؛ اشربه ٣٢ ؛ جه اشربه ١٣ ؛ طس ٢٢٢٠

٣ – تلاميذ أبي النضرة : قتادة . حم ٣/٢٣ ؛ ٩٠ ؛ م اشربه ٤٤

٤ – تلاميذ بشر بن حرب : حماد . طس ٢١٧٢

(٢) ابن عباس . وروى عنه : ١ – ابو جمرة ٢ – أبو الحكم ٣ – ابن جبير ٤ – ابن المسيب ٥ – أنس ٦ – عكرمة ٧ – قيس ٨ – الحكم بن عتيبة .

١ – تلاميذ أبي جمرة :

أ – بسطام بن مسلم طك ٥/٢٧٤ ب

ب – حماد م اشربه ٣٩ ؛ د اشربه ٧ ؛ طك ٥/٢٧٣ ب

ج – شعبة حم ١/٢٢٨ ؛ الجعد ١٥١

د – عباد بن عباد ن ايمان ٢٥ ؛ د اشربه ٧

هـ – معمر حم ١/٤ – ٣٣٣

٢ – تلاميذ أبي الحكم وعنه : سلمة بن كهيل . حم ١/٢٧ ؛ طك ٥/٢٦٢ ب

٣ – تلاميذ ابن جبير :

أ – أبو بشر حم ١/٢٩١

ب – حبيب بن أبي عمرة حم ١/٢٧٦ ؛ ٣٠٤ ؛ م اشربه ٤٠ ؛ ٤١

ج – سلمة بن ابي عطاء طك ٥/٢٥١ ب

د – منصور بن حيان م اشربه ٤٧ ؛ ن اشربه ٣٥

٤ – تلاميذ ابن المسيب : قتادة حم ١/٣٦١

٥ – تلاميذ انس : أسماء بنت يزيد ن اشربه ٣٥

٦ – تلاميذعكرمه :

أ – حسين بن عبد الله يعلى ١٣٧ ب

ب – قتادة حم ٣٦١/١

٧ – تلاميذقيس : علي بن جذيمة د اشربه ٧ ؛ طلك ١/٢٥٤/٥

٨ – تلاميذيحيى بن عمرالبهراني : الحكم بن عتيبة . حم ٣٤١/١ ؛ م اشربه ٤٢

(٣) ابن عمر . وروى عنه :

١ – أبو الزبير ٢ – ابن المسيب ٣ – زاذان

٤ – سعيد بن المحارب ٥ – طاووس ٦ – عقبة بن حريث

٧ – عمرو بن دينار ٨ – محارب بن دثار ٩ – معروف بن بشير

١٠ – نافع .

١ – تلاميذ ابي الزبير : زهير طس ١٩١٧

٢ – تلاميذابن المسيب : عبد الخالق حم ٧٨/٢ ؛ م اشربه ٥٨

٣ – تلاميذزاذان : عمروبن مرة طس ١٩٣٩ انظر حم ٥٦/٢ أيضاً

٤ – تلاميذسعيد بن المحارب : عبد الله ن اشربة ٣٣

٥ – تلاميذطاوس :

أ – ابن طاوس حم ٣٥/٢

ب – ابراهيم بن ميسرة ن اشربه ٣٠

٦ – تلاميذعقبة بن حريث : شعبة حم ٤٤/٢ ؛ ٤ – ٧٣ ؛ م اشربه٥٥ ؛ طس١٩١١

٧ – تلاميذعمرو بن دينار : زكريا بن اسحاق طلك ١/٣١١/٥

٨ – تلاميذمحارب بن دثار : شعبة حم ٣/٢-٤٢ ؛ ٥٨ ؛ م اشربه ٥٤ ؛ طس ١٩٣٤

٩ – تلاميذمعروف بن بشير : قرة بن خالد طط ٨٦/١ ب

١٠ – تلاميذنافع :

أ – اسامة م اشربه ٤٩

ب – أيوب حم ٤٨/٢ ؛ م اشربه ٤٩

ج – عبيد الله حم ٥٤/٢ ؛ م اشربه ٤٩

د – الليث م اشربه ٤٩ ؛ جه اشربه ١٣

هـ – مالك ط اشربه ٥ ؛ م اشربه ٤٨

(٤) ام سلمة . عمار الدهني – امرأة مجهولة – ام سلمة حم ٣١٤/٦

(٥) انس بن مالك : روى عنه :

١ – الزهري ٢ – عمارة بن عاصم ٣ – المختار بن الفلفل

١ – تلاميذ الزهري :

أ – أيوب بن موسى طط ٢٣/١ ب

ب – سفيان حم ١١٠/٣ ؛ م اشربه ٣١ ؛ يعلى ١٧٠ ب

ج – الليث م اشربه ٣٠؛ ن اشربه ٣١
د – معمر حم ١٦٥/٣
٢ – تلاميذ عمارة بن عاصم : محمد بن اسماعيل حم ١٦٧/٣ ؛ طط ١/٨٥/١
٣ – تلاميذ المختار بن الفلفل :
أ – ابن ادريس حم ١١٩/٣
ب – زهير حم ١٥٤/٣
(٦) بريدة : وروى عنه : ١ – عبد الله بن بريدة ٢ – سليمان بن بريدة .
١ – تلاميذ عبد الله بن بريده : عطاء الخراساني طك ١/٧٨/١ – ب
٢ – تلاميذ سليمان بن بريده :
أ – أبو هباب حم ٣٥٩/٥
ب – محارب بن دثار داشربه ٧
(٧) ثوبان : يزيد بن ربيعة – أبو الاشعث – عنه . طك ١/٩٦ ب – ١/٩٧
(٨) جابر : روى عنه أبو الزبير وعنه :
أ – أبو خيثمة زهير بن معاوية م اشربه ٥٩ ؛ الجعد ٣٤١
ب – ابن جريج م اشربه ٦٠ ؛ ن اشربه ٣٨
ج – حرب بن أبي العالية طس ١٧٣٩
د – حماد حم ٣٥٦/٣
ه – عبد الملك بن أبي سليمان حم ٣٠٤/٣ ، ٣٥٧ ، ن اشربه ٣٨
(٩) الحكم الغفاري : ابو تميمة – دلجة بن قيس – عنه . طك ١/٢١٢/١
(١٠) سمرة : ورقاء بن إياس – علي بن ربيعة – عنه . حم ١٧/٥ ؛ طك ٢٠٥/٤ ب
(١١) عائذ بن عمرو : شعبة – أبو شمر الضبعي – عنه . حم ٦٤/٥ ؛ ٦٥
(١٢) عائشة : وروى عنها : ١ – أبو سلمة ٢ – ام ثلجة ٣ – اسود ٤ – ثمامة بن حزم ٥ – جميلة بنت عباد ٦ – عبد خير ٧ – عبد الله بن شماس ٨ – عبد الله بن معقل ٩ – القاسم بن محمد ١٠ – معاذة البصرية ١١ – هنيدة بنت شريك .
١ – تلاميذابي سلمة : ثمامة بن الكلاب . حم ٢٤٢/٦
٢ – تلاميذ أم ثلجة : يزيد بن أبي زياد . طط ١/٢٩٢/١
٣ – تلاميذاسود : ابراهيم . حم ١١٥/٦ ؛ ١٧٢ ؛ ٢٠٣ ؛ م اشربه ٣٥ ؛ ٣٦ طس ١٣٧٦ ؛ الجعد ٩٥ ؛ يعلى ٢٠٥ ب ؛ طط ١٦٨/١ ب
٤ – تلاميذثمامة بن حزم : القاسم بن الفضل . م اشربه ٣٧ ؛ ن اشربه ٣٤
٥ – تلاميذ جميلة بنت عباد : عون بن صالح البارقي . ن اشربه ٣٣
٦ – تلاميذعبد خير : خالد بن علقمة . حم ٢٤٤/٦ وانظر أيضاً طس ١٥٣٨
٧ – تلاميذ عبد الله بن شماس : عبد الله بن عمران . حم ٩٧/٦
٨ – تلاميذ عبد الله بن معقل : الأشعث . حم ٨٠/٦ ؛ ٩٨ ؛ ١٢٣

٩ – تلاميذالقاسم بن محمد : ابن زيد ن اشربه ٢٥
١٠ – تلاميذ معاذة : اسحاق بن سويد م اشربه ٣٨ ؛ ن اشربه ٣٤
١١ – تلاميذهنيدة بنت شريك : عبد الملك القيسي ن اشربه ٣٤
(١٣) عبد الرحمن بن يعمر : شعبة – بكير بن عطاء – عنه جه اشربه ١٣
(١٤) عبد الله بن جابر العبدي : الحـاث بن مرة – نفيس – حم ٤٤٦/٥ ؛ بغداد ٢٠٨/٨
(١٥) عبد الله بن الزبير : سلمة بن كهيل – أبو الحكم – عنه حم ٢٧/١
(١٦) عبد الله بن المغفل : عاصم الاحول – الفضل بن يزيد الرقاشي – عنه حم ٨٦/٤ ؛ ٨٧ ؛ ٥٧/٥
(١٧) علي بن ابي طالب : روى عنه :
١ – الحارث بن سويد ٢ – صعصعة بن صوحان ٣ – عبد الرحمن بن أبي ليلى.
١ – تلاميذ الحارث بن سويد : ابراهيم التيمي حم ٨٣/١ ؛ ١٤٠ ؛ م اشربه ٣٤ ؛ ن اشربه ٣١؛ يعلى ٣٧ ب
٢ – تلاميذصعصعة بن صوحان : مالك بن عمير حم ١١٩/١ ؛ وانظر أيضاً د اشربه ٧
٣ – تلاميذعبد الرحمن بن أبي ليلى : مسلم الأعور يعلى ٣٧ ب
(١٨) عمران بن حصين : أبو التياح – حفص الليثي – عنه حم ٤٤٣/٤
(١٩) ميمونة : عبد الله بن محمد بن عقيل – سليمان بن يسار – عنها حم ٣٣٣/٦
(٢٠) احد اعضاء وفد عبد القيس : عوف – زيد بن عدي – احد اعضاء الوفد حم ٢٠٦/٤ ؛ واشربة ٧

مقارنة الروايات :

اتفق عامة الرواة على ان رسول الله صلى الله عليه وسلم منع استعمال بعض الاوعية التي كانت تستعمل لصناعة المسكرات . فقال بعضهم : نهى عن المزفت والحنتم والنقير .
وقال الآخرون نهى عن الدباء والمزفت
وورد في بعض الروايات نهى عن الجرار الخضر والدباء .

أسماء الرواة :

الطبقة الأولى :

١ – أبو هريرة ٢ – أبو سعيد الخدري ٣ – ابن عباس
٤ – ابن عمر ٥ – ام سلمة ٦ – أنس
٧ – بريدة ٨ – ثوبان ٩ – جابر
١٠ – الحكم الغفاري ١١ – سمرة ١٢ – عائذ
١٣ – عائشة ١٤ – عبد الرحمن بن يعمر ١٥ – عبد الله بن جابر

١٦ – عبد الله بن الزبير ١٧ – عبد الله بن المغفل ١٨ – علي
١٩ – عمران بن حصين ٢٠ – ميمونة
٢١ – وفد عبد القيس (احد الأعضاء)

الطبقة الثانية :

١ – ابن جبير الكوفي ٢ – ابن سيرين البصري ٣ – ابن المسيب المدني
٤ – اسود الكوفي ٥ – ابو الأشعث ٦ – ابو الحكم الكوفي
٧ – ابو جمرة البصري ٨ – أبو الزبير المكي ٩ – ابو سلمة المدني
١٠ – ابو شمر الضبعي ١١ – أبو صالح المدني ١٢ – ابو المتوكل البصري
١٣ – أبو النضرة البصري ١٤ – أخو عبد الحكم البصري ١٥ – ام ثلجة
١٦ – امرأة مجهولة ١٧ – انس البصري ١٨ – بشر بن حرب البصري
١٩ – بكير بن عطاء الكوفي ٢٠ – ثمامة بن حزم البصري ٢١ – جميلة بنت عباد
٢٢ – الحارث بن سويد الكوفي ٢٣ – حفص البصري ٢٤ – دجلة بن قيس
٢٥ – زاذان ٢٦ – الزهري المدني ٢٧ – زيد بن عدي
٢٨ – سعيد بن محارب ٢٩ – سليمان بن بريده المروزي ٣٠ – سليمان بن يسار المدني
٣١ – شهر بن حوشب الشامي ٣٢ – صعصعة بن صوحان الكوفي ٣٣ – طاووس اليماني
٣٤ – عبد خير ٣٥ – عبد الرحمن المدني ٣٦ – عبد الرحمن بن ابي ليلى الكوفي
٣٧ – عبد الله بن بريدة المروزي ٣٨ – عبد الله بن الشماس المصري
٣٩ – عبد الله بن المغفل الكوفي ٤٠ – عراك بن مالك المدني ٤١ – عقبة بن حريث الكوفي
٤٢ – عكرمة المدني ٤٣ – علي بن ربيعة الكوفي ٤٤ – عمارة بن عاصم
٤٥ – عمرو بن دينار المكي ٤٦ – الفضل بن يزيد الرقاشي البصري
٤٧ – القاسم بن محمد المدني ٤٨ – قيس بن حبتر الكوفي ٤٩ – مجاهد المكي
٥٠ – محارب بن دثار الكوفي ٥١ – محمد بن زياد المدني ٥٢ – المختار بن الفلفل الكوفي
٥٣ – معاذة البصرية ٥٤ – معروف بن بشير ٥٥ – نافع المدني
٥٦ – نفيس البصري ٥٧ – هنيدة بنت شريك البصرية
٥٨ – يحيى بن يعمر البهراني

الطبقة الثالثة :

١ – ابن ادريس الكوفي ٢ – ابن جريج المكي ٣ – ابن زيد
٤ – ابن طاووس اليماني ٥ – ابو اسحاق ٦ – ابو بشر الكوفي
٧ – أبو تميمة البصري ٨ – أبو التياح البصري ٩ – أبو خباب
١٠ – ابراهيم التيمي الكوفي ١١ – ابراهيم بن ميسرة الطائفي ١٢ – اسامة المدني
١٣ – اسحاق بن سويد البصري ١٤ – اسماء بنت يزيد البصرية ١٥ – اشعث الكوفي

١٦ – ايوب بن موسى المكي ١٧ – ايوب السختياني البصري ١٨ – بسطام بن مسلم البصري
١٩ – ثمامة المدني ٢٠ – الحارث بن مرة البصري ٢١ – حبيب بن ابي عمرة الكوفي
٢٢ – حرب بن ابي العالية البصري ٢٣ – الحسين ٢٤ – الحسين بن عبدالله المدني
٢٥ – حفص بن خالد الشامي ٢٦ – الحكم بن عتيبة الكوفي ٢٧ – حماد البصري
٢٨ – خالد بن علقمة ٢٩ – زكريا بن اسحاق المكي ٣٠ – زهير الكوفي ابوخيثمة
٣١ – الزهري المدني ٣٢ – سفيان المكي ٣٣ – سلمة بن أبي عطاء
٣٤ – سلمة بن كهيل الكوفي ٣٥ – سهيل المدني ٣٦ – شعبة الواسطي
٢٧ – عاصم الأحول البصري ٣٨ – عبد الحكم البصري ٣٩ – عباد بن عباد البصري
٤٠ – عبد الخالق البصري ٤١ – عبد الله
٤٢ – عبد الله بن أبي سلمة الماجشون المدني ٤٣ – عبد الله بن أبي عمران المكي
٤٤ – عبدالله بن محمد بن عقيل المدني ٤٥ – عبدالله بن عون البصري ٤٦ – عبيد الله المدني
٤٧ – عبد الملك العرزمي الكوفي ٤٨ – عبد الملك القيسي ٤٩ – عطاء الخراساني
٥٠ – عمار الدهني الكوفي ٥١ – عمرو بن مرة الكوفي ٥٢ – علي بن بذيمة الجزري
٥٣ – العلاء المدني ٥٤ – عوف ٥٥ – عون بن صالح
٥٦ – القاسم بن الفضل البصري ٥٧ – قتادة البصري ٥٨ – قرة بن خالد البصري
٥٩ – الليث المصري ٦٠ – مالك المدني ٦١ – مالك بن عمير الكوفي
٦٢ – المثنى البصري ٦٣ – محارب بن دثار الكوفي ٦٤ – محمد بن اسماعيل
٦٥ – محمد بن عمرو المدني ٦٦ – مسلم الأعور الكوفي ٦٧ – معمر اليمني
٦٨ – منصور بن حيان ٦٩ – هشام المدني ٧٠ – ورقاء الكوفي
٧١ – يحيى اليمامي ٧٢ – يزيد بن ابراهيم التستري ٧٣ – يزيد بن أبي زياد
٧٤ – يزيد بن ربيعة .

وروده في مسند ابن حنبل : ٨ مرات عن طريق أبي هريرة و ٤٩ مرة عن طريق الآخرين .

الحديث رقم (٢٨)

الرواة عن أبي هريرة :

تلاميذ أبي صالح : سهيل وعنه :

١ – الدراوردي	خزيمة ١٩٥ ب
٢ – خالد بن عبد الله	م جمعة ٦٧
٣ – سفيان	الحميدي ٩٧٦ ؛ م جمعة ٦٩ ؛ خزيمة ١٩٥ ب
٤ – جرير	ن جمعة ٤٢ ؛ م جمعة ٦٩ ؛ خزيمة ١٩٥ ب
٥ – عبد الله بن ادريس	حم ٢/٢٤٩ ؛ ٤٤٢ ؛ جه اقامة ٩٥ ؛ م جمعة ٦٨ ؛ بغداد ٨/٨٥

٦ – اسماعيل بن زكريا	د صلاة ٢٣٧
٧ – عاصم	حم ٤٩٩/٢
٨ – ابو عوانة	طس ٢٤٠٦
٩ – عبد العزيز بن المختار	الأصل/٢٨

الشواهد :

لم أجد له متابعاً ولا شاهداً

مقارنة الروايات :

تلامذة سهيل متفقون فيما بينهم .

أسماء الرواة :

الطبقة الأولى :

١ – أبو هريرة

الطبقة الثانية :

١ – أبوصالح .

الطبقة الثالثة :

١ – سهيل .

وروده في مسند ابن حنبل : ٣ مرات عن طريق ابي هريرة .

الحديث رقم (٢٩)

الرواة عن أبي هريرة :

١ – تلاميذ أبي صالح : سهيل وعنه :

١ – ابن جريج	الكامل ١٣٦/٢ ب
٢ – الداروروي	م سلام ١٣
٣ – جرير	م سلام ١٣
٤ – روح بن القاسم	طط ١/٤١/١
٥ – زهير	حم ٢٦٣/٢ ؛ الجعد ٣٤٧
٦ – شريك	كامل ١٣٦/٢ ب
٧ – شعبة	حم ٣٤٦/٢ ؛ ٤٥٩ ؛ د ادب ٣٨ ؛ طس ٢٤٢٤
٨ – سفيان	حم ٤٤٤/٢ ؛ ٥٢٥ ؛ م سلام ١٣
٩ – عبد العزيز بن المختار	الأصل /٢٩
١٠ – معمر	حم ٢٦٦/٢

الشواهد :

١ – أبو عبد الرحمن الجهني   ٢ – ابن عمر   ٣ – أبو بصرة الغفاري

(١) ابو عبد الرحمن الجهني : يزيد بن أبي حبيب – مرثد بن عبد الله – عنه .   حم ٢٣٣/٣ ؛
جه ادب ١٣ ؛ سعد ٧١/١/٤ ؛ يعلى ٥٩ ب

(٢) ابن عمر ؛ عبد الله – نافع – عنه . سعد ١٢٠/٢/٤ (طلب رد السلام من اليهود)

(٣) أبو بصرة الغفاري : يزيد بن أبي حبيب – مرثد بن عبد الله – عنه .   حم ٣٩٦/٦ ؛
طك ١/١٤١/١ ؛ ١/١٤١ ب

يوجد الحديث في مصدر شيعي ايضا . الكافي ٢/٩-٦٤٨

مقارنة الروايات :

لم أجد متابعاً لسهيل .

أما الروايات عن سهيل متفقة في المعنى وفي الكلمات إلى حد كبير . جاء في بعض الروايات : « اذا لقيتموهم » وفي الأخرى : « اذا لقيتم اهل الكتاب » . وروى زهير : « اذا لقيتموهم » فسأله علي بن الجعد: «هل هم اليهود والنصارى؟ فقال زهير : «لا : هم المشركون». الجعد ٣٤٧

أما الروايات عن الصحابة الآخرين ففيه: إني راكب غدا الى اليهود فلا تبدؤهم بالسلام . سعد ٧١/١/٤

أسماء الرواة :

الطبقة الأولى :

١ – أبو هريرة   ٢ – ابن عمر   ٣ – ابو بصرة الغفاري

٤ – ابو عبد الرحمن الجهني

الطبقة الثانية :

١ – أبو صالح   ٢ – مرثد بن عبد الله   ٣ – نافع

الطبقة الثالثة :

١ – سهيل   ٢ – عبد الله   ٣ – يزيد بن أبي حبيب

الرواية عن أكثر من شيخ : في الطبقة الثانية، مرثد بن عبد الله روى عن أكثر من شيخ.

وروده في مسند ابن حنبل: ٦ مرات عن طريق أبي هريرة ومرة واحدة عن طريق الآخرين.

الحديث رقم (٣٠)

الرواة عن أبي هريرة :

١ – أبو سلمة   ٢ – أبو صالح السمان   ٣ – أبو صالح النبهان

٤ – أبو سعيد	٥ – الاعرج	٦ – حيان
٧ – طاووس	٨ – عبد الرحمن بن ابي عمرة	٩ – أبو العلاء عبدالرحمن
١٠ – محمد بن زياد	١١ – همام	١٢ – الوليد بن رباح

١ – تلاميذ أبي سلمة : محمد حم ٥٠١/٢

٢ – تلاميذ أبي صالح :

أ – الاعمش حم ٤٨٠/٢ ؛ م البر ٣٠ ؛ طص ٢١٠

ب – أبو بكر بن عياش طط ١/٥٣/١

ج – عاصم حم ٥١٢/٢

د – سهيل وعنه :

١ – عبد العزيز بن المختار الأصل /٣٠

٢ – وهيب حم ٣٨٩/٢ ؛ م البر ٣١

٣ – تلاميذ أبي صالح النبهان : سفيان حم ٢٨٨/٢ ؛ ٣٩٣

٤ – تلاميذ أبي سعيد : داود بن قيس حم ٢٧٧/٢ ؛ ٣٦٠ ؛ الكشي ١٦٣ ب

٥ – تلاميذ الاعرج :

أ – أبو الزناد حم ٢٨٧/٢ ؛ ٤٦٥ ؛ ٥١٧ ؛ ط حسن الخلق ١٥ ؛ م البر ٢٨ ؛ د ادب ٤٧

ب – جعفر بن ربيعة خ نكاح ٤٥

٦ – تلاميذ حيان : سليم بن حيان حم ٤٧٠/٢ ؛ ٢-٤٩١ ؛ طس ٥٣٣

٧ – تلاميذ طاووس :

أ – ابن طاووس حم٣٤٢/٢ ؛ خ فرائض ٢

ب – الليث حم ٥٣٩/٢

٨ – عبد الرحمن : العلاء م البر ٢٩

٩ – عبد الرحمن بن أبي عمرة :

هلال بن علي حم ٤٨٢/٢

١٠ – تلاميذ محمد بن زياد حم ٤٤٦/٢ ؛ ٤٦٩

١١ – تلاميذ همام : معمر حم ٣١٢/٢ ؛ خ ادب ٥٧

١٢ – تلاميذ الوليدبن رباح : كثير بن زيد حم ٣٩٤/٢

الشواهد :

١ – أبو بكر ٢ – أبو أيوب الانصاري ٣ – ابن عباس ٤ – أنس بن مالك .

(١) أبو بكر الصديق : سليم بن عامر – أوسط بن اسماعيل – عنه . حم ٣/١ ؛ ٥ ؛ ٧ ؛ حميدي ٧ ؛ جه دعاء ٥ .

(٢) أبوأيوب الأنصاري : الزهري – عطاء بن يزيد الليثي – عنه . طص ٦-٥٥

(٣) ابن عباس : الزهري – عبيد الله بن عبد الله – عنه . طص ٦ـ٥٥ ؛ طط ١/١٧١/١-ب

(٤) أنس بن مالك : روى عنه ١ – قتادة ٢ – الزهري

١ – قتادة وعنه :

أ – ابان	حم ٣/٢٨٣
ب – شعبة	حم ٣/٢٠٩ ؛ ٢٧٧ ؛ م البر ٢٤

٢ – الزهري وعنه :

أ – ابن جريج	ابن جريج ١/١٢٣
ب – ابن أبي ذئب	طس ٢٠٩١
ج – ابن عيينة	م البر ٢٣ ؛ طس ٢٠٩١ ؛ يعلى ١٦٨ ب
د – الزبيري	م البر ٢٣
هـ – زمعة	طس ٢٠٩١
و – شعيب	حم ٣/٢٢٥ ؛ خ ادب ٥٧
ز – عبد الرحمن بن اسحاق	يعلى ١/١٧١
ح – عبيد الله بن عمر	طط ٢/١٩٨ ب
ط – مالك	ط حسن الخلق ١٤ ؛ خ ادب ٦٢ ؛ م البر ٢٣
ي – معمر	حم ٢/١٩٩ ؛ م البر ٢٣
ك – يونس	م البر ٢٣

يوجد هذا الحديث في مصدر اباضي أيضاً . شرح مسند الربيع ٣/٥٠٧ ؛ ٥١٢.

مقارنة الروايات :

الرواة متفقون في المعنى وكذلك في الالفاظ مع حذف كلمة أو أخرى .

أسماء الرواة :

الطبقة الأولى :

١ – أبو هريرة	٢ – أبو بكر	٣ – أبو أيوب الانصاري
٤ – ابن عباس	٥ – أنس	

الطبقة الثانية :

١ – أبو سلمة	٢ – أبوصالح السمان	٣ – أبوصالح النبهان
٤ – أبو سعيد	٥ – الاعرج	٦ – أوسط بن اسماعيل
٧ – حيان	٨ – طاووس	٩ – عبد الرحمن أبو العلاء
١٠ – عبد الرحمن بن أبي عمرة	١١ – عطاء بن يزيد الليثي	١٢ – محمد بن زياد
١٣ – الزهري	١٤ – قتادة	١٥ – همام
١٦ – عبيد الله بن عبد الله	١٧ – الوليد بن رباح .	

الطبقة الثالثة :

١ – ابن جريج	٢ – ابن أبي ذئب	٣ – ابان
٤ – أبو الزناد	٥ – أبو بكر بن عياش	٦ – ابن طاووس
٧ – جعفر بن ربيعة	٨ – حماد بن سلمة	٩ – داود بن قيس
١٠ – الزبيدي	١١ – زمعة	١٢ – سفيان
١٣ – سليم بن حيان	١٤ – سليم بن عامر	١٥ – شعيب
١٦ – شعبة	١٧ – عاصم	١٨ – العلاء
١٩ – عبد العزيز بن المختار	٢٠ – عبد الرحمن بن اسحاق	٢١ – عبد الله بن عمر
٢٢ – ليث	٢٣ – مالك	٢٤ – محمد
٢٥ – معمر	٢٦ – كثير بن زيد	٢٧ – هلال بن علي
٢٨ – وهيب	٢٩ – يونس	٣٠ – الزهري .

الرواة عن أكثر من شيخ :

الزهري يروي عن أربعة شيوخ . وكأنه الراوي الوحيد عن المصدرين وكذلك معمر وسفيان يرويان عن أكثر من شيخ .

وروده في مسند ابن حنبل :

٢٠ مرة عن طريق أبي هريرة و ٨ مرات عن طريق الآخرين .

الحديث رقم (٣١)

الرواة عن أبي هريرة : ١ – أبو صالح

١ – تلاميذ أبي صالح :

أ – الاعمش	م ذكر ٦٣ ؛ ت دعوات ٦٧
ب – سهيل وعنه :	
١ – ابن عياش	حم ٤٠٤/٢
٢ – خالد الطحان	م ذكر ٦١ ؛ ت دعوات ١٩
٣ – عبد العزيز بن المختار	جه دعاء ١٥ ؛ الأصل ٣١
٤ – وهيب	حم ٣٨١/٢

الشواهد :

١ – عائشة . (١) عائشة : الشعبي – مسروق – عنها . يعلى ١/٢١٨

مقارنة الروايات :

الرواة متفقون في المعنى إلا بعض الكلمات مع التغيير في الترتيب أحياناً .

سماء الرواة :

الطبقة الأولى :

١ – أبو هريرة ٢ – عائشة .

الطبقة الثانية :

١ – أبو صالح ٢ – مسروق .

الطبقة الثالثة :

١ – الأعمش ٢ – سهيل ٣ – الشعبي .

وروده في مسند ابن حنبل : مرتين عن أبي هريرة .

الحديث رقم (٣٢)

الرواة عن أبي هريرة :

١ – أبو صالح ٢ – اسحاق ٣ – سعيد ٤ – صالح مولى التوأمة ٥ – رجل غير مسمى .

١ – تلاميذ أبي صالح : سهيل وعنه :

١ – حماد	حم ٥١٥/٢ ؛ ٥٢٧
٢ – عبد العزيز بن المختار	الأصل ٣٢
٣ – وهيب	حم ٣٨٩/٢
٢ – تلاميذ اسحاق : سعد بن أبي سعد	حم ٤٣٢/٢
٣ – تلاميذ سعيد : ابن عجلان	الحميدي ١١٥٨
٤ – تلاميذ صالح :	
أ – ابن أبي ذئب	حم ٤٥٣/٢
ب – زياد بن سعد	حم ٤٥٩/٢
ج – سفيان	حم ٤٤٦/٢ ؛ ٤٨١
٥ – تلاميذ رجل غير مسمى :	
محمد بن عمرو بن علقمة	حم ٤٩٤/٢

الشواهد :

لم أجد له شاهداً ويوجد هذا الحديث في مصدر شيعي أيضاً الكافي ٤٩٧/٢

مقارنة الروايات :

الرواة متفقون في المعنى وكذلك في أكثر الالفاظ .

أسماء الرواة :

الطبقة الأولى :

١ – أبو هريرة

الطبقة الثانية :

١ – أبوصالح	٢ – اسحاق	٣ – سعيد
٤ – صالح	٥ – رجل غير مسمى	

الطبقة الثالثة :

١ – ابن أبي ذئب	٢ – ابن عجلان	٣ – زياد بن سعد
٤ – سفيان	٥ – سهيل	٦ – محمد بن عمرو بن علقمة

وروده في مسند ابن حنبل : ٩ مرات عن طريق أبي هريرة .

الحديث رقم (٣٣)

الرواة عن أبي هريرة :

١ – أبوصالح ٢ – ابن المسيب .

١ – تلاميذ أبي صالح : سهيل وعنه :

١ – خالد	دى اطعمه ٢٧
٢ – زهير	حم ٢٦٣/٢ ؛ ٥٣٧ ؛ الجعد ٣٤٧ ؛ د اطعمه ٥٣
٣ – عبد العزيز	جه اطعمه ٢٢ ؛ الأصل ٣٣

٢ – تلاميذ ابن المسيب : الزهري حم ٣٤٤/٢

الشواهد :

١ – فاطمة .

(١) فاطمة : فاطمة بنت الحسين – الحسين بن علي – عنها جه اطعمه ٢٢

يوجد هذا الحديث في مصدر شيعي أيضاً . علل الشرائع ٢٤٣/٢

مقارنة الروايات :

الرواة متفقون في المعنى وإلى حد كبير في الألفاظ .

أسماء الرواة :

الطبقة الأولى :

١ – أبو هريرة ٢ – فاطمة

الطبقة الثانية :

١ – أبو صالح	٢ – ابن المسيب	٣ – الحسين بن علي .

الطبقة الثالثة :

١ – الزهري　　　　٢ – سهيل　　　　٣ – فاطمة

وروده في مسند ابن حنبل : ٣ مرات عن طريق أبي هريرة .

الحديث رقم (٣٤)

الرواة عن أبي هريرة : ١ – أبو صالح

تلاميذ أبي صالح :

أ – الأعمش	خ دعوات ٦٦
ب – سهيل وعنه :	
١ – حماد بن سلمة	المستدرك ١/٤٩٥
٢ – زهير	حم ٢/٣٥٨
٣ – عبد العزيز	الأصل /٣٤
٤ – وهيب	م ذكر٢٥ ؛ طس ٢٤٣٤

الشواهد :

١ – جابر بن عبد الله ٢ – عبد الله بن عباس .

(١) جابر بن عبد الله : عمر بن عبد الله – أيوب بن خالد – عنه . المستدرك ١/٤٩٤ ؛ طط ١/١٣٩ ب ؛ الكشي ١٢٣ ب

(٢) عبد الله بن عباس : عمر بن ذر – مجاهد – عنه . طس ٢٢٢

مقارنة الروايات :

الرواة عن أبي هريرة متفقون في المعنى وفي الالفاظ إلى حد كبير جداً . اما رواية جابر وعبد الله بن عباس فتتفق كلتاهما مع رواية أبي هريرة في مجمل المعنى .

أسماء الرواة :

الطبقة الأولى :

١ – أبو هريرة　　　　٢ – جابر بن عبد الله　　　　٣ – عبد الله بن عباس .

الطبقة الثانية :

١ – أبوصالح　　　　٢ – أيوب　　　　٣ – مجاهد .

الطبقة الثالثة :

١ – الأعمش　　　　٢ – سهيل　　　　٣ – عمر بن ذر

٤ – عمر بن عبد الله .

الرواية عن أكثر من شيخ : لا توجد .

وروده في مسند ابن حنبل: مرة واحدة عن طريق أبي هريرة .

الحديث رقم (٣٥)

الرواة عن أبي هريرة :

١ – أبو صالح :

تلاميذ أبي صالح : سهيل وعنه :

١ – أبو اسحاق	حم ٣٩٩/٢
٢ – ابراهيم بن محمد	م امارة ١٣١
٣ – حماد	حم ٢٦٣/٢ ؛ ٣٥٣
٤ – عبد العزيز	الأصل ٣٥
٥ – محمد بن عجلان	حم ٣٤٠/٢ ؛ طص ٨٢

الشواهد :

لا أعرف له متابعاً ولا شاهداً .

مقارنة الروايات :

الرواة متفقون في المعنى وإلى حد كبير في الالفاظ أيضاً .

أسماء الرواة :

الطبقة الأولى :

١ – أبو هريرة

الطبقة الثانية :

١ – أبو صالح .

الطبقة الثالثة :

١ – سهيل

وروده في مسند ابن حنبل : ٤ مرات عن طريق أبي هريرة .

الحديث رقم (٣٦)

الرواة عن أبي هريرة :

١ – أبو سلمة ٢ – أبو صالح ٣ – سعيد بن يسار ٤ – القاسم بن محمد .

١ – تلاميذ أبي سلمة : محمد بن عمرو حم ٥٤١/٢

٢ – تلاميذ أبي صالح :

أ – زيد بن أسلم — خ زكاة ٨ ؛ م زكاة ٦٤

ب – مسلم بن أبي مريم — خ زكاة ٨

ج – عبد الله بن دينار — خ توحيد ٢٣ ؛ زكاة ٨

د – سهيل وعنه :

١ – خالد — حم ٣٨٢/٢

٢ – روح بن القاسم — م زكاة ٦٤ ؛ طط ١/٤١/١

٣ – سليمان بن بلال — م زكاة ٦٤

٤ – عبد العزيز — الأصل /٣٦

٥ – وهيب — حم ٢/٢-٣٨١

٦ – يعقوب بن عبد الرحمن — حم ٤١٩/٢ ؛ م زكاة ٦٤

٣ – تلاميذ سعيد بن يسار :

ا – ابن عجلان — حم ٤١٨/٢ ؛ ٤٣١ ؛ الحميدي ١١٥٤

ب – سعيد بن أبي سعيد — حم ٥٣٨/٢ ؛ ن ٤٨ ؛ م زكاة ٦٣ ؛ جه زكاة ٢٨

ج – عبد الله بن دينار — حم ٣٣١/٢ ؛ خ توحيد ٣٢ ؛ زكاة ٨

د – يحيى بن سعيد — دى زكاة ٣٥

٤ – تلاميذ القاسم بن محمد : عباد — حم ٤٧١/٢

الشواهد :

١ – عائشة

(١) عائشة : ثابت – القاسم بن محمد – عنها . حم ٢٥١/٦

يوجد هذا الحديث في مصدر زيدي أيضاً مسند زيد ١٩٩

مقارنة الروايات :

الرواة متفقون في المعنى وكذلك في أكثر الكلمات .

أسماء الرواة :

الطبقة الأولى :

١ – أبو هريرة .   ٢ – عائشة .

الطبقة الثانية :

١ – أبو سلمة   ٢ – أبوصالح   ٣ – سعيد بن يسار

٤ – القاسم بن محمد .

الطبقة الثالثة :

١ – ابن عجلان   ٢ – ثابت   ٣ – زيد بن أسلم

٤ – سعيد بن أبي سعيد	٥ – سهيل	٦ – عبد الله بن دينار
٧ – محمد بن عمرو	٨ – مسلم بن أبي مريم	٩ – يحيى بن سعيد
١٠ – عباد .		

الرواية عن أكثر من شيخ : عبد الله بن دينار والقاسم بن محمد يرويان عن أكثر من شيخ

وروده في مسند ابن حنبل : ٩مرات عن طريق أبي هريرة ومرة واحدة عن طريق عائشة.

الحديث رقم (٣٧)

الرواة عن أبي هريرة :

١ – أبو صالح

تلاميذ أبي صالح : سهيل وعنه :

١ – أبو عوانة	حم ٤٨٣/٢ ؛ م سلام ٣١
٢ – جرير	جه ادب ٢٢
٣ – حماد	حم ٣٤٢/٢ ؛ ٥٢٧ ؛ د ادب ٢٨
٤ – زهير	حم ٢٦٣/٢ ؛ الجعد ٣٤٧ ؛ دى استئذان ٢٥
٥ – سفيان	حم ٤٤٦/٢ ؛ ٤٤٧
٦ – عبد العزيز بن محمد	م سلام ٣١
٧ – عبد العزيز بن المختار	الأصل /٣٧
٨ – معمر	حم ٢٨٣/٢
٩ – هاشم	حم ٥٣٧/٢
١٠ – وهيب	حم ٣٨٩/٢

الشواهد :

١ – وهب بن حذيفة ٢ – أبوسعيد الخدري

(١) وهب بن حذيفة : محمد بن يحيى – واسع بن حبان – عنه . حم ٤٢٢/٣ ؛ ت ٩٩/٢

(٢) أبوسعيد الخدري : محمد بن يحيى – واسع بن حبان – عنه . حم ٣٢/٣

مقارنة الروايات :

الرواة متفقون في المعاني وكذلك في الكلمات إلى حد كبير جداً .

أسماء الرواة :

الطبقة الأولى :

١ – أبو هريرة	٢ – وهب بن حذيفة	٣ – أبو سعيد الخدري

الطبقة الثانية :

١ - أبو صالح　　　　٢ - واسع بن حبان

الطبقة الثالثة :

١ - سهيل　　　　٢ - محمد بن يحيى .

الرواية عن أكثر من شيخ: واسع بن حبان روى عن أكثر من شخص .

وروده في مسند ابن حنبل: ٩ مرات عن طريق أبي هريرة .

الحديث رقم (٣٨)

الرواة عن أبي هريرة :

١ - أبوصالح

تلاميذ أبي صالح :

أ - الأعمش	م الذكر ٣٨ ؛ د ادب ٦٠ ؛ جه مقدمة ١٧ ؛ ت حدود ٣ ؛ البر ١٩
ب - محمد بن المنكدر	حم ٥١٤/٢ انظر أيضاً حم ٢٩٦/٢ ؛ ٥٠٠
ج - سهيل وعنه :	
١ - ابن عياش	حم ٤٠٤/٢
٢ - حماد	حم ٥٢٢/٢
٣ - روح	م البر ٧١ ؛ طط ١/٤٢/١
٤ - عبد العزيز بن المختار	الأصل /٣٨
٥ - وهيب	حم ٣٩٨/٢ ؛ م البر ٧٢ ؛ طس ٢٤٢٧

الشواهد :

١ - أبو أيوب الانصاري ٢ - أبو علقمة ٣ - ابن عمر ٤ - عائشة ٥ - مسلمة بن مخلد .

(١) أبو أيوب الانصاري : أبو سعيد الاعمى - عطاء - عنه . حم ٦٢/٤ ؛ ٣٧٥/٥ ؛ الحميدي ٣٨٤ .

(٢) أبو علقمة : مالك بن دينار - علقمة المزني - عنه . طط ١/٨١/٢

(٣) ابن عمر : الزهري - سالم - عنه . حم ٩١/٢ ؛ خ مظالم ٣ ؛ م البر ٥٨ ؛ د ادب ٣٨ ؛ ت حدود ٣

(٤) عائشة : داود - عروة - عنها . راهويه ١/١٠١

(٥) مسلمة بن مخلد : محمد بن المنكدر - أبو أيوب - عنه . حم ١٠٤/٤ .

(٦) يوجد الحديث في مصدر شيعي أيضاً . الكافي ٤٢٨/٢ .

الطبقة الثالثة :

الروايات متفقة في المعاني وكذلك متقاربة في الكلمات .

أسماء الرواة :

الطبقة الأولى :

١ – أبو هريرة	٢ – أبو أيوب	٣ – أبو علقمة
٤ – ابن عمر	٥ – عائشة	٦ – مسلمة بن مخلد .

الطبقة الثانية :

١ – أبو صالح	٢ – أبو أيوب	٣ – سالم
٤ – عطاء	٥ – علقمة	٦ – عروة .

الطبقة الثالثة :

١ – أبو سعيد	٢ – الأعمش	٣ – الزهري
٤ – سهيل	٥ – داود	٦ – مالك بن دينار
٧ – محمد بن المنكدر .		

الرواة عن أكثر من شيخ : أبو أيوب ومحمد بن المنكدر يرويان عن اكثر من شيخ.

ادراجه في مسند ابن حنبل : ٤ مرات عن طريق أبي هريرة .

الحديث رقم (٣٩)

الرواة عن أبي هريرة : ١ – أبو صالح

تلاميذ أبي صالح :

أ – الأعمش	الاعمش /١٠
ب – سلم بن أبي مريم	الحميدي ٩٧٥ ؛ ط حسن الخلق ١٨ ؛ م البر ٣٦ ؛ ابن وهب ٤٣ .
ج – سهيل وعنه :	
١ – أبو غسان	الجعد ٣٩٣
٢ – جرير	م البر ٣٥
٣ – الدراوروي	م البر ٣٥
٤ – عبد العزيز بن المختار	الأصل /٣٩
٥ – مالك	حم ٢/٤٠٠ ؛ ٤٦٥ ؛ ابن وهب ٤١ ؛ م البر ٣٥ ؛ ط حسن الخلق ١٧ .

٦ – محمد بن رفاعة　　حم ٢/٣٢٦ وانظر ت البر ٧٦
٧ – معمر　　حم ٢/٢٦٨ ؛ يعلى ٣٠٦ ب
٨ – وهيب　　حم ٢/٢٨٩ ؛ طس ٢٤٠٣
١ – ابن مسعود ٢ – اسامة بن زيد .

الشواهد :

(١) ابن مسعود : علي بن يزيد – القاسم بن عبد الرحمن – عنه – ابن وهب ٤٢

(٢) اسامة بن زيد . عمر بن الحكم – مولى قدامة بن مظعون – عنه . سعد ٤/٢/٥٠ .

مقارنة الروايات :

اتفقت الروايات معنى وهي متقاربة في الالفاظ . وحديث اسامة اخصر من الأصل .

أسماء الرواة :

الطبقة الأولى :

١ – أبو هريرة　　٢ – ابن مسعود　　٣ – اسامة

الطبقة الثانية :

١ – أبو صالح　　٢ – القاسم بن عبد الرحمن　　٣ – مولى قدامة بن مظعون

الطبقة الثالثة :

١ – الأعمش　　٢ – سلم بن أبي مريم　　٣ – سهيل
٤ – علي بن يزيد　　٥ – عمر بن الحكم .

الرواية عن أكثر من شيخ : لا توجد .

وروده في مسند ابن حنبل : ٥ مرات عن طريق أبي هريرة .

الحديث رقم (٤٠)

الرواة عن أبي هريرة :

١ – أبوصالح ٢ – أبوسلمة ٣ – عجلان .

١ – تلاميذ أبي صلاح : سهيل وعنه :
أ – جرير　　م مساقاة ١٤١
ب – عبد العزيز بن المختار　　الأصل /٤٠
ج – وهيب　　حم ٢/٣٨٨ ؛ طس ٢٤١٠
٢ – تلاميذ أبي سلمة : عمر بن أبي سلمة　　حم ٢/٣٨٧
٣ – تلاميذ عجلان : ابن عجلان　　حم ٢/٤٣٢

الشواهد :

١ – أبو مالك الاشعري　　٢ – ابن عمر　　٣ – الحكم بن الحارث

٤ – سعيد بن زيد ٥ – عائشة ٦ – المسور بن مخرمة
٧ – يعلى بن مرة .

(١) أبو مالك الأشعري : عبد الله بن محمد بن عقيل – عطاء بن يسار – عنه . طك١/٢٣٣/١
(٢) ابن عمر : موسى بن عقبة – سالم – عنه . خ بدء الخلق .
(٣) الحكم بن الحارث . محمد بن حمران – عطية – عنه . طص ٢٤٨ .
(٤) سعيد بن زيد :
الحارث بن عبد الرحمن – أبو سلمة – عنه . حم ١٨٨/١ ؛ ١٩٠ ؛ يعلى ٦٠ ب
الوليد بن عبد الله – أبو الطفيل – عنه . طط ١٧٠/١ ب ، طص ٥-٥٤
العلاء بن عبد الرحمن – عباس بن سهل – عنه . م مساقاة ١٣٧ ؛ طك ١/٢٦/١
هشام – عروة – عنه . خ بدء الخلق ٢ ؛ م مساقاة ١٣٩ ؛ ١٤٠ ؛ يعلى ٦٠ ب
عمر بن محمد – عن ابيه – عنه م مساقاة ١٣٨ ، يعلى ١/٦٠
طلحة بن عبد الله – عبد الرحمن بن سهل – عنه . حم ١٨٩/١ ؛ دى بيوع ٦٤ ؛ يعلى ١/٦٠ ؛ الكشي ١/٤٩ ؛ انظر أيضاً حم ١٨٧/١ ؛ ١٨٨ ؛ ١٨٩
(٥) عائشة : محمد بن ابراهيم – أبو سلمة – عنها . خ بدء الخلق ٢ ؛ م مساقاة ١٤٢ ؛ طط ١/١٣٩/١
(٦) المسور بن مخرمة . محمد بن مسلم الطائفي – عمرو بن دينار – عنه. طك ٢٤٦/١٠ ب
(٧) يعلى بن مرة : الربيع بن عبد الله – ايمن بن نائل – عنه . الكشي ١/٤٩
الشعبي – ايمن بن نائل – عنه . طص ٢١٩

مقارنة الروايات :

اتفق الرواة في المعنى وكذلك في أكثر الكلمات .

أسماء الرواة :

الطبقة الأولى :

١ – أبو هريرة ٢ – أبو مالك الاشعري ٣ – ابن عمر
٤ – الحكم بن الحارث ٥ – سعيد بن زيد ٦ – عائشة
٧ – المسور بن مخرمة ٨ – يعلى بن مرة .

الطبقة الثانية :

١ – أبو سلمة ٢ – أبو صالح ٣ – أبو الطفيل
٤ – أيمن بن نائل ٥ – سالم ٦ – عجلان

٧ – عطاء بن يسار ٨ – عطية ٩ – عبد الرحمن بن سهل
١٠ – عباس بن سهل ١١ – عمرو بن دينار ١٢ – عروة ١٣ – محمد

الطبقة الثالثة :

١ – ابن عجلان ٢ – الحارث بن عبد الرحمن ٣ – سهيل
٤ – الشعبي ٥ – طلحة بن عبد الله ٦ – عبدالله بن محمد بن عقيل
٧ – عمر بن أبي سلمة ٨ – عمر بن محمد ٩ – الربيع بن عبد الله
١٠ – العلاء بن عبد الرحمن ١١ – محمد بن حمران ١٢ – محمد الطائفي
١٣ – محمد بن ابراهيم ١٤ – موسى بن عقبة ١٥ – الوليد بن عبد الله
١٦ – هشام .

الرواية عن أكثر من شيخ : ابو سلمة يروي عن أكثر من شيخ .

وروده في مسند ابن حنبل : ٣مرات عن طريق أبي هريرة و ٥ مرات عن طريق الآخرين.

الحديث رقم (٤١)

الرواة عن أبي هريرة :

١ – أبو صالح ٢ – أبو العلاء .

١ – تلاميذ أبي صالح :

أ – زيد بن أسلم — د ادب ٦٠

ب – سمى — حم ٥٣٣/٢ ؛ م البر ١٢٧ ؛ امارة ١٦٤ ؛ ط جماعه ٦ ؛ خ اذان ٣٢ ؛ ت البر ٣٨

ج – سهيل وعنه :

١ – اسماعيل — حم ٤٠٤/٢ مختصراً

٢ – سفيان — حم ٢٨٦/٢ ؛ الحميدي١١٤٠

٣ – عبد العزيز بن المختار — الأصل ٤١

وهيب — حم ٣٤١/٢

٢ – تلاميذ أبي العلاء : العلاء — حم ٤٨٥/٢

الشواهد :

يوجد هذا الحديث في مصدر اباضي ايضا مسند الربيع ٩٩/٢ ولم أجد له شاهداً . ولكن قال الترمذي في البر ٣٨ : وفي الباب عن ابن عباس وابي برزة .

مقارنة الروايات :

اتفق الرواة في المعنى وكذلك في الكلمات الى حد كبير جداً ما عدى رواية زيد بن أسلم ففيها بعض الزيادات .

أسماء الرواة :

الطبقة الأولى :

١ – أبو هريرة .

الطبقة الثانية :

١ – أبوصالح ٢ – أبو العلاء

الطبقة الثالثة :

١ – زيد بن أسلم ٢ – سمى ٣ – سهيل ٤ – العلاء

الرواية عن أكثر من شيخ : لا توجد .

وروده في مسند بن حنبل : ٥ مرات عن طريق أبي هريرة .

الحديث رقم (٤٢)

الرواة عن ابي هريرة :

١ – أبو صالح .

تلاميذ أبي صالح : سهيل وعنه :

أ – حماد	حم ٢/٣٣٧
ب – عبد العزيز بن محمد	حم ٢/٣٧٨ ؛ ت ثواب ٢
ج – عبد العزيز بن المختار	الأصل /٤٢
د – معمر	حم ٢/٢٨٤
هـ – وهيب	حم ٢/٣٨٨
و – يعقوب	م مسافرين ٢١٢

الشواهد :

١ – ابن عمر ٢ – ابن مسعود ٣ – زيد بن خالد الجهني .

(١) ابن عمر . عبيد الله – نافع – عنه . م مسافرين ٢٠٨ ؛ جه اقامة ١٨٦

(٢) ابن مسعود . سلمة بن كهيل – أبو الاحوص – عنه موقوفاً . دى فضائل القرآن ١٣ ؛ طك ٥/٢٩/١

(٣) زيد بن خالد الجهني . عبد الملك بن أبي سلبيمان – عطاء – عنه . الكشي ٣٣ ب .

مقارنة الروايات :

لم أجد متابعاً لسهيل في هذه الرواية : اتفق رواة حديث أبي هريرة في المعنى وكذلك في عامة الالفاظ ويوجد نصف الحديث من هذه الرواية عند ابن عمر والنصف الآخر عند ابن مسعود .

أسماء الرواة :

الطبقة الأولى :

١ – أبو هريرة ٢ – ابن عمر ٣ – ابن مسعود

٤ – زيد بن خالد الجهني .

الطبقة الثانية :

١ – أبو صالح ٢ – أبو الأحوص ٣ – عطاء

٤ – نافع .

الطبقة الثالثة :

١ – سلمة بن كهيل ٢ – سهيل ٣ – عبد الملك بن ابي سليمان

٤ – عبيد الله .

الرواية عن أكثر من شيخ: لا يوجد .

وروده في مسند ابن حنبل: ٤ مرات عن طريق أبي هريرة .

الحديث رقم (٤٣)

الرواة عن أبي هريرة :

١ – أبو صالح

تلاميذ أبي صالح : سهيل وعنه :

أ – حماد	حم ٢/٣٤٢ ؛ ٣٦٣ ؛ طس ٢٤٢٨
ب – زهير	حم ٢/٣٥٨
ج – عبد العزيز بن المختار	الأصل/٤٢
د – يعقوب	م فتن ٤٤

الشواهد :

لم أجد له متابعاً ولا شاهداً .

مقارنة الروايات :

اتفق الرواة معنى وكذلك في أكثر الكلمات .

أسماء الرواة :

الطبقة الأولى :

١ – أبو هريرة .

الطبقة الثانية :

١ – أبو صالح .

الطبقة الثالثة :

١ – سهيل .

وروده في مسند ابن حنبل : ٣ مرات

الحديث رقم (٤٤)

الرواة عن أبي هريرة :

١ – أبو صالح .

تلاميذ أبي صالح : سهيل وعنه :

أ – حماد — حم ٢/٢٦٢

ب – عبد العزيز بن المختار — الأصل ٤٤

الشواهد :

لم أجد له متابعاً ولا مشاهداً .

مقارنة الروايات :

اتفق الرواة معنى ولفظاً .

أسماء الرواة :

الطبقة الأولى :

١ – أبو هريرة .

الطبقة الثانية :

١ – أبو صالح .

الطبقة الثالثة :

١ – سهيل .

وروده في مسند ابن حنبل : مرة واحدة .

الحديث رقم (٤٥)

الرواية عن أبي هريرة :

١ – أبو سلمة ٢ – أبو صالح .

١ – تلاميذ أبي سلمة : محمد بن عمرو حم ٢/٤٤١ ؛ يعلى ٢٧٢ ب

٢ – تلاميذ أبي صالح :

أ – الأعمش — م ايمان ٢١٠ وانظر أيضاً طس ٢٤٠١

ب – سهيل وعنه :

١ – جرير	م ايمان ٢٠٩
٢ – عبد العزيز بن المختار	الأصل/٤٥

الشواهد :

(١) ابن مسعود : ابراهيم – علقمة – عنه . م ايمان ٢١١

مقارنة الروايات :

اتفق الرواة عن أبي هريرة في المعنى وكذلك في أكثر الكلمات . أما رواية ابن مسعود فتتفق مع رواية أبي هريرة في المعنى .

أسماء الرواة :

الطبقة الأولى :

١ – أبو هريرة ٢ – ابن مسعود

الطبقة الثانية :

١ – أبوسلمة ٢ – أبو صالح ٣ – علقمة

الطبقة الثالثة :

١ – ابراهيم ٢ – الأعمش ٣ – سهيل

٤ – محمد بن عمرو .

الرواية عن أكثر من شيخ: لا توجد .

وروده في مسند ابن حنبل: مرة واحدة عن طريق أبي هريرة .

الحديث رقم (٤٦)

الرواة عن أبي هريرة :

١ – أبو صالح ٢ – زرارة بن أبي أوفى

١ – تلاميذ أبي صالح : سهيل وعنه :

أبو عوانة	حم ٣٤٣/٢
بشر بن المفضل	م لباس ١٠٣
حماد	حم ٣٢٧/٢
خالد	حم ٣١١/٢
زهير	حم ٢-٣/٢٦٢ ؛ ٥٣٧ ؛ الجعد ٣٤٧ ؛ دىاستئذان ٤٤
شريك	حم ٣٩٢/٢ ؛ ٤٤٤ ؛ ٤٧٦
عبد العزيز بن محمد	م لباس ١٠٣ ؛ ت جهاد ٢٥
عبد العزيز بن المختار	الأصل ٤٦

٢ – تلاميذ زرارة بن أبي أوفى: قتادة حم ٢/٣٨٥؛ ٤١٤ ؛ راهويه ١/٤٥

الشواهد :

١ – أبو طلحة ٢ – ام حبيبة ٣ – ام سلمة ٤ – عائشة .

(١) أبوطلحة : عبيد الله بن عبد الله – ابن عباس – عنه . طك ٣/٢٨ ب ؛ ١/٢٩

بشير بن سعيد – زيد بن خالد – عنه . طك ٣/١/٢٩

بكير بن سعيد – زيد بن خالد – عنه . طك ٣/١/٢٩

(٢) أم حبيبة : يزيد بن أبي حبيب – عراك – سالم بن عبد الله – أبوالجراح – عنها . ١٦ ب نسخة الليث

نافع – سالم بن عبد الله – ابو الجراح – عنها حم ٦/٣٢٦

انظر أيضاً دى استئذان ٤٤

(٣) أم سلمة : زهير – أبو الزبير – عنها . الجعد ٣٣٦

ابن جريج – سلمان بن بابية – عنها . ن زينة ٥٤

(٤) عائشة : ابن جريج – بنانة – عنها . حم ٦/٢٤٢ ؛ د خاتم ٦

مقارنة الروايات :

اتفق الرواة في المعنى وكذلك في الكلمات إلى حد كبير مع تقديم وتأخير مثل : « كلب » او « جرس » و « جرس ولا كلب » أو « كلب ولا جرس » ..

أسماء الرواة :

الطبقة الأولى :

١ – أبو هريرة	٢ – أبو طلحة	٣ – ام حبيبة
٤ – ام سلمة	٥ – عائشة .	

الطبقة الثانية :

١ – أبو الزبير	٢ – أبو صالح	٣ – أبو زرارة
٤ – أبو الجراح	٥ – ابن عباس	٦ – زيد بن خالد
٧ – سلمان بن بابية	٨ – بنانة .	

الطبقة الثالثة :

١ – ابن جريج	٢ – بشر بن سعيد	٣ – زهير
٤ – سالم	٥ – سهيل	٦ – بكير بن سعيد
٧ – سعيد بن يسار	٨ – عبيد الله بن عبد الله	٩ – قتادة .

الرواية عن أكثر من شيخ : ابن جريج يروي عن أكثر من شيخ .

وروده في مسند ابن حنبل: ١٠ مرات عن طريق أبي هريرة . ومرتين عن طريق الآخرين .

الحديث رقم (٤٧)

الرواة عن أبي هريرة :

١ – أبوزرعة ٢ – أبو صالح ٣ – الأعرج .

١ – تلاميذ أبي زرعة : عمارة بن القعقاع خ جهاد ٩٤

٢ – تلاميذ أبي صالح : سهيل وعنه :

عبد العزيز بن المختار	الأصل/٤٧
يعقوب	حم ٤١٧/٢ ؛ م فتن ٨٢ ؛ حم ٥٣٠/٢

الشواهد :

(١) ابن عمر :

الزهري– سالم – عنه	خ مناقب ٢٥ ؛ م فتن ٨١
عمر بن حمزة – سالم – عنه	م فتن ٨٠ ؛ يعلى ٢٥٦ ب
مالك – نافع – عنه	خ جهاد ٩٤
عبيد الله – نافع – عنه	م فتن ٧٩

مقارنة الروايات :

اتفق الرواة معنى والى حد كبير لفظاً . وتوجد الزيادة في حديث أبي هريرة إلا شجرة الخ ..

أسماء الرواة :

الطبقة الأولى :

١ – أبو هريرة ٢ – ابن عمر

الطبقة الثانية :

١ – أبو زرعة ٢ – أبوصالح ٣ – الاعرج

٤ – سالم ٥ – نافع .

الطبقة الثالثة :

١ – أبو الزناد ٢ – الزهري ٣ – سهيل

٤ – عبيد الله ٥ – عمارة بن القعقاع ٦ – عمر بن حمزة

٧ – مالك .

الرواية عن أكثر من شيخ : لا توجد .

وروده في مسند ابن حنبل : مرتين عن طريق أبي هريرة .

الحديث رقم (٤٨)

الرواة عن ابـــي هريرة :

١ – أبو صالح ٢ – أبو يونس .

١ – تلاميذ أبي صالح : سهيل وعنه :

عبد العزيز بن المختار	الأصل/٤٨
يعقوب	حم ٤١٧/٢ ؛ م زكاة ٦٠

٢ – تلاميذ ابي يونس : عمرو بن الحارث . م زكاة ٦١

الشواهد :

١ – أبو موسى الأشعري ٢ – حارثة بن وهب .

(١) ابوموسى الأشعري : بريد – أبو بردة – عنه . م زكاة ٥٩

(٢) حارثة بن وهب : شعبة –معبد بن خالد– عنه . حم ٣٠٦/٤ ؛ خ زكاة٩ ؛ م زكاة ٥٨

مقارنة الروايات :

تفق الرواة معنى ولفظاً إلى حد كبير . إلا انه ورد في رواية حارثة تصدقوا فانه يأتي عليكم زمان . لم يذكروا لا تقوم الساعة ...

اسماء الرواة :

الطبقة الاولى:

١ – أبوهريرة ٢ – أبو موسى ٣ – حارثة بن وهب

الطبقة الثانية :

١ – أبوبردة ٢ – أبوصالح ٣ – أبويونس

٤ – معبد بن خالد .

الطبقة الثالثة :

١ – بريد ٢ – سهيل ٣ – شعبة

٤ – عمرو بن الحارث .

الرواية عن أكثر من شيخ : لا توجد .

وروده في مسند ابن حنبل: مرة واحدة عن طريق أبي هريرة ومرة واحدة عن طريق الآخرين.

كيفية تفرع الأسانيد :

مع مراعاة أحاديث نسخة سهيل بن أبي صالح ، يمكن توزيع الأحاديث من حيث تفرع الأسانيد الى الأنواع الآتية :

١ - أبو هريرة الراوي الوحيد للحديث . وله تلميذ واحد ولتلميذه تلميذ واحد وليس له شاهد من رواية الصحابة الآخرين .

ويندرج تحت هذا النوع الأحاديث الآتية : ١١ ؛ ٢٨ ، ٣٥ ، ٤٣ ، ٤٤ = ٥

٢ - أبو هريرة له تلميذ واحد وله شاهد من رواية الصحابة الآخرين .

ويندرج تحت هذا النوع الأحاديث الآتية : ١ ، ٢ ، ١٣ ، ١٤ ، ٢٩ ، ٣١ ، ٣٤ ، ٣٧ ، ٣٨ ، ٣٩ ، ٤٢ = ١١

٣ - أبو هريرة له تلامذة عديدون وله شواهد من رواية الصحابة الآخرين .

ويندرج تحت هذا النوع الأحاديث الآتية : - ٣ ، ٤ ، ٥ ، ٦ ؛ ٧ ، ٨ ، ٩ ، ١٠ ، ١٢ ؛ ١٥ ؛ ١٦ ؛ ١٧ ؛ ١٨ ؛ ١٩ ؛ ٢٠ ؛ ٢١ ؛ ٢٢ ؛ ٢٣ ؛ ٢٤ ؛ ٢٥ ؛ ٢٦ ، ٢٧ ، ٣٠ ؛ ٣٢ ؛ ٣٣ ؛ ٣٦ ، ٤٠ ؛ ٤١ ، ٤٥ ؛ ٤٦ ؛ ٤٧ ؛ ٤٨ ؛= ٣٢ حديثاً.

ولمزيد من التوضيح ، انظر الرسوم البيانية في الصفحات القادمة .

رسوم بيانيَّة

لتحمّل الأحاديث عن رَسول الله صلى الله عليه وسَلم
وتفرع أسَانيدها الى الطبقة الثالثة

الحديث رقم (11) يمثل المجموعة الأولى

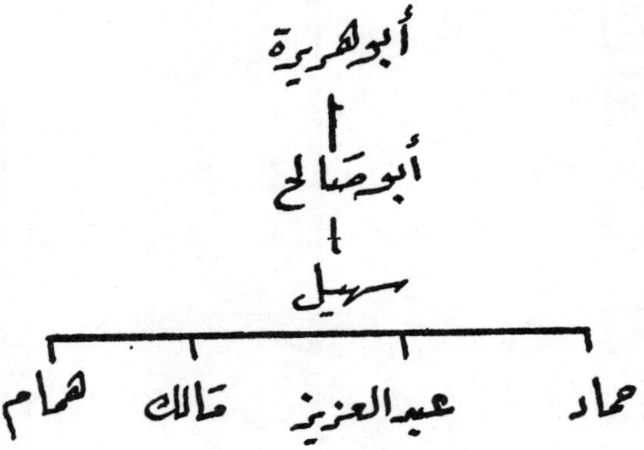

الحديث رقم (1) يمثل المجموعة الثانية

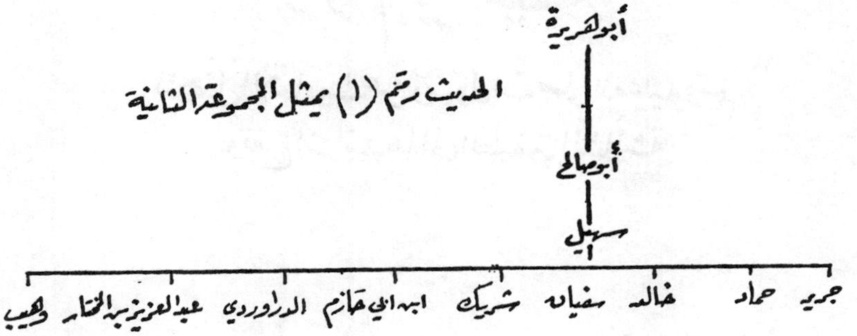

الشواهد

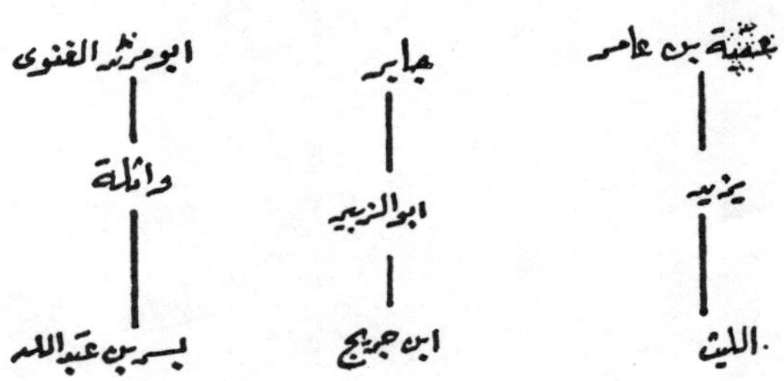

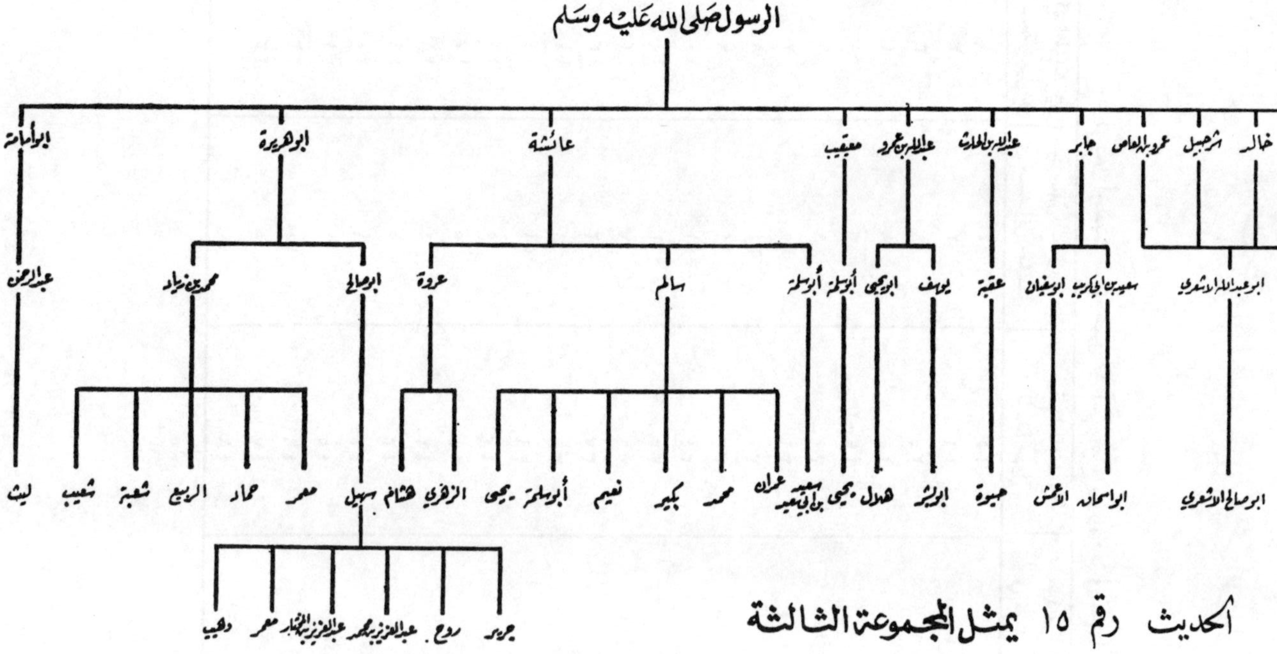

الحديث رقم ١٥ يمثل المجموعة الثالثة

جدول يبين أحاديث نسخة سهيل بن أبي صالح وورودها في مسندا بن حنبل

رقم الحديث في نسخة سهيل	عدد مرات وروده في مسند ابن حنبل	رقم الحديث في نسخة سهيل	عدد مرات وروده في مسند ابن حنبل
١	٤	٢٥	٥
٢	٢	٢٦	١١
٣	٩	٢٧	٨
٤	٨	٢٨	٣
٥	٣	٢٩	٦
٦	٩	٣٠	٢٠
٧	١٥	٣١	٢
٨	٢٤	٣٢	٩
٩	٤	٣٣	٣
١٠	١	٣٤	١
١١	٣	٣٥	٤
١٢	٧	٣٦	٩
١٣	٢	٣٧	٩
١٤	١	٣٨	٤
١٥	١١	٣٩	٥
١٦	٥	٤٠	٣
١٧	٥	٤١	٥
١٨	٤	٤٢	٤
١٩	٥	٤٣	٣
٢٠	١	٤٤	١
٢١	١	٤٥	١
٢٢	١٠	٤٦	١٠
٢٣	٥	٤٧	٢
		٤٨	١

أحاديث
عبيد الله بن عمر
عن نافع

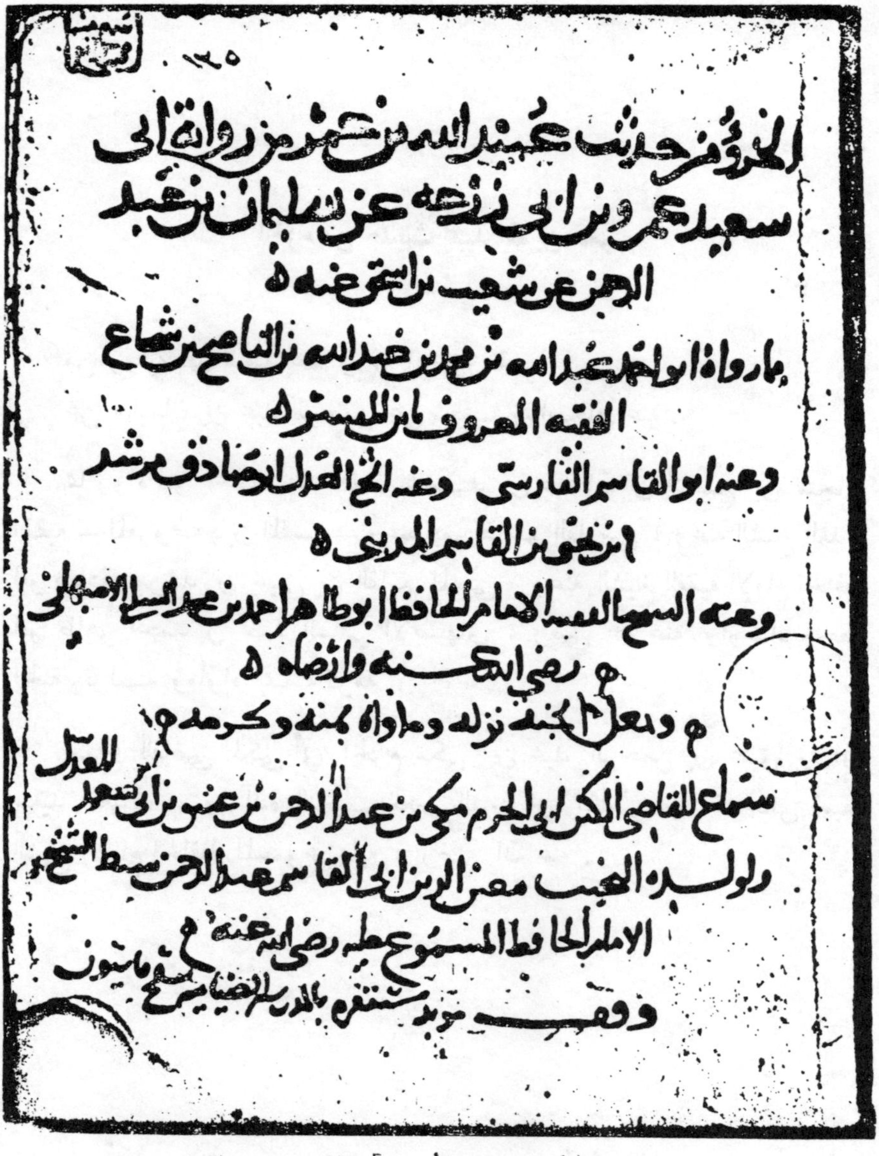
الجزء من حديث عبيد الله بن عمر من رواية ابي
سعيد عمرو بن ابي نفيعة عن سليمان بن عبد
الرحمن عن شعيب بن اسحق عنه
بما رواه ابو احمد عبد الله بن محمد بن عبد الله بن الناصح بن شجاع
الفقيه المعروف بابن المفسر
وعنه ابو القاسم الفارسي وعنه الشيخ العدل ابو الصادق مرشد
ابن يحيى بن القاسم المديني
وعنه الشيخ الفقيه الامام الحافظ ابو طاهر احمد بن محمد السلفي الاصبهاني
رضي الله عنه وارضاه
وجعل الجنة نزله ومأواه بمنه وكرمه
سماع للقاضي الاكمل ابي المكارم مكي بن عبد الرحمن بن عتيق بن ابي سعد العدل
ولولده النجيب معين الدين ابي القاسم عبد الرحمن سبط الشيخ
الامام الحافظ المسموع عليه رضي الله عنه
وقف مؤبد يستقر بالمدرسة الضيائية بسفح قاسيون

راموز الصفحة الأولى من مخطوطة أحاديث عبيدالله بن عمر عن نافع

الجزء من حديث عبيد الله بن عمر

من رواية ابي سعيد عمرو بن ابي زرعة ،
عن سليمان بن عبد الرحمن عن شعيب بن اسحاق عنه .

مما رواه ابو احمد عبد الله بن محمد بن عبد الله بن الناصح بن شجاع الفقيه – المعروف بابن المفسر – وعنه ابو القاسم الفارسي ، وعنه الشيخ العدل ابو صادق مرشد بن يحيى بن القاسم المديني ، وعنه الشيخ الفقيه الإمام الحافظ ابو طاهر احمد بن محمد السلفي الاصبهاني ، رضي الله عنه وارضاه وجعل الجنة نزله ومأواه بمنه وكرمه .

سماع للقاضي المكنى أبي الحرم مكي بن عبد الرحمن بن عتيق بن ابي سعيد المعدّل ، ولولده النجيب معين الدين ابي القاسم عبد الرحمن سبط الشيخ الإمام الحافظ المسموع عليه ، رضي الله عنه .

بِسْمِ اللَّهِ الرَّحْمَنِ الرَّحِيمِ

اخبرنا الشيخ الفقيه الإمام العالم الحافظ شيخ الاسلام أوحد الانام فخر الأئمة مفتي السنة ، ابو طاهر احمد بن محمد بن احمد بن محمد بن ابراهيم السلفي الاصبهاني قراءة عليه ، وانا اسمع في ربيع الاول سنة ست وسبعين وخمسمائة .

قال : انا ابو صادق مرشد بن يحيى بن القاسم المديني المعدل بقراءتي عليه في ذي الحجة سنة خمس عشرة وخمسمائة بالفسطاط .

انا ابو القاسم علي بن محمد بن علي الفارسي ، قراءة ابي الحسن علي بن بقي وانا اسمع في شهر رمضان سنة اربعين واربعمائة .

اخبرنا ابو احمد عبد الله بن محمد بن عبد الله بن ناصح بن شجاع المعروف بابن المفسر : حدثني ابو سعيد بن ابي زرعة عمرو بن عبد الرحمن بن عمرو ، قراءة عليّ سنة اثنتين وتسعين ومائتين .

قال : حدثنا سليمان بن عبد الرحمن سنة اثنتين وثلاثين ومائتين .

قال : حدثنا شعيب بن اسحاق القرشي .

نا عبيد الله بن عمر بن حفص .

1 — عن نافع ان عبد الله بن عمر : « لم يكن يرى باساً ان يغسل الرجل رأسه بالخطمى » [1] .

---

(1) في الأصل ، بعده بخط مغاير « قبل ان يحلق » .

١٢ – حدثني عمرو ثنا سليمان ثنا شعيب ثنا عبيد الله عن عبد الرحمن عن القاسم ان عمر رضي الله عنه قال لاهل مكة : « ما لكم يا اهل مكة ! يقدم الناس محرمين شعثاً غبراً وانتم مدهنون . اذا رأيتم الهلال فاحرموا . »

١٣ – حدثني عمرو ثنا سليمان ثنا شعيب ثنا عبيد الله عن نافع ان عبدالله ابن عمر رضي الله عنه اخبره ان رجلا سأل رسول الله ﷺ عن صلاة الليل ، فقال : « يصلي أحدكم بالليل مثنى مثنى فاذا خشي ان يصبح يصلي واحدة فلتوتر له ما قد صلى » .

وقال : « اجعلوا آخر صلاتكم بالليل وتراً » .

١٤ – حدثني عمرو ثنا سليمان نا شعيب نا عبيد الله عن نافع أنّ عبد الله اسرع السير مرة فجمع بين المغرب والعشاء بعد ما غاب الشفق بساعة فكلموه في ذلك فقال (١٣٧ ب) فقال [١] : « اني رأيت رسول الله ﷺ يصنع ذلك ، اذا جد به السير » .

١٥ – حدثني عمرو نا سليمان نا شعيب نا عبيد الله عن نافع ان عبد الله اخبره انه سمع رسول الله ﷺ يقول :

« أنّ الذي تفوته صلاة العصر كأنما وتر ماله وأهله » .

١٦ – حدثني عمرو نا سليمان نا شعيب نا عبيد الله عن نافع ان عبد الله « كان يصلي على بعيره السبحة اينما توجه به » . ويخبر ان رسول الله ﷺ كان يصنع ذلك .

وذكر ان ابن عمر كان يوتر عليه .

١٧ – حدثني عمرو نا سليمان نا شعيب نا عبيد الله عن نافع ان عبد الله اخبره انه سمع رسول الله ﷺ يقول :

« اذا جاء احدكم الى الجمعة فليغتسل » .

---

(١) تكررت كلمة « فقال » مرتين . انظر سببه في الصفحة ٢٧٦ بالجزء الانكليزي

٢ - حدثني عمرو: نا سليمان : نا شعيب نا عبيد الله (٣٦١/ب) عن نافع أنّ عبد الله كان يغتسل ، اذا رمى الجمار .

٣ - حدثني عمرو ثنا سليمان ثنا شعيب ثنا عبيد الله عن نافع ان عبد الله كان يكره المنطقة للمحرم .

٤ - حدثني عمرو ثنا سليمان ثنا شعيب ثنا عبيد الله عن نافع : ان عبد الله كان يقول : «ليس في شيء من الدفعتين تحريك، الا في بطن محسر قدر رمية بحجر» .

٥ - حدثني عمرو ثنا سليمان ثنا شعيب ثنا عبيد الله عن نافع ان عبد الله كان يقول : « حرم الرجل فيما فوق ذقنه ، وحرم المرأة في وجهها » .

٦ - حدثني عمرو ثنا سليمان ثنا شعيب ثنا عبيد الله عن نافع ان عبد الله كان اذا نحر هدية قال : « بسم الله والله اكبر ، واذا اشعر قال مثل ذلك »[1]

٧ - حدثني عمرو ثنا سليمان ثنا شعيب ثنا عبيد الله عن نافع : ان عبد الله كان اذا اراد ان ينحر هديه صف ايديهما قياماً ووجهها الى القبلة .

٨ - حدثني عمرو ثنا سليمان ثنا شعيب ثنا عبيد الله عن نافع : ان عبدالله كان لا يرى الهدى الا ما قلد واشعر وسيق ووقف » .

٩ - حدثني عمرو ثنا سليمان ثنا شعيب ثنا عبيد الله عن نافع : انعبد الله كان يقول : « ما استيسر من الهدى ، البدنة دون البدنة ، والبقرة دون البقرة»

١٠ - حدثني عمرو ثنا سليمان ثنا شعيب ثنا عبيدالله عن نافع : أنّ عبد الله (١٣٧ / ١) : « كان يمشي ذاهباً وراجعاً إلى الجمار » .

١١ - حدثني عمرو ثنا سليمان حدثنا شعيب ثنا عبيد الله عن نافع ان عبد الله : « احرم من مكة ثلاث مرات . مرتين [2] قبل الهلال ومرة حين يصرخ الى منى » .

---

(١) بهامش الأصل « فعل »　　(٢) في الأصل « مرتين مرتين » بالتكرار .

١٨ ـ حدثني عمرو نا سليمان نا شعيب نا عبيد الله عن نافع ان عبد الله قال : « بينا رسول الله ﷺ قائم يصلي للناس رأى نخامة في قبلة المسجد فحتّها ثم نهى الناس ان ينتخم احدهم اذا كان في الصلاة قبل وجهه » .

قال : « ان الله سبحانه قبل وجه احدكم اذا كان في الصلاة فلا ينتخم احدكم قبل وجهه اذا كان في الصلاة » .

١٩ ـ حدثني عمرو نا سليمان نا شعيب نا عبيد الله عن نافع ان عبد الله ابن عمر قال : « صليت مع رسول الله ﷺ (١٣٨/١) قبل الظهر سجدتين ، وبعدها سجدتين ، وبعد الجمعة سجدتين [١] وبعد المغرب سجدتين وبعد العشاء سجدتين . فاما المغرب والعشاء والجمعة ففي بيته » .

٢٠ ـ حدثني عمرو نا سليمان نا شعيب نا عبيد الله عن نافع ان عبد الله اخبره : « ان حفصة بنت عمر رضي الله عنها اخبرته : « ان رسول الله ﷺ كان يصلي سجدتين خفيفتين حين يتبين الفجر قبل الصلاة » .

٢١ ـ حدثني عمرو نا سليمان نا شعيب نا عبيد الله عن نافع ان عبد الله اخبره ان رسول الله ﷺ دخل الكعبة هو واسامة بن زيد وعثمان بن طلحة وبلال . فمكث في البيت فأطال ثم خرج فدخل عبد الله على اثره والناس .

قال فسألت بلالا : « اين صلى رسول الله ﷺ ؟ » فقال «بين العمودين» : المقدمين » .

وقال : « نسيت ان اسأله كم صلى ؟ » . وهما : « اليمانيان » .

٢٢ ـ حدثني عمرو نا سليمان نا شعيب نا عبيد الله عن نافع ان عبد الله اخبره ان رسول الله ﷺ قال « صلوا في بيوتكم ولا تتخذوها [٢] قبوراً » .

٢٣ ـ حدثني عمرو نا سليمان نا شعيب نا عبيد الله عن نافع ان عبد الله

(١) في الأصل « قبل الظهر سجدتين وبعد الجمعة سجدتين وبعدها سجدتين وبعد المغرب سجدتين ... »

(٢) في الاصل ولا اتخذوها.

قال : « صليت مع رسول الله ﷺ بمنى (١٣٨ ب) سجدتين حتى هلك ﷺ ثم مع ابي بكر رضي الله عنه حتى هلك ، ثم مع عمر رضي الله عنه حتى هلك ثم مع عثمان رضي الله عنه صدراً من خلافته » .

٢٤ — حدثني عمرو نا سليمان نا شعيب نا عبيد الله عن نافع ان عبد الله اخبره ان رسول الله ﷺ : « كان اذا خرج الى مكة صلى في مسجد الشجرة ، واذا رجع صلى بذي الحليفة ببطن الوادي ، وبات بها حتى يصبح .

٢٥ — حدثني عمرو نا سليمان نا شعيب نا عبيد الله عن نافع ان عبد الله: كان اذا قدم من مكة دخل عشاء المدينة ، واذا قدم مكة بات بذي طوى ، فلم يدخل الا بكرة ، كما كان يدخل رسول الله ﷺ .

٢٦ —حدثني عمرو نا سليمان نا شعيب نا عبيد الله عن نافع عن عبد الله ابن عمر ان رسول الله ﷺ كان يصلي في الاضحى والفطر ثم يخطب بعد الصلاة .

٢٧ — حدثني عمرو نا سليمان نا شعيب نا عبيد الله عن نافع عن صفية بنت ابي عبيد ان عمر بن الخطاب رضي الله عنه : كتب الى امراء الاجناد يأمرهم ان يصلوا الصبح والنجوم بادية مشتبكة ، والظهر اذا زالت الشمس الى ان يكون ظل كل شيء مثله ، والعصر والشمس مرتفعة بيضاء نقية . قدر ما يسير الراكب (٢/١٣٩) فرسخين ، والمغرب حين تغرب الشمس وينظر الى الليل ، والعشاء حين يغيب الشفق ، فان شغلتم فيما بينكم وبين ثلث الليل . ألا ، ولا تشغلوا عن الصلاة . فمن رقد بعد فلا ارقد الله عينيه . ثم من رقد فلا ارقد الله عينيه . ثم من رقد فلا ارقد الله عينه » .

٢٨ — حدثني عمرو نا سليمان نا شعيب نا عبيد الله عن نافع : ان عبدالله كان يقصر الصلاة الى خيبر .

وانه اخبره سالم : انه قصر مرة الى ذات النصب ، وهي على اربعة برد .

٢٩ – حدثني عمرو نا سليمان نا شعيب نا عبيد الله عن نافع : ان عبد الله صلى غداة جمع صلاة الصبح قبل طلوع الفجر ثم عاد لصلاته بعد طلوع الفجر .

٣٠ – حدثني عمرو نا سليمان نا شعيب نا عبيد الله عن نافع : ان عبد الله اخبره انهم اريح عليهم الثلج في غزوة أذربيجان ستة اشهر يقصرون الصلاة .

٣١ – حدثني عمرو نا سليمان نا شعيب نا عبيد الله عن نافع ان سالماً اخبره ان عبد الله دعى بوضوء [1] فتوضأ مرة وهو في سفر بعد ان ارتفعت الشمس ثم صلى .

قال سالم فقلت له : « إن هذه الصلاة ما كنت رأيتك تصليها » .

قال : « اني ذكرت اني مسست ذكري قبل الصلاة بعد ان توضأت فنسيت ان اعود للوضوء فذكرتها الآن ، فعدت لصلاتي .

٣٢ – (١٣٩ب) حدثني عمرو نا سليمان نا شعيب نا عبيد الله عن نافع ان عبد الله : كان يكبر اذا وضع جبهته في الصلاة .

٣٣ – حدثني عمرو نا سليمان نا شعيب نا عبيد الله عن نافع : ان عبد الله كان يسجد في النجم ، واقرأ باسم ربك الذي خلق ، الا ان يكون في صلاة مفروضة فانه يركع .

٣٤ – حدثني عمرو نا سليمان نا شعيب نا عبيد الله عن نافع : ان عبد الله كان قرأ في المغرب مرة بيسين ، وانه كان يقرأ في العشاء بالذين كفروا ، وانا فتحنا لك .

٣٥ – حدثني عمرو نا سليمان نا شعيب نا عبيد الله عن نافع ان عبد الله

---

(١) في الأصل « بضو » .

اخبره : ان عمر بن الخطاب رضي الله عنه كان اذا خرج الى الصلاة نادى في المسجد فقال : « اياكم واللغط » ، وانه كان يقول : «ارتفعوا في اعلى المسجد»

٣٦ – حدثني عمرو نا سليمان نا شعيب نا عبيد الله عن نافع : ان عبد الله كان يقول : « من صلى وراء الإمام كفته قراءته ، وان كان يقرأ في الظهر في اربعتهن وفي العصر في اربعتهن ، وفي سجدتين من المغرب وفي سجدتين من العشاء ، فاذا صلى احدكم وحده فليقرأ » .

٣٧ – حدثني عمرو نا سليمان نا شعيب نا عبيد الله عن نافع : ان عبد الله كان اذا سجد السجدتين الاوليين من الظهر او العصر او المغرب او العشاء ، اذا جلس قال :

بسم الله التحيات لله والصلوات لله الزاكيات ١٤٠/١ لله السلام على النبي ورحمة الله وبركاته ، السلام علينا وعلى عباد الله الصالحين . شهدت ان لا اله الا الله . وشهدت ان محمداً رسول الله ، ثم يجلس ما بدأ له . فاذا قام كبر فاذا سجد السجدتين الاخيرتين جلس ، وقال : بسم الله التحيات لله الصلوات لله الزاكيات لله ، ولم يسلم : شهدت ان لا اله الا الله وشهدت ان محمداً رسول الله حتى يجعل التسليم آخر صلاته . فاذا سلم الإمام وقال السلام على النبي ورحمة الله وبركاته السلام علينا وعلى عباد الله الصالحين ، ويرد على الإمام ثم يسلم على من كان على يمينه ، فاذا سلم عليه احد من قبل شماله سلم عليه .

٣٨ – حدثني عمرو نا سليمان نا شعيب نا اسحاق نا عبيد الله بن عمر عن نافع : انه سمع ابا هريرة يكبر في الأضحى والفطر في السجدة الاولى سبعاً وفي الآخرة خمساً قبل القراءة ، في الركعتين جميعاً ، سوى التكبيرتين اللتين ركع بهما .

٣٩ – حدثني عمرو نا سليمان نا شعيب نا عبيد الله عن نافع عن صفية بنت ابي عبيد ان عمر كان يقرأ في الصبح بالسورة التي ذكر فيها يوسف ، والذي ذكر فيها اصحاب الكهف ونحوهما من السور .

٤٠ ــ (١٤٠ ب) حدثني عمرو نا سليمان نا شعيب نا عبيد الله عن نافع : ان عبد الله بن عمر كان اذا فاته من الصلاة شيء مع الإمام مما يقرأ فيه فانه حين يسلم الإمام قام فقرأ فيما بقي .

٤١ ــ حدثني عمرو نا سليمان نا شعيب نا عبيد الله عن نافع : ان عبد الله اشتكى حتى اغمي عليه يوماً وليلة ، فلم يعد لصلاته .

٤٢ ــ حدثني عمرو نا سليمان نا شعيب نا عبيد الله عن نافع : ان عبد الله كان اذا صلى رفع عمامته عن جبهته على الارض .

٤٣ ــ حدثني عمرو نا سليمان نا شعيب نا عبيد الله عن نافع : ان عبد الله اتى بابن ابنه صبياً مولوداً قد توفي فصلى عليه عبد الله في داره ثم امر به فاحتمل الى البقيع فدفن .

٤٤ ــ حدثني عمرو نا سليمان نا شعيب نا عبيد الله عن نافع : ان عبد الله كان لا يقدم من سفر الا دخل المسجد فركع ركعتين ثم سلم على رسول الله ﷺ وعلى ابي بكر وعلى عمر رضي الله عنهما عند القبر .

٤٥ ــ حدثني عمرو نا سليمان نا شعيب نا عبيد الله عن نافع : ان عبد الله كان اذا ابتدأ الصلاة رفع يديه واذا اراد الركوع رفع يديه ، واذا رفع رأسه من الركعة للسجود رفع يديه واذا قام من الركعتين كبر ورفع يديه .

٤٦ ــ حدثني عمرو نا سليمان نا شعيب نا عبيد الله عن نافع : ان عبد الله كان يجمع الصلاة هو ونافع ليس معهما احد .

٤٧ ــ حدثني عمرو نا سليمان نا شعيب نا عبيد الله عن نافع : ان عبد الله كان (١٤١/أ) يحمل الجنازة ثم يدخل المسجد فيصلي ولا يتوضأ .

٤٨ ــ حدثني عمرو نا سليمان نا شعيب نا عبيد الله عن نافع : ان عبد الله كان يصلي مع الناس اذا جمعوا بين الصلاتين ليلة المطر ، وهما المغرب والعشاء قبل ان يغيب الشفق .

٤٩ ـ حدثني عمرو نا سليمان نا شعيب نا عبيد الله عن نافع : ان عبد الله كان يصلي وهو مريض وهو جالس لا يرفع الى جبهته شيئاً ، ولكنه يؤمى برأسه . وذلك اذا غلب فلم يستطع ان يسجد وهو جالس .

٥٠ ـ حدثني عمرو نا سليمان نا شعيب نا عبيد الله عن نافع عن ابن عمر : ان عمر رضي الله عنه لم يكن يكبر للناس في الصلاة حتى يعدلوا الصفوف ويوكل بذلك رجالا .

٥١ ـ حدثني عمرو نا سليمان نا شعيب نا عبيد الله عن نافع . ان عبد الله كان يقول : « اذا وضع أحدكم جبهته الى الارض فليضع كفيه واذا رفع رأسه فليرفعهما ، فان اليدين تسجدان كما يسجد الوجه . »

٥٢ ـ حدثني عمرو نا سليمان نا شعيب نا عبيد الله عن نافع : ان عبد الله كان ليلة بمكة يصلي والسماء مغيمة ، فخشي الصبح فاوتر بواحدة ثم انه انكشف الغيم ورأى عليه ليلا ، فشفع بواحدة ، ثم صلى ركعتين ركعتين ، فلما جلس خشي الصبح اوتر بواحدة .

٥٣ ـ حدثني عمرو نا سليمان نا شعيب نا عبيد الله عن نافع : ان عبد الله كان يقصر الصلاة ما لم (١٤١ ب) يجمع اقامة .

٥٤ ـ حدثني عمرو نا سلمان نا شعيب نا عبيد الله عن نافع : ان عبد الله عن نافع : ان عبد الله اقام بمكة عشراً يقصر الصلاة .

٥٥ ـ حدثني عمرو نا سليمان نا شعيب نا عبيد الله عن نافع : ان عبد الله كان يقول : «صلاة الخوف أن يقوم الامام ويقوم طائفة وراءه ويقوم طائفة بينه وبين العدو ثم يصلي (١) بهم ركعة ، ثم ينصرف فيقوم مقام الأخرى . وتأتي الطائفة الاخرى فيصلي بهم ركعة ثم يسلم الإمام ، ثم تتم الطائفتان لأنفسهما ركعة ركعة » .

٥٦ ـ حدثني عمرو نا سليمان نا شعيب نا عبيد الله عن نافع قال :

---

(١) في الأصل « صلى » .

« رأيت في رداء عبد الله دماً فنزعته عنه ورديته ردائي فصلى كما هو » .

٥٧ ــ حدثني عمرو نا سليمان نا شعيب نا عبيد الله عن نافع ان عبد الله كان يقول : « اذا صلى الرجل في بيته ثم أتى المسجد والإمام يصلي فليصل معه الا المغرب والصبح فلا يعود لهما . »

٥٨ ــ حدثني عمرو نا سليمان نا شعيب نا عبيد الله عن نافع : ان عبد الله لم يكن يصلي قبل صلاة العيد ولا بعدها .

٥٩ ــ حدثني عمرو نا سليمان نا شعيب نا عبيد الله عن نافع : ان عبد الله مر على رجل وهو يصلي فسلم عليه فرد عليه الرجل كلاماً فرجع اليه عبد الله فقال : « اذا كان احدكم في الصلاة فسُلِّم عليه فلا يتكلم وليشر اشارة » .

٦٠ ــ حدثني عمرو نا سليمان نا (١/١٤٢) شعيب نا عبيد الله عن نافع : ان عبد الله كان يقول : « لا يقطع الصلاة شيء . وادرأ عنك ما استطعت » .

٦١ ــ حدثني عمرو نا سليمان نا شعيب نا عبيد الله عن نافع : ان عبد الله كان ينصرف من الصلاة اذا رأى الدم قليله وكثيره .

٦٢ ــ حدثني عمرو نا سليمان نا شعيب نا عبيد الله عن نافع : ان عبدالله كان يُسَبِّح ثماني ركعات قبل الظهر وبعدها اربعة ، وانه كان لا يرى باساً ان يصلي الرجل اربعاً في سبحة النهار ، لا يسلم بينهما إلا بتشهد .

٦٣ ــ حدثني عمرو نا سليمان نا شعيب نا عبيد الله عن نافع : ان عبد الله كان يصلي الفريضة ثم يسبح في مقامه الذي صلى فيه .

٦٤ ــ حدثني عمرو نا سليمان نا شعيب نا عبيد الله عن نافع : ان عبد الله ربما كان يتكلم في صلاة الليل بعد السجدتين ثم يصلي واحدة يؤتر بها .

٦٥ ــ حدثني عمرو نا سليمان نا شعيب نا عبيد الله عن نافع : « ان عبد الله كان يفتتح ام الكتاب في الصلاة ببسم الله الرحمن الرحيم واذا افتتح السورة فعل مثل ذلك ».

٦٦ ــ حدثني عمرو نا سليمان نا شعيب نا عبيد الله عن نافع : ان عبد الله كان يخرج الى الغابة وهو على بريد من المدينة فلا يقصر ولا يفطر .

٦٧ ــ حدثني عمرو نا سليمان نا شعيب نا عبيد الله عن نافع : « ان عبد الله كان يقعى (١٤٢ ب) بين السجدتين . »

٦٨ ــ حدثني عمرو نا سليمان نا شعيب نا عبيد الله عن نافع : « ان عبد الله لم يكن يصلي الا وهو متزر » .

وكان يقول : « من صلى في ثوب واحد فليتزر به » .

٦٩ ــ حدثني عمرو نا سليمان نا شعيب نا عبيد الله عن نافع : « ان عبد الله كان يجلس في الصلاة ، يفترش في الصلاة ثم يجلس عليهما » .

٧٠ ــ حدثني عمرو نا سليمان نا شعيب نا عبيد الله عن نافع : « ان عبد الله طلق امرأة له وهي حائض تطليقة واحدة ، فسأل عمر رسول الله ﷺ قال : ان عبد الله طلق امرأته وهي حائض ، فأمر رسول الله ﷺ ان يراجعها حتى تطهر ، ثم تحيض عنده حيضة اخرى ثم يمهلها حتى تطهر من حيضتها الاخرى ، ثم يطلقها ان شاء قبل أن يمسها . فتلك العدة التي أمر الله عز وجل ان يطلق لها النساء » .

٧١ــ حدثني عمرو نا سليمان نا شعيب نا عبيد الله عن نافع :
إن عبد الله كان يقول : « إذا طلق الرجل أمرأته ــ التي لم يدخل بها ــ ثلاثا فلا تحل له حتى تنكح زوجاً غيره » .

٧٢ ــ حدثني عمرو نا سليمان نا شعيب نا عبيد الله عن نافع قال : حدثني محمد بن أياس بن البكير أنه أتى عاصم بن عمر وعبد الله الزبير فقال: « أن طيري هذا نكح أبنة عزلة ثم طلقها ثلاثا قبل أن يدخل بها ، فقال ابن الزبير : أذهب فاني قد (١/١٤٣) تركت أبا هريرة وعبد الله بن عباس عند عائشة رضي الله عنها . فاستفتهم . ثم آتت فأخبرنا، فزعموا : أن محمد بن اياس قال : جئتهم فسألتهم ، فقال أبن عباس لابي هريرة : « أفته » ، . فقال : « لاتحل له حتى تنكح زوجاً غيره » .

وقالت عائشة : « مثل ذلك » ؛ وقال ابن عباس لابي هريرة : « طبقت الفتوى »
٧٣- حدثني عمرو نا سليمان نا شعيب نا عبيد الله عن نافع :

« أن عبد الله أخبره أن ربيع أبنة معوذ اخبرته أنها اختلفت من زوجها على عهد عثمان رضي الله عنه ، فذهب عمها معاذ بن عفراء إلى عثمان فقال : أن ابنة معوذ قد اختلفت من زوجها اليوم أفتنتقل ؟ فقال عثمان : نعم لتنتقل ، فليس عليها عدة ، غير أنها لا تنكح حتى تحيض حيضة واحدة . فقال عبد الله : « فعثمان أكبرنا واعلمنا » .

٧٤- حدثني عمرو نا سليمان نا شعيب نا عبيد الله عن نافع :

أن عبد الله كان يقول : « إن التي يولى منها زوجها ، اذا مرت أربعة أشهر فلا تصلح له أن يمسكها الا كما أمره الله سبحانه ، إما يمسكها بمعروف ، أو يسرحها باحسان » .

٧٥- حدثني عمرو نا سليمان نا شعيب نا عبيد الله عن نافع « أن عبد الله أتته مولاة لامرأته اختلعت من زوجها بكل شيء لها ، وبكل ثوب عليها إلا درعها فلم ينكر ذلك عليها عبد الله . »

٧٦- حدثني عمرو نا سليمان نا شعيب نا (١٤٣ب) عبيد الله عن نافع : أن عبد الله كان يقول : « لكل مطلقة متاع التي تطلق واحدة واثنتين وثلاثاً الا أن تكون امرأة طلقها زوجها قبل أن يمسها فحبسها فريضتها . فان لم يكن فرض لها فليس لها الا المتعة » .

٧٧- حدثني عمرو نا سليمان نا شعيب نا عبيد الله عن نافع : أن عبد الله كان يقول : « إذا طلقت المرأة البتة فإنها تأتي المسجد ولا تبيت الا في بيتها ، والمتوفي عنها تزور ولا تبيت إلا في بيتها » .

٧٨- حدثني عمرو نا سليمان نا شعيب نا عبيد الله عن نافع : أن

عبد الله بن عمر كان يقول : « إذا طلقت المرأة تطليقة أو تطليقتين فانها لا تخرج إلا بأذن زوجها حتى تحل من عدتها » .

٧٩- حدثني عمرو نا سليمان نا شعيب نا عبيد الله عن نافع : « أن عبد الله بن الزبير طلق امرأة له ثم كتمها قريباً من سنة ثم آذنها بعد ذلك بالطلاق فخطبت فقال قائل : « حتى تقضي عدتها » ، فذكر ذلك لعبد الله بن عمر فقال : « بئس ما صنع ابن الزبير بكتمانه إياها » ، فقال عبد الله بن عمر : « لا عدة عليها ، إنما العدة من يوم موت الزوج أو يطلق . »

٨٠- حدثني عمرو نا سليمان نا شعيب نا عبيد الله عن نافع : أن عمر قبض أبنه عاصم بن عمر بعد ما طلق أمه . فاقبلت جدته الشموس بنت أبي عامر فانطلقت به ، فذكر ذلك لعمر فلحقها على فرس فاراد أن ينزع الغلام منها. فمنعته[1] فتساوقا إلى ابي بكر الصديق رضي الله عنه في ذلك فامره أبو بكر [2] أن يدع الغلام عند أمه (١/١٤٤) فتكون هي تحضنه ففعل عمر » .

٨١- حدثني عمرو نا سليمان نا شعيب نا عبيد الله عن نافع : أن سليمان بن يسار أخبره أن ابن الاحوص في عهد معاوية رضى الله عنه بالشام طلق أمرأته ثم مرض فمات وهي في آخر حيضتها لم تطهر منها بعد فكتب معاوية بن أبي سفيان إلى زيد بن ثابت يسأله عن ذلك فقال له زيد : « لا ترثه ولا يرثها . وقد برئت منه ، وبرئ منها » .

قال نافع : وكان عبد الله بن عمر يقول : مثل ذلك .

٨٢- حدثني عمرو نا سليمان نا شعيب نا عبيد الله عن نافع : أن عبد الله أخبره أن رسول الله ﷺ : « فرّق بين رجل وامرأته من الانصار ، قذف أمرأته فاحلفهما وفرق بينهما . »

---

(١) في الأصل « فنعه » .
(٢) في الأصل « فأمره عمر أبو بكر » .

٨٣– حدثني عمرو نا سليمان نا شعيب نا عبيد الله عن نافع : أن عبد الله كان يقول : « اذا طلق العبد الحرة فطلاقه ثنتان ، وتعتد ثلاثا وإذا طلق الحر الامة فطلاقه أثنتان وتعتد أثنتين » .

٨٤– حدثني عمرو نا سليمان نا شعيب نا عبيد الله عن نافع : أن سلمى [١] أبنة أبي حفص بن المغيرة وكانت تحت عبد الله ابن أبي ربيعة فطلقها تطليقة ، فتزوجها عمر بن الخطاب ، فدخل عليها فوضع خمارها ونقض ثيابها ثم دخل على حفصة أم المؤمنين فقالت : ياأبت تزوجت أبنة أبي حفص ؟ فقال نعم . فقالت (١٤٤ب) : فاني لا أخالها بارة قال : فلولا الولد ما نكحت النساء ففارقها ، وقد رأى برأسها قرعا كرهه . فرجعت إلى عبد الله بن أبي ربيعة » .

٨٥– حدثني عمرو نا سليمان نا شعيب نا عبيد الله عن نافع : « أن رجلا جاء إلى عبد الله فقال : أني طلقت أمراتي ثلاثا وهي حائض . قال عصيت ربك وفارقتك أمرأتك »

٨٦– حدثني عمرو نا سليمان نا شعيب نا عبيد الله عن نافع أن عبد الله كان يقول : « إذا نكح الرجل عبده طائعاً فليس بيده فراق بينهما ».

٨٧– حدثني عمرو نا سليمان نا شعيب نا عبيد الله عن نافع : « أن عبد الله طلق أمرأته صفية تطليقة ، ثم كان لا يدخل عليها إلا بأذن . وكانت طريقهما واحد فصرف طريقه عنها » .

٨٨– حدثني عمرو نا سليمان نا شعيب نا عبيد الله عن نافع أن عبد الله قال : « وذكر يوم عاشوراء » ، فقال رسول الله ﷺ : « يوم كانت تصومه الجاهلية فمن أحب منكم أن يصومه فليصمه ومن أحب أن يدعه فليدعه » .

---

(١) في الأصل « سليمان »

٨٩ـ حدثني عمرو نا سليمان نا شعيب نا عبيد الله عن نافع : أن عبد الله كان يقول : « من لم يجمع الصيام من الليل فلا يصم » .

٩٠ـ حدثني عمرو نا سليمان نا شعيب نا عبيد الله عن نافع أن عبد الله كان يقول : « لان أفطر في رمضان في السفر أحب إلى من أن اصوم ».

٩١ـ حدثني عمرو نا سليمان نا شعيب نا عبيد الله عن نافع : أن عبد الله قال : « لو أن المؤذن أذن بالصلاة وانا بين (١٤٥/١) رجلى أمرأتي لاغتسلت ثم أتممت صومي .

٩٢ـ حدثني عمرو نا سليمان نا شعيب نا عبيد الله عن نافع : « أن عبد الله أخبره أن رسول الله ﷺ : ذكر رمضان فاشار بيده فعقف أبهامه فقال : أنما الشهر تسع وعشرون ليلة ولكن لا تصوموا حتى تروه ، ولا تفطروا حتى تروه » .

وكان عبد الله يبعث إذا خلى من شعبان تسع وعشرون ليلة من ينظر اليه ، فان رآه أصبح صائماً فان رأى سحاباً يحول دون منظره أو قترة أصبح صائماً ، وان لم ير شيئاً تحول دونه ولم يره لم يصم . وكان لا يفطر حتى يفطر الناس .

٩٣ـ حدثني عمرو نا سليمان نا شعيب نا عبيد الله عن نافع : أن عبد الله كان يقول : « من أدركه رمضان وعليه رمضان شيء فليطعم عن [1] كل يوم مسكيناً مدا من حنطة » .

٩٤ـ حدثني عمرو نا سليمان نا شعيب نا عبيد الله عن نافع : أن عبد الله كان يقول : « لا يفرق بين قضاء رمضان ، ولا يقطع بينه » .

٩٥ـ حدثني عمرو نا سليمان نا شعيب نا عبيد الله عن نافع : « أن عبد الله أخبره : أن الرجل الذي يذرعه القيء وهو صائم ، أنه يتم صومه ، وان استقاء متعمداً فقد أفطر » .

٩٦ـ حدثني عمرو نا سليمان (١٤٥ب) نا شعيب نا عبيد الله عن نافع :

---

(١) في الاصل :فليطعم كان كل يوم

أن عبد الله كان يقول : « من أفطر في رمضان وهو مريض ثم مات قبل أن يقضي فليطعم عنه كل يوم أفطره مسكيناً ، مدا من حنطة » .

٩٧- حدثني عمرو نا سليمان نا شعيب نا عبيد الله عن نافع : « أن عبد الله كان ينهي عن القبلة والمباشرة والرجل صائم » .

٩٨- حدثني عمرو نا سليمان نا شعيب نا عبيد الله عن نافع : « أن عبد الله كان يصدق المرأة من بناته وبنات أخيه الف دينار ، فيجعل لها منها قريبا من أربعمائة دينار حلياً . »

٩٩- حدثني عمرو نا سليمان شعيب نا عبيد الله قال : وسألت نافعا عن زكاته فقال كان عبدالله يقول : ليس فيه زكاة

١٠٠-حدثني عمرو نا سليمان نا شعيب نا عبيد الله عن نافع أن عبد الله كان يقول : « لا يجب في المال صدقة حتى يحول عليه الحول » .

١٠١-حدثني عمرو نا سليمان نا شعيب نا عبيد الله قال : حدثني نافع : « أنه كانت عند عبد الله أموال اليتامى يليهم فنستسلفها لتحرزها في الهلاك ثم يخرج صدقتها من اموالهم » .

١٠٢-حدثني عمرو نا سليمان نا شعيب نا عبيد الله عن نافع : « أن جيشاً غنموا في زمان رسول الله (١/١٤٦) ﷺ طعاماً وعسلاً فلم يؤخذ منهم الخمس » .

١٠٣-حدثني عمرو نا سليمان نا شعيب نا عبيد الله عن نافع : « أن عبد الله أخبره : أن رسول الله ﷺ فرض زكاة الفطر صاعا من تمر أو صاعاً من شعير عن العبد والحر والذكر والانثى والصغير والكبير ، »

قال نافع : فعدل الناس ذلك بنصفه من الحنطة .

١٠٤-حدثني عمرو نا سليمان نا شعيب نا عبيد الله عن نافع : عن عبد الله أن رسول الله ﷺ : « نهى عن بيع الثمار حتى تبدوا صلاحها ، ونهى عن المزابنة ،

والمزابنة أن يبيع الرجل ثمر حائطه بتمر كيلا أن كانت نخلا أو زبيباً أو كرماً أو زرعاً . ما كان نهى عن بيعه بكيل مسمّى ».

١٠٥ـ حدثني عمرو نا سليمان نا شعيب نا عبيد الله عن نافع : أن عبد الله قال أخبرني زيد بن ثابت أن رسول الله ﷺ رخص في بيع العرايا بخرصها كيلا .

١٠٦ـ حدثني عمرو نا سليمان نا شعيب نا عبيد الله عن نافع : أن عبد الله أخبره أن أبا لبابة أخبره أن رسول الله ﷺ نهى عن قتل الجنان الا أن يكون الابتر التي في (١٤٦ب) البيوت .

١٠٧ـ حدثني عمرو نا سليمان نا شعيب نا عبيد الله عن نافع أن سايبه اخبرته أن عائشة رضي الله عنها زوج النبى ﷺ قالت : « أن رسول الله ﷺ نهى عن الجنان الا أن يكون الابترو ذا الطفيتين فانهما يخطفان الابصار ، يقتلان في ما في بطون النساء ، فمن تركها فليس مني » .

١٠٨ـ حدثني عمرو نا سليمان نا شعيب نا عبيد الله عن نافع أن عبد الله أخبره أن رسول الله ﷺ ذكر المسيح بين ظهرى الناس ، فقال : « أن الله ليس باعور ، الا أن المسيح الدجال أعور عين اليمنى كأن عينه طافية » .

١٠٩ـ حدثني عمرو نا سليمان نا عبيد الله عن نافع أن عبد الله كان يقول : قال رسول الله ﷺ :

« ألا كلكم راع وكلكم مسئول عن رعيته ، ألا والامير الذي على الناس راع وهو مسئول عن رعيته عنهم . والرجل راع على أهله وهو مسئول عنهم وأمرأة الرجل راعية على بيت بعلها وولده وهي مسئولة عنهم . وعبد الرجل راع على مال سيده وهو مسئول عنه (١٤٧ / ١) ألا وكلكم راع وكلكم مسئول عن رعيته . »

١١٠ـ حدثني عمرو نا سليمان نا شعيب نا عبيد الله عن نافع أن عبد الله

اخبره أن رسول الله ﷺ أدرك عمر بن الخطاب وهو في ركب وهو يحلف بابيه حتى جاء رسول الله ﷺ فقال :

« ألا أن الله ينهاكم أن تحلفوا بآبائكم ، فليحلف حالف بالله أو ليسكت»

١١١– حدثني عمرو نا سليمان نا شعيب نا عبيد الله عن نافع : « أن عبد الله كان يكري المزارع ، فحدث أن رافع بن خديج يأثر عن رسول الله ﷺ أنه نهى عن ذلك .

قال نافع : فخرج اليه عبد الله على البلاط وأنا معه ، فسأله فقال : رافع نعم ؛ نهى رسول الله ﷺ عن كراء المزارع . »

فترك كراءها عبد الله .

١١٢–حدثني عمرو نا سليمان نا شعيب نا عبيد الله عن نافع :

أن عبد الله كان يقول : « قد علمت أنها قد كانت تكرى في عهد رسول الله ﷺ المزارع على أن لرب الأرض ما على الربيع الساقي وطائفة من التبن لا أدري كم هي . »

١١٣–حدثني عمرو نا سليمان نا شعيب نا عبيد الله (١٤٧ب) عن نافع أن سالماً أخبره أن مولى أم حبيبة زوج رسول [١] الله ﷺ اخبر عبد الله أن أم حبيبة رضي الله عنها أخبرته أن رسول الله ﷺ قال :

« لا تصحب الملائكة رفقة فيها جرس . »

١١٤–حدثني عمرو نا سليمان نا شعيب نا عبيد الله عن نافع أن عبد الله أخبره أن رسول الله ﷺ قال :

« الرويا الصالحة جزء من سبعين جزءا من النبوة » .

١١٥–حدثني عمرو نا سليمان نا شعيب نا عبيد الله عن نافع أن عبد الله

---

(١) كلمة « رسول » سقطت من الأصل .

أخبره أن رجلا سأل رسول الله ﷺ ، وهو على المنبر ، فقال : يا رسول الله ما ترى في أكل الضب ؟ قال : « لا آكله ولا أحرمه . »

١١٦–حدثني عمرو نا سليمان نا شعيب نا عبيد الله عن نافع أن عبد الله أخبره أن رسول الله ﷺ قال : « كل متبايعين أحدهما على صاحبه بالخيار ما لم يفترقا . قال : ويكون خياراً . »

١١٧–حدثني عمرو نا سليمان نا شعيب نا عبيد الله عن نافع أن عبد الله أخبره (١٤٨ / ١) أن رسول الله ﷺ قال :

« من حمل علينا السلاح فليس منا » .

١١٨–حدثني عمرو نا سليمان نا شعيب نا عبيد الله عن نافع أن زيد بن عبد الله أخبره : أن عبد الله بن عبد الرحمن بن أبي بكر رضي الله عنه أخبره : أن أم سلمة زوج النبي ﷺ أخبرته : أنها سمعت رسول الله ﷺ وهو يقول :

« أن الذي يشرب في آنية الفضة أنما يجرجر في بطنه نار جهنم » .

١١٩–حدثني عمرو نا سليمان نا شعيب نا عبيد الله عن نافع أن عبد الله أخبره أن رسول الله ﷺ : « نهى عن بيع الطعام اذا اشتراه أحدكم حتى يستوفيه ويقبضه » .

١٢٠–حدثني عمرو نا سليمان نا شعيب نا عبيد الله عن نافع أن عبد الله أخبره أن رسول الله ﷺ قال :

« أن الذي يقتني كلبا الا كلب ماشية أو كلب صيد فانه ينقص أجره كل يوم قيراطان . وانه كان يأمر بالكلاب أن تقتل » .

١٢١–حدثني عمرو نا سليمان نا شعيب نا عبيد الله عن نافع أن عبد الله أخبره أن رسول الله ﷺ (١٤٨ب) قال :

«لا يبيع أحدكم على بيع أخيه ولا يخطب على خطبة أخيه حتى يأذن له».

١٢٢ ـ حدثني عمرو نا سليمان نا شعيب نا عبيد الله عن نافع أن عبد الله كان يقول: «نهى رسول الله ﷺ عن مواشي الناس أن تحلب بغير أذن أربابها،

يقول: أيحب أحدكم أن يؤتى إلى مشربيته التي فيها طعامه فيكسر بابها فينتشل ما فيها من الطعام؟ فانما ضروع مواشيهم فيها طعام أحدكم فلا يحتلبن أحد ماشية أحد بغير أذنه».

١٢٣ ـ حدثني عمرو نا سليمان نا شعيب نا عبيد الله عن نافع أن عبد الله أذن ليلة وهو بضحنان بالعشاء في ليلة باردة، فقال صلوا في رحالكم.

ثم ذكر أن رسول الله ﷺ: كان يأمر المنادي فينادى بالصلاة، ثم ينادى في أثرها بضجنان(١): أن صلوا في الليلة الباردة أو الليلة المطيرة في السفر».

١٢٤ ـ حدثني عمرو نا سليمان نا شعيب نا (١٤٩ / ١) عبيد الله حدثني نافع أن سعيد بن أبي هند أخبره أن أبا موسى الاشعرى قال:
قال رسول الله ﷺ:

«أحل لبس الحربر والذهب لاناث أمتي وحرم على ذكورها».

١٢٥ ـ حدثني عمرو نا سليمان نا شعيب نا عبيد الله عن نافع أن عبد الله قال: «الخلية والبرية والبتة ثلاث».

١٢٦ ـ حدثني عمرو نا سليمان نا شعيب نا عبيد الله عن نافع أن عبد الله أخبره «أن عمر بن الخطاب رضي الله عنه خلفه على امرأته وكانت قد طافت يوم النحر بالبيت ثم حاضت بعد أن طافت يوم النحر».

فامره عمر رضى الله عنه بحبسها بمكة حتى تطهر. (٢)

١٢٧ ـ حدثني عمرو نا سليمان نا أبو الوليد بن مسلم نا عبد الله بن العلاء

---

(١) في الاصل: بصحتان. وما ذكرنا من «صحع مسلم». وضجنان: جبيل قريب من مكة

(٢) بالهامش «آخر حديث العمري»

وغيره انهما سمعا بلال بن سعد يحدث عن أبيه سعد أنه قيل : « يا رسول الله ما للخليفة من بعدك (١٤٩ب) قال : مثل الذي لي ، ما عدل في الحكم واسقط في القسط فمن لم يفعل(١) ذلك فليس مني ». قال : يريد الطاعة في طاعة الله عز وجل والمعصية في معصية الله عز وجل .

بلغ مقابلة بحسب الطاقة

آخره والحمد لله رب العلمين وصلاته على سيدنا محمد نبيه وآله وصحبه وسلم تسليما .

وكان الفراغ من نسخه يوم السبت التاسع والعشرون من ربيع الاول سنة ست وسبعين وخمسمائة .

وكتب عبد الغني بن أبي عبد الله محمد بن أبي (٢) المقبري .

ياخير مطلوب ويا خير طالب

أغفر لصاحبه نعم والكاتب

وحسبنا الله ونعم الوكيل .

---

(١) في الاصل : فمن فعل ذلك .

(٢) في الاصل : كلمتان مطموستان

تعليقات على أحاديث عبيد الله بن عمر

الحديث رقم / ١	ط حج ٧
الحديث رقم / ٣	ط حج ١٢
الحديث رقم / ٤	ط حج ١٧٧
الحديث رقم / ٥	ط حج ١٣ و ١٥
الحديث رقم / ٦	ط حج ١٤٦
الحديث رقم / ٧	ط حج ١٤٥
الحديث رقم / ٨	ط حج ١٤٦
الحديث رقم / ٩	ط حج ١٦٠ . وليس فيه «دون البدنة» و «دون البقرة»
الحديث رقم / ١٢	ط حج ٤٩
الحديث رقم / ١٣	ط صلاة الليل ١٣ ؛ جويرية / ٤٧
الحديث رقم / ١٤	ط قصر الصلاة ٣ ؛ جويرية / ٤٩
الحديث رقم / ١٥	ط وقوت الصلاة ٢١ ؛ جويرية / ٥٤
الحديث رقم / ١٦	ط قصر الصلاة ٢٦ . رواه عن عبد الله بن دينار عن ابن عمر
الحديث رقم / ١٧	ط جمعة ٥ ؛ جويرية / ٤٠
الحديث رقم / ١٨	ط القبلة ٤ ؛ جويرية / ١٦
الحديث رقم / ١٩	ط قصر الصلاة ٦٩ ؛ جويرية / ٥٠
الحديث رقم / ٢٠	ط صلاة الليل ٢٩ ؛ جويرية / ٤٨
الحديث رقم / ٢١	جويرية ٥٢
الحديث رقم / ٢٥	ط حج ٦ جزء منه فقط
الحديث رقم / ٢٦	ط عيدين ٣ عن طريق الزهري
الحديث رقم / ٢٧	ط وقوت الصلاة ٦

الحديث رقم / ٢٨	ط سفر ١٢ و ١٣
الحديث رقم / ٣١	ط طهارة ٦٣
الحديث رقم / ٣٦	ط صلاة ٢٦ و ٤٣
الحديث رقم / ٣٧	ط صلاة ٥٤
الحديث رقم / ٣٨	ط عيدين ٩
الحديث رقم / ٤٠	ط صلاة ٣٢
الحديث رقم / ٤٥	ط صلاة ٢٠
الحديث رقم / ٤٨	ط قصر الصلاة ٥ .وليس فيه قبل ان يغيب الشفق
الحديث رقم / ٤٩	ط قصر الصلاة ٧٤
الحديث رقم / ٥٠	ط قصر الصلاة ٤٤
الحديث رقم / ٥١	ط قصر الصلاة ٦٠
الحديث رقم / ٥٢	ط صلاة الليل ١٩
الحديث رقم / ٥٤	ط قصر الصلاة ١٧
الحديث رقم / ٥٥	ط صلاة الخوف ٣
الحديث رقم / ٥٧	ط صلاة الجماعة ١٢ ما معناه
الحديث رقم / ٥٨	ط عيدين / ١٠
الحديث رقم / ٥٩	ط قصر الصلاة ٧٦
الحديث رقم / ٦٤	ط صلاة الليل ٢٠
الحديث رقم / ٦٦	ط قصر الصلاة ١٤
الحديث رقم / ٧٠	ط طلاق ٥٣ ؛ جويرية / ٦٠
الحديث رقم / ٧٣	ط طلاق ٣٣ مع بعض الاختلاف
الحديث رقم / ٧٦	ط طلاق ٤٥
الحديث رقم / ٧٧	ط طلاق ٩٠
الحديث رقم / ٨١	ط طلاق ٥٦ و ٥٨
الحديث رقم / ٨٢	ط طلاق ٣٥ وفيه بعض الزيادات ، جويرية / ٣٤
الحديث رقم / ٨٣	ط طلاق ٥٠ نحوه .
الحديث رقم / ٨٦	ط طلاق ٥١
الحديث رقم / ٨٧	ط طلاق ٦٥ نحوه
الحديث رقم / ٨٨	جويرية / ١٧ .
الحديث رقم / ٨٩	ط صيام ٥ وفيه قبل الفجر بدلا عن «من الليل»..
الحديث رقم / ٩٠	ط صيام ٢٥ نحوه
الحديث رقم / ٩٤	ط صيام ٤٥

الحديث رقم / ٩٥	ط صيام ٤٧ نحوه
الحديث رقم / ٩٧	ط صيام ٢٠
الحديث رقم / ١٠٣	ط زكاة ٥٢ ؛ جويرية / ٧
الحديث رقم / ١٠٤	ط بيوع ١٠ و ٢٣ ؛ جويرية / ١٤
الحديث رقم / ١٠٥	ط بيوع ١٣
الحديث رقم / ١٠٦	ط . استئذان ؛ وليس فيه « إلا الابتر » ولم يذكر عبد الله في السند .
الحديث رقم / ١٠٧	ط استئذان ٣٢ . وليس فيه عن عائشة ؛ جويرية/٦٥
الحديث رقم / ١٠٨	جويرية / ٢٣
الحديث رقم / ١٠٩	جويرية / ٥
الحديث رقم / ١١٠	أخرجه مالك في الموطأ كما في تجريد التمهيد لابن عبد البر . رقم / ٥٨١ ؛ جويرية / ٤
الحديث رقم / ١١٤	جويرية / ١٩
الحديث رقم / ١١٥	جويرية / ٢٤
الحديث رقم / ١١٦	اخرجه مالك في الموطأ كما في تجريد التمهيد لابن عبد البر . رقم / ٥٥٢ ؛ جويرية / ٢٥
الحديث رقم / ١١٧	جويرية / ٥٥
الحديث رقم / ١١٨	ط صفة النبي / ١١ ؛ جويرية ٥٦
الحديث رقم / ١١٩	ط بيوع ٤٠
الحديث رقم / ١٢٠	ط استئذان ١٣ و ١٤ ؛ جويرية / ٥٦
الحديث رقم / ١٢١	جويرية / ٢٦
الحديث رقم / ١٢٢	ط استئذان ١٧ ؛ جويرية ٢٧
الحديث رقم / ١٢٣	أخرجه مالك في الموطأ كما في تجريد التمهيد لابن عبد البر . رقم / ٥٤١ ؛ جويرية / ٥١
الحديث رقم / ١٢٥	ط طلاق ٧

أحاديث أبي اليمان الحكم بن نافع
عن شعيب بن أبي حمزة
عن الزهري

جزء فيه أحاديث أبي اليمان الحكم بن نافع و
أحاديث إسناده وأحاديث يحيى بن معين
وغيره رواية الشيخ الإمام الكامل أبي منصور
عبد الرحيم بن محمد بن أحمد الشيرازي حرسها الله عن الشيخ
أبي بكر محمد بن الحسين بن أحمد بن محمد بن الليث الشاهد رحمه الله

راموز الصفحة الاولى من أحاديث أبي اليمان الحكم بن نافع عن شعيب بن أبي حمزه عن الزهري

جزء فيه أحاديث أبي اليمان الحكم بن نافع

وأحاديث أبي ذوالة وأحاديث يحيى بن معين وغيره رحمهم الله

رواية الشيخ الامام الحاكم أبي منصور عبدالرحيم بن محمد بن أحمد الشرابي حرسه الله

عن الشيخ أبي بكر محمد بن الحسن بن أحمد بن بن محمد بن الليث الشاهد رحمه الله

بسم الله الرحمن الرحيم

أخبرنا الشيخ الامام الحاكم أبو منصور عبد الرحيم بن محمد بن أحمد بن يحيى الشرابي بقراءتي عليه في صفر سنة تسع عشرة وخمسمائة .

قال اخبرنا الشيخ أبو بكر محمد بن الحسن بن أحمد بن محمد بن الليث الشاهد الصفار قراءة عليه في شهر رمضان سنة ست واربعين واربعمائة . قال أنا أبو الفضل محمد بن عبد الله بن محمد بن خميروية الكرابيسي نا أبو الحسن علي بن محمد بن عيسى الخزاعى الحكاني نا أبو اليمان الحكم بن نافع ، أخبرني شعيب بن أبي حمزة .

١ ــ عن الزهرى حدثني عروة بن الزبير أن عائشة زوج النبي ﷺ قالت : كان عتبة بن ابي وقاص عهد إلى أخيه سعد بن أبي وقاص أن يقبض اليه ابن وليدة زمعة . وقال عتبة أنه ابنى .

فلما قدم رسول الله ﷺ زمن الفتح أخذ سعد بن وليدة زمعة ، فاقبل به إلى رسول الله ﷺ واقبل معه عبد بن زمعة ، فقال سعد يا رسول الله هذا ابن أخي عهد اليّ به أنه ابنه . وقال عبد بن زمعة يا رسول الله هذا أخي ابن زمعة ، وولد على فراشه ، فنظر رسول الله ﷺ إلى ابن وليدة زمعة ، فاذا هو أشبه الناس بعتبة بن أبي وقاص . فقال رسول الله ﷺ هو لك يا عبد بن زمعة ، من أجل انه ولد على فراش أبيه ، وقال رسول الله ﷺ

احتجبي منه يا سودة بنت زمعة مما رأى من شبهه بعتبة بن أبي وقاص» . وسودة بنت زمعة زوج النبى ﷺ .

٢ ـ حدثنا أبو اليمان أخبرني شعيب عن الزهري قال حدثني عروة بن الزبير أن عائشة زوج النبى ﷺ قالت . قال رسول الله ﷺ : « الولد للفراش وللعاهر الحجر » . وكان أبو هريرة يصيح بذلك .

٣ ـ حدثنا أبو اليمان أخبرني شعيب عن الزهرى اخبرني عروة بن الزبير أن هشام بن حكيم بن حزام وجد عياض بن غنم وهو على حمص . شمس اناسا من نبط في أداء الجزية . فقال له هشام ما هذا يا عياض ؟ أني سمعت رسول الله ﷺ يقول :

« أن الله تعالى يعذب الذين يعذبون الناس في الدنيا » .

(٧١ / ب) حدثنا أبو اليمان اخبرني شعيب عن الزهرى اخبرني عروة بن الزبير أن زينب بنت أبي سلمة وامها أم سلمة زوج النبى ﷺ اخبرته أن أم حبيبة بنت أبي سفيان أخبرتها أنها قالت : قلت يا رسول الله انكح اختي أبنة أبي سفيان . قالت : فقال لي رسول الله ﷺ أو تحبين ذلك؟ قالت ، فقلت : يا رسول الله! نعم: ولست لك بمخلية واحب من يشركني في خير اختي . قالت . فقال رسول الله ﷺ : ان ذلك لا تحل لي . قالت فقلت والله يا رسول الله انا لنتحدث أنك تريد أن تنكح درة بنت أبي سلمة فقال ابنت أم سلمة ؟ قالت فقلت نعم . فقال والله لو انها لم تكن ربيبتي في حجرتي ما حلت لي . انها لابنة أخي من الرضاعة . ارضعتني وابا سلمة ثويبة . فلا تعرضن عليّ بناتكن ولا اخواتكن .

قال عروة وثويبة مولاة أبي لهب . كان أبو لهب أعتقها . فارضعت رسول الله ﷺ . فلما مات أبو لهب اريه بعض أهله في النوم بشر وخيبة . فقالت له ماذا لقيت ؟ فقال أبو لهب لم الق بعدكم رخاء غير أني قد سقيت

في هذه مني بعتاقتي ثويبة . واشار الى النقيرة التي بين الابهام والتي تليها من الاصابع .

٥ ـ حدثنا أبو اليمان اخبرني شعيب عن الزهرى اخبرني عروة بن الزبير أن عائشة قالت لقد رأيت رسول الله ﷺ يقوم على باب حجرتي والحبشة يلعبون بالحراب في المسجد وانه ليسترني بردائه لكي أنظر إلى لعبهم ثم يقوم من أجلي حتى أكون أنا الذي املّ فانصرف . فاقد روا قدر الجارية الحديثة السن الحريصة على اللهو .

٦ ـ حدثنا أبو اليمان أخبرني شعيب عن الزهري اخبرني عروة بن الزبير أن عائشة قالت كان أبو بكر نحلني جادَّ عشرين وسقا من ماله . فلما حضرته الوفاة جلس فاحتبى ثم قال : أما بعد أي بنية، فان أحب الناس إليَّ غنى بعدي لانت وان أعز الناس عليَّ فقرا بعدي لانت(١/٧٢). واني كنت نحلتك جداد عشرين وسقا من مالي . فوددت والله أنك كنت جدتيه واحتزتيه ولكن انما هو اليوم مال الوارث وانما هو اخواك واختاك فقالت : قلت أي ابتاه هذه اسماء فمن الاخرى ؟. فقال : ذو بطن بنت خارجة، أراها جارية. قالت ، فقلت : لو أعطيتني ما بين كذا إلى كذا لرددته اليك. قالت، وقلت حين نزل به : من لا يزال دمعه مقنعاً... فانه يوم مدقوق. قالت : فقال أبو بكر وهو يجود بنفسه : أي بنية ليس كذلك، ولكن قولي :وجاءت سكرة الموت بالحق ذلك ما كنت منه تحيد .

٧ ـ حدثنا أبو اليمان أخبرني شعيب عن الزهرى قال كان عروة الزبير يقول يرد من جنف الحي التأجل في حياته ما يرد من جنف الميت وصيته عند وفاته .

٨ ـ حدثنا أبو اليمان أخبرني شعيب عن الزهرى أخبرني عروة بن الزبير أنه سأل عائشة عن قول الله تعالى «حتى اذا استياس الرسول وظنوا انهم قد كذبوا ، أكُذِبوا أم كُذِّبوا . قالت بل كُذِّبوا . قال : فقلت :

لقد استيقنوا أن قومهم قد كذّبوهم وما هو بالظن . فقالت : أجل عمري لقد استيقنوا بذلك.قال، فقلت : فلعلها وظنوا أنهم قد كُذبوا. فقالت: معاذ الله. لم تكن الرسل لتظن ذلك بربها. قال،فقلت: ما هذه الآية؟ قالت: هم اتباع الرسل الذين آمنوا بهم وصدقوهم طال عليهم البلاء واستأخر عنهم النصر حتى اذا استيأس الرسل من قومهم وظنوا أن أتباعهم الذين آمنعوا بهم قد كذّبوهم جاءهم نصر الله عند ذلك [1] .

٩ –حدثنا أبو اليمان أخبرني شعيب عن الزهرى قال كان عروة بن الزبير يحدث أنه سأل عائشة عن قول الله تعالى « وان خفتم الا تقسطوا في اليتامى فانكحوا ما طاب لكم من النساء مثنى وثلاث ورباع فان خفتم ألا تعدلوا فواحدة أو ما ملكت أيمانكم » . قالت عائشة رضى الله عنها وعن أبيها هي اليتيمة تكون في جحر وليها فيرغب في جمالها ومالها ويريد أن يتزوجها (٧٢/ب) بأدنى من سنة نسائها. فنهوا عن نكاحهن إلاأن يقسطوا لهن في اكمال الصداق . وامروا بنكاح من سواهن من النساء . قالت عائشة ثم استفتى الناس رسول الله ﷺ. فأنزل الله تعالى«يستفتونك في النساء قل الله يفتيكم فيهن» الآية. قالت عائشة فبيّن الله لهم في هذه الآية أن اليتيمة اذا كانت ذات جمال ومال رغبوا في نكاحها ولم تلحقوها بسنة نسائها في اكمال الصداق. وإذا كانت مرغوباً عنها في قلة الجمال والمال تركوها والتمسوا غيرها من النساء .

قالت عائشة : فكما تركوها حين يرغبون عنها ، فليس لهم أن ينكحوها إذا رغبوا فيها إلا أن يقسطوا لها ويعطوها حقها الأوفى من الصدق .

١٠–حدثنا أبو اليمان أخبرني شعيب عن الزهرى حدثني عروة بن الزبير أن عائشة قالت : استأذن على أفلح أخو أبي قعيس بعد ما أنزل الحجاب فقلت له : لا آذن لك حتى استأذن رسول الله ﷺ ، فان أخا أبي القعيس ليس هو أرضعني ولكن أرضعتني أمرأة أبي القعيس . قالت فدخل عليّ رسول الله

(١) بالهامش رواه خ عن أبي اليمان ورواه م عن أبي بكر بن اسحاق عن أبي اليمان .

ﷺ فقلت : يا رسول الله أن أفلح أخا أبي القعيس، استأذن عليّ فأبيت أن آذن له حتى أستأذنك في ذلك . فقال لي رسول الله ﷺ : ومـــا يمنعك أن تأذني لعمك ؟. فقلت : يا رسول الله! أن الرجل ليس هو أرضعني، ولكن أرضعتني امرأة . فقالت قال رسول الله ﷺ : ائذني له فإنه عمك . تربت يمينك . قال عروة فبذلك كانت تقول : حرموا من الرضاعة ما تحرمون من النسب .

١١–حدثنا أبو اليمان أخبرني شعيب عن الزهري أخبرني عروة بن الزبير أن حذيفة بن اليمان وهو أحد بنى عبس قاتل مع رسول الله ﷺ هو وأبوه اليمان يوم أحد ، فأخطأ المسلمون يومئذ بأبيه يحسبونه من العدو فتواشقوه بأسيافهم . فطفق حذيفة يقول: أبي أبي. فلم ينههم قوله حتى قتلوه. فقال حذيفة عند ذلك: يغفر الله لكم وهو أرحم الراحمين .

فبلغت النبي ﷺ فزاد حذيفة عنده خيراً .

١٢– (١/٧٣) حدثنا أبو اليمان أخبرني شعيب عن الزهري أخبرني عروة بن الزبير عن عائشة أن أبا حذيفة بن عتبة بن ربيعة بن عبد شمس ، وكان ممن اشهد بدراً مع رسول الله صلى ﷺ تبنى سالما وزوجه بنت أخيه هند بنت الوليد بن عتبة وهو مولى لامرأة من الأنصار ، كما تبنى النبي ﷺ زيداً ، وكان من تبنى رجلا في الجاهلية دعاه الناس اليه وورث من ميراثه حتى أنزل الله تعالى في ذلك «ادعوهم لآبائهم هو أقسط عند الله . فان لم تعلموا آباءهم فإخوانكم في الدين ومواليكم » . فردوا إلى آبائهم فمن لم يعلم له أب كان مولاً وأخاً في الدين» . فجاءت سهلة بنت سهيل بن عمرو القرشي ثم العامري ، وهي امرأة أبي حذيفة ، إلى النبي ﷺ فقالت :

يا رسول الله إنا كنا نرى سالماً ولداً ، وكان يأوي معي ومع أبي حذيفة في بيت واحد ويراني فضلاً ، وقد أنزل الله تعالى ما قد علمت ، فكيف ترى ؟ يا رسول الله ! فقال لها رسول الله ﷺ أرضعيه ، فأرضعته خمس

رضعات فكان بمنزلة ولدها من الرضاعة . فبذلك كانت عائشة تأمر بنات اخوتها وبنات أخواتها أن يرضعن من أحبت عائشة أن يريها ويدخل عليها ، وان كان كبيراً ، خمس رضعات ثم يدخل عليها . وأبت أم سلمة وسائر أزواج النبي ﷺ أن يدخلن عليهن بتلك الرضاعة أحداً من الناس حتى يرضع في المهد وقلن لعائشة رضي الله عنهن أجمعين والله ما ندري لعلها رخصة لسالم من رسول الله ﷺ من دون الناس .

١٣ـ حدثنا أبو اليمان أخبرني شعيب عن الزهري أخبرني عروة بن الزبير أن عائشة قالت : قال رسول الله ﷺ «ما من مصيبة تصيب المسلم الا كفّر الله عنه بها حتى الشوكة تشاكها » .

١٤ـ حدثنا أبو اليمان أخبرني شعيب عن الزهري حدثني عروة بن الزبير عن عائشة قالت : جاءت امرأة رفاعة القرظي إلى رسول الله ﷺ وأنا جالسة عنده وأبو بكر فقالت : يا رسول الله: إني كنت تحت رفاعة فطلقني فبت طلاقي (٧٣ ب) فتزوجت بعده عبدالرحمن بن الزبير وانه ما معه يا رسول الله إلا مثل الهدبة ، وأخذت هدبة من جلبابها . قالت فسمع خالد بن سعيد قولها بالباب لم يوذن له . قالت فقال خالد : يا أبا بكر ألا تنه هذه عما تجهر به عند رسول الله ﷺ . وقالت لا والله ما يزيد رسول الله ﷺ على التبسم قالت فقال رسول الله ﷺ : لعلك تريدين أن ترجعي إلى رفاعة؟ لا.حتى يذوق عسيلتك وتذوقي عسيلته ، وكانت سنة بعده .

١٥ـ حدثنا أبو اليمان أخبرني شعيب عن الزهري أخبرني عروة بن الزبير أن عائشة كانت تقول : « حرموا من الرضاعة ما تحرمون من النسب » .

١٦ـ حدثنا أبو اليمان أخبرني شعيب عن الزهري عن عروة بن الزبير أن زينب بنت أبي سلمة حدثته أن أم حبيبة بنت أبي سفيان حدثتها عن زينب بنت جحش أن رسول الله ﷺ دخل عليها فزعا يقول لا إله إلا الله ويل للعرب من شر قد اقترب. فتح اليوم من ردم ياجوج وماجوج مثل هذه وحلق بأصبعه

– الابهام والتي تليها – قالت زينب ، فقلت : يا رسول الله : أنهلك وفينا الصالحون ؟ فقال : نعم اذا كثر الخبث .

١٧–حدثنا أبو اليمان أخبرني شعيب عن الزهري أخبرني عروة بن الزبير أن زينب بنت أبي سلمة وأمها أم سلمة زوج النبي ﷺ أخبرته أن أمها أم سلمة قالت سمع النبي ﷺ جلبة خصام عند بابه ، فخرج إليهم ، فقال إنما أنا بشر وانه يأتيني الخصم فلعل بعضهم أن يكون أبلغ من بعض فأقضي له بذلك وأحسب أنه صادق فمن قضيت له بحق مسلم فانما هو قطعة من نار فليأخذها أو ليدعها .

١٨–حدثنا أبو اليمان أخبرني شعيب عن الزهري قال: قال عروة بن الزبير، قالت عائشة: كان رسول الله ﷺ وهو صحيح (١/٧٤) يقول: إنه لم يقبض نبي قط حتى يرى مقعده من الجنة. ثم يحي. فلما اشتكى وحضره القبض. ورأسه على فخذ عائشة ، غشي عليه . فلما أفاق ، شخص بصره نحو سقف البيت . ثم قال « اللهم الرفيق الأعلى » .

قالت عائشة فقلت اذاً لا يجاورنا ، وعرفت أنه حديثه الذي كان يحدثنا وهو صحيح .

١٩–حدثنا أبو اليمان أخبرني شعيب عن الزهري أخبرني عروة بن الزبير، أن عائشة زوج النبي ﷺ أخبرته أن أبا بكر حين حضرته الوفاة قال « اغسلوا ثوبي هذين – اللذين كان يلبس – فكفنوني فيهما ، فإن الحي هو أفقر إلى الجديد من الميت » .

٢٠–حدثنا أبو اليمان أخبرني شعيب عن الزهري حدثني سعيد بن المسيب وأبو سلمة بن عبد الرحمن أن أبا هريرة كان يحدث أن رسول الله ﷺ :

كان يدعو في الصلاة حين يقول « سمع الله لمن حمده . ربنا ولك الحمد » ثم يقول وهو قائم قبل أن يسجد : « اللهم أنج الوليد بن الوليد وسلمة بن

هشام وعياش بن أبي ربيعة والمستضعفين من المؤمنين . اللهم اشدد وطأتك مضر واجعلها كسني يوسف » . ثم يقول « الله أكبر » .

٢١–حدثنا أبو اليمان أخبرني شعيب عن الزهري أخبرني سعيد بن المسيب وأبو سلمة بن عبد الرحمن أن أبا هريرة قال: سمعت رسول الله ﷺ يقول: « تفضل صلاة الجمع صلاة أحدكم وحده بخمسة وعشرين جزءاً ، وتجتمع ملائكة الليل وملائكة النهار في صلاة الفجر » .

ثم يقول أبو هريرة : اقرأوا إن شئتم «إن قرآن الفجر كان مشهوداً ».(١)

٢٢–حدثنا أبو اليمان أخبرني شعيب عن الزهري أخبرني سعيد بن المسيب وأبو سلمة بن عبد الرحمن أن عبد الله بن عمرو بن العاص قال :

أخبر رسول الله ﷺ أني أقول : « لأصومن النهار ولأقومن الليل ما عشت له » . فقلت له قد قلت : « بأبي أنت وأمي » . قال : « فإنك لا تستطيع ذلك فصم وافطر ونم. وصم من الشهر ثلاثة أيام، فإن الحسنة بعشر أمثالها، وذلك مثل صيام الدهر». قال فقلت : « أني أطيق أفضل من ذلك » . قال : «فصم (١/٧٤) يوماً وأفطر يوماً، وذلك صوم داوود، وهو أعدل الصيام». قال فقلت « أني أطيق أفضل من ذلك » . قال فقال رسول الله ﷺ: « لا أفضل من ذلك».

٢٣–حدثنا أبو اليمان أخبرني شعيب عن الزهري أخبرني سعيد بن المسيب أن أبا هريرة قال سمعت رسول ﷺ يقول : « مثل المجاهد في سبيل الله ، – والله أعلم بمن يجاهد في سبيله – كمثل الصائم القائم . وتوكل الله للمجاهد في سبيله بأن يتوفيه ، فيدخله الجنة ، أو يرجعه سالماً بما نال من أجر أو غنيمة » .

٢٤–حدثنا أبو اليمان أخبرني شعيب عن الزهري أخبرني سعيد بن المسيب أن أبا هريرة قال سمعت رسول الله ﷺ يقول : « والذي نفسي بيده ، لولا أن رجالا من المؤمنين لا تطيب أنفسهم أن يتخلفوا عني ولا أجد ما أحملهم عليه ، ما تخلفت عن سرية تغزو في سبيل الله ، والذي نفسي بيده لوددت أني

(١) في الأصل : وقران الفجر قران الفجر كان مشهودا .

أقتل في سبيل الله ثم أحيي ، ثم أقتل ثم أحيي ثم أقتل ثم أحيي ثم أقتل » .

٢٥–حدثنا أبو اليمان أخبرني شعيب عن الزهري أخبرني سعيد بن المسيب أن أبا هريرة أخبره أن رسول الله ﷺ قال : « أمرت أن أقاتل الناس حتى يقولوا لا إله إلا الله . فمن قال لا إله إلا الله فقد عصم مني نفسه وماله إلا بحقه ، وحسابه على الله تعالى » .

٢٦–حدثنا أبو اليمان أخبرني شعيب عن الزهري حدثني سعيد بن المسيب قال : قال أبو هريرة سمعت رسول الله ﷺ يقول : « ما من بني آدم من مولود إلا يمسه الشيطان حين يولد فيستهل صارخاً من مس الشيطان غير مريم وابنها ».

ثم يقول أبو هريرة اقرءوا أن شئتم « إني أعيذها بك وذريتها من الشيطان الرجيم » .

٢٧–حدثنا أبو اليمان أخبرني شعيب عن الزهرى أخبرني سعيد بن المسيب أن أبا هريرة قال سمعت رسول الله ﷺ يقول : « لا تقوم الساعة حتى تضطرب اليات نساء دوس على ذي الخلصة » . وذو الخلصة طاغية دوس الذي كانوا يعبدونه[1] في الجاهلية .

٢٨– حدثنا أبو اليمان أخبرني شعيب عن الزهري (١/٧٥) حدثني سعيد بن المسيب أن عبد الله بن عمرو قال « المقسطون في الدنيا على منابر من نور يوم القيامة بين يدي الرحمن لما أقسطوا له في الدنيا » .

٢٩–حدثنا أبو اليمان أخبرني شعيب عن الزهري أخبرني سعيد بن المسيب وعطاء بن يزيد الليثي أن أبا هريرة أخبرهما أن الناس قالوا : « يا رسول الله هل نرى ربنا يوم القيامة ؟ » فقال رسول الله ﷺ : « هل تمارون في القمر ليلة البدر ليس دونه سحاب ؟ » قالوا لا يارسول الله. قال : « فإنكم ترونه ». وذكر الحديث بطوله .

٣٠– حدثنا أبو اليمان أخبرنى شعيب عن الزهري أخبرني سعيد بن المسيب

---

(١) في الاصل يعبدون

أبا هريرة قال شهدنا مع رسول الله ﷺ خيبر فقال رسول الله ﷺ لرجل ممن معه يدعي بالاسلام أن هذا من أهل النار . فلما حضر القتال قاتل الرجل أشد القتال حتى إذا كثر به الجراح فأثبتّه ، فجاء رجل من أصحاب رسول الله ﷺ فقال يا رسول الله أرأيت الرجل الذي ذكرت من أهل النار قد والله قاتل في سبيل الله أشد القتال و كثرت به الجراح . فقال رسول الله ﷺ « أما انه من من أهل النار » . فكان بعض الناس يرتاب ، فبينما هو على ذاك ، وجد الرجل ألم الجراح فأهوى يده إلى كنانته فاستخرج منه أسهماً فانتحر بها . فاشتد رجال من المسلمين إلى رسول الله ﷺ فقالوا « يارسول الله قد صدق الله حديثك . قد انتحر فلان فقتل نفسه ، فقال رسول الله ﷺ « يا بلال قم فأذن لا يدخل الجنة الا مؤمن . إن الله تعالى يؤيد هذا الدين بالرجل الفاجر » .

٣١–حدثنا أبو اليمان أخبرني شعيب عن الزهري أخبرني سعيد بن المسيب عن أبيه أنه قال لما حضرت أبا طالب الوفاة جاءه رسول الله ﷺ فوجد عنده أبا جهل وعبد الله بن أبي أمية بن المغيرة فقال رسول الله ﷺ لأبي طالب « أي عم قل لا إله إلا الله . كلمة أحاج لك بها عند الله » . قال أبو جهل وعبد الله ابن أبي أُمية « أترغب من ملة عبد المطلب ؟ » ، فلم يزل رسول الله ﷺ يعرضها عليه ويعاندانه بتلك المقالة حتى قال أبو طالب آخر ما كلمهم به على ملة عبد المطلب. وأبى أن يقول لا إله إلا الله ، (٧٥ ب) فقال رسول الله ﷺ أما والله لأستغفرن لك ما لم أنه عنك » . فأنزل الله تعالى « ما كـان للنبي والذين آمنوا أن يستغفروا للمشركين ولو كانوا أولي قربى من بعد ما تبين لهم أنهم أصحاب الجحيم » . وأنزل الله في أبي طالب فقال لرسوله « إنك لا تهدي من أحببت ولكن الله يهدي من يشاء » .

٣٢–حدثنا أبو اليمان أخبرني شعيب عن الزهري أخبرني سعيد بن المسيب أن أبا هريرة قال سمعت رسول الله ﷺ يقول : « يدخل الجنة من أمتي زمرة هي سبعون ألفا تضيء وجوههم إضاءة القمر ليلة البدر » . فقام عكاشة بن

محصن الاسدي يرفع نحره عليه فقال : يـا رسول الله ادع الله أن يجعلني منهم » . فقـال رسول الله ﷺ : « اللهم اجعلـه منهم » . ثم قام رجل من الأنصار فقال يا رسول الله ادع الله أن يجعلني منهم . فقال رسول الله ﷺ : « سبقك بها عكاشة » .

٣٣—حدثنا أبو اليمان أخبرني شعيب عن الزهري قال سمعت سعيد بن المسيب يقول : أن البحيرة التي تمنع درها للطواغيت فلا يحلبها أحد من الناس ، والسائبة : التي كانو يسيبونها لآلهتهم فلا يحمل عليها شيء . قال وقال أبو هريرة : سمعت رسول الله ﷺ يقول « رأيت عمرو الخزاعي يجر قصبه في النار وكان أول من سيب السوائب » . وذكر الحديث .

٣٤—حدثنا أبو اليمان أخبرني شعيب عن الزهري أخبرني سعيد بن المسيب أن طعام البحر ما يبس منه فتزود في السفر ثم تلا هذه الآية (أحل لكم صيد البحر وطعـامه متاعاً لكم وللسيارة) قال سعيد « صيده ما كان عريضاً ، وطعامه ما يتزود به السيارة » .

٣٥—حدثنا أبو اليمان أخبرني شعيب عن الزهري قال قال سعيد بن المسيب نزلت هذه الآية « ولكل جعلنا موالي مما ترك الوالدان والأقربون » . في الذين كانوا يتبنون رجالا غير أبنائهم ويورثونهم . فأنزل الله عز وجل لهم أن يجعل لهم نصيباً في الوصية ، ورد الله الميراث إلى الموالي في الرحم والعصبة وأبى أن يجعل للمدعين ميراثاً ممن ادعاهم وتبناهم ولكن جعل لهم نصيباً في الوصية مكان ما تعاقدوا عليه في الميراث الذي رد الله عليهم فيه أمرهم .

٣٦—حدثنا أبو اليمان أخبرني شعيب عن الزهري أخبرني سعيد بن المسيب وسليمان بن يسار أن السنة في هاتين الآيتين اللتين ذكر الله فيهما نشوز المرء وإعراضه عن امرأته في قوله وان امرأة خافت من بعلها نشوزا او اعراضا الى تمام الآيتين ، وآثر عليها ، قال : من الحق أن يعرض عليها أن يطلقها أو تستقر عنده على ما كانت عليه من أثر في القسم من نفسه وماله ، فان استقرت عنده على ذلك وكرهت أن يطلقها ، فلا حرج عليه فيما آثره عليها به من ذلك ،

فان لم يعرض عليها الطلاق وصالحها على أن يعطيها من ماله ما يرضى به وتقر عنده على الاثرة في القسم من ماله ونفسه صلح له ذلك وجاز صلحها عليه وذلك ذكر سعيد وسليمان الصلح الذي قال الله تعالى « فلا جناح عليهما أن يصالحا بينهما صلحاً والصلح خير » . وذكر الحديث بطوله .

٣٧–حدثنا أبو اليمان أخبرني شعيب عن الزهري أخبرني سعيد بن المسيب وأبو سلمة بن عبد الرحمن أن أبا هريرة قال أنكم تقولون أن أبا هريرة يكثر الحديث عن رسول الله ﷺ ، وتقولون ما للمهاجرين لا يحدثون عن رسول الله ﷺ مثل حديث أبي هريرة وان إخوتي من المهاجرين كان يشغلهم الصفق في الأسواق ، وكان يشغل إخوتي من الأنصار عمل أموالهم. وكنت امرءاً مسكيناً من مساكين الصفة ، ألزم رسول الله ﷺ على ملء البطن فأحضر حين يغيبون ، وأعي حين ينسون ، وقد قال رسول الله ﷺ في حديث يحدثه يوماً : « إنه لن يبسط أحد ثوبه حتى أقضي مقالتي هذه ثم يجمع اليه ثوبه ، إلا وعى ما أقول » . فبسطت نمرة عليّ حتى اذا قضى رسول الله ﷺ مقالته ، جمعتها إلى صدري فما نسيت من مقالة رسول الله ﷺ تلك من شيء .

٣٨–حدثنا أبو اليمان أخبرني شعيب عن الزهري أخبرني سعيد بن المسيب وأبو سلمة بن عبد الرحمن (٧٦ ب) أن أبا هريرة قال قام رسول الله ﷺ حين أنزل الله عليه «وأنذر عشيرتك الأقربين» . فقال يا معشر قريش، أشتروا أنفسكم من الله لا أغني عنكم من الله شيئاً. يا بني عبد مناف، لا أغني عنكم من الله شيئاً. يا عباس بن عبد المطلب، لا أغني عنك من الله شيئا. يا صفية عمة رسول الله ﷺ، لا أغني عنك من الله شيئا . يا فاطمة بنت محمد سليني ما شئت لا أغني عنك من الله شيئا » .

٣٩–حدثنا أبو اليمان أخبرني شعيب عن الزهري حدثني سعيد بن المسيب أن أبا هريرة قال سمعت رسول الله ﷺ يقول : جاء أهل اليمن هم أرق أفئدة وأضعف قلوبا. الايمان يمان والحكمة يمانية. السكينة في أهل الغنم والفخر والخيلاء

في الفدادين أهل الوبر _قبل مطلع الشمس » .

٤٠ـحدثنا أبو اليمان أخبرني شعيب عن الزهرى أخبرني أبو سلمة بن عبد الرحمن أن أبا عبد الرحمن أن أبا هريرة قال : قال رسول الله ﷺ : « يأتي الشيطان أحدكم في صلاته فيهبس عليه حتى لا يدري كم صلّ . فاذا وجد أحدكم ذلك فليسجد سجدتين وهو جالس » . فاعلمنا أنهما قبل التسليم بسجود رسول الله ﷺ حين سجد في الجلوس قبل أن يسلم .

٤١ـحدثنا أبو اليمان أخبرني شعيب عن الزهري أخبرني أبو سلمة بن عبد الرحمن أنه أخبره أبو سفيان بن سعيد بن الأخنس عن أم حبيبة زوج النبي ﷺ ، وهي خالة أبي سفيان بن سعيد أنها قالت في سويق شربه عندها يوماً، إي ابن إختي توضّأ، فان رسول الله ﷺ قال : « توضئوا مما مستة النار».

٤٢ـحدثنا أبو اليمان شعيب عن الزهري أخبرني أبو سلمة بن عبد الرحمن أن أبا هريرة قال : « نهى رسول الله ﷺ عن الوصال فقال له رجل من المسلمين : « فانك يا رسول الله تواصل » : فقال « وأيكم مثلي أني أبيت فيطعمني ربي ويسقيني » . فلما أبوا أن ينتهوا عن الوصال ، واصل بهم يوماً ثم يوماً رأوا الهلال فقال « لو تأخر لزدتكم » (١/٧٧). كالتنكيل لهم حين أبوا أن ينتهوا .

٤٣ـحدثنا أبو اليمان أخبرني شعيب عن الزهري حدثني أبو سلمة بن عبد الرحمن أن أبا هريرة قال : قال رسول الله ﷺ : « لكل نبي دعوة . فأريد إن شاء الله أن أختبىء دعوتي شفاعة لأمتي يوم القيامة » .

٤٤ـحدثنا أبو اليمان أخبرني شعيب عن الزهري أخبرني أبوسلمة بن عبد الرحمن أنه سمع حسان بن ثابت الأنصاري يستشهد أبا هريرة : « أنشدك الله هل سمعت رسول الله ﷺ يقول : يا حسان أجب عن رسول الله ﷺ ، اللهم أيده بروح القدس » . قال أبو هريرة : « نعم » .

٤٥ـ حدثنا أبو اليمان أخبرني شعيب عن الزهري أخبرني أبو سلمة بن عبد الرحمن وسعيد بن المسيب أن أبا هريرة قال : « استب رجل من المسلمين ورجل من اليهود ، فقال المسلم : « والذي اصطفى محمداً على العالمين » ، في قسم يقسم به . فقال اليهودي : « والذي اصطفى موسى على العالمين » . فرفع المسلم عند ذلك يده فلطم اليهودي . فذهب اليهودي إلى رسول الله ﷺ فأخبره بالذي كان من أمره وأمر المسلم . فقال رسول الله ﷺ : « لا تخيروني على موسى ، فان الناس يصعقون فأكون أول من يفيق ، فاذا موسى باطش بجانب العرش . فلا أدري أكان فيمن صعق فأفاق قبلي ، أم كان ممن استثناه [1] الله تعالى » .

٤٦ـ حدثنا أبو اليمان أخبرني شعيب عن الزهرى حدثني أبو سلمة بن عبد الرحمن أن أبا هريرة قال : « قال رسول الله ﷺ حين أراد قدوم مكة : « منزلنا غداً إن شاء الله بخيف بني كنانة ، حيث تقاسموا على الكفر » .

٤٧ـ حدثنا أبو اليمان أخبرني شعيب عن الزهري أخبرني أبو سلمة بن عبد الرحمن أن عائشة قالت : « قال رسول الله ﷺ : « يا عائشة هـذا جبريل عليه السلام، وهو يقرأ عليك السلام». فقلت : « وعليه السلام ورحمة الله » . وقالت عائشة : « وهو يرى ما لا أرى».

٤٨ـ (٧٧ ب) [حدثنا] أبو اليمان أخبرني شعيب عن الزهري حدثني أبو سلمة بن عبد الرحمن أن أبا هريرة قال: «سمعت رسول الله ﷺ يقول: «أنما يشد الرحل إلى ثلاثة مساجد، إلى المسجد الحرام، ومسجدكم هذا، وايليا» .

٤٩ـ حدثنا أبو اليمان أخبرني شعيب عن الزهري حدثني أبو سلمة بن عبد الرحمن وابو عبد الله الأغر صاحب أبا هريرة أن أبا هريرة أخبرهما أن رسول الله ﷺ قال : « ينزل ربنا كل ليلة حين يبقى ثلث الليل الآخر إلى

---

(١) في الاصل « استثنى الله تعالى »

السماء الدنيا فيقول من يدعوني فاستجيب له ، من يستغفرني فأغفر له ، من يسألني فأعطيه حتى الفجر » .

٥٠ ـ حدثنا أبو اليمان أخبرني شعيب عن الزهري نا أبو سلمة بن عبد الرحمن أن أبا هريرة قال : قال رسول الله ﷺ :

« ستكون فتن . القاعد فيها خير من القائم ، والقائم فيها خير من الماشي ، والماشي فيها خير من الساعي . من تشرف لها يستشرف له . فمن وجد منها ملجأ أو معاذاً فليعذ به » .

٥١ ـ حدثنا أبو اليمان أخبرني شعيب عن الزهري أخبرني أبو سلمة بن عبد الرحمن أن أبا هريرة قال : قال رسول الله ﷺ :

« لا تقوم الساعة حتى تقتتل فئتان دعواهما واحد » .

٥٢ ـ حدثنا أبو اليمان أخبرني شعيب عن الزهري أخبرني أبو سلمة بن عبد الرحمن أن أبا هريرة قال : سمعت رسول الله ﷺ يقول :

« من أطاعني فقد أطاع الله ، ومن عصى أميري فقد عصاني » .

٥٣ ـ حدثنا أبو اليمان أخبرني شعيب عن الزهري أخبرني أبو سلمة بن عبد الرحمن أن أبا هريرة قال : سمعت رسول الله ﷺ يقول :

« الفخر والخيلاء في الفدادين أهل الوبر والسكينة في أهل الغنم .والإيمان يمان والحكمة يمانية » .

٥٤ـ حدثنا أبو اليمان أخبرني شعيب عن الزهرى أخبرني أبو سلمة بن عبد الرحمن أن عبد الله ين عدى بن الحراء الزهرى أخبره أنه سمع رسول الله ﷺ يقول وهو واقف بالجذوة في سوق مكة :

« انك لخير أرض الله ، وأحب ارض الله الى الله . ولولا أني أخرجت منك ما خرجت.»

٥٥ـ حدثنا أبو اليمان أخبرني شعيب عن الزهرى قال قال أبو سلمة

عبد الرحمن وعبد الله بن عبد الله بن عيتبة بن مسود أنهما يحدثان أنهما سمعا أبا هريرة يقول : قال رسول الله ﷺ وهو في مجلس عظيم من المسلمين :

« أحدثكم بخير دور الانصار ؟ » . قالوا : نعم يا رسول الله » . قال رسول الله ﷺ : « بنو عبد الأشهل ، وهم رهط سعد بن معاذ » . قالوا : « ثم من يا رسول الله ؟ » . قال : « ثم بني النجار » . قالوا : « ثم من يا رسول الله ؟ » . قال : « ثم بنو الحارث بن الخزرج » . قالوا : « ثم من يا رسول الله ؟ » . قال : « ثم بنو ساعد » . قالوا : « ثم من يا رسول الله ؟ » قال : « ثم في كل دور الأنصار خير » .

فقام سعد بن عبادة وكان سيد ساعدة مغضبا فقال : « سمانا في آخر أربعة أذور وازاد كلام رسول الله ﷺ . فقال له رجل من القوم : « اجلس ، ألا ترض أن يسمى قومك في الأربعة الأذور التي سمى فمن ترك فلم يسم أكثر ممن سمي » . فانتهى سعد بن عبادة عن كلام رسول الله حين قالوا ذلك .

٥٦ ــ حدثنا أبو اليمان أخبرني شعيب عن الزهري حدثني أبو سلمة بن عبد الرحمن أنه سمع أبا هريرة يقول : « قال رسول الله ﷺ :

« اشتكت النار الى ربها تعالى فقالت يا رب أكل بعضي بعضاً ، فأذن لها بنفسين ، نفس في الشتاء ، ونفس في الصيف ، وهو أشد ما تجدون من الحر ، وأشد ما تجدون من الزمهرير » .

٥٧ ــ حدثنا أبو اليمان أخبرني شعيب عن الزهري أخبرني أبو سلمة بن عبد الرحمن قال قال أبو هريرة : « سمعت رسول الله ﷺ يقول :

« والله اني لأستغفر وأتوب في اليوم أكثر من سبعين مرة » .

٥٨ ـ حدثنا أبو اليمان أخبرني شعيب عن الزهري أخبرني أبو سلمة بن عبد الرحمن أن أبا هريرة قال : « قام رسول الله ﷺ في الصلاة ، وقمنا معه . فقال اعرابي وهو في الصلاة : « اللهم ارحمني ومحمداً ، ولا ترحم معنا أحدا ». فلما سلم رسول الله ﷺ قال للأعرابي : «لقد حجرت واسعاً،» يريد رحمـــة الله .

٥٩ـ حدثنا أبو اليمان أخبرني شعيب عن الزهري أخبرني أبو سلمة بن عبد الرحمن أن أبا مالك الليثي أخبره عن عبد الرحمن بن عوف أنه سمع رسول الله ﷺ يقول : (قال الله تعالى : « أنا الرحمن وأنا خلقت الـــرحم وشققت لها من اسمي فمن وصلها وصلته ومن قطعها قطعته وثبته . »

٦٠ـ حدثنا أبو اليمان أخبرني شعيب عن الزهري أخبرني أبو سلمة بن عبد الرحمن أن أبا هريرة قال سمعت رسول الله ﷺ يقول للشونيز : « عليكم بهذه الحبة السوداء ، فان فيها شفاء من كل شيء إلا السام يعني الموت » .

٦١ـ حدثنا أبو اليمان أخبرني شعيب عن الزهري أخبرني أبو سلمة بن عبد الرحمن أن عائشة زوج النبي ﷺ أخبرته أن رسول الله ﷺ جاءها حين أمر الله أن يخير أزواجه . قالت عائشة فبدأ بي رسول الله ﷺ فقال : « أني ذاكر لك أمراً ، فلا عليك ألا تستعجلي حتى تستأمري أبويك . قالت وقد علم أن أبوي لم يكونا ليأمراني بفراقه . قالت ثم قال رسول الله ﷺ أن الله تعالى قال : « يا أيها النبي قل لأزواجك إن كنتن تردن الحياة الدنيا إلى تمام لآيتين . قالت : فقلت له : ففي أي هذا أستأمر أبوي ؟ فاني أريد الله ورسوله والدار الآخرة .

٦٢ـ حدثنا أبو اليمان أخبرني شعيب عن الزهري أخبرني أبو سلمة بن عبد الرحمن أن أبا سعيد الخدري قال : بينا نحن عند رسول الله ﷺ وهو يقسم قسما ، أتاه ذوالخويصرة وهورجل من بني تميم. فقال: يا رسول الله اعدل.

فقال: « ويحك ومن يعدل إذا لم أعدل فقد خبت وخسرت أن لم أكن (١/٧٩) أعدل. فقال عمر بن الخطاب : يا رسول الله ائذن لي فيه أضرب عنقه. فقال رسول الله ﷺ: «دعه فان له أصحاباً يحقر أحدكم صلاته مع صلاتهم وصيامه مع صيامهم. يقرءون القرآن لا يجاوز تراقيهم. يمرقون من الاسلام كما يمرق السهم من الرمية، ينظر إلى نصله فلا يوجد فيه شيء ثم ينظر إلى نصبه وهو قد فلا يوجد فيه شيء. ثم ينظر إلى قدده فلا يوجد فيه شيء. قد سبق الفرث والدم. آيتهم رجل أسود إحدى عضديه مثل ثدى المرأة أو مثل البضعة تدردر، يخرجون على خير فرقة من الناس. »

قال أبو سعيد : « فأشهد أني سمعت هذا من رسول الله ﷺ، وأشهد أن على بن أبي طالب قاتلهم. وأنا معه. فأمر بذلك الرجل فالتمس، فأتى به حتى نظرت اليه على نعت رسول الله ﷺ الذي نعته ».

٦٣—حدثنا أبو اليمان أخبرني شعيب عن الزهري أخبرني أبو سلمة بن عبد الرحمن أن عائشة قالت : سئل رسول الله ﷺ عن البتع ونبيذ العسل— كان أهل اليمن يشربونه — فقال رسول الله ﷺ: « كل شراب أسكر حرام ».

٦٤—حدثنا أبو اليمان أخبرني شعيب عن الزهري أخبرني أبو سلمة بن عبد الرحمن وسعيد بن المسيب أن أبا هريرة قال : أتى رجل من أسلم رسول الله ﷺ وهو في المسجد فناداه فقال: يا رسول الله أن الآخر زنى — يعني نفسه — فأعرض عنه رسول الله ﷺ فتنحّا لشق وجهه الذي أعرض قبله. فقال : يا رسول الله أن الآخر زنى. فأعرض عنه رسول الله ﷺ، فتنحّا لشق وجهه الذي أعرض قبله فقال : يا رسول الله أن الآخر زنى. فأعرض عنه رسول الله ﷺ فتنحّا له الرابعة. فلما شهد على نفسه أربع مرات. دعاه رسول الله ﷺ فقال : هل بك من جنون ؟ فقال : لا، فقال رسول الله ﷺ: «اذهبوا به فارجموه ». وكان قد أحصن.

قال الزهري، فأخبرني من سمع جابر بن عبد الله الأنصاري قال: كنت

فيمن رجمه ، فرجمناه في المصلى (٧٩/ب) في المدينة ، فلما أذلقته الحجارة حمز حتى أدركناه بالحرة فرجمناه حتى مات .

٦٥ــحدثنا أبو اليمان أخبرني شعيب عن الزهرى أخبرني أبو سلمة بن عبد الرحمن أن عائشة زوج النبي ﷺ أخبرته أن رسول الله ﷺ حين توفي سجي ببرد حرة . فصدق ذلك عندي حديث علي بن الحسن أن رسول الله ﷺ كفن في ثوب حبرة .

٦٦ــحدثنا أبو اليمان أخبرني شعيب عن الزهري أخبرني أبو سلمة بن عبد الرحمن أن جابر بن عبد الله أخبره أن رسول الله ﷺ قضى أنه من أعمر رجلاً عمرى له ولعقبه فانها للذي أعمرها قد بتها من صاحبها الذي أعطاها وقع من مواريث الله وحقه .

٦٧ــحدثنا أبو اليمان أخبرني شعيب عن الزهري أنا سعيد بن المسيب أن أبا هريرة قال : سمعت رسول الله ﷺ يقول : « جعل الله الرحمة مائة جزء فأمسك عنده تسعاً وتسعين وأنزل في الأرض جزء واحد فمن ذلك الجزء يتراحم الخلق حتى ترفع الفرس حافرها عن ولدها خشية أن تصيبه » .

٦٨ــحدثنا أبو اليمان أخبرني شعيب عن الزهري أخبرني سعيد بن المسيب أنه سمع أبا هريرة يقول : أتى رسول الله ﷺ ليلة أسري به بايليا بقدحين خمر ولبن فنظر اليهما ثم أخذ اللبن . فقال له جبريل عليه السلام : « الحمد لله الذي هداك للفطرة لو أخذت الخمر لغوت أمتك » .

٦٩ــحدثنا أبو اليمان أخبرني شعيب عن الزهري أخبرني عقبة بن سويد الأنصاري أنه سمع أباه وكان من أصحاب رسول الله ﷺ قال : قفلنا مع رسول الله ﷺ من غزوة خيبر فلما بدء له أحد . قال رسول الله ﷺ « الله أكبر جبل يحبنا ونحبه » .

٧٠ــحدثنا أبو اليمان أخبرني شعيب عن الزهري أخبرني أبو سلمة أن

أبا هريرة قال : سمعت رسول الله ﷺ يقول : «إذا اشتد الحر ، فأبردوا عن الظهر . فان شدة الحر من فيح جهنم . »

٧١–حدثنا أبو اليمان أخبرني شعيب عن الزهرى أنا أبو سلمة أن أبا هريرة قال : سمعت رسول الله ﷺ (١/٨٠) يقول : «إذا أقيمت الصلاة فلا تأتوها تسعون. واتوها تمشون وعليكم السكينة، فما أدركتم فصلوا وما فاتكم فأتموا » .

٧٢–حدثنا أبو اليمان أخبرني شعيب عن الزهري أخبرني أبو سلمة وأبو عبد الله الأغر صاحب أبي هريرة أن أبا هريرة أخبرهما أن رسول الله ﷺ قال : « مشي المهجر إلى الصلاة كمثل الذي يهدي البدنة ثم الذي على أثره كالذي يهدي البقرة ثم الذي على أثره كالذي يهدي الشاة ثم الذي على أثره كالذي يهدي الدجاجة ثم الذي على أثره كالذي يهدي البيضة . »

آخر أحاديث أبي اليمان
وصلى الله على محمد وآله أجمعين

تعليقات على أحاديث أبي اليمـــان

الحديث رقم /١	ط أقضية ٢ ؛ الحميدي / ٢٣٨ . وفيه قيل لسفيان فان مالكاً يقول « وللعاهر الحجر ». فقال سفيان « لكنا لم نحفظ عن الزهري انه قال في هذا الحديث »
الحديث رقم /٢	ط أقضية ٢ ؛ الحميدي /١٠٨٥ . وانظر تخريج هذا الحديث في نهاية هذا التعليق .
الحديث رقم /٦	ط أقضية/٤٠ .
الحديث رقم /١٠	ط رضاع ٣ مختصراً وكذلك الحميدي /٢٢٩
الحديث رقم /١٢	ط رضاع ١٢.
الحديث رقم /١٤	الحميدي /٢٢٦ وفيه قيل لسفيان فان مالكا لا يرويه عن الزهري انما يرويه عن المسوربن رفاعة فقال سفيان لكنا قد سمعنا من الزهري كما قصصناه عليكم أنظر ط نكاح ١٧ . وفيه الحديث عن المسور .
الحديث رقم /١٦	الحميدي /٣٠٨ .
الحديث رقم /٢٠	الحميدي /٩٣٩ .
الحديث رقم /٢١	ط صلاة الجماعة ، جزء منه .
الحديث رقم /٣٧	الحميدي /١١٤٢ عن طريق الزهري – الاعرج – ابي هريرة .
الحديث رقم /٤٠	ط سهوا ؛ الحميدي /٩٤٧ . قد أخرج كلاهما إلى قوله فليسجد سجدتين وهو جالس
الحديث رقم /٤١	الحميدي/٨٩٨. ويقول سفيان انه اختلط عليه هذا الحديث.
الحديث رقم /٤٤	الحميدي /١١٠٥ وفيه الزهري عن ابن المسيب .
الحديث رقم /٤٨	الحميدي /٩٤٣ وفيه الزهري عن ابن المسيب .
الحديث رقم /٤٩	ط القرآن ٣٠ . ولم يذكر فيه ابا سلمة .

الحديث رقم /٥٦	الحميدي /٩٤٢ . وفيه الزهري عن ابن المسيب .
الحديث رقم /٥٨	الحميدي /٩٣٨ ببعض الزيادات والاختلاف وفيه الزهري عن ابن المسيب .
الحديث رقم /٦٠	الحميدي /١١٠٧ .
الحديث رقم /٦٣	ط أشربه ٩ ؛ الحميدي ٢٨١ . وفيه قيل لسفيان فان مالكا وغيره يذكرون البتع . فقال : ما قال لنا ابن شهاب البتع . إلا كما قلت لك .
الحديث رقم /٦٤	ط حدود ٢ ؛ و ٤ موقوفا .
الحديث رقم /٦٦	ط أقضية ٤٣ .
الحديث رقم /٧٠	الحميدي /٩٤٢ عن طريق ابن‌المسيب . وفيه بعض الزيادات
الحديث رقم /٧١	الحميدي /٩٣٥ . وفيه عن الزهري سعيد بن المسيب.
الحديث رقم /٧٢	الحميدي ٩٣٤ . عن طريق‌ابن المسيب وفيه : قيل لسفيان انهم يقولون في هذا الحديث « عن الاغر عن أبي هريرة ». قال سفيان : ما سمعت الزهري ذكر الاغر قط. ما سمعته يقول إلا عن سعيد أنه أخبره عن أبي هريرة .

تخريج

الحديث رقم ١ و ٢ « الولد للفراش وللعاهر الحجر »

الرواة عن أبي هريرة :

١ – ابو رافع. ٢ – ابو سلمة. ٣ – ابن المسيب.

١ – تلاميذ ابي رافع : خلاس حم ٤٩٢/٢

٢ – تلاميذ ابي سلمة وابن المسيب : الزهري حم ٢٣٩/٢ ؛ ٢٨٠

٣ – تلاميذ ابن المسيب : محمد بن زياد حم ٢٣٩/٢ ؛ ٢٨٠

الشواهد :

١ – ابو امامة الباهلي ٢ – ابو مسعود ٣ – عبادة بن الصامت

٤ – عثمان ٥ – عائشة ٦ – عبد الله بن عمرو بن العاص

٧ – عمر بن الخطاب ٨ – عمرو بن خارجة

(١) ابو امامة الباهلي . اسماعيل بن عياش – شرحبيل بن مسلم – عنه . حم ٢٦٧/٥

(٢) ابو مسعود . عيسى بن أسيد – عبد الرحمن بن زيد – عنه . طك – ١/٥٨/٩

(٣) عبادة بن الصامت . موسى بن عقبة – اسحاق بن يحي – عنه . حم ٣٢٦/٥

(٤) عثمان. الحسن بن سعد – رباح – عنه حم٥٩/١ ؛ ٦٥ ؛ ٦٩ انظر ايضا حم١٠٤/١

(٥) عائشة : – الزهري – عروة – عنها حم ١٢٩/٦ ؛ ٢٠٠ ؛ ٢٣٧ ؛ ٢٤٧
خ خصومات ٦ ؛ أحكام ٢٩؛ بيوع ٣ ؛ ١٠٠
وصايا ٤ ؛ حدود ٢٣ ؛ الفرائض ٢٨ ؛ الحميدي
٢٣٨ ؛ ١٠٨٥ ؛ طس ١٤٤٤؛ ط أقضية ٢٠ .

(٦) عبد الله بن عمرو بن العاص . عمرو بن شيعب عن أبيه عن جده . حم ١٧٩/٢ ؛ ٢٠٧

(٧) عمر بن الخطاب. يزيد بن أبي زياد – ابو زياد – عنه. حم ٢٥/١ ؛ انظر أيضا يعلى ١٦ ب

(٨) عمرو بن خارجة : –

شهر بن حوشب – عبد الرحمن بن غنم – عمرو بن خارجة .حم ١٨٦/٤ ؛ ٧-١٨٦ ؛ ١٨٧ ؛ ٢٣٨؛ ٢٣٩ ؛ موصلي ١/٨٧ طك ١/٦/٩

٩ – يوجد الحديث في مصدر زيدي مسند زيد ٣٣٦

١٠ – وفي مصدر إباضي كذلك شرح مسند الربيع . ٣/٤-٣٠٣

وذكر شارح مسند الربيع نقلا عن ابن عبد البر أنه قد روى الحديث بضعة وعشرين نفساً من الصحابة . شرح مسند الربيع ٣٠٤/٣

مقارنة الروايات :

اتفق الرواة لفظا ومعنى . إلا أن أكثر الروايات ذكرت :

« الولد للفراش وللعاهر الحجر » . وذكرت بعض الروايات الفقره الاولى فقط كما وردت في رواية الأثلب بدل الحجر .

أسماء الرواة :

الطبقة الاولى : ١ – ابو هريرة ٢ – ابو امامة الباهلي ٣ – ابو مسعود ٤ – عبادة بن الصامت ٥ – عثمان ٦ – عائشة ٧ – عبد الله بن عمر ٨ – عمرو بن الخطاب ٩ – عمرو بن خارجة.

الطبقة الثانية : ١ – ابو رافع ٢ – ابو زياد ٣ – ابو سلمة ٤ – ابن المسيب ٥ – اسحاق بن يحيى ٦ – رباح ٧ – شرحبيل بن مسلم ٨ – شعيب ٩ – عبد الرحمن بن زيد ١٠ – عبد الرحمن بن غنم ١١ – عروة .

الطبقة الثالثة : ١ – اسماعيل بن عياش ٢ – الحسن بن سعد ٣ – خلاس ٤ – الزهري ٥ – شهر بن حوشب ٦ – عمرو بن شعيب ٧ – عيسى بن اسيد ٨ – محمد بن زياد ٩ – موسى بن عقبة ١٠ – يزيد بن أبي زياد .

الرواية عن أكثر من شيخ : في الطبقة الثالثة يروي الزهري عن أكثر من شخص وكأنه الراوي الوحيد عن عروة .

ادراجه في مسند ابن حنبل :

٥ مرات عن طريق ابي هريرة و ١٨ مرة عن طريق الآخرين .